ACCA

Paper F6

Taxation

Complete text

Finance Act 2009
for 2010 examination sittings

British library cataloguing-in-publication data

A catalogue record for this book is available from the British Library.

Published by:
Kaplan Publishing UK
Unit 2 The Business Centre
Molly Millars Lane
Wokingham
Berkshire
RG41 2QZ

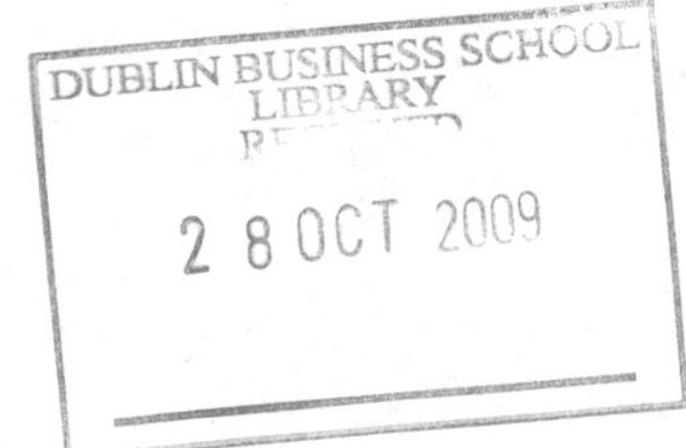

ISBN 978-1-84710-727-5

The text in this material and any others made available by any Kaplan Group company does not amount to advice on a particular matter and should not be taken as such. No reliance should be placed on the content as the basis for any investment or other decision or in connection with any advice given to third parties. Please consult your appropriate professional adviser as necessary. Kaplan Publishing Limited and all other Kaplan group companies expressly disclaim all liability to any person in respect of any losses or other claims, whether direct, indirect, incidental, consequential or otherwise arising in relation to the use of such materials.

Printed in the UK by CPI William Clowes, Beccles NR34 7TL.

Acknowledgements

We are grateful to the Association of Chartered Certified Accountants and the Chartered Institute of Management Accountants for permisssion to reproduce past examination questions. The answers have been prepared by Kaplan Publishing.

EXCITING EXTRA ONLINE RESOURCES INCLUDED

REF ONLY

H

SO T… …WHERE

IN ADDITION T… …ENABLES YOU TO BENEFIT FROM… …TUDY MATERIALS:

- An online ve… …t of the expandable content and… …ercises
- Fixed Online…
- Test History… …results
- Interim and F…

And you can acce… …ere using your EN-gage account.

How to access you…

If you are a Kaplan Financial…	…and these extra resources will …d to register again, as this … was completed when you enrolled. If you are having problems accessing online materials, please ask your course administrator.
If you purchased through Kaplan Flexible Learning or via the Kaplan Publishing website	You will automatically receive an e-mail invitation to EN-gage online. Please register your details using this e-mail to gain access to your content. If you do not receive the e-mail or book content, please contact Kaplan Flexible Learning.
If you are already a registered EN-gage user	Go to www.EN-gage.co.uk and log in. Select the 'add a book' feature and enter the ISBN number of this book and the unique pass key at the bottom of this card. Then click 'finished' or 'add another book'. You may add as many books as you have purchased from this screen.
If you are a new EN-gage user	Register at www.EN-gage.co.uk and click on the link contained in the e-mail we sent you to activate your account. Then select the 'add a book' feature, enter the ISBN number of this book and the unique pass key at the bottom of this card. Then click 'finished' or 'add another book'.
Your Code and Information	**This code can only be used once** for the registration of one book online. This registration will expire when the final sittings for the examinations covered by this book have taken place. Please allow one hour from the time you submitted your book details for us to process your request.

bi2F-4Stl-NAeT-Muwn

For technical support, please visit www.EN-gage.co.uk

Contents

Paper Introduction

How to Use the Materials

These Kaplan Publishing learning materials have been carefully designed to make your learning experience as easy as possible and to give you the best chances of success in your examinations.

The product range contains a number of features to help you in the study process. They include:

(1) Detailed study guide and syllabus objectives

(2) Description of the examination

(3) Study skills and revision guidance

(4) Complete text or essential text

(5) Question practice

The sections on the study guide, the syllabus objectives, the examination and study skills should all be read before you commence your studies. They are designed to familiarise you with the nature and content of the examination and give you tips on how to best to approach your learning.

The **complete text or essential text** comprises the main learning materials and gives guidance as to the importance of topics and where other related resources can be found. Each chapter includes:

- The **learning objectives** contained in each chapter, which have been carefully mapped to the examining body's own syllabus learning objectives or outcomes. You should use these to check you have a clear understanding of all the topics on which you might be assessed in the examination.
- The **chapter diagram** provides a visual reference for the content in the chapter, giving an overview of the topics and how they link together.
- The **content** for each topic area commences with a brief explanation or definition to put the topic into context before covering the topic in detail. You should follow your studying of the content with a review of the example. These are worked examples which will help you to understand better how to apply the content for the topic.
- **Test your understanding** sections provide an opportunity to assess your understanding of the key topics by applying what you have learned to short questions. Answers can be found at the back of each chapter.

- **Summary diagrams** complete each chapter to show the important links between topics and the overall content of the paper. These diagrams should be used to check that you have covered and understood the core topics before moving on.
- **Question practice** is provided at the back of each text.

Icon Explanations

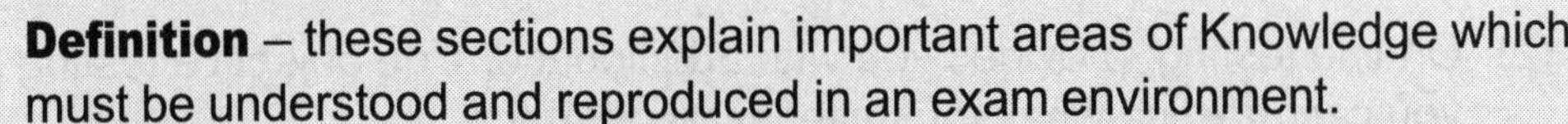

Definition – these sections explain important areas of Knowledge which must be understood and reproduced in an exam environment.

Key Point – identifies topics which are key to success and are often examined.

Expandable Text – within the online version of the work book is a more detailed explanation of key terms, these sections will help to provide a deeper understanding of core areas. Reference to this text is vital when self studying.

Test Your Understanding – following key points and definitions are exercises which give the opportunity to assess the understanding of these core areas. Within the work book the answers to these sections are left blank, explanations to the questions can be found within the online version which can be hidden or shown on screen to enable repetition of activities.

Example – to help develop an understanding of topics and the test your understanding exercises the illustrative examples can be used.

Exclamation Mark – this symbol signifies a topic which can be more difficult to understand, when reviewing these areas care should be taken.

On-line subscribers

Our on-line resources are designed to increase the flexibility of your learning materials and provide you with immediate feedback on how your studies are progressing.

If you are subscribed to our on-line resources you will find:

(1) On-line referenceware: reproduces your Complete or Essential Text on-line, giving you anytime, anywhere access.

(2) On-line testing: provides you with additional on-line objective testing so you can practice what you have learned further.

(3) On-line performance management: immediate access to your on-line testing results. Review your performance by key topics and chart your achievement through the course relative to your peer group.

Ask your local customer services staff if you are not already a subscriber and wish to join.

Syllabus

Paper background

The aim of ACCA Paper F6, **Taxation**, is to develop knowledge and skills relating to the tax system as applicable to individuals, single companies and groups of companies.

Objectives of the syllabus

- Explain the operation and scope of the tax system.
- Explain and compute the income tax liabilities of individuals.
- Explain and compute the corporation tax liabilities of individual companies and groups of companies.
- Explain and compute the chargeable gains arising on companies and individuals.
- Explain and compute the effect of national insurance contributions on employees, employers and the self employed.
- Explain and compute the effects of value added tax on incorporated and unincorporated businesses.
- Identify and explain the obligations of tax payers and/or their agents and the implications of non-compliance.

Core areas of the syllabus

- The UK tax system.
- Income tax liabilities.
- Corporation tax liabilities.
- Capital gains.
- National insurance contributions.
- Value added tax.
- The obligations of tax payers and/or their agents.

Syllabus objectives

We have reproduced the ACCA's syllabus below, showing where the objectives are explored within this book. Within the chapters, we have broken down the extensive information found in the syllabus into easily digestible and relevant sections, called Content Objectives. These correspond to the objectives at the beginning of each chapter.

Syllabus learning objective	Chapter reference
A THE UK TAX SYSTEM	
1 The overall function and purpose of taxation in a modern economy	
(a) Describe the purpose (economic, social, etc) of taxation in a modern economy.[2]	
2 Different types of taxes	
(a) Identify the different types of capital and revenue tax.[1]	1
(b) Explain the difference between direct and indirect taxation.[2]	1
3 Principal sources of revenue law and practice	
(a) Describe the overall structure of the UK tax system. [1]	1
(b) State the different sources of revenue law.[1]	1
(c) Appreciate the interaction of the UK tax system with that of other tax jurisdictions.[2]	1
4 Tax avoidance and tax evasion	
(a) Explain the difference between tax avoidance and tax evasion. [1]	1
(b) Explain the need for an ethical and professional approach.[2]	1

Excluded topics:

Anti-avoidance legislation.

B **INCOME TAX LIABILITIES**

1 The scope of income tax

(a) Explain how the residence of an individual is determined.[1] 2

Excluded topics:

The treatment of a person who comes to the UK to work or a person who leaves the UK to take up employment overseas.

Foreign income, non-residents and double taxation relief.

Income from trusts and settlements.

2 Income from employment

(a) Recognise the factors that determine whether an engagement is treated as employment or self-employment.[2] 4

(b) Recognise the basis of assessment for employment income.[2] 4

(c) Compute the income assessable.[2] 4

(d) Recognise the allowable deductions, including travelling expenses.[2] 4

(e) Discuss the use of the statutory approved mileage allowances.[2] 4

(f) Explain the PAYE system.[2] 13

(g) Identify P11D employees.[2] 4

(h) Compute the amount of benefits assessable.[2] 4

(i) Explain the purpose of a dispensation from HM Revenue & Customs.[2] 4

(j) Explain how charitable giving can be made through a payroll deduction scheme.[1] 4

Excluded topics:

The calculation of a car benefit where emission figures are not available.

Share and share option incentive schemes for employees.

Payments of the termination of employment, and other lump sums received by employees.

3 Income from self employment

(a) Recognise the basis of assessment for self employment income.[2] 5

(b) Describe and apply the badges of trade.[2] 5

(c) Recognise the expenditure that is allowable in calculating the tax-adjusted trading profit.[2] 5

(d) Recognise the relief that can be obtained for pre-trading expenditure.[2] 5

(e) Compute the assessable profits on commencement and on cessation.[2] 8

(f) Change of accounting date

(i) Recognise the factors that will influence the choice of accounting date.[2] 8

(ii) State the conditions that must be met for a change of accounting date to be valid.[1] 8

(iii) Compute the assessable profits on a change of accounting date.[2] 8

(g) Capital allowances

(i) Define plant and machinery for capital allowances purposes.[1] 6

(ii) Compute writing down allowances, and the annual investment allowance.[2] 6

(iii) Compute capital allowances for motor cars.[2] 6

(iv) Compute balancing allowances and balancing charges.[2] 6

(v) Recognise the treatment of short-life assets.[2] 6

(vi) Explain the treatment of assets included in the special rate pool.[2] 6

(vii) Define an industrial building for industrial buildings allowance purposes.[1] 7

(viii) Compute industrial buildings allowance for new buildings.[2] 7

(h) Relief for trading losses

(i) Understand how trading losses can be carried forward.[2] 10

(ii) Explain how trading losses can be carried forward following the incorporation of a business.[2] 10

(iii) Understand how trading losses can be claimed against total income and chargeable gains. [2] 10

(iv) Explain and compute the relief for trading losses in the early years of a trade.[1] 10

(v) Explain and compute terminal loss relief.[1] 10

(i) Partnerships and limited liability partnerships

(i) Explain how a partnership is assessed to tax.[2] 9

(ii) Compute the assessable profits for each partner following a change in the profit-sharing ratio. [2] 9

(iii) Compute the assessable profits for each partner following a change in the membership of the partnership.[2] 9

(iv) Describe the alternative loss relief claims that are available to partners.[1] 10

(v) Explain the loss relief restriction that applies to the partners of a limited liability partnership.[1] 10

Excluded topics:

The 100% allowance for expenditure on renovating business premises in disadvantaged areas, flats above shops and water technologies.

Capital allowances for agricultural buildings, patents, scientific research and know-how.

Enterprise zones.

Apportionment in order to determine the rate of writing-down allowance where a period of account spans 6 April 2008 (1 April 2008 for companies).

Apportionment in order to determine the amount of annual investment allowance where a period of account spans 6 April 2008 (1 April 2008 for companies).

Apportionment in order to determine the rate of industrial building writing down allowance where a limited company's chargeable period falls into two financial years.

The calculation of industrial buildings allowance on the purchase of a secondhand industrial building.

Investment income of a partnership.

The allocation of notional profits and losses for a partnership.

Farmers averaging of profits.

The averaging of profits for authors and creative artists.

Loss relief for shares in unquoted trading companies.

4 Property and investment income

(a) Compute property business profits.[2] 3

(b) Explain the treatment of furnished holiday lettings.[1] 3

(c) Describe rent-a-room relief. [1] 3

(d) Compute the amount assessable when a premium is received for the grant of a short lease.[2] 3

(e) Understand how relief for a property business loss is given. [2] 3

(f) Compute the tax payable on savings income.[2] 2 & 3

(g) Compute the tax payable on dividend income.[2] 2 & 3

(h) Explain the treatment of individual savings accounts (ISAs) and other tax exempt investments.[1] 3

5 The comprehensive computation of taxable income and income tax liability

(a) Prepare a basic income tax computation involving different types of income.[2] 2

(b) Calculate the amount of personal allowance available to people aged 65 and above. [2] 2

(c) Compute the amount of income tax payable.[2] 2

(d) Explain the treatment of interest paid for a qualifying purpose.[2] 2

(e) Explain the treatment of gift aid donations.[1] 2

(f) Explain the treatment of property owned jointly by a married couple, or by a couple in a civil partnership.[1] 2

Excluded topics:

The blind person's allowance and the married couple's allowance.
Tax credits.
Maintenance payments.
The income of minor children.

6 The use of exemptions and reliefs in deferring and minimising income tax liabilities

(a) Explain and compute the relief given for contributions to personal pension schemes, using the rules applicable from 6 April 2006.[2] 11

(b) Describe the relief given for contributions to occupational pension schemes, using the rules applicable from 6 April 2006.[1] 11

(c) Explain how a married couple or couple in a civil partnership can minimise their tax liabilities.[2] 3

Excluded topics:

The conditions that must be met in order for a pension scheme to obtain approval from HM Revenue & Customs.
The enterprise investment scheme.
Venture capital trusts.

C **CORPORATION TAX LIABILITIES**

1 The scope of corporation tax

(a) Define the terms 'period of account', 'accounting period', and 'financial year'.[1] 18

(b) Recognise when an accounting period starts and when an accounting period finishes.[1] 18

(c) Explain how the residence of a company is determined.[2] 18

Excluded topics:

Investment companies.
Close companies.
Companies in receivership or liquidation.
Reorganisations.
The purchase by a company of its own shares.
Personal service companies.

2 Profits chargeable to corporation tax

(a) Recognise the expenditure that is allowable in calculating the tax-adjusted trading profit.[2] 19

(b) Explain how relief can be obtained for pre-trading expenditure.[1] 19

(c) Compute capital allowances (as for income tax).[2] 19

(d) Compute property business profits.[2] 19

(e) Explain the treatment of interest paid and received under the loan relationship rules.[1] 19

(f) Explain the treatment of gift aid donations.[2] 19

(g) Understand how trading losses can be carried forward.[2] 21

(h) Understand how trading losses can be claimed against income of the current or previous accounting periods.[2] 21

(i) Recognise the factors that will influence the choice of loss relief claim.[2] 21

(j) Explain how relief for a property business loss is given.[1] 21

(k) Compute profits chargeable to corporation tax.[2] 18 & 19

Excluded topics:

Research and development expenditure.
Non-trading deficits on loan relationships.
Relief for intangible assets.

3 The comprehensive computation of corporation tax liability

(a) Compute the corporation tax liability and apply marginal relief.[2] 18

(b) Explain the implications of receiving franked investment income.[2] 18

(c) Explain how exemptions and reliefs can defer or minimise corporation tax liabilities.[2] 20-23

Excluded topics:

The corporate venturing scheme.

4 The effect of a group corporate structure for corporation tax purposes

(a) Define an associated company and recognise the effect of being an associated company for corporation tax purposes. [2] 22

(b) Define a 75% group, and recognise the reliefs that are available to members of such a group.[2] 22

(c) Define a 75% capital gains group, and recognise the reliefs that are available to members of such a group.[2] 22

(d) Compare the tax treatment of an overseas branch to an overseas subsidiary.[2]

(e) Calculate double taxation relief for withholding tax.[2] 23

(f) Explain the basic principles of the transfer pricing rules.[2] 23

Excluded topics:

Relief for trading losses incurred by an overseas subsidiary.
Consortia.
Pre-entry gains and losses.
The anti-avoidance provisions where arrangements exist for a company to leave a group.
The tax charge that applies where a company leaves a group within six years of receiving an asset by way of a no gain/no loss transfer.
Controlled foreign companies.
Foreign companies trading in the UK.
Expense relief in respect of overseas tax.
Double taxation relief for underlying tax.
The carry back and carry forward of unrelieved foreign tax, or any aspect of the on-shore pooling rules.
Transfer pricing transactions not involving an overseas company.

5 The use of exemptions and reliefs in deferring and minimising corporation tax liabilities. (The use of such exemptions and reliefs is implicit within all of the above sections 1 to 4 of part C of the syllabus, concerning corporation tax.)

D **CHARGEABLE GAINS**

1 The scope of the taxation of capital gains

(a)	Describe the scope of capital gains tax.[2]	14
(b)	Explain how the residence and ordinary residence of an individual is determined.[2]	14
(c)	List those assets which are exempt.[1]	14

Excluded topics:

Assets situated overseas and double taxation relief.
Partnership capital gains.

2 The basic principles of computing gains and losses.

(a)	Compute capital gains for both individuals and companies.[2]	14 & 20
(b)	Calculate the indexation allowance available to companies.[2]	14 & 20
(c)	Explain the treatment of capital losses for both individuals and companies.[1]	14 & 20
(d)	Explain the treatment of transfers between a husband and wife or between a couple in a civil partnership.[2]	15
(e)	Compute the amount of allowable expenditure for a part disposal.[2]	15
(f)	Explain the treatment where an asset is damaged, lost or destroyed, and the implications of receiving insurance proceeds and reinvesting such proceeds.[2]	15

Excluded topics:

The capital gains tax rules that applied up to 5 April 2008.
Small part disposals of land.
Losses in the year of death.
Relief for losses incurred on loans made to traders.
Negligible value claims.

3	**Gains and losses on the disposal of movable and immovable property**	
	(a) Identify when chattels and wasting assets are exempt. [1]	15
	(b) Compute the chargeable gain when a chattel is disposed of. [2]	15
	(c) Calculate the chargeable gain when a wasting asset is disposed of.[2]	15
	(d) Compute the exemption when a principal private residence is disposed of.[2]	17
	(e) Calculate the chargeable gain when a principal private residence has been used for business purposes.[2]	17
	(f) Identify the amount of letting relief available when a principal private residence has been let out.[2]	17
	Excluded topics: The disposal of leases and the creation of sub-leases.	
4	**Gains and losses on the disposal of shares and securities**	
	(a) Calculate the value of quoted shares where they are disposed of by way of a gift.[2]	16
	(b) Explain and apply the identification rules as they apply to individuals and to companies, including the same day, nine day,and thirty day matching rules.[2]	16 & 20
	(c) Explain the pooling provisions.[2]	16 & 20
	(d) Explain the treatment of bonus issues, rights issues, takeovers and reorganisations.[2]	16 & 20
	(e) Explain the exemption available for gilt-edged securities and qualifying corporate bonds [1]	16
	Excluded topics: A detailed question on the pooling positions for shares as they apply to limited companies The small part disposal rules applicable to rights issues. Substantial shareholdings. Gilt-edged securities and qualifying corporate bonds other than the fact that they are exempt.	
5	**The computation of the capital gains tax payable by individuals**	
	(a) Compute the amount of capital gains tax payable.[2]	14

6 The use of exemptions and reliefs in deferring and minimising tax liabilities arising on the disposal of capital assets

(a) Explain and apply entrepreneurs' relief as it applies to individuals.[2] 17

(b) Explain and apply rollover relief as it applies to individuals and companies.[2] 17 & 20

(c) Explain and apply holdover relief for the gift of business assets.[2] 17

(d) Explain and apply the incorporation relief that is available upon the transfer of a business to a company.[2] 17

Excluded topics:
Reinvestment relief.
Entrepreneurs' relief for associated disposals.

E NATIONAL INSURANCE CONTRIBUTIONS

1 The scope of national insurance

(a) Describe the scope of national insurance.[1] 12

2 Class 1 and Class 1A contributions for employed persons

(a) Compute Class 1 NIC.[2] 12

(b) Compute Class 1A NIC.[2] 12

Excluded topics:
The calculation of directors' national insurance on a month-by-month basis.
Contracted out contributions.

3 Class 2 and Class 4 contributions for self-employed persons

(a) Compute Class 2 NIC.[2] 12

(b) Compute Class 4 NIC.[2] 12

Excluded topics:
The offset of trading losses against non-trading income.

F	**VALUE ADDED TAX**		
1	The scope of value added tax (VAT)		
	(a)	Describe the scope of VAT.[2]	25
	(b)	List the principal zero-rated and exempt supplies.[2]	25
2	The VAT registration requirements		
	(a)	Recognise the circumstances in which a person must register for VAT.[2]	25
	(b)	Explain the advantages of voluntary VAT registration.[2]	25
	(c)	Explain the circumstances in which pre-registration input VAT can be recovered.[2]	25
	(d)	Explain how and when a person can deregister for VAT.[1]	
	Excluded topics: Group registration.		
3	The computation of VAT liabilities		
	(a)	Explain how VAT is accounted for and administered.[2]	26
	(b)	Recognise the tax point when goods or services are supplied. [2]	25
	(c)	List the information that must be given on a VAT invoice. [1]	26
	(d)	Explain and apply the principles regarding the valuation of supplies.[2]	25
	(e)	Recognise the circumstances in which input VAT is non-deductible.[2]	25
	(f)	Compute the relief that is available for impairment losses on trade debts.[2]	25
	(g)	Explain the circumstances in which the default surcharge, and default interest will be applied.[1]	26
	Excluded topics: Imports, exports and trading within the European Community. Partial exemption. In respect of property and land: leases, do-it-yourself builders, and a landlord's option to tax. Penalties apart from those listed here (repeated misdeclarations are excluded).		

4 The effect of special schemes

(a) Describe the cash accounting scheme, and recognise when it will be advantageous to use the scheme.[2] — 26

(b) Describe the annual accounting scheme, and recognise when it will be advantageous to use the scheme.[2] — 26

(c) Describe the flat rate scheme, and recognise when it will be advantageous to use the scheme.[2] — 26

Excluded topics:

The second-hand goods scheme.
The capital goods scheme.
The special schemes for retailers.

G THE OBLIGATIONS OF TAX PAYERS AND/OR THEIR AGENTS

1 The systems for self-assessment and the making of returns

(a) Explain and apply the features of the self-assessment system as it applies to individuals.[2] — 13

(b) Explain and apply the features of the self-assessment system as it applies to companies.[2] — 24

2 The time limits for the submission of information, claims and payment of tax, including payments on account

(a) Recognise the time limits that apply to the filing of returns and the making of claims.[2] — 13 & 24

(b) Recognise the due dates for the payment of tax under the self-assessment system.[2] — 13

(c) Compute payments on account and balancing payments/repayments for individuals.[2] — 13

(d) Explain how large companies are required to account for corporation tax on a quarterly basis.[2] — 24

(e) List the information and records that taxpayers need to retain for tax purposes.[1] — 13 & 24

Excluded topics:

The payment of CGT by annual instalments.

3 The procedures relating to enquiries, appeals and disputes

(a)	Explain the circumstances in which HM Revenue & Customs can enquire into a self-assessment tax return.[2]	13 & 24
(b)	Explain the procedures for dealing with appeals and disputes.[1]	13 & 24

4 Penalties for non-compliance

(a)	Calculate interest on overdue tax. [2]	13 & 24
(b)	State the penalties that can be charged.[2]	13 & 24

The superscript numbers in square brackets indicate the intellectual depth at which the subject area could be assessed within the examination.

Level 1 (knowledge and comprehension) broadly equates with the Knowledge module.

Level 2 (application and analysis) with the Skills module.

Level 3 (synthesis and evaluation) to the Professional level.

However, lower level skills can continue to be assessed as you progress through each module and level.

The Examination

Examination format

The paper will be predominantly computational and will have five questions, all of which will be compulsory.

- Questions 1 and 2 will be for a total of 55 marks with one of the questions being for 30 marks and the other for 25 marks.

  Question 1 will focus on income tax and question 2 will focus on corporation tax.

- Question 3 will be for 20 marks, and will focus on chargeable gains (either personal or corporate).
- Questions 4 and 5 will be on any area of the syllabus and will be for 15 marks and 10 marks respectively.

There will always be at a minimum of 10 marks on value added tax on any paper. These marks will normally be included within question 1 or 2 although there might be a separate question on value added tax.

National insurance contributions will not be examined as a separate question, but may be examined in any question involving income tax or corporation tax.

Groups and overseas aspects of corporation tax will only be examined in Question 2, and will account for no more than one third of the marks available for that question.

Chargeable gains can be examined in questions other than Question 3, for example as part of a corporation tax or business income tax scenario.

Any of the five questions might include the consideration of issues relating to the minimisation or deferral of tax liabilities.

Total marks: 100

Total time allowed: 3 hours plus 15 minutes reading and planning time.

Paper-based examination tips

Spend the reading time of the examination reading the paper carefully.

Divide the time you spend on questions in proportion to the marks on offer. One suggestion **for this examination** is to allocate 1.8 minutes to each mark available, so a 10-mark question should be completed in approximately 18 minutes.

Unless you know exactly how to answer the question, spend some time planning your answer. Stick to the question and tailor your answer to what you are asked. Pay particular attention to the verbs in the question.

Spend the last five minutes reading through your answers and making any additions or corrections.

If you **get completely stuck** with a question, leave space in your answer book and return to it later.

If you do not understand what a question is asking, state your assumptions. Even if you do not answer in precisely the way the examiner hoped, you should be given some credit, if your assumptions are reasonable.

You should do everything you can to make things easy for the marker. The marker will find it easier to identify the points you have made if your answers are legible.

Computations: It is essential to include all your workings in your answers. Many computational questions require the use of a standard format. Be sure you know these formats thoroughly before the exam and use the layouts that you see in the answers given in this book and in model answers.

Reports, memos and other documents: some questions ask you to present your answer in the form of a report or a memo or other document. So use the correct format – there are easy marks to gain here.

Study skills and revision guidance

This section aims to give guidance on how to study for your ACCA exams and to give ideas on how to improve your existing study techniques.

Preparing to study

Set your objectives

Before starting to study decide what you want to achieve – the type of pass you wish to obtain. This will decide the level of commitment and time you need to dedicate to your studies.

Devise a study plan

Determine which times of the week you will study.

Split these times into sessions of at least one hour for study of new material. Any shorter periods could be used for revision or practice.

Put the times you plan to study onto a study plan for the weeks from now until the exam and set yourself targets for each period of study - in your sessions make sure you cover the course, course assignments and revision.

If you are studying for more than one paper at a time, try to vary your subjects as this can help you to keep interested and see subjects as part of wider knowledge.

When working through your course, compare your progress with your plan and, if necessary, re-plan your work (perhaps including extra sessions) or, if you are ahead, do some extra revision/practice questions.

Effective studying

Active reading

You are not expected to learn the text by rote, rather, you must understand what you are reading and be able to use it to pass the exam and develop good practice. A good technique to use is SQ3Rs – Survey, Question, Read, Recall, Review:

(1) **Survey the chapter** – look at the headings and read the introduction, summary and objectives, so as to get an overview of what the chapter deals with.

(2) **Question** – whilst undertaking the survey, ask yourself the questions that you hope the chapter will answer for you.

(3) **Read** through the chapter thoroughly, answering the questions and making sure you can meet the objectives. Attempt the exercises and activities in the text, and work through all the examples.

(4) **Recall** – at the end of each section and at the end of the chapter, try to recall the main ideas of the section/chapter without referring to the text. This is best done after a short break of a couple of minutes after the reading stage.

(5) **Review** – check that your recall notes are correct.

You may also find it helpful to re-read the chapter to try to see the topic(s) it deals with as a whole.

Note-taking

Taking notes is a useful way of learning, but do not simply copy out the text. The notes must:

- be in your own words
- be concise
- cover the key points
- be well-organised
- be modified as you study further chapters in this text or in related ones.

Trying to summarise a chapter without referring to the text can be a useful way of determining which areas you know and which you don't.

Three ways of taking notes:

(1) **Summarise the key points of a chapter.**

(2) **Make linear notes** – a list of headings, divided up with subheadings listing the key points. If you use linear notes, you can use different colours to highlight key points and keep topic areas together. Use plenty of space to make your notes easy to use.

(3) **Try a diagrammatic form** – the most common of which is a mind-map. To make a mind-map, put the main heading in the centre of the paper and put a circle around it. Then draw short lines radiating from this to the main sub-headings, which again have circles around them. Then continue the process from the sub-headings to sub-sub-headings, advantages, disadvantages, etc.

Highlighting and underlining

You may find it useful to underline or highlight key points in your study text - but do be selective. You may also wish to make notes in the margins.

Revision

The best approach to revision is to revise the course as you work through it. Also try to leave four to six weeks before the exam for final revision. Make sure you cover the whole syllabus and pay special attention to those areas where your knowledge is weak. Here are some recommendations:

Read through the text and your notes again and condense your notes into key phrases. It may help to put key revision points onto index cards to look at when you have a few minutes to spare.

Review any assignments you have completed and look at where you lost marks – put more work into those areas where you were weak.

Practise exam standard questions under timed conditions. If you are short of time, list the points that you would cover in your answer and then read the model answer, but do try to complete at least a few questions under exam conditions.

Also practise producing answer plans and comparing them to the model answer.

If you are stuck on a topic find somebody (a tutor) to explain it to you.

Read good newspapers and professional journals, especially ACCA's Student Accountant – this can give you an advantage in the exam.

Ensure you **know the structure of the exam** – how many questions and of what type you will be expected to answer. During your revision attempt all the different styles of questions you may be asked.

Further reading

You can find further reading and technical articles under the student section of ACCA's website.

RATES AND ALLOWANCES

Supplementary instructions given in the examination

1. **Calculations and workings need only be made to the nearest £.**
2. **All apportionments should be made to the nearest month.**
3. **All workings should be shown.**

The following tax rates and allowances are to be used

INCOME TAX

		%
Basic rate	£1 – £37,400	20
Higher rate	£37,401 and above	40

A starting rate of 10% applies to savings income where it falls within the first £2,440 of taxable income.

Personal allowances

Personal allowance	Standard	£6,475
Personal allowance	65 – 74	£9,490
Personal allowance	75 and over	£9,640
Income limit for age related allowances		£22,900

Car benefit percentage

The base level of CO_2 emission is 135 grams per kilometre.
A lower rate of 10% applies to cars with CO_2 emissions of 120 grams per kilometre or less.

Car fuel benefit

The base level figure for calculating car fuel benefit is £16,900.

Pension scheme limits

Annual allowance £245,000

The maximum contribution that can qualify for tax relief without any earnings is £3,600.

Authorised mileage rates: cars

Up to 10,000 miles	40p
Over 10,000 miles	25p

Capital allowances

Plant and machinery		%
Writing down allowance	– General rate	20
	– Special rate pool	10
First year allowance	– Low emission cars (CO_2 emissions of less than 110 grams per kilometre)	100
Annual investment allowance for the first £50,000 of expenditure		100

Motor cars		
CO_2 emissions up to 110 gm/km	FYA	100
CO_2 emissions between 111 and 160 gm/km	WDA	20
CO_2 emissions above 160 gm/km	WDA	10

Industrial buildings	
Writing down allowance	2

CORPORATION TAX

Financial Year	*2007*	*2008*	*2009*
Small companies rate	20%	21%	21%
Full rate	30%	28%	28%
Lower limit	£300,000	£300,000	£300,000
Upper limit	£1,500,000	£1,500,000	£1,500,000
Marginal relief fraction	1/40	7/400	7,400

Marginal relief

(M – P) × I/P × Marginal relief fraction

VALUE ADDED TAX

Standard rate	Up to 31 December 2009	15.0%
	From 1 January 2010	17.5%
Registration limit		£68,000
Deregistration limit		£66,000

CAPITAL GAINS TAX

Rate of tax		18%
Annual exemption		£10,100
Entrepreneurs' relief	– Lifetime limit	£1,000,000
	– Relief factor	4/9ths

NATIONAL INSURANCE CONTRIBUTIONS
(not contracted out rates)

		%
Class 1 Employee	£1 – £5,715 per year	Nil
	£5,716 – £43,875 per year	11.0
	£43,876 and above	1.0
Class 1 Employer	£1 – £5,715 per year	Nil
	£5,876 and above per year	12.8
Class 1A		12.8
Self employed		
Class 2	£2.40 per week	
Class 4	£1 – £5,715 per year	Nil
	£5,716 – £43,875 per year	8.0
	£43,876 and above per year	1.0

RATES OF INTEREST

Official rate of interest:	4.75%
Interest on underpaid tax	2.50% (assumed)
interest on overpaid tax	Nil% (assumed)

TIME LIMITS FOR ELECTIONS AND CLAIMS

The following tables summarise the key time limits for elections and claims. These tables are not given in the examination.

Note that the section numbers are given for reference purposes only; students are not required to know or quote section numbers in the examination.

Income tax

Election / claim	Time limit	For 2009/10
Agree the amount of trading losses to carry forward (s83 ITA 2007)	4 years from the end of the tax year in which the loss arose	5 April 2014
Current and prior year set-off of trading losses against total income and chargeable gains (s64 ITA 2007) (s261B TCGA 1992)	12 months from 31 January following the end of the tax year in which the loss arose	31 January 2012
Three year carry back of trading losses in the opening years (s72 ITA 2007)	12 months from 31 January following the end of the tax year in which the loss arose	31 January 2012
Three year carry back of terminal trading losses in the closing years (s89 ITA 2007)	4 years from the end of the last tax year of trading	5 April 2014

National Insurance Contributions

Election / claim	Time limit	For 2009/10
Class 1 primary and secondary – pay days	14 days after the end of each tax month under PAYE system	19th of each month
Class 1 A NIC – pay day	19 July following end of tax year	19 July 2010
Class 2 NICs – pay days	Monthly by direct debit or quarterly invoicing	
Class 4 NICs – pay days	Paid under self assessment with income tax	

Capital gains tax

Election / claim	Time limit	For 2009/10
Replacement of business asset relief for individuals (Rollover relief)	4 years from the end of the tax year in which the disposal occurred	5 April 2014
Holdover relief of gain on the gift of a business asset (Gift relief)	4 years from the end of the tax year in which the disposal occurred	5 April 2014
Entrepreneurs' relief	12 months from 31 January following the end of the tax year in which the disposal occurred	31 January 2012
Determination of principal private residence	2 years from the acquisition of the second property	

Self assessment – individuals

Election / claim	Time limit	For 2009/10
Self assessment	1st instalment: 31 January in the tax year	31 January 2010
Pay days for income tax and Class 4 NIC	2nd instalment: 31 July following the end of the tax year	31 July 2010
	Balancing payment: 31 January following the end of the tax year	31 January 2011
Self assessment Pay day for CGT	31 January following the end of the tax year	31 January 2011
Self assessment Filing dates: If return issued by 31 October in the tax year	Paper return: 31 October following end of tax year	31 October 2010
	Electronic return: 31 January following end of tax year	31 January 2011

Filing dates: If return issued after 31 October in the tax year	3 months from the date of issue of the return	
Retention of records Business records Personal records	 5 years from 31 January following the end of the tax year 12 months from 31 January following the end of the tax year	 31 January 2016 31 January 2012
HMRC right of repair (i.e. to correct mistakes)	9 months from the date the return was filed	
Taxpayers right to amend a return	12 months from 31 January following the end of the tax year	31 January 2012
Taxpayers error or mistake claim	4 years from the end of the tax year	5 April 2014
HMRC can open an enquiry	12 months from the actual submission of the return	
HMRC can raise a discovery assessment		
No careless or deliberate behaviour	4 years from the end of the tax year	5 April 2014
Tax lost due to careless behaviour	6 years from the end of the tax year	5 April 2016
Tax lost due to deliberate behaviour	20 years from the end of the tax year	5 April 2030
Taxpayers right of appeal against an assessment	30 days from the assessment – appeal in writing	

Corporation tax

Election / claim	**Time limit**
Replacement of business asset relief for companies (Rollover relief)	4 years from the end of the chargeable accounting period in which the disposal occurred
Agree the amount of trading losses to carry forward (s393(1) ICTA 1988)	4 years from the end of the chargeable accounting period in which the loss arose

Current year set-off of trading losses against total profits (income and gains) and 12 month carry back of trading losses against total profits (income and gains) (s393(A) ICTA 1988)	2 years from the end of the chargeable accounting period in which the loss arose
Election for transfer of capital gains and losses to other group companies	2 years from the end of the chargeable accounting period in which the disposal occurred by the company actually making the disposal

Self assessment – companies

Election / claim	**Time limit**
Self assessment Pay day for small and medium companies	9 months and one day after the end of the chargeable accounting period
Self assessment Pay day for large companies	Instalments due on 14th day of: – Seventh – Tenth – Thirteenth, and – Sixteenth month after the start of the chargeable accounting period
Self assessment Filing dates	Later of: – 12 months from the end of the chargeable accounting period – 3 months form the issue of a notice to deliver a corporation tax return
Companies error or mistake claim	4 years from the end of the chargeable accounting period
HMRC can open an enquiry	12 months from the actual submission of the return
Retention of records	6 years from the end of the chargeable accounting period

Value added tax

Election / claim	Time limit
Compulsory registration – Historic test Notify HMRC Charge VAT – Future test Notify HMRC Charge VAT	 – 30 days from end of the month in which the threshold was exceeded – Beginning of the month following the month in which the threshold was exceeded – 30 days from the date it is anticipated that the threshold will be exceeded – the date it is anticipated that the threshold will be exceeded (i.e. the beginning of the 30 day period)
Compulsory deregistration	30 days from cessation
Filing of VAT return and payment of VAT	End of month following the return period

hapter

1

The UK tax system

Chapter learning objectives

Upon completion of this chapter you will be able to:

- describe the purpose (economic, social etc.) of taxation in a modern economy
- identify the different types of capital and revenue tax
- explain the difference between direct and indirect taxation
- describe the overall structure of the UK tax system
- explain the different sources of tax law
- appreciate the interaction of the UK tax system with overseas tax systems
- define the terms tax avoidance and tax evasion and recognise the difference between them
- recognise the purpose of the professional and ethical framework in which the accountant operates.

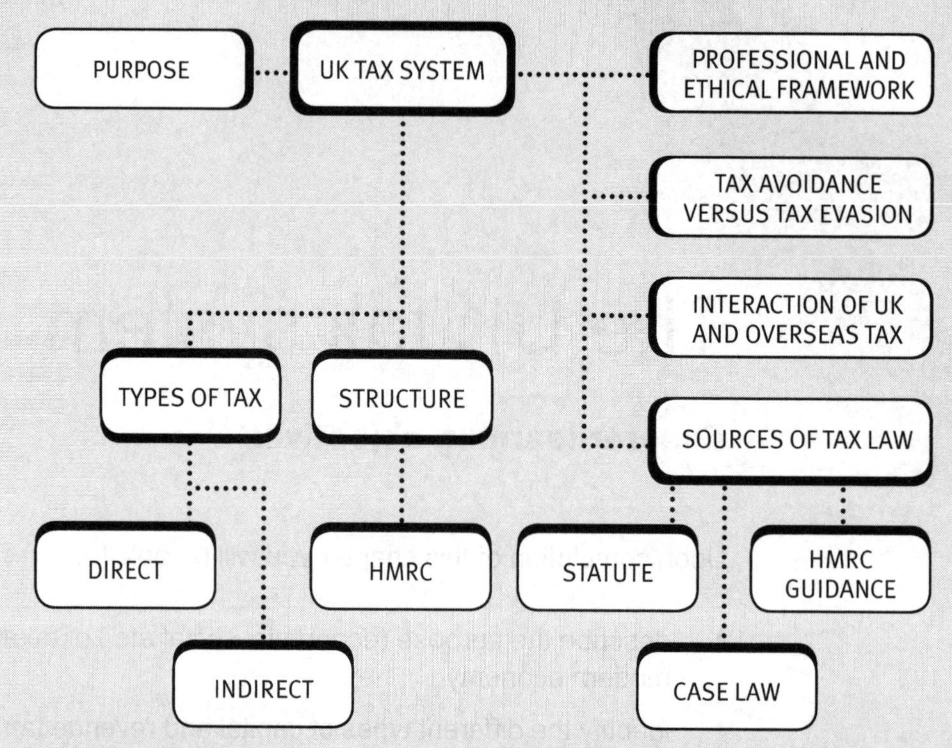

Purpose of taxation

Economic

- The system of taxation and spending by government impacts on the economy of a country as a whole.
- Taxation polices have been used to influence many economic factors such as inflation, employment levels, imports/exports.
- It is also used to direct the economic behaviour of business and individuals.
  - The current UK tax system encourages:

    (1) individual saving habits by offering tax incentives on savings accounts such as Individual Savings Accounts (ISAs)

    (2) charitable donations by offering tax relief through the Gift Aid scheme

    (3) entrepreneurs and investors by offering tax relief for investments in specified schemes.

  - The current UK tax system discourages:

    (1) motoring by imposing fuel duties

    (2) smoking and alcoholic drinks by imposing significant taxes on these items

    (3) environmental pollution by imposing a variety of taxes such as landfill tax, climate change levy and linking CO_2 emissions to the taxation of company cars.

- As government objectives change, taxation policies are altered accordingly.

Social justice

The type of taxation structure imposed has a direct impact on the accumulation and redistribution of wealth within a country.

The main taxation principles are listed below. The arguments for and against each of these are often the matter of significant political debate.

Progressive taxation

- As income rises the proportion of taxation raised also rises.

  For example: 10% on £10,000 of income and 30% on £30,000 of income. Income tax is an example of a progressive tax.

Regressive taxation

- As income rises the proportion of taxation paid falls.

  For example, the tax on a litre of petrol is the same regardless of the level of income of the purchaser.

  This is a regressive tax as it represents a greater proportion of income for a lower income earner than a high income earner.

Proportional taxation

- As income rises the proportion of tax remains constant.

  For example, 10% of all earnings regardless of the level.

Ad Valorem principle

- A tax calculated as a percentage of the value of the item.

  For example, 15% VAT on most goods sold in the UK.

1 Types of tax

The UK tax system, administered by HM Revenue and Customs (HMRC), comprises a number of different taxes. The following taxes are examinable.

Income tax

- Payable by individuals on their earnings (e.g. self-employment and employment) and investment income.

National insurance contributions (NICs)

- Payable by individuals who are either employed or self-employed.
- Also payable by businesses (e.g. sole trader, company) in relation to their employees.

Capital gains tax

- Payable by individuals on the disposal of capital assets.
- Capital assets include land, buildings and shares, but could include smaller items, such as antiques.

Corporation tax

- Payable by companies on all their income and gains.

Value added tax (VAT)

- Payable on the supply of goods and services to the final consumer.

2 Direct versus indirect taxation

Direct taxation

- The taxpayer pays direct taxes directly to the Government.
- They are based on income/profits and the more that is earned/received, the more tax is paid.
- Examples of direct taxes include income tax, corporation tax, capital gains tax.

Indirect taxation

- An indirect tax is collected from the taxpayer via an intermediary such as a retail shop.
- The intermediary then pays over the tax collected to the Government.
- An example of indirect taxation is VAT. The consumer pays VAT to the supplier, who then pays it to the Government.

3 Structure of the UK tax system

HM Revenue and Customs

- HM Revenue and Customs is a single body that controls and administers all areas of UK tax law.

Commissioners

- Heading up HMRC are the Commissioners whose main duties are:
  - to implement statute law
  - to oversee the process of UK tax administration.
- To enable the effective running of HMRC across the country, the main body is divided into:
  - District offices
  - Accounting and payments offices.

District offices

- The Commissioners appoint Officers of HM Revenue and Customs to implement the day-to-day work of HMRC.
- There are several hundred district offices covering all areas of the UK.

Accounts and payments offices

- Accounts and payments offices concentrate on the collection and payment of tax liabilities.

4 Sources of tax law

The basic rules of the UK tax system have been established from the following main sources:

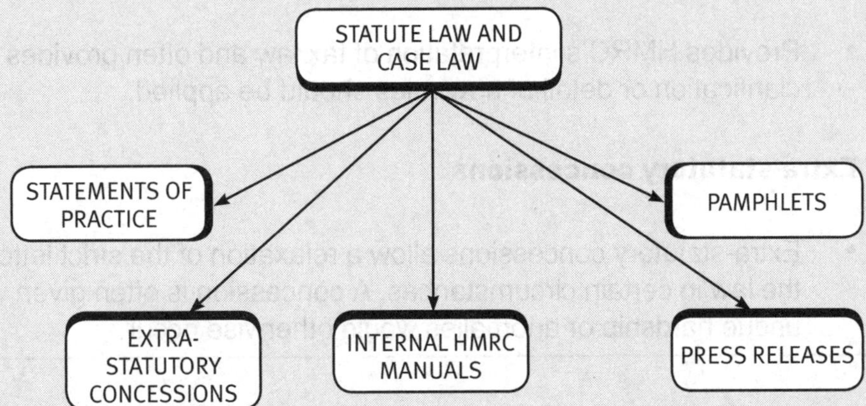

Sources of tax law

Tax legislation/statutes

- Tax legislation/statutes are law and therefore adherence is mandatory.
- Tax legislation is updated each year by the annual Finance Act that follows from the proposals made by the Chancellor of the Exchequer in his annual Budget statement.
- Statutory instruments are issued where detailed notes are required on an area of tax legislation.

Case law

- Case law refers to the decisions made in tax cases brought before the courts.
- Often the case challenges current tax legislation or argues a certain interpretation of the tax law should be applied.
- These rulings are binding and therefore provide guidance on the interpretation of tax legislation.

HMRC guidance

- As the tax legislation can be complex to understand and open to misinterpretation, further guidance is issued by HMRC in order to:
  - explain how to implement the law
  - give their interpretation of the law.
- The main types of guidance are listed below.

Statements of Practice

- Provides HMRC's interpretation of tax law and often provides clarification or detail of how rules should be applied.

Extra-statutory concessions

- Extra-statutory concessions allow a relaxation of the strict letter of the law in certain circumstances. A concession is often given where undue hardship or anomalies would otherwise occur.

Internal guidance manuals

- HMRC's own manuals, produced for their staff, giving guidance on interpretation of the law, are also available to the general public.

Press releases

- Provide details of a specific tax issue that has arisen in the year.

Pamphlets

- Aimed at the general public and provide explanations of various tax issues in non-technical language.

Interaction of UK and overseas tax systems

Due to the differing tax systems in overseas countries, it is possible that an individual or company could be taxed under two different systems on the same income.

Double taxation relief

Agreements between most countries have been established to decide how a particular individual/company should be taxed.

- These are known as bilateral double taxation treaties.
- Such treaties take precedence over domestic UK tax law and either:
  - exempt certain overseas income from tax in the UK, or
  - provide relief where tax is suffered in two countries on the same income.
- Where no such treaty exists, the UK system still allows for relief to be given where double tax is paid.

Further detail of the operation of the double taxation relief system for companies is found in Chapter 23. Double taxation relief for individuals is not examinable.

Influence of the European Union (EU)

- One of the aims of the EU is to remove barriers and distortions due to different economic and political policies imposed in different member states.
- Although EU members do not have to align their tax systems, members can agree to jointly enact specific laws, known as Directives.
- To date the most important of these has been agreements regarding VAT. EU members have aligned their VAT **policies** according to European legislation. They have not however aligned their **rates** of VAT.
- Many cases have been brought before the European Court of Justice regarding the discrimination of non-tax residents by the UK tax system, some of which have resulted in changes to UK tax law.

5 Tax avoidance versus tax evasion

The difference between tax avoidance and evasion is important due to the legal implications.

Tax evasion

- The term tax evasion summarises any action taken to evade taxes by illegal means.
- The main forms of tax evasion are:
  - suppressing information, e.g. failing to declare taxable income to HMRC
  - submitting false information, e.g. claiming expenses that have not been incurred.
- Tax evasion is an illegal activity and carries a risk of criminal prosecution (fines and/or imprisonment).

Tax avoidance

- Tax avoidance is using the taxation regime to one's own advantage by arranging your affairs to minimise your tax liability.
- It is legal and does not entail misleading HMRC, e.g. making tax savings by investing in ISAs.
- The term is also used to describe tax schemes that utilise loopholes in the tax legislation.
- HMRC have now introduced disclosure obligations regarding tax schemes that involve declaring the details of such schemes to HMRC.

Test your understanding 1

State which of the following is tax evasion:

- Selling a capital asset in May 2009 instead of March 2009 to ensure that the gain is taxed in a later tax year.
- Altering a bill of £700 to read £7,000 on your tax return.
- Moving taxable interest into a tax free ISA account.

6 Professional and ethical guidance

The ACCA 'Professional Code of Ethics and Conduct' has already been covered in your earlier studies. A reminder of the key points is given in expandable text.

Fundamental principles

The ACCA expects its members to:

- adopt an ethical approach to work, employers and clients
- acknowledge your professional duty to society as a whole
- maintain an objective outlook, and
- provide professional, high standards of service, conduct and performance at all times.

To meet these expectations the ACCA 'Code of Ethics and Conduct' sets out five fundamental principles, which members should abide by:

- Integrity
- Objectivity
- Professional competence and due care
- Confidentiality
- Professional behaviour.

Integrity

- Members should act in a straightforward and honest manner in all professional and business judgements.

Objectivity

- Members should not allow bias, conflicts of interest or the influence of others to override objectivity.

Professional competence and due care

- Members have an ongoing duty to maintain professional knowledge and skills to ensure that a client/employer receives competent, professional service based on current developments.
- Members should be diligent and act in accordance with applicable technical and professional standards when providing professional services.

Confidentiality

- Members should respect the confidentiality of information acquired as a result of professional and business relationships and should not disclose any such information to third parties unless:
  - they have proper and specific authority, or
  - there is a legal or professional right or duty to disclose, e.g. Money laundering.
- Confidential information acquired as a result of professional and business relationships, should not be used for the personal advantage of members or third parties.

Professional behaviour

- Members should refrain from any conduct that might bring discredit to the profession.

Advise on taxation issues

A person advising either a company or an individual on taxation issues has duties and responsibilities towards both:

- his client, and
- HM Revenue and Customs.

7 Chapter summary

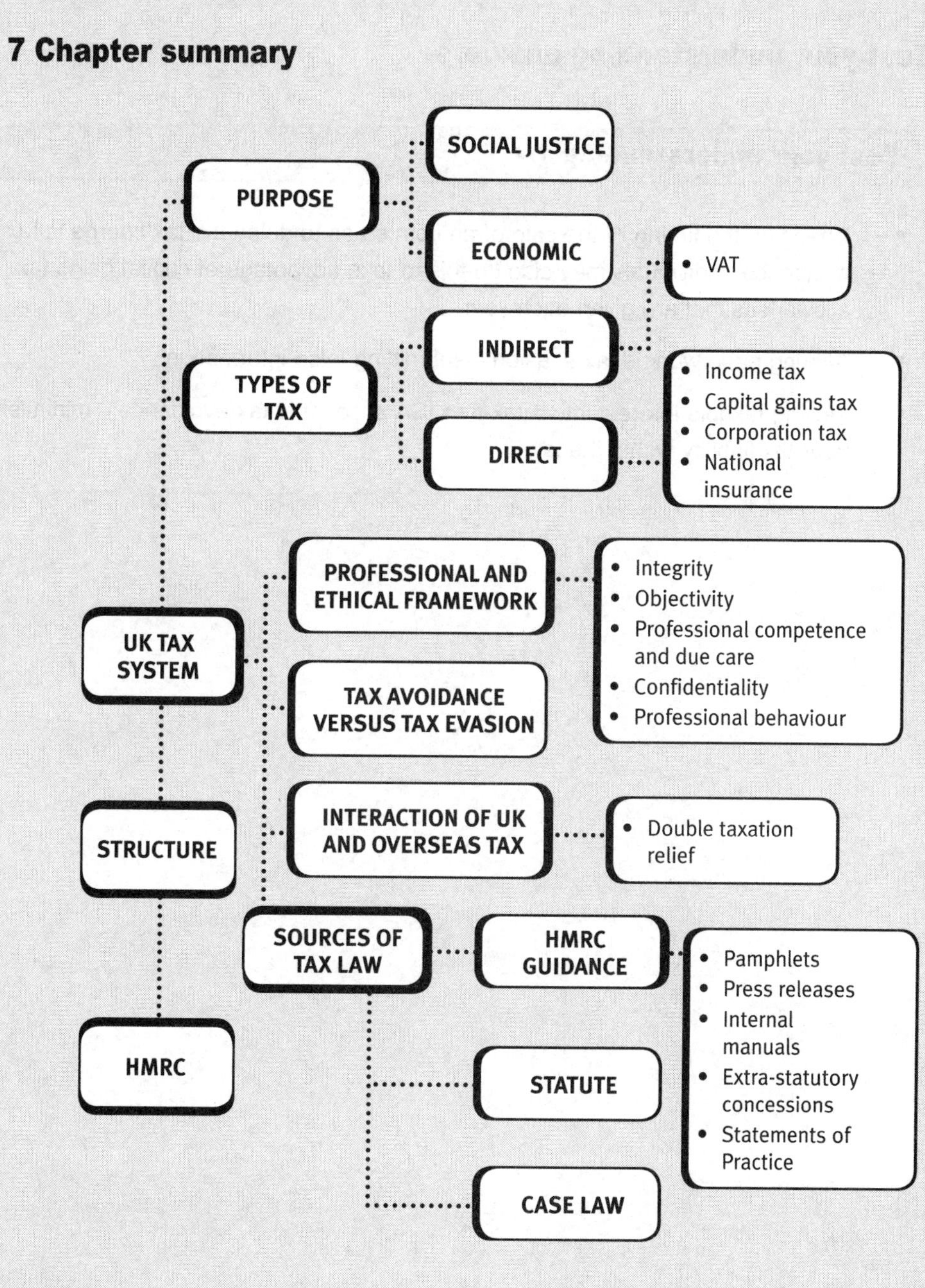

Test your understanding answers

Test your understanding 1

- Changing the timing of the sale of an item so as to delay the tax charge is tax avoidance. Individuals may also do this to take advantage of capital gains tax allowances that are given each year.
- Altering paperwork is tax evasion – submitting false information.
- Moving taxable interest into a tax-free ISA account is tax avoidance – minimising your tax liability within the law.

hapter

2

Basic income tax computation

Chapter learning objectives

Upon completion of this chapter you will be able to:

- identify the scope of income tax and those assessable
- explain how the residence of an individual is determined
- recognise the different types of taxable income for an individual
- calculate the income tax liability arising on different types of income
- distinguish between income tax liability and income tax payable
- recognise qualifying reliefs deductible from total income and explain the tax treatment
- explain the tax treatment of charitable donations
- select and calculate personal age allowances in a variety of situations.

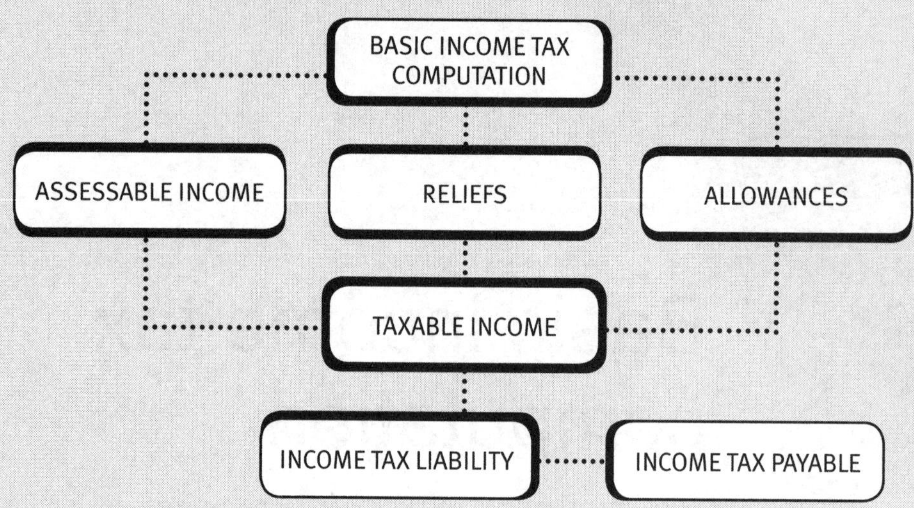

1 The principles of income tax

Introduction

This and the following eight chapters deal in detail with the way in which individuals, whether they are employed, self-employed or simply in receipt of investment income, are assessed to income tax.

Income tax is an important topic as it will be the focus of question one in the examination which will be for either 25 marks or 30 marks.

This chapter sets out the basis upon which individuals are assessed to income tax and explains how an individual's income tax liability is calculated.

Basis of assessment

Individuals are assessed to income tax on their income arising in a tax year.

- A tax year is the year ended on 5 April and is labelled by the calendar years it straddles.
- The year from 6 April 2009 to 5 April 2010, is referred to as the tax year 2009/10.

Personal allowances

Every taxpayer is entitled to a basic personal allowance (PA).

- The PA is an amount of tax-free income that every taxpayer is entitled to each tax year.
- The basic PA in 2009/10 is £6,475.
- Personal allowances are dealt with in more detail in section 7.

Assessable persons

Each individual is required to pay income tax on his or her taxable income for each tax year. The implications of this are:

- all individuals, including children, are chargeable to income tax
- both spouses within a married couple are treated as separate individuals for the purposes of income tax.

Husband and wife

There are special rules governing the allocation of income between spouses where assets are jointly owned:

- Generally, income generated from assets jointly owned will be split 50:50 between spouses regardless of the actual percentage ownership.
- Where jointly owned assets are held other than in a 50:50 ratio, an election can be made to HM Revenue & Customs (HMRC) for the income to be taxed on the individual spouses according to their actual percentage ownership.
- Civil partnerships are treated in the same way as married couples

Civil partnership

Civil partners are same-sex couples who are registered as a civil partnership under the Civil Partnership Act 2004.

Children

Although a child under the age of 18 is a taxable person, their income typically falls short of their personal allowance in any tax year and therefore no tax liability actually arises on their income.

Tax status of an individual

- All persons resident, ordinarily resident and domiciled in the UK are assessed to UK tax on their worldwide income.

Definition of residence

- Broadly, a person is deemed resident in the UK for a tax year if they are present in the UK for a period of six months or more.

Residence

An individual is UK resident if:

- he or she is physically present in the UK for a period (or periods) of six months or more in any tax year, or
- he or she has made frequent and substantial visits to the UK.

Visits of (in aggregate) three months a year, on average, for four consecutive years are regarded as 'frequent and substantial'.

Definition of ordinary residence

An individual's ordinary residence is the place where he normally resides as opposed to his place of occasional residence.

Ordinary residence implies residence with some degree of continuity, ignoring incidental or temporary absences.

Ordinary residence

- An individual who has previously been resident and ordinarily resident in the UK may still be regarded as UK ordinarily resident for a year that he spends wholly overseas if it is their intention to return to the UK.
- An individual must be absent from the UK for at least three years before they will be regarded as having lost their ordinarily residence status.

Definition of domicile

An individual's domicile is basically his permanent home.

In the F6 examination, for income tax, in computational questions the individual will be resident, ordinarily resident and domiciled in the UK.

2 Taxable income

Basic pro forma

The first stage of the income tax computation is to have a short statement summarising all taxable income.

- All income is included **gross** in the computation.
- Any exempt income identified can be excluded.

Income tax computation – 2009/10

	£
Earned income	
Trading income	X
Employment income	X
Property income	X
Investment income	
Building society interest (× 100/80)	X
Bank interest (× 100/80)	X
UK dividends (× 100/90)	X
	—
Total income	X
Less: Reliefs	(X)
	—
Net income	X
Less: Personal allowance (PA)	(X)
	—
Taxable income	X
	—

Classification of income

There are a number of different sources of income. For example:

- Income earned from employment and self-employment.
- Income arising from the ownership of property.
- Investment income.
- Income exempt from income tax.

It is important to classify each source of income correctly as the tax rules are different for each source.

All taxable income is included in the income tax computation **gross**.

- Some income, such as employment income and bank interest will have had some tax deducted at source.
- Where a net figure is given, the income must be grossed up before being included in the income tax computation.

Earned income

Earned income can be generated in the following ways:

- The profit of a trade, profession or vocation of a self-employed individual is assessed as trading income.
- Earnings derived from an office or employment are assessed as employment income.

Property and investment income

Sources of property and investment income include:

- Property income – typically rental income, but also includes other items such as the income element of a premium on granting a short lease.
- Savings income – usually bank and building society interest. This can be received either net (of 20% income tax) or gross. In both cases it is the gross amount that is included in the tax computation. Credit is given for any tax paid at source in the calculation of income tax payable.
- Dividend income is received net of a 10% tax credit. The grossed up amount (amount received × 100/90) is included in the income tax computation.

Exempt income

Examples of exempt income include:

- Income from certain National Savings products.
- Gaming, lottery and premium bonds winnings.
- Income received from an Individual Savings Account (ISA).
- Some social-security benefits.

Reliefs

Reliefs are deductible from an individual's total income. They include certain payments that an individual makes and certain losses that may be incurred by an individual.

Reliefs are considered in more detail in section 5.

3 Income tax liability

Pro forma – income tax liability computation

The second stage of the income tax computation is to compute the income tax liability on the taxable income.

- Different rates of tax apply dependent upon the type of income.

	£		£
Other income			
On the first £37,400	37,400	@ 20%	X
On excess over £37,400	X	@ 40%	X
Other income	X		
On savings income	X	@ 20/40%	X
On dividend income	X	@10/32.5%	X
Income tax liability			X

Rates of income tax

The rates of income tax for 2009/10 are as follows:

- a basic rate of 20% applies to the first £37,400 of taxable income
- a higher rate of 40% applies where taxable income exceeds £37,400.

These rates are supplied to you in the examination.

These rates apply to all income except dividend income. Special rates of tax apply to dividend income.

The income tax rates for all sources of income for 2009/10 are:

Level of income	Other income	Savings income	Dividend income
Basic rate band (first £37,400)	20%	20% (see note below)	10%
Higher rate (excess over £37,400)	40%	40%	32.5%

The income tax liability is calculated in a strict order.

The order in which income tax is applied is as follows:

(1) Other income

(2) Savings income

(3) Dividend income

Note: Special rates may apply to savings income if it falls within the first £2,440 of taxable income.

The special rates for savings and dividend income are considered in more detail in Chapter 3.

Example 1 - Income tax liability

Tony has assessable trading income of £19,535 and employment income of £3,000 for 2009/10. He does not have any savings income or dividend income.

Calculate Tony's income tax liability for 2009/10.

Answer to example 1

	£
Trading income	19,535
Employment income	3,000
Total income	22,535
Less: Personal allowance	(6,475)
Taxable income	16,060
Income tax liability (£16,060 × 20%)	3,212

Example 2 - Income tax liability

Teresa has assessable trading income of £43,765 and employment income of £4,000 for 2009/10. She does not have any savings income or dividend income.

Calculate Teresa's income tax liability for 2009/10.

Answer to example 2

			£
Trading income			43,765
Employment income			4,000
			———
Total income			47,765
Less: Personal allowance			(6,475)
			———
Taxable income			41,290
			———
Income tax	£		
Basic rate	37,400	x 20%	7,480
Higher rate	3,890	x 40%	1,556
	———		
	41,290		
	———		———
Income tax liability			9,036
			———

Test your understanding 1

(1) Andrew has income from self-employment of £15,000 and employment income of £2,500.

(2) Alice has income from self-employment of £36,000 and employment income of £21,000.

Assume that neither taxpayer has any other source of income in 2009/10

Calculate the income tax liabilities of Andrew and Alice for 2009/10.

4 Income tax payable

Income tax payable

Certain forms of income, such as:

- savings
- dividends
- most employment income

are received after income tax has been deducted at source.

In determining taxable income, all income has been included in the income tax computation gross.

The income tax liability is then calculated on the gross taxable income.

To avoid the double payment of income tax, credit is then given as the final element of the income tax computation, in order to arrive at how much of the income liability is still payable as follows:

	£
Income tax liability	X
Less: Tax credits on dividends	(X)
Tax deducted from savings income	(X)
PAYE on employment income	(X)
	——
Income tax payable	X
	——

The income tax payable is the amount due to be paid by the taxpayer. It will be collected via the self-assessment system (see Chapter 13).

In the event that the amount of tax paid during the year is greater than the amount actually due, a refund will be given via the self-assessment system.

In summary:

- **Income tax liability:**
  - The total income tax due on the taxpayer's total gross income, after deducting reliefs and personal allowances.
- **Income tax payable:**
  - The final tax bill to be paid via self-assessment after deducting credits for any tax already suffered/paid at source.

Example 3 - Income tax payable

Akram has assessable trading income of £41,535 and employment income of £9,000 (gross), for 2009/10. He does not have any savings income or dividend income. He suffered tax at source on his employment income (PAYE) of £590.

Calculate Akram's income tax payable for 2009/10.

Answer to example 3

Income tax computation – 2009/10

		£
Trading income		41,535
Employment income		9,000
Total income		50,535
Less: Personal allowance		(6,475)
Taxable income		44,060
Income tax	£	
Basic rate	37,400 x 20%	7,480
Higher rate	6,660 x 40%	2,664
	44,060	
Income tax liability		10,144
Less: PAYE		(590)
Income tax payable		9,554

Test your understanding 2

Waqar provides you with the following information for 2009/10:

Salary	£28,000
Trading income	£20,000

He has no other sources of income for the year, although he does notify you that he suffered £4,390 PAYE, during 2009/10.

Calculate Waqar's income tax payable for 2009/10.

5 Reliefs against total income

Introduction

Tax relief is given for certain losses incurred and payments made by an individual.

- Relief is given by deducting the losses/payments from total income.
- Losses are covered in detail in Chapter 10.
- The only payments deductible from total income which are examinable are certain qualifying interest payments.
- In order to maximise the use of reliefs, qualifying interest payments should be deducted from total income in priority to losses incurred.

Interest payments

Relief is given for interest paid on loans incurred to finance expenditure for a qualifying purpose.

There are a number of qualifying purposes to which the loan must be applied. The only ones relevant to your examination are as follows:

- **Employees:** The purchase of plant or machinery by an employed person for use in his employment.
- **Partners:** The purchase of a share in a partnership, or the contribution to a partnership of capital or a loan. The borrower must be a partner in the partnership. A loan taken out by a partner for the purchase of plant or machinery for use in the partnership, also qualifies.

Relief is given by deducting the amount of interest **paid** in a tax year from total income.

Example 4 - Reliefs against total income

Anwar and Barry each have total income of £50,000 none of which is savings or dividend income. They made the following payments during 2009/10.

- Anwar made interest payments during the year totalling £2,000 on his mortgage for his principal private residence.
- Barry made interest payments of £2,000 on a loan to invest in a partnership in which he is a partner.

Calculate the income tax liability for Anwar and Barry for 2009/10.

Answer to example 4

Income tax computations – 2009/10

				Anwar	Barry
				£	£
Total income				50,000	50,000
Less Reliefs: Qualifying interest paid					(2,000)
Net income				50,000	48,000
Less: Personal allowance				(6,475)	(6,475)
Taxable income				43,525	41,525
Income tax	£	£			
Basic rate	37,400	37,400	x 20%	7,480	7,480
Higher rate	6,125	4,125	x 40%	2,450	1,650
	43,525	41,525			
Income tax liability				9,930	9,130

Note: Mortgage interest paid for a principal private residence is not qualifying interest and therefore not deductible as a relief.

Test your understanding 3

Emmanuel provides the following information in respect of 2009/10:

	£
Employment income	29,600
Trading income	19,000
Qualifying interest payment	4,000

He notifies you that PAYE suffered was £4,190, for 2009/10.

Calculate Emmanuel's income tax payable for 2009/10.

6 Charitable giving

Introduction

Tax relief is available for charitable giving in one of two ways:

- Donations under the Gift Aid scheme.
- Payroll giving.

Donations under the Gift Aid scheme are covered below and the payroll giving scheme is covered in Chapter 4.

Donations under the Gift Aid scheme

For those who wish to make gifts of money to charity, the Gift Aid scheme is available. The scheme operates as follows:

- Donations made under the scheme attract relief at the donor's highest rate of tax.
- There are no minimum or maximum contribution limits, and gifts can either be one-off or a series of donations.
- The payments must be made with basic rate tax deducted at source. Effectively providing basic rate tax relief at the time the payment is made.
- The basic rate tax is claimed by the charity from HMRC.

Basic rate taxpayers – obtain the tax relief at the time of payment, by only paying 80% of the amount due.

Higher rate taxpayers – relief comes in two parts:

- 20% tax relief is granted at the time the payment is made, as above.
- Additional higher rate relief is obtained by adding the gross amount of the donation to the basic rate band in the income tax liability calculation.

The effect of extending the basic rate band is that income equivalent to the value of the gross donation is taxed at 20%, rather than 40%, giving the additional 20% tax relief that the higher rate taxpayer is entitled to.

Example 5 - Donations under Gift Aid scheme

Brenda earns £50,000 each year and makes a donation of £3,600 to the RSPB under the Gift Aid scheme.

Calculate Brenda's income tax liability for 2009/10.

Answer to example 5

Income tax computation – 2009/10

			£
Employment income			50,000
Less: Personal allowance			(6,475)
Taxable income			43,525
Income tax	£		
Basic rate – extended (W)	41,900	x 20%	8,380
Higher rate	1,625	x 40%	650
	43,525		
Income tax liability			9,030

Working: Extended basic rate band

	£
Basic rate band	37,400
Plus Gross Gift Aid donation (3,600 x 100/80)	4,500
Extended basic rate band	41,900

Test your understanding 4

Both Paul and Peter earn £46,995 a year. Peter makes donations of £2,000 (net), declaring them to be under the Gift Aid scheme.

Calculate the income tax payable for both for 2009/10.

7 Personal allowances

Every taxpayer (including children) is entitled to a personal allowance (PA).

- The amount for 2009/10 is £6,475.
- The PA is deducted from the taxpayer's net income from the different sources of income in the following order:
  (1) Other income
  (2) Savings income
  (3) Dividend income
- Surplus personal allowances are lost, they cannot be set against capital gains nor can they be transferred to any other taxpayer.
- There is no restriction to the PA where the individual is only alive for part of the year (i.e. full allowance available in year of birth or death).

Age allowance

Taxpayers aged 65 and over at any time in the year of assessment, are entitled to a higher rate of personal allowance.

- Those **aged 65 – 74** are entitled to an increased personal allowance, £9,490 in 2009/10.
- Those **aged 75 and over** get the highest rate personal allowance, £9,640 in 2009/10.
- The allowance is given for the year of assessment in which the 65th or 75th birthday falls, even if the taxpayer dies before the birthday.
- The allowance is given to attempt to provide some protection for those on lower incomes.
- An income restriction operates to reduce the level of the allowances, where the taxpayer's net income reaches a certain level. This is set at £22,900 for 2009/10.
- The reduction in allowances is calculated as:
  - **50% × (Net income – £22,900)**
  - This formula gives a progressive reduction in the personal age allowance. However, the allowance can never fall below the basic personal allowance of £6,475 for 2009/10.

Example 6 - Personal allowances

Calculate the age allowance in the following situations.

At the end of 2009/10:

- Dennis will be 71 and has net income of £23,750
- Nora will be 90 and has net income of £25,400
- Peter will be 80 and has net income of £30,900

Answer to example 6

	Dennis	**Nora**	**Peter**
Age at the end of the tax year:	71	90	80
	£	£	£
Personal age allowance	9,490	9,640	9,640
Less: Restriction			
50% × (£23,750 – £22,900)	(425)		
50% × (£25,400 – £22,900)		(1,250)	
50% × (£30,900 – £22,900) = £4,000 restricted			(3,165)
Personal age allowance	9,065	8,390	6,475

Test your understanding 5

Identify the personal allowances available in 2009/10, to the following individuals:

Taxpayer	Date of birth	Net income
Vera	4 June 1936	£17,000
Agatha	15 March 1933	£24,000
Henry	20 August 1923	£25,000
Leon	7 September 1941	£29,000

8 Chapter summary

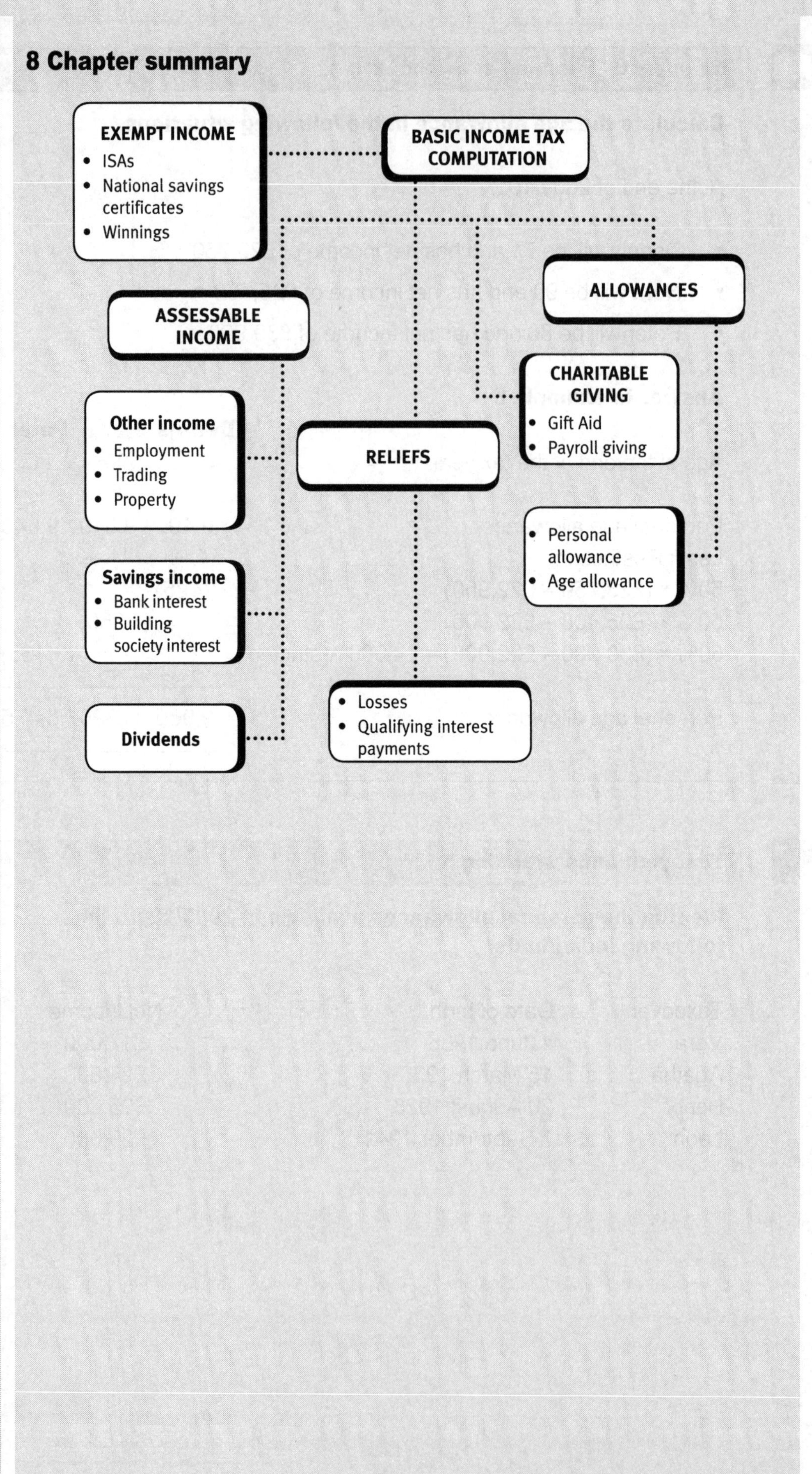

Test your understanding answers

Test your understanding 1

Andrew
Income tax computation – 2009/10

	£
Trading income	15,000
Employment income	2,500
Total income	17,500
Less: Personal allowance	(6,475)
Taxable income	11,025
Income tax liability (£11,025 x 20%)	2,205

Alice
Income tax computation – 2009/10

			£
Trading income			36,000
Employment income			21,000
Total income			57,000
Less: Personal allowance			(6,475)
Taxable income			50,525
Income tax	£		
Basic rate	37,400	x 20%	7,480
Higher rate	13,125	x 40%	5,250
	50,525		
Income tax liability			12,730

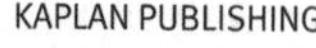

Test your understanding 2

Waqar

Income tax computation – 2009/10

			£
Trading income			28,000
Employment income			20,000
Total income			48,000
Less: Personal allowance			(6,475)
Taxable income			41,525
Income tax	£		
Basic rate	37,400	x 20%	7,480
Higher rate	4,125	x 40%	1,650
	41,525		
Income tax liability			9,130
Less: PAYE			(4,390)
Income tax payable			4,740

Test your understanding 3

Emmanuel

Income tax computation – 2009/10

			£
Employment income			29,600
Trading income			19,000
Total income			48,600
Less Reliefs: Qualifying interest			(4,000)
Net income			44,600
Less: Personal allowance			(6,475)
Taxable income			38,125
Income tax	£		
Basic rate	37,400	x 20%	7,480
Higher rate	725	x 40%	290
	38,125		
Income tax liability			7,770
Less: PAYE			(4,190)
Income tax payable			3,580

Test your understanding 4

Peter and Paul

Income tax computations – 2009/10

					Paul	**Peter**
					£	£
Income					46,995	46,995
Less: PA					(6,475)	(6,475)
Taxable income					40,520	40,520
Income tax	£	£				
	37,400	39,900	(W)	x 20%	7,480	7,980
	3,120	620		x 40%	1,248	284
	40,520	40,520				
Income tax liability					8,728	8,228

Despite having the same income, Peter's income tax liability is £500 lower than Paul's.

This represents the additional 20% tax saving on the gross payment of £2,500 (£2,000 x 100/80) to the charity.

Working: Peter's basic rate band is extended:

£37,400 + (£2,000 × 100/80) = £39,900

Test your understanding 5

Personal age allowances

	Vera	Agatha	Henry	Leon
Age at the end of the tax year:	73	77	86	68
	£	£	£	£
Personal age allowance	9,490	9,640	9,640	9,490
Less: Restriction				
No restriction required	Nil			
50% × (£24,000 – £22,900)		(550)		
50% × (£25,000 – £22,900)			(1,050)	
50% × (£29,000 – £22,900)				(3,015)
= £3,050 restricted				
Personal age allowance	9,490	9,090	8,590	6,475

chapter

3

Property and investment income

Chapter learning objectives

Upon completion of this chapter you will be able to:

- identify savings income
- calculate tax on savings income
- compute the tax payable on dividend income
- recognise the basis for computing property business profits
- explain the rules for allowing expenses and identify the key deductions from property business profits
- demonstrate the reliefs available for a property business loss
- compute the amount assessable when a premium is received for the grant of a short lease
- define when a letting qualifies as furnished holiday lettings
- explain the differences between furnished holiday lettings and normal furnished lettings
- explain when rent a room relief applies
- recognise investments which produce tax free income
- explain the key features of an Individual Savings Account
- explain how a married couple or a couple in a civil partnership can minimise their tax liabilities.

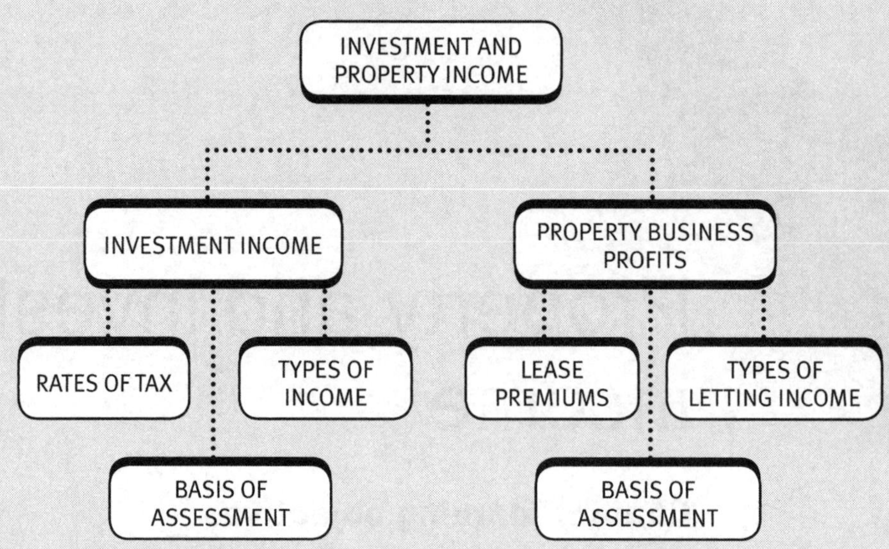

1 Introduction

The primary source of income for most taxpayers is derived from earnings, either from employment or self-employment. These are covered in detail in Chapters 4 to 10.

This chapter covers the taxation of income from investments. The main sources of investment income are:

- Savings income.
- Dividend income.
- Property income.

However, some investments are exempt from income tax. The following tax efficient investments are also covered in this chapter:

- Individual Savings Accounts (ISAs).
- National savings products.
- Premium bonds.

2 Savings income

The main types of savings income are bank and building society interest.

Basis of assessment

Banks and building societies pay interest to individuals net of 20% tax.

An individual is taxed on the grossed up amount of the actual savings income **received in a tax year**.

- The gross amount of interest is calculated as:

interest received × 100/80

- The 20% tax is retained by the bank or building society and then paid direct to HMRC on behalf of the individual taxpayer.

Where the tax suffered on bank and building society interest exceeds the individual's tax liability, it is repaid via the self-assessment process (see Chapter 13).

Rates of tax on savings

Savings income is normally taxed in the same way as 'other income' at the basic and higher rates of tax (20% and 40%).

However, a starting rate of tax of 10% will apply to the first £2,440 of savings income in certain limited circumstances.

- In determining at what rate to tax the savings income, the income is treated as the next slice of a taxpayer's income after his 'other income' (i.e. employment income, trading income and property income) has been taxed.
- The new 10% starting rate will only apply where savings income falls into the first £2,440 of taxable income.

Therefore, a taxpayer with taxable savings income will be taxed according to the level of their 'other income' as follows:

'Other income'		**Savings income taxed at**
None	First £2,440 of taxable savings income	10%
	Next £34,960	20%
	Balance above £37,400	40%
Below £2,440	Taxable savings income falling into the first £2,440	10%
	Next £34,960	20%
	Balance above £37,400	40%
In excess of £2,440	The 10% rate is not applicable	
	Taxable savings income falling into the first £37,400	20%
	Balance above £37,400	40%

The taxpayer has 20% deducted at source, therefore:

- if the recipient is a basic rate taxpayer, there is no additional tax liability to pay on this income. Whilst the income will be recorded gross in the tax computation, the tax paid at source will fully meet the liability
- if the account holder only pays tax at the starting rate (10%) he or she will be entitled to a refund
- for higher rate taxpayers, an additional liability falls due.

Income tax computation

Where an individual has different sources of income, set up the following pro forma using different columns for the different types of income.

This will ensure that you:

- calculate the income tax liability on the different sources of income in the correct order, and
- apply the correct rates of income tax.

Income tax computation – 2009/10

	Total	Other income	Savings income	Dividends
	£	£	£	£
Employment income	X	X		
Trading profits	X	X		
Property income	X	X		
Interest (× 100/80)	X		X	
Dividends (×100/90)	X			X
Total income	X	X	X	X
Less Reliefs	(X)	(X)		
Net income	X	X	X	X
Personal allowance	(6,475)	(6,475)		
Taxable income	X	X	X	X

Test your understanding 1

Jamie received bank interest of £1,600 during 2009/10.

Calculate his income tax payable if his income from employment during 2009/10 was:

(a) £25,000

(b) £45,000

(c) £7,350

Set off of reliefs and personal allowances

Personal allowances (PAs) and reliefs are deducted from income in the following order:

(1) Other income.

(2) Savings income.

(3) Dividend income.

This is because the basic rate of tax on other income and savings income (20%) is higher than the corresponding lower rate of tax on dividends (10%). Deducting PAs and reliefs in this order produces the highest tax saving.

Example 1 - Set off of reliefs and personal allowances

Simon earned employment income off of £6,900 and received building society interest of £6,000 (net) in 2009/10. He paid qualifying interest of £100 during the year. PAYE of £93 was deducted from his employment income.

Calculate the income tax repayable to Simon.

Answer to example 1

Income tax computation – 2009/10

	Total	Other income	Savings income
	£	£	£
Employment income	6,900	6,900	–
Savings income (£6,000 × 100/80)	7,500	–	7,500
Total income	14,400	6,900	7,500
Less: Interest paid	(100)	(100)	
Net income	14,300	6,800	7,500
Less: Personal allowance	(6,475)	(6,475)	–
Taxable income	7,825	325	7,500

Income tax	£		£
Other income – basic rate	325	x 20%	65
Savings income – starting rate	2,115	x 10%	211
	2,440		
Rest of savings income – basic rate	5,385	x 20%	1,077
	7,825		
Income tax liability			1,353
Less: PAYE			(93)
Tax credit on savings income (£7,500 at 20%)			(1,500)
Income tax repayable			(240)

The savings income is partly taxed at the starting rate of 10%, with the balance taxed at the basic rate of 20%.

Here, tax is repayable because the tax credits exceed the tax liability.

Example 2 - Income tax payable or repayable

Patrick has total income in 2009/10 of:

(a) £3,000

(b) £33,000

(c) £45,000

This includes £1,600 (net) of savings income. Patrick has no dividend income.

Calculate Patrick's income tax payable or repayable for the year.

Answer to example 2

(a) Total income £3,000

Income tax computation – 2009/10

	Total	Other income	Savings income
	£	£	£
Other income	1,000	1,000	
Savings income (£1,600 × 100/80)	2,000		2,000
Total income	3,000	1,000	2,000
Less: Personal allowance	(3,000)	(1,000)	(2,000)
Taxable income	Nil	Nil	Nil
Income tax liability			Nil
Less: Tax credit on savings income (£2,000 × 20%)			(400)
Income tax repayable			(400)

(b) Total income £33,000

Income tax computation – 2009/10

	Total	Other income	Savings income
	£	£	£
Other income	31,000	31,000	
Savings income (£1,600 × 100/80)	2,000		2,000
Total income	33,000	31,000	2,000
Less: Personal allowance	(6,475)	(6,475)	–
Taxable income	26,525	24,525	2,000

Income tax	£		£
Other income – basic rate	24,525	x 20%	4,905
Savings income – basic rate	2,000	x 20%	400
	26,525		
Income tax liability			5,305
Less: Tax credit on savings income (£2,000 × 20%)			(400)
Income tax payable			4,905

(c) Total income £42,000

Income tax computation – 2009/10

	Total	Other income	Savings income
	£	£	£
Other income	43,000	43,000	
Savings income (£1,600 × 100/80)	2,000		2,000
Total income	45,000	43,000	2,000
Personal allowance	(6,475)	(6,475)	–
Taxable income	38,525	36,525	2,000

Income tax	£		£
Other income – basic rate	36,525	x 20%	7,305
Savings income – basic rate	875	x 20%	175
	37,400		
Savings income – higher rate	1,125	x 40%	450
	38,525		
Income tax liability			7,930
Less: Tax credit on savings income (£2,000 × 20%)			(400)
Income tax payable			7,530

3 Dividend income

Dividends received from a company are charged to income tax in the tax year in which they are received.

The receipt date is taken as the date on the dividend voucher.

Tax treatment of dividends

As with savings income, dividends are received net. However for dividends, the process differs slightly:

- Dividends are deemed to be received net of a notional tax credit of 10%. Therefore, any dividends received must be grossed up by 100/90 prior to inclusion within the income tax computation as follows:

Dividend received × 100/90

- As with savings income, the tax credit is available to be set against the taxpayer's tax liability.
- However, as the tax credit is notional (i.e. the paying company does not actually make any payment to HMRC on the shareholder's behalf), it can only be used to reduce the taxpayer's income tax liability.
- It is not possible to reclaim this tax credit in cash should it exceed the tax liability for the year.
- Tax credits on dividends are set off, against a taxpayer's income tax liability, in priority to all other tax credits, including PAYE.

Rates of tax on dividends

The following rates of tax apply to dividend income:

Dividends falling into the:	Rate of tax
Basic rate band (first £37,400)	10%
Higher rate (over £37,400)	32.5%

There are special rules applicable to the taxation of dividends:

- If the recipient is a basic rate taxpayer, there is no additional liability to pay or refund to claim on any dividend income received.
- For higher rate taxpayers, an additional liability falls due.

In calculating the income tax liability, dividends are treated as the top slice of income (above 'other income' and 'savings income').

If dividends fall above the higher rate threshold, then they are taxed at the special higher rate of 32.5%, with a notional tax credit of 10% suffered at source.

Example 3 - Dividend income

Jeremy earned employment income of £14,000 and received dividends of £6,750 in 2009/10. PAYE of £1,505 was deducted in respect of the employment income.

Calculate the income tax payable for 2009/10.

Answer to example 3

The dividends are treated as the highest part of Jeremy's income.

As he is only a basic rate taxpayer, all the dividends will be taxed at 10%.

Income tax computation – 2009/10

	Total	Other income	Dividend income
	£	£	£
Employment income	14,000	14,000	
Dividends (£6,750 × 100/90) (Note 1)	7,500		7,500
	———	———	———
Total income	21,500	14,000	7,500
Less: PA (Note 2)	(6,475)	(6,475)	–
	———	———	———
Taxable income	15,025	7,525	7,500
	———	———	———

			£
Income tax			
Other income	7,525	x 20%	1,505
Dividend income (Note 3)	7,500	x 10%	750
	———		
	15,025		
	———		———
Income tax liability			2,255
Less: Tax credit on dividend (Note 4)			(750)
PAYE on employment income			(1,505)
			———
Income tax payable			Nil
			———

Notes:

(1) Remember that dividends are always deemed to have been received net of a 10% tax credit and must be grossed up by 100/90, before including in the tax computation.

(2) Note that the PA is deducted from 'other income' as this results in the highest tax saving.

(3) The 10% rate is charged on dividend income to the extent that it falls within the basic rate band.

(4) The dividend credit can never create a refund; at best it can reduce the income tax liability to £nil. It is set off in priority to other tax credits and PAYE.

Example 4 - Dividend income

Jacob earned employment income of £27,900 and received dividends of £15,750 in 2009/10. PAYE of £4,285 was paid in respect of the employment income.

Calculate the income tax payable.

Answer to example 4

Income tax computation – 2009/10

	Total	Other income	Dividend income
	£	£	£
Employment income	27,900	27,900	
Dividends (£15,750 × 100/90) (Note)	17,500		17,500
Total income	45,400	27,900	17,500
Less: Personal allowance	(6,475)	(6,475)	–
Taxable income	38,925	21,425	17,500

Income tax			
Other income – basic rate	21,425	x 20%	4,285
Dividend income – basic rate (Note)	15,975	x 10%	1,597
	37,400		
Dividend income – higher rate	1,525	x 32.5%	496
	38,925		
Income tax liability			6,378
Less: Tax credit on dividend			(1,750)
PAYE on employment income			(4,285)
Income tax payable			343

Note: The dividends are treated as the highest part of Jacob's income. The first £15,975 of the gross dividend falls into the basic rate band, and is taxed at the lower rate of 10%, the remaining £1,525 (£17,500 – £15,975) falls into the higher rate band, and is taxed at the higher rate of 32.5%.

Example 5 - Dividend income

Simone received dividends of £6,075 in 2009/10. She received no other income during the year.

Calculate the income tax payable/repayable.

Answer to example 5

Income tax computation – 2009/10

	£
Dividends (£6,075 × 100/90)	6,750
Less: Personal allowance	(6,475)
Taxable income	275
Income tax liability (£275 at 10%)	27
Less: Tax credit on dividends (£275 at 10%) (Note)	(27)
Income tax payable	Nil

Note: The tax credit on the dividends in excess of the tax liability is not repayable and therefore lost.

Test your understanding 2

Emily has income in 2009/10 as follows:

Employment income	£39,600
Bank interest received	£1,600
Dividends received	£2,700

PAYE deducted in the year is £6,625

Calculate Emily's income tax payable for the year.

Example 6 - Comprehensive scenarios

Gordon Lamont, a single man, received dividend income of £1,350 and bank interest of £300 (net), in 2009/10. He also has trading income.

Assume his trading income in 2009/10 is as follows:

Situation:	£
A	3,970
B	8,600
C	45,745

Calculate the income tax payable/repayable for each situation.

Answer to example 6

Situation A

Income tax computation – 2009/10

	Total	Other income	Savings income	Dividend income
	£	£	£	£
Trading income	3,970	3,970		
Bank interest (£300 × 100/80)	375		375	
Dividends (£1,350 × 100/90)	1,500			1,500
Total income	5,845	3,970	375	1,500
Less: Personal allowance (restricted)	(6,475)	(3,970)	(375)	(1,500)
Taxable income	Nil	Nil	Nil	Nil

Income tax	Nil
Less: Tax credit on Dividend income (Note)	Nil
Tax credit on Savings income	(75)
Income tax repayable	(75)

Note: The tax credit on the dividend income is only available to reduce a liability; it cannot create a refund.

Situation B

Income tax computation – 2009/10

	Total	Other income	Savings income	Dividend income
	£	£	£	£
Trading income	8,600	8,600		
Savings (£300 × 100/80)	375		375	
Dividends (£1,350 × 100/90)	1,500			1,500
Total income	10,475	8,600	375	1,500
Less: PA	(6,475)	(6,475)		
Taxable income	4,000	2,125	375	1,500

Income tax	£		£
Other income – basic rate	2,125	x 20%	425
Savings income – starting rate	315	x 10%	31
	2,440		
Rest of savings income – basic rate	60	x 20%	12
Dividend income – basic rate	1,500	x 10%	150
	4,000		
Income tax liability			618
Less: Tax credit on dividend			(150)
Tax credit on savings			(75)
Income tax payable			393

Situation C

Income tax computation – 2009/10

	Total	Other income	Savings income	Dividend income
	£	£	£	£
Trading income	45,745	45,745		
Savings (£300 × 100/80)	375		375	
Dividends				
(£1,350 × 100/90)	1,500			1,500
Total income	47,620	45,745	375	1,500
Less: Personal allowance	(6,475)	(6,475)		
Taxable income	41,145	39,270	375	1,500

Income tax	£		£
Other income – basic rate	37,400	x 20%	7,480
Other income – higher rate	1.870	x 40%	748
	39,270		
Savings income – higher rate	375	x 40%	150
Dividend income – higher rate	1,500	x 32.5%	488
	41,145		
Income tax liability			8,866
Less: Tax credit on dividend			(150)
Tax credit on savings			(75)
Income tax payable			8,641

Test your understanding 3

Susan has the following income and outgoings for 2009/10:

	£
Trading income	11,615
Employment income (gross)	13,000
Savings income (amount received)	2,800
Dividend income (amount received)	1,800
Qualifying interest (amount paid)	1,000

PAYE of £1,305 was deducted from the employment income.

Calculate Susan's income tax payable Susan's for 2009/10.

4 Property income

Introduction

For the purposes of the examination, you are required to be able to deal with the following:

- Property business profits arising from the rental/lease of property.
- The premium received on the grant of a short lease.
- Profits arising from the commercial letting of furnished holiday accommodation.
- Rental income received from the rent a room scheme.

Property business profit – basis of assessment

The key assessment rules for property business profits are as follows:

- The assessable income from land and buildings for each tax year is computed as:

	£
Rental income	X
Less: related expenses	(X)
	—
Assessable income	X
	—

- If the landlord lets more than one property, the assessable amount for each year is the aggregate of the profits and losses from all properties (except furnished holiday lettings – see later).
- The rental income and related expenses are assessable/deductible on an accruals basis. Accordingly, the due dates for payment of rent and actual payment dates are irrelevant.
- All calculations in the examination are made to the nearest month.

Example 7 - Property income

Hembery owns a property that was let for the first time on 1 July 2009.

The rent of £5,000 pa is paid alternatively:

(a) quarterly in advance

(b) quarterly in arrears.

Hembery paid allowable expenses of £200 in December 2009 (related to redecoration following a burst pipe), and of £400 in May 2010, (related to repair work which was completed in March 2010).

Calculate his property business profit for 2009/10.

Answer to example 7

	£	£
Rent accrued (9/12 × £5,000) (Note 1)		3,750
Expenses		
Redecoration	200	
Repairs (Note 2)	400	
		(600)
Property business profit		3,150

Notes:

(1) The rent under each alternative is the same – the accruals basis of assessment means the rents accrued between 6 April 2009 to 5 April 2010. The actual payment terms or payment dates are irrelevant.

(2) As the work was completed in March 2010 under the accruals basis the expenditure is deductible in 2009/10, the period in which the work was undertaken, and not when the expenditure is paid.

Property business profit – allowable deductions

The expenses allowable against the rental income are computed under the normal rules for the assessment of trading income. These are discussed more fully in Chapter 5.

The main rules are as follows:

- To be allowable, the expenses must have been incurred **wholly** and **exclusively** for the **purposes of the property business.** This covers items such as:
  - insurance
  - agents fees and other management expenses
  - repairs
  - interest on a loan to acquire or improve the property.
- Irrecoverable debts are allowable. If a tenant leaves without paying the outstanding rent, the amount owed can be deducted as an expense.
- Relief is available for any expenditure incurred before letting commenced, under the normal pre-trading expenditure rules (see Chapter 5).
- Capital expenditure is not normally an allowable deduction. The main distinction between capital and revenue expenditure is between improvements and repairs.
  - Repairs expenditure would normally be allowable.
  - Improvement expenditure is not allowable.

Distinction between repairs and capital expenditure

Caution is required where an item is in need of repair.

For example, the replacement of kitchen units with similar standard units would normally be regarded as a repair. However, had the new units been state of the art new kitchen units, the expenditure would probably have been regarded as an improvement.

- Depreciation may be charged in accounts as a means of writing off the cost of capital expenditure over the life of an asset. Depreciation is not an allowable deduction.
- Normal capital allowances (see Chapter 6) cannot be claimed for expenditure on plant and machinery for use in a dwelling house. However, a form of capital allowances known as the 'renewals basis' can be claimed for furnished accommodation.

Renewals basis

- The renewals basis allows relief for the expense of renewing furniture to the same standard.
- The original cost and any improvement element in a replacement is disallowed.
- The detailed record keeping requirements of this method of relief normally discourage its use in practice.

Wear and tear allowance

The renewals basis of giving relief for capital expenditure is normally replaced by a 'wear and tear' allowance, which is calculated as (10% of the rent received).

If the landlord pays the council tax or water rates on the property, the wear and tear allowance is calculated as 10% of the rent received, net of these expenses.

Wear and tear allowance

= 10% × (rents received – council tax – water rates)

Example 8 - Property income

Giles owns a cottage that he lets out furnished at an annual rent of £3,600, payable monthly in advance.

During 2009/10, he incurs the following expenditure:

May 2009	Replacement of one broken kitchen unit with a unit of similar standard	£275
June 2009	Insurance for year from 5 July (previous year £420)	£480
November 2009	Drain clearance	£380
May 2010	Redecoration (work completed in March 2010)	£750

The tenant had vacated the property during June 2009, without having paid the rent due for June. Giles was unable to trace the defaulting tenant, but managed to let the property to new tenants from 1 July 2009.

Calculate the property business profit for 2009/10, assuming Giles claims the 10% wear and tear allowance.

Answer to example 8

Property business profit – 2009/10

	£	£
Rent accrued		3,600
Expenses		
Repair to kitchen units (Note)	275	
Irrecoverable debt – June 2009 rent (1/12 × £3,600)	300	
Insurance (3/12 × £420 + 9/12 × £480)	465	
Drain clearance	380	
Redecoration	750	
Wear and tear = 10% × rent received		
10% × (£3,600 – £300)	330	
		(2,500)
Property business profit		1,100

Note: The replacement of a kitchen unit with one of a similar standard would normally be treated as an allowable repair.

Test your understanding 4

Eastleigh acquired two properties on 1 June 2009, that were first let on 1 July 2009.

Property A is let unfurnished for an annual rent of £4,000, payable quarterly in advance. Eastleigh incurred the following expenditure in respect of this property.

20.6.09	Repairs to roof following a storm on 15 June	£1,600
29.6.09	Insurance for year ended 31.5.10	£420
1.2.10	Repainting exterior	£810

Property B is let furnished for an annual rent of £5,000, payable quarterly in arrears. The tenants were late in paying the amount due on 31 March 2010 – this was not received until 15 April 2010.

Eastleigh incurred the following expenditure in respect of this property in 2009/10.

4.6.09	Letting expenses paid to agent	£40
29.6.09	Insurance for year ended 31.5.10	£585

Calculate Eastleigh's property business profit for 2009/10.

Property business losses

If rental income for a particular year is less than the allowable expenditure, a loss arises.

- If the landlord owns more than one property, the profits and losses on all the properties are aggregated to calculate the assessable income for the year. This effectively provides instant loss relief.
- If there is an overall loss on all properties, the property income assessment for the year will be £nil.
- Any unrelieved loss is carried forward indefinitely and offset against the first available future property business profits.

Example 9 - Property losses

Sheila owns three properties that were rented out. Her assessable income and allowable expenses for the two years to 5 April 2010 were:

Property	1	2	3
	£	£	£
Income			
2008/09	1,200	450	3,150
2009/10	800	1,750	2,550
Expenses			
2008/09	1,850	600	2,800
2009/10	900	950	2,700

Calculate Sheila's property business profit/(loss) for 2008/09 and 2009/10.

Answer to example 9

Property	1	2	3	Total
	£	£	£	£
2008/09				
Income	1,200	450	3,150	4,800
Less: Expenses	(1,850)	(600)	(2,800)	(5,250)
Profit/(loss)	(650)	(150)	350	(450)
Property business profit				Nil
Loss carried forward				450
2009/10				
Income	800	1,750	2,550	5,100
Less: Expenses	(900)	(950)	(2,700)	(4,550)
Profit/(loss)	(100)	800	(150)	550
Less: Loss brought forward				(450)
Property business profit				100

Note: There is no need to calculate the profit/(loss) on each property separately. One computation amalgamating all income and expenses is all that is required.

Example 10 - Property income and losses

For many years Tom Jones has owned six houses in Upland Avenue that are available for letting unfurnished. The following details have been provided by the client:

Property number	21	23	25	38	40	67
	£	£	£	£	£	£
Rent due for y/e 5.4.10	2,080	1,820	2,340	1,300	1,300	2,080
Insurance due for y/e 5.4.10	280	220	340	150	150	140

Tom employs a gardener to look after all the properties, and pays him £1,200 a year. There are also accountancy charges of £480 a year; both of these costs are allocated equally to each property.

Numbers 23 and 40, had new tenancies in the year. The cost of advertising for tenants was £50, in respect of number 23 and £100 for number 40. The new tenant at number 23 took over immediately the old tenant moved out. Unfortunately, the old tenant at Number 40 defaulted on rent of £350, due before the new tenant moved in.

During the year Tom had to replace the boiler in number 40, at a cost of £800. During the year he also had to replace the water tank at number 21, at a cost of £100 and a replacement roof for number 25, cost him £5,000.

Tom has loans outstanding on each of the six properties and pays interest of £500 per year on each loan.

(a) **Explain how relief for a property business loss can be obtained.**

(b) **Calculate Tom's property business loss for 2009/10 and state how it will be relieved.**

Answer to example 10

(a) **Relief for property business losses**

Where a taxpayer owns numerous properties, accounts will normally be prepared for each property for each tax year, resulting in either a profit or loss in each case. These are automatically offset against each other for the tax year to ascertain the property business profit or loss for the year.

Where the aggregated total is a loss, this is carried forward indefinitely, to be offset against the first available future aggregate property business profits.

(b) **Property business loss – 2009/10**

	£	£
Rents accrued (£2,080 + £1,820 + £2,340 + £1,300 + £1,300 + £2,080)		10,920
Expenses payable		
Insurance (£280 + £220 + £340 + £150 + £150 + £140)	1,280	
Gardener	1,200	
Accountancy	480	
Advertising (£50 + £100)	150	
Repairs (£100 + £5,000 + £800)	5,900	
Irrecoverable debt	350	
Interest (£500 × 6)	3,000	
		(12,360)
Property loss		(1,440)
Assessable property income for 2009/10		Nil

Notes:

(1) It is not necessary to consider profits and losses on each property individually, the accounts could be drawn up to show the total rents, expenses etc. for all the properties, instead of property by property.

(2) The replacement of the boiler, water tank and roof are taken to be necessary replacements with assets of a similar kind and will therefore normally be treated as allowable revenue expenditure. Had there been an element of improvement in the expenditure, some or all of the expenditure may be disallowed as capital in nature.

5 Premiums received on the grant of a short lease

Premiums

A premium is a lump sum payment made by the tenant to the landlord in consideration for the granting of a lease.

Short lease

A short lease is a lease for a period of less than or equal to 50 years.

- Part of the premium received in respect of the granting of a short lease is assessed on the landlord as property business income in the year the lease is granted.
- The amount assessable as property business income is:

	£
Premium	X
Less: Premium × 2% × (duration of lease – 1)	(X)
Property business income	X

Duration of lease = number of **complete** years (ignore part of a year).

Example 11 - Premiums received on the grant of a short lease

Rodney granted a 21-year lease to Charles on 1 July 2009, for a premium of £10,500.

Calculate the amount assessable on Rodney as property business income in 2009/10.

Answer to example 11

	£
Premium	10,500
Less: £10,500 × 2% × (21 – 1)	(4,200)
Property business income – 2009/10	6,300

Test your understanding 5

Albert grants an 18-year lease to Derek for £26,000, on 6 September 2009.

Calculate the amount assessable on Albert as property business income for 2009/10.

Grant of a sub-lease

Where a tenant is granted a short lease on a property and then grants a sub-lease to a subtenant, any premium received from the subtenant is charged on the tenant as property business income under the normal rules for granting leases.

However, if the tenant originally paid a premium to the landlord on the granting of its own lease (known as the head lease), relief is given as follows:

$$\text{Taxable premium for head lease} \times \frac{\text{Duration of sub -lease}}{\text{Duration of head lease}}$$

Example 12 - Grant of a sub-lease

On 1 August 2001 Victor granted a lease to Alex for a period of 20 years. Alex paid a premium of £20,000.

On 1 August 2009 Alex granted a sublease to Max for a period of 5 years. Max paid a premium of £24,000.

Calculate the property business income assessable on Alex in 2009/10.

Answer to example 12

	£
Premium received re sub-lease	24,000
Less: £24,000 × 2% × (5 – 1)	(1,920)
	22,080
Less: Relief for premium paid re head lease (W) £12,400 × 5/20	(3,100)
Property business income – 2009/10	18,980

Working: Premium paid on head lease

The premium assessed on the landlord in respect of the head lease is:

	£
Premium received	20,000
Less: £20,000 × 2% × (20 – 1)	(7,600)
Premium assessed on Victor	12,400

Test your understanding 6

Sasha granted a lease to Irina for a period of 25 years on 1 June 2004. Irina paid a premium of £32,000.

On 1 May 2009 Irina granted a sublease to Anna for a period of 7 years. Anna paid a premium of £21,000.

Calculate the property business income assessable on Irina in 2009/10.

6 Furnished holiday lettings

Introduction

Profits arising from the commercial letting of furnished holiday accommodation is still assessable as property business income but it is treated as though the profits arose from a single and separate trade.

As a result, separate records regarding these properties have to be kept.

There are specific rules and reliefs that apply to such properties.

Qualifying conditions

The letting will only be treated as furnished holiday accommodation if it meets the following conditions:

- The property is situated in the UK or an EEA country.
- It is let furnished.
- The letting is on a commercial basis with a view to the realisation of profits.
- It is available for commercial letting, to the public generally, as holiday accommodation for not less than 140 days a year.

- The accommodation is actually let for at least 70 days a year (excluding periods of 'long-term occupation' – see below).
- Where a taxpayer owns more than one property, the 70 days test is satisfied if the average number of days for which the properties are let in the year is at least 70.
- The property must not be let for periods of 'long-term occupation' in excess of 155 days in a year.

Long-term occupation is defined as a period of more than 31 consecutive days when the property is let to the same person.

It is possible for the property to be let to the same person for more than 31 days, however, when aggregating all such periods of longer term occupation (which could be a few periods of letting to different persons), the total must not exceed 155 days.

Tax treatment of furnished holiday lettings

Any profits from commercially let furnished holiday accommodation remain assessable as property income.

However, the profits are treated as arising from a separate trade carried on by the landlord, and are not pooled with other rental property.

The following advantages and reliefs thereby become available:

- Relief may be claimed for any losses sustained as if they were trading losses and not property business losses. The losses can therefore be offset against other income and not just other property income (see Chapter 10).
- The profits are treated as relevant earnings for the purposes of relief for personal pension scheme contributions (see Chapter 11).
- Capital gains tax roll-over relief and entrepreneurs' relief is available (see Chapter 17).
- Normal capital allowances will be available in respect of plant and machinery. This will usually be more beneficial than the wear and tear allowance or the renewals basis.

Note that it has been announced in FA2009 that these special furnished holiday lettings rules will be repealed in 2010/11.

7 Rent a room relief

Introduction

If an individual lets furnished accommodation in his or her main residence, and the income is liable to tax as property income or trading income, a special exemption applies.

Gross annual rental receipts are equal to or less than £4,250

- If the gross annual rental receipts are £4,250 or below, they will be exempt from tax.
- The individual's limit of £4,250 is reduced by half to £2,125 if, during a particular tax year, any other person(s) also received income from letting accommodation in the property while the property was the first person's main residence.
- This rule allows a married couple taking in lodgers to either have all the rent paid to one spouse (who will then have the full limit of £4,250), or to have the rent divided between the spouses (and each spouse will then have a limit of £2,125).
- An individual may elect to ignore the exemption for a particular year, for example, if a loss is incurred when taking account of expenses.

Gross annual rental receipts are more than £4,250

- If the gross annual rental receipts are more than £4,250, an individual may choose between:
  - paying tax on the excess of his gross rent over £4,250
  - being taxed in the normal way on the profit from letting (rent less expenses).

Summary: Assess lower of:

Method 1 – Normal assessment		Method 2 – Rent a room relief	
	£		£
Rental income	X	Rental income	X
Less Expenses	(X)	Less Rent a room relief	(4,250)
Less Wear and tear allowance	(X)		
	—		—
Profit	X	Profit	X
	—		—

8 Tax-free investments

Introduction

The following investment income is tax-free:

- Income from an Individual Savings Account (ISA).
- Proceeds of National Savings Certificates.
- Premium bond, national lottery, betting winnings.

The objective of these products is to enable the taxpayer to invest and create tax efficient income streams.

Individual savings accounts

Individual savings accounts (ISAs) are the most common form of tax efficient investment. They can be opened by any individual aged 16 or over who is resident and ordinarily resident in the UK.

An ISA offers the following tax reliefs:

- Income (interest and dividends) is received free of income tax.
- Disposals of investments within an ISA are free of capital gains tax.

There is no minimum holding period, so withdrawals can be made from the account at any time.

There are two types of ISAs:

- **Cash ISAs**

  This includes bank and building society accounts, as well as those National Savings products where the income is not exempt from tax.

- **Stocks and shares ISAs**

  Investment is allowed in shares and securities listed on a stock exchange anywhere in the world.

Qualifying stocks and shares include:

- Ordinary shares.
- Fixed interest preference shares and convertible preference shares.
- Fixed interest corporate bonds and convertible bonds with at least five years to run until maturity.
- Gilts with at least five years to run until maturity.
- Investments in unit trusts, investment trusts and open-ended investment companies.

Unlisted shares and shares traded on the alternative investment market do not qualify.

ISA annual subscription limits

For the tax year 2009/10, there is an annual subscription limit based on age and a stipulated maximum amount that can be invested in a cash ISA as follows:

Age	Total limit	Maximum cash ISA limit
	£	£
50 and over	10,200	5,100
Under 50	7,200	3,600

The balance of the annual total limit not invested in a cash ISA may be invested in a stocks ISA.

Note that husbands and wives each have their own limits.

ISA account providers

Savers have a choice of account providers and account formats. They can take out separate accounts for cash ISA and stocks and shares ISA with the same provider, or with different providers.

National savings

National savings offer a variety of products. The taxation treatment of National Savings products is as follows:

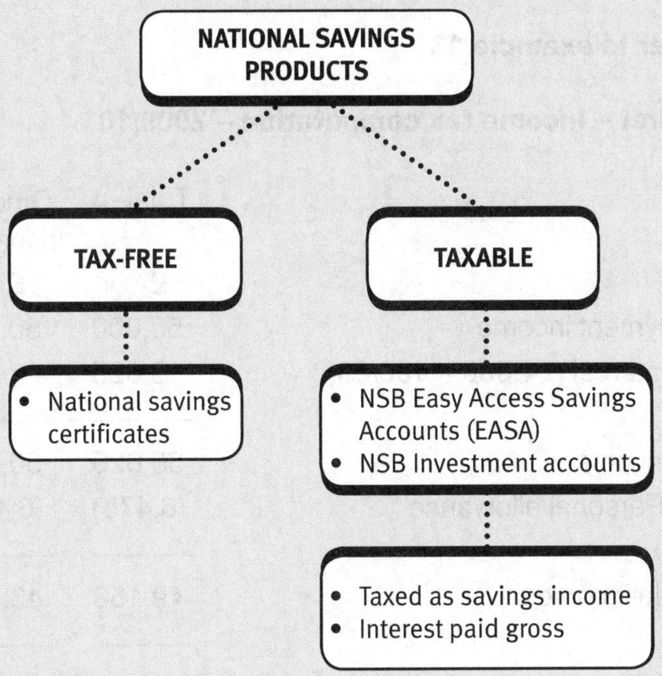

9 Husband and wife planning

Individual spouses have their own personal allowances and income tax rate bands.

Where one spouse is not fully utilising their allowances or basic rate tax band a married couple can transfer income generating assets between them, at no tax cost, to minimise their joint tax liability.

These rules also apply to partners within a Civil Partnership.

Example 13 - Husband and wife planning

Margaret is married to Alfred. She is aged 45 and has employment income of £50,000 pa. She has various bank accounts from which she receives interest of £4,500 each year.

Alfred, aged 52, earns £20,000 trading profits from self-employment each year. He has no other income.

Calculate the couple's income tax liability for 2009/10 and advise how they could have saved tax by better organising their investments.

Answer to example 13

Margaret – Income tax computation – 2009/10

	Total	Other income	Savings income
	£	£	£
Employment income	50,000	50,000	
Bank interest (£4,500 × 100/80)	5,625		5,625
Total income	55,625	50,000	5,625
Less: Personal allowance	(6,475)	(6,475)	
Taxable income	49,150	43,525	5,625

Income tax:			
	£		£
Other income – basic rate	37,400	x 20%	7,480
Other income – higher rate	6,125	x 40%	2,450
	43,525		
Savings income – higher rate	5,625	x 40%	2,250
	49,150		
Income tax liability			12,180

Alfred – Income tax computation – 2009/10

	£
Trading income	20,000
Less Personal allowance	(6,475)
Taxable income	13,525
Income tax liability (£13,525 x 20%)	2,705

Tax saving advice

Margaret is a higher rate taxpayer and has paid tax on her investment income at the rate of 40% in 2009/10. Alfred, however, is a basic rate taxpayer.

If the bank accounts had been in Alfred's name he would have paid tax on the interest at 20% thus saving the couple tax of £1,125 (£5,625 × 20%).

Alternatively Margaret could take advantage of an ISA and invest £3,600. The interest would be tax free. If some of the bank account is in Alfred's name he could also transfer £5,100 into an ISA.

10 Chapter summary

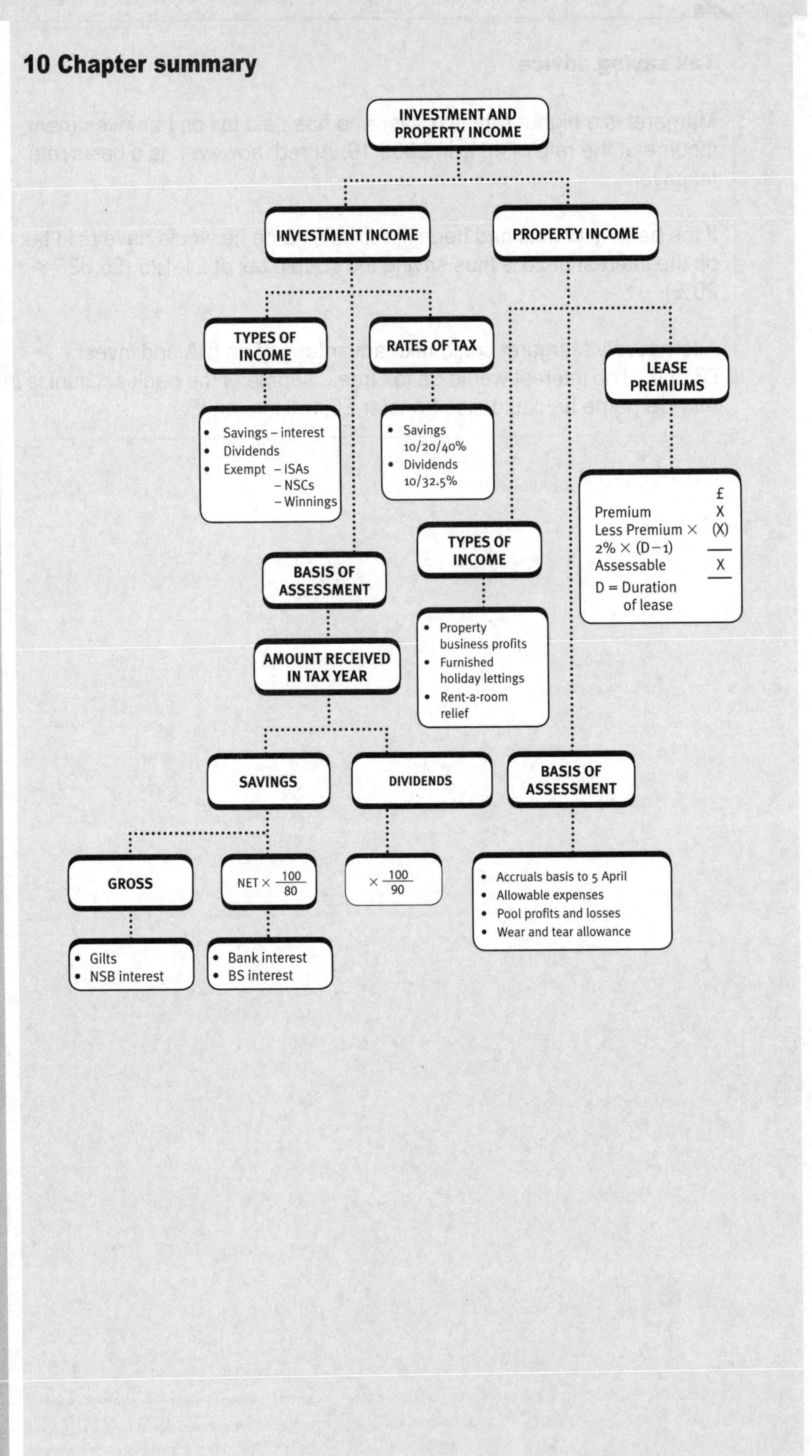

INVESTMENT AND PROPERTY INCOME
INVESTMENT INCOME
PROPERTY INCOME
TYPES OF INCOME
RATES OF TAX
• Savings – interest
• Dividends
• Exempt – ISAs – NSCs – Winnings
• Savings 10/20/40%
• Dividends 10/32.5%
BASIS OF ASSESSMENT
AMOUNT RECEIVED IN TAX YEAR
SAVINGS
DIVIDENDS
GROSS
NET × 100/80
× 100/90
• Gilts
• NSB interest
• Bank interest
• BS interest
LEASE PREMIUMS
£
Premium X
Less Premium × 2% × (D−1) (X)
Assessable X
D = Duration of lease
TYPES OF INCOME
• Property business profits
• Furnished holiday lettings
• Rent-a-room relief
BASIS OF ASSESSMENT
• Accruals basis to 5 April
• Allowable expenses
• Pool profits and losses
• Wear and tear allowance

Test your understanding answers

Test your understanding 1

Jamie

(a) **Employment income – £25,000**

Income tax computation – 2009/10

	Total	Other income	Savings income
	£	£	£
Employment income	25,000	25,000	
Savings income (£1,600 × 100/80)	2,000		2,000
Total income	27,000	25,000	2,000
Less: Personal allowance	(6,475)	(6,475)	
Taxable income	20,525	18,525	2,000

Income tax			
Other income – basic rate	18,525	x 20%	3,705
Savings income – basic rate	2,000	x 20%	400
	20,525		
Income tax liability			4,105
Less: Tax credit on savings income (£2,000 × 20%)			(400)
Income tax payable			3,705

Note: The starting rate for savings income is not applicable as 'other income' exceeds the £2,440 band limit. Savings income, to the extent it falls in the basic rate band, is assessed at 20%.

(b) **Employment income – £45,000**

	Total	Other income	Savings income
	£	£	£
Employment income	45,000	45,000	
Savings income (£1,600 × 100/80)	2,000		2,000
Total income	47,000	45,000	2,000
Less: Personal allowance	(6,475)	(6,475)	–
Taxable income	40,525	38,525	2,000

Income tax			
Other income – basic rate	37,400	x 20%	7,480
Other income – higher rate	1,125	x 40%	450
	38,525		
Savings income – higher rate	2,000	x 40%	800
	40,525		
Income tax liability			8,730
Less: Tax credit on savings income (£2,000 × 20%)			(400)
Income tax payable			8,330

Note: In this situation, the starting rate for savings income is not applicable and the savings income falls in the higher rate band. It is therefore assessed at 40%. The deduction for the amount already paid is given, and the additional liability of £400 is settled via the self-assessment process.

(c) **Employment income – £7,350**

Income tax computation – 2009/10

	Total		Other income	Savings income
	£		£	£
Employment income	7,350		7,350	
Savings income (£1,600 × 100/80)	2,000			2,000
Total income	9,350		7,350	2,000
Personal allowance	(6,475)		(6,475)	–
Taxable income	2,875		875	2,000
Income tax				
Other income – basic rate	875	x 20%		175
Savings income – starting rate	1,565	x 10%		156
	2,440			
Rest of savings income – basic rate	435	x 20%		87
	2,875			
Income tax liability				418
Less: Tax credit on savings income (£2,000 × 20%)				(400)
Income tax payable				18

Note: The starting rate band for savings income is firstly reduced by other income before being applied to savings income.

Test your understanding 2

Emily

Income tax computation – 2009/10

	Total	Other income	Savings income	Dividend income
	£	£	£	£
Employment income	39,600	39,600		
Savings (£1,600 × 100/80)	2,000		2,000	
Dividends (£2,700 × 100/90)	3,000			3,000
Total income	44,600	39,600	2,000	3,000
Less: PA	(6,475)	(6,475)		
Taxable income	38,125	33,125	2,000	3,000

Income tax	£		£
Other income – basic rate	33,125	x 20%	6,625
Savings income – basic rate	2,000	x 20%	400
Dividend income – basic rate	2,275	x 10%	227
	37,400		
Dividend income – higher rate	725	x 32.5%	236
	38,125		
Income tax liability			7,488
Less: Tax credit on dividend			(300)
PAYE on employment income			(6,625)
Tax credit on interest			(400)
Income tax payable			163

Test your understanding 3

Susan

Income tax computation – 2009/10

	Total	Other income	Savings income	Dividend income
	£	£	£	£
Trading income	11,615	11,615		
Employment income	13,000	13,000		
Savings (£2,800 × 100/80)	3,500		3,500	
Dividends (£1,800 × 100/90)	2,000			2,000
Total income	30,115	24,615	3,500	2,000
Less Reliefs: Interest paid	(1,000)	(1,000)		
Net income	29,115	23,615	3,500	2,000
Less: PA	(6,475)	(6,475)		–
Taxable income	22,640	17,140	3,500	2,000

Income tax	£		£
Other income – basic rate	17,140	x 20%	3,428
Savings income – basic rate	3,500	x 20%	700
Dividend income – basic rate	2,000	x 10%	200
	22,640		
Income tax liability			4,328
Less: Tax credit on dividend			(200)
PAYE on employment income			(1,305)
Tax credit on interest			(700)
Income tax payable			2,123

Whilst the presentation above is the one that you have become used to, the columnar approach takes longer, time that may be valuable in the exam. It is possible to complete the computation with a single column and then separate the income, in the liability calculation at the foot of the computation.

Only use this approach however if you are totally comfortable that you will be able to correctly identify the different sources of income and apply the correct tax rates.

Susan

Income tax computation – 2009/10

	£
Trading income	11,615
Employment income	13,000
Other income	24,615
Savings income (£2,800 × 100/80)	3,500
Dividend income (£1,800 × 100/90)	2,000
Total income	30,115
Less: Reliefs: Interest paid	(1,000)
Net income	29,115
Less: Personal allowance	(6,475)
Taxable income	22,640

Analysis of income:	£
Other income (£22,640 – £3,500 – £2,000)	17,140
Savings	3,500
Dividends	2,000

Income tax computation = as before

Test your understanding 4

Eastleigh

Property business profit – 2009/10

Property A	£	£
Rent (9/12 × £4,000)		3,000
Less: Insurance (10/12 × £420)	350	
Repainting exterior	810	
Roof repairs (pre-trading expenditure)	1,600	
		(2,760)
Profit		240
Property B		
Rent (9/12 × £5,000)		3,750
Less: Insurance (10/12 × £585)	488	
Letting expenses	40	
		(528)
		3,222
Wear and tear allowance (10% × £3,750)		(375)
Profit		2,847
Property business profit (£240 + £2,847)		3,087

Test your understanding 5

Albert

	£
Premium	26,000
Less: £26,000 × 2% × (18 - 1)	(8,840)
Property business income	17,160

Test your understanding 6

Irina

	£
Premium received re sub-lease	21,000
Less: £21,000 × 2% × (7 – 1)	(2,520)
	18,480
Less: Relief for premium paid re head lease (W) £16,640 × 7/25	(4,659)
Property business income – 2009/10	13,821

Working: Premium paid on head lease

The premium assessed on the landlord (Sasha) in respect of the head lease is:

	£
Premium received	32,000
Less: £32,000 × 2% × (25 – 1)	(15,360)
Premium assessed on Sasha	16,640

chapter

4

Employment income

Chapter learning objectives

Upon completion of this chapter you will be able to:

- recognise the factors that determine whether an engagement is treated as employment or self-employment
- state the basis of assessment for income from employment
- list the statutory allowable employment income deductions, including an explanation of how charitable giving can be made through a payroll deduction scheme
- determine when travel expenses are allowable
- explain the basis for other allowable employment income expenses
- determine when the statutory approved mileage allowance is due and calculate it
- explain the purpose of a dispensation from HM Revenue and Customs
- recognise the general principles in calculating benefits
- recognise the exempt benefits
- calculate the benefits assessable on all employees
- explain the basis of determining whether an individual is a P11D employee and state the effect
- calculate the benefits arising on an employer-provided vehicle
- identify the circumstances when the provision of a loan will result in an employee benefit and calculate the loan interest benefit
- calculate the employee benefit where an asset is provided for private use
- calculate the benefit when an asset is transferred to an employee
- calculate the benefit(s) when accommodation is provided to an employee
- given details of a remuneration package calculate the employment income assessable.

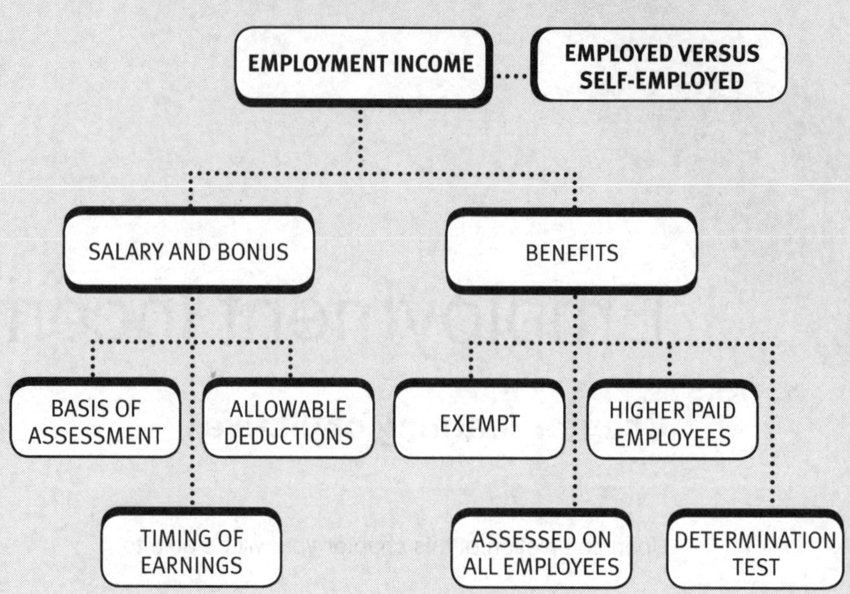

1 The scope of employment income

Employment or self-employment?

The distinction between employment and self-employment is fundamental:

- an employee is taxable under the employment income provisions
- a self-employed person is assessed on the profits derived from his trade, profession or vocation, under the trading income provisions.

The following principles, laid down by statute and case law decisions, are important matters to be taken into account in deciding whether a person is employed or self-employed.

The primary test of an employment is the nature of the contract that exists:

Nature of contract	Status
'of service'	employment
'for services'	self-employment

However, even in the absence of a written contract of service any of the following matters would corroborate the existence of such a contract, and, therefore, employment:

- an obligation by the employer to offer work and an obligation by the employee to undertake the work offered. An employee would not normally be in a position to decline work when offered
- the employer controls the manner and method of the work

- the individual is entitled to benefits normally provided to employees such as sick pay and holiday pay
- the individual is committed to work a specified number of hours at certain fixed times, and is paid by the hour, week or month
- the engagement is for a long period of time
- the individual does not provide his own equipment
- the individual is obliged to work personally and exclusively for the employer, and cannot hire his own helpers
- the work performed by the individual is an integral part of the business of the employer, and not merely an accessory to it
- the economic reality of self-employment is missing – namely the financial risk arising from not being paid an agreed, regular, remuneration
- the individual cannot profit from sound management.

There is much case law on this area. However, note that an important case concerning a vision mixer who was engaged under a series of short-term contracts in the film industry, made the following fundamental points:

- It is necessary to look at the overall picture by examining a number of criteria, and
- No one factor is conclusive.

In this particular case, like many persons engaged in a profession or specialised vocation, he did not have all the trappings of a business, and did not supply his own equipment. However, the number of separate engagements was held to be a deciding factor in the decision to treat him as self-employed.

2 Basis of assessment

Assessable earnings

- All directors and employees are assessed on the amount of earnings received in the year of assessment (the **receipts basis**).
- The term 'earnings' includes not only cash wages or salary, but also bonuses, commission, round sum allowances and benefits made available to the employee by the employer.

The date earnings are received

The date of receipt is the **earlier** of the following:

- Actual payment of, or on account of, earnings.
- Becoming entitled to such a payment.

In the case of directors, who are in a position to manipulate the timing of payments, there are extra rules. They are deemed to receive earnings on the **earliest** of four dates; the two general rules set out above, and the following two rules:

- when sums on account of earnings are credited in the accounts
- where earnings are determined:
  - before the end of a period of account = the end of that period
  - after the end of a period of account = date the earnings are determined.

3 Deductibility of expenses from employment income

General rule

Expenditure will only be deductible if it is incurred **wholly**, **exclusively** and **necessarily** in the **performance of duties**.

General rule for employment income expenses

- In the performance of the duties.

This aspect of the test means that there is no deduction for expenditure incurred beforehand, to gain the requisite knowledge or experience to do the work. So, for example, the cost of attending evening classes by a schoolteacher has been disallowed.

- Necessarily.

For expenditure to comply with this test, it must be an inherent requirement of the job, not something imposed by the employee's circumstances. Thus an employee with poor eyesight was unable to deduct the cost of spectacles. In other words, to be necessary expenditure, each and every person undertaking the duties would have to incur it.

- Wholly and exclusively.

To be deemed wholly and exclusively incurred, such expenditure must be made with the sole objective of performing the duties of the employment.

Two examples show this distinction:

- If an employee is required to wear clothes of a high standard for his employment and so purchases them, the expenditure is not deductible. The employee's clothes satisfy both professional and personal needs.
- Expenditure on a home telephone can be partly deductible. Business calls are made 'wholly and exclusively' and so are deductible. But, on the same reasoning as applied to the clothes, no part of the line rental for a home phone may be deducted.

Expenditure allowed by statute

A deduction for certain types of expenditure is specifically permitted by statute as follows:

- contributions to registered pension schemes (within certain limits) (see Chapter 11)
- fees and subscriptions to professional bodies and learned societies, provided that the recipient is approved for the purpose by HMRC, and its activities are relevant to the individual's employment
- payments to charity made under a payroll deduction scheme, operated by an employer
- expenditure on travel and other expenditure, is deductible to the extent that it complies with very stringent rules.
- capital allowances are available for plant and machinery necessarily provided by an employee for use in his or her duties.

Capital allowances

Capital allowances are available for plant and machinery necessarily provided by an employee for use in his or her duties. For example, capital allowances will be available where an employee uses his own computer for business use. Allowances will be restricted to the proportion of business use (see Chapter 6).

Payroll deduction scheme

- Under the payroll deduction scheme an employee authorises his employer to make deductions from his salary and pay the amounts over to specified charities.

- There is no limit on the amount of donations that an employee can make under the scheme.
- The donations are deducted from the employee's gross pay before tax (PAYE) is applied to his taxable pay.

Travel expenditure

Travel expenses may be deducted only where they:

- are incurred necessarily in the performance of the duties of the employment; or
- are attributable to the necessary attendance at any place by the employee in the performance of their duties.

Relief is not given for the cost of journeys that are ordinary commuting or for the cost of private travel.

- Ordinary commuting is the journey made each day between home and a permanent workplace.
- Private travel is a journey between home and any other place that an employee does not have to be, for the purposes of work.

Travel expenditure

- Relief is available for travelling expenditure where an employee travels to visit a client. Where such travel is integral to the performance of the duties, it is allowable. This will include travel undertaken by commercial travellers and service engineers who move from place to place during the day.
- No relief is given for travelling between two separate employments. However, if an employee has more than one place where duties have to be performed for the same employer, then travelling expenses between them are allowable.

In addition, the following rules apply for travel to a temporary workplace:

- Relief is given where an employee travels directly from home to a temporary place of work.
- A temporary workplace is defined as one where an employee goes to perform a task of limited duration, or for a temporary purpose.
- A place of work will not be classed as a temporary workplace, where an employee works there continuously for a period which lasts, or is expected to last, more than 24 months.

- Where an employee passes their normal permanent workplace on the way to a temporary workplace, relief will still be available provided the employee does not stop at the normal workplace, or any stop is incidental, e.g. to pick up some papers.
- An employee may travel to a temporary workplace without that journey being significantly different from his or her normal commuting. This may be the case where the temporary workplace is situated near the permanent workplace, and in these circumstances relief is denied.

4 Approved mileage allowance (AMA)

Allowable rates

Employees who use their own motor cars for business purposes are normally paid a mileage allowance by their employer. HMRC publish approved mileage rates which are tax allowable as follows:

First 10,000 miles pa	40p
Over 10,000 miles pa	25p

- Details of the approved mileage allowance (AMA) will be given in the tax rates and allowances.
- If the mileage allowance paid by the employer is within the AMA:
= no benefit arises
- Where payments made to the employee > the AMAs:
= the excess will be assessed on the employee as a benefit.
- Where the payment to the employee < the AMA:
= the employee can make a claim to deduct the difference from their employment income.

Example 1 - Approved mileage allowance

An employee uses her own 1,800 cc motor car for business travel. During 2009/10, she drove 13,000 miles on business. Her employer paid her 30p per mile.

Calculate the expense claim for 2009/10 that can be made against taxable employment income.

Answer to example 1

The mileage allowance of £3,900 (13,000 at 30p) will be received tax free, but in addition, the employee can make an expense claim of £850 as follows:

	£
10,000 miles at 40p	4,000
3,000 miles at 25p	750
Allowable amount	4,750
Mileage allowance received	(3,900)
Expense claim	850

The £850 can be deducted in arriving at the individual's assessable employment income for 2009/10.

Test your understanding 1

John has travelled 12,000 business miles in 2009/10, in his own car. His employer pays him 38p per mile for each business mile.

(a) **Calculate how much of the mileage allowance is taxable.**

(b) **Explain how your answer would differ, if John's employer paid 35p per mile.**

Test your understanding 2

Underwood is employed as an insurance salesman at a monthly salary of £950. In addition to his basic salary, he receives a bonus that is paid in May each year, and which is related to the sales achieved by Underwood in the year to the previous 31 October. His bonuses are as follows:

Bonus for year to:	Paid during:	£
31 October 2007	May 2008	1,920
31 October 2008	May 2009	1,260
31 October 2009	May 2010	2,700

Underwood made the following payments in respect of his employment in 2009/10.

	£
Contribution to occupational pension scheme	342
Subscription to Chartered Insurance Institute	100
Payroll deduction scheme (in favour of Oxfam)	200

Compute Underwood's assessable income from employment for 2009/10.

P11D Dispensations

Where an employee is reimbursed with business related expenses, (e.g. for rail fares for business trips), the employer should report the expenses to HMRC on the employee's P11D. The reimbursed expenses are treated as taxable employment income and the employee must then make a claim for a deduction against his employment income for the business related expenses in his tax return.

An employer can reduce the administrative burden associated with reporting and recording business related expenses paid to employees, by getting approval in advance that specified expenses do not need to be reported to HMRC. This process is referred to as obtaining a dispensation from HMRC.

The impact of obtaining a dispensation is that it permits:

- The employer to omit information from forms such as the P11D, which would otherwise require reporting.
- It saves employees claiming a deduction in their tax returns for expenses that they have received in reimbursement for expenses incurred wholly, exclusively and necessarily, in the performance of their duties.

The employer is required to apply in advance for permission to make such payments and, upon receiving approval from HMRC, can continue to apply the dispensation until further notice.

5 Employment benefits

Introduction

In addition to salary, the term 'earnings' within the scope of income tax also covers benefits received by the employee.

There are three main types of benefits:

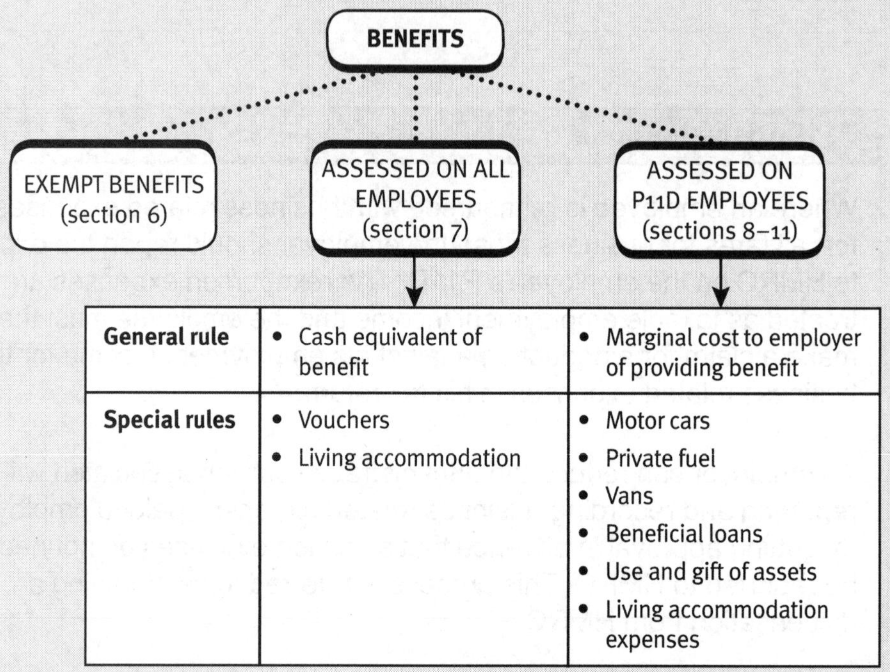

	ASSESSED ON ALL EMPLOYEES (section 7)	ASSESSED ON P11D EMPLOYEES (sections 8–11)
General rule	• Cash equivalent of benefit	• Marginal cost to employer of providing benefit
Special rules	• Vouchers • Living accommodation	• Motor cars • Private fuel • Vans • Beneficial loans • Use and gift of assets • Living accommodation expenses

6 Exempt benefits

There are a significant number of benefits that the employer can provide to the employee, that do not attract a tax charge.

Of these the most commonly examined include:

- An employer's contribution to a registered pension scheme.
- The use of subsidised on-site restaurant or canteen facilities, provided they are available for all employees.
- Luncheon vouchers up to a value of 15p per working day.
- The provision of a car parking space provided at or near the place of work, including the reimbursement of the cost of such a parking place.
- The provision of one mobile telephone by the employer to an employee.

- Certain benefits aimed at encouraging employees to travel to work other than by private car. This exemption includes work buses, subsidies to public bus services, and the provision of bicycles and cycling safety equipment.
- Christmas parties, annual dinner dances, etc. for staff generally, provided they are of modest cost (up to £150 pa per head).
- Workplace nurseries for child care.
- A payment of up to £55 per week to an approved child carer. However, the provision of cash allowances or vouchers to meet child care expenses with non-approved carers are taxable.
- Relocation and removal expenses up to £8,000.
- Expenses incurred by employees whilst away overnight on company business.
- Home worker's additional household expenses of up to £3 per week (£156 per tax year) can be paid tax-free without the need for any supporting evidence.

Further exempt benefits

Further exempt benefits include:

- Home worker's additional household expenses:
  For higher amounts than £156 per tax year to be exempt, it is necessary to have supporting evidence that the payments are wholly in respect of additional household expenses incurred by the employee, in carrying out his duties at home.
- Entertainment provided for an employee, by reason of his or her employment, by a genuine third party, e.g. a ticket or seat at a sporting or cultural event provided by a business contact or client, to generate goodwill.
- Gifts received, by reason of his or her employment, from genuine third parties, provided the cost from any one source does not exceed £250 in a tax year.
- Long service awards in kind (e.g. gold watches) are exempt up to a cost of £50 for each year of service of 20 years or more.
- Provision of travel, accommodation and subsistence during public transport disruption caused by industrial action.
- Employer funded training. Where the expenses of training are paid for by the employer, no taxable benefit arises on the employee.

- Medical insurance for treatment and medical services where the need for treatment arises while abroad in the performance of employment duties.
- Security assets and services. Where a security asset or security service is provided by reason of employment, or where reimbursement is made for the cost of such measures.
- Recreational or sporting facilities. No benefit arises on the provision of such facilities by a person's employer (directly or indirectly).
- Welfare counselling for employees provided the service is available to employees generally.
- Pension's advice for employees. The advice must cost no more than £150 per employee per year and must be available to all employees.
- Employee liability insurance. Liability insurance is aimed at protecting an employee from a work-related liability.
- Provision by employers of eye care tests and/or corrective glasses for VDU use by their employees, provided they are made available to all employees.

This is an extremely comprehensive list and in reality, the examiner is likely to refer to one or two within a question that you will be expected to identify as exempt.

Workplace nurseries

The employer must be responsible for the finance and management of the nursery for it to qualify.

The nursery must either be at the workplace or at other non-domestic premises.

Facilities that are run jointly with other employers or local authorities and similar facilities for older children after school or during school holidays, also qualify.

Relocation and removal expenses

- No assessable benefit arises on payment or reimbursement of removal expenses and benefits, provided that the following criteria are met:

- the expenses are incurred in connection with either a totally new employment, or a new role with the existing employer; or
- a change in the location at which the employee's duties are carried out. In either case it must be necessary for the employee to acquire a new principal private residence, as a commute to the new place of work would not be viable.

- The costs met or reimbursed must be qualifying expenses. These include costs of disposing of the first house, travel and subsistence when looking for a new house, removal expenses and interest on a bridging loan whilst the employee owns both the old and new homes.
- The expenditure must be incurred by the end of the tax year following the one in which the employment change occurred.

Expenses incurred overnight on business

- This includes where employers pay personal expenses, such as telephone calls home, laundry etc. for employees who stay away from home on business.
- No benefit arises on these expenses provided that they fall below the de minimis limit of £5 per night in the UK and £10 per night overseas.
- If an amount above the limit is paid, the whole amount is taxable.

7 Benefits assessable on all employees

The general rule of valuing the benefit:

- **cash equivalent value** on disposal to a third party is used
- unless there are specific statutory rules for valuing a benefit.

Specific rules have been established for a number of benefits that are assessable on all employees:

- Vouchers and credit tokens.
- Living accommodation.

Vouchers and credit tokens

Vouchers are broadly documents with which an individual can obtain goods and services.

The provision of vouchers is assessed as follows:

Cash vouchers	• Subject to tax and PAYE when given to employee • No further benefit arises
Non-cash vouchers	• Benefit = cost of providing voucher • Exception = vouchers to provide exempt benefits (e.g. luncheon vouchers up to 15p per day, child care vouchers up to £55 per week) • Excess over exempt limit = benefit
Credit token (e.g. company credit card)	• Benefit = value of goods and services bought for private use

No assessable benefit arises where the employee can show that the use of vouchers or credit tokens was wholly, exclusively and necessarily in the performance of the duties of his or her employment.

For example, where a voucher for travel for business purposes is provided, no benefit arises.

Living accommodation

Where an employee is provided with living accommodation as a result of his employment, the benefit is assessed as follows:

	Benefit arising
All properties: Basic charge	Higher of: • the accommodation's **annual value**, and • the rent actually paid by the employer.
'Expensive' living accommodation	(Cost of providing the accommodation – £75,000) × the appropriate percentage This is charged in addition to the basic charge.

Annual value

The annual value is assumed to be the rateable value of the property. This figure will always be given to you in the examination.

Expensive living accommodation

An additional benefit arises where the 'cost of the accommodation' provided exceeds £75,000.

- The 'cost of providing the accommodation' is calculated as:

	£
Original cost (or market value – see below)	X
Add: Capital improvements prior to the start of the current tax year	X
	—
Cost of providing accommodation	X
	—

- The appropriate percentage is the official rate of interest (ORI) in force at the start of the tax year. For 2009/10, the ORI is 4.75% and will be provided in the examination.
- Where the employer acquired the accommodation more than **six years** before first providing it to the employee, the calculation of the additional benefit uses the property's **market value when first provided** to the employee, rather than the original cost.
- It is important to note that regardless of the market value, an additional benefit is only imposed if the 'cost of providing the accommodation' exceeds £75,000.

The total living accommodation benefits can be reduced by:

- any amount paid by the employee towards meeting the employer's cost of providing the benefit
- the extent that the accommodation is used wholly, exclusively and necessarily for business purposes
- any periods during the tax year that the property is not available to the employee.

Job-related accommodation

There is no assessable benefit if the accommodation is job-related.

To be defined as job related, the property must be provided for one of the following reasons:

- Where it is necessary for the proper performance of the employee's duties (e.g. a caretaker).
- Where it will enable the better performance of the employee's duties and (for that type of employment) it is customary (e.g. hotel-worker).
- Where there is a special threat to the employee's security and he resides in the accommodation as part of special security arrangements.

Exception for directors

A director can only claim one of the first two exemptions if he is a full-time working director and has no material interest in the company (broadly, material interest means more than 5% of the company's ordinary share capital).

Example 2 - Benefits assessable on all employees

Jack was provided with a house to live in by his employer. It cost them £200,000 in June 2005 and has an annual value of £3,000 pa. Assume the official rate of interest is 4.75%.

Calculate the assessable benefit assuming the accommodation is not job-related.

Answer to example 2

	£	£
Basic charge:		
Higher of		
(i) annual value	3,000	
(ii) rent paid by employer	Nil	
	———	3,000
Expensive living accommodation charge		
(£200,000 – £75,000) × 4.75%		5,937
		———
Taxable benefit		8,937
		———

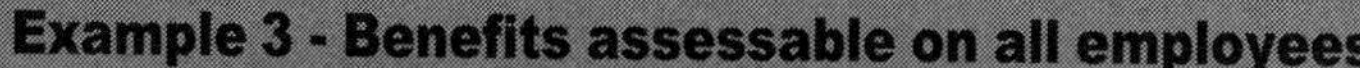

Example 3 - Benefits assessable on all employees

The house cost £90,000, when acquired in June 2004; it has an annual value of £1,700.

Since this time the following improvements have taken place:

Date of expenditure:	Type of expenditure:	£
February 2005	Conservatory	15,000
August 2007	Redecoration	2,000
July 2009	Garage extension	10,000

Its market value was as follows:

April 2009	200,000
June 2009	165,000

The accommodation is not job-related and Sachin pays a rent of £100 per month to his employer.

(a) **Calculate the amount assessable for 2009/10 in the following situations:**

(i) **Sachin moved in during June 2009.**

(ii) **Sachin moved in during June 2009, but the property was actually acquired by his employer in June 2001.**

(b) **For each of the scenarios above and assuming Sachin remains in the property, with no further improvements than the ones referred to above, what will be the cost of providing the accommodation for calculating the expensive accommodation charge for 2010/11?**

Assume an official rate of interest of 4.75%.

Answer to example 3

(a) **Assessable benefits for accommodation – 2009/10**

(i) **Property acquired June 2004**

	£	£
Basic charge		
Higher of (i) annual value	1,700	
(ii) rent paid by employer	Nil	
		1,700
Expensive living accommodation charge (W1)		
(£105,000 – £75,000) × 4.75%		1,425
		3,125
Restriction for part-year occupation		
(June 2009 – March 2010) (10/12 × £3,125)		2,604
Less: Contributions paid by employee		
(10 months)		(1,000)
Taxable benefit		1,604

(ii) **Property acquired June 2001**

	£	£
Basic charge		
Higher of		
(i) annual value	1,700	
(ii) rent paid by employer	Nil	
		1,700
Expensive living accommodation charge (W2)		
(£165,000 – £75,000) × 4.75%		4,275
		5,975
Restriction for part-year occupation		
(10/12 × £5,975)		4,979
Less: Contributions paid by employee		
(10 months)		(1,000)
Taxable benefit		3,979

(b) **Cost of providing accommodation – 2010/11**

	Scenario (a)(i)	Scenario (a)(ii)
	£	£
Original cost + improvements (W1)	105,000	
Market value (W2)		165,000
Garage extension (July 2009)	10,000	10,000
	115,000	175,000

Workings

(W1) **Cost of providing accommodation – 2009/10**

	£
Cost (June 2004)	90,000
Improvements:	
Conservatory (Feb 2005)	15,000
Redecoration (Aug 2007) (Note 1)	Nil
Extension (July 2009) (Note 2)	Nil
Cost of providing accommodation	105,000

(W2) **Market value**

As Sachin has moved in more than 6 years after the employer acquired the property, the cost is the market value at the date the property was made available to Sachin, i.e. £165,000. The cost of the conservatory is already accounted for in the market value as at June 2009.

As in scenario (a)(i) the improvements that take place in 2009/10 do not come into the calculation until the following year.

Notes:

(1) The redecoration does not represent capital expenditure and therefore is not included in the calculation.

(2) Only those improvements up to the start of the tax year are included, as this expenditure does not take place until July 2009, it will not be included in the calculation until 2010/11.

Test your understanding 3

Paolo lives in a furnished company flat that cost his employers £105,000 in June 2004. The annual value (i.e. gross rateable value) of the flat is £2,500 and he pays his employers rent of £100 a month. The accommodation is not job-related.

Calculate Paolo's taxable benefit for 2009/10.

Assume the official rate of interest is 4.75%.

8 Benefits assessable on P11D employees and directors

Principles of assessment

Special provisions apply to:

- employees earning at a rate of £8,500 p.a. or more, and
- directors.

These are sometimes referred to as 'P11D employees'.

General rule

The general rule is that the assessable amount of the benefit is:

- the **cost of providing** the benefit
- unless there are specific statutory rules for valuing a benefit.

Under case law, the 'cost of providing' the benefit has been held to mean the **additional or marginal cost** incurred by the employer – not a proportion of the total cost.

This principle is particularly relevant where employer's provide in-house benefits, such as free tickets for employees of a bus company, or airline, reduced fees for children of school teachers in a public school.

Specific rules

Specific rules have been established for the following benefits that are assessable on P11D employees:

- Motor cars and vans (section 9).
- Private fuel (section 9).
- Beneficial loans (section 10).

- Use and gift of assets (section 11).
- Living accommodation expenses (section 12).

Note that:

- An employee is deemed to be provided with a benefit, not only when it is provided to him directly, but also when it is provided to a member of his family or household.
- To be taxed under these principles, a benefit must be provided to the employee by reason of his employment.

P11D employees

The benefits provided to employees earning at a rate of £8,500 pa or more, are reported to HMRC on form P11D. The term 'P11D employee' is therefore sometimes used to denote an employee earning at a rate of £8,500 pa. The term 'higher-paid' employee can also be used.

Directors are automatically subject to the benefits regime for those earning at a rate of over £8,500 pa, unless he or she:

- earns less than £8,500 pa,
- has no material interest in the company (5% of ordinary share capital), **and**
- is a full-time working director of the company.

The threshold income level

The calculation to ascertain whether a person reaches the threshold income level of £8,500 p.a. is as follows:

	£
Salary	X
Benefits assessable on all employees	X
Benefits assessable only on P11D employees	X
	—
	X
Less: Pension contributions	(X)
Payroll giving donations to charity	(X)
	—
Total earnings (for test purposes)	X
	—

Note that:

- There is no reduction in this calculation for any expenses incurred, apart from contributions to registered pension funds and charitable donations, under an approved payroll deduction scheme.
- In reality, it is likely that the vast majority of employees receiving benefits, would fall within the category of being a P11D employee. However, the examiner retains the right to test this area of the law to determine whether they are or not.

9 Motor cars, vans and private fuel

Motor cars

The company car is one of the benefits most widely provided for employees.

Where a company car is available to the employee for private use a taxable benefit arises, calculated as follows:

	£
(List price when new) × appropriate %	X
Less: Employee contributions for the private use of the car	(X)
Assessable benefit	X

List price

The list price of a car is calculated as follows:

- Price (including taxes) appropriate for the car on the assumption that it is sold in the UK, as an individual sale in the retail market, on the day before the car's first registration. Consequently employees of large companies cannot benefit from bulk discounts their employer might negotiate.
- Plus the value of all accessories and extras fitted at the time of issue, plus the cost of any added subsequently.
- Less any capital contributions up to £5,000, made by the employee towards the capital cost of the car.
- Subject to a maximum price (after deducting any employee capital contribution) of £80,000.

Appropriate percentage

The car benefit charge is a fixed percentage of the car's list price. The percentage to be applied is determined by the CO_2 emissions of the car.

CO_2 emissions per km	Petrol car %	Diesel car %
120 grams or less	10	13
121 – 135 grams	15	18
Each complete additional 5 grams emission above 135 grams	An additional 1% is added to the 15% or 18% up to a maximum % of 35%	

Note that the maximum % that can be applied to any car is 35%.

Employee contributions

- A reduction is made from the car benefit where the employee makes a financial contribution towards the running costs, as a condition of the car being available for his private use.
- This should not be confused with a capital contribution made towards the purchase cost of the car, which is deducted from the list price on which the percentage car benefit is based.

Additional points to note

- The car benefit is reduced proportionately where the car is unavailable for part of the tax year because it was first provided or ceased to be provided part-way through a tax year.
- This is also relevant where an employee changes their car during the year when a separate calculation needs to be performed in respect of each car.
- Where the car is unavailable for a period during the tax year (but was available both before and after, e.g. if it was under repair after a crash), the benefit charge is again proportionately reduced. However, the reduction applies only if the car was unavailable for a continuous period of at least 30 days.
- The charge for cars available for private use takes into account all of the running expenses of the vehicle, so there is no additional taxable benefit when the employer pays for insurance, road fund licence, maintenance etc.
- If a chauffeur is provided with the car however, it constitutes an additional benefit.
- A separate benefit charge is made for private car fuel (see below).

- When more than one car is made available simultaneously to an employee, the benefit in respect of the second car is computed in exactly the same way as set out above.

Example 4 - Benefits assessable on P11D employees

Boris is provided with a company car which has CO_2 emissions of 205 g/km.

Identify the % to be used in calculating the assessable benefit arising on the provision of the company car.

Explain the difference if the car provided to Boris had a diesel engine.

Answer to example 4

	%
Basic % for petrol car	15
Plus (205 – 135) × 1/5	14
Appropriate %	29

If Boris's car had a diesel engine, the charge will be increased by 3% to 32%.

Note that if the CO_2 emissions of the car were 209 g/km the starting point of the calculation would still be 205 g/km as you always round down the g/km to the nearest full number divisible by 5.

Test your understanding 4

Louis is provided with a company car by his employer. It has a carbon dioxide emission rate of:

(1) 167 g/km.

(2) 128 g/km.

(3) 232 g/km.

(4) 119 g/km.

Calculate the appropriate percentage assuming the car runs on petrol or diesel.

Pool cars

There is no assessable benefit if the car provided is a pool car.

To qualify as a pool car, all of the following conditions must be met during the tax year in question:

- The car must be used by more than one employee (and not usually by one employee to the exclusion of the others).
- It must not normally be kept overnight at or near the residence of any of the employees making use of it.
- Any private use by an employee must be merely incidental to his or her business use of it.

Example 5 - Benefits assessable on P11D employees

During 2009/10 Fashionable plc provided the following employees with company motor cars:

(1) Amanda was provided with a new diesel powered company car on 6 August 2009. The motor car has a list price of £13,500 and an official CO_2 emission rate of 127 g/km.

(2) Betty was provided with a new petrol powered car throughout 2009/10. The motor car has a list price of £16,400 and an official CO_2 emission rate of 193 g/km.

(3) Charles was provided with a new petrol powered car throughout 2009/10. Fashionable plc purchased the car for £21,000 and Charles was required to contribute £3,000 towards the purchase cost. The motor car has a list price of £22,600 and an official CO_2 emission rate of 254 g/km. Charles paid the company £1,200 during 2009/10 for the private use of the motor car.

Calculate the car benefit assessable on each of the above employees of Fashionable plc in 2009/10.

Answer to example 5

Amanda	£
Benefit: (£13,500 × 18%) (W1)	2,430
Less: Reduction for non-availability (W2)	(810)
Assessable benefit	1,620
Betty	
Benefit: (£16,400 × 26%) (W3)	4,264
Charles	
Benefit: (£19,600 × 35%) (W4)	6,860
Less: Payment for use of car (W5)	(1,200)
Assessable benefit	5,660

Workings

(W1) The CO_2 emissions are below the base level figure of 135 g/km, above 120 g/km, so the relevant percentage is 18% (15% plus a 3% charge for a diesel car).

(W2) Reduction for non-availability

The motor car was not available for four months of 2009/10, so the benefit is reduced by £810 (£2,430 × 4/12).

Alternatively, the benefit can be time apportioned and calculated more quickly for the 8 months the car was available as follows: (£13,500 x 18% x 8/12) = £1,620

(W3) Appropriate percentage

	%
Basic % for petrol car	15
Plus (190 – 135) × 1/5	11
	26

The CO_2 emissions figure of 193 is rounded down to 190 so that it is divisible by 5. The minimum percentage of 15% is increased in 1% steps for each 5 g/km above the base level.

(W4) The car benefit is based on the list price of the car. The price paid for the car by the company is not relevant.

Charles has contributed £3,000 towards the purchase price of the car. As this is less than £5,000, the capital contribution of £3,000 is deducted from the list price of the car upon which the benefit is calculated. The price on which the car benefit is calculated is £19,600 (£22,600 – £3,000).

The CO_2 emissions are above the base level of 135 g/km.

	%
Basic % for petrol car	15
Plus (230 – 135) × 1/5	23
	38
Restricted to	35

(W5) The contributions by Charles for the private use of the car reduce the assessable benefit.

Test your understanding 5

Sue is provided with a 2,000cc petrol driven car by her employer. The emission rate shown on the registration document is 201 grams of carbon dioxide per kilometre and the list price of the car when new was £16,000. During 2009/10, Sue drove 3,000 business miles and paid her employer £2,000 in respect of her private use of the car.

Paul is provided with a 2,300cc diesel powered car by his employer. The list price of the car when new was £36,000. During 2009/10, Paul drove 28,000 business miles. The emission rating of the car is 237g/km.

Calculate the benefit taxable on Sue and Paul for 2009/10.

Private fuel

In addition to the provision of the motor car, some employees also have all (or part) of their fuel for private mileage paid for by their employer.

This is an entirely separate benefit from the provision of the car, and the rules are as follows:

- The benefit where car fuel is provided for private motoring in a car provided by reason of a person's employment is also based on the CO_2 emissions of the car.
- The fuel benefit is calculated as a percentage of a base figure, which is set each year. The base figure for 2009/10 is £16,900. The base figure of £16,900 will be given in the tax rates and allowances section of the examination paper.

- The CO_2 percentage used in the calculation of the car benefit is also used to calculate the fuel benefit charge. The percentage will therefore range from 15% to 35% (10% or 13% for low emission cars).
- The fuel benefit is proportionately reduced where the fuel itself is only provided for part of the tax year.

Fuel provided for part of the tax year

However, it is not possible to opt in and out of the fuel benefit charge.

If, for example, fuel is provided from 6 April to 30 September 2009, then the fuel benefit for 2009/10 will only be charged for six months as the provision of fuel has permanently ceased.

If fuel is provided from 6 April to 30 September 2009, and then again from 1 January to 5 April 2010, the fuel benefit will not be reduced since the cessation was only temporary.

- No reduction is made to the fuel benefit for payments made by the employee unless he or she pays for all fuel used for private motoring. In that case there would be no fuel benefit.
- The fuel benefit only applies to vehicles for which there is a car benefit charge. It does not therefore apply to pool cars.

Example 6 - Benefits assessable on P11D employees

Continuing with the situations set out in Example 5 Fashionable plc.

Amanda was provided with fuel for private use between 6 August 2009 and 5 April 2010.

Betty was provided with fuel for private use between 6 April and 31 December 2009.

Charles was provided with fuel for private use between 6 April 2009 and 5 April 2010. He paid Fashionable plc £600 during 2009/10, towards the cost of private fuel, although the actual cost of this fuel was £1,000.

Calculate the car fuel benefit assessable on each of the above employees of Fashionable plc in 2009/10.

Answer to example 6

Amanda	£
Benefit: (£16,900 × 18%)	3,042
Less: Reduction for non-availability (W1)	(1,014)
Assessable benefit	2,028

Betty	
Benefit: (£16,900 × 26%)	4,394
Less: Reduction for non-availability (W2)	(1,099)
Assessable benefit	3,295

Charles	
Benefit: (£16,900 × 35%) (W3)	5,915

Workings

(W1) Reduction for non-availability:

The motor car was not available for four months of 2009/10, so the benefit is reduced by £1,014 (£3,042 × 4/12).

Alternatively the benefit can be time apportioned and calculated more quickly for the 8 months fuel was provided:

£16,900 x 18% x 8/12 = £2,028

(W2) Reduction for non-availability:

Fuel was not available for three months of 2009/10, so the benefit is reduced by £1,099 (£4,394 × 3/12).

Alternatively the benefit is calculated as: (£16,900 x 26% x 9/12) = £3,295

(W3) There is no reduction for the contribution paid by Charles towards the cost of private fuel, since he did not reimburse the full cost of the private fuel.

Test your understanding 6

Charles took up employment with Weavers Ltd on 1 July 2009. His remuneration package included a 5 year-old 2,500cc petrol-driven car with a list price of £24,000. He took delivery of the car on 1 August 2009. The car has CO_2 emissions of 220 g/km. As a condition of the car being made available to him for private motoring, Charles paid £100 per month for the car and £50 per month for petrol.

Weavers Ltd incurred the following expenses in connection with Charles's car:

Servicing	£450
Insurance	£780
Fuel (of which £1,150 was for business purposes)	£2,500
Maintenance	£240

Calculate Charles's assessable benefits for 2009/10 in connection with his private use of the car.

Test your understanding 7

Joan was employed as sales manager of Wilt Ltd from 1 August 2009 at a salary of £60,000 pa. From 1 November 2009, the company provided her with a 1,800cc car, the list price of which was £15,000 and the emission rate was 164 g/km. Up to 5 April 2010, she drove 6,000 miles of which 4,500 were for private purposes. The company paid for all running expenses.

Between 1 November 2009 and 31 January 2010, the company paid for all petrol usage including private use. Joan made a contribution to her employer of £15 per month towards the provision of the petrol for her private use. From 1 February 2010 her employer only paid for business use petrol.

Calculate Joan's taxable earnings for 2009/10.

Vans

The benefit rules for vans are different from those for the motor car. They are as follows:

- The benefit for the private use of a van for 2009/10 is a flat rate scale charge of **£3,000 p.a.**
- No benefit arises where the private use of a van is insignificant. When determining the level of private use, journeys between home and work are ignored. This is not the case for cars.
- Proportionate reductions in the scale charge are made where a van is unavailable (using the same definition as for cars) for part of the tax year.
- A reduction in the benefit is made for payments by the employee for the private use of the van.
- Where employees share the private use of the van, the scale charge is divided equally between the employees who made any private use of the van during the tax year, regardless of the amount of private use.
- In addition a benefit of **£500 p.a.** arises where fuel is provided for private mileage.

10 Beneficial loans

Introduction

Beneficial loans are those made to an employee below the **official rate** of interest. The examiner will assume that 4.75% applies throughout 2009/10.

Employees are liable to a benefit charge on:

	£
Interest that would be payable on the loan (had interest been charged at the official rate)	X
Less: Interest actually paid in respect of the tax year	(X)
	—
Assessable benefit	X
	—

- An exemption for small loans applies where all an employee's cheap or interest free loans (excluding loans which qualify for tax relief) total no more than £5,000.
- There are two methods of calculating the benefit:
  - **The simple (or average) method** – this uses the average balance of the loan outstanding during the year.

    (Balance outstanding at beginning of tax year + Balance outstanding at end of tax year) x 1/2

    If the loan was taken out or redeemed during the tax year, that date is used instead of the beginning or end of the tax year.
  - **The accurate (or precise) method** – this calculates the benefit day by day on the balance actually outstanding.

  Either the taxpayer or HMRC can decide that the precise method should be used.
- If an interest free or cheap loan is used for a purpose that fully qualifies for tax relief (e.g. loan to buy plant used wholly for employment), then there is no benefit.
- If all or part of a loan to an employee (whether or not made on low-interest or interest-free terms) is written off, the amount written off is treated as a benefit and charged to income tax.

Example 7 - Beneficial loans

Daniel was granted a loan of £35,000 by his employer on 31 March 2009, to help finance the purchase of a yacht. Interest is payable on the loan at 3% pa.

On 1 June 2009, Daniel repaid £5,000 and on 1 December 2009, he repaid a further £15,000. The remaining £15,000 was still outstanding on 5 April 2010. Daniel earns £30,000 pa.

Calculate the assessable benefit for 2009/10 using:

(a) **the average method**

(b) **the precise method.**

Answer to example 7

(a) Average method

	£	£
(£35,000 + £15,000) x 1/2 × 4.75%		1,187
Less: Interest paid		
6.4.09 – 31.5.09 : (£35,000 × 3% × 2/12)	175	
1.6.09 – 30.11.09: (£30,000 × 3% × 6/12)	450	
1.12.09 – 5.4.10: (£15,000 × 3% × 4/12)	150	
		(775)
Benefit		412

(b) Precise method

	£
6.4.09 – 31.5.09: (£35,000 × 4.75% × 2/12)	277
1.6.09 – 30.11.09: (£30,000 × 4.75% × 6/12)	712
1.12.09 – 5.4.10: (£15,000 × 4.75% × 4/12)	237
	1,226
Less: Interest paid (as above)	(775)
Benefit	451

In this situation HMRC could opt for the precise method, although they would probably accept £412 as the difference is not significant.

Test your understanding 8

Bob is loaned £10,000, interest free, by his employer on 6 August 2008. He repaid £2,000 on 6 September 2009.

Calculate the amount taxable on Bob in 2009/10.

Assume an official rate of interest of 4.75%.

Exemption for commercial loans

There is an exemption for loans made to employees on commercial terms by employers who lend to the general public e.g. banks. The exemption will apply where:

- the loans are made by an employer whose business includes the lending of money
- loans are made to employees on the same terms and conditions as are available to members of the public
- a substantial number of loans on these terms are made to public customers.

11 Assets provided to employees

Private use of an asset provided by the employer

The general rule that applies to the provision of assets (other than cars and vans) is that an employee is taxed on an annual benefit of:

20% of an asset's market value at the time it is first provided.

- Where the employer rents the asset made available to the employee instead of buying it, the employee is taxed on the rental paid by the employer, rather than 20% of market value **if** the rental is the higher figure.
- Payments made by the employee for the use of the asset reduce (or eliminate) the taxable benefit.
- The provision of one mobile phone to an employee is an exempt benefit. The above rules however, will apply to any additional mobile phones provided.
- These rules do not apply to cars, vans and living accommodation. As we have already seen special rules apply to the provision of these assets.

Example 8 - Use of assets

An employee is provided with a computer by his employer, which cost £800.

Compute the benefit arising on the employee. How does your answer vary if the employer rents the computer for £200 pa?

Answer to example 8

The benefit taxed as employment income is £160 (£800 × 20%). The benefit is assessed for **each** tax year in which it is provided (not just the one in which it was first made available).

In the event that the company rents the computer for £200 p.a. rather than owns it as the rent is higher than the general rule calculation, it will be the rent paid that is assessed on the employee.

Gifts of assets

If an employer purchases a new asset and gives it to an employee immediately, the employee is taxed on the cost to the employer.

Private use followed by gift of the asset

Where an asset is used by an employee and then subsequently given to that employee, the employee is taxed on the higher of:

	£	£
Asset market value when gifted		X
		—
Asset market value at the time it was **first made available** to the employee	X	
Less: The benefits assessed on the employee during the time he or she had the use of it, but did not own it	(X)	
	—	X
		—

If applicable, any amount paid for the asset by the employee is deducted from either figure in the above calculation.

The purpose of the special rule for gifts of used assets is to prevent employees gaining from gifts of assets that depreciate in value rapidly once they are used.

Where the asset being given to an employee is a used car or van, the above rules do not apply. Instead, the benefit is the market value at the date of transfer.

Example 9 - Use of assets

Brian's employer, X Ltd, purchased a dishwasher for his use on 1 June 2008, costing £600. On 6 April 2009, X Ltd gave the dishwasher to Brian (its market value then being £150).

Calculate the benefit assessable on Brian on the basis of:

(a) the circumstances as set out above

(b) if Brian paid X Ltd £100 for the dishwasher.

Answer to example 9

(a) **Sale for nil proceeds**	£
Market value when first made available to Brian	600
Less: Benefit already assessed 2008/09:	
(£600 × 20% × 10/12)	(100)
Taxable benefit on gift: 2009/10	500

The benefit is £500 since this is greater than the dishwasher's market value when given to Brian (£150).

(b) **Sale of dishwasher to Brian for £100**	£
Benefit as calculated in (a) above	500
Less: Price paid	(100)
Taxable benefit on gift: 2009/10	400

Brian would also have been taxed on the benefits of using the dishwasher in 2008/09.

Note: Where the benefit is provided for only part of a tax year the benefit is reduced proportionately.

Test your understanding 9

A suit costing £300 was purchased for Bill's use by his employer on 6 April 2008. On 6 August 2009, the suit is purchased by Bill for £20, when the market value was £30. Bill earns £30,000 pa.

Calculate the amounts taxable on Bill for each of the tax years affected by the information above.

12 Expenses connected with living accommodation

In addition to the benefit charges outlined in section 7 (which apply to living accommodation provided to all employees):

- expenses connected with living accommodation (such as lighting and heating) are also taxable on higher paid employees where the cost is met by his employer.

Job-related accommodation

Where the employee's accommodation is job-related, there is a limit on this additional living accommodation expenses benefit.

The limit applies to the following types of expense:

- Heating, lighting and cleaning.
- Repairing, maintaining or decorating the premises.
- Furniture and other goods normal for domestic occupation.

The assessable benefit for the expenses is limited to 10% of net earnings (i.e. employment income excluding this benefit for living accommodation).

Example 10 - Expenses connected with living accommodation

Amy is a hotel manager and is provided with accommodation. Her salary is £25,000. She has other employment benefits of £500 and makes payments into her employer's registered occupational pension scheme of £2,000 pa.

The accommodation has an annual value of £1,500 and cost her employer £90,000 four years ago. The accommodation contains furniture which cost the employer £10,000 four years ago (when she first occupied the accommodation). The employer pays all of her household bills totalling £1,000.

(a) **Calculate the taxable benefit for 2009/10, assuming the accommodation is not job-related.**

(b) **Explain how the taxable benefit will differ if the accommodation is job-related. You are not required to calculate the benefit.**

Assume the official rate of interest is 4.75%.

Answer to example 10

(a) **Taxable benefit – not job-related accommodation**

	£
Basic charge – Annual value	1,500
Expensive accommodation charge	
(£90,000 – £75,000) × 4.75%	712
Provision of services – furniture (20% × £10,000)	2,000
– household bills	1,000
Total benefit	5,212

Note: Be careful when calculating the accommodation benefit. Before starting to calculate consider all the factors that can impact the calculation (e.g. is it job related, does it cost more than £75,000, is it owned or rented by the employer?)

(b) **Job related accommodation**

If the accommodation is job related, there will be:

- No basic charge.
- No expensive accommodation charge.
- The provision of services benefit will be restricted to 10% of Andy's net earnings.

13 Comprehensive examples

Example 11 - Employment benefits

Mr Darcy, managing director of the Pemberley Trading Co Ltd, is paid an annual salary of £36,000 and also bonuses based on the company's performance. Pemberley Trading Co Ltd's accounting year ends on 31 December each year and the bonuses are normally determined and paid on 31 May thereafter. In recent years bonuses have been:

	£
Year to 31 December 2007	4,000
Year to 31 December 2008	8,000
Year to 31 December 2009	4,000

Mr Darcy uses a company car (3,500cc) purchased in 2003, at its list price of £20,000. Running expenses, including diesel paid by the company, were £2,600 in the year. The car has CO_2 emissions of 225 g/km.

Compute Mr Darcy's income tax liability for 2009/10. Briefly give reasons for your treatment of items included or excluded, in arriving at his taxable income.

Answer to example 11

Mr Darcy – Income tax computation – 2009/10

	£
Salary	36,000
Bonus (Note 1)	8,000
	44,000
Car benefit (£20,000 × 35%) (W)	7,000
Car fuel benefit (£16,900 × 35%) (Note 2)	5,915
Total income	56,915
Less: Personal allowance (PA)	(6,475)
Taxable income	50,440

	£	£
Basic rate	37,400 x 20%	7,480
Higher rate	13,040 x 40%	5,216
	50,440	
Income tax liability		12,696

Notes: Explanation of treatment

(1) Under the receipts basis for directors the bonus is treated as received, and therefore taxed, when it is determined. Thus the bonus determined in May 2009, is taxable in 2009/10.

(2) A fuel benefit will arise if Mr Darcy is provided with fuel for private motoring. It has been assumed that this is the case.

Working: Car benefit percentage

	%
Basic % for diesel car	18
Plus (225 – 135) x 1/5	18
	36

The maximum percentage of 35% therefore applies.

Test your understanding 10

Mr Drake is employed as the sales director of Drakemain Ltd at a salary of £20,000 pa.

Details of expenses and benefits paid by his employer for the year ended 5 April 2010, are as follows:

	£
Entertainment expenses reimbursed	683
Travelling and subsistence expenses	
(including £385 rail fares home to office)	826
Motor car benefit	4,800
Gross annual value of company house	650
Medical subscription	409
Home telephone (calls)	160
Private fuel – taxable benefit	4,200
	11,728

You are given the following further information.

(1) £10 per month is deducted from Mr Drake's net salary to cover his private use of the motor car and £40 per month as rent for the house.

(2) Mr Drake paid the council tax on the company house in the year 2009/10. This amounted to £325.

(3) The telephone installed in the company house is used only 40% for business.

(4) Unless otherwise indicated, all expenses reimbursed to Mr Drake were incurred for business purposes.

(5) The company purchased a TV on 6 April 2008 and allowed Mr Drake the use of it for the whole of the years ended 5 April 2009 and 2010. The set was then given to him on 5 April 2010. The set cost £500 and was worth £150 in April 2010.

Calculate Mr Drake's taxable employment income for 2009/10.

Test your understanding 11

Mrs Cornell is a senior executive with Berkeley plc. Her salary is £20,000 pa. In the tax year 2009/10 her employers will make the following benefits available to her:

(1) A Ford Granada 2,300cc motor car from 6 October 2009. Its list price will be £18,000 in October 2009 and its CO_2 emissions will be 189 g/km. The company will pay all running expenses including private diesel.

(2) She will continue to have the use of a stereo system owned by the company which cost £2,000 two years ago and which is kept at her home.

(3) Berkeley plc has provided Mrs Cornell with a television for her personal use since 6 April 2007 when it cost £1,200. On 6 April 2009 the television was sold to Mrs Cornell for £225 when its market value was £375.

(4) Berkeley plc provided Mrs Cornell with an interest-free loan of £30,000 on 1 January 2009. She will repay £10,000 of the loan on 30 June 2009. The loan is not used for a qualifying purpose.

In addition she has been offered the choice of luncheon vouchers of £2 per day (for 200 working days) or free meals worth £3 per day in the company's canteen (for 200 working days). Meals are available free of charge to all other employees.

After making the most tax efficient choice in respect of the lunch facilities, calculate the total value for taxation purposes of the benefits Mrs Cornell will receive for the tax year 2009/10.

Test your understanding 12

Basil Ransom is managing director of Boston plc. He is also a substantial shareholder in the company.

The company's accounts show the following information:

Years ended 30 April:	2008	2009	2010
	£	£	£
Salary, as managing director	13,620	43,560	44,100
Performance bonus	10,000	15,000	18,000

The performance bonus is determined and paid in the July following the accounting year end.

Mr Ransom has the use of a 2,800cc Porsche motor car with a list price of £34,000. The CO_2 emissions were 242g/km. All petrol and expenses were paid by the company. Mr Ransom drove a total of 18,000 miles in 2009/10, of which 10,000 were for private purposes.

He reimbursed the company £50 in respect of private petrol.

Mr Ransom also has had the use of a company house since 6 April 2009, whose annual value is £1,200 and which is provided rent free. The house had cost £90,000 in 2002 and its market value in April 2009 was £135,000.

The company pays private medical insurance for all its employees. Mr Ransom's share of the group premium was £320 for 2009/10. In June 2009 he needed to have treatment following a motor accident and the cost to the insurance company was £1,720.

In 2009/10 Mr Ransom was reimbursed £1,500 in respect of business travelling in the UK.

Calculate the assessable earnings of Mr Ransom for 2009/10 after his claim for a deduction from employment income.

14 Chapter summary

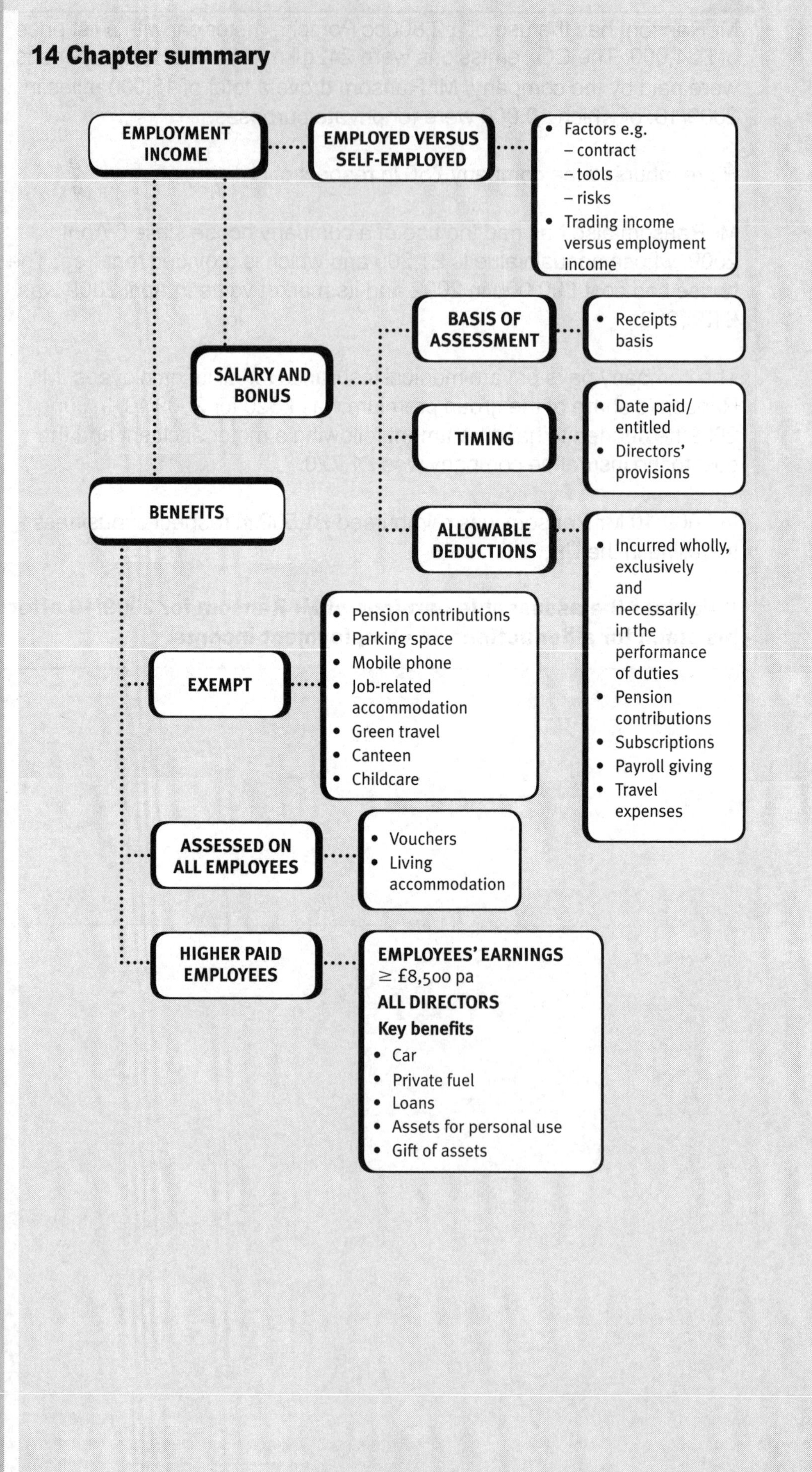

Test your understanding answers

Test your understanding 1

John

(a) **Taxable amount**

	£	£
Income (12,000 × 38p)		4,560
Less: Allowable expenses		
10,000 × 40p	4,000	
2,000 × 25p	500	
		(4,500)
Taxable amount		60

(b) **If employer paid 35p**

If John's employer paid 35p per mile, the total paid would be 12,000 × 35p = £4,200.

John could deduct the shortfall of £300 (£4,500 – £4,200) from his employment income, as an allowable expense.

Test your understanding 2

Underwood

	£	£
Basic salary (£950 × 12)		11,400
Bonus paid in May 2009 (receipts basis)		1,260
		12,660
Less: Allowable expenses		
Subscription	100	
Pension contribution	342	
Payroll deduction scheme	200	
		(642)
Taxable employment income		12,018

Test your understanding 3

Paolo

Assessable benefit for accommodation – 2009/10

	£
Basic charge – annual value (no rent paid by employer)	2,500
Expensive living accommodation charge	
(£105,000 – £75,000) × 4.75%	1,425
	3,925
Less: Contribution by employee (£100 × 12)	(1,200)
Taxable benefit	2,725

Test your understanding 4

Louis

CO_2 emissions		**Petrol %**	**Diesel %**
167 g/km	Basic %	15	18
	Plus (165 – 135) x 1/5	6	6
		21	24
128 g/km	Basic %	15	18
232 g/km	Basic %	15	18
	Plus (230 – 135) x 1/5	19	19
		34	37
	Restricted to maximum		35%
119 g/km	Basic % – low emission car	10	13

Test your understanding 5

Sue

	£
£16,000 × 28% (W)	4,480
Less: Contribution	(2,000)
Benefit	2,480

Working: Appropriate %

	%
Basic % for petrol car	15
Plus (200 – 135) x 1/5	13
	28

Paul

Benefit = £36,000 × 35% (W) = £12,600

Working: Appropriate %

	%
Basic % for diesel car	18
Plus (235 – 135) x 1/5	20
	38
Restricted to	35

Note that the amount of business mileage driven is not relevant to the calculation.

Test your understanding 6

Charles

	£
Car benefit: (£24,000 × 32% (W1) x 8/12 (W2))	5,120
Less: Payment for use (W3)	(800)
	4,320
Fuel benefit: (£16,900 × 32% (W4) x 8/12 (W2))	3,605
Total assessable benefits	7,925

Workings

(W1) Appropriate %

	%
Basic % for petrol car	15
Plus (220 – 135) x 1/5	17
	32

(W2) Reduction for non-availability of car

Car first made available on 1 August 2009, therefore not available for 4 months of 2009/10. It has been available for 8 months.

(W3) Payment for use

Payment made for 8 months @ £100/month = £800.

(W4) Car fuel

The fuel benefit is calculated using the same percentage as the car benefit of a fixed amount, which is £16,900 for 2009/10. Same proportionate reduction for non-availability applies as for car benefit charge.

Note: Charles cannot deduct the £50 per month paid for petrol and does not qualify for a reduction of the fuel scale charge, because he does not pay for all fuel used for private motoring.

Test your understanding 7

Joan

	£
Salary (£60,000 × 8/12)	40,000
Car benefit (£15,000 × 20% (W1) x 5/12)	1,250
Fuel benefit (£16,900 × 20% × 3/12 (W2))	845
Taxable earnings	42,095

Workings

(W1) Appropriate %

	%
Basic % for petrol	15
Plus (160 – 135) x 1/5	5
	20

The car has only been available for 5 months.

(W2) The petrol was only provided for 3 months in 2009/10. The contribution towards the cost of private petrol does not reduce the fuel benefit, as the cost was not reimbursed in full.

Test your understanding 8

Bob

(a) Average method

	£
4.75% × ½ × (£10,000 + £8,000)	427
Interest paid by employee	–
Taxable benefit	427

(b) Precise method

	£
6.4.09 – 5.9.09: (£10,000 × 4.75% × 5/12)	198
6.9.09 – 5.4.10: (£8,000 × 4.75% × 7/12)	222
	420

In this situation, whilst Bob can opt for the precise method it is likely he will accept an assessment of £427.

Test your understanding 9

Bill

	£	£
2008/09		
Annual value (20% × £300)		60
2009/10		
Annual value (20% × £300) × 4/12		20
Assessment upon gift, greater of:		
Suit's current market value	30	
Less: Price paid by employee	(20)	
	10	
Suit's original market value	300	
Less: Taxed in respect of use to date:		
2008/09	(60)	
2009/10	(20)	
	220	
Less: Price paid by employer	(20)	
	200	200
Amount assessable in 2009/10		220

Note: Essentially, Bill has received a £300 suit for £20 and been assessed on taxable income of £280 (£60 + £220).

Test your understanding 10

Mr Drake

	£	£
Salary		20,000
Expenses and benefits		11,728
		31,728
Less: Entertaining (disallowed in the employer's tax computation)	683	
Travelling, etc. (other than home to office)	441	
Telephone (£160 less private 60%)	64	
Payments for accommodation (£40 per month)	480	
Payments for use of company car	120	
		(1,788)
		29,940
Benefit for use of TV (20% of £500)		100
Benefit for gift of TV (£500 – £100 – £100)		300
Employment income assessment		30,340

Note: Council tax is the personal liability of Mr Drake. If his employer met the cost, it would be taxed on Mr Drake as a benefit.

Test your understanding 11

Mrs Cornell

	£
Car (W1)	2,520
Fuel (W2)	2,366
Stereo system (20% × £2,000)	400
Television (W3)	495
Beneficial loan (W4)	1,068
Lunch facility (W5)	Nil
Taxable benefits – 2009/10	6,849

Workings

(W1) **Car benefit**

	%
Base % for diesel car	18
(185 - 135) = (50 ÷ 5)	10
	28

Car benefit = (28% × £18,000) = £5,040

Time apportion benefit as the car was only available from 6 October 2009: (£5,040 × 6/12) = £2,520

(W2) **Fuel benefit**

(28% × £16,900) = £4,732

Time apportion as only available from 6 October 2009 (£4,732 × 6/12) = £2,366

(W3) **Television**

Greater of:	£
(1) Original cost less benefits assessed	
£1,200 – (£240 + £240)	720
(2) Current market value	375

	£
Original cost less benefits assessed	720
Less: Amount paid to employer	(225)
Assessable benefit	495

(W4) **Beneficial Loan**

	£
Average method	
(£30,000 + £20,000) × ½ × 4.75%	1,187
Precise method	
£30,000 × 3/12 (April/May/June) × 4.75%	356
£20,000 × 9/12 (July to March) × 4.75%	712
	1,068

Therefore Mrs Cornell should elect for the precise method.

(W5) **Lunch facilities**

Luncheon vouchers	
200 days × (£2 - 15p)	£370
Canteen: 200 days × £3/day	Exempt

Test your understanding 12

Basil Ransom

Assessable earnings – 2009/10

	£
Salary (1/12 × £43,560 + 11/12 × £44,100)	44,055
Performance bonus (received in July 2009)	15,000
Benefits:	
Car benefit (35% × £34,000) (W1)	11,900
Fuel benefit (35% × £16,900) (W1)	5,915
Living accommodation:	
Annual value	1,200
Expensive accommodation charge	
(£135,000 - £75,000) × 4.75% (W2)	2,850
Private medical insurance	320
Reimbursed expenses	1,500
	82,740
Less: Deduction from employment income claim	(1,500)
Assessable earnings	81,240

Workings:

(W1) **Car and fuel percentage**

	%
Basic % for petrol car	15
(240 – 135) = (105 ÷ 5)	21
	36 Restricted to 35%

There is no deduction for the reimbursement of part of the cost of the private petrol provided.

(W2) **Accommodation**

The house was acquired by the employer more than six years before it was made available to the employee, therefore the market value at the date it was provided to Mr Ransom is used instead of the cost.

chapter

5

Income from self-employment

Chapter learning objectives

Upon completion of this chapter you will be able to:

- state the basis of assessment for income from self-employment
- describe and apply the badges of trade
- prepare the tax adjusted trading profit/loss
- recognise the relief that can be obtained for pre-trading expenditure.

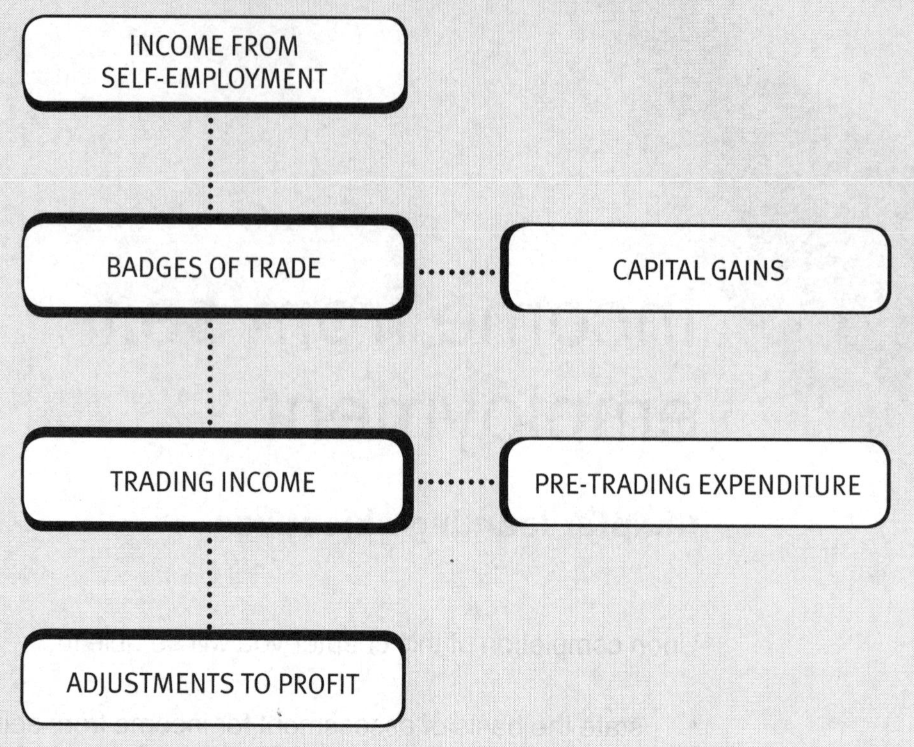

1 Introduction

Trading income

The profits of an unincorporated trader arising from a trade, profession or vocation are assessed as trading income. Typically these individuals are referred to as self-employed or sole traders.

Basis of assessment

The profits of an unincorporated business are assessed on a **current year basis (CYB)**.

This means the profits assessed in a tax year are those of the **twelve month accounting period ending in that tax year**.

Test your understanding 1

A sole trader prepares his accounts to 31 December 2009.

In which tax year will the profits be assessed?

The detailed basis of assessment rules are covered in more detail in Chapter 8.

2 Badges of trade

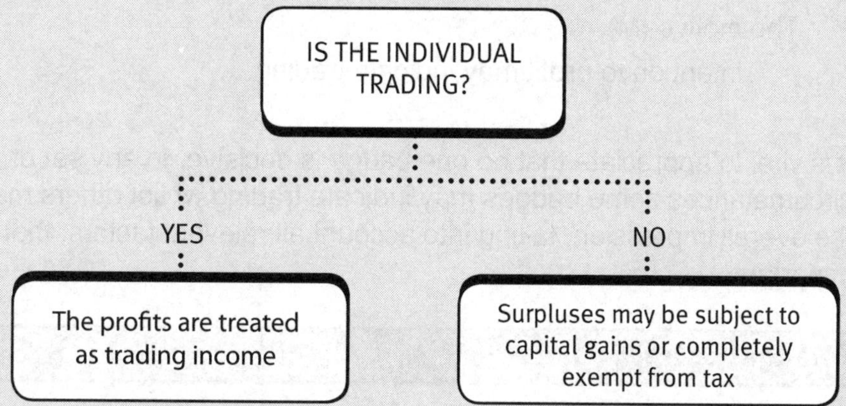

To determine whether an individual is trading, a number of tests, known as the 'badges of trade', are considered.

Nature of trade

'Trade includes every trade, manufacture, adventure or concern in the nature of trade.'

Although the above is the statutory definition of a trade, in practice it is not a very helpful one. What constitutes a trade has been reviewed numerous times by the Courts and the criteria have been developed and are set out by a Royal Commission. These criteria which should be considered are known as the 'badges of trade'.

The badges of trade which are used to determine if an activity is in the nature of a trade are as follows (and can be remembered by using the mnemonic 'SOFIRM'):

- The subject matter of the transaction (S).
  - are the goods of a type normally used for trading?
- The length of the period of ownership (O).
  - short period of ownership is more likely to indicate trading.
- The frequency of similar transactions by the same person (F).
  - frequent transactions indicate trading.
- Supplementary work, improvements and marketing (I).
  - work performed on goods to make them more marketable indicates trading.

- The circumstances/reason for the sale (R).
  - forced sale indicates not trading.
- The motive (M).
  - intention to profit may indicate trading.

It is vital to appreciate that no one badge is decisive. In any set of circumstances some badges may indicate trading whilst others may not. It is the overall impression, taking into account all relevant factors, that is important.

Badges of trade

Subject matter of the transaction (S)

The type of goods involved in a transaction is relevant in deciding the nature of the transaction. An asset is said to have been acquired for one of three reasons:

- an investment – in which case it is capital in nature and not subject to income tax
- goods for the private use of the individual (or family) – therefore not subject to tax
- stock in trade – therefore a trading transaction and subject to income tax.

Normally, to be considered as an investment, the goods must either be income producing (such as land or shares), or liable to be held for aesthetic reasons (such as works of art).

So, when an individual acquired 1,000,000 rolls of toilet paper and resold them at a profit, he was held not to have acquired them for private use, not acquired and resold an investment and consequently was judged to have made a trading profit.

The length of the period of ownership (O)

As a general rule, the longer the period between the date of acquisition and the date of disposal of an asset, the greater the likelihood that the transaction will not be treated as trading in nature.

Care must be taken in applying this principle and in particular the nature of the asset has to be taken into account.

For instance, it would be necessary to hold land for far longer than quoted shares to obtain the benefit of this rule, since normally the market in land operates much more slowly than that in shares.

The frequency of similar transactions by the same person (F)

As was seen in the toilet rolls case above, a single transaction may be enough for a person to be regarded as trading. However, the usual situation is that the more often similar transactions are entered into, the more likely they will be regarded as trading activities.

Again the nature of the assets involved is important:

- A taxpayer was held to be trading on the evidence of over 200 Stock Exchange sales and purchases over a period of three years.
- A director of a spinning company was engaged in buying the shares of mill-owning companies and then selling the assets of the companies (asset stripping). One transaction of this kind might have been regarded as capital in nature, but when he had done the same thing four times over, he was held to be trading.

Supplementary work, improvements and marketing (I)

Supplementary work done on an asset to make it more marketable before it is sold is an indication of trading.

For example, the purchase of brandy in bulk and subsequent blending and re-casking before resale was held to be a trade.

The circumstances/reason for the sale (R)

A forced sale to raise cash for an emergency is an indication that the transaction was not of a trading nature.

Similarly, an individual who deliberately purchases goods is more likely to be regarded as trading than one who acquires them accidentally, for example, by inheritance or by gift.

The motive (M)

The more obvious an individual's intention to profit from a transaction the more likely it is that it will be viewed as trading.

For example, an individual purchased a large quantity of silver bullion as a hedge against the devaluation of sterling. The profit resulting from its resale was regarded as a trading profit, on the basis that the motive for the transaction was to make a profit in sterling terms.

It is important to appreciate, however, that the absence of a profit motive does not of itself preclude the transaction from being treated as trade.

3 Adjusting the accounting profit

The net profit per the financial accounts and the taxable trading profit figure are rarely the same figure.

For example, HMRC will not allow all accounting expenses for tax purposes. Therefore, a number of adjustments need to be made to the accounting profit for tax purposes in order to calculate the taxable trading profit (tax-adjusted trading profit).

Adjustments

There are four types of adjustment that need to be made to move from accounting profit to the tax-adjusted trading profit as follows:

Reason for adjusting profits	Adjustment required to arrive at tax-adjusted trading profit
Expenditure which tax law prevents from being an allowable deduction may have been charged in the profit and loss account.	**Add back** to the accounting profit.
Taxable trading income may not be included in the profit and loss account.	**Add back** to the accounting profit.
Expenditure that is deductible for tax purposes may not be charged in the profit and loss account.	**Deduct** from accounting profit.
Income may be included in the profit and loss account that is not taxable as trading income.	**Deduct** from accounting profit.

Pro forma – Tax adjusted trading profit

	£	£
Net profit per accounts		X
Add: Expenditure not allowable for taxation purposes	X	
Taxable trading income not credited in the accounts	X	
	—	X
		—
		X
Less: Expenditure not charged in the accounts but allowable for the purposes of taxation	X	
Income included in the accounts that is not taxable as trading income	X	
Capital allowances (see Chapters 6 & 7)	X	
	—	(X)
		—
Tax-adjusted trading profit		X
		—

Before considering the adjustments in detail, three important points need to be emphasised:

- We are only calculating the taxable trading profit here. The fact that an item of income (such as rental income) is excluded in calculating the tax-adjusted trading profit, does not mean that it is not taxable. It just means that it is not taxable as trading income. As we saw in Chapter 3, rental income is taxable as property business income and comes into the income tax computation as a separate source of income.
- The starting point in deciding whether or not an adjustment is necessary, is that the principles of normal commercial accountancy apply unless overridden by tax law (i.e. if allowed for accounting, it is allowed for tax **unless** there is a proivision in tax law requiring an adjustment).

4 Non-deductible expenditure

Non-deductible/disallowable expenditure is the most common form of adjustment. The following are the main examples that you can expect to come across in the examination.

Expenditure not incurred wholly and exclusively for trading purposes

The general rule to follow in deciding whether expenditure is an allowable deduction from trading profits is that only expenditure incurred **wholly and exclusively for the purposes of the trade** is allowable.

Expenditure may be disallowed because:

- it is too remote from the purposes of the trade – the remoteness test
- it has more than one purpose and one of them is not trading – the duality principle.

Remoteness test and duality principle

Remoteness test

Expenditure is regarded as being too remote from the trade, when it is incurred in some other capacity than that of trading. For example, normal accountancy and compliance taxation fees are allowable, but the cost of any personal tax advice work is not.

Duality principle

- The duality principle is best illustrated by decided cases:
  - A self-employed trader was unable to eat lunch at home and claimed the extra cost of eating out as a tax deduction. It was held that the expenditure was not allowable. The duality of purpose lay in the fact that the taxpayer needed to eat to live, not just to work.
  - A self-employed barrister was refused a tax deduction for her expenditure on the black clothing necessary for court appearances. It was held that the expenditure had been for her personal as well as professional needs.
- Where expenditure has been incurred for both trading and non-trading purposes, a deduction can be claimed for the business use proportion, provided it can be separately identified. This is particularly relevant to expenditure on motor cars, where business and private mileage can be identified.

Appropriations

Appropriations are the withdrawal of funds from a business (i.e. profit extraction rather than expenses incurred in earning them) and, as such, are disallowed expenses. The most common examples are:

- A business owner's salary.
- Interest paid to the owner on capital invested in the business.

- Drawings made by a sole trader or partner.
- Any private element of expenditure relating to the owner's motor car, telephone etc.

Example 1 - Non-deductible expenditure

Jim is a self-employed solicitor. During the year ended 31 December 2009, Jim drove a total of 20,000 miles and his motor expenses amounted to £10,800.

Each working day Jim drives from his home to his office, which is ten miles away. He works five days a week and 50 weeks a year.

Jim drove 1,500 miles on a holiday in August 2009, but for the rest of the year his wife's car was used for private journeys. Jim's wife owns her own car, and is not involved in Jim's business.

Calculate the amount of Jim's motor expenses that are allowable.

Answer to example 1

Jim's motor expenses will be apportioned according to his proportion of business mileage to total mileage for the year.

Travel from home to work and back is classed as private mileage, so Jim's total private mileage is 6,500 miles (10 × 5 × 50 × 2 + 1,500). His business mileage is therefore 13,500 miles (20,000 - 6,500).

Of the motor expenses, £7,290 (£10,800 × 13,500/20,000) is allowable and £3,510 (£10,800 × 6,500/20,000) is disallowed.

Excessive salary paid to a sole trader's family

- Business owners (especially sole traders) often employ their spouses or members of their families in their business.
- Any salary paid to the family of the owner of an unincorporated business will be allowable provided it is not excessive. In other words, it must be remuneration at the commercial rate for the work performed. Any excessive salary payments are disallowed.

Test your understanding 2

Sheila is in business running her own advertising agency. Her husband Richard has given up work to look after their daughter who was born three years ago.

Until 2009 Sheila employed a part-time typist, who was paid £4,500 pa, but the typist then left and Sheila could not find a suitable replacement. Richard therefore agreed to do Sheila's typing at home. During the year ended 5 April 2010, Sheila paid Richard a salary of £10,000.

Explain the probable adjustment in calculating the tax-adjusted trading income for the year ended 5 April 2010.

Interest payable

- Interest on borrowings such as business account overdrafts, credit cards or hire purchase contracts, is an allowable trading expense calculated on an accruals basis.
- For unincorporated businesses, interest paid on overdue tax is never allowable and likewise interest received on overpaid tax is not taxable.

Capital expenditure

- Expenditure on capital assets is not an allowable trading expense. Any expense in the form of depreciation, loss on sale of fixed assets or the amortisation of a lease is also disallowed for tax purposes.
- The distinction between revenue expenditure (allowable) and capital expenditure (disallowable) is not always clear-cut. This is especially the case when deciding if expenditure is in respect of a repair to an asset (revenue expenditure) or is an improvement (capital expenditure).

Repair v Improvement

Whilst you are not required to know the legal cases from which the following decisions were reached, it is important to understand the legal principles behind case decisions regarding capital expenditure as this will help with exam questions:

- The cost of initial repairs in order to make an asset usable is not deductible.

  For example, a taxpayer failed to obtain a deduction for repair work on a newly bought ship, in order to make the ship seaworthy prior to using it.

- The cost of initial repairs is deductible if the asset can be put into use before any repairs are carried out.

  For example, a taxpayer obtained a deduction for the cost of renovating newly acquired cinemas. The work was to make good normal wear and tear and the purchase price was not reduced to take account of the necessary repair work.

- The treatment of restoration costs is another disputed area. To be allowable, it needs to be proven that the restoration renews a subsidiary part of an asset.

  For example, the replacement of a factory chimney, was held to be a repair to the factory.

  Where it is deemed as the renewal of a separate asset it is treated as non-allowable capital expenditure.

  For example, the replacement of an old stand with a new one at a football club, was held to be expenditure on a new asset and thus capital expenditure.

- Expenditure on plant and machinery and industrial buildings attracts capital allowances. They are effectively a form of depreciation allowance for tax purposes. Capital allowances are covered in detail in Chapters 6 and 7.

Car leasing

- Rental and lease charges payable in respect of leased motor cars are allowable where the CO_2 emissions of the car are 160 g/km or less.
- Where CO_2 emissions exceed 160 g/km, 15% of the rental/lease charges are disallowed.

Example 2 - Expensive car leasing

Roger enters into a leasing contract for a motor car with CO_2 emissions of 168 g/km, paying £8,000 pa in rental charges.

Calculate the amount of the rental charge that is disallowed.

Answer to example 2

Disallowable rental charge = (15% × £8,000) = £1,200

Subscriptions and donations

- Trade or professional association subscriptions are normally deductible since they will be made wholly and exclusively for the purposes of the trade.
- In the case of charitable donations they must meet three tests to be allowable:
  - First, they must be wholly and exclusively for trading purposes (for example, promoting the business name).
  - Second, it must be local and reasonable in size in relation to the business making the donation.
  - Third, it must be made to an educational, religious, cultural, recreational or benevolent organisation.
- If the donation is disallowed but the payment was made to a charity, the taxpayer can instead claim relief under the Gift Aid provisions.
- Subscriptions and donations to political parties are not deductible.
- Non-charitable gifts are not allowable, except as set out below.

Entertaining and gifts

- Entertainment expenditure is disallowed.
- The only exception is for expenditure relating to employees, provided it is not incidental to the entertainment of others.

Gifts to employees

- Gifts to employees are normally treated as allowable trading expenditure.
- Care must be taken, however, as the gift may fall within the benefit rules and be assessed on the employee as employment income.

Gifts to customers

- Gifts to customers are only allowable if:
  - they cost less than £50 per recipient per year; and
  - the gift is not of food, drink, tobacco or vouchers exchangeable for goods; and
  - the gift carries a conspicuous advertisement of the business making the gift.
- The cost of a gift that does not meet these conditions is disallowed.
- If the total of gifts in the tax year exceeds £50, it is the full cost of the item that is disallowable, not just the excess.

Legal and professional charges

In order to determine whether legal and professional charges are allowable, it is important to review the reasons for the business incurring the costs.

As a general principle, where expenditure is incurred for the purposes of the trade, the expenditure is allowable. Examples include:

- legal fees chasing trading debts
- charges incurred in defending the title to fixed assets.

Where expenditure is of a capital nature, it is disallowable. For example:

- Fees associated with acquiring new fixed assets
- There are the following exceptions:
  - Fees and other costs of obtaining long-term debt finance are allowable for a sole trader.
  - The cost of registering patents is allowable.
  - The expense of renewing a short lease (i.e. less than 50 years) is allowable, although the legal expenses incurred on the initial granting of the lease are not.

Impaired debts and allowances for debtors

The following are allowable items:

- The write-off of a trade debt (therefore, the recovery of a trade debt previously written-off is taxable).
- An allowance for trade debtors to reflect the potential irrecoverability or impairment of debtors, provided it is calculated in accordance with UK generally accepted accounting practice (UK GAAP). Again, the reduction in an allowance for trade debtors is taxable income.

The following items are disallowable:

- The write-off of a non-trade debt (e.g. a loan to a customer or a former employee).

Example 3 - Impaired debtor and allowance for debtor

The profit and loss account of Mary for the year ended 30 June 2009, includes a figure for impaired debts of £200. This is made up as follows:

	£	£
Trade debts written-off		500
Loan to former staff written-off		200
Allowance for impaired debtors		
As at 1 July 2008	900	
As at 30 June 2009	700	
		(200)
Trade debts recovered		(400)
Loan to supplier written-off		250
Loan to a customer recovered		(150)
		200

The loan to supplier written-off relates to a loan to a supplier with cash flow problems. The loan to the customer recovered is in respect of a loan written-off two years ago.

Calculate the adjustment required in preparing Mary's tax adjusted trading profit.

Answer to example 3

	£
Loan to former staff written-off	200
Loan to supplier written-off	250
	450
Less: Loan to customer recovered	(150)
Amount to add back to profit	300

To be allowed, debt write-offs must be in respect of normal trade debts. The recovery of such debts already written-off is taxable.

The write-off of other debts is not allowable when computing trading profit. Their recovery, after being written-off, is not taxable and will therefore not be included in the tax adjusted trading profit.

Amounts charged or credited to the profit and loss account in respect of allowances for trade debts are allowable deductions against trading profits.

Other items

Set out below is a list of some other items you may encounter and a brief description of how to treat each.

Type of expenditure	Treatment	Notes
Provisions for future costs (e.g. provision for future warranty costs)	Allow	Provided they are calculated in accordance with UK GAAP and their estimation is sufficiently accurate
Compensation for loss of office paid to an employee	Allow	Only if for benefit of trade
Counselling services for redundant employees	Allow	
Damages paid	Allow	Only if paid in connection with trade matter
Defalcations (e.g. theft/ fraud)	Allow	Only if by employee, not the business owner/director
Educational courses	Allow	Only if for trade purposes
Fines	Disallow	Unless parking fines incurred on business by employee, but not business owner/director
Payment that constitutes a criminal offence	Disallow	
Pension contributions to registered pension scheme	Allow	Provided paid (not accrued) by the year end
Premiums for insurance against an employee's death or illness	Allow	
Redundancy pay in excess of the statutory amount	Allow	On the cessation of trading the limit is 3 × the statutory amount
Removal expenses	Allow	Provided not an expansionary move
Salaries accrued at year end	Allow	Provided paid not more than 9 months after year end

Test your understanding 3

For each item of income or expenditure state whether you need to adjust for the item for tax purposes by adding or deducting an amount from the accounting profit.

Item of expenditure/income	**Add back/deduct**
Drawings of the proprietor	
£45,000 salary paid to the proprietor's spouse. Typical market rate is estimated at £15,000	
Subscription to golf club where sole trader might meet/entertain clients	
Legal fees to acquire a short lease (7 years)	
Trade related NVQ training course for apprentice employee	

5 Other adjustments

Taxable trading income not included in the profit and loss account

This adjustment is normally only needed when a trader removes goods from the business for his or her own use.

- The trader is treated as making a sale to himself based on the selling price of the goods concerned.
- Note that this rule does not apply to the supply of services.

The adjustment required depends on the treatment in the accounts:

- if the trader has accounted for the removal of the goods, he will have adjusted for the cost element, therefore for tax purposes the profit element of the transaction needs to be added in the adjustment of profits computation
- if the trader has not accounted for the removal of the goods, the full selling price must be added in the adjustment of profits computation.

Example 4 - Goods for own use

A car dealer removes a vehicle from the business for his own personal use. It had originally cost the business £10,000 and has a market value of £12,500. No entries have been made in the accounts to reflect this transaction, other than the original purchase.

Explain the adjustment, if any, that should be made to the car dealer's accounts, for tax purposes, to reflect the above transaction.

Answer to example 4

The tax-adjusted trading profit must reflect the transaction as if the owner has sold the vehicle to himself based on the selling price of the goods concerned.

In determining the adjustment required, it is important to identify the entries made in the accounts to date. In this example, only the original cost has been recorded, therefore the adjustment is to add the market value £12,500 to the accounting profit to arrive at the tax-adjusted trading profit.

If the removal of the vehicle had been accounted for, only the profit element of £2,500 would need to be added to the accounting profit to arrive at the tax-adjusted trading profit.

Deductible expenditure not charged in the profit and loss account

- The most important item of deductible expenditure not charged in the profit and loss account is the figure for capital allowances. These are deductible as if they were a trading expense. Capital allowances are covered in detail in Chapters 6 and 7.
- In addition to this, other examples include:
  - Allowable trading element of lease premiums paid on short leases.
  - Where a business owner uses their private residence partly for business purposes. For example, uses a room in their private house as an office, the business portion of running expenses is allowable.
  - Business calls from the private telephone of the sole trader.
  - Expenses that are wholly and exclusively for the trade that have been met from the private funds of the owner.

Short lease premiums

- When a landlord receives a premium for the grant of a short lease a proportion of the lease premium is charged to income tax as a property income (see Chapter 3).

- Where a business pays a premium for a short lease, for premises which he uses in his business, he is entitled to deduct a proportion of the amount assessable on the landlord in calculating his taxable trading profit. This will not be reflected in the accounts. However, the cost of the lease will be charged in the profit and loss accounts in an annual amortisation charge.

The adjustments required for the lease are therefore as follows:

- Add back: the amortisation charged in the accounts (disallowable as capital).
- Deduct: allowable proportion of the lease premium.

The allowable deduction for the trader is the property business income element of the premium (see Chapter 3) spread evenly over the period of the lease.

The property business income assessable on the landlord is calculated as:

P – (P × 2% × (D – 1))

Where:

P = total premium
D = duration of lease in years.

Example 5 - Lease premium

Lawrie prepares accounts to 31 March. On 1 April 2009 he paid a premium of £25,200 for the grant of a 21-year lease on business premises.

Calculate the deduction Lawrie can claim in his tax-adjusted trading profit.

Answer to example 5

	£
Premium	25,200
Less (£25,200 × 2% × (21 – 1))	(10,080)
Amount assessed on landlord	15,120

The annual allowable trading deduction for Lawrie is therefore £720 (£15,120 × 1/21) each year.

This deduction is time apportioned for the year ended 31 March 2010, if the premium had not been paid at the start of the accounting period.

Example 6 - Use of home for business

Sam is in business as a central heating engineer. She uses one room of her five-room house as an office, and no adjustment has been made in her accounts for the year ended 5 April 2010, in respect of this.

Sam has listed her household expenses relating to the year ended 5 April 2010, as follows:

	£
Electricity	400
Gas	250
Rates	450
Television repairs	50
Groceries	600
Video rental	200
Mortgage interest on £20,000 mortgage	900

Calculate the amount Sam can claim as a trading expense for her use of an office at home.

Answer to example 6

Sam uses one room out of five as an office and therefore it is appropriate to allow one fifth of her expenses that relate to running the home.

Sam's television repairs, groceries and video rental are all of a private nature and are therefore not allowable.

The total of the remaining items is £2,000 (£400 + £250 + £450 + £900).

Therefore, Sam's deductible trading expense for the use of the office is £400 (£2,000 × 1/5).

Income included in the profit and loss account that is not taxable trading income

There are three categories of income which need to be adjusted for as follows:

- Capital receipts (which may be treated as chargeable gains – see Chapter 14). In addition, any profit on the sale of a capital asset should also be deducted in calculating the tax adjusted trading profit.
- Other forms of income (such as savings income or dividends) must be deducted in arriving at the taxable trading profit. However, they may be subject to income tax by being included elsewhere in an individual's income tax computation.
- Income that is exempt from tax (such as interest received on overpaid income tax).

6 Relief for pre-trading expenditure

Any revenue expenditure, incurred in the **seven years** before a business commences to trade, is treated as an expense on the day that the business starts trading.

Example 7 - Relief for pre-trading expenditure

Able commenced trading on 1 April 2009. He had spent £6,000 in the previous six months advertising the fact that he was about to start trading.

Explain how the expenditure of £6,000 on advertising treated for tax purposes.

Answer to example 7

The £6,000 advertising expenditure is treated as a trading expense as if it had been incurred on 1 April 2009.

7 Comprehensive example

Test your understanding 4

On 1 June 2009 William Wise, aged 38, commenced in self-employment running a retail clothing shop.

William's profit and loss account for the year ended 31 May 2010:

	£	£
Gross profit		139,880
Administration expenses:		
Depreciation	4,760	
Light and heat (Note 1)	1,525	
Motor expenses (Note 2)	4,720	
Repairs and renewals (Note 3)	5,660	
Rent and rates (Note 1)	3,900	
Professional fees (Note 4)	2,300	
Wages and salaries (Note 5)	83,825	
		(106,690)
Other operating expenses (Note 6)		(2,990)
Net profit		30,200

Notes:

(1) **Private accommodation**

William and his wife live in a flat that is situated above the clothing shop. Of the expenditure included in the profit and loss account for light, heat, rent and rates, 40% relates to the flat.

(2) **Motor expenses**

During the year ended 31 May 2010, William drove a total of 12,000 miles, of which 9,000 were for private journeys.

(3) **Repairs and renewals**

The figure of £5,660 for repairs and renewals includes £2,200 for decorating the clothing shop during May 2009, and £1,050 for decorating the private flat during June 2009. The building was in a usable state when it was purchased.

(4) **Professional fees**

	£
Accountancy	700
Legal fees in connection with the purchase of the shop	1,200
Debt collection	400
	2,300

Included in the figure for accountancy is £250 in respect of capital gains tax work.

(5) **Wages and salaries**

The figure of £83,825 for wages and salaries includes the annual salary of £15,500 paid to William's wife. She works in the clothing shop as a sales assistant. The other sales assistants doing the same job are paid an annual salary of £11,000.

(6) **Other operating expenses**

The figure of £2,990 for other operating expenses, includes £640 for gifts to customers of food hampers costing £40 each, £320 for gifts to customers of pens carrying an advertisement for the clothing shop costing £1.60 each, £100 for a donation to a national charity, and £40 for a donation to a local charity's fête. The fête's programme carried a free advertisement for the clothing shop.

(7) **Goods for own use**

During the year ended 31 May 2010, William took clothes out of the shop for his personal use without paying for them. The cost of these clothes was £460, and they had a selling price of £650.

(8) **Plant and machinery**

The capital allowances available for the year ended 31 May 2010 are £13,060.

Calculate William's tax adjusted trading profit for the year ended 31 May 2010.

8 Chapter summary

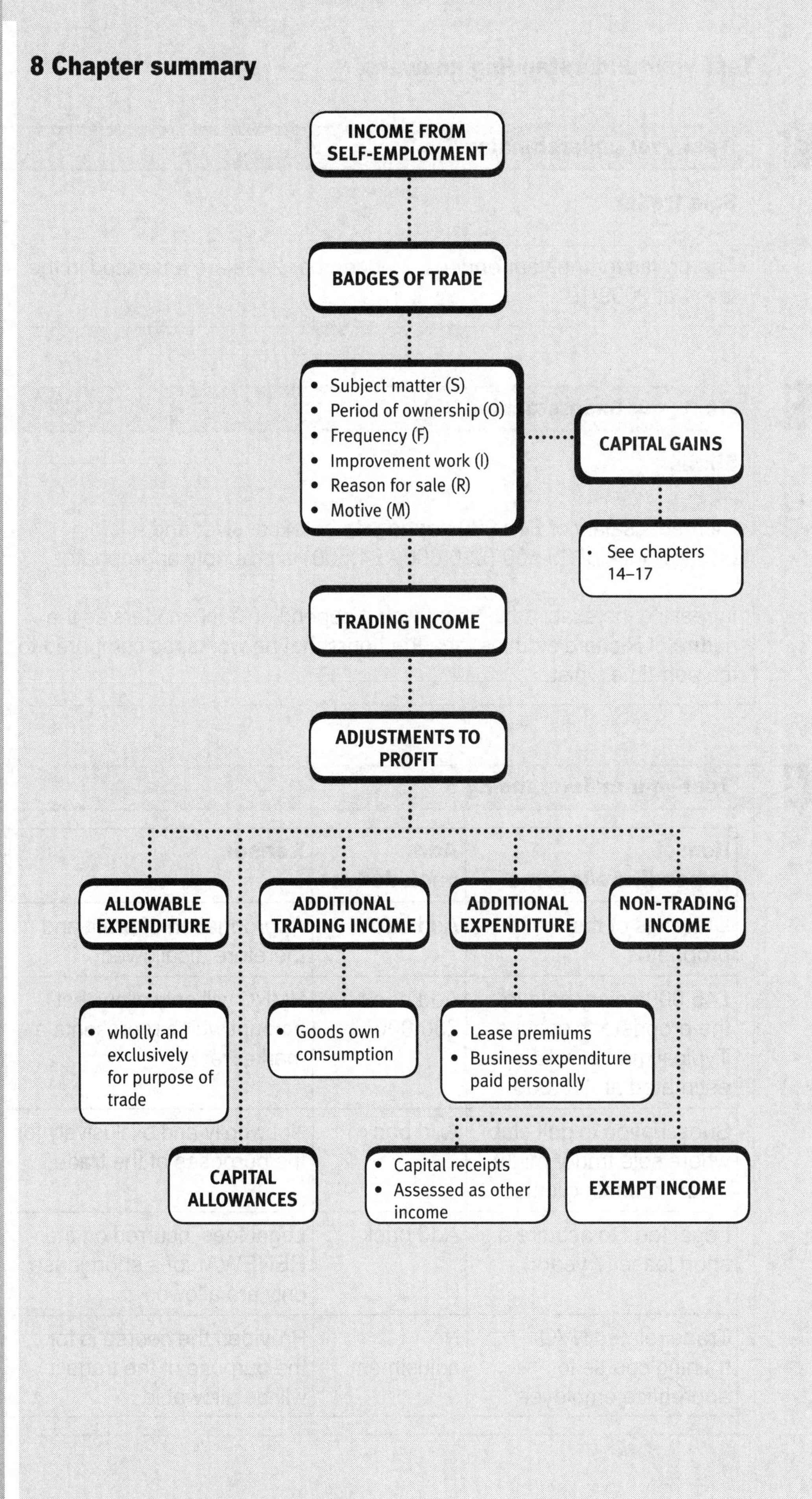

Test your understanding answers

Test your understanding 1

Sole trader

The profits for the year ended 31 December 2009 are assessed in the tax year 2009/10.

Test your understanding 2

Sheila

Richard's salary of £10,000 appears to be excessive, and a disallowance of £5,500 (£10,000 - £4,500) is probably appropriate.

In real life the exact adjustment would depend on such matters as the nature of Richard's duties, and the hours that he works, as compared to the part-time typist.

Test your understanding 3

Item of expenditure/income	Add back/deduct	Reason
Drawings of the proprietor	Add back	Appropriation of profit and therefore disallowed
£45,000 salary paid to the proprietor's spouse. Typical market rate is estimated at £15,000	Add back £30,000	HMRC will only allow that amount which represents a market rate
Subscription to golf club where sole trader might meet/entertain clients	Add back	Not wholly and exclusively for the purposes of the trade
Legal fees to acquire a short lease (7 years)	Add back	Legal fees incurred on the RENEWAL of a short lease only are allowed
Trade related NVQ training course for apprentice employee	No adjustment	Provided the course is for the purpose of the trade it will be allowable

Test your understanding 4

William Wise

Tax adjusted trading profit for the year ended 31 May 2010

	£	£
Net profit as per accounts		30,200
Add: Items debited in accounts not allowed for tax purposes		
Depreciation	4,760	
Light and heat (40% × £1,525)	610	
Motor expenses (9,000/12,000 × £4,720)	3,540	
Capital gains tax work	250	
Purchase of new shop	1,200	
Rent and rates (40% × £3,900)	1,560	
Decorating private flat	1,050	
Gift of food hampers	640	
Donation to national charity	100	
Excessive remuneration to William's wife (£15,500 – £11,000)	4,500	
Goods own consumption	650	
		18,860
Adjusted trading profit		49,060
Less: Capital allowances (given)		(13,060)
Tax adjusted trading profit		36,000

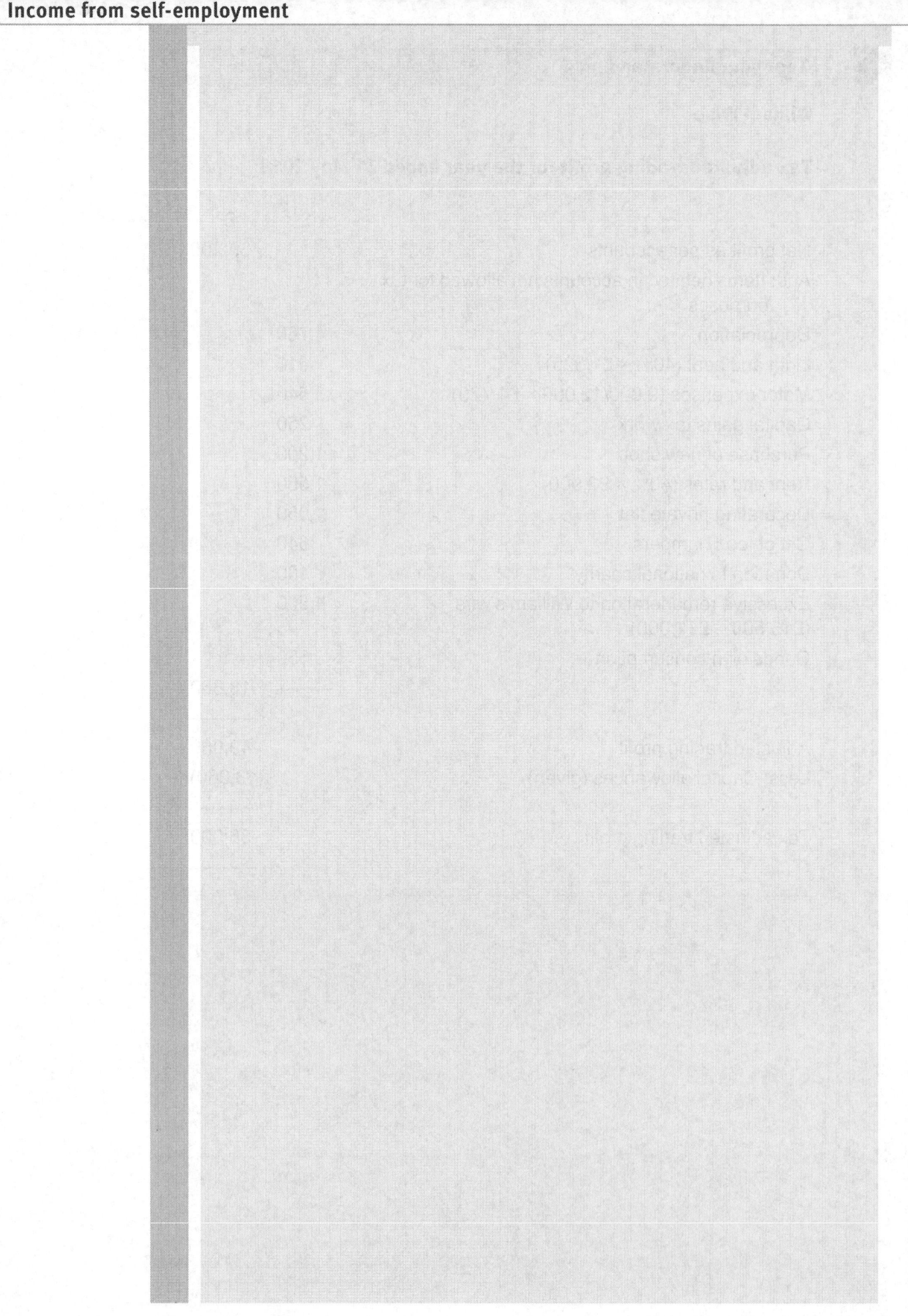

chapter

6

Capital allowances: Plant and machinery

Chapter learning objectives

Upon completion of this chapter you will be able to:

- define plant and machinery for capital allowance purposes
- compute writing down allowances for an accounting period
- compute First Year allowances (FYAs) available
- compute the Annual Investment Allowance (AIA) available for certain types of expenditure
- compute capital allowances for motor cars
- compute balancing allowances and balancing charges
- recognise the impact of private use of an asset on capital allowances
- recognise treatment of short-life assets
- explain the treatment of assets included in the special rate pool.

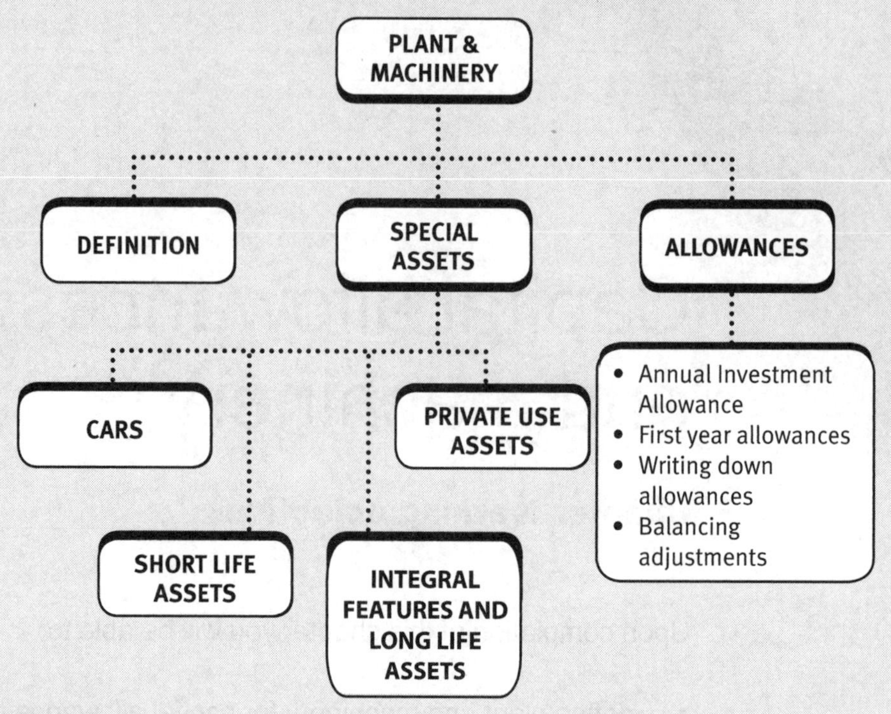

1 Eligibility

Purpose

Capital allowances are provided to give a business tax relief for capital expenditure on qualifying assets over the life of those assets.

Remember that depreciation charged in the accounts is not an allowable deduction in computing taxable trading profits; capital allowances are given instead.

The capital allowances covered in the F6 syllabus are for expenditure on:

- plant and machinery
- industrial buildings and qualifying hotels (see Chapter 7).

Who may claim capital allowances?

Capital allowances are available to persons who buy **qualifying assets** for use in a trade or profession.

Qualifying expenditure

Capital allowances are given on the original cost of a capital asset and all subsequent qualifying expenditure of a capital nature, such as improvements.

Relief for capital allowances

Capital allowances are:

- deducted as a trading expense in calculating the tax-adjusted trading income
- calculated for a trader's period of account (i.e. the period for which they draw up accounts).

2 Meaning of plant and machinery

Definition

'Machinery' has a commonly understood meaning. It includes all machines, computers, office equipment, etc.

The term 'plant' however, is not clearly defined in the tax legislation. HMRC has however codified some rules based on decided Court cases and has specifically deemed certain types of expenditure to be plant and machinery.

Key principles

The key principles to apply in deciding the appropriate treatment of a capital purchase is to consider the function that the asset performs for the business:

Does the asset perform:	This means that the asset is:	Plant and machinery?
An active function	Apparatus **with which** the business is carried on	Yes
A passive function	The setting **in which** the business is carried on	No

Assets deemed to be plant

There are certain types of expenditure that would not be thought of as plant using the above key principles, but are to be treated as plant by specific legislation.

These include:

- capital expenditure incurred in complying with fire regulations
- the cost of alterations to buildings needed for the installation of plant
- expenditure on acquiring computer software.

Assets deemed not to be plant

Statute also makes it clear that land, buildings and structures cannot be plant for capital allowance purposes.

Summary

Determining what is and what is not plant can be difficult in practice.

In the exam the most common examples of plant and machinery that you will come across are:

- computers and software
- machinery
- cars and lorries
- office furniture
- moveable partitions
- air-conditioning
- alterations of buildings needed to install plant and machinery.

Definition of plant and machinery

The original interpretation of plant and machinery was provided in the case of Yarmouth v France (1887). Plant was said to include:

'Whatever apparatus is used by a businessman for carrying on his business – not his stock-in-trade that he buys or makes for sale – but all goods and chattels, fixed or moveable, live or dead, which he keeps for permanent employment in his business.'

This is obviously a very far-reaching definition. It includes not only the obvious items of plant and machinery, but also such items as moveable partitions, office furniture and carpets, heating systems, motor vehicles, computers, lifts and any expenditure incurred to enable the proper functioning of the item, such as reinforced floors or air conditioning systems for computers.

The Courts' interpretation of 'plant'

The original definition of plant has been subsequently refined by the Courts.

In particular, the key test that has been applied is a functional one. It asks whether the item is simply part of the setting or premises in which the trade is carried on or is it something with which the trade is carried on?

In essence, if it is part of the setting or premises it is not plant, and thus no capital allowances are available, but if it fulfils a function it is plant.

The dividing line between an asset that is functional and one that is merely part of the setting in which the trade is carried on, is not always clear. Examples below show how the Courts have reacted to claims for capital allowances in these circumstances:

- A canopy covering petrol pumps at a petrol station was held to be part of the setting and not plant and machinery (it did not assist in serving petrol to customers).
- False ceilings in a restaurant were held not to be plant (all they did was hide unsightly pipes).
- Swimming pools at a caravan park were held to be plant and machinery (the caravan park as a whole was the setting but the pool and its associated pumping and filtering equipment had an active role of providing leisure apparatus).

Plant and buildings

There are statutory provisions that state that land, buildings and structures cannot be plant.

The provisions also give detailed lists of items associated with buildings that are part of the building, and are not deemed to be plant.

The term 'buildings' includes:

- walls, floors, ceilings, doors, windows and stairs
- mains services and systems of water, electricity and gas.

The following however may fall within the definition of a building but will nevertheless normally qualify as plant:

- electrical, cold water and gas systems provided mainly to meet the particular requirements of the trade, or to serve particular machinery used for the purposes of the trade
- space or water heating systems, systems of ventilation and air cooling, and any ceiling or floor comprised in such systems
- manufacturing or processing equipment, storage equipment, display equipment, counters, check outs and similar equipment
- cookers, washing machines, dishwashers, refrigerators and similar equipment
- wash basins, sinks, baths, showers, sanitary ware and similar equipment
- furniture and furnishings

- lifts, escalators and moving walkways
- sprinkler equipment and fire alarm systems
- movable partition walls
- decorative assets provided for the enjoyment of the public in a hotel, restaurant or similar trade
- advertising hoardings, signs and similar displays.

3 Calculating the allowances

The general pool (or main pool)

Generally expenditure on plant and machinery becomes part of a pool of expenditure upon which capital allowances are claimed. Normally capital allowances are not calculated on individual assets.

- Most items of plant and machinery purchased are included within the general pool (also known as the main pool).
- Some motor cars are also included in the general pool, namely:
  - Cars purchased before 6 April 2009 costing ≤ £12,000
  - Cars purchased on/after 6 April 2009 with CO_2 emissions between 111 g/km and 160 g/km

  The detailed rules relating to all types of cars are covered in section 5.

- When an addition is made, the purchase price increases the value of the pool.
- When an asset is disposed of, the pool value is reduced by the sale proceeds.

Certain items are not included in the general pool. For unincorporated businesses, these are:

- motor cars purchased pre 6 April 2009 costing more than £12,000 (i.e. 'expensive' cars)
- motor cars purchased on/after 6 April 2009 with CO_2 emissions below 110 g/km or in excess of 160 g/km
- assets that are used partly for private purposes by the owner of the business
- expenditure incurred on short-life assets where an election to de-pool is made
- expenditure incurred on items that form part of the 'special rate pool'.

These exceptional treatments are dealt with later in this chapter.

The Annual Investment Allowance (AIA)

The Annual Investment Allowance (AIA) is a 100% allowance for the first £50,000 of expenditure incurred by a business on plant and machinery.

The key rules for the allowance are as follows:

- available to **all** businesses regardless of size;
- available on acquisitions of general plant and machinery and acquisitions of 'special rate pool' items (see later);
- **not** available on any cars;
- limited to a maximum of £50,000 expenditure incurred in each accounting period of 12 months in length;
- for long and short accounting periods the £50,000 allowance is pro-rated;
- not available in the accounting period in which the trade ceases.

Where a business spends more than £50,000 in a 12 month accounting period on assets qualifying for the AIA:

- the expenditure above the £50,000 limit will qualify for further allowances (see below).

Note also that:

- the taxpayer does not have to claim all / any of the AIA if he does not want to
- any unused AIA can not be carried forward or carried back, the benefit of the allowance is just lost.

Example 1 - AIA

Matthew commenced trading on 1 May 2009. In his first year of trading he made the following purchases:

Plant and machinery for the factory he rented	£120,000
Office furniture and equipment	£35,000
A car with CO_2 emissions of 138 g/km for his manager	£11,000

(a) **Calculate Matthew's annual investment allowance for the year ended 30 April 2010 and state how much is eligible for further allowances.**

(b) **What if Matthew did not purchase the plant and machinery?**

Answer to example 1

(a) Year ended 30 April 2010

	£	General pool £
Additions:		
Not qualifying for AIA:		
Car (CO_2 emissions < 160 g/km)		11,000
Qualifying for AIA:		
Plant and machinery	120,000	
Office furniture	35,000	
	155,000	
Less AIA (Maximum)	(50,000)	
		105,000
Eligible for further allowances (see below)		116,000

(b) If Matthew did not purchase the plant and machinery

	£	General pool £
Additions:		
Not qualifying for AIA:		
Car (CO_2 emissions < 160 g/km)		11,000
Qualifying for AIA:		
Office furniture	35,000	
Less AIA (Note)	(35,000)	
		Nil
Eligible for further allowances (see below)		11,000

Note: The unused AIA of £15,000 (£50,000 – £35,000) is lost.

Further allowances available:

- Expenditure on plant and machinery in the main pool not qualifying for AIA will qualify for writing down allowances (WDA)
- Expenditure on plant and machinery in the main pool qualifying for AIA but falling above the £50,000 AIA limit will qualify for further allowances as follows:

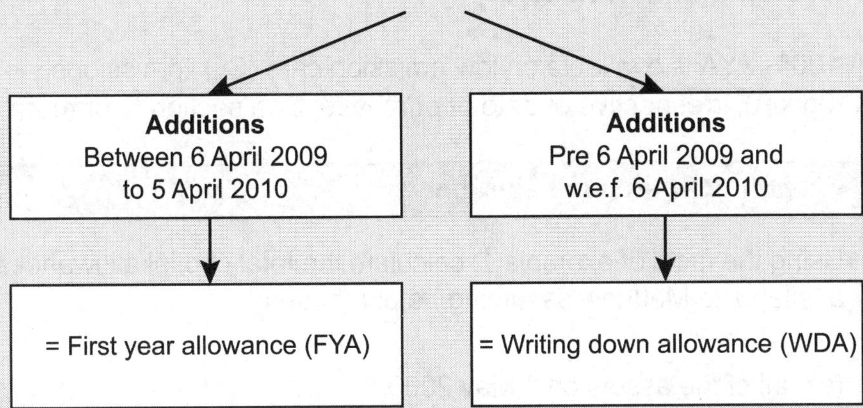

Note that the business can choose the expenditure against which the AIA is matched.

It will therefore be most beneficial for the AIA to be allocated against expenditure in the following order:

(1) Expenditure eligible for the WDA

(2) Expenditure eligible for the temporary 40% FYA

First year allowance (FYA)

Two types of FYA are available:

(1) Temporary FYA on plant and machinery

(2) FYA on low emission cars

Temporary FYA on plant and machinery

A temporary FYA of 40% is available for expenditure on main pool items that are not covered by the AIA.

The rules are as follows:

- Only applies to expenditure between 6 April 2009 to 5 April 2010
- Main pool items only

- Not available on cars (but see low emission car rules below)
- FYA given instead of the WDA in the year of purchase (i.e. can not have both the FYA and WDA on that expenditure in the first year)
- Unlike the AIA and WDA, the FYA is never pro-rated for accounting periods of greater or less than 12 months
- FYA not available in the accounting year in which the trade ceases.

FYA on low emission cars

A 100% FYA is available on low emission cars (CO_2 emissions < 110g/km), irrespective of date of purchase. See section 5 for more detail.

Example 2 - First year allowances

Using the facts of example 1, calculate the total capital allowances available to Matthew assuming he purchased:

(a) all of the assets on 1 May 2009

(b) the plant and machinery on 16 April 2010.

Answer to example 2

(a) **All assets purchased on 1 May 2009**

		General pool	Allowances
y/e 30 April 2010	£	£	£
Additions:			
Not qualifying for AIA or FYA:			
Car (CO_2 between 111 – 160 g/km)		11,000	
Qualifying for AIA and FYA:			
Plant and machinery	120,000		
Office furniture	35,000		
	155,000		
Less: AIA	(50,000)		50,000
	105,000	11,000	
Less: WDA (20% x £11,000) (Note)		(2,200)	2,200
Less: FYA (40% x £105,000)	(42,000)		42,000
		63,000	
TWDV c/f		71,800	
Total allowances			94,200

Note: The WDA must be calculated on the main pool before the FYA as the WDA is not available on the balance of the plant and machinery expenditure that is eligible for both the AIA and FYA.

(b) **Purchased the plant and machinery on 16 April 2010**

		General pool	Allowances
y/e 30 April 2010	£	£	£
Additions:			
Not qualifying for AIA or FYA:			
Car (CO_2 between 111 – 160 g/km)		11,000	
Qualifying for AIA but not FYA:			
Purchases w.e.f. 6 April 2010			
Plant and machinery	120,000		
Less: AIA (Maximum)	(50,000)		50,000
	———	70,000	
Qualifying for AIA and FYA:			
Purchases before 6 April 2010			
Office furniture	35,000		
Less: AIA (Maximum already used)	(Nil)		
	———		
	35,000		
		———	
		81,000	
Less: WDA (20% x £81,000)		(16,200)	16,200
Less: FYA (40% x £35,000)	(14,000)		14,000
	———	21,000	
		———	
TWDV c/f		85,800	
		———	———
Total allowances			80,200
			———

Writing down allowances (WDA)

- An annual WDA of 20% is given on a reducing balance basis
- It is given on:
  - the unrelieved expenditure in the pool brought forward at the beginning of the period of account (i.e. tax written down value) (TWDV).
  - any additions on which the AIA is not available
  - any additions pre 6 April 2009 and w.e.f. 6 April 2010, not covered by the AIA
  - after taking account of disposals
- The TWDV brought forward includes all prior expenditure, less allowances already claimed.
- Note that the WDA is not available on additions between 6 April 2009 to 5 April 2010, as these are eligible for the AIA and temporary 40% FYA instead.

Example 3 - Writing down allowances

Grace commenced trading on 1 August 2009. Her trading profits, adjusted for tax purposes but before capital allowances, are as follows:

	£
Year ended 31 July 2010	59,500
Year ended 31 July 2011	31,200

On 9 November 2009, she bought plant and machinery for £60,000 and a motor car with CO_2 emissions of 131 g/km for £6,500.

Calculate Grace's tax-adjusted trading profit for both years.

Answer to example 3

Taxable trading income

	Adjusted trading profit	Capital allowances (W)	Tax-adjusted trading profit
	£	£	£
y/e 31 July 2010	59,500	(55,300)	4,200
y/e 31 July 2011	31,200	(2,240)	28,960

Working: Capital allowances computation

		General pool	Allowances
y/e 31 July 2010	£	£	£
Additions:			
Not qualifying for AIA or FYA:			
Car (CO_2 between 111 – 160 g/km)		6,500	
Qualifying for AIA and FYA:			
Plant and machinery	60,000		
Less: AIA	(50,000)		50,000
	10,000		
Less: WDA (20% x £6,500)		(1,300)	1,300
Less: FYA (40% x £10,000)	(4,000)		4,000
		6,000	
TWDV c/f		11,200	
Total allowances			55,300
y/e 31 July 2011			
Less: WDA (20%)		(2,240)	2,240
TWDV c/f		8,960	
Total allowances			2,240

Test your understanding 1

Gayle commenced trading on 1 May 2009. Her trading profits, adjusted for tax purposes but before capital allowances, are as follows:

Year ended 30 April 2010	£60,500
Year ended 30 April 2011	£54,000

On 1 May 2009, Gayle acquired plant and machinery for £53,000 and a new motor car with CO_2 emissions of 156 g/km for £10,000.

Calculate Gayle's tax-adjusted trading profit for both years.

Short or long periods of account

- The AIA and WDAs are given for periods of account (i.e. the period for which a trader draws up accounts). The £50,000 AIA and the percentage of 20% is based on a period of account of 12 months.
- Shorter or longer periods of account result in the allowances being pro-rated.
- If the period of account exceeds 18 months it must be split into a 12-month period and a second period of account to deal with the remaining months.
- The most common occasion for a business having a non 12-month period of account is at the start of trading.

Example 4 - WDA: Long period of account

Giles commenced trading on 1 August 2009. His trading profits, adjusted for tax purposes but before capital allowances, are as follows:

14-month period ended 30 September 2010	£128,000
Year ended 30 September 2011	£135,000

On 1 November 2009, he bought plant and machinery for £56,000 and a motor car with CO_2 emissions of 149 g/km for £9,800.

Calculate his tax-adjusted trading profit for each of the periods of trading.

Answer to example 4

Period ended	Adjusted trading profit	Capital allowances (W)	Tax adjusted trading profit
	£	£	£
30 September 2010	128,000	(58,287)	69,713
30 September 2011	135,000	(1,503)	133,497

Working: Capital allowances computation

		General pool	Allowances
14 m/e 30 September 2010	£	£	£
Additions:			
Not qualifying for AIA or FYA:			
Car (CO_2 between 111 – 160 g/km)		9,800	
Qualifying for AIA and FYA:			
Plant and machinery	56,000		
Less: AIA (Note)	(56,000)		56,000
	Nil		
Less: WDA (20% × £9,800 × 14/12)		(2,287)	2,287
Less: FYA (40% × £Nil)	(Nil)		Nil
		Nil	
TWDV c/f		7,513	
Total allowances			58,287
y/e 30 September 2011			
Less: WDA (20%)		(1,503)	1,503
TWDV c/f		6,010	
Total allowances			1,503

Note: The AIA is pro-rated to £58,333 (£50,000 x 14/12) and therefore all of the £56,000 expenditure is eligible for the allowance in the 14 months ended 30 September 2010. The unused allowance is lost.

Both the AIA and the WDA are pro-rated to reflect the 14 month-period.

Test your understanding 2

Graham commenced trading on 1 May 2009. His trading profits, adjusted for tax purposes but before capital allowances, are as follows:

	£
4-month period ended 31 August 2009	32,000
Year ended 31 August 2010	45,000

On 1 May 2009, he bought plant and machinery for £18,000 and a motor car with CO_2 emissions of 129 g/km for £11,500.

Calculate the tax-adjusted trading profit for each of the periods of trading.

Length of ownership in the period of account

It is important to distinguish between the length of the period of account and the date of acquisition of the asset during the period:

- The WDA is never restricted by reference to the length of ownership of an asset in the period of account.
- If a business prepares accounts for the year ended 31 March 2010, the same WDA is given whether an asset is purchased on 10 April 2009 or on 31 March 2010.

  This is because it is ownership of an asset on the last day of the period of account that determines whether the allowance is available, not the length of ownership.

4 Sale of plant and machinery

At the point an asset is sold or scrapped the following steps are taken:

- The disposal value (sale proceeds) is deducted from the total of: (TWDV brought forward on the pool plus additions brought into the general pool).
- Note the additions are:
  - additions not qualifying for either the AIA or FYA, and
  - additions qualifying for AIA but not FYA (i.e. if purchased before 6 April 2009 or after 5 April 2010).
- The WDA for the year is then calculated on the remaining figure, and the temporary FYA is calculated after the WDA is deducted.

- If sale proceeds exceed the original cost of the asset, the sale proceeds deducted from the pool are restricted to the original cost of the asset. An excess of sale proceeds over original cost may then be taxed as a chargeable gain.

- Therefore on a disposal always deduct from the pool the lower of the sale proceeds and the original cost.

Example 5 - Sale of plant and machinery

Glyn prepares accounts to 31 May. In the year to 31 May 2010, the following transactions took place:

5 June 2009	Plant sold (originally purchased for £8,000) for £1,200
3 September 2009	Plant purchased for £53,000

Compute the capital allowances for the year ended 31 May 2010, assuming that the TWDV on 1 June 2009, was £10,000.

Answer to example 5

Glyn – Capital allowances computation

		General pool	Allowances
	£	£	£
y/e 31 May 2010			
TWDV b/f		10,000	
Additions:			
Qualifying for AIA and FYA:			
Plant and machinery	53,000		
Less: AIA	(50,000)		50,000
	3,000		
Disposal (lower of cost and SP)		(1,200)	
		8,800	
Less: WDA (20% x £8,800)		(1,760)	1,760
Less: FYA (40% x £3,000)	(1,200)		1,200
		1,800	
TWDV c/f		8,840	
Total allowances			52,960

Balancing charges

If, on disposal of an asset in the pool, disposal proceeds exceed the pool balance brought forward, the excess allowances previously given will be recovered and charged to tax by means of a balancing charge.

A balancing charge is added to the taxable trading profit.

Balancing allowances

The following rules apply:

- The basic idea underlying capital allowances is that the business will over time obtain relief for the actual cost of an asset to the business (i.e. cost less sale proceeds (if any)).
- When the business is permanently discontinued, and there is still a balance of unrelieved expenditure in the pool, a business can claim relief for the unrelieved balance by way of a balancing allowance.
- The only time a balancing allowance will arise in the general pool is when the trade is permanently discontinued.
- A balancing allowance is computed by reference to the excess of the pool balance at the end of the final period of account over the sale proceeds received on the ultimate disposal of plant and machinery.
- No AIA, FYAs or WDAs are available in the final period of account.

Test your understanding 3

Gene has previously prepared accounts to 31 July. He decided to cease to trade on 31 December 2010, after a period of ill health.

The following transactions have recently taken place:

21.6.10	Plant sold (originally purchased for £2,000) for £320
10.9.10	Plant purchased for £4,000

On the completion of the sale of his business, Gene received £5,400 for his plant and machinery. No item was sold for more than its original cost.

The WDV on 1 August 2009, was £9,000.

Compute the capital allowances for the year ended 31 July 2010, and the period ended 31 December 2010.

Test your understanding 4

Gloria has owned and run her own business for many years. She prepares accounts to 30 June each year. During the year ended 30 June 2010, the following transactions took place:

21 July 2009	Purchased a motor car with CO_2 emissions of 145 g/km for £11,000.
14 October 2009	Sold a piece of plant for £3,000, she had paid £15,000 for this when she acquired it.
31 March 2010	Purchased plant for £19,500.

The TWDV at 1 July 2009, was £21,000.

Compute the capital allowances for the year ended 30 June 2010.

5 Motor cars

Motor cars purchased pre 6 April 2009

Inexpensive cars

Motor cars costing £12,000 or less were included in the general pool unless:

- the motor car is used by the owner of the business partly for private purposes
- the car is a low emission car.

Note that the AIA and FYA are not available against expenditure on cars, whether or not they are included in the general pool.

Expensive cars

Where cars cost more than £12,000:

- The cost of a motor car was put into a separate pool.
- The capital allowances on each 'expensive' car is separately computed.

In the examination, there may be an existing expensive car used in the business.

If so, the TWDV b/f will be given and the allowances are computed as follows:

- The AIA is not available and the FYA is not available.
- The WDA is available but is restricted to a maximum (for a 12-month period of account) of £3,000.
- Once the motor car has a written down value of below £15,000, the WDA will be computed in the normal way (i.e. 20% of TWDV) but the motor car remains in its separate column of the computation. It must not be brought into the general pool.
- When each 'expensive' motor car is sold, a balancing allowance or charge must be computed on the difference between the TWDV and the sale proceeds.

Note that in the exam there will not be a purchase of a new expensive car.

Example 6 - Motor cars

Glenda prepares accounts to 30 April. At 1 May 2009, the TWDVs are as follows:

General pool	£21,200
Expensive motor car	£16,600

The following transations took place during the two years ended 30 April 2011:

25.08.09	Purchased a motor car with CO_2 emissions of 153 g/km for £10,600
11.10.10	Purchased plant and machinery for £61,000
15.12.10	Sold the expensive motor car for £9,400

Calculate the capital allowances for the two years to 30 April 2011.

Answer to example 6

Capital allowances computation

		General pool	Expensive car	Allowances
	£	£	£	£
y/e 30 April 2010				
TWDV b/f		21,200	16,600	
Additions:				
Not qualifying for AIA or FYA:				
Car (CO_2 between 111 – 160 g/km)		10,600		
		31,800		
Less: WDA (20% x £31,800)		(6,360)		6,360
WDA (maximum)			(3,000)	3,000
TWDV c/f		25,440	13,600	
Total allowances				9,360
y/e 30 April 2011				
Additions:				
Qualifying for AIA and FYA:				
Plant and machinery	61,000			
Less: AIA	(50,000)			50,000
	11,000			
Disposal (lower of cost and SP)			(9,400)	
		25,440	4,200	
Balancing allowance			(4,200)	4,200
Less: WDA (20% x £25,440)		(5,088)		5,088
Less: FYA (40% x £11,000)	(4,400)			4,400
		6,600		
TWDV c/f		26,952		
Total allowances				63,688

Test your understanding 5

Glen prepares accounts to 31 January. At 1 February 2009, the TWDVs are as follows:

General pool	£43,500
Expensive motor car	£14,500

The following transactions took place during the year ended 31 January 2010:

10.5.09	Purchased plant for £53,300
25.6.09	Purchased a motor car with CO_2 emissions of 147 g/km for £10,600
15.1.10	Sold expensive motor car for £9,400

Calculate the capital allowances for the year to 31 January 2010.

Low emission motor cars

Low emission cars were treated differently, as follows:

- Expenditure on low emission cars by all businesses were eligible for a 100% first year allowance.
- A low emission car is one which emits 110 or less grams per kilometre of carbon dioxide (i.e. CO_2 emissions ≤ 110 g/km).

Remember that:

- The AIA is not available on any type of car.
- The relief for FYA is calculated as follows:
  - In the period of acquisition, a 100% FYA is given instead of the WDA.
  - Unlike the WDA, the FYA is not pro-rated for periods of greater or less than 12 months.
  - FYAs are not given in the final period of trading.

Motor cars purchased on/after 6 April 2009

The treatment of motor cars purchased on/after 6 April 2009 depends on its CO_2 emissions as follows:

CO_2 emissions	Description	Treatment in capital allowances computation:
≤ 110 g/km	Low emission	Treated in the same way as before 6 April 2009 (see above)
111 – 160 g/km	Standard emission	Included in general pool as an addition not qualifying for AIA or FYA (as seen in previous examples)
> 160 g/km	High emission	Include in the 'special rate pool' (see section 8)

Note however that:

- Motor cars with an element of private use, regardless of their date of purchase, are treated separately (see section 6).

Test your understanding 6

Gwen runs a business preparing accounts to 5 April. The TWDV on the general pool on 6 April 2009 was £11,000 and on the expensive car: £18,000.

During the year ended 5 April 2010 the following transactions took place:

25 May 2009	Purchased plant for £59,000
31 August 2009	Purchased two cars for £13,000 each, one with CO_2 emissions of 100 g/km, the other 146 g/km
30 March 2010	Sold plant for £4,600 (originally purchased for £9,500)

Calculate the capital allowances for the year ended 5 April 2010.

6 Assets with private use by the owner of the business

Where an asset is used by the owner of the business, partly for business and partly for private purposes:

- only the business proportion of the available capital allowances are available as a tax deduction.

The following rules must be followed when computing capital allowances:

- The cost of the privately used asset is not brought into the general pool, but must be the subject of a separate computation.
- The AIA, FYA or WDA on the asset is based on its full cost but only the business proportion of any allowance is actually deductible in computing the taxable trading profit.
- Note that if applicable, the business can choose the expenditure against which the AIA is matched.
- It will therefore be most beneficial for the AIA to be allocated against the general pool expenditure rather than any private use asset as only the business proportion of any AIA available can be claimed.
- However note that in examinations the assets most commonly used for private purposes are cars, which are not eligible for the AIA.
- Motor cars with private use are treated separately, regardless of the date of purchase and CO_2 emissions.
- On disposal of the asset, a balancing adjustment is computed by comparing sale proceeds with the TWDV. There is a balancing charge if there is a profit, and a balancing allowance if there is a loss.
- Having computed the balancing adjustment, the amount assessed or allowed is then reduced to the business proportion.
- Where the asset concerned is an expensive motor car, WDAs are first restricted to the £3,000 limit and then the business proportion of £3,000 is actually given as an allowance.
- Private use by an employee of an asset owned by the business has no effect on the business's entitlement to capital allowances.

Example 7 - Assets with private use by the owner of the business

George runs a business and prepares his accounts to 5 April. As at 6 April 2009, the tax written down values are as follows:

General pool	£11,700
Expensive motor car (used 60% for private purposes by George)	£11,600

The following transactions took place in the year ended 5 April 2010:

- Purchased plant for £68,500
- Purchased a motor car with CO_2 emissions of 158 g/km for £16,000
- Sold the expensive motor car for £5,500
- Purchased a motor car with CO_2 emissions of 136 g/km for £9,400 (used 45% for private purposes by George)

Calculate the capital allowances for the year to 5 April 2010.

Answer to example 7

Capital allowances computation

		General pool	Expensive Car (BU 40%)	Private use car (BU 55%)	Business use	Allow-ances
	£	£	£	£	%	£
y/e 5 April 2010						
TWDV b/f		11,700	11,600			
Additions:						
Not qualifying for AIA or FYA:						
Car (CO_2 between 111 – 160 g/km)		16,000				
Private use car				9,400		
Qualifying for AIA and FYA:						
Plant and machinery	68,500					
Less: AIA	(50,000)					50,000
	18,500					
Disposal (lower of Cost and SP)			(5,500)			
		27,700	6,100	9,400		
Balancing allowance			(6,100)		× 40%	2,440
Less: WDA (20% x £27,700)		(5,540)				5,540
WDA (20% x £9,400)				(1,880)	× 55%	1,034
Less: FYA (40% x £18,500)	(7,400)					7,400
		11,100				
TWDV c/f		33,260		7,520		
Total allowances						66,414

Test your understanding 7

Georgina runs a small business and prepares accounts to 5 April. At 6 April 2009, the TWDVs are as follows:

	£
General pool	21,200
Expensive motor car (used 30% for private purposes by Georgina)	13,600

The following transactions took place during the year ended 5 April 2010:

10.5.09	Purchased plant for £6,600
25.6.09	Purchased a motor car with CO_2 emissions of 134 g/km for £17,000
15.2.10	Sold the expensive motor car for £9,400
16.2.10	Purchased a motor car with CO_2 emissions of 116 g/km for £10,600 (used 40% for private purposes by Georgina)
14.3.10	Purchased a motor car with CO_2 emissions of 107 g/km for £11,750

Calculate the capital allowances for the year to 5 April 2010.

7 Short-life assets

Purpose

The short-life asset election exists to enable businesses to accelerate capital allowances on certain qualifying expenditure.

Qualifying expenditure

For the purposes of the exam, all plant and machinery, with the exception of motor cars, constitute eligible expenditure, where it is the intention to sell or scrap the item within four years of the end of the period of account in which the asset is acquired.

Process for computation

The following steps must be taken:

- Each short-life asset is the subject of a separate column within the capital allowances computation.

- On disposal within four years of the end of the period of account in which the asset was acquired, a separate balancing allowance or balancing charge is calculated.
- An election (written application to HMRC) must be made to enable assets to be treated separately in the capital allowances computation as short-life assets. This is known as de-pooling.
- This election must be made by the first anniversary of 31 January following the end of the tax year in which the trading period of expenditure ends.
- If no disposal has taken place within four years of the end of the period of account in which the acquisition took place, the unrelieved balance is transferred to the general pool. The transfer takes place in the first period of account following the four-year anniversary.
- However, note that the AIA is available against short life assets and the business can choose the expenditure against which the AIA is matched.
- If eligible for the AIA, there will be no expenditure left to "de-pool" and the short life asset election will not be made.
- If there is expenditure in excess of the maximum £50,000 on expenditure eligible for the AIA, it may be advantageous for the AIA to be allocated against the general pool expenditure rather than a short life asset and for the short life asset election to be made.
- Expenditure in excess of the AIA that is depooled is eligible for the FYA of 40% in the year of purchase, and the WDA in subsequent years.
- It will be advantageous to make the election if it is anticipated that a balancing allowance will arise within the following four accounting periods.

Example 8 - Short-life assets

Gina has traded for many years preparing accounts to 31 March each year. The TWDV on the general pool was £15,000 on 1 April 2009.

In May 2009, she acquired a new machine costing £10,000. She anticipated that the machine would last two years and she eventually sold it on 30 June 2011, for £1,750.

In August 2009, she acquired general plant and machinery for £52,000.

Calculate the allowances available for each year, illustrating whether or not an election to treat the new machine as a short life asset would be beneficial.

Answer to example 8

Gina – Capital allowances computation – without making a short life asset election

		General pool	Allowances
	£	£	£
y/e 31 March 2010			
TWDV b/f		15,000	
Additions:			
Qualifying for AIA and FYA:			
Plant and machinery (£52,000 + £10,000)	62,000		
Less: AIA	(50,000)		50,000
	12,000		
Less: WDA (20% x £15,000)		(3,000)	3,000
Less: FYA (40% x £12,000)	(4,800)		4,800
		7,200	
TWDV c/f		19,200	
Total allowances			57,800
y/e 31 March 2011			
Less: WDA (20% x £19,200)		(3,840)	3,840
TWDV c/f		15,360	
Total allowances			3,840
y/e 31 March 2012			
Disposal (lower of Cost and SP)		(1,750)	
		13,610	
Less: WDA (20% x £13,610)		(2,722)	2,722
TWDV c/f		10,888	
Total allowances			2,722

Gina – Capital allowances computation – with a short life asset election

		General pool	Short life asset	Allowances
	£	£	£	£
y/e 31 March 2010				
TWDV b/f		15,000		
Additions:				
Qualifying for AIA and FYA:				
Plant and machinery	52,000		10,000	
Less: AIA	(50,000)		(Nil)	50,000
	2,000		10,000	
Less: WDA (20% x £15,000)		(3,000)		3,000
Less: FYA (40% x £2,000 / £10,000)	(800)		(4,000)	4,800
		1,200		
TWDV c/f		13,200	6,000	
Total allowances				57,800
y/e 31 March 2011				
Less: WDA (20% x £13,200 / £6,000)		(2,640)	(1,200)	3,840
TWDV c/f		10,560	4,800	
Total allowances				3,840
y/e 31 March 2012				
Disposal (lower of cost and SP)			(1,750)	
		10,560	3,050	
Balancing allowance			(3,050)	3,050
Less: WDA (20% x £10,560)		(2,112)		2,112
TWDV c/f		8,448		
Total allowances				5,162

The total allowances claimed without making the election are £64,362 (£57,800 + £3,840 + £2,722). In the event Gina makes the election, the allowances available for the three years are £66,802 (£57,800 + £3,840 + £5,162)

Note that the election just accelerates the allowances available and only changes the timing of the allowances. The total allowances available will eventually be the same, however, without the election, it will take considerably longer to get there relief.

Therefore, if not covered by the AIA, it is recommended that the short life treatment is taken but only if it is expected that a balancing allowance can be accelerated. It is not advantageous to accelerate a balancing charge.

8 Special rate pool

The 'special rate pool' is a pool of qualifying expenditure that operates in the same way as the general pool except that:

- the WDA is 10% for a 12 month period (rather than 20%)
- the temporary FYA of 40% is not available.

Note that:

- the AIA is available against this expenditure (except on high emission cars) and
- the business can choose the expenditure against which the AIA is matched.

It will therefore be most beneficial for the AIA to be allocated against expenditure in the following order:

(1) the 'special rate pool' (as assets in the 'special rate pool' are not eligible for the temporary FYA, they are only eligible for 10% WDA, whereas general plant and machinery is eligible for the FYA of 40%).

(2) the general pool

(3) short life assets

(4) private use assets.

Qualifying expenditure

The 'special rate pool' groups together expenditure incurred on the following type of assets:

- long-life assets
- 'integral features' of a building or structure
- thermal insulation of a building
- high emission cars (CO_2 emissions > 160 g/km) purchased on/after 6 April 2009.

Long-life assets

Long-life assets are defined as plant and machinery with:

- a total cost of at least £100,000 (for a 12-month period) and
- an expected working life of 25 years or more.
  - Examples of long-life assets might include aircraft used by an airline and agricultural equipment used by a farm.
  - The 25 year working life is from the time that the asset is first brought into use, to the time that it ceases to be capable of being used. It is not sufficient to just look at the expected life in the hands of the current owner.

Where the business spends less than £100,000 pa on long-life assets, they are treated as normal additions in the general pool.

The following can never be classed as long-life assets:

- Motor cars.
- Plant and machinery situated in a building that is used as a retail shop, showroom, hotel or office.

Integral features of a building or structure and thermal insulation

'Integral features of a building or structure' include expenditure incurred on the following:

- electrical (including lighting) systems;
- cold water systems;
- space or water heating systems;
- powered systems of ventilation, air cooling or air purification;
- lifts and escalators.

Thermal insulation in all business buildings (except residential buildings in a property business) is also included in the special rate pool.

Example 9 - Long-life assets

Apple runs a manufacturing business and prepares her accounts to 31 March each year. As at 1 April 2009, the tax written down values are as follows:

	£
General pool	103,000
Expensive motor car	16,200

During the year ended 31 March 2010 Apple incurred the following expenditure:

- Spent £120,000 on a new air-conditioning system for the factory which is expected to last 30 years.
- Purchased a new computer and related software for £25,000 and £5,000 respectively.
- Spent £15,000 on a new packing machine. Apple also incurred £4,000 on alterations to the factory in order to accommodate the new machine.
- Purchased a new car with CO_2 emissions of 168 g/km for £28,000.

In addition she sold old machinery for £10,000 (original cost £60,000).

Calculate the capital allowances available to Apple for the year ended 31 March 2010.

Answer to example 9

Capital allowances computation

		General pool	Special rate pool	Expensive car	Allow-ances
	£	£	£	£	£
y/e 31 March 2010					
TWDV b/f		103,000	Nil	16,200	
Additions:					
Not qualifying for AIA or FYA:					
Car (CO_2 > 160 g/km)			28,000		
Qualifying for AIA but not FYA:					
Long life asset (Note 1)	120,000				
Less: AIA (Max) (Note 2)	(50,000)				50,000
	———		70,000		
Qualifying for AIA and FYA:					
Computer and software	30,000				
Machine (Note 3)	19,000				
	———				
	49,000				
Less: AIA (Note 2)	(Nil)				
	———				
	49,000				
Disposal (lower of Cost and SP)		(10,000)			
		———	———	———	
		93,000	98,000	16,200	
Less: WDA (20% x £93,000)		(18,600)			18,600
WDA (10% x£98,000)			(9,800)		9,800
WDA (restricted to max)				(3,000)	3,000
Less: FYA (40% x £49,000)	(19,600)				19,600
	———	29,400			
		———	———	———	
TWDV c/f		103,800	88,200	13,200	
		———	———	———	———
Total allowances					101,000
					———

Notes:

(1) The air-conditioning unit has an expected life of more than 25 years and is therefore a long-life asset. As Apple has incurred more than £100,000 on such assets in the year the air-conditioning unit is included in the 'special rate pool' and WDAs are restricted to 10%.

(2) The AIA is allocated to the additions in the 'special rate pool' in priority to the additions in the general pool. The maximum £50,000 is therefore all allocated to the special rate pool and there is no AIA available against the general pool expenditure.

(3) Software and the cost of altering buildings to accommodate plant are specifically deemed by statute to be items of general plant and machinery.

9 The small pool WDA

Where the balance immediately before the calculation of the WDA:

- on the general and/or 'special rate' pool
- is ≤ £1,000 (see below)

the balance can be claimed as a small pool WDA and immediately written off in that year.

Note that the **£1,000 limit** is for a **12 month accounting period**, it is therefore pro rated for long and short accounting periods.

The claim is optional. However, the taxpayer will want to claim the maximum allowances available and reduce the balance on the pool to £Nil.

Test your understanding 8

Angelina is in business as a sole trader and prepares accounts to 31 March each year.

During the year ending 31 March 2010 she purchased the following:

15 May 2009	Purchased new office furniture for £13,800.
2 June 2009	Purchased a new car (with CO_2 emissions of 127 g/km) for £10,000 which Angela will use 20% of the time for private purposes.
10 June 2009	Installed a new water heating system in her business premises at a cost of £15,000 and a new lighting system at a cost of £20,000.

In addition on 1 July 2009 she sold office equipment for £10,000 (original cost £18,000).

As at 1 April 2009 the tax written down value on her general pool was £10,800.

Calculate Angelina's capital allowances for the year ended 31 March 2010.

10 Summary of computational technique

- Capital allowances are an important element of the syllabus and are certain to appear in the exam, within at least one of the questions.
- To be successful answering these questions, it is vital to use a methodical approach to work through the information in the question.
- Always follow the approach to computational questions outlined below and always ensure that you answer the question using the following pro-formas amended to reflect the particular circumstances of the question.

Approach to computational questions

For plant and machinery capital allowances, adopt the following step-by-step approach:

(1) Read the information in the question and decide how many columns / pools you will require.

(2) Draft the layout and insert the TWDV b/f (does not apply in a new trade).

(3) Insert additions not eligible for the AIA or FYAs into the appropriate column taking particular care to allocate cars into the correct column according to cost or CO_2 emissions as relevant.

(4) Insert additions eligible for the AIA in the first column, then allocate the AIA to the additions.

Allocate the AIA to 'special rate pool' additions in priority to additions of plant and machinery in the general or special asset pools.

Within the general pool, allocate the AIA to expenditure that does not qualify for a 40% FYA in priority.

(5) Any 'special rate pool' additions in excess of the AIA must be added to the 'special rate pool' column to increase the balance available for 10% WDA.

Any general pool expenditure, in excess of the AIA, which has been incurred between 6.4.09 to 5.4.10 should be carried forward to the FYA section as it qualifies for 40% FYA.

Otherwise the excess should be added to the general pool to increase the balance qualifying for 20% WDA.

(6) Deal with any disposal by deducting the lower of cost or sale proceeds.

(7) Work out any balancing charge / balancing allowance for assets in individual pools.

Remember to adjust for any private use.

(8) Consider if the small pools WDA applies to the general pool and / or the 'special rate pool'.

(9) Calculate the WDA on each of the pools at the appropriate rate (20% or 10%). Remember to:

- time apportion if the accounting period is not 12 months
- adjust for any private use if an unincorporated business (not relevant for companies)

(10) Insert additions eligible for FYAs - the balance of any general pool expenditure (excluding cars) in excess of the AIA will get a FYA of 40% (the balance should then be transferred to the general pool) and any cars with emissions of 110 g/km or less will get 100% FYA.

(11) Calculate the TWDV to carry forward to the next accounting period and add the allowances column.

(12) Deduct the total allowances from the tax adjusted trading profits.

Proforma capital allowances computation

	Notes		General pool	Special rate pool	Short life asset	Private use asset (Note 3)	Expensive car (Note 1)	Allowances
		£	£	£	£	£	£	£
TWDV b/f			X	X	X		X	
Additions:								
Not qualifying for AIA or FYA:	(2)							
Cars (111-160 gm/km)			X					
Cars (over 160 gm/km)				X				
Car with private use						X		
Qualifying for AIA but not FYA:								
Special rate pool expenditure		X						
Less AIA (Max £50,000 in total)	(4)	(X)						X
Transfer balance to special rate pool				X				
Plant and machinery (purchased pre 6.4.09 and post 5.4.10)		X						
Less AIA (Max £50,000 in total)		(X)						
Transfer balance to general pool			X					
Qualifying for AIA and FYA:								
Plant and machinery (purchased between 6.4.09 and 5.4.10)		X						
Less AIA (Max £50,000 in total)		(X)						X
Balance of AIA qualifying expenditure (see below)	(5)	B						
Disposals (lower of original cost or sale proceeds)			(X)		(X)			
			X	X	X	X		
BA / (BC)					X / (X)			X / (X)
Small pools WDA	(6)							
WDA at 20%			(X)					X
WDA at 20% (max £3,000)	(1)						(X)	X
WDA at 10%				(X)				X
WDA at 10%/20% (depending on emissions)						(X) × BU%		X
Additions qualifying for FYAs:								
Balance of AIA qualifying expenditure (see B above)	(5)							
eligible for FYA at 40%		(X)	X					
Low emission cars (up to 110 gm/km)		X						
Less FYA at 100%		(X)						X
			Nil					
TWDV c/f			X	X		X	X	
Total allowances								X

Notes to the proforma capital allowances computation

(1) Cars purchased before 6 April 2009 (sole traders and partnerships) continue to be dealt with under the old rules.

The F6 examiner has confirmed that questions may have an 'old' expensive car with a TWDV b/f, however he will not have the purchase of a car pre 6 April 2009. This means that:

- Cars costing over £12,000 (expensive cars), have a separate pool and attract a WDA of 20% subject to a maximum of £3,000 per annum.
- Cars costing £12,000 or less are included as 'general' pool TWDV b/f, and attract a WDA of 20%.
- Private use cars are de-pooled and only the business proportion of allowances can be claimed
- Low emission cars (CO_2 emissions of 110 g/km or less) are eligible for 100% FYAs.

(2) Cars purchased on/after 6 April 2009 (sole traders and partnerships) are pooled according to their CO_2 emissions into either the 'general' or 'special rate' pool.

Low emission cars continue to receive 100% FYA.

(3) Cars with private use are de-pooled regardless of the date of purchase, and only the business proportion of allowances can be claimed. However, the date of purchase (pre or post April 2009) is important in determining the rate of WDA available.

(4) Allocate the AIA to the 'special rate' pool expenditure in priority to plant and machinery assets as a WDA of only 10% is available on the 'special rate' pool as opposed to 20% available on 'general' pool items.

(5) Pre April 2009, expenditure qualifying for AIA in the general pool but exceeding the level of AIA available, was eligible for a WDA of 20%. However, with effect from April 2009, expenditure qualifying for AIA in the general pool but exceeding the level of AIA available, is eligible for a FYA at 40% provided it is purchased in the year ending 5 April 2010 (sole traders and partnerships).

(6) Small pools WDA: can claim up to a maximum WDA of £1,000 but on the general pool and/or 'special rate pool' only.

(7) The taxpayer does not have to claim all or any of the AIA or WDA.

11 Comprehensive examples

Example 10 - Comprehensive example

Ashley runs a manufacturing business and prepares accounts to 30 April each year.

During the year ending 30 April 2010 Ashley incurred the following expenditure:

1 May 2009	Spent £120,000 on a new air-conditioning system for the factory which is expected to last 30 years.
1 June 2009	Purchased new machinery for £40,000.
3 June 2009	Purchased a car with CO_2 emissions of 109 g/km for £17,000.
15 July 2009	Purchased a new car for with CO_2 emissions of 146 g/km for £18,000.

In addition on 1 July 2009 Ashley sold an old machine for £10,000 (original cost £15,000) and the expensive car for £7,000, which had originally cost £15,000.

As at 1 April 2009 the tax written down values were as follows:

General pool	£64,000
Expensive car	£9,000

Calculate Ashley's capital allowances for the year ended 30 April 2010.

Answer to example 10

Capital allowances computation

		General pool	Special rate pool	Expensive car	Allow-ances
	£	£	£	£	£
y/e 30 April 2010					
TWDV b/f		64,000	Nil	9,000	
Additions:					
Not qualifying for AIA or FYA:					
Car (CO_2 emissions 146 g/km)		18,000			
Qualifying for AIA but not FYA:					
Integral features	120,000				
Less: AIA (Max)	(50,000)				50,000
	———		70,000		
Qualifying for AIA and FYA:					
Plant and machinery	40,000				
Less: AIA (Max used)	(Nil)				
	———				
	40,000				
Disposal (lower of Cost and SP)		(10,000)		(7,000)	
		———	———	———	
		72,000	70,000	2,000	
Balancing allowance				(2,000)	2,000
Less: WDA (20% x £72,000)		(14,400)			14,400
WDA (10% x £70,000)			(7,000)		7,000
Less: FYA (40% x £40,000)	(16,000)				16,000
	———	24,000			
Car (CO_2 < 110 g/km)	17,000				
Less: FYA (100%)	(17,000)				17,000
	———	Nil			
		———	———	———	
TWDV c/f		81,600	63,000	Nil	
		———	———	———	———
Total allowances					106,400
					———

Note: The AIA is allocated to the additions in the 'special rate pool' (WDA 10%) in priority to the additions in the general pool (WDA 20%).

Test your understanding 9

On 1 January 2010, Gordon commenced in self-employment running a music-recording studio. He prepared his first set of accounts for the 3 months to 31 March 2010.

The following information relates to the 3 months of trading to 31 March 2010:

(1) The tax adjusted trading profit for the period is £22,590. This figure is before taking account of capital allowances.

(2) Gordon purchased the following assets:

		£
1 January 2010	Recording equipment	21,625
15 January 2010	Motor car with CO_2 emissions of 162 g/km (used by Gordon – 60% business use)	15,800
20 February 2010	Motor car with CO_2 emissions of 156 gkm (used privately by employee – 20% private use)	10,400
4 March 2010	Recording equipment (expected to be scrapped in 2 years)	3,250

Calculate Gordon's taxable trading income for the period ended 31 March 2010.

12 Chapter summary

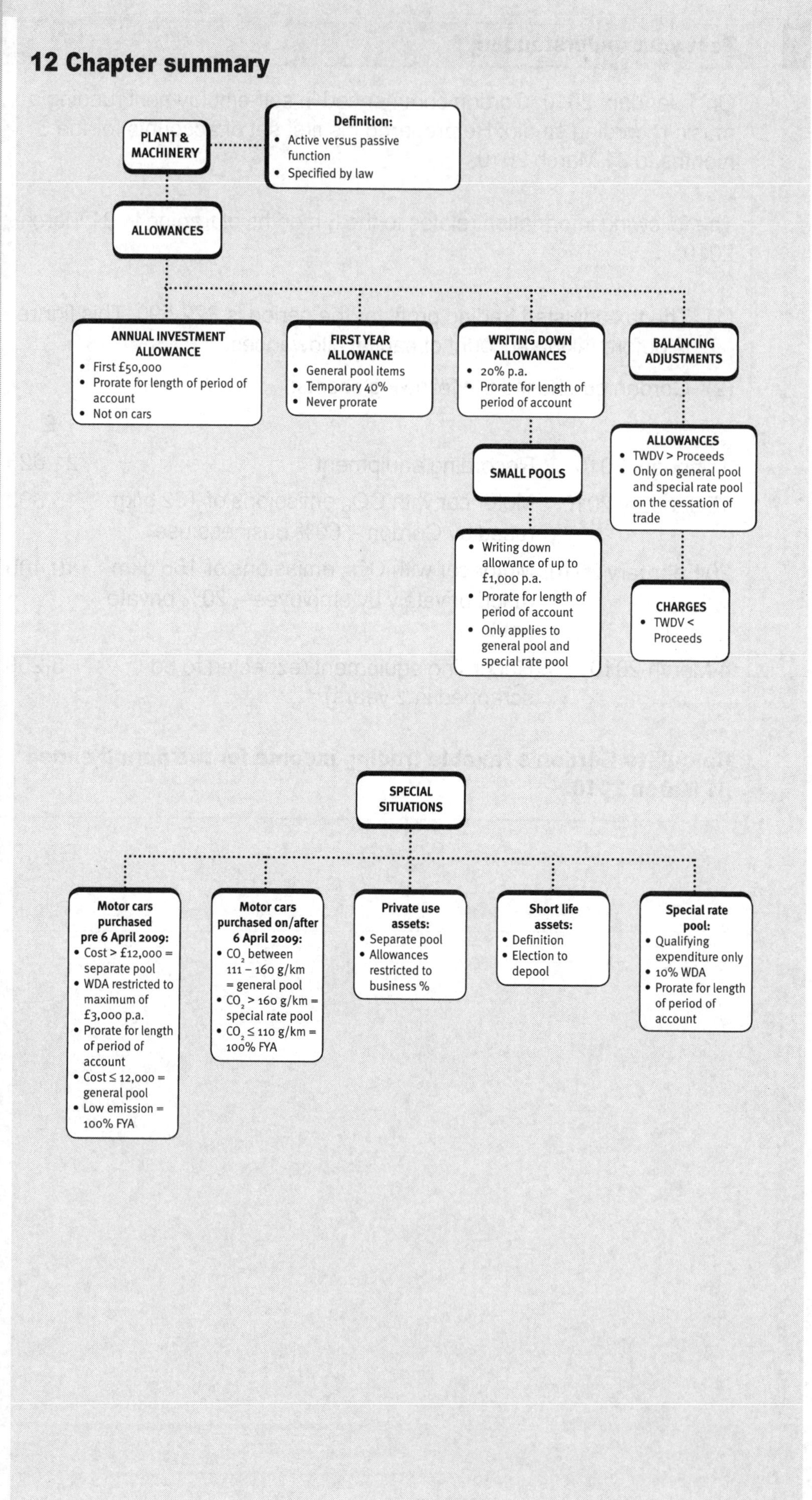

Test your understanding answers

Test your understanding 1

Gayle

Taxable trading income

	Adjusted profit	Capital allowances (W)	Tax-adjusted trading profit
	£	£	£
y/e 30 April 2010	60,500	(53,200)	7,300
y/e 30 April 2011	54,000	(1,960)	52,040

Working: Capital allowances computation

		General pool	Allowances
	£	£	£
y/e 30 April 2010			
Additions:			
Not qualifying for AIA or FYA:			
Car (CO_2 between 111 – 160 g/km)		10,000	
Qualifying for AIA and FYA:			
Plant and machinery	53,000		
Less: AIA	(50,000)		50,000
	3,000		
Less: WDA (20% x £10,000)		(2,000)	2,000
Less: FYA (40% x £3,000)	(1,200)		1,200
		1,800	
TWDV c/f		9,800	
Total allowances			53,200
y/e 30 April 2010			
Less: WDA (20% x £9,800)		(1,960)	1,960
TWDV c/f		7,840	
Total allowances			1,960

Test your understanding 2

Graham

Trading income assessments

	Adjusted trading profit	Capital allowances (W)	Tax adjusted trading profit
	£	£	£
P/e 31 August 2009	32,000	(17,967)	14,033
Y/e 31 August 2010	45,000	(2,307)	42,693

Working: Capital allowances computation

		General pool	Allowances
4 m/e 31 August 2009	£	£	£
Additions:			
Not qualifying for AIA or FYA:			
Car (CO_2 between 111 – 160 g/km)		11,500	
Qualifying for AIA and FYA:			
Plant and machinery	18,000		
Less: AIA (Note)	(16,667)		16,667
	1,333		
Less: WDA (20% × £11,500 × 4/12)		(767)	767
Less: FYA (40% × £1,333)	(533)		533
		800	
TWDV c/f		11,533	
Total allowances			17,967
y/e 31 August 2010			
Less: WDA (20% × £11,533)		(2,307)	2,307
TWDV c/f		9,226	
Total allowances			2,307

Note: The maximum AIA is pro-rated to £16,667 (£50,000 x 4/12). The AIA and the WDA are pro-rated for the 4 month period.

Test your understanding 3

Gene

Capital allowances computation

	General pool	Total allowances
	£	£
Year ended 31 July 2010		
TWDV b/f	9,000	
Disposals (lower of cost or sale proceeds)	(320)	
	8,680	
WDA (20% x £8,680)	(1,736)	1,736
TWDV c/f	6,944	
Total allowances		1,736
Period ended 31 December 2010		
Additions:		
Not qualifying for AIA or FYA (Note)		
Plant and machinery	4,000	
	10,944	
Disposals (lower of cost or sale proceeds)	(5,400)	
	5,544	
Balancing allowance	(5,544)	5,544
Total allowances		5,544

Note: There is no AIA, FYA or WDA available in the final period of account.

Test your understanding 4

Gloria

Capital allowances computation

	£	General pool £	Total allowances £
Year ended 30 June 2010			
TWDV b/f		21,000	
Additions:			
Not qualifying for AIA or FYA:			
Car (111 - 160 g/km)		11,000	
Qualifying for AIA and FYA:			
Plant and machinery	19,500		
Less AIA (Note)	(19,500)		19,500
	Nil		
		32,000	
Disposals (lower of cost or sale proceeds)		(3,000)	
		29,000	
Less: WDA (20% × £29,000)		(5,800)	5,800
Less: FYA (40% × £Nil)	(Nil)		
		(Nil)	
TWDV c/f		23,200	
Total allowances			25,300

Test your understanding 5

Glen

Capital allowances computation

		General pool	Expensive car	Allowances
	£	£	£	£
y/e 31 January 2010				
TWDV b/f		43,500	14,500	
Additions:				
Not qualifying for AIA or FYA:				
Car (CO_2 between 111 – 160 g/km)		10,600		
Qualifying for AIA and FYA:				
Plant and machinery	53,300			
Less: AIA	(50,000)			50,000
	3,300			
Disposal (lower of cost and SP)			(9,400)	
		54,100	5,100	
Balancing allowance			(5,100)	5,100
Less: WDA (20% x £54,100)		(10,820)		10,820
Less: FYA (40% x £3,300)	(1,320)			1,320
		1,980		
TWDV c/f		45,260		
Total allowances				67,240

Test your understanding 6

Gwen

Capital allowances computation

		General pool	Expensive car	Allowances
y/e 5 April 2010	£	£	£	£
TWDV b/f		11,000	18,000	
Additions:				
Not qualifying for AIA or FYA:				
Car (CO_2 between 111 – 160 g/km)		13,000		
Qualifying for AIA and FYA:				
Plant and machinery	59,000			
Less: AIA	(50,000)			50,000
	9,000			
Disposal (lower of cost and SP)		(4,600)		
		19,400	18,000	
Less: WDA (20% x £19,400)		(3,880)		3,880
WDA (maximum)			(3,000)	3,000
Less: FYA (40% x £9,000)	(3,600)			3,600
		5,400		
Low emission car (CO_2 < 110 g/km)	13,000			
Less: FYA (100%)	(13,000)			13,000
		Nil		
TWDV c/f		20,920	15,000	
Total allowances				73,480

Notes:

(1) There is no balancing allowance in the general pool except in the period when trade is permanently discontinued. A WDA is claimed on the unrelieved expenditure after recording the disposal.

(2) The low emission car is dealt with at the end of the computation as it is not eligible for either the AIA or a WDA. It is eligible for 100% FYA.

Test your understanding 7

Georgina

Capital allowances computation

		General pool	Expensive Car (BU 70%)	Private use car (BU 60%)	Business use	Allow-ances
	£	£	£	£	%	£
y/e 5 April 2010						
TWDV b/f		21,200	13,600			
Additions:						
Not qualifying for AIA or FYA:						
Car (CO_2 between 111 – 160 g/km)		17,000				
Private use car				10,600		
Qualifying for AIA and FYA:						
Plant and machinery	6,600					
Less: AIA	(6,600)					6,600
	Nil					
Disposal (lower of Cost and SP)			(9,400)			
		38,200	4,200	10,600		
Balancing allowance			(4,200)		× 70%	2,940
Less: WDA (20% x £38,200)		(7,640)				7,640
WDA (20% x £10,600)				(2,120)	× 60%	1,272
Less: FYA (40%)	(Nil)					
		Nil				
Additions:						
Qualifying for FYA						
Car (CO_2 < 110 g/km)	11,750					
Less: FYA (100%)	(11,750)					11,750
		Nil				
TWDV c/f		30,560		8,480		
Total allowances						30,202

Test your understanding 8

Angelina

Capital allowances computation

		General pool	Special rate pool	Private use car (BU 80%)	Business use	Allow-ances
	£	£	£	£	%	£
y/e 31 March 2010						
TWDV b/f		10,800	Nil			
Additions:						
Not qualifying for AIA or FYA:						
Private use car				10,000		
Qualifying for AIA but not FYA:						
Integral features	35,000					
Less: AIA	(35,000)					35,000
	———		Nil			
Qualifying for AIA and FYA:						
Plant and machinery	13,800					
Less: AIA (Max)	13,800					
	———	Nil				13,800
Disposal (lower of Cost and SP)		(10,000)				
		800	Nil	10,000		
Less: Small pool WDA		(800)				800
Less: WDA (10% x £Nil)			(Nil)			Nil
WDA (20% x £10,000)				(2,000)	× 80%	1,600
TWDV c/f		Nil	Nil	8,000		
Total allowances						51,200

Note: The AIA is allocated to the additions in the 'special rate pool' (WDA 10%) in priority to the additions in the general pool (WDA 20%).

Test your understanding 9

Gordon

Period ended 31 March 2010

	£
Adjusted profit	22,590
Less: Capital allowances (W1)	(18,207)
Trading profit	4,383

(W1) Capital allowances computation

		General pool	Short life asset	Private use car	Business use	Allow-ances
P/e 31 March 2010	£	£	£	£	%	£
Additions:						
Not qualifying for AIA or FYA:						
Car (CO_2 156 g/km) (Note 1)		10,400				
Private use car				15,800		
Qualifying for AIA and FYA:						
Equipment	21,625		3,250			
Less: AIA (Max) (Note 2)	(12,500)		(Nil)			12,500
	9,125		3,250			
		10,400		15,800		
Less: WDA (20% × £10,400 × 3/12)		(520)				520
WDA (10% × £15,800 × 3/12) (CO_2 > 160 g/km)				(395)	× 60%	237
Less: FYA (40% × £9,125)	(3,650)		(1,300)			4,950
		5,475				
TWDV c/f		15,355	1,950	15,405		
Total allowances						18,207

Private use by an employee is not relevant. A separate private use asset column is only required where there is private use by the owner of the business.

The AIA is pro-rated for the three month period. The maximum allowance is therefore £12,500 (£50,000 x 3/12). The AIA is allocated to the general plant and machinery in priority to the short life asset.

chapter

7

Capital allowances: Industrial buildings allowances

Chapter learning objectives

Upon completion of this chapter you will be able to:

- recognise qualifying and non-qualifying expenditure for industrial buildings allowance purposes
- compute the industrial buildings allowances for a new building used solely for industrial purposes

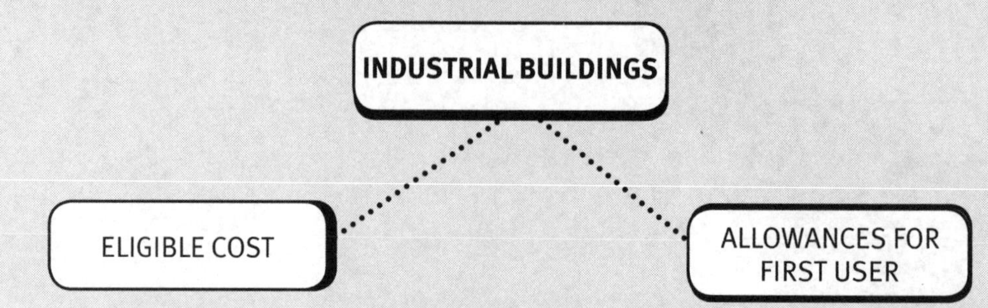

1 Introduction

The purpose of industrial buildings allowances (IBAs) is to provide the business with tax relief for the acquisition of qualifying industrial buildings.

The relief is given as follows:

- IBAs are deducted as a trading expense in calculating the tax-adjusted trading profit.
- IBAs are calculated for a trader's period of account (i.e. the period for which they draw up accounts).

2 Definition of an industrial building

Qualifying industrial buildings are those used for the purposes of a qualifying trade. The more important of these qualifying trades are:

- a trade carried on in a mill, factory or similar premises
- a trade in the manufacture of goods or materials or the subjection of goods or materials to any process
- a trade in the storage of:
  - goods or materials used for manufacturing purposes, or which are to be subjected to any process
  - finished goods or materials that have been manufactured or subjected to any process.

In addition, the following structures are also industrial buildings:

- Any building or structure provided by the company carrying on one of the above trades for the welfare of its employees, for example, a canteen or workplace nursery.
- A drawing office used for the preparation of plans for manufacturing or processing operations.
- Qualifying hotels. The conditions to be satisfied are given in expandable text.

Qualifying hotels

Provided that a hotel meets all the following four conditions, it is treated as an industrial building:

- The building must be a hotel.
- The hotel must be open for at least four months (120 days) in the season (1 April to 31 October each year).
- When open in the season, the hotel must have at least ten bedrooms that are available for short-term letting to the public (not more than 30 days per letting).
- When open in the season, the services provided for guests must normally include breakfast, evening meal, room cleaning and the making of beds.

Excluded buildings

Buildings specifically excluded from being industrial buildings are:

- dwelling houses
- retail or wholesale premises
- showrooms
- offices.

3 Qualifying cost of construction

- The qualifying cost of an industrial building includes only that expenditure actually incurred in its construction.

- The cost of the land (and the incidental expenses associated with acquiring the land) does not qualify for IBAs.
- As well as the actual cost of constructing the building the following are also qualifying elements of the construction cost:
  - costs in connection with the land that are preliminary to construction do qualify, including:
    (1) the preparation of the site in order to lay foundations
    (2) cutting, tunnelling and levelling the land in connection with the construction.
  - professional fees, notably those of architects, incurred as part of the construction project.
  - capital expenditure on alterations to an existing industrial building.

- Where part of a building is not used for a qualifying purpose and the expenditure on that non-industrial part does not exceed 25% of the total qualifying cost of the whole building, then IBAs will be given on the cost of the whole building.
- If the non-industrial part represents more than 25%, IBAs will only be given on the industrial cost element.
- The total cost of constructing a qualifying building is eligible for IBAs (subject to the rule on non-qualifying parts of a building) if built by or for the trader.
- If the building was acquired after construction (but before use) the eligible cost depends on the type of vendor:
  - When purchased from a builder the eligible expenditure is the purchase price (including the builder's profit margin).
  - For any other vendor the eligible cost is always the lower of the purchase price and the construction expenditure incurred.

Example 1 - Qualifying cost of construction

Harry erected a factory for use in his manufacturing business. The total construction cost of £370,000, was apportioned as follows:

	£
Freehold land	60,000
Cutting and levelling of site	2,000
Construction of building comprising:	
Employees' canteen	12,000
General offices	29,000
Factory	267,000
	370,000

Calculate the expenditure qualifying for IBAs.

Answer to example 1

	£
Total cost	370,000
Less: Land	(60,000)
Cost of construction of whole building	310,000

The cost of the non-qualifying part of the building (i.e. the general offices) of £29,000 does not exceed 25% of the cost of the whole building of £310,000. Therefore, IBAs are available on the cost of the whole building.

If the general offices had actually cost say £100,000, then as a proportion of the qualifying cost (£100,000/£310,000) is 32.258% > 25% and hence would be disallowed.

In this situation, the eligible cost would be £210,000.

Test your understanding 1

Harriet acquired a new factory at a cost of £409,300, on 1 January 2007. It was brought into industrial use on the same day. The total cost was made up as follows:

	£
Land	90,000
Levelling the land	10,000
Architects' fees	25,000
Air-conditioning system	19,300
Strengthened concrete floor to support machinery	10,200
General offices	62,500
Factory	192,300
	409,300

(a) **Compute the expenditure qualifying for IBAs.**

(b) **Compute the qualifying expenditure if the general offices had cost £82,500 and the total spend remains as above at £409,300.**

4 Calculating industrial buildings allowances for a new building

Writing down allowance (WDA)

The following rules apply:

- WDAs for industrial buildings are given on a straight-line basis on the eligible cost of the qualifying building.
- The rate of WDA for 2009/10 for individuals is 2%.

- Companies also qualify for IBAs and are entitled to the 2% WDA for the year ended 31 March 2010.
- The WDA is proportionately reduced where the period of account is less than 12 months.

- A WDA is given provided the building is in use as an industrial building at the end of the period of account.

Sale of buildings

Where a building is disposed of there are no capital allowance implications for the vendor, other than he will cease to claim IBAs in the period of account in which the building is disposed of.

Example 2 - Calculating IBAs for a new building

Assume the expenditure on industrial buildings was as in the previous illustration, Harry. The factory was completed and paid for on 1 June 2006 and taken into use on 1 August 2006. Harry prepares accounts to 31 March.

Harry was entitled to total IBAs of £34,100 up to 31 March 2009.

On 1 August 2010, the factory was sold for £500,000 (including £100,000 for the land), to Henry.

Explain the IBAs available to Harry for the years ended 31 March 2010 and 2011.

Answer to example 2

Qualifying expenditure incurred (June 2006) = £310,000

	£
Up to year ended 31 March 2009	34,100
Year ended 31 March 2010	
WDA (2% × £310,000)	6,200
Total allowances	40,300

Year ended 31 March 2011

The building was not in use on 31 March 2011 (sold 1 August 2010) and therefore no allowances are available in the year to 31 March 2011.

Test your understanding 2

Henrietta incurred £300,000 on the purchase of a new industrial building on 1 January 2008. It was taken into industrial use on 1 February 2008. Henrietta prepares accounts to 31 March each year.

On 15 August 2010 the building was sold for £424,000 including £109,000 for the land.

Calculate the IBAs available to Henrietta for the years 31 March 2010 and 2011.

5 Comprehensive example

Example 3 - Comprehensive example

Chris commenced to trade on 1 January 1992 and prepares his accounts regularly to 31 March each year.

He acquired a new industrial building on 1 September 2004 and brought it into use immediately. The total cost of £112,500, was made up as follows:

	£
Land	12,500
Site clearance	2,500
Foundation	7,500
General office	5,000
Drawing (design) office	2,500
Canteen	3,750
Accounts office	4,500
Other allowable costs	74,250
Total expenditure	112,500

On 1 July 2010 Chris sold the building to Freddy for £130,000.

Compute the IBAs available to Chris for the years ended 31 March 2010 and 2011.

Answer to example 3

Chris

		£
Total cost		112,500
Less: Land		(12,500)
Potential qualifying cost		100,000 × 25% = £25,000
General office	£5,000	
Accounts office	£4,500	
Total	£9,500	
= Less than £25,000 and therefore allowed		
Qualifying cost		100,000

Allowances

y/e 31 March 2010

WDA (2% x £100,000)	£2,000

y/e 31 March 2011

No allowances – building sold 1.7.10	Nil

6 Chapter summary

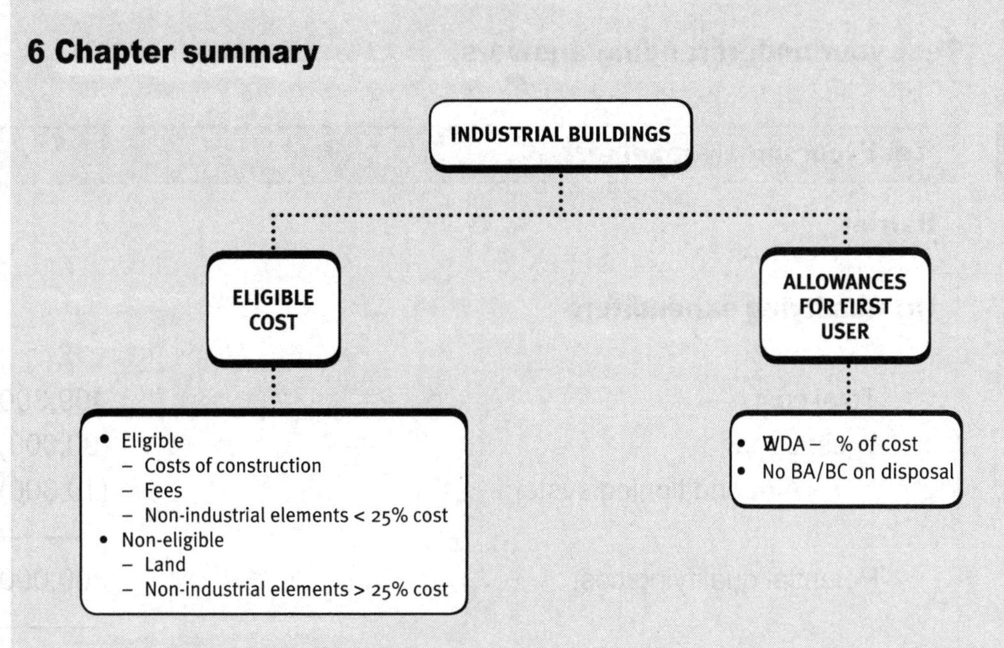

Test your understanding answers

Test your understanding 1

Harriet

(a) Qualifying expenditure

	£
Total cost	409,300
Less: Land	(90,000)
Air-conditioning system	(19,300)
Potential qualifying cost	300,000
£300,000 × 25% = £75,000	
General office £62,500 = less than £75,000	
Therefore qualifying cost	300,000

(b) If general offices cost £82,500

General office £82,500 = more than £75,000 therefore not allowed	
Therefore qualifying cost (£300,000 – £82,500)	217,500

Test your understanding 2

Henrietta

Qualifying expenditure incurred (Jan 2008) = £300,000

Year ended 31 March 2010

WDA (2% × £300,000)	£6,000

Year ended 31 March 2011

No allowances – building sold 15.08.10	Nil

hapter

8

Sole traders: Basis of assessment

Chapter learning objectives

Upon completion of this chapter you will be able to:

- Recognise the basis of assessment for income from self-employment
- Compute the assessable trading profits for a new business
- Compute the assessable trading profits on cessation of a business
- Recognise the factors that will influence the choice of accounting date for a new business
- State the conditions that must be met for a change of accounting date to be valid
- Compute the assessable profits on a change of accounting date

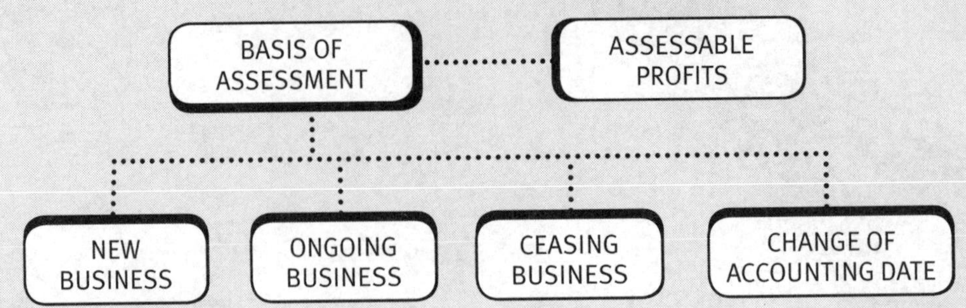

1 Introduction

Once the tax-adjusted trading profit has been calculated for a period of account, it is important to identify in which tax year it will be assessed.

- Income tax is charged for a tax year or year of assessment which runs from 6 April to the following 5 April.
- Since traders do not necessarily prepare their accounts to coincide with the tax year, there needs to be a system for attributing profits earned in a period of account to a particular tax year.

The profit-earning (or loss-making) period of account that is attributed to a particular tax year is known as the 'basis period' for that tax year.

- In the examination, where the apportionment of trading profits into different tax years is required, the apportionment should be performed on a monthly basis as shown in all the illustrations below.

2 Ongoing year rules

Basic principles

The basic rule is:

- The profits for a year of assessment are the tax-adjusted trading profits for the 12 month period of account ending in that year.
- This is sometimes referred to as the current year basis of assessment (or CYB for short).

Test your understanding 1

A sole trader prepares his accounts to 31 December each year. He has been operating for several years.

State which profits will be assessed in 2009/10.

Test your understanding 2

Jerry prepares accounts to 30 September annually. His recent taxable trading profits have been as follows:

	£
Year to 30 September 2008	20,000
Year to 30 September 2009	22,000

State in which tax years will these profits be assessed.

3 Opening year rules

Assuming a business starts to trade on 1 January 2009 and prepares accounts for calendar years, the first tax year it is trading is in 2008/09.

However, the first accounting period will not end until 31 December 2009 and using the basic principle above this period will not be taxed until 2009/10.

In order to ensure that there is an assessment for each tax year that a business is trading, the following special provisions apply:

Year 1 The actual profits from commencement of trading to the following 5 April are assessed to tax in the first tax year (known as the **actual basis** of assessment).

Year 2 If there is a 12 month period of account ending in the second tax year, then this is the basis period (CYB).

Otherwise apply the following rules:

Period of account	**Basis of assessment**
The period of account ending in the second tax year is:	
– **LESS than 12 months**	First 12 months of trading.
– **MORE than 12 months**	Twelve months ended on the new permanent accounting date.
There is **no period of account** ending in the second tax year.	Actual profits arising between 6 April and 5 April.

Year 3 Assess the 12 months ending with the accounting date in that year.

Example 1 - Opening year rules

Jenny commenced trading on 1 January 2009 and prepared her first set of accounts to 31 December that year. Her tax-adjusted trading profits were £12,000 for the y/e 31 December 2009.

Explain which profits will be assessed in Jenny's first two tax years.

Answer to example 1

First tax year

The profits assessed for 2008/09 will be the actual profits falling in the first tax year on a pro rata basis.

Tax year	Basis period	Calculation	Assessable profits
2008/09	01.01.09 - 05.04.09	(3/12 × £12,000)	£3,000

Second tax year

In the second tax year there is a 12 month period of account ending in the tax year. The current year basis can therefore be applied.

Tax year	Basis period	Assessable profits
2009/10	CYB (y/e 31 December 2009)	£12,000

You will notice that in the two years above, the profits for the period 1 January to 5 April (£3,000) have been assessed twice.

These are referred to as **overlap profits**.

Overlap profits

- Profits that are assessed in more than one tax year are known as the overlap profits.
- Overlap profits arise in every scenario at commencement of trade other than when the trader opts to take a 31 March year-end.
- The overlap profits are carried forward and are normally deducted from the assessment for the period in which the business ceases.
- Whilst this does mean that the trader will get relief for overlap profits, relief may not be obtained for many years if the business continues for a long while.
- Overlap profits may also be relieved when a business changes its accounting date (see section 7).

Test your understanding 3

Rob started to trade on 1 September 2008 and prepared his first accounts for the year ended 31 August 2009. His tax-adjusted trading profits were £18,000 in that year.

Calculate his assessable profits for 2008/09 and 2009/10.

Identify the months that have been taxed more than once and the overlap profits arising.

Summary of opening year rules

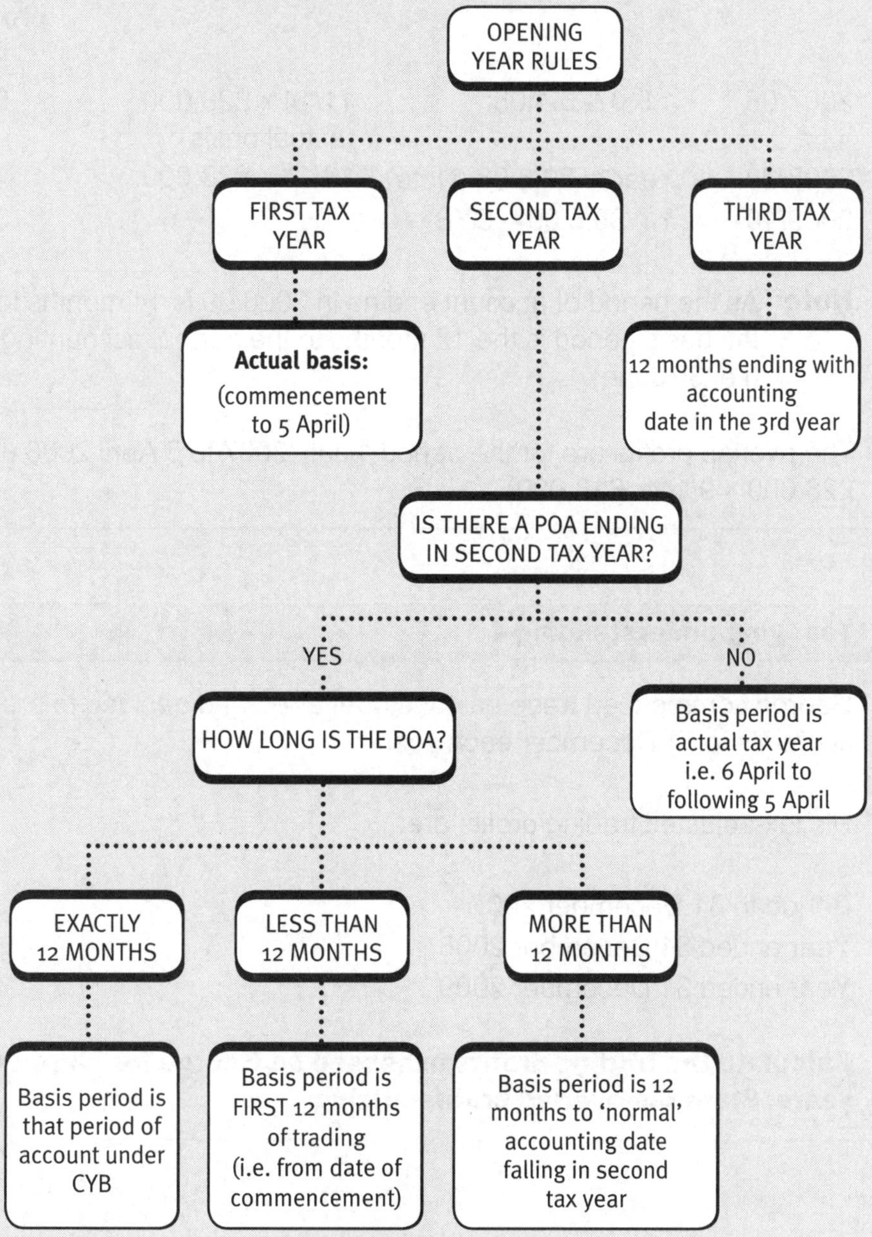

- OPENING YEAR RULES
  - FIRST TAX YEAR → **Actual basis:** (commencement to 5 April)
  - SECOND TAX YEAR → IS THERE A POA ENDING IN SECOND TAX YEAR?
    - YES → HOW LONG IS THE POA?
      - EXACTLY 12 MONTHS → Basis period is that period of account under CYB
      - LESS THAN 12 MONTHS → Basis period is FIRST 12 months of trading (i.e. from date of commencement)
      - MORE THAN 12 MONTHS → Basis period is 12 months to 'normal' accounting date falling in second tax year
    - NO → Basis period is actual tax year i.e. 6 April to following 5 April
  - THIRD TAX YEAR → 12 months ending with accounting date in the 3rd year

Example 2 - Opening year rules

Arthur commenced trading on 1 May 2007. He prepares accounts to 30 June each year. His tax-adjusted trading profits were as follows:

Period ended 30.6.08	£28,000
Year ended 30.6.09	£30,000

Calculate Arthur's trading income assessments for his first three tax years and his overlap profits.

Answer to example 2

Tax year	Basis period	Calculation	Assessable profits
			£
2007/08	1.5.07- 5.4.08:	11/14 x £28,000 (actual basis)	22,000
2008/09	Year to 30.6.08 (Note)	12/14 x £28,000	24,000
2009/10	Y/e 30.6.09 – CYB		30,000

Note: As the period of account ending in 2008/09 is 14 months long, the basis period is the 12 months to the normal accounting date (i.e. 30 June).

The overlap profits are for the period 1 July 2007 to 5 April 2008 (i.e. £28,000 × 9/14 = £18,000).

Test your understanding 4

George commenced trade on 1 October 2006 and decided to prepare accounts to 31 December each year.

His tax-adjusted trading profits are:

	£
Period to 31 December 2007	30,000
Year ended 31 December 2008	36,000
Year ended 31 December 2009	40,000

Calculate the trading profits assessed on George for all relevant years. State the overlap profits arising.

Example 3 - Opening year rules

Pattie commenced trading on 1 September 2007. She prepared accounts to 30 June 2008 and annually thereafter.

Her tax-adjusted trading profits for the first two periods were as follows:

Period ended 30 June 2008	£30,000
Year ended 30 June 2009	£48,000

Calculate Pattie's trading income assessments for her first three tax years and her overlap profits.

Answer to example 3

Tax year	Basis period	Calculation	Assessable profits
			£
2007/08	1.9.07 - 5.4.08	(£30,000 × 7/10) (actual)	21,000
2008/09	1.9.07 - 31.8.08	(£30,000 + (2/12 × £48,000) (Note)	38,000
2009/10	y/e 30.6.09 – CYB		48,000

Note: Because the accounting date ending in the second year of assessment is less than 12 months after the commencement of trading, the basis of assessment is the first 12 months of trading.

Overlap profits = £29,000: £21,000 (1.9.07 to 5.4.08) and £8,000 (1.7.08 to 31.8.08: 2/12 × £48,000).

Test your understanding 5

Fred commenced a new trade on 1 June 2006 and decided that his normal accounting date would be 30 April each year.

Given below are the tax-adjusted trading profits since commencement:

Period to 30 April 2007	£11,000
Year ended 30 April 2008	£18,000
Year ended 30 April 2009	£22,000

Calculate the trading profits assessable on Fred for all relevant years and his overlap profits.

Example 4 - Opening year rules

Cordelia commenced trading on 1 July 2007. She prepared accounts to 30 April 2009 and annually thereafter. Her tax-adjusted trading profits for the first two periods were as follows:

Period ended 30.04.09	£55,000
Year ended 30.04.10	£32,000

Calculate Cordelia's trading income assessments for her first three tax years and her overlap profits.

Answer to example 4

Tax year	**Basis period**	**Calculation**	**Assessable profits**
			£
2007/08	(01.07.07 – 05.04.08)	£55,000 × 9/22 (actual)	22,500
2008/09	(06.04.08 – 05.04.09)	£55,000 × 12/22 (Note 1)	30,000
2009/10	(Year to 30.04.09)	£55,000 × 12/22 (Note 2)	30,000
2010/11	(Year to 30.04.10)	CYB	32,000

Notes:

(1) Because there is no accounting date in the second year of assessment, the basis of assessment is the actual basis for the period from 6.4.08 to 5.4.09.

(2) In year three, the basis period is the profits of the 12-months ending with the accounting date in that year.

Overlap profits: £27,500 (01.05.08 to 05.04.09 = 11/22 × £55,000)

Test your understanding 6

Maria commenced business on 1 January 2006 and prepared her first accounts for the period to 30 June 2007, and thereafter to 30 June in each year.

Her tax-adjusted trading profits have been:

Period to 30 June 2007	£27,000
Year ended 30 June 2008	£30,000
Year ended 30 June 2009	£40,000

Calculate the trading profits assessed on Maria for all relevant years. State the overlap profits.

4 Closing year rules

- The objective in the final year of assessment is to ensure that any profits not previously assessed are assessed here.
- Any overlap profits from commencement are deducted from the assessment for the final year.
- The easiest approach to identify the basis period of assessment for the final tax year is:
  - Identify the tax year in which the trade ceases. This is the last year that profits must be assessed.
  - For the immediately preceding tax year, identify the assessment under normal CYB rules.
  - All profits after this period of account will not have been assessed and so fall into the assessment for the final tax year of trade.
  - Remember to deduct overlap profits in this final assessment.

Example 5 - Closing year rules

Michael ceased trading on 31 March 2010. His tax-adjusted trading profits for the final three periods of trading are as follows:

Year ended 30.4.08	£40,000
Year ended 30.4.09	£42,000
Period ended 31.3.10	£38,000

He has unrelieved overlap profits of £27,000.

Calculate Michael's final two trading income assessments.

Answer to example 5

The final year of assessment is 2009/10, the year in which trade ceases.

		£
2008/09	CYB (Year to 30.4.08)	40,000
2009/10	Final year: all profits not yet assessed (23 months from 1.5.08 to 31.3.10) (£42,000 + £38,000)	80,000
	Less Overlap profits	(27,000)
	Final assessable amount	53,000

Test your understanding 7

Major, who has been trading for many years, decides to cease trading on 31 December 2009. Major regularly prepared accounts to 30 June in each year.

The recent tax-adjusted trading profits have been:

	£
Period to 31 December 2009	6,000
Year ended 30 June 2009	12,000
Year ended 30 June 2008	15,000
Year ended 30 June 2007	20,000
Year ended 30 June 2006	18,000

The overlap profits on commencement were £7,500.

Calculate the trading profits that will be assessed on Major for all tax years affected by the above accounts.

Test your understanding 8

Benny commenced to trade on 1 July 2004 and prepared his first accounts to 31 August 2005 and thereafter to 31 August annually. Benny ceased to trade on 31 December 2009.

Given below are the tax adjusted trading profits for all the relevant periods:

	£
Period ended 31 August 2005	10,500
Year ended 31 August 2006	18,000
Year ended 31 August 2007	22,500
Year ended 31 August 2008	31,500
Year ended 31 August 2009	27,000
Period ended 31 December 2009	8,400
	117,900

Compute the trading profits that will have been assessed on Benny for each tax year.

5 Choice of accounting date

Options available

There are various factors to consider in identifying the accounting date that a business adopts:

- An accounting date of just after, rather than just before, 5 April (such as 30 April) will ensure the maximum interval between earning profits and having to pay the related tax liability.
- However, an accounting date just after 5 April will result in increased overlap profits upon the commencement of trading. Although there is relief for overlap profits, there may be a long delay before relief is obtained.
- Alternatively an accounting date of just before 5 April, such as 31 March, will give the shortest interval between earning profits and having to pay the related tax liability. However, there will be no overlap profits.

6 Change of accounting date – conditions

Provided certain conditions are met, an unincorporated business is allowed to change its accounting date. There may be tax advantages in doing so, or the change may be made for commercial reasons. For example, it may be easier to take stock at certain times of the year.

The detailed conditions and consequences of failing to meet the conditions are covered in expandable text.

Conditions to be met for a valid change

A change in accounting date will only be valid if the following conditions are met:

- The change of accounting date must be notified to HMRC on or before 31 January following the tax year in which the change is to be made.
- The first accounts to the new accounting date must not exceed 18 months in length.
- If the period between the old accounting date and the proposed new accounting date is longer than 18 months, then two sets of accounts will have to be prepared.
- There must not have been another change of accounting date during the previous five tax years. This condition may be ignored if HMRC accept that the present change is made for genuine commercial reasons.

Failure to meet the conditions

If the conditions are not met, the old accounting date will continue to apply. If accounts are prepared to the new accounting date, then the figures will have to be apportioned accordingly.

7 Change of accounting date – calculations

Calculation of assessable profits

If the conditions are met, then the period of account for the tax year in which the change of accounting date is made, will either be less than or more than 12 months in length.

Change of accounting date – calculations

A trader has previously prepared accounts to 30 June. If he changes his accounting date to 30 September, the next set of accounts are going to be for either 3 or 15 months.

However, all basis of assessments other than for the first and final tax years must be of 12 months in duration.

As the latest period of account will not be, the assessment will either be made up to 12 months, by creating further overlap profits, or reduced back to 12 months by relieving earlier overlap profits.

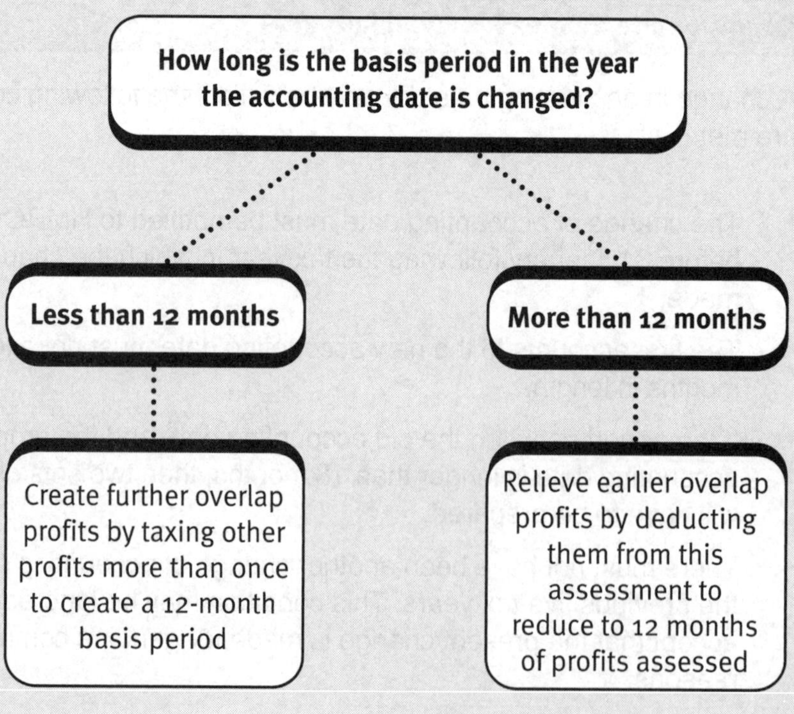
How long is the basis period in the year the accounting date is changed?
Less than 12 months
More than 12 months
Create further overlap profits by taxing other profits more than once to create a 12-month basis period
Relieve earlier overlap profits by deducting them from this assessment to reduce to 12 months of profits assessed

New date is earlier in the tax year

Where the new accounting date is earlier in the tax year than the old one, the basis period for the tax year of change will be the **12 month period ending with the new accounting date**.

This will result in some profits being assessed more than once. Overlap profits will therefore arise, which are treated in exactly the same way as overlap profits arising on the commencement of trade.

Example 6 - New date earlier - short period

Andrea, a sole trader, has always prepared her accounts to 31 March. She decides to change her accounting date to 30 June by preparing accounts for the three-month period to 30 June 2009.

Andrea's tax-adjusted trading profits are as follows:

	£
Year ended 31 March 2009	60,000
Three months to 30 June 2009	20,000
Year ended 30 June 2010	85,000

Calculate Andrea's trading income assessments for 2008/09 to 2010/11.

Answer to example 6

Note that the new accounting date (June) is earlier in the tax year than the previous accounting date (March).

The tax year of change is the year in which accounts to the new accounting date are prepared. The basis period for the tax year of change is the 12 months to the new accounting date.

The trading profits assessable will be as follows:

Tax year	Basis period	Assessable profits
		£
2008/09	Year to 31.3.09 (Normal CYB)	60,000
2009/10	12-month period to new accounting date of 30.6.09	
	Year to 31.3.09: (£60,000 × 9/12)	45,000
	Period to 30.6.09	20,000
		65,000
2010/11	Year to 30.6.10 (CYB)	85,000

Note: The change in accounting date has created further overlap profits of £45,000, as the 9 months to 31 March 2009 are assessed in both 2008/09 and 2009/10. The overlap profits will be offset in the final year of assessment.

As well as moving to an earlier date in the tax year with a short accounting period, it is possible to do this with a long accounting period.

Example 7 - New date earlier - long period

If Andrea had instead prepared accounts for the 15-month period to 30 June 2010, then the result would have been virtually the same. Assume the tax adjusted profit for the 15-month period ended 30 June 2010 is £105,000.

Calculate Andrea's trading income assessments for 2008/09 to 2010/11.

Answer to example 7

The tax year in which the change takes place is still 2009/10 as Andrea does not adopt her normal 31 March year-end here.

Because all the criteria are met, she is allowed to adopt the new accounting date in this year, preparing accounts for the 12 months to the new accounting date – 30 June.

Tax year	Basis period	Assessable profits
		£
2008/09	Year to 31.3.09 (Normal CYB)	60,000
2009/10	12-month period to new accounting date of 30.6.09	
	Year to 31.3.09: (£60,000 × 9/12)	45,000
	Period to 30.6.10: (£105,000 × 3/15)	21,000
		66,000
2010/11	Year to 30.6.10: (£105,000 × 12/15)	84,000

Overlap profits still arise in respect of the nine months to 31 March 2009, as before = £45,000.

New date is later in the tax year

Where the new accounting date is later in the tax year than the old one the basis period for the tax year of change will be the period ending with the new accounting date.

As the resulting basis period may be more than 12 months, a corresponding proportion of any overlap profits that arose upon the commencement of trading are offset against the assessable profits.

Again, it is possible to have either a short accounting period creating the new date, or a long period.

Example 8 - New date later - long period

Peter, a sole trader, commenced trading on 1 July 2006, and has always prepared his accounts to 30 June. He has now decided to change his accounting date to 30 September by preparing accounts for the 15-month period to 30 September 2009.

Peter's tax-adjusted trading profits are as follows:

	£
Year ended 30 June 2007	18,000
Year ended 30 June 2008	24,000
Period ended 30 September 2009	30,000
Year ended 30 September 2010	36,000

Calculate Peter's trading income assessments for 2006/07 to 2010/11.

Answer to example 8

The tax year of change is the tax year in which accounts are prepared to the new accounting date (i.e. 2009/10). As the new accounting date is later in the tax year, the basis period is the period ending with the new accounting date.

Tax year	Basis period	Assessable profits
		£
2006/07	1.7.06 to 5.4.07: Actual (£18,000 × 9/12)	13,500
2007/08	Year to 30.6.07: CYB	18,000
2008/09	Year to 30.6.08: CYB	24,000
2009/10	15 months period to 30.9.09	30,000
	Less: Overlap profits (£13,500 × 3/9)	(4,500)
		25,500
2010/11	Year to 30.9.10: CYB	36,000

The overlap profits on commencement of trade are £13,500, representing the 9 months (1.7.06 to 5.4.07) that have been taxed twice.

In 2009/10 the period of account is 15 months. No assessment can be for more than 12 months and in this case, Peter is allowed to offset three months' worth of his overlap profits.

The remaining 6 months of overlap profits are carried forward as normal and available for relief, either on a further change in accounting date, or on the cessation of trade.

8 Chapter summary

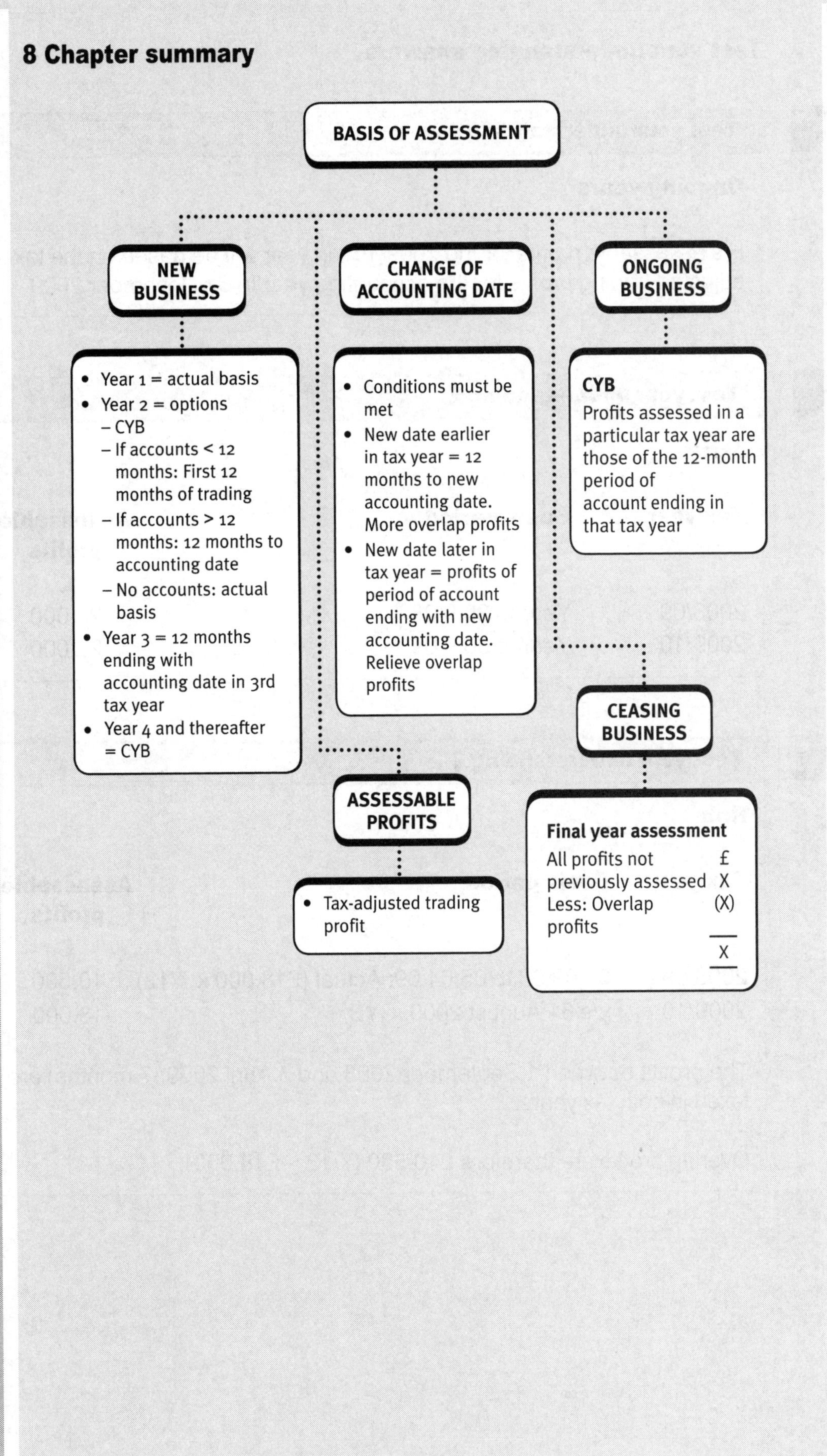

BASIS OF ASSESSMENT
NEW BUSINESS
CHANGE OF ACCOUNTING DATE
ONGOING BUSINESS
• Year 1 = actual basis
• Year 2 = options
– CYB
– If accounts < 12 months: First 12 months of trading
– If accounts > 12 months: 12 months to accounting date
– No accounts: actual basis
• Year 3 = 12 months ending with accounting date in 3rd tax year
• Year 4 and thereafter = CYB
• Conditions must be met
• New date earlier in tax year = 12 months to new accounting date. More overlap profits
• New date later in tax year = profits of period of account ending with new accounting date. Relieve overlap profits
CYB
Profits assessed in a particular tax year are those of the 12-month period of account ending in that tax year
CEASING BUSINESS
ASSESSABLE PROFITS
• Tax-adjusted trading profit
Final year assessment
All profits not previously assessed £ X
Less: Overlap profits (X)
X

Test your understanding answers

Test your understanding 1

Ongoing years

His assessable profits for the 2009/10 tax year will be based on the tax-adjusted trading profits for the accounting year to 31 December 2009.

Test your understanding 2

Jerry

Tax year	Basis period	Assessable profits
		£
2008/09	Year to 30.9.08	20,000
2009/10	Year to 30.9.09	22,000

Test your understanding 3

Rob

Tax year	Basis period	Assessable profits
		£
2008/09	01.09.08 to 05.04.09: Actual (£18,000 x 7/12)	10,500
2009/10	y/e 31 August 2009: CYB	18,000

The profits between 1 September 2008 and 5 April 2009 (7 months) are taxed in both tax years.

Overlap profits are therefore £10,500 (7/12 × £18,000).

Test your understanding 4

George

Tax year	Basis period	Assessable profits
		£
2006/07	01/10/06 to 05/04/07: Actual (6/15 × £30,000)	12,000
2007/08	01/01/07 to 31/12/07: 12 months ending on accounting date (12/15 × £30,000)	24,000
2008/09	y/e 31/12/08: CYB	36,000
2009/10	y/e 31/12/09: CYB	40,000

Overlap profits: £6,000, i.e. 1/1/07 to 5/4/07 (3/15 × £30,000)

Test your understanding 5

Fred

Tax year	Basis period	Assessable profits
		£
2006/07	01/06/06 to 05/04/07: Actual (10/11 × £11,000)	10,000
2007/08	01/06/06 to 31/05/07: First 12 months (£11,000 + (1/12 × £18,000))	12,500
2008/09	y/e 30/04/08: CYB	18,000
2009/10	y/e 30/04/09: CYB	22,000

As the period of account ending in the second year is less than 12 months long, the basis period is the first 12 months of trading.

Overlap profits = £11,500
i.e. 01/06/06 to 05/04/07 (£10,000) and 01/05/07 to 31/05/07 (1/12 × £18,000).

Test your understanding 6

Maria

Tax year	**Basis period**	**Assessable profits**
		£
2005/06	01/01/06 to 05/04/06: Actual (3/18 × £27,000)	4,500
2006/07	06/04/06 to 05/04/07: Actual (12/18 × £27,000) (Note)	18,000
2007/08	01/07/06 to 30/06/07: 12m to the accounting date (12/18 × £27,000)	18,000
2008/09	y/e 30/06/08: CYB	30,000
2009/10	y/e 30/06/09: CYB	40,000

Note: There is no period of account ending in the second year. The profits are therefore assessed on the actual basis.

Test your understanding 7

Major

Tax year	**Basis period**	**Assessable profits**
		£
2006/07	y/e 30/06/06: CYB	18,000
2007/08	y/e 30/06/07: CYB	20,000
2008/09	y/e 30/06/08: CYB	15,000
2009/10	01/07/08 to 31/12/09: FINAL - anything not yet taxed (£12,000 + £6,000 – £7,500)	10,500

The final year of assessment is 2009/10, the year in which trade ceases.

Test your understanding 8

Benny

Tax year	Basis period	Assessable profits
		£
2004/05	01/07/04 to 05/04/05: Actual (9/14 × £10,500)	6,750
2005/06	01/09/04 to 31/08/05: 12m to accounting date (12/14 × £10,500)	9,000
2006/07	y/e 31/08/06: CYB	18,000
2007/08	y/e 31/08/07: CYB	22,500
2008/09	y/e 31/08/08: CYB	31,500
2009/10	01/09/08 to 31/12/09: FINAL - anything not yet taxed (£27,000 + £8,400 – £5,250)	30,150
		117,900

Overlap profits: 01/09/04 to 05/04/05 = 7/14 × £10,500 = £5,250

Note that over the life of the business the total profits of £117,900 have been assessed to tax.

chapter

9

Partnerships

Chapter learning objectives

Upon completion of this chapter you will be able to:

- explain how a partnership is assessed to tax
- show the allocation of profits/losses between partners for the period of account
- show the allocation of profits/losses between partners for the period of account following a change in the profit-sharing ratio
- calculate the assessable profit for ongoing/new and ceasing partners.

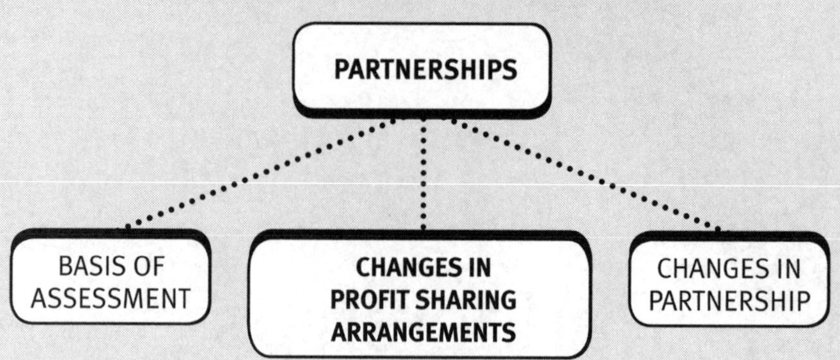

1 Introduction

Definition

- A partnership is a body of persons carrying on business together with a view to profit (Partnership Act 1890).

Basis of assessment

- Each partner is taxed individually, despite the partnership being a single trading entity.
- Each partner is assessed on his share of the partnership profits as if he were a sole trader.
- To determine a partner's assessable profits:
  - firstly, the trading profits per the partnership accounts are adjusted for tax purposes as for a sole trader (see Chapter 5).
  - secondly, the tax-adjusted trading profits of the partnership are allocated to the individual partners.
  - finally, apply the basis of assessment rules to determine the partner's assessable profits in a tax year (see Chapter 8).

2 The allocation of profits and losses

The computation of partnership profits and losses

- The principles of computation of a partnership's total tax-adjusted trading profits for a period of account are the same as those for a sole trader.
- Partners' salaries and interest on capital are not deductible expenses, since these are an allocation of profit.

The allocation of the profit or loss

- The tax-adjusted trading profit or loss is allocated (divided) between the partners according to their profit-sharing arrangements for that period of account.
- Partners may be entitled to salaries (a fixed allocation of profit) and interest on capital. The balance of profits will be allocated in the profit-sharing ratio (PSR).
- Whether it is described as salary, interest on capital or profit share, the total allocated to a partner is assessable as trading income.

Example 1 - The allocation of profits and losses

Dan and Phil have been in partnership for a number of years. The partnership agreement provides that each should take a salary of £25,000, 5% interest on capital balances at the start of the accounting period and then split the profit remaining 60:40 in Phil's favour.

Calculate the trading income assessable for each partner for 2009/10, if the tax-adjusted trading profits for the year ended 30 September 2009, were £74,000.

Their respective capital balances at 1 October 2008, were

Phil	£75,000
Dan	£60,000

Answer to example 1

Year ended 30 September 2009	Total	Phil	Dan
	£	£	£
Salary	50,000	25,000	25,000
Interest on capital (£75/60k × 5%)	6,750	3,750	3,000
	56,750	28,750	28,000
Balance (£74,000 – £56,750) (60:40)	17,250	10,350	6,900
Total allocation of partnership profits	74,000	39,100	34,900

The allocated profit represents each partner's share of their profits for this period of account. Each partner's allocated share of the profit is then assessed to tax on the individual partners as trading income using the basis of assessment rules for a sole trader.

Trading income assessment – 2009/10
(CYB = Year ended 30 September 2009)

Phil	£39,100
Dan	£34,900

Test your understanding 1

Paul and Art have been in partnership for many years preparing accounts to 31 December each year.

The partnership agreement provides Paul with a salary of £3,000 and Art is entitled to 15% interest on his capital balance at the start of the period. His capital balance was £27,000 on 1 January 2009. Paul and Art agreed to split any remaining profits equally.

Calculate Paul and Art's share of profits, if in the year ended 31 December 2009, the trading profits as adjusted for tax were £30,000.

Partnership capital allowances

Capital allowances are calculated in the same way as for a sole trader:

- Capital allowances are deducted as an expense in calculating the tax-adjusted trading profit or loss of the partnership. The profit allocated between the partners is therefore after deducting capital allowances.
- Individual partners cannot claim capital allowances on their own behalf.
- If assets are owned privately (such as motor cars), then the business proportion of such assets must be included in the partnership's capital allowances computation. The total capital allowances are then deducted as an expense.

3 Changes in profit-sharing ratio

The profit-sharing ratio may change for a number of reasons:

- The existing partners decide to allocate profits in a different way. This may be as a result of a change in duties, seniority or simply by agreement of the parties concerned.
- The membership of a partnership may change as the result of the admission, death or retirement of a partner.
- Provided that there is at least one partner common to the business before and after the change, the partnership will automatically continue.
- Where there is a change in membership, the commencement or cessation basis of assessment rules will apply to the individual partner who is joining or leaving the partnership only.

4 The effect of a change in the profit-sharing ratio

- If a partnership changes its basis of profit-sharing during a period of account, then the accounting period is split, with a different allocation of profits in the different parts.

Example 2 - The effect of a change in the profit-sharing ratio

David and Peter are in partnership. Their tax-adjusted trading profit for the year ended 30 September 2009, was £16,500.

Up to 30 June 2009, profits were shared between David and Peter 3:2, after paying annual salaries of £3,000 and £2,000 respectively.

From 1 July 2009, profits are shared 2:1 after paying annual salaries of £6,000 and £4,000.

Show the trading income assessments for David and Peter for 2009/10.

Answer to example 2

	Total	David	Peter
	£	£	£
1.10.08 to 30.6.09			
(Profits £16,500 × 9/12 = £12,375)			
Salaries (9/12)	3,750	2,250	1,500
Balance (3:2)	8,625	5,175	3,450
	12,375	7,425	4,950
1.7.09 to 30.9.09			
(Profits £16,500 × 3/12 = £4,125)			
Salaries (3/12)	2,500	1,500	1,000
Balance (2:1)	1,625	1,083	542
	4,125	2,583	1,542
Total allocation of partnership profits	16,500	10,008	6,492

Trading income assessments – 2009/10
(CYB = Year ended 30 September 2009):

David	£10,008
Peter	£6,492

Test your understanding 2

John and Major have been in partnership for many years preparing accounts to 31 December.

Their profit-sharing arrangement provides for salaries of £4,500 and £3,000 pa and the balance in the ratio of 3:2 respectively.

From 1 July 2009, John will receive a salary of £9,000 pa and Major a salary of £6,000 pa, with the balance in the ratio 2:1 in John's favour. Their recent tax-adjusted trading profits for the accounting year ended 31 December 2009, are £24,800.

Show the division of profits for the relevant period of account and the trading income assessment to be raised on each partner for 2009/10.

5 Commencement and cessation

Changes in membership

The normal opening year and closing year basis of assessment rules apply upon commencement and cessation of a partnership.

- A change in the membership of the partnership will normally affect only the partner joining or leaving.

Commencement

The normal commencement rules apply for the partner being admitted to the partnership.

The steps taken are:

- Identify the start date of the new partner.
- Allocate the profits between the old and new partner(s):
  - If the new start date is part way through the period of account, the allocation of profits will need to be split between the two periods concerned.
  - If the new partner joins at the start of a new period of account, profits in the period will be allocated throughout using the new PSR.
- Determine the assessable trading profits for the tax year.
  - For those partners common to the old and new partnerships, there will be no change in the method of calculating their assessable trading income and the normal CYB approach applies.
  - For the partner joining, they must apply the opening year rules, as for the sole trader in Chapter 8. A partner will be treated as commencing when he or she joins the partnership.
  - Each partner has his or her own overlap profits, available for overlap relief.

Example 3 - Commencement and cessation

Alex, Arsene and Jose have been in partnership for a number of years. Their recent results have been as follows:

	£
Year ended 30 September 2008	103,500
Year ended 30 September 2009	128,000

The relationship is often fractious and there have been a number of disputes over the years. In an attempt to improve the dynamics, on 1 January 2009, Rafa was admitted to the partnership.

Profits had been shared equally, after allocating salaries and interest on capital, prior to the admission of Rafa.

Partner	Salary	Capital balance	Interest on capital
	£	£	
Alex	15,000	100,000	5%
Arsene	12,000	80,000	5%
Jose	10,000	40,000	5%

Rafa's admission changed the profit-sharing arrangements as follows:

Partner	Salary	Capital balance	Interest on capital	Profit share
	£	£		
Alex	20,000	100,000	5%	35%
Arsene	18,000	80,000	5%	30%
Jose	15,000	40,000	5%	25%
Rafa	10,000	Nil	n/a	10%

The projected result for year ended 30 September 2010, is a profit of £140,000.

Calculate the assessable trading income for each of the partners from 2008/09 to 2010/11.

Answer to example 3

Step 1: Allocate the tax-adjusted trading profits for each accounting period between the partners

	Total	Alex	Arsene	Jose	Rafa
	£	£	£	£	£
Y/e 30.9.08					
Salary	37,000	15,000	12,000	10,000	
Interest at 5% on capital	11,000	5,000	4,000	2,000	
PSR	55,500	18,500	18,500	18,500	
Total	103,500	38,500	34,500	30,500	
Y/e 30.9.09					
1.10.08 –31.12.08					
(Profits £128,000 × 3/12 = £32,000)					
Salary (3/12)	9,250	3,750	3,000	2,500	
Interest at 5% (× 3/12)	2,750	1,250	1,000	500	
PSR	20,000	6,667	6,667	6,666	
	32,000	11,667	10,667	9,666	
1.1.09 –30.9.09					
(Profits £128,000 × 9/12 = £96,000)					
Salary (9/12)	47,250	15,000	13,500	11,250	7,500
Interest at 5% (× 9/12)	8,250	3,750	3,000	1,500	Nil
PSR (35:30:25:10)	40,500	14,175	12,150	10,125	4,050
	96,000	32,925	28,650	22,875	11,550
Total	128,000	44,592	39,317	32,541	11,550
Y/e 30.9.10					
Salary	63,000	20,000	18,000	15,000	10,000
Interest at 5% on capital	11,000	5,000	4,000	2,000	Nil
PSR (35:30:25:10)	66,000	23,100	19,800	16,500	6,600
Total	140,000	48,100	41,800	33,500	16,600

Step 2: Compute each partner's assessable trading profits.

Alex, Arsene and Jose will be assessed on a CYB for each tax year.

	Alex	Arsene	Jose
	£	£	£
2008/09	38,500	34,500	30,500
2009/10	44,592	39,317	32,541
2010/11	48,100	41,800	33,500

Rafa will be treated as commencing on 1 January 2009.

Tax year	Basis period	Assessable profits
		£
2008/09	1 January 2009 to 5 April 2009 (£11,550 × 3/9)	3,850
2009/10	First 12 months (£11,550 + ((£16,600 × 3/12))	15,700
2010/11	Year ended 30 September 2010	16,600

He will carry forward overlap profits of £8,000 (£3,850 + 4,150).

Note: This question tests knowledge of a wide range of issues in relation to partnerships. It is unlikely that such a wide range of issues would be tested in a single question in the examination.

Test your understanding 3

Able and Bertie have been in partnership since 1 July 2007 preparing their accounts to 30 June each year. On 1 July 2009, Carol joins the partnership. Profits are shared equally.

The partnership's tax-adjusted trading profits are as follows:

	£
Year ended 30 June 2008	10,000
Year ended 30 June 2009	13,500
Year ended 30 June 2010	18,000

Show the amounts assessed on the individual partners for 2007/08 to 2010/11.

Cessation

As for commencement, the normal rules for a sole trader are applied to a partner leaving a partnership.

The steps taken are:

- Identify the partner ceasing to be a member.
- Allocate the profits, remembering that if this is part-way through the period of account it will affect the profit-sharing ratio for that period of account and this will need to be calculated in two parts.
- For the partners continuing, use the normal CYB method of assessment.
- For the partner ceasing, use the closing year rules and deduct any overlap profits they have available.

Example 4 - Commencement and cessation

Ball, Sphere, Globe and Bauble have been in partnership for a number of years, drawing up accounts to 30 September each year. The profit sharing arrangements have been as follows:

Partner	Annual salary	Capital balance	Interest on capital	Profit share
	£	£		
Ball	20,000	100,000	5%	35%
Sphere	18,000	80,000	5%	30%
Globe	15,000	40,000	5%	25%
Bauble	10,000	Nil	n.a.	10%

Ball has decided to resign as a partner at the end of March 2010.

The existing salary and interest arrangements will remain in place, but the balance of the profit will then be split equally between the three remaining partners.

Profits for the year end 30 September 2009 and 2010 are expected to be £180,000 and £210,000 respectively.

Calculate the assessable trading profits of each partner for 2009/10 and 2010/11. Ball informs you he had £15,000 of overlap profits from commencement.

Answer to example 4

Profits for year end 30 September 2009 and 2010, are expected to be £180,000 and £210,000 respectively.

	Total	Ball	Sphere	Globe	Bauble
	£	£	£	£	£
Y/e 30.9.09					
Salary	63,000	20,000	18,000	15,000	10,000
Interest at 5% on capital	11,000	5,000	4,000	2,000	Nil
PSR (35:30:25:10)	106,000	37,100	31,800	26,500	10,600
Total	180,000	62,100	53,800	43,500	20,600
Y/e 30.9.10					
1.10.09 – 31.3.10					
(Profits £210,000 × 6/12 = £105,000)					
Salary (6/12)	31,500	10,000	9,000	7,500	5,000
Interest at 5% (× 6/12)	5,500	2,500	2,000	1,000	Nil
PSR (35:30:25:10)	68,000	23,800	20,400	17,000	6,800
	105,000	36,300	31,400	25,500	11,800
1.4.10 – 30.9.10					
(Profits £210,000 × 6/12 = £105,000)					
Salary (6/12)	21,500	Nil	9,000	7,500	5,000
Interest at 5% (6/12)	3,000	Nil	2,000	1,000	Nil
PSR (1:1:1)	80,500	Nil	26,834	26,833	26,833
	105,000	Nil	37,834	35,333	31,833
Total	210,000	36,300	69,234	60,833	43,633

Sphere, Globe and Bauble will continue to be assessed on CYB:

	Sphere	Globe	Bauble
	£	£	£
2009/10	53,800	43,500	20,600
2010/11	69,234	60,833	43,633

Ball will be treated as ceasing to trade on 31 March 2010, his share of the partnership profits will be as follows:

Tax year	Basis period	Assessable profits
		£
2009/10	Year ended 30 September 2009	62,100
	Period ended 31 March 2010	36,300
		98,400
	Less: Overlap relief	(15,000)
	Assessable trading income	83,400

Test your understanding 4

Continuing the TYU3 above with Able, Bertie and Carol.

After suffering a period of ill health, Bertie plans to retire on 31 December 2010.

Profits for year ended 30 June 2011, are expected to be £24,000.

The profit-sharing ratio will remain unchanged until Bertie retires. Thereafter it will be split 65:35 in Able's favour.

Calculate Bertie's assessable trading income for 2010/11 and Able and Carol's assessable trading income for 2011/12.

6 Chapter summary

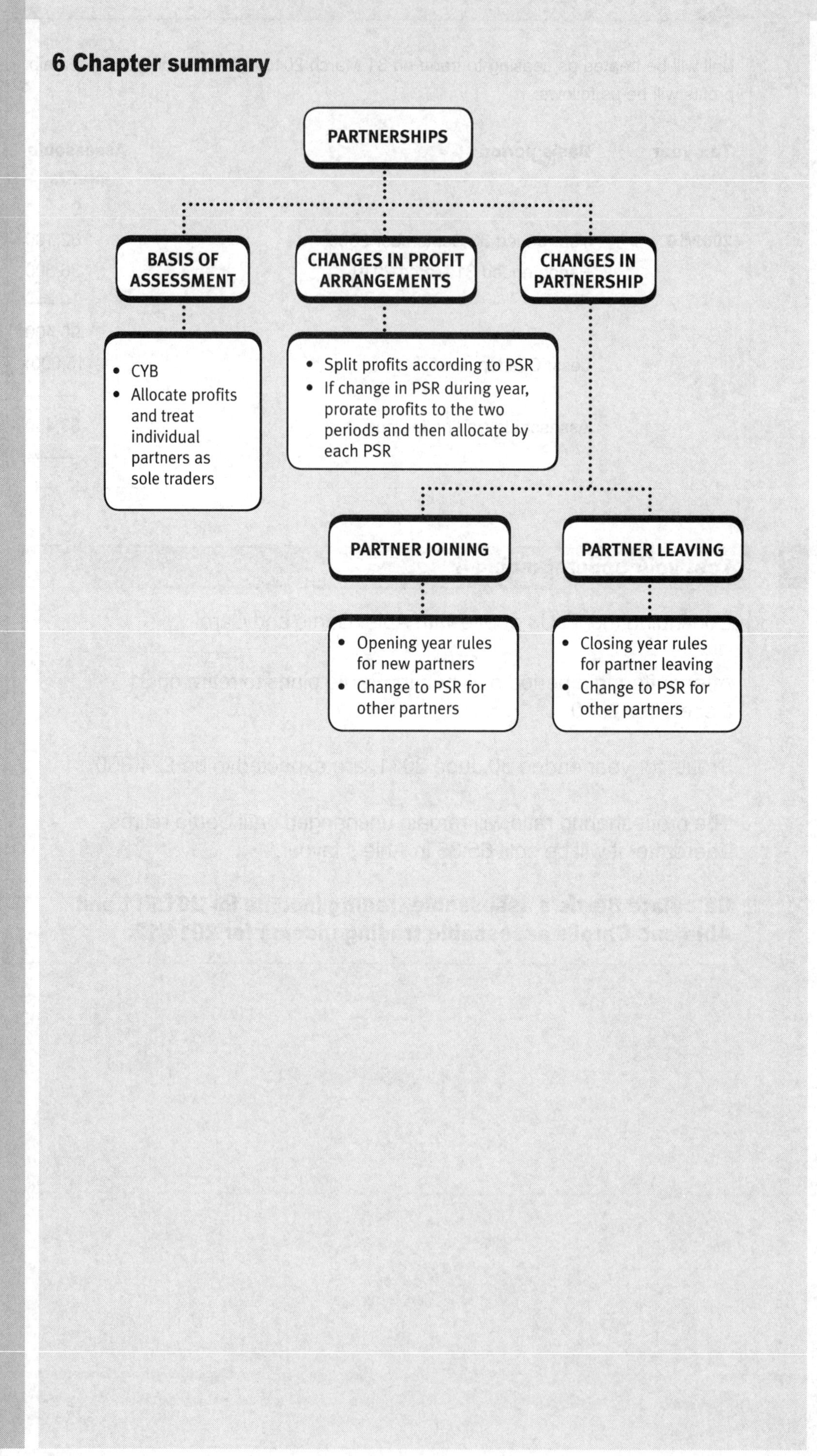

Test your understanding answers

Test your understanding 1

Paul and Art

Year ended 31 December 2009	Total	Paul	Art
	£	£	£
Salary	3,000	3,000	
Interest on capital (£27,000 × 15%)	4,050		4,050
	7,050	3,000	4,050
Balance (£30,000 – £7,050) (50:50)	22,950	11,475	11,475
Allocation of partnership profits	30,000	14,475	15,525

Trading income assessment for 2009/10
(CYB, Year ended 31 December 2009)

Paul	£14,475
Art	£15,525

Test your understanding 2

John and Major

	Total	John	Major
	£	£	£
1.1.09 to 30.6.09			
(Profits £24,800 × 6/12 = £12,400)			
Salaries (6/12)	3,750	2,250	1,500
Balance (3:2)	8,650	5,190	3,460
	12,400	7,440	4,960
1.7.09 to 31.12.09			
(Profits £24,800 × 6/12 = £12,400)			
Salaries (6/12)	7,500	4,500	3,000
Balance (2:1)	4,900	3,267	1,633
	12,400	7,767	4,633
Total allocation of partnership profits	24,800	15,207	9,593

Trading income assessments for 2009/10
(CYB Year ended 31 December 2009):

John	£15,207
Major	£9,593

Test your understanding 3

Able and Bert

Step 1: Allocate the tax-adjusted trading profits for accounting periods between the partners.

	Total	Able	Bertie	Carol
	£	£	£	£
Y/e 30.6.08	10,000	5,000	5,000	
Y/e 30.6.09	13,500	6,750	6,750	
Y/e 30.6.10	18,000	6,000	6,000	6,000

Step 2: Compute each partner's assessable trading profits, as though they were a sole trader.

Able and Bertie will both be assessed as follows, based upon a commencement on 1 July 2007:

Tax year	**Basis period**	**Assessable profits**
		£
2007/08	1 July 2007 to 5 April 2008 (£5,000 × 9/12)	3,750
2008/09	Year ended 30 June 2008	5,000
2009/10	Year ended 30 June 2009	6,750
2010/11	Year ended 30 June 2010	6,000

They will each carry forward overlap profits of £3,750 in respect of the period 1 July 2007 to 5 April 2008.

Carol will be treated as commencing on 1 July 2009, and will be assessed on her share of the partnership profits as follows:

Tax year	**Basis period**	**Assessable profits**
		£
2009/10	1 July 2009 to 5 April 2010 (£6,000 × 9/12)	4,500
2010/11	Year ended 30 June 2010	6,000

She will carry forward overlap profits of £4,500 in respect of the period 1 July 2009 to 5 April 2010.

Test your understanding 4

Able, Bertie and Carol

Profits will be allocated between the partners as follows:

	Total	Able	Bertie	Carol
Y/e 30 June 2011	£	£	£	£
1.7.10 – 31.12.10				
£24,000 × 6/12 (1/3:1/3:1/3)	12,000	4,000	4,000	4,000
1.1.11 – 30.6.11				
£24,000 × 6/12 (65:35)	12,000	7,800	–	4,200
Total	24,000	11,800	4,000	8,200

Able and Carol will both be assessed on the current year basis:

Tax year	Basis period	Able	Carol
		£	£
2011/12	Year ended 30 June 2011	11,800	8,200

Bertie will be treated as ceasing to trade on 31 December 2010. His final tax year of trade is 2010/11.

Tax year	Basis period	Assessable profits
		£
2010/11	Year ended 30 June 2010 (see TYU 3)	6,000
	Period ended 31 December 2010	4,000
		10,000
	Less: Overlap relief	(3,750)
	Assessable trading income	6,250

chapter

10

Trading losses for individuals

Chapter learning objectives

Upon completion of this chapter you will be able to:

- understand how to calculate a trading loss for a tax year
- explain how trading losses can be carried forward for an ongoing business
- demonstrate when a trading loss can be used against total income and chargeable gains
- explain how a trading loss can be relieved in the early years of a trade
- explain the extended carry back loss relief against trading profits
- calculate a terminal loss
- explain how a terminal loss can be relieved
- demonstrate the optimum use of trading loss reliefs
- describe the alternative loss relief claims that are available to partners
- explain the loss relief restriction to the partners of a limited liability partnership
- identify the circumstances when trading losses can be carried forward and used on the incorporation of a business.

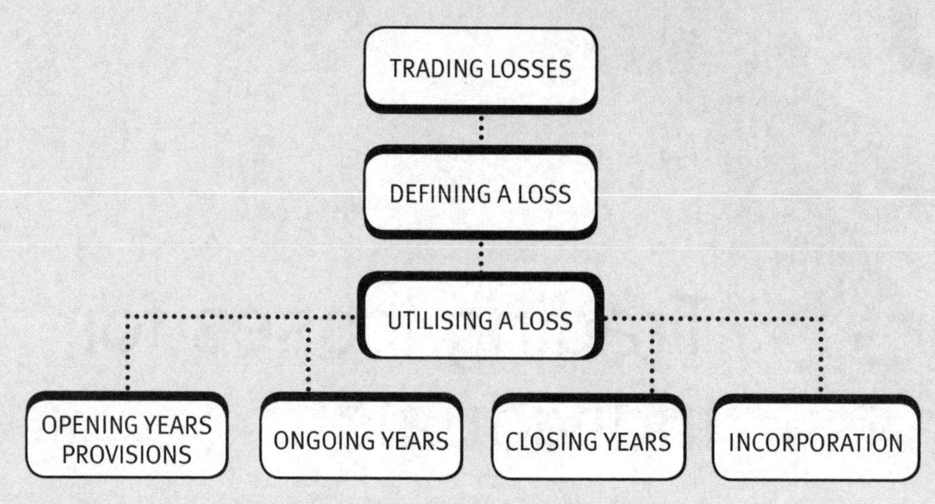

1 Introduction

Identifying a trading loss

A trading loss arises when the normal tax adjusted trading profit computation gives a negative result.

A trading loss can occur in two situations, as follows:

	£	£
Tax adjusted trading profit / (loss) before capital allowances	X	(X)
Less: Plant and Machinery Allowances	(X)	(X)
Industrial Buildings Allowances	(X)	(X)
Trading loss	(X)	(X)

Note that:

- capital allowances are taken into account in calculating the amount of the trading loss available for relief
- capital allowances:
  - can increase a tax adjusted trading loss; and
  - can turn a tax adjusted trading profit into a trading loss.

Where a trading loss occurs:

- the individual's trading income assessment will be £Nil
- a number of loss relief options are available to obtain relief for the loss.

Loss relief options

The main reliefs available for a trading loss, as explained in the following sections, are as follows:

- Carry forward against future trading profits (section 3)
- Relief against total income (section 4)
- Opening year loss relief against total income (section 6)
- Terminal loss relief against previous trading profits (section 7)

2 Loss relief options in ongoing years

If an individual makes a trading loss in the ongoing years, they initially have to decide whether to claim relief against total income or carry forward all of the loss.

The choices can be summarised as follows:

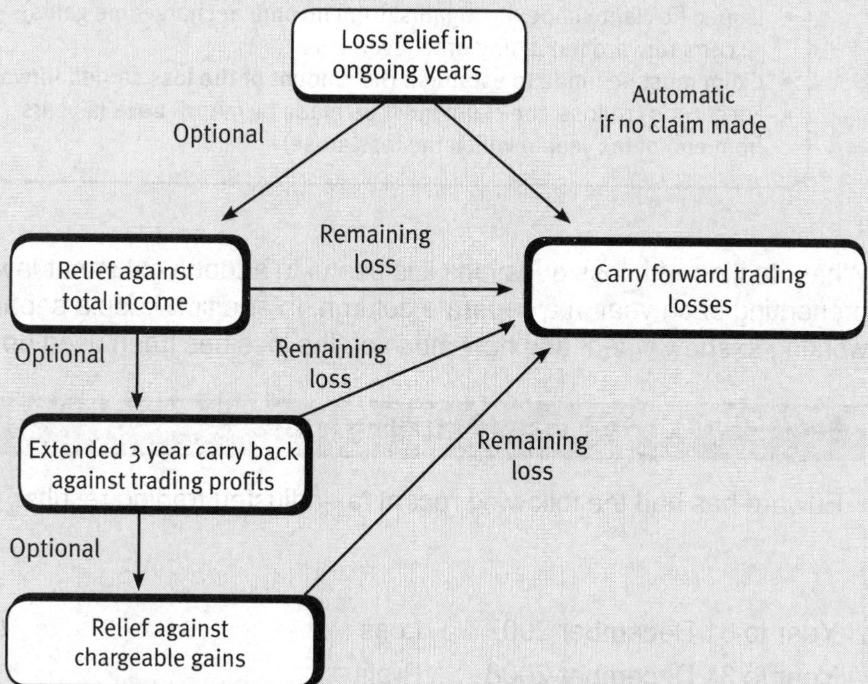

Where a claim against total income is made, any remaining loss is automatically carried forward unless the individual then makes a claim to:

- set the loss against chargeable gains, or
- extend the loss carry back against trading profits of the previous three years.

Note that a claim against gains and the extended carry back claim can only be made after a claim against total income has been made.

3 Carry forward of trading losses

Principles of the relief

The key rules are as follows:

Carry forward trading losses

- **Automatic relief**
- **Carry forward** against
  - **First available**
  - **Trading profits**
  - Of the **same trade**
- Can carry forward indefinitely
- But **must set off maximum amount** possible each year, no partial claims allowed
- If no specific claim made:
  - carry all loss forward
- If specific claim made (i.e. against total income or chargeable gains):
  - carry forward remaining unrelieved loss
- Claim must be made to **establish the amount of the loss** carried forward
- For a 2009/10 loss, the claim must be made by **5 April 2014** (4 years from end of tax year in which the loss arose)

When dealing with loss questions it is useful to adopt a columnar layout, presenting each year in a separate column. In addition keep a separate working to show when, and how much of, the loss has been used up.

Example 1 - Carry forward of trading losses

Edward has had the following recent tax-adjusted trading results:

		£
Year to 31 December 2007	Loss	(5,000)
Year to 31 December 2008	Profit	3,000
Year to 31 December 2009	Profit	10,000

Assuming that Edward wishes to carry the loss forward, calculate his assessable trading profits for 2007/08 to 2009/10 inclusive.

Answer to example 1

	2007/08	2008/09	2009/10
	£	£	£
Trading income	Nil	3,000	10,000
Less: Loss relief b/f (W)	Nil	(3,000)	(2,000)
Net trading income	Nil	Nil	8,000

Working – Loss memorandum

	£
Trading loss – year to 31 December 2007	5,000
Less: Used in 2008/09	(3,000)
Less: Used in 2009/10	(2,000)
Loss carried forward to 2010/11	Nil

Test your understanding 1

Michael has been trading for many years as a retailer. His recent tax-adjusted trading results are as follows:

		£
Year to 31 August 2007	Loss	(9,000)
Year to 31 August 2008	Profit	6,000
Year to 31 August 2009	Profit	19,000

Michael has had no other sources of income.

Calculate Michael's assessable trading income for 2007/08 to 2009/10, assuming he carries the loss forward.

Carry forward loss relief is useful as:

- the taxpayer gets the potential of an unrestricted period over which to utilise the available loss, providing that he continues to trade and makes subsequent future profits from the same trade.

However, there are a number of disadvantages to carrying losses forward:

- In a prolonged difficult period for a business, relief may take a long time to materialise.
- Obtaining relief in a later period is less advantageous from the perspective of cash flow and time value of money.
- There is no certainty about the levels of future trading profits and whether it will be possible to utilise the loss.

Consequently taxpayers are likely to consider the alternative loss reliefs available.

4 Loss relief against total income

Introduction

The alternative loss relief claims available are as follows.

A taxpayer making a loss in 2009/10 has the option to make:

- a claim against **total income**.

Then, if any loss remains, they can make:

- an extended claim against **trading profits**, and/or
- a claim against **chargeable gains**.

However, note that the latter two options are only possible after a claim against total income has been made.

Relief against total income is **optional** but if claimed it permits the taxpayer to relieve trading losses against the **total income** of the:

- 'tax year of the loss', **and/or**
- previous tax year.

Tax year of loss

The 'tax year of the loss' is the tax year in which the loss making period ends.

For example: a loss for the year ended 31 December 2009 arises in the tax year 2009/10.

Therefore, the 'tax year of the loss' is 2009/10.

The loss can then be set off against total income in

- 2009/10, and/or
- 2008/09.

Example 2 - Loss relief against total income

Graham's recent tax-adjusted results are as follows:

		£
Year to 31 December 2008	Profit	10,000
Year to 31 December 2009	Loss	(6,000)
Year to 31 December 2010	Profit	12,000

Explain how Graham can utilise the loss in respect of the year to 31 December 2009 assuming he claims to offset it against his total income.

Answer to example 2

The loss of £6,000 arises in the tax year 2009/10.

Relief is available for the loss against total income in 2009/10 and/or 2008/09.

Obtaining relief for the loss

Due to the wording "and/or", the taxpayer has five key options to consider:

(1) against total income of the year of the loss, followed by a claim against total income of the previous year; or

(2) against total income of the previous year, followed by a claim against total income of the current year; or

(3) against total income of the year of the loss only

(4) against total income of the previous year only

(5) make no claim and carry all of the loss forward.

In the case of the first four options, any unrelieved loss can be carried forward.

However, a key point to note is that if relief against total income is claimed, the taxpayer must set off the **maximum amount possible** for a given year; a partial claim is not allowed.

Other points to note:

- Qualifying interest payments (see Chapter 2) are also deducted from total income. In order not to waste the relief for interest payments, these should be deducted from total income in priority to losses.
- Personal allowances are deducted from net income (i.e. total income after deducting reliefs). Therefore, a claim against total income may involve wasting personal allowances.
- The two years available for potential claims are treated separately and thus a claim is required for each year.
- A written claim must be made within one year of 31 January following the end of the tax year of loss. For a 2009/10 loss the claim must be made by 31 January 2012.
- A taxpayer may have losses for two consecutive tax years and wish to relieve both against total profits. In these circumstances the total income of a year is relieved by the loss of that year, in priority to the loss carried back from the following year.

Example 3 - Loss against total income

Derek's recent tax-adjusted trading results are as follows:

		£
Year ended 31 July 2007	Profit	18,000
Year ended 31 July 2008	Loss	(43,200)
Year ended 31 July 2009	Profit	13,000
Year ended 31 July 2010	Profit	15,000

Derek's other income each year is £12,000 (gross).

Show Derek's net income for all tax years affected by the above results assuming:

(a) **No claim is made against total income for the trading loss.**

(b) **Full claims against total income are to be made to obtain relief as early as possible.**

Answer to example 3

(a) **No relief against total income** – If no claim is made against total income, the trading loss of 2007/08 is carried forward against future trading profits.

	2007/08	2008/09	2009/10	2010/11
	£	£	£	£
Trading profits	18,000	Nil	13,000	15,000
Less: Loss relief b/f	–	–	(13,000)	(15,000)
	18,000	Nil	Nil	Nil
Other income	12,000	12,000	12,000	12,000
Net income	30,000	12,000	12,000	12,000

Working – Loss memorandum

	£
Loss in y/e 31 July 2008	43,200
Less: Used in 2009/10	(13,000)
Less: Used in 2010/11	(15,000)
Loss relief carry forward to 2011/12	15,200

(b) **Full claims against total income** – Claims against total income can only be made for 2007/08 and/or 2008/09 and any balance is carried forward.

	2007/08	2008/09	2009/10	2010/11
	£	£	£	£
Trading income	18,000	Nil	13,000	15,000
Less: Loss relief b/f	–	–	(1,200)	–
	18,000	Nil	11,800	15,000
Other income	12,000	12,000	12,000	12,000
Total income	30,000	12,000	23,800	27,000
Less: Loss relief	(30,000)	(12,000)	–	–
Net income	Nil	Nil	23,800	27,000

Working – Loss memorandum

	£
Loss in y/e 31 July 2008	43,200
Less: Used in 2007/08	(30,000)
Less: Used in 2008/09	(12,000)
Loss to carry forward	1,200
Less: Used in 2009/10	(1,200)
Loss to carry forward	Nil

Test your understanding 2

Adrian's recent results have been:

		£
Year ended 31 December 2008	Profit	34,000
Year ended 31 December 2009	Loss	(48,000)
Year ended 31 December 2010	Profit	6,800

In 2008/09, Adrian has other income of £5,000. In 2009/10, he had other income of £6,000 and he paid qualifying interest of £2,500. In 2010/11 he had other income of £7,000.

Show how relief for the loss would be given against total income, assuming that Adrian makes claims to the extent that they are beneficial. State the amount of the remaining loss, if any.

Assume the 2009/10 tax rates and allowances continue in the future.

Extended carry back against trading profits

If any loss remains after a claim against total income, a taxpayer can make:

- an extended claim against **trading profits** (see below), and/or
- a claim against **chargeable gains** (section 5).

However, note that the latter two options are only possible after a claim against total income has been made.

The normal claim against total income permits trading losses to be offset against total income of the tax year of loss and/or the preceding tax year.

For losses incurred in 2008/09 or 2009/10 there is an additional relief available so that **up to £50,000** of loss can be carried back against **trading profits** of the two tax years before the preceding tax year.

The extended relief will operate as follows:

- Trade losses of 2008/09 or 2009/10 can be subject to an extended carry back claim, although for examination purposes you will not have to deal with losses arising in 2008/09.
- The extended relief is optional and does not have to be claimed.
- A claim against total income must be made for the loss first, before an extended carry back claim can be made.
- The taxpayer has the usual choice of whether to claim one year or both years for the claim against total income.
- The claim need not be made if the taxpayer has no income in the two years of a possible claim; he does not have to claim in both years before an extended claim can be made.
- If a loss remains after the normal claim has been made against total income, then:
  - the loss can be carried back
  - against **trade profits**
  - of the **three years** preceding the loss.
- The carry back to the preceding year is unlimited.
- A **maximum** of **£50,000** can be carried back for two further years.
- The carry back is on a **LIFO basis**.
- Hence a loss of 2009/10 can be carried back against trade profits firstly of 2008/09 (if the claim against total income did not include that year) then 2007/08 and finally 2006/07.
- This is an extra relief and does not affect the ability of the taxpayer to use the loss in any other way that they choose.
- These rules also apply to losses on furnished holiday lettings which are treated as trade losses.

Test your understanding 3

Gertrude has been in business for many years and until recently her business had been profitable. The results for the last four years, as adjusted for tax purposes, are as follows:

Year ended 30 September 2006	£72,000
Year ended 30 September 2007	£39,000
Year ended 30 September 2008	£28,000
Year ended 30 September 2009	£92,000 loss

Gertrude has £5,500 of property business income each year but no other income.

Show how Gertrude could obtain relief for her loss as efficiently as possible.

Assume the 2009/10 tax rates and allowances apply throughout.

5 Relief of trading losses against chargeable gains

If any loss remains after a claim against total income, a taxpayer can make:

- an extended claim against trading profits (see above), and/or
- a claim against chargeable gains.

Relief against chargeable gains is **optional** but if claimed it permits the taxpayer to relieve trading losses against the **gains** in the same years as a claim against total income, i.e. in the:

- 'tax year of the loss', and/or
- previous tax year.

A claim may be made in:

- either year in isolation, or
- both years, in any order.

The relief operates as follows:

- A trader is permitted to set trading losses against chargeable gains, provided:
  - the total income of the year in question has been reduced to zero, and
  - unrelieved losses remain.
- There is no need to make a claim against total income for the previous year but relief against chargeable gains is only granted if total income has been reduced to nil in the same tax year.
- There is no need to make an extended carry back claim for the relief to be available.
- If claimed, the unrelieved trading loss, is treated as a current year capital loss.
- It takes precedence over both the CGT annual exemption and any capital losses brought forward.

A key point to note is that if a claim is made against chargeable gains, the taxpayer must set off the **maximum amount** possible for a given year; a partial claim is not allowed.

The maximum amount is the lower of:

- the remaining loss, or
- chargeable gains in the year **after** the deduction of current year capital losses **and** brought forward capital losses.

The loss relief is offset as follows:

	£
Chargeable gains in year	X
Less: Capital losses in year	(X)
	X
Less: Trading loss relief (subject to the maximum amount)	(X)
Less: Capital losses b/f	(X)
Net chargeable gains before annual exemption	X

Other points to note:

- The annual exemption is deducted after this relief, therefore a claim may result in wasting the annual exemption.
- The two years available for potential claims are treated separately and thus a claim is required for each year.
- A written claim is required in the same time period as for a claim against total income (i.e. within one year of 31 January following the end of the tax year of loss). For a 2009/10 loss the claim must be made by 31 January 2012.

Test your understanding 4

Charles made a trading profit of £3,000 in the year ended 31 December 2009 and a trading loss of £14,000 the following year.

He has other income of £4,500 (gross) in 2009/10 and also realised chargeable gains of £16,000 and capital losses of £5,000 in that tax year.

Calculate the amounts that remain in charge to tax for 2009/10, assuming that Charles claims loss relief against both total income and gains for that year, but makes no claims in respect of any other year.

The procedure for dealing with questions involving losses

As seen in the previous examples and test your understandings, the following procedure should be adopted when answering questions:

(1) Determine the tax adjusted profits and losses after capital allowances for each accounting period.

(2) Determine when losses arise and therefore when loss relief is available (i.e. in which tax years).

(3) Set up a proforma income tax computation for each tax year side by side and leave spaces for the loss set off to be inserted later.

(4) Set up a loss memo working for each loss to show how it is utilised.

(5) If more than one loss – consider in chronological order.

(6) Consider each option – be prepared to explain the options, the consequences of making a claim, the advantages and disadvantages.

(7) Set off losses according to the requirements of the question, or in the most beneficial way if it is a tax planning question.

6 Relief for trading losses in the opening years

Introduction

The options available in the opening years of trade are exactly the same as those available to an ongoing business, with one extra option to carry back losses three years against total income.

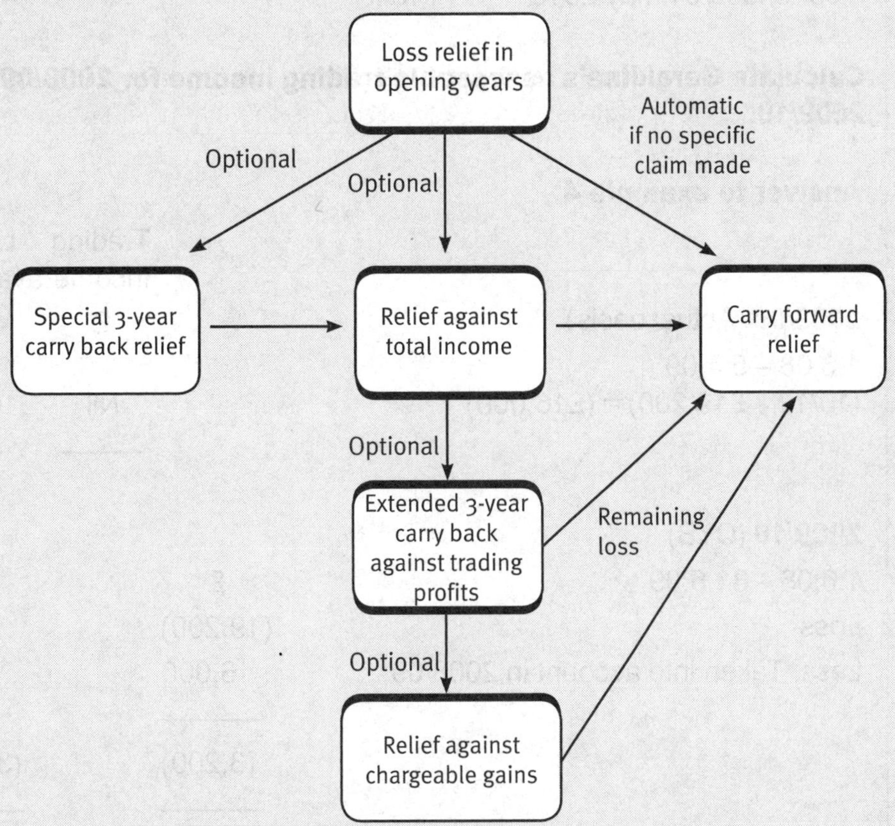

If an individual makes a trading loss in the opening years, they therefore have to initially decide whether to claim normal relief against total income, special opening year loss relief or carry forward the loss.

Relief against total income in opening years

If relief is claimed against total income for an opening year loss, the rules are the same as in any other years. However note that:

- It is vital to remember that a loss may only be relieved once.
- There is no such thing as overlap losses.
- If, in the opening years, a loss has been taken into account in one tax year, it is treated as nil when calculating the assessment for the next tax year.

Example 4 - Loss relief against total income in opening years

Geraldine starts trading on 1 June 2008. Her results, as adjusted for tax purposes, are:

		£
Year ended 31 May 2009	Loss	(19,200)
Year ended 31 May 2010	Profit	48,000

Calculate Geraldine's assessable trading income for 2008/09 and 2009/10.

Answer to example 4

		Trading income	Loss available
2008/09 (Actual basis)		£	£
1.6.08 – 5.4.09			
(10/12 × £19,200) = (£16,000)		Nil	16,000
2009/10 (CYB)			
1.6.08 – 31.5.09	£		
Loss	(19,200)		
Less: Taken into account in 2008/09	16,000		
	(3,200)		(3,200)

Test your understanding 5

Georgina started trading on 1 May 2006. The results of her initial periods of trading were as follows:

		£
Year ended 30 April 2007	Loss	(36,000)
Year ended 30 April 2008	Profit	30,000
Year ended 30 April 2009	Profit	35,000

Calculate Georgina's assessable trading income and available loss for each year affected by the above results.

Extended carry back relief in opening years

The extended relief claim is not possible in the first two years of business, and is unlikely to be made in the third year.

This is because the relief is against trading profits of the three years preceding the year of the loss, when profits are likely to be minimal.

The extended carry back is therefore unlikely to feature in opening year questions.

Special opening year loss relief

As an alternative to, or in addition to, a claim against total income the taxpayer can make a special opening year loss relief claim.

The relief operates as follows:

Special opening year relief against total income

- Optional claim
- Applies to loss arising in any of **first 4 years** of trading
- If claimed, set loss against
  - **total income**
  - **in 3 tax years** before tax year of loss
  - on a FIFO basis (i.e. earliest year first)
- There is no need for the trade to have been carried on in the earlier years
- **One claim** covers all 3 years
- For example:
  Loss in y/e 31.12.09 (2009/10) will be set off in:
  1. 2006/07
  2. 2007/08
  3. 2008/09
- If claimed
  - Must set off **maximum amount possible**
  - Cannot restrict set-off to preserve the personal allowance
  - Therefore, the benefit of the personal allowance may be wasted if a claim is made
- Relief must be claimed in writing
- For 2009/10 loss, the claim must be made by 31 January 2012

Example 5 - Relief for trading losses in opening years

Caroline started her business on 1 July 2008. Her trading results, as adjusted for tax purposes, for the first two years are as follows:

		£
Year ended 30 June 2009	Loss	(12,000)
Year ended 30 June 2010	Profit	2,500

Before becoming self-employed, Caroline had been employed as a dressmaker. Her remuneration from this employment, which ceased on 30 September 2007, for recent years, was:

2007/08	£6,678
2006/07	£11,860
2005/06	£11,330

Caroline has other income of £4,500 (gross) pa.

Calculate the taxable income for all years after claiming special opening year loss relief.

Assume the 2009/10 tax rates and allowances apply throughout.

Answer to example 5

Taxable income computations

	2005/06	2006/07	2007/08	2008/09
	£	£	£	£
Employment income	11,330	11,860	6,678	–
Other income	4,500	4,500	4,500	4,500
Total income	15,830	16,360	11,178	4,500
Less: Loss relief (W)	(9,000)	(3,000)	–	–
Net income	6,830	13,360	11,178	4,500
Less: PA	(6,475)	(6,475)	(6,475)	(6,475)
Taxable income	355	6,885	4,703	Nil

	2009/10	2010/11
	£	£
Trading income (W)	Nil	2,500
Other income	4,500	4,500
Total income	4,500	7,000
Less: Personal Allowance	(6,475)	(6,475)
Taxable income	Nil	525

Notes

(1) Under the special opening year loss relief rules, the loss of 2008/09 of £9,000 is set initially against total income of 2005/06. Any loss remaining would have been set automatically against total income of 2006/07 and finally against total income of 2007/08.

(2) The loss of 2009/10 of £3,000 is set initially against total income of 2006/07 before relieving 2007/08 and 2008/09 (had any loss remained).

(3) There is no requirement that the trade be carried on in the earlier year for which a claim is made.

Workings: New business – assessments/loss relief

Tax year	Basis period	Loss relief	Assessable profits
		£	£
2008/09	1.7.08– 5.4.09 (9/12 × £12,000)	9,000	Nil
2009/10	y/e 30.6.09 (£12,000 – £9,000)	3,000	Nil
2010/11	y/e 30.6.10		2,500

Test your understanding 6

Knight started a business on 1 May 2007. His taxable trade profits are as follows:

		£
Year ended 30 April 2008	Profit	6,120
Year ended 30 April 2009	Loss	(28,480)
Year ended 30 April 2010	Profit	7,630

Prior to commencing in business Knight had been in salaried employment.

His employment earnings for 2005/06 and 2006/07 were £9,400 and £13,660 respectively. In addition he enjoys savings income amounting to £1,700 (gross) each year.

Show how Knight will obtain relief for the loss if he makes a claim for special opening year loss relief.

7 Terminal loss relief

Introduction

The options available in the closing years of trade are exactly the same as those available to an ongoing business, except that:

- the option to carry forward losses is not available as there will be no further trading profits once the trade ceases
- an extra option for terminal loss relief is available
- an additional option for incorporation relief is available if the business is ceasing because it is being incorporated.

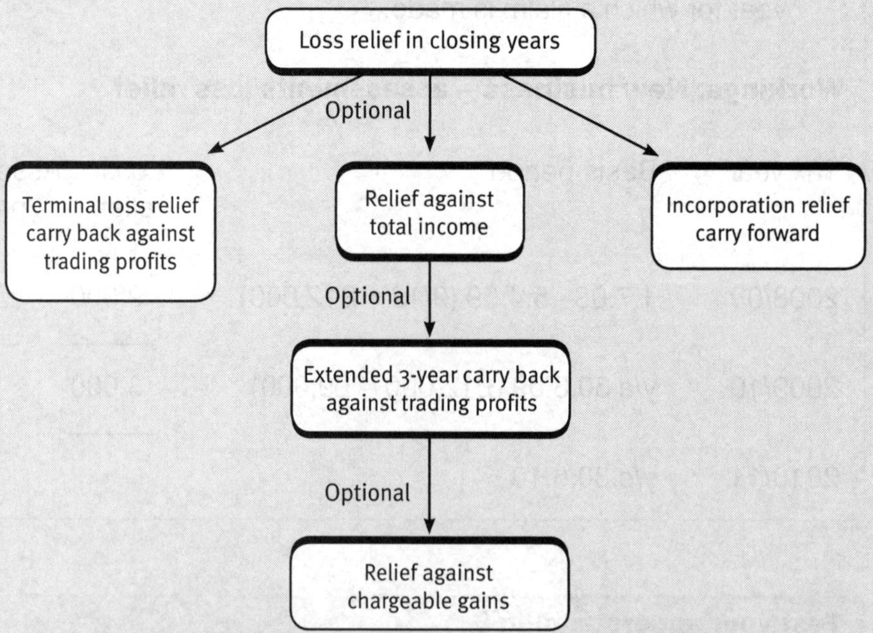

If an individual makes a trading loss in the closing years, they therefore have to initially decide whether to claim relief against total income (and then possibly offset against gains).

If there are remaining losses, the individual can claim terminal loss relief.

Terminal loss relief

The relief operates as follows:

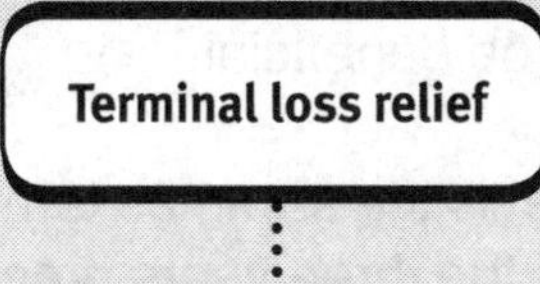

- **Optional** claim
  - however will normally be claimed
  - otherwise the benefit of the loss will be lost
- The relief is to set the **'terminal loss'** against **'trading income'**
  - of the **last tax year** (if any), and then
  - **carry back three tax years**
  - on a **LIFO basis**
- The terminal loss is the **loss of the last 12 months** (see below)
- The relief must be **claimed in writing**
- For 2009/10 loss, the claim must be made by **5 April 2014** (i.e. within 4 years of the end of the last tax year of trading)

The calculation of the terminal loss

The terminal loss is the loss of the **last 12 months of trading** and is calculated as follows:

	£
6 April before cessation to the date of cessation	
(1) Actual trading loss in this period (ignore if a profit)	X
(2) Overlap profits not yet relieved	X
12 months before cessation to 5 April before cessation	
(3) Actual trading loss in this period (ignore if a profit)	X
	——
Terminal loss	X
	——

Note that in the closing years, it is not compulsory to make a claim against total income before claiming terminal loss relief.

However, where losses included in the above terminal loss calculation have already been relieved under another claim (i.e. against total income or chargeable gains), the amount of the terminal loss must be reduced.

Extended carry back relief in closing years

It is possible to claim the extended carry back relief in the closing years.

However it is unlikely to be beneficial.

This is because the relief is the same as terminal loss relief (i.e. set off against trading profits of the three years preceding the year of the loss) but with terminal loss relief there is no £50,000 maximum restriction.

In addition, terminal loss relief is available for the losses of the last 12 months trading, not just the loss of the last tax year.

Test your understanding 7

Yves ceased trading on 30 June 2009. His final period of trade was the nine months to 30 June 2009 and beforehand he prepared accounts annually to 30 September. His tax-adjusted trading results are as follows:

		£
Nine months to 30.6.09	Loss	(7,200)
Year to 30.9.08	Profit	100
Year to 30.9.07	Profit	7,300
Year to 30.9.06	Profit	7,500

There was overlap relief of £1,800 brought forward.

Yves had no other sources of income.

Calculate the terminal loss available to Yves and show how relief may be obtained for it.

8 Choice of loss reliefs

Utilising loss relief

When planning relief for trading losses, careful consideration needs to be given to the personal circumstances of the individual.

Tax advice should aim to satisfy the following goals of a taxpayer:

- Obtain tax relief at the highest marginal rate of tax.
- Obtain relief as soon as possible.
- Ensure the taxpayer's personal allowances are not wasted, if possible.

It may not be possible to satisfy all of these aims, for example:

- in order to get a higher rate of relief, the taxpayer may have to waste their personal allowance
- carrying losses forward may give a higher rate of relief, but the cash flow implications of claiming relief now rather than waiting for relief, may be more important to the taxpayer.

The specific circumstances faced by the taxpayer will help to determine which of these is most important.

Factors to consider

In understanding the position of the taxpayer, it is important to understand the comparative features of the various reliefs.

Income relieved	Timing of relief	Flexibility
Total income - normal claim (possibly also extended carry back and chargeable gains relief)	Current and/or previous tax year	Either, neither or both tax years (in either order). All or nothing.
Total income - special opening years claim	Preceding three tax years on a FIFO basis	Only in opening years. All or nothing. Can be used with a normal claim against total income
Future trading income	As soon as possible in future	None

Choice of loss relief

Although the reliefs against total income (normal relief and special opening year relief), obtain relief more quickly than relief by carry forward, they frequently involve loss of personal allowances.

However, for a large loss that will eliminate several years' modest trading profits, there is no point in choosing to carry forward a loss if there is no non-trading income in those future years to obtain relief for personal allowances. All that will have happened is that future personal allowances rather than current ones will be wasted.

The taxpayer can choose when to claim relief against total income, that is, in the tax year of the loss; or the preceding year, as the legislation does not dictate that either takes priority.

After a claim against total income is made, the extended carry back relief is available and may give a high rate of tax relief, an immediate repayment and possibly a repayment supplement. However it is not possible unless a claim against total income is made. It may therefore be advantageous to make such a claim in order to get the benefit of the extended carry back relief.

If neither a current nor a previous year claim against total income appears appropriate, look at the chargeable gains position.

Where the taxpayer has made a large chargeable gain, a claim against it may be appropriate. Since the claim can only be made once total income for the year is reduced to zero, it will generally involve wasting at least one year's personal allowance.

9 Partnership losses

The allocation of trading losses

Trading losses are allocated between partners in exactly the same way as trading profits.

Loss relief claims available

Claims available to partners are the same as those for sole traders.

- A partner joining a partnership may be entitled to claim opening year loss relief, where a loss is incurred in the first four tax years of his membership of the partnership.

  This relief would not be available to the existing partners.

- A partner leaving the partnership may be entitled to claim for terminal loss relief.

  Again, this relief would not be available to the partners remaining in the partnership.

Test your understanding 8

Diane, Lynne and John are in partnership preparing their accounts to 5 April. During 2009/10, John left the partnership and Rose joined in his place.

For the year ended 5 April 2010, the partnership made a tax-adjusted loss of £40,000.

State the loss relief claims that will be available to the partners.

Example 6 - Partnership loss

Jake and Milo have been in partnership together since 1998, but ceased trading on 30 September 2009.

The tax-adjusted trading profits and losses for the final four years before allocation between the partners are as follows:

		£
2006/07	Profit - y/e 30.9.06	15,000
2007/08	Profit - y/e 30.9.07	14,000
2008/09	Profit - y/e 30.9.08	11,200
2009/10	Loss - y/e 30.9.09	(33,500)

Profits and losses have always been shared 40% to Jake and 60% to Milo.

Jake is single and had no other income or outgoings.

Milo is single and also has no other income or outgoings apart from bank interest of £4,350 (gross) received on 1 December 2009 from investing a recent inheritance. He has a chargeable gain of £23,400 for 2009/10 in respect of the disposal of an asset on 18 July 2009.

Assume that the 2009/10 rates and allowances apply to all years. Ignore overlap relief.

(a) **Advise the partners of the possible ways of relieving the partnership loss for 2009/10.**

(b) **Advise the partners as to which loss relief claims would be the most beneficial.**

(c) **After taking into account the advice in (b), calculate the partners' taxable income for 2006/07 to 2009/10.**

Answer to example 6

(a) **Options for relieving loss** – There are two possible ways to relieve the partnership loss:

(1) A claim can be made against total income for 2009/10 and/or 2008/09.

Subject to this claim being made, it would then be possible to extend the carry back claim against trading profits of 2007/08 and 2006/07 and/or claim against chargeable gains of the same year.

(2) Terminal loss relief can be claimed.

The tax-adjusted trading profits will be split between the partners:

	Jake 40%	Milo 60%
	£	£
2006/07	6,000	9,000
2007/08	5,600	8,400
2008/09	4,480	6,720
2009/10	(13,400)	(20,100)

(b) **Most beneficial relief**

The most beneficial loss relief claim available to Jake would appear to be a terminal loss claim, as he has no other income or gains.

Milo could also make a terminal loss claim, but this would waste his personal allowances for several years. He would be advised to make a claim against his total income of £4,350 for 2009/10, which wastes his personal allowance in that year, but then allows a claim against his chargeable gains of £23,400 for 2009/10.

(c) **Jake – Taxable income**

	2006/07	2007/08	2008/09	2009/10
	£	£	£	£
Trading income	6,000	5,600	4,480	Nil
Less: Terminal loss	(3,320)	(5,600)	(4,480)	(Nil)
Net income	2,680	Nil	Nil	Nil
Less: PA (restricted)	(2,680)	–	–	–
Taxable income	Nil	Nil	Nil	Nil

Milo – Taxable income

	2006/07	2007/08	2008/09	2009/10
	£	£	£	£
Trading income	9,000	8,400	6,720	Nil
Bank interest	–	–	–	4,350
Total income	9,000	8,400	6,720	4,350
Less: Loss relief	–	–	–	(4,350)
Net income	9,000	8,400	6,720	Nil
Less: PA	(6,475)	(6,475)	(6,475)	–
Taxable income	2,525	1,925	245	Nil

Limited liability partnerships (LLP)

An LLP is a special type of partnership where the amount that each partner contributes towards the partnership losses, debts and liabilities is limited by agreement.

The taxation implications of an LLP are as follows:

- It is generally taxed in the same way as all other partnerships.
- The normal loss reliefs are available.
- However, the losses that may be set against income **not** deriving from the partnership is limited to the amount of capital that the partner has contributed to the partnership.

Test your understanding 9

Rob and Linda are partners in a limited liability partnership (LLP) to which they contributed capital of £45,000 and £15,000 respectively.

The LLP prepares its accounts to 31 March each year and Rob and Linda share profits and losses 2:1. For the year to 31 March 2010, the LLP made a trading loss of £60,000.

State the amount of the loss available to Rob and Linda to off set against total income in 2009/10.

10 Businesses transferred to companies

When an unincorporated business ceases, the individual will seek to obtain relief from any losses as soon as possible.

They will therefore consider relief against total income and against chargeable gains first, then claim terminal loss relief. Normally, if there are any unrelieved losses remaining after these claims, the loss is lost.

However, where the business is ceasing because it is being incorporated, these unrelieved losses can be relieved against future income derived from the company.

The key rules relating to the relief are as follows:

Incorporation relief against future income from the company

- Incorporation relief is available where an unincorporated business
  - is **transferred to a company**
  - **'wholly or mainly'** in exchange **for shares,** and
  - the company is controlled by the former owner of the business
- 'Wholly or mainly' it usually taken to mean that **at least 80%** of the consideration received from the business from the company is in the form of shares
- The relief is to **carry the losses forward**
  - indefinitely
  - provided the owner retains the shares throughout the whole tax year in which the loss relief is given, and
  - provided the company continues to carry on the trade of the former unincorporated business
- Losses are **set against**
  - the **first available income** the individual derives **from the company** (e.g. salary, interest, dividends)
  - Set off against types of income from the company in any order
  - Most beneficial order will be from employment income first, then savings income, then dividends
- Note that the losses cannot be set against the future profits of the company

11 Chapter summary

TRADING LOSSES

DETERMINING A LOSS

- Use same calculation rules as for adjustment to profits
- Loss is the negative outcome
- Trading income = £nil
- No overlap losses

UTILISING A LOSS

OPENING YEARS

- Carry forward relief – as below
- Relief against total income – as below
- Extended carry back relief – as below
- Relief against chargeable gains – as below
- Special opening year relief
  - carry back 3 years
  - loss of any of first four tax years of trade
  - against total income
  - FIFO basis

ONGOING YEARS

- Carry forward relief
  - carry forward
  - first available future trading income
- Relief against total income
  - current and/or previous years
  - againat total income
- Extended carry back relief
  - three years preceding year of loss
  - LIFO basis
  - maximum £50,000
  - against trading income only
  - after claim against total income
- Relief against chargeable gains
  - current and/or previous years
  - against chargeable gains
  - after claim against total income

CLOSING YEARS

- Relief against total income – as below
- Terminal loss relief:
  - current and 3-year carry back
  - LIFO basis
  - against trading income only
- Incorporation relief:
  - carry forward
  - first available future income derived from company

Test your understanding answers

Test your understanding 1

Michael	2007/08	2008/09	2009/10
	£	£	£
Trading income	Nil	6,000	19,000
Less: Loss relief b/f (W)	Nil	(6,000)	(3,000)
Net trading income	Nil	Nil	16,000

Working – Loss memorandum

	£
Trading loss – year to 31 August 2007	9,000
Less: Used in 2008/09	(6,000)
Less: Used in 2009/10	(3,000)
Loss carried forward to 2010/11	Nil

Test your understanding 2

Adrian

Year of the loss = 2009/10

Relief against total income in: 2009/10 and /or 2008/09.

	2008/09	2009/10	2010/11
	£	£	£
Trading income	34,000	Nil	6,800
Less: Loss relief b/f (W)	–	–	(6,800)
	34,000	Nil	Nil
Other income	5,000	6,000	7,000
Total income	39,000	6,000	7,000
Less: Qualifying interest paid	Nil	(2,500)	Nil
	39,000	3,500	7,000
Less: Loss relief (W)	(39,000)	–	–
Net income	Nil	3,500	7,000
Less: PA (Note)	–	(3,500)	(6,475)
Taxable income	Nil	Nil	525

Working – Loss memorandum

	£
2009/10 – loss of y/e 31.12.09	48,000
Less: Used in 2008/09	(39,000)
Loss carried forward	9,000
Less: Used in 2010/11	(6,800)
Loss carried forward to 2011/12	2,200

Note: A claim for relief against total income in 2009/10 is not beneficial as the income is already covered by the personal allowance. Therefore if a claim is made in this year it would needlessly utilise the loss, waste the personal allowance for that year and save no tax.

However, a claim in 2008/09 will achieve a tax saving and will obtain relief for the loss as soon as possible. The personal allowance in that year is wasted, however relief sooner rather than later and at a higher rate of tax is preferable to carrying forward a loss and waiting for the relief.

The best course of action will depend on the personal circumstances of each case but as a general principle there is no point in claiming relief against total income where personal allowances already cover all or most of the total income.

Test your understanding 3

Gertrude

Computation of taxable income

	2006/07	2007/08	2008/09	2009/10
	£	£	£	£
Trading income	72,0000	39,000	28,000	Nil
Extended carry back relief	(11,000)	(39,000)	(Nil)	
	61,000	Nil	28,000	
Property income	5,550	5,500	5,500	5,500
Total income	66,500	5,500	33,500	5,500
Less: Loss relief	-	-	(33,500)	Nil
Net income	66,500	5,500	Nil	5,500
Less: PA	(6,475)	(5,500)	-	(5,500)
Taxable income	60,025	Nil	Nil	Nil

Working - Loss memorandum

	£
Loss for year ending 30 September 2009	92,000
Less: Relief against total income:	
2009/10 (no claims as income covered by PA)	Nil
2008/09	(33,500)
	58,500
Less: Extended carry back relief claims:	
2007/08	(39,000)
2006/07 (£50,000 max – £39,000)	(11,000)
Loss remaining to carry forward	8,500

Note: The claim against total income could be made in 2009/10 instead of 2008/09. This would waste the 2009/10 PA, but would mean only £28,000 of loss would be utilised against trading income in 2008/09. In this example there is no net effect, however the choice of year for the claim could be significant if there are varying levels of other income.

Test your understanding 4

Charles

Income tax computation – 2009/10

	£
Trading income (y/e 31.12.09)	3,000
Other income	4,500
Total income	7,500
Less: Loss relief	(7,500)
Taxable income	Nil

Chargeable gains computation – 2009/10

Chargeable gains	16,000
Less: Capital losses – current year	(5,000)
Net chargeable gains	11,000
Less: Trading loss relief (W)	(6,500)
Net chargeable gains before annual exemption	4,500

Note: As a result of the claims, Charles' personal allowance and part of the annual annual exemption are wasted.

Working - Loss memorandum

	£
Loss for year ending 31 December 2009	14,000
Less: Used in 2009/10 against total income	(7,500)
	6,500
Less: Used in 2009/10 against chargeable gains	(6,500)
Loss carried forward	Nil

Test your understanding 5

Georgina

		Trading income	Loss available
2006/07 (Actual basis)		£	£
1.5.06 – 5.4.07			
11/12 × (£36,000) = (£33,000)		Nil	33,000
2007/08 (CYB)	£		
Year ended 30 April 2007	36,000		
Less: Used in 2006/07	(33,000)		
	(3,000)	Nil	3,000
2008/09 (CYB)			
Year ended 30 April 2008		30,000	Nil
2009/10 (CYB)			
Year ended 30 April 2009		35,000	Nil

Test your understanding 6

Knight

	Loss available	Trading income
	£	£
2007/08		
(1 May 2007 – 5 April 2008) (£6,120 × 11/12)		5,610
2008/09		
(Year ended 30 April 2008)		6,120
2009/10		
(Year ended 30 April 2009)	28,480	Nil
2010/11		
(Year ended 30 April 2010)		7,630

Note: 2009/10 is the 'tax year of the loss'. Therefore, the loss of £28,480 is set off against total income of 2006/07 first, then 2007/08, and finally 2008/09.

	2006/07	2007/08	2008/09
	£	£	£
Trading income	Nil	5,610	6,120
Employment income	13,660	Nil	Nil
Savings income	1,700	1,700	1,700
Total income	15,360	7,310	7,820
Less: Loss relief	(15,360)	(7,310)	(5,810)
Net income	Nil	Nil	2,010

Working – Loss memorandum

	£
Trading loss	28,480
Less: Used in 2006/07	(15,360)
Less: Used in 2007/08	(7,310)
Less: Used in 2008/09	(5,810)
	Nil

Test your understanding 7

Yves

	2006/07	2007/08	2008/09	2009/10
	£	£	£	£
Trading income	7,500	7,300	100	Nil
Less: TLR (W2)	(iii) (1,575)	(ii) (7,300)	(i) (100)	Nil
Net income	5,925	Nil	Nil	Nil

Workings

(W1) Calculation of terminal loss

	£
6.4.09 to 30.6.09: Actual loss (3/9 × £7,200)	2,400
1.7.08 to 5.4.09: Actual loss	
(6/9 × £7,200) – (3/12 × £100)	4,775
Overlap relief	1,800
Terminal loss	8,975

(W2) Terminal loss relief (TLR)

The terminal loss is then relieved on a LIFO basis in the final year of assessment and the previous three years, against the trading profits.

Test your understanding 8

Diane, Lynne and John

All the partners will be entitled to relief against total income, as well as the option to extend the relief against chargeable gains or the additional three year loss carry back.

All the partners except John will be entitled to carry forward loss relief.

John will be entitled to terminal loss relief since he has ceased trading.

Rose will be entitled to claim special opening years relief since she has commenced trading.

Diane and Lynne will not be entitled to terminal loss relief or special opeing year loss relief.

Test your understanding 9

Rob and Linda

Rob will be entitled to £40,000 (£60,000 × 2/3) of the loss arising in the year ended 31 March 2010. This figure is less than the capital that he has contributed of £45,000 and the full amount of the loss (£40,000) is therefore available to be offset against Rob's non-partnership income for 2009/10.

Linda will be entitled to £20,000 (£60,000 × 1/3) of the loss arising in the year ended 31 March 2010.

The amount of the loss, which may be set against income not deriving from the partnership in 2009/10, is however limited to £15,000, being the amount of capital that she has contributed to the LLP.

The balance of the loss, £5,000 (£20,000 – £15,000), can only be claimed against partnership income, for example by carry forward.

chapter

11

Pensions

Chapter learning objectives

Upon completion of this chapter you will be able to:

- explain the basis for calculating the maximum annual contributions to a registered pension scheme for an individual
- calculate the tax relief available and explain how relief for pension contributions is given
- explain the concept of the lifetime allowance and the implications of the allowance being exceeded.

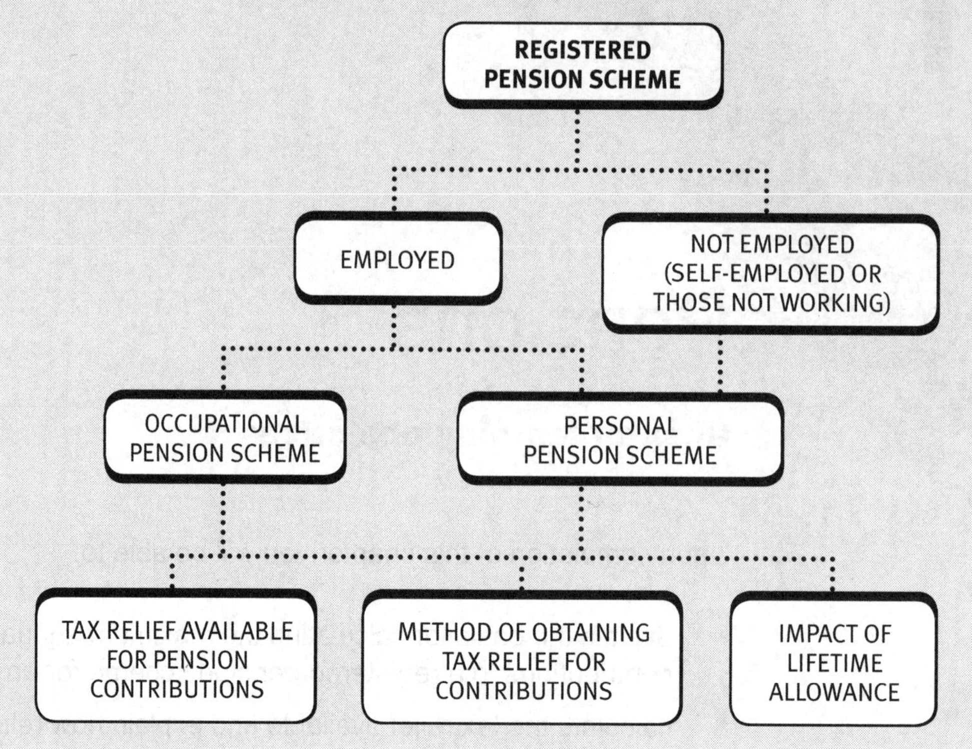

1 Types of registered pension schemes

Introduction

An individual can set up an investment of funds to provide an income during his retirement in a tax-efficient way by making payments into a registered pension scheme.

A pension scheme is a savings plan for retirement that enjoys special tax privileges, but only if the scheme is registered with HMRC.

Investing in a registered pension scheme is a long-term investment and is very tax efficient for the following reasons:

- The individual obtains tax relief on the contributions made into the scheme.
- Where an employer contributes into the scheme, tax relief for the employer contributions is available without there being a taxable benefit for the employee.
- Registered pension scheme funds can grow tax-free as the scheme is exempt from income tax and capital gains tax.
- On retirement, part of the funds can be withdrawn as a tax-free lump sum.

The two main types of registered pension schemes available are:

- Occupational pension schemes
- Personal pension schemes.

If self-employed or unemployed, the individual can only set up a personal pension scheme.

If employed, the individual may:

- join an occupational pension scheme if one is provided by his employer, or
- choose not to join the employer's scheme and set up a personal pension scheme, or
- contribute into both his employer's occupational scheme and set up a personal pension scheme.

Occupational pension schemes

An occupational pension scheme is a scheme set up by an employer for the benefit of his employees.

Employers may use an insurance company to provide a pension scheme for its employees, or it may set up its own self-administered pension fund.

Contributions into occupational schemes may be made by the employer, and the employee.

Occupational pension schemes

Registered occupational pension schemes may be 'defined benefit' or 'money purchase' schemes.

Under a **defined benefit scheme** :

- the benefits obtained on retirement are linked to the level of earnings of the employee.

Under a **money purchase scheme** (also known as a 'defined contribution' scheme):

- the benefits obtained depend upon the performance of the investments held by the pension fund.

Personal pension schemes

Personal pension schemes can be established by **any** individual:

- the employed
- the self-employed
- those not working (including children).

Contributions into personal pension schemes may be made by:

- the individual, and
- any third party on behalf of the individual (for example the employer, a spouse, parent or grandparent).

Personal pension schemes are usually 'money purchase' schemes administered by financial institutions on behalf of the individual.

Overview of the tax relief rules for registered pension schemes

- The **amount** of tax relief available for pension contributions is the same regardless of whether the scheme is an occupational or personal pension scheme.
- The **method** of obtaining tax relief for the contributions is different depending on whether the scheme is an occupational or a personal pension scheme.
- Once the funds are invested in the scheme, all registered pension schemes are governed by the same rules.

2 Tax relief for pension contributions

The relief for contributions made by individuals

Tax relief is available for pension contributions if both:

- the pension scheme is a registered scheme
- the individual is resident in the UK and aged under 75.

Regardless of the level of earnings, an individual may make pension contributions of **any amount** into either:

- a pension scheme, or
- a number of different pension schemes.

However, **tax relief** is only available for a **maximum annual amount** each tax year.

The total maximum annual gross contribution for which an individual can obtain tax relief is calculated as follows.

The higher of:

- £3,600, and
- 100% of the individual's 'relevant earnings', chargeable to income tax in the tax year.

Relevant earnings includes taxable trading profits, employment income and furnished holiday lettings but not investment income.

- The above maximum limit applies to the total gross contributions made into all schemes where:
  - an employee contributes to both an occupational and a personal pension scheme, or
  - an individual contributes into more than one personal pension scheme.
- An individual with no relevant earnings can still obtain tax relief on gross contributions of up to £3,600 p.a. This figure will be provided in the examination.

Example 1 - Maximum tax relief for individuals

The following individuals made gross pension contributions into a personal pension scheme in 2009/10:

	Pension contributions (gross)	Relevant earnings
	£	£
Amy	2,500	Nil
Brenda	6,000	Nil
Caroline	36,000	75,000
Deborah	96,000	75,000

Explain the maximum amount of pension contribution for which tax relief is available for each individual in 2009/10.

Answer to example 1

	Tax relief	Explanation
Amy	£2,500	Relief = contributions made as they are below the maximum annual amount of £3,600 (higher of £3,600 and £nil).
Brenda	£3,600	Contributions (£6,000) exceed the maximum annual amount (higher of £3,600 and £nil). Relief = restricted to maximum annual amount of £3,600.
Caroline	£36,000	Relief = contributions made (£36,000) as they are below the maximum annual amount of £75,000 (higher of £3,600 and £75,000).
Deborah	£75,000	Contributions (£96,000) exceed the maximum annual amount (higher of £3,600 and £75,000). Relief = restricted to the annual maximum amount of £75,000.

The tax charge on contributions in excess of the annual allowance

As we have seen tax relief for pension contributions is restricted to the **maximum annual amount**.

In addition however, a tax charge is levied on the individual if the total of all contributions on which tax relief has been obtained exceed an **annual allowance** of £245,000 for 2009/10.

This limit will be provided in the examination.

The tax charge is a **40% income tax charge**, which is:

- added to the individual's income tax liability in his income tax computation, and
- paid through the self-assessment system.

Note that there is no income tax charge where excess contributions have **not** qualified for tax relief.

Therefore, the combined total of all contributions paid into an individual's registered pension scheme(s) **for which tax relief is obtained** is compared with the £245,000 limit.

Combined contributions

The total contributions paid into the scheme are:

- Contributions made by the individual within the maximum annual amount (see above).
- Contributions made by other individuals (for example: spouse, parents, grandparents) that have obtained tax relief.
- All contributions made by an employer.

In Example 1 above:

- The £75,000 is taken into account to calculate whether or not there is an annual allowance charge for Deborah (not the gross contributions of £96,000 she paid into the scheme).
- The £75,000 would be added to any contributions made by her employer or other third parties to decide whether the annual allowance charge should be levied.

Summary

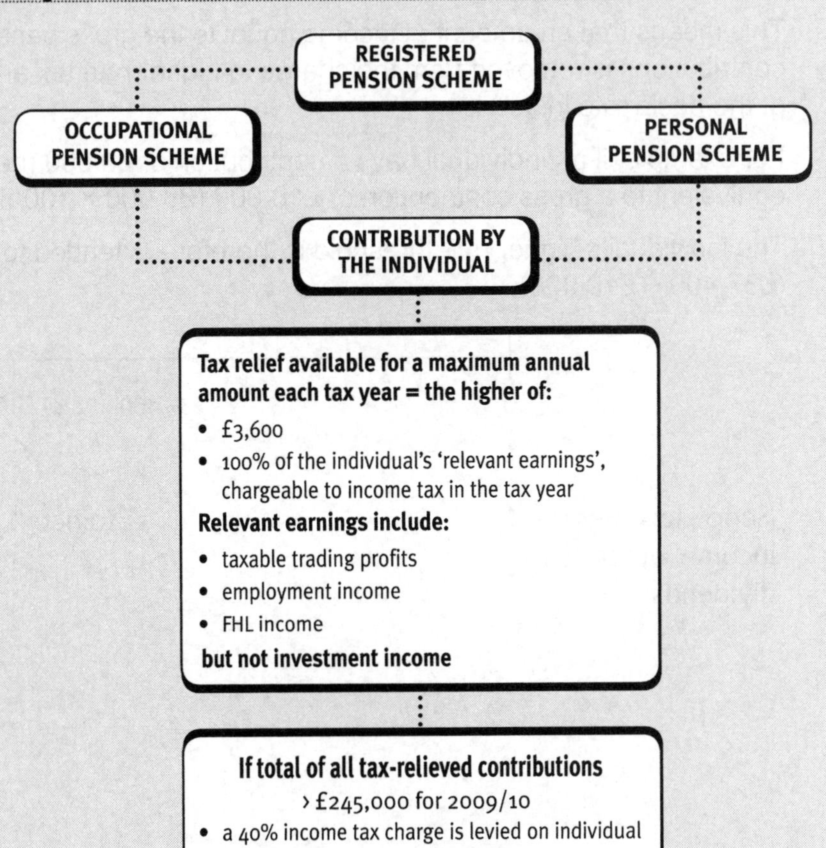

3 The method of obtaining relief for pension contributions

Personal pension schemes

The method of obtaining tax relief for contributions into a personal pension scheme is the same whether they are made by an employee, a self-employed individual or an individual who is not working.

Relief is given as follows:

Basic rate tax relief

- Basic rate tax relief is automatically given by deduction at source when contributions are paid, as an individual makes contributions net of the basic rate of income tax (20%).
- Contributions into a personal pension scheme benefit from basic rate tax relief, even if the taxpayer is paying tax at the starting rate, higher rate or not paying tax at all.

Higher rate tax relief

- For higher rate taxpayers, basic rate relief of 20% is given at source (as above) and higher rate relief is given by extending the basic rate tax band by the gross amount of pension payments paid in the tax year.
- This means that an amount of income equal to the gross pension contributions is removed from the charge to higher rate tax and is taxed at the basic rate instead.
- For example, if an individual pays a contribution of £8,000 (net), this is equivalent to a gross contribution of £10,000 (£8,000 × 100/80).
- The individual's higher rate threshold is therefore extended to £47,400 (£37,400 + £10,000).

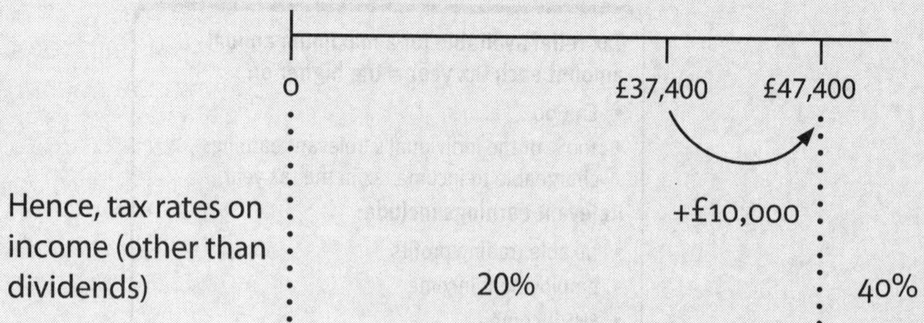

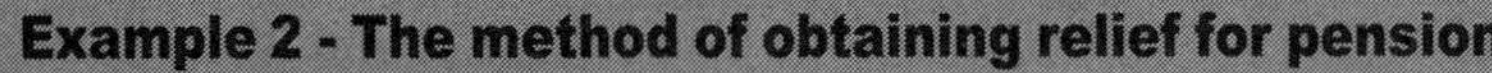

Example 2 - The method of obtaining relief for pension

The following individuals made gross pension contributions into a personal pension scheme in 2009/10.

	Pension contributions (gross)	Trading profits
	£	£
Andy	5,000	Nil
Brad	5,000	20,000
Cindy	25,000	20,000
Don	40,000	85,000
Ed	100,000	85,000

Explain how tax relief for the pension contributions will be given in 2009/10 for each individual and calculate the income tax liability of Don and Ed for 2009/10.

Answer to example 2

Andy

- As Andy has no earnings he will obtain tax relief on a maximum gross amount of £3,600.
- He will obtain basic rate tax relief at source of £720 (£3,600 × 20%) and pay £4,280 (£5,000 – £720) to the pension scheme.

Brad

- Brad's pension contributions are less than his earnings for the year and he will therefore receive tax relief on the full amount of the contribution.
- He will obtain basic rate tax relief at source of £1,000 (£5,000 × 20%) and pay £4,000 (£5,000 – £1,000) to the pension scheme.
- As Brad is not a higher rate taxpayer no adjustment is required in his income tax computation.

Cindy

- The tax relief available on Cindy's pension contributions is restricted to 100% of her earnings, i.e. £20,000.
- She will obtain basic rate tax relief at source of £4,000 (£20,000 × 20%) and pay £21,000 (£25,000 – £4,000) to the pension scheme.
- As Cindy is not a higher rate taxpayer no adjustment is required in her income tax computation.

Don

- Don's pension contributions are less than his earnings; he will therefore receive tax relief on the full amount of the contribution.
- He will obtain basic rate tax relief at source of £8,000 (£40,000 × 20%) and pay £32,000 (£40,000 – £8,000) to the pension scheme.
- Higher rate tax relief will be given by extending the basic rate band by £40,000 from £37,400 to £77,400.

Don's income tax computation for 2009/10 will be:

		£
Trading income		85,000
Less: Personal allowance		(6,475)
Taxable income		78,525
	£	
Basic rate	77,400 @ 20%	15,480
Higher rate	1,125 @ 40%	450
	78,525	
Income tax liability		15,930

Ed

- The tax relief available on Ed's pension contributions is restricted to 100% of his earnings, i.e. £85,000.
- He will obtain basic rate tax relief at source of £17,000 (£85,000 × 20%) and pay £83,000 (£100,000 – £17,000) to the scheme.
- Higher rate tax relief will be given by extending the basic rate band by £85,000 from £37,400 to £122,400.

Ed's income tax computation for 2009/10 will be:

	£
Trading income	85,000
Less: Personal allowance	(6,475)
Taxable income	78,525
Income tax (£78,525 × 20%)	15,705

Example 3 - Contributions in excess of the annual allowance

Julie has been a self-employed interior designer for a number of years. In the year to 31 March 2010 she made taxable trading profits of £296,000. Julie made a gross contribution of £250,000 into her personal pension scheme in 2009/10.

Explain how tax relief will be obtained for the pension contribution made by Julie and calculate her income tax liability.

Answer to example 3

Julie can obtain tax relief for a pension contribution up a maximum of 100% of her earnings (i.e. £296,000 in 2009/10). She will therefore obtain relief on the gross contribution of £250,000.

Julie will have paid the pension contribution net of basic rate tax of £50,000 (£250,000 × 20%) and paid £200,000 (£250,000 – £50,000) into the pension scheme.

As a higher rate taxpayer, higher rate relief is obtained by extending the basic rate band by £250,000 from £37,400 to £287,400.

However Julie's gross contributions of £250,000 have exceeded the annual allowance of £245,000. She will therefore have an additional income tax liability of £2,000 (£250,000 – £245,000 = £5,000 × 40%).

Julie's income tax computation for 2009/10 will be:

			£
Trading income			296,000
Less: Personal allowance			(6,475)
Taxable income			289,525
Income tax liability	£		
Basic rate	287,400	@ 20%	57,480
Higher rate	2,125	@ 40%	850
	289,525		
			58,330
Annual allowance charge	5,000	@ 40%	2,000
Income tax liability			60,330

Occupational pension schemes

Where employees make pension contributions into an occupational pension scheme, payments are made gross and tax relief is given at source by the employer through the PAYE system, as an allowable deduction against employment income.

Tax relief is given at basic and higher rates of tax depending on the individual's level of income as follows:

- The employer will deduct the pension contribution from the individual's earned income, before calculating income tax under the PAYE system.
- Tax relief is therefore automatically given at both the basic and higher rate at source.

Test your understanding 1

Henry is employed by Lloyd Ltd on an annual salary of £80,000 pa. He is a member of the company's occupational pension scheme.

Henry pays 3% and Lloyd Ltd pays 5% of his salary into the scheme each year. He has no other income.

Calculate Henry's income tax liability for 2009/10, showing how tax relief is obtained for his pension contributions.

Contributions made by employers into registered pension schemes

Contributions paid by an employer into a registered pension scheme are:

- tax deductible in calculating the employer's taxable trading profits, provided the contributions are paid for the purposes of the trade, and
- an exempt employment benefit for the employee, and
- added to the pension contributions paid by the employee on which tax relief is given to determine whether the annual allowance has been exceeded and an income tax charge levied.

Employer contributions as a trading deduction into a reg. pension

The deduction against the employer's trading profits is given in the accounting period in which the contribution is **paid**; the accounting treatment is not followed.

Therefore, in the adjustment to profit computation:

- add back any amount charged in the profit and loss account, and
- deduct the amount paid in the accounting period.

Test your understanding 2

Hugh is a self-employed builder, who prepares accounts to September each year. His recent tax-adjusted trading profits have been:

	£
Year ended 30 September 2008	140,000
Year ended 30 September 2009	150,000

Hugh's wife, Holly, has employment income from a part-time job of £3,500 pa.

They also have a joint bank account on which they earned interest of £5,000 (gross) in 2009/10.

During the year to 5 April 2010, Hugh paid £79,400 into his registered personal pension scheme. Holly paid £2,600 into her employer's registered occupational pension scheme and Holly's employer contributed a further £4,500.

Calculate how much of the pension contributions made by Hugh, Holly and Holly's employer in 2009/10 will obtain tax relief and explain how the tax relief will be obtained.

Test your understanding 3

Marcus has been employed for many years.

In 2009/10 Marcus earned £302,500 and made a gross contribution of £256,000 into his personal pension scheme.

Calculate Marcus' income tax liability for 2009/10.

Summary

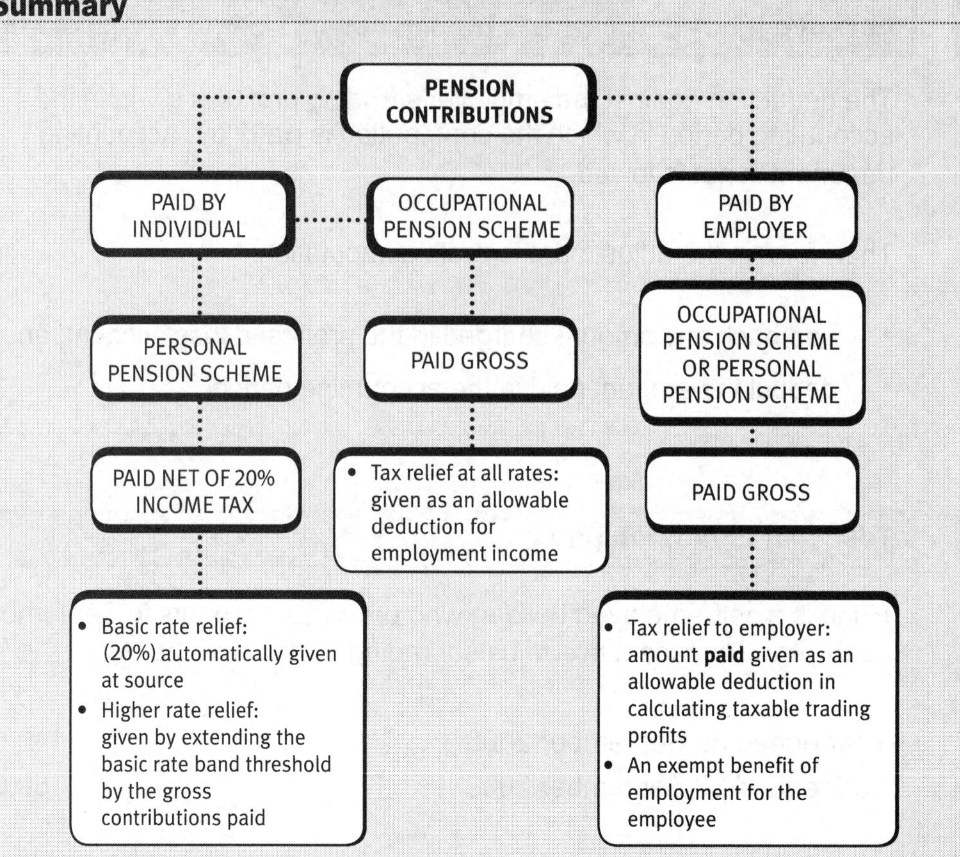
PENSION CONTRIBUTIONS
PAID BY INDIVIDUAL
OCCUPATIONAL PENSION SCHEME
PAID BY EMPLOYER
PERSONAL PENSION SCHEME
PAID GROSS
OCCUPATIONAL PENSION SCHEME OR PERSONAL PENSION SCHEME
PAID NET OF 20% INCOME TAX
• Tax relief at all rates: given as an allowable deduction for employment income
PAID GROSS
• Basic rate relief: (20%) automatically given at source
• Higher rate relief: given by extending the basic rate band threshold by the gross contributions paid
• Tax relief to employer: amount paid given as an allowable deduction in calculating taxable trading profits
• An exempt benefit of employment for the employee

4 The lifetime allowance

There is no restriction on the **total** contribution that an individual may make into a registered pension scheme. There is only a limit upon the annual contributions upon which **tax relief** will be available.

Once invested, funds in a registered pension scheme each year will be accumulated and can grow in value, tax free, as the scheme is:

- exempt from income tax in respect of any income earned from the assets invested
- exempt from capital gains tax in respect of any capital disposals made by the trustees over the life of the scheme.

However, there is a maximum limit to the amount that an individual can accumulate in a pension scheme tax-free, known as the 'lifetime allowance'.

Lifetime allowance

The lifetime allowance is:

- £1.75 million for 2009/10
- considered when a member becomes entitled to withdraw benefits out of the scheme (for example, when he becomes entitled to take a pension and/or lump sum payment).

If the value of the pension fund exceeds the lifetime allowance:

- an additional income tax charge arises on the excess fund value (i.e. the excess value above £1.75 million).

The detail rules for the income tax charge is not examinable.

5 Chapter summary

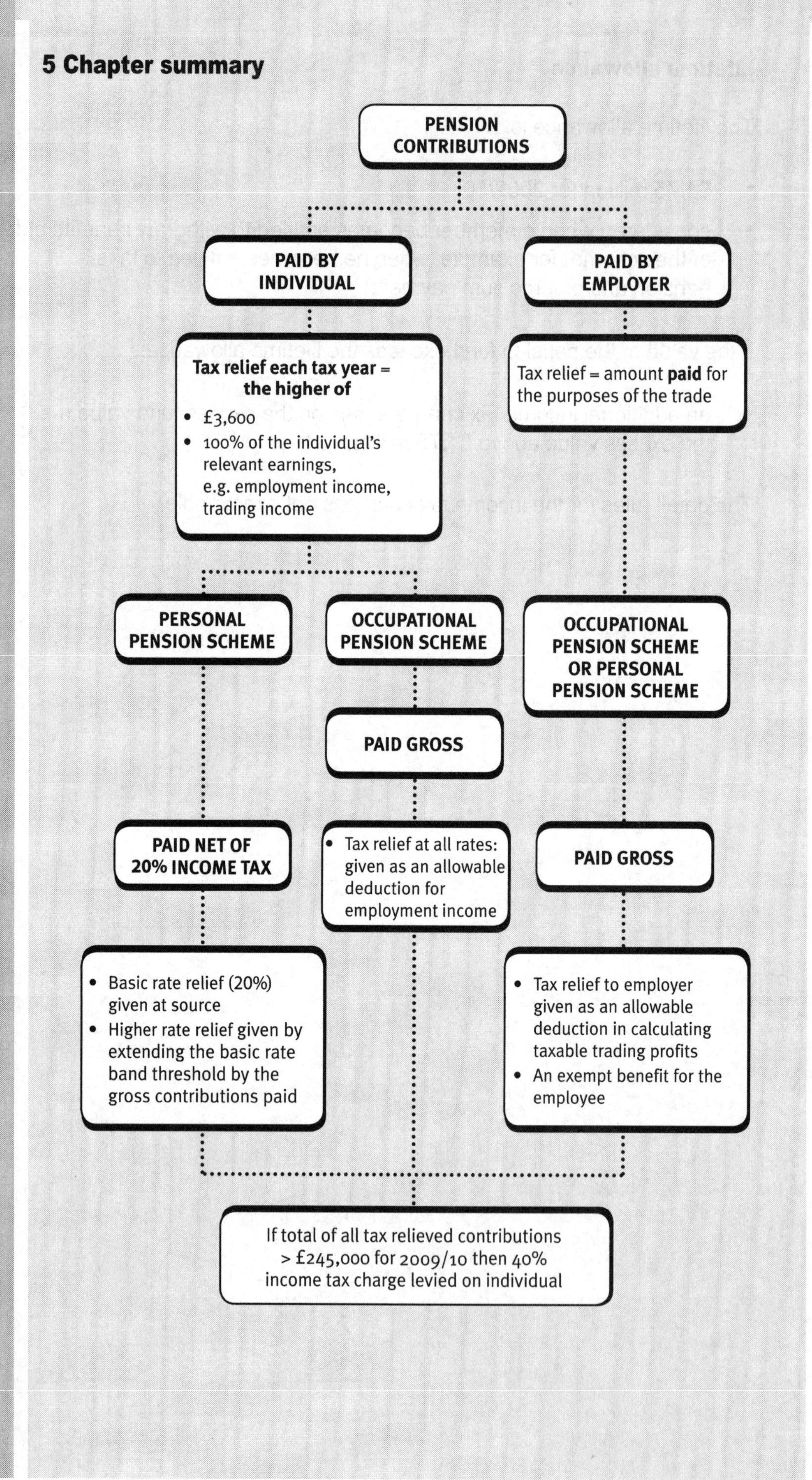
PENSION CONTRIBUTIONS
PAID BY INDIVIDUAL
PAID BY EMPLOYER
Tax relief each tax year = the higher of
• £3,600
• 100% of the individual's relevant earnings, e.g. employment income, trading income
Tax relief = amount paid for the purposes of the trade
PERSONAL PENSION SCHEME
OCCUPATIONAL PENSION SCHEME
OCCUPATIONAL PENSION SCHEME OR PERSONAL PENSION SCHEME
PAID GROSS
PAID NET OF 20% INCOME TAX
• Tax relief at all rates: given as an allowable deduction for employment income
PAID GROSS
• Basic rate relief (20%) given at source
• Higher rate relief given by extending the basic rate band threshold by the gross contributions paid
• Tax relief to employer given as an allowable deduction in calculating taxable trading profits
• An exempt benefit for the employee
If total of all tax relieved contributions > £245,000 for 2009/10 then 40% income tax charge levied on individual

Test your understanding answers

Test your understanding 1

Henry

Income tax computation – 2009/10

		£
Salary		80,000
Less: Employee's pension contributions (3%)		(2,400)
Employment income		77,600
Less: Personal allowance		(6,475)
Taxable income		71,125
Income tax	£	
Basic rate	37,400 @ 20%	7,480
Higher rate	33,725 @ 40%	13,490
	71,125	
Income tax liability		20,970

Note: The employer's contribution into his pension scheme is an exempt employment benefit and is therefore not taxable income for Henry.

Test your understanding 2

Hugh

- Hugh can obtain tax relief for a pension contribution of up to a maximum of 100% of his earnings in 2009/10.
- His earnings are his assessable trading profits for 2009/10, i.e. £150,000 (year ended 30 September 2009).
- Unearned income such as bank interest is not included.
- Hugh will have paid the pension contribution net of basic rate tax of £19,850 (£79,400 × 20/80).
- The gross pension contribution is £99,250 (£79,400 × 100/80).
- As a higher rate taxpayer, higher rate tax relief is obtained by extending the basic rate band threshold by £99,250 from £37,400 to £136,650.

Holly

- Holly can obtain tax relief for a gross pension contribution of up to a maximum of the higher of £3,600 or 100% of her employment earnings in 2009/10 (i.e. £3,500).
- Her gross pension contribution of £2,600 is less than £3,600, therefore she can obtain tax relief for all £2,600 contributions paid.
- Holly's employer will deduct the gross contribution of £2,600 from her employment income before calculating her income tax liability under PAYE.
- Holly's employer's contributions of £4,500 are a tax free benefit.

Holly's employer

- Holly's employer will obtain tax relief for all of the £4,500 contribution made into the occupational pension scheme.
- Relief is given as an allowable deduction in the calculation of the employer's taxable trading profits.

Test your understanding 3

Marcus

- Marcus can obtain tax relief for a gross pension contribution of up to a maximum of 100% of his earnings (i.e. £302,500 in 2009/10).
- However, he only made a gross contribution of £256,000. Tax relief is therefore available on the full contribution of £256,000.
- Marcus will have paid the pension contribution net of basic rate tax of £51,200 (£256,000 × 20%) and paid £204,800 (£256,000 × 80%) into the pension scheme.
- As a higher rate taxpayer, higher rate relief is obtained by extending the basic rate band threshold by £256,000 from £37,400 to £293,400.
- However the gross contributions paid into the scheme on which tax relief has been given in 2009/10 of £256,000 exceeds the annual allowance of £245,000.
- Marcus will therefore have an additional income tax liability in 2009/10 of £4,400 (£256,000 – £245,000 = £11,000 × 40%).

Marcus' income tax computation for 2009/10 will be:

		£
Employment income		302,500
Less: Personal allowance		(6,475)
Taxable income		296,025
Income tax	£	
Basic rate	293,400 @ 20%	58,680
Higher rate	2,625 @ 40%	1,050
	296,025	
		59,730
Add: Annual allowance charge (£11,000 × 40%)		4,400
Income tax liability		64,130

chapter

12

National insurance

Chapter learning objectives

Upon completion of this chapter you will be able to:

- identify the different types of National Insurance Contributions (NICs) and the persons who are liable
- define earnings for the purposes of Class 1 NICs
- calculate the Class 1 NIC primary and secondary liabilities on earnings
- state how and when Class 1 NICs are collected
- explain the basis of the Class 1A NIC charge and calculate the amount of Class 1A NICs payable
- state how and when Class 1A NICs are payable
- calculate Class 2 NICs for relevant self-employed persons
- explain how Class 2 NICs are collected
- identify the relevant earnings for Class 4 NICs and calculate the liability
- demonstrate the mechanism for the payment of Class 4 NICs
- calculate the total NIC liability for a self-employed person.

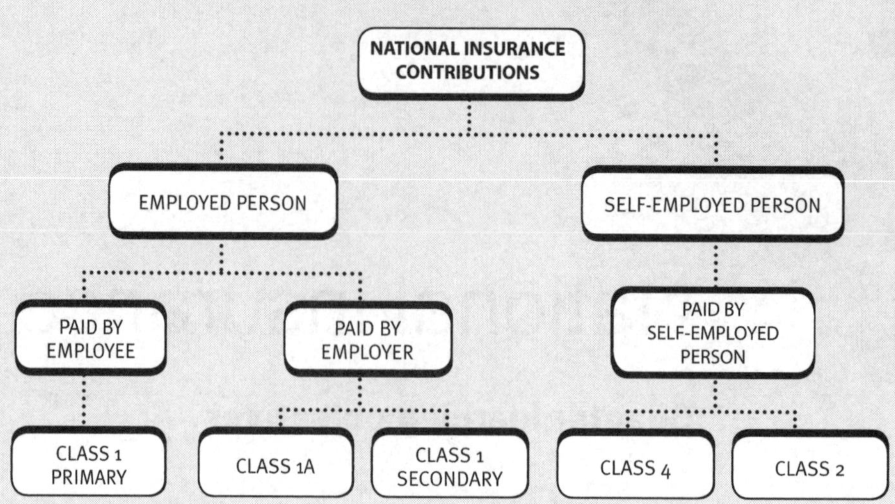

1 Classes of National Insurance Contributions

The amount of National Insurance Contribution (NIC) a person pays and the payment of contributions depend on the class of contribution.

The main classes and persons who are liable are as follows:

Class of contribution	Basis of assessment	Person liable
Class 1 primary	A percentage-based contribution levied on employee earnings in excess of £5,715 for 2009/10	Employee
Class 1 secondary		Employer
Class 1A	A percentage-based contribution levied on assessable benefits provided to employees	Employer
Class 2	A flat rate weekly contribution	Self-employed
Class 4	A percentage-based contribution levied on taxable trading profits in excess of £5,715 for 2009/10	Self-employed

Example 1 - Classes of NICs

Nicholas has been self-employed for many years. He employs a full-time salesman and six part-time employees. Nicholas' taxable trading profits for 2009/10 are £86,000.

The salesman earns a salary of £14,000 p.a. and is provided with a company car. The remaining members of staff earn £3,000 p.a.

Explain which classes of NICs are payable by Nicholas.

Answer to example 1

Nicholas will pay:

(1) Flat rate Class 2 contributions in respect of his self-employed business.

(2) Class 4 contributions in respect of his self-employed business based on his taxable trading profits as they are in excess of £5,715.

(3) Class 1 secondary contributions as Nicholas is an employer. The contributions will be based on the salesman's salary of £14,000 as his earnings are in excess of £5,715.

(4) Class 1A contributions based on the assessable employment benefit arising from the provision of a company car to the salesman.

Notes

(1) No NICs are payable in respect of the remaining six part-time staff members as they each earn less than £5,715 p.a.

(2) The salesman is liable to pay Class 1 primary contributions based on his salary of £14,000.

Example 2 - Classes of NICs

Stephen works for Camberley Cars Ltd on a part-time basis earning a salary of £19,000 pa. He is provided with a company car; petrol for both business and private mileage; and a place is provided for his daughter at the company's workplace nursery while he is working for them.

Stephen also runs a small bed and breakfast business from his home. In the year to 31 March 2010 his taxable trading profit from the business is £10,300.

Explain which classes of NICs are payable by Stephen and Camberley Cars Ltd in respect of 2009/10.

Answer to example 2

Stephen will pay:

(1) Class 1 primary contributions based on his salary from Camberley Cars Ltd of £19,000 as his earnings are in excess of £5,715.

(2) Flat rate Class 2 contributions in respect of his bed and breakfast business.

(3) Class 4 contributions in respect of his bed and breakfast business based on his taxable trading profits as they are in excess of £5,715.

Camberley Cars Ltd will pay:

(1) Class 1 secondary contributions based on Stephen's salary of £19,000 as his earnings are in excess of £5,715.

(2) Class 1A contributions based on the assessable employment benefit arising from the provision of a company car and private petrol to Stephen.

Note: Class 1A contributions are not required in respect of the provision of a nursery place as it is an exempt benefit.

2 NICs payable in respect of employees

The following NICs are payable in respect of employees:

- Class 1 primary contributions
- Class 1 secondary contributions
- Class 1A contributions.

Class 1 primary and secondary NICs

Both the primary Class 1 contribution paid by the employee and the secondary contribution paid by the employer are a percentage-based contribution levied on the 'gross earnings' of the employee in excess of £5,715 for 2009/10.

The definition of earnings for Class 1 NIC purposes

'Earnings' for the purpose of Class 1 NICs consists of **any** remuneration derived from the employment and paid in **cash** or assets which are readily convertible into cash.

The calculation of Class 1 NICs is based on **gross earnings** with **no allowable deductions** (i.e. earnings before deductions that are allowable for income tax purposes, such as employee occupational pension scheme contributions and subscriptions to professional bodies).

Gross earnings **includes**:

- wages, salary, overtime pay, commission or bonus
- sick pay, including statutory sick pay
- tips and gratuities paid or allocated by the employer

- payment of the cost of travel between home and work
- vouchers (exchangeable for cash or non-cash items, such as goods).

'Gross earnings' **does not include**:

- exempt employment benefits (e.g. employer contributions into a pension scheme, a mobile phone, etc.) (see chapter 4)
- most taxable **non-cash benefits** except remuneration received in the form of financial instruments, readily convertible assets and non-cash vouchers (see above)
- tips received from customers
- mileage allowance received from the employer provided it does not exceed the HMRC approved allowance mileage rate of 40p per mile
- business expenses paid for or reimbursed by the employer, including reasonable travel and subsistence expenses.

Note that dividends are not subject to NICs, even if they are drawn by a director/shareholder in place of a monthly salary.

Example 3 - Definition of Class 1 earnings

Janet and John are employed by Garden Gnomes Ltd. Their remuneration for 2009/10 is as follows:

	Janet	John
	£	£
Salary	30,000	55,000
Bonus	Nil	4,000
Car benefit	Nil	3,950
Employer's occupational pension scheme contribution	2,300	4,575
Employee's occupational pension scheme contribution	1,650	3,800

Calculate Janet and John's 'gross earnings' for Class 1 NIC purposes.

Answer to example 3

	Janet	John
	£	£
Salary	30,000	55,000
Bonuses	Nil	4,000
Gross earnings for Class 1 NICs	30,000	59,000

Notes

(1) The employer's pension contributions are excluded as they are an exempt benefit.

(2) The employee's pension contributions are ignored as these are not deductible in calculating earnings for NIC purposes.

(3) The car benefit is excluded as it is a non-cash benefit which will be assessed to Class 1A NICs, not Class 1.

Eligible employees

Class 1 contributions are payable where the individual:

- is employed in the UK, and
- is aged 16 or over, and
- has earnings in excess of the lower earnings threshold of £5,715 for 2009/10.

Class 1 primary contributions

Class 1 primary contributions are payable by employees:

- aged 16 or over until
- attaining pensionable age (65 for a man, 60 for a woman).

The employer is responsible for calculating the amount of Class 1 primary NICs due and deducting the contributions from the employee's wages. Note that Class 1 primary contributions:

- are not an allowable deduction for the purposes of calculating the individual employee's personal income tax liability
- do not represent a cost to the business of the employer, as they are ultimately paid by the employee. Therefore, they are not a deductible expense when calculating the employer's taxable trading profits.

Calculating Class 1 primary contributions

Primary contributions are normally calculated by reference to an employee's earnings period:

- if paid weekly, the contributions are calculated on a weekly basis
- if paid monthly, the contributions are calculated on a monthly basis.

In the examination, the Class 1 NIC limits are usually shown on an annual basis and Class 1 NIC calculations should therefore be performed on an annual basis unless you are clearly told otherwise.

The primary contributions payable are calculated as:

- 11% on gross earnings between £5,715 and £43,875
- 1% on gross earnings in excess of £43,875

Earnings period

The annual earnings thresholds can be used to calculate the rate of Class 1 NICs payable where the employee's wages or salary does not fluctuate during the year.

However, where an employee's salary fluctuates during the year:

- the calculations must be performed on an earnings period basis
- the annual limits are divided into weekly or monthly thresholds.

The apportioned lower limit is £110 per week (£5,715/52) or £476 per month (£5,715/12); and the upper limit is £844 a week (£43,875/52) or £3,656 a month (£43,875/12).

Class 1 secondary contributions

Class 1 secondary contributions are payable by employers in respect of employees:

- aged 16 or over
- until the employee ceases employment.

There is no upper age limit for employer contributions, the employer is liable in full even if the employee is above pensionable age.

Secondary contributions are an additional cost of employment and are a deductible expense when calculating the employer's taxable trading profits.

Calculating Class 1 secondary contributions

Secondary contributions are calculated by reference to an employee's earnings period.

In the examination, Class 1 NIC calculations should be performed on an annual basis unless you are clearly told otherwise.

Secondary contributions are calculated as:

- 12.8% on all gross earnings above £5,715.

Note that there is:

- no upper earnings limit
- no change in rate of NIC payable for employer contributions.

Example 4 - Class 1 NICs

Millie is employed by Blue Forge Ltd and is paid an annual salary of £43,000. Millie is also provided with the following taxable benefits:

	£
Company car	5,000
Vouchers for the local gym	2,000

Calculate the employee's and the employer's Class 1 NIC liability due for 2009/10.

Answer to example 4

Class 1 NICs are due on annual earning of £45,000 (salary £43,000 and vouchers £2,000). The company car is a non-cash benefit and is therefore not subject to Class 1 NICs.

	£
Employee's Class 1 NICs	
(£43,875 – £5,715) @ 11%	4,198
(£45,000 – £43,875) @ 1%	11
	4,209
Employer's Class 1 NICs	
(£45,000 – £5,715) × 12.8%	5,028

Test your understanding 1

Alex is paid £7,950 per year and Betty is paid £44,440 per year.

Calculate the employee's and the employer's Class 1 NIC liability due for 2009/10.

Company directors

Special rules apply to company directors to prevent the avoidance of NICs by paying low weekly or monthly salaries, and then taking a large bonus in a single week or month.

Therefore, when an employee is a company director, his Class 1 NICs are calculated as if he had an annual earnings period.

Payment of Class 1 contributions

The administration and payment of Class 1 NICs is carried out by the employer as follows:

- The employer is responsible for calculating the amount of Class 1 primary and secondary contributions at each pay date.
- Primary contributions are deducted from the employee's wages or salary by the employer and paid to HMRC on the employee's behalf.
- The total primary and secondary contributions are payable by the employer to HMRC, along with income tax deducted from the employees under PAYE.
- The payment is normally due on the 19th of each month (i.e. due not later than 14 days after the end of each PAYE month).
- The specific payment rules for very small employers and those paying electronically are covered in detail in Chapter 13.

Class 1A NICs

Employers are required to pay Class 1A contributions on 'taxable benefits' provided to employees earning at a rate of £8,500 pa and directors (i.e. higher paid employees).

No Class 1A contributions are payable in respect of:

- exempt benefits
- benefits already treated as earnings and assessed to Class 1 NICs, such as remuneration received in the form of non-cash vouchers (see above).

The contributions are calculated as:

- 12.8% on the value of the taxable benefits.

Class 1A contributions are an additional cost of employment and are a deductible expense when calculating the employer's taxable trading profits.

Example 5 - Class 1A NICs

Simon is employed by Dutton Ltd at an annual salary of £52,000.

He was provided with a company car throughout 2009/10 that had a list price of £15,000. The car has CO_2 emissions of 193 g/km. Petrol for both business and private mileage is provided by his employer.

Calculate the employee's and the employer's Class 1 and Class 1A NIC liabilities due for 2009/10.

Answer to example 5

(a) Class 1 NICs

Employee's Class 1 NICs	£
(£43,875 – £5,715) x 11% (maximum)	4,198
(£52,000 – £43,875) x 1%	81
	4,279
Employer's Class 1 NICs	
(£52,000 – £5,715) x 12.8%	5,924

(b) Class 1A NICs

Simon's taxable benefits for Class 1A purposes are as follows:

Company motor car	£
15% + ((190 – 135) / 5) = 26% × £15,000	3,900
Private fuel provided by company (26% × £16,900)	4,394
Taxable benefits for Class 1A	8,294
Employer's Class 1A NICs (£8,294 at 12.8%)	1,062

Test your understanding 2

Sally is paid £25,000 per year and had taxable benefits for 2009/10 of:

	£
Company motor car	5,250
Private fuel provided by company	4,200
Beneficial loan	2,600
Vouchers to be used at the local department store	250

The company also provided Sally with a mobile phone, which cost £135.
Contributions into her personal pension scheme were as follows:

Employer's contribution	£2,540
Employee's contribution	£1,380

Calculate the employee's and the employer's Class 1 and Class 1A NIC liabilities due for 2009/10.

Payment of Class 1A contributions

Class 1A contributions are payable to HMRC by 19 July following the end of the tax year (i.e. by 19 July 2010 for 2009/10).

Summary

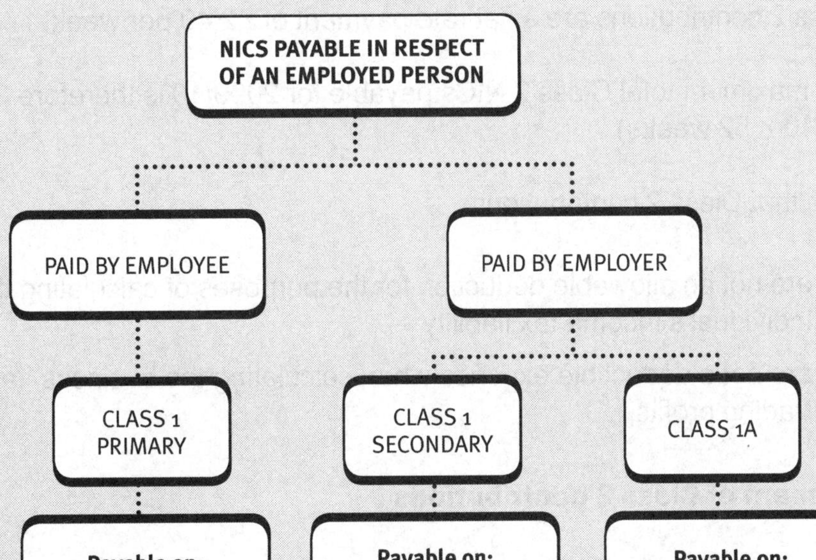

3 NICs payable in respect of self-employed individuals

The following NICs are payable by self-employed individuals:

- Class 2 contributions
- Class 4 contributions.

Class 2 contributions

Class 2 contributions are payable by individuals:

- aged 16 or over until
- attaining pensionable age (65 for a man, 60 for a woman).

Amount payable

Class 2 contributions are a flat rate payment of £2.40 per week.

The maximum total Class 2 NICs payable for 2009/10 is therefore £125 (£2.40 × 52 weeks).

Note that Class 2 contributions:

- are not an allowable deduction for the purposes of calculating the individual's income tax liability
- are not a deductible expense when calculating the business' taxable trading profits.

Payment of Class 2 contributions

Class 2 contributions are collected by HMRC on a monthly basis by direct debit, or by quarterly billing in arrears.

Class 4 contributions

In addition to Class 2 NICs, a self-employed individual may also be liable to Class 4 NICs.

Class 4 contributions are payable by self-employed individuals who:

- at the start of the tax year, are aged 16 or over.

They continue to pay **until**:

- the end of the tax year in which they attain pensionable age (65 for a man, 60 for a woman).

Class 4 NICs are a percentage-based contribution levied on the 'profits' of the individual in excess of £5,715 for 2009/10.

Note that Class 4 contributions:

- are not an allowable deduction for the purposes of calculating the individual's income tax liability
- are not a deductible expense when calculating the business' taxable trading profits.

The definition of Class 4 profits

'Profits' for the purposes of Class 4 NICs consists of:

- the taxable trading profits of the individual that are assessed for income tax after deducting trading losses (if any).

Note that 'profits' for Class 4 NICs are **before** deducting the individual's personal allowance that is available for income tax purposes.

If the individual has more than one business, the aggregate of all profits from all self-employed occupations are used to calculate the Class 4 NIC liability.

Calculating Class 4 NICs

The contributions payable are calculated as:

- 8% on profits between £5,715 and £43,875
- 1% on profits in excess of £43,875.

Example 6 - Class 4 NICs

James has been trading as a self-employed painter and decorator since 1998. His taxable trading profits for 2009/10 are £56,000 and he has trading losses brought forward of £10,000.

His wife, Poppy, is a part-time mobile hairdresser. Her taxable trading profits for 2009/10 are £6,560.

Calculate the Class 4 NICs payable by James and Poppy for 2009/10.

Answer to example 6

James	£
Taxable trading profits for 2009/10	56,000
Less: Trading losses brought forward	(10,000)
Profits for Class 4 purposes	46,000

Class 4 NICs	£
(£43,875 – £5,715) × 8% (maximum)	3,053
(£46,000 – £43,875) × 1%	21
	3,074

Poppy – Class 4 NICs	
(£6,560 – £5,715) × 8%	68

Test your understanding 3

Jack is a self-employed builder who has been in business for many years and prepares accounts to 31 March each year.

His taxable trading profit for the year ended 31 March 2009 is £46,850.

Calculate Jack's Class 2 and Class 4 NICs liability for 2009/10.

Payment of Class 4 contributions

Class 4 contributions are paid to HMRC at the same time as the individual's income tax due under self assessment, as follows:

Payment	Due date	Amount
Payments on account	• 31 January in the tax year (i.e. 31.1.2010 for 2009/10) • 31 July following the end of the tax year (i.e. 31.7.10 for 2009/10)	Two equal instalments of: • 50% of the amount paid by self assessment in the preceding year
Balancing payment	• 31 January following the end of the tax year (i.e. 31.1.11 for 2009/10)	Under or overpayment for the year

The detailed administration and payment rules are covered in Chapter 13.

Summary

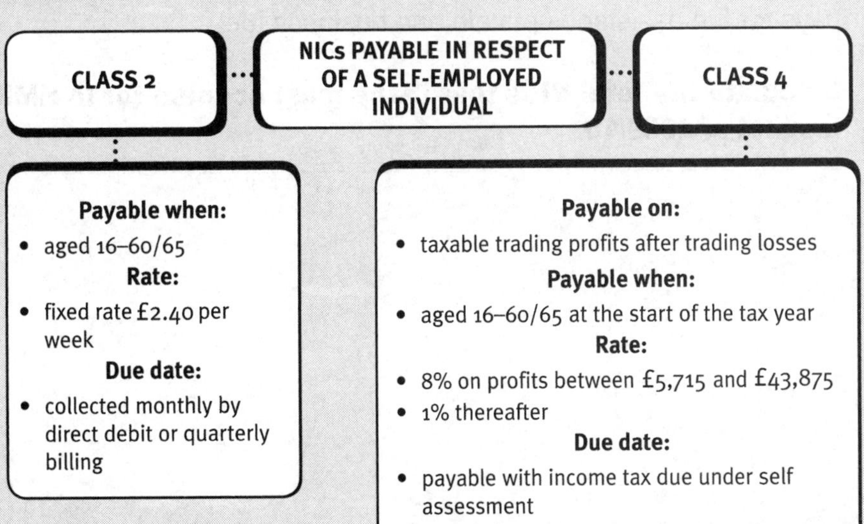

CLASS 2
NICs PAYABLE IN RESPECT OF A SELF-EMPLOYED INDIVIDUAL
CLASS 4
Payable when:
• aged 16–60/65
Rate:
• fixed rate £2.40 per week
Due date:
• collected monthly by direct debit or quarterly billing
Payable on:
• taxable trading profits after trading losses
Payable when:
• aged 16–60/65 at the start of the tax year
Rate:
• 8% on profits between £5,715 and £43,875
• 1% thereafter
Due date:
• payable with income tax due under self assessment

4 Total NICs payable by a self-employed individual

A self-employed individual pays both Class 2 and Class 4 NICs in respect of his trading profits.

In addition, if the self-employed individual employs staff, he will be required to account for:

- Class 2 and Class 4 NICs in respect of his trading profits
- Class 1 primary, Class 1 secondary and Class 1A NICs in respect of earnings and benefits provided to employees.

Test your understanding 4

Diane has been a self-employed computer consultant for many years. Her taxable trading profits for 2009/10 are £50,000.

Diane employs a full-time personal assistant at a salary of £15,800 p.a. She also provides the assistant with a diesel-engined company car, which has a list price of £13,500 and CO_2 emissions of 161 g/km. Diane pays for the assistant's private and business fuel.

Calculate the total NICs that Diane must account for to HMRC in respect of 2009/10.

5 Chapter summary

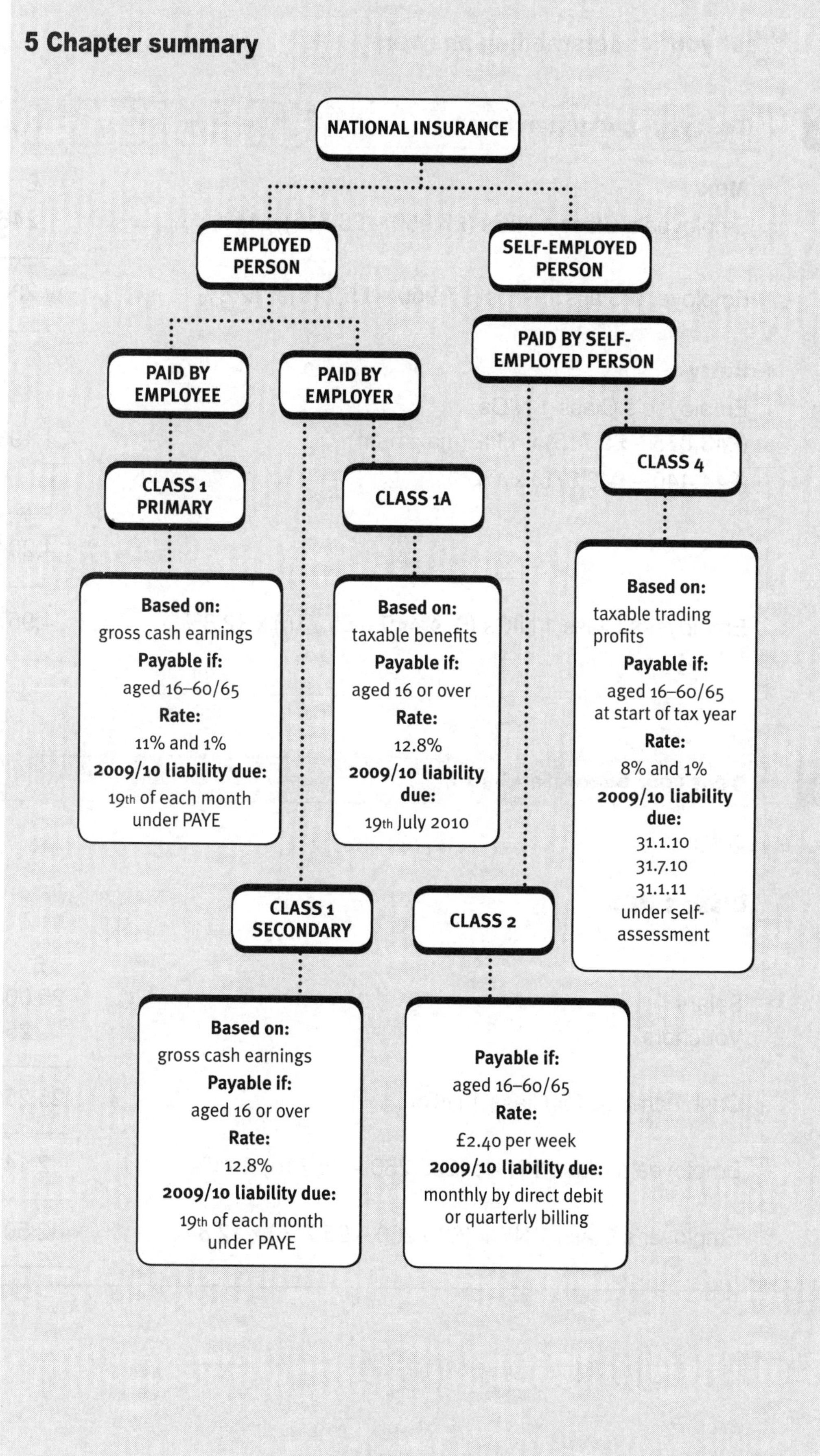

Test your understanding answers

Test your understanding 1

Alex	£
Employee's Class 1 NICs (£7,950 – £5,715) x 11%	246
Employer's Class 1 NICs (£7,950 – £5,715) x 12.8%	286
Betty	
Employee's Class 1 NICs	
(£43,875 – £5,715) x 11% (maximum)	4,198
(£44,440 – £43,875) x 1%	6
	4,204
Employer's Class 1 NICs (£44,440 – £5,715) x 12.8%	4,957

Test your understanding 2

Sally

Class 1 NICs

	£
Salary	25,000
Vouchers	250
Cash earnings for Class 1 NICs	25,250
Employee's Class 1 NICs (£25,250 – £5,715) x 11%	2,149
Employer's Class 1 NICs (£25,250 – £5,715) x 12.8%	2,500

Notes

(1) The provision of one mobile phone per employee, and employer pension contributions, are excluded as they are exempt benefits.

(2) The employee pension contributions are not allowable deductions in calculating earnings for NIC purposes.

(3) The car, fuel and beneficial loan benefits are excluded as they are non-cash benefits which are assessed to Class 1A NICs, not Class 1.

Class 1A NICs

	£
Company motor car	5,250
Private fuel provided by company	4,200
Beneficial loan	2,600
Taxable benefits for Class 1A	12,050
Employer's Class 1A NICs (£12,050 at 12.8%)	1,542

Test your understanding 3

Jack	£
Class 2 NICs (£2.40 × 52 weeks)	125
Class 4 NICs	
(£43,875 – £5,715) × 8% (maximum)	3,053
(£46,850 – £43,875) × 1%	30
	3,083

Test your understanding 4

Diane

(1) Flat rate Class 2 contributions in respect of the business.

Class 2 NICs	
(£2.40 × 52 weeks)	£125

(2) Class 4 contributions in respect of the business based on taxable trading profits as they are in excess of £5,715.

Class 4 NICs	£
(£43,875 – £5,715) × 8% (maximum)	3,053
(£50,000 – £43,875) × 1%	61
	3,114

(3) Class 1 secondary contributions as Diane is an employer, based on her personal assistant's salary of £15,800.

Employer's Class 1 NICs	
(£15,800 – £5,715) x 12.8%	£1,291

(4) Class 1A contributions based on the benefit arising from the provision of a company car to the personal assistant.

	£
Company motor car	
18% + ((160 – 135) / 5) = 23% × £13,500	3,105
Private fuel provided (23% × £16,900)	3,887
Taxable benefits for Class 1A	6,992

Employer's Class 1A NICs	
(£6,992 at 12.8%)	895

(5) Class 1 primary contributions are levied on the personal assistant. However, it is Diane's responsibility to deduct the NICs from the assistant's salary and pay them to HMRC along with the Class 1 secondary contributions on the 19th of each month.

Employee's Class 1 NICs

(£15,800 – £5,715) x 11%	£1,109

Summary

	£
Class 2	125
Class 4	3,114
Class 1 secondary	1,291
Class 1A	895
Diane's total liability	5,425
Class 1 primary	1,109
Total amount Diane must account for to HMRC	6,534

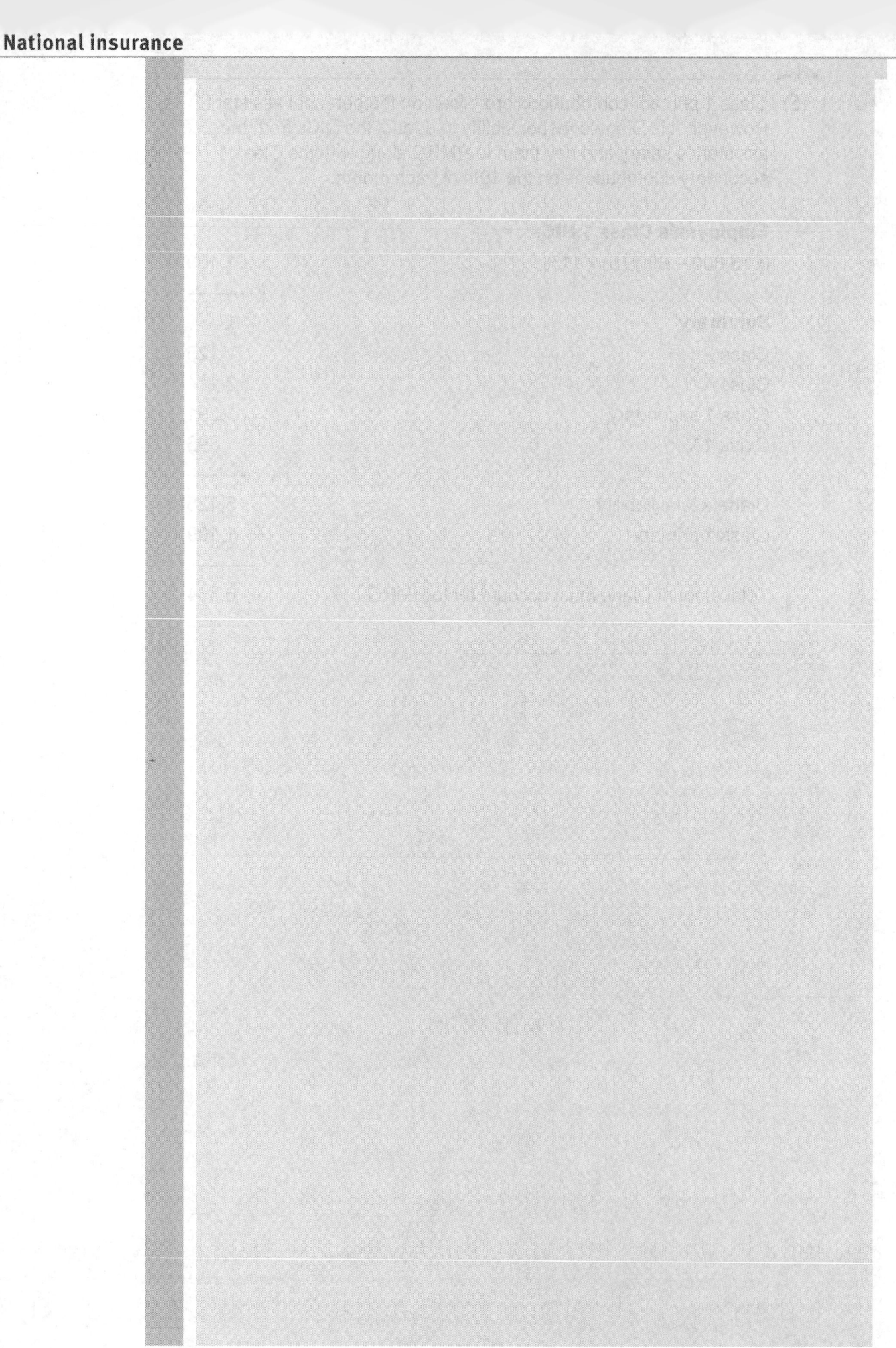

chapter

13

Tax administration for individuals

Chapter learning objectives

Upon completion of this chapter you will be able to:

- explain the self-assessment system as it applies to individuals
- state the time limits for notifying a liability and filing a return
- state the penalties for late submission of returns and notifying HMRC of liability
- list the information and records that the taxpayer needs to retain for tax purposes together with the retention period
- state the due dates for payment of tax under self-assessment
- compute payments on account and balancing payments/repayments
- state the effect of making a late payment on account/balancing payment
- calculate interest on overdue tax
- state the penalties that can be charged on a late payment of tax
- determine the time limits for key claims
- explain the circumstances in which HMRC can enquire into a self-assessment tax return
- describe the procedures for dealing with appeals and disputes
- explain the PAYE system
- list the key PAYE forms and explain their purpose.

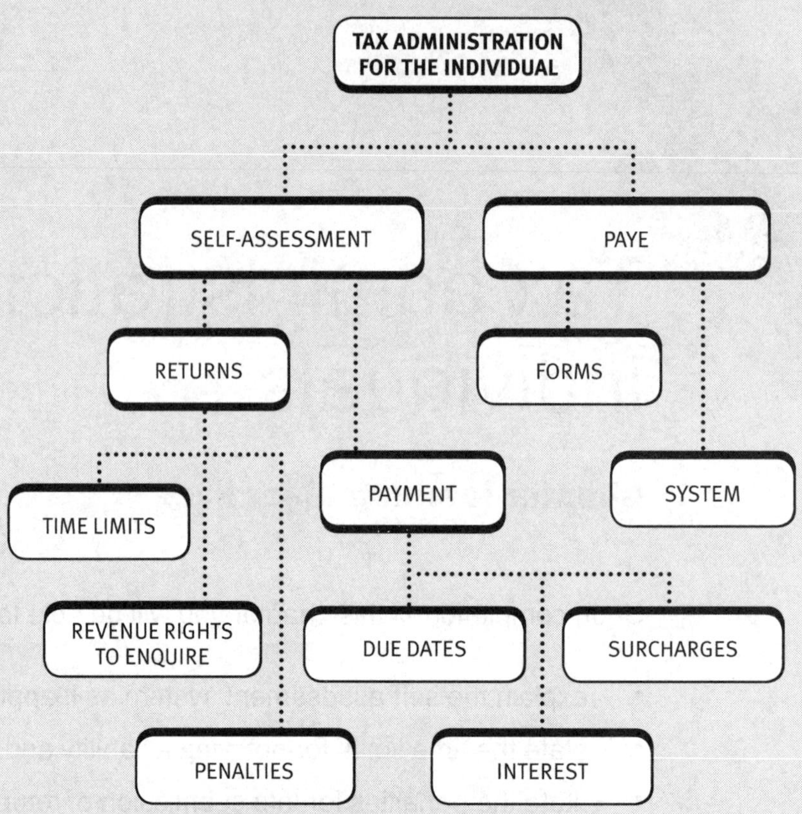

1 The self-assessment system

Introduction

The key aspects of the self-assessment system for the individual are as follows.

- The onus is placed on the taxpayer to calculate his or her own tax liability.
- The taxpayer will be sent a self-assessment tax return annually.
- Different filing deadlines exist for paper and electronic (online) returns.
- The final due date for the payment of the year's income tax, Class 4 NIC and CGT liability is 31 January following the end of the tax year to which it relates.
- Interim payments on account may be required on 31 January in the tax year and 31 July following the tax year for certain taxpayers.

The self-assessment tax return

The filing deadline for the 2009/10 self-assessment tax return depends on how the return is filed.

The filing deadline is the later of:

- 31 October 2010 for a paper return
- 31 January 2011 for an electronic (online) return (known as the filing date)
- three months after the issue of the return.

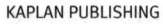

Content of tax return

The return comes in two parts.

- In the first part, the taxpayer needs to provide all the information required to calculate his tax liability for the year.

  This will be some or all of:
  - taxable income from all sources
  - any capital gains for the tax year concerned
  - reliefs and allowances.

  Self-employed people: The return includes a section for standardised accounts information.

  Employees: Generally pay their tax liability under PAYE and often a self-assessment tax return will not be required as there is no further tax liability.

  Partnerships: Although partners are dealt with individually, a partnership return will have to be completed to aid self-assessment on the individual partners. This will give details of the partners, and includes a partnership statement detailing the partnership's tax-adjusted income and how this is allocated between the partners.

- In the second part of the return, there is a section for the taxpayer to calculate his or her own tax liability (hence the term 'self-assessment'). This self-assessment is required even if the tax due is £Nil or if a repayment is due.

- Where a return is filed electronically a calculation of the tax liability is automatically provided as part of the online filing process.
- Where a paper return is submitted the taxpayer has the option of requesting HMRC to calculate the tax liability on behalf of the taxpayer provided the return is submitted by the 31 October deadline. The calculation by HMRC is treated as a self-assessment on behalf of the taxpayer.
- Note that in this situation, HMRC makes no judgement of the accuracy of the figures included in the return, but merely calculates the tax liability based on the information submitted.
- HMRC normally communicate with the taxpayer by issuing a statement of account.

  The statement of account sets out:

  – the tax charges
  – any charges of interest or surcharges (see later)
  – any payments already made by the taxpayer.

  The statement is not a notice to pay but merely a reminder of the taxpayer's indebtedness.

Amendments to the return

Either party may amend the return:

- HMRC may correct any obvious errors or mistakes within nine months of the date that the return is filed with them. These would include arithmetical errors or errors of principle. This does not mean that HMRC has necessarily accepted the return as accurate.
- The taxpayer can amend the return within 12 months of 31 January following the end of the tax year. For 2009/10, amendments must therefore be made by 31 January 2012. Note that the deadline is the same regardless of whether the return is filed on paper or electronically.

If an error is discovered at a later date then the taxpayer can make an error or mistake claim (see later) to recover any tax overpaid.

Notification of chargeability

Self-assessment places the onus on the taxpayers, therefore:

- Taxpayers who do not receive a return are required to notify HMRC if they have income or chargeable gains on which tax is due.
- The time limit for notifying HMRC of chargeability is six months from the end of the tax year in which the liability arises.
- Notification is not necessary if there is no actual tax liability. For example, if the income or capital gain is covered by allowances or exemptions.
- A standard penalty may arise for failure to notify chargability (see section 5).

Penalty for failure to submit a return

HMRC can impose fixed penalties and tax geared penalties for the failure to submit a return, depending on the length of the delay.

See section 5 for the detail on the penalties that can be imposed.

Determination of tax due if no return is filed

Where a self-assessment tax return is not filed by the filing date, HMRC may determine the amount of tax due. The impact of this is:

- The determination is treated as a self-assessment by the taxpayer.
- The determination can only be replaced by the actual self-assessment when it is submitted by the taxpayer.
- There is no appeal against a determination, which therefore encourages the taxpayer to displace it with the actual self-assessment.
- A determination can be made at any time within three years of the filing date.

Records

Taxpayers are required to keep and preserve records necessary to make a correct and complete return.

For a business (including the letting of property), the records that must be kept include:

- all receipts and expenses
- all goods purchased and sold
- all supporting documents relating to the transactions of the business, such as accounts, books, contracts, vouchers and receipts.

These taxpayers (i.e. the self-employed), must keep all their records (not just those relating to the business) until five years from 31 January following the end of the tax year. For 2009/10 records must therefore be retained until 31 January 2016.

For other taxpayers, they are likely to have many fewer records, but should keep evidence of income received such as dividend vouchers, P60s, copies of PIIDs and bank statements.

The records for these taxpayers must be retained until the later of:

- 12 months after the 31 January filing date (31 January 2012 for 2009/10)
- the date on which an enquiry into the return is completed
- the date on which it becomes impossible for an enquiry to be started.

A penalty may be charged for failure to keep or retain adequate records.

The maximum penalty is only likely to be imposed in the most serious cases such as where a taxpayer deliberately destroys his records in order to obstruct an HMRC enquiry.

See section 5 for the detail on penalties which can be imposed.

2 Payment of tax

Introduction

A taxpayer will be required to settle liabilities by 31 January following the end of the tax year for:

- income tax
- national insurance
- capital gains.

For 2009/10 this is 31 January 2011.

Payments on account

For certain taxpayers, payments on account (POAs) may also be required.

If the taxpayer had an income tax liability in the previous year in excess of any tax deducted at source, a POA is normally required for the following year.

The exceptions to this are if:

- the relevant amount for the previous year is less than £1,000 or
- more than 80% of the income tax liability for the previous year was met by deduction of tax at source.

The impact of these provisions is that most employed people will not have to make POAs, since at least 80% of their tax liability is paid through PAYE.

For those taxpayers who are required to make POAs, the dates for 2009/10 are:

- first POA – 31 January 2010
- second POA – 31 July 2010.

Any remaining liability is then settled on the 31 January 2011 due date.

The POAs are only for:

- income tax
- Class 4 National Insurance Contributions (NICs).

No POAs are ever required for capital gains tax.

The POAs are calculated using the previous year's tax liability. Therefore the POAs for 2009/10 are based on the tax liability for 2008/09.

This is referred to as the relevant amount and is calculated as:

	£
Total tax liability for the year	X
Less: Amounts paid at source (income tax and Class 4 NICs)	
e.g. PAYE, tax on bank and building society interest, dividend tax credits	(X)
	—
Relevant amount	X
	—

Note: No POAs are required if there is no relevant amount in the previous year. A taxpayer who commences self-employment on 1 May 2009 will not have to make POAs for 2009/10, since he or she will not have a relevant amount for 2008/09.

Example 1 - Payment of tax

Roderick, who is 47, is required to make payments on account of his 2009/10 tax liability. His income tax payable for 2008/09 was £5,100. Of this, £1,250 was collected via PAYE.

What are Roderick's POAs in respect of his 2009/10 income tax liability?

Answer to example 1

The relevant amount for the previous year is £3,850 (£5,100 – £1,250). As this is > £1,000 and > 20% of the total tax liability (20% × £5,100 = £1,020), POAs are required.

The amounts payable as POAs are based on an **equal** division of the relevant amount for the previous year's tax payable, hence £3,850 × 1/2 = £1,925.

Roderick is required to make two POAs of £1,925 on 31 January 2010 and 31 July 2010.

Test your understanding 1

Ahmed's tax liability for 2008/09 was as follows:

	£
Income tax	9,400
Less: Tax deducted at source	(2,100)
	7,300
Class 4 NIC	700
CGT	3,500
Total tax liability	11,500

Calculate the POAs for 2009/10.

Claims to reduce POAs

- At any time before 31 January following the tax year, a taxpayer can claim to reduce the POAs.
- A taxpayer would claim to reduce the POAs if he expected the actual income tax and Class 4 NIC liability (net of tax deducted at source) for 2009/10 to be lower than 2008/09.
- The claim must state the grounds for making the claim.

Following a claim to reduce POAs:

- The POAs will be reduced.
- Each POA will be for half the reduced amount, unless the taxpayer claims that there is no tax liability at all.
- If POAs are paid before a claim is made, then HMRC will refund the overpayment.

Incorrect claims to reduce POAs

A taxpayer should only claim to reduce POAs if the tax liability (net of tax deducted at source) for the current year is expected to be less than the POAs based on the previous years relevant amount.

In the event that the claim is incorrect and the actual tax liability for the current year turns out to be higher than the original POAs, then the following consequences arise:

- Interest will be charged on the tax underpaid.
- A penalty may be charged if a taxpayer fraudulently or negligently claims to reduce POAs. See section 5 for the detail on penalties which can be imposed.
- A penalty will not be sought in cases of innocent error. The aim is to penalise taxpayers who claim large reductions in payments on account without any foundation to the claim.

Balancing payments

The balancing payment is due on 31 January following the tax year. For 2009/10 this will be 31 January 2011.

The balancing payment is calculated as:

	£	£
Total tax liability for the year (Income tax, Class 4 NIC and CGT)		X
Less: Amounts deducted at source	X	
Less: POAs	X	
	—	(X)
		—
Balancing payment		X
		—

- It is possible that a balancing repayment will be due, in which case HMRC will repay the amount of tax overpaid.
- Where the amount of tax due changes as a result of an amendment to the self-assessment (by either the taxpayer or HMRC), any additional tax due must be paid within 30 days of the notice of amendment if this is later than the normal due date.

Example 2 - Payment of tax

Continuing the example of Roderick from above. You now learn that his final liability for 2009/10 has been agreed as £7,629. Of this amount £1,635 has been collected via the PAYE system.

State the total amount payable by Roderick on 31 January 2011 and what the payments relate to.

Answer to example 2

The payment made on 31 January 2011 will comprise two parts:

- the balancing payment for 2009/10
- first POA for 2010/11.

The balancing payment for 2009/10 will be based on the final liability for 2009/10 less amounts collected at source and the POAs already made.

	£
2009/10 IT liability	7,629
Less: PAYE	(1,635)
Less: POAs	(3,850)
	———
Final payment	2,144
	———

The first POA for 2010/11 will be 50% of the relevant amount using the 2009/10 position.

	£
2009/10 IT liability	7,629
Less: PAYE	(1,635)
Relevant amount	5,994

The first POA is (£5,994 × 1/2) = £2,997

Summary:	£
Balancing payment 2009/10	2,144
First POA 2010/11	2,997
Total payable 31 January 2011	5,141

Test your understanding 2

Peter's tax liability for 2009/10 is as follows:

	£
Income tax	10,800
Less: Tax deducted at source	(2,500)
	8,300
Class 4 NIC	800
CGT	4,600
Total tax liability	13,700

He made POAs of £8,000 in respect of 2009/10.

Identify the balancing payment to be made for 2009/10, the first POA for 2010/11 and state the due date for payment of both.

3 Interest and surcharges

The interest rate will be provided in the Tax Rates and Allowances section of the exam.

For the June 2010 and December 2010 exams, the rate to use is 2.5% pa.

Interest on tax paid late

Interest will automatically be charged if any tax is paid late.

Interest can arise in respect of:

- payments on account
- balancing payments
- any tax payable following an amendment to a self-assessment
- any tax payable following a discovery assessment.

The date from which interest runs depends on the payment made late:

- For POAs, interest runs from the due date of the relevant POA (i.e. 31 January in the tax year or 31 July following it).
- In other instances, interest runs from 31 January following the tax year to the date of payment. This is the case even if the tax was not actually due until a later date (i.e. following the amendment of the self-assessment).

The only exception to this is where the return was issued late, in which case the due date will be three months after the issue of the return if this is later.

Interest is charged on penalties from the date they become due to the date that they are paid. The actual interest charge is calculated for the period from the due date to the day before actual payment takes place.

Example 3 - Interest and surcharges

A taxpayer pays his 2009/10 POAs on 15 March 2010 and 10 August 2010. The balancing payment is paid on 15 April 2011.

Identify the payments that will attract interest and state the period for which interest will be charged.

Answer to example 3

Interest will be charged as follows:

- first POA: from 31 January 2010 to 14 March 2010
- second POA: from 31 July 2010 to 9 August 2010
- balancing payment: from 31 January 2011 to 14 April 2011.

Test your understanding 3

Rodney was due to make the following payments of tax for 2009/10.

Due Date	Payment	Actual date of payment
31 January 2010	£2,100	28 February 2010
31 July 2010	£2,100	31 August 2010
31 January 2011	£1,000	31 March 2011

Identify the periods for which interest will be charged. Calculate the amount of interest payable assuming a 2.5% interest rate.

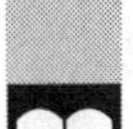

Interest on incorrect claims to reduce POAs

- Interest will be charged where an excessive claim is made to reduce POAs.
- The charge is based on the difference between the amounts actually paid and the amounts that should have been paid. The amount that should have been paid is the lower of:
  - the original POAs based on the relevant amount for the previous year
  - 50% of the final tax liability (excluding CGT, and net of tax deducted at source) for the current year.

Interest runs from the due dates of 31 January in the tax year and 31 July following the tax year to the date of payment. The date of payment will be 31 January following the tax year when the balancing payment is due, unless the balancing payment is made late.

Example 4 - Interest and surcharges

A taxpayer's relevant amount for 2008/09 is £5,000 (POAs for 2009/10 are therefore £2,500), but a claim is made to reduce the POAs to £1,000 each. These payments are made on time.

Subsequently the taxpayer identifies the actual tax liability (net of tax deducted at source) for 2009/10 to be £4,500. The correct balancing payment (i.e. £4,500 – £2,000 = £2,500) is paid on 31 January 2011.

Identify the amounts on which interest is to be charged and state the period(s) for which interest will be charged.

Answer to example 4

POAs should have been reduced to £2,250 (£4,500 × 1/2) rather than £1,000. Interest will therefore be charged as follows:

- on £1,250 from 31 January 2010 to 30 January 2011
- on £1,250 from 31 July 2010 to 30 January 2011.

Example 5 - Interest and surcharges

Herbert's POAs for 2009/10 based on his income tax liability for 2008/09 were £4,500 each. However, Herbert made a claim to reduce these amounts to £3,500. He made his interim POAs for 2009/10 as follows:

Payment	£	Date
First POA	3,500	29 January 2010
Second POA	3,500	12 August 2010

When Herbert's eventual liability for 2009/10 was agreed, it was as follows:

Income tax liability	£10,000
Capital gains	£2,500

Herbert paid the balance of the tax due £5,500 on 19 February 2011.

Identify the amounts on which interest is to be charged and state the period(s) for which interest will be charged.

Answer to example 5

POAs should not have been reduced, therefore the amounts that should have been paid, on each of the due dates was £4,500.

First POA:

£3,500 is paid on time.

Interest charge therefore only levied on £1,000 that should also have been paid.

Levied for the period 31 January 2010 to 18 February 2011.

Second POA:

£3,500, as well as being the wrong amount, was also paid late.

On £3,500, interest charged 31 July 2010 to 11 August 2010.

On the additional £1,000, interest levied for the period 31 July 2010 to 18 February 2011.

On balancing payment:

Income tax of £9,000 (£4,500 × 2) has been dealt with above, so it is only the remaining £1,000 that will incur an interest charge, from 31 January 2011 to 18 February 2011.

Capital gains tax of £2,500 incurs interest from 31 January 2011 to 18 February 2011.

Interest paid on overpayments of tax

Interest may be paid by HMRC on any overpayment of tax. The rate changes throughout the year according to the economic circumstances.

The interest rate will be provided in the Tax Rates and Allowances section of the exam.

For the June 2010 and December 2010 exams the rate to use is Nil%.

If applicable, interest runs from the later of:

- the due date
- the actual payment date

to the date of repayment.

Where interest is paid, it is only paid on the amount of tax that should have been paid (i.e. deliberate overpayments will not attract interest).

Surcharge on unpaid tax

Interest on tax paid late is not a penalty, since it merely compensates for the advantage of paying late. Therefore, to further encourage compliance, surcharges can also be imposed where income tax, Class 4 NIC or CGT is paid late.

The surcharge does not apply to POAs.

Surcharges are calculated as follows:

- Where a balancing payment is not paid until more than 28 days after the due date (31 January following the tax year), a surcharge equal to 5% of the tax unpaid is imposed.
- A further 5% surcharge arises if the tax is still unpaid after six months.

Where additional tax becomes due as a result of an amendment to a self-assessment, a surcharge is only imposed if the additional tax is not paid within 28 days of the due date for the amendment (30 days after the amendment).

Note: This last provision differs from interest that runs from the normal due date; 31 January following the tax year.

There is also an interest charge on the surcharge, if the surcharge is not paid within 30 days of the date that it is imposed.

A surcharge may be mitigated by HMRC, for example if there is a reasonable excuse for the non-payment of the tax. Insufficiency of funds is not a reasonable excuse.

Example 6 - Interest and surcharges

A taxpayer's balancing payment due for 2009/10 is £5,000. Only £1,200 of this was paid on 31 January 2011.

Set out the interest and surcharges that will be payable and state the implication of continued non-payment of the liability.

Answer to example 6

Interest

Interest will be charged on £3,800 from 31 January 2011 to the date of payment.

Surcharges

A surcharge of £190 (£3,800 at 5%) will be due if the tax of £3,800 is not paid by 28 February 2011.

A further surcharge of £190 will be due if the tax is not paid by 31 July 2011.

In the event that either of the surcharges are not paid within 30 days of their issue, interest will be assessed on these amounts as well.

Test your understanding 4

Rowena's final tax payable (after credits but before payments on account) is computed for 2009/10 as follows:

Income tax	£6,000
Capital gains tax	£3,000

POAs of £4,000 in total were made on the relevant dates. The balance of the tax due was paid as follows:

Income tax	1 March 2011
Capital gains tax	1 April 2011

Calculate the interest and surcharges due. Assume the rate of interest on unpaid tax is 2.5%.

4 Claims

Introduction

- A claim for a relief, allowance or repayment must be quantified at the time that the claim is made. For example, if loss relief is claimed, then the amount of the loss must be stated.
- Wherever possible the taxpayer must include claims in his or her self-assessment tax return.

Claims for earlier years

Certain claims will relate to earlier years. The most obvious example of this is the claiming of loss relief for earlier years.

The basic rule is that such a claim is:

- established in the later year
- calculated based on the tax liability of the earlier year.

This means that the tax liability for the earlier year is not adjusted. Instead, the tax reduction resulting from the claim will be set off against the tax liability for the later year. The logic behind this is that it avoids re-opening self-assessments for earlier years.

If the taxpayer does make a claim in the return for the later year, the HMRC will refund the tax due.

As the claim is only quantified by reference to the earlier year, POAs that are based on the relevant amount for the earlier year, will not change.

Example 7 - Claims for earlier years

A taxpayer's relevant amount for 2008/09 is £4,400. In 2009/10 the taxpayer makes a trading loss of £1,000, and makes a claim to offset this against his total income of 2008/09.

Explain how the taxpayer will receive the tax refund arising as a result of the relief for the loss arising in 2009/10.

Answer to example 7

The taxpayer's POAs for 2009/10 are £2,200 (£4,400 × 1/2), and these will not change as a result of the loss relief claim.

The tax refund due will be calculated at the taxpayer's marginal income tax rate(s) for 2008/09. The tax refund due will either be set off against the 2009/10 tax liability, thereby affecting the balancing payment on 31 January 2011, or if there is insufficient tax left owing, HMRC will make a refund.

Error or mistake claims

Where an assessment is excessive due to an error or mistake in a return, the taxpayer can claim relief.

The claim must be made within four years of the end of the tax year concerned. For 2009/10 an error or mistake claim must be made by 5 April 2014.

A claim can be made in respect of errors made, and mistakes arising from not understanding the law.

5 Enquiries into returns

HMRC's right of enquiry

HMRC have the right to enquire into the completeness and accuracy of any self-assessment tax return.

The enquiry may be made as a result of any of the following:

- a suspicion that income is undeclared
- deductions being incorrectly claimed
- other information in HMRC's possession
- being part of a random review process.

Additional points:

- HMRC do not have to state a reason for the enquiry and are unlikely to do so.
- An enquiry can be made even if HMRC calculated a taxpayer's tax liability.
- HMRC must give written notice before commencing an enquiry.
- The written notice must be issued within 12 months of the date the return is filed with HMRC. Once this deadline is passed, the taxpayer can normally consider the self-assessment for that year as final.

Enquiry procedures

HMRC can demand that the taxpayer produces any or all of the following:

- documents
- accounts
- other written particulars
- full answers to specific questions.

The information requested by HMRC should be limited to that connected with the return.

The taxpayer has 30 days to comply with the request. An appeal can be made against the request.

The enquiry ends when HMRC gives written notice that it has been completed. The notice will state the outcome of the enquiry.

The closure notice must include either:

- confirmation that no amendments are required
- HMRC's amendments to the self-assessment.

The taxpayer has 30 days to appeal against any amendments by HMRC. The appeal must be in writing.

Discovery assessment

HMRC must normally begin enquiries into a self-assessment return within 12 months of the date the return is filed, however a discovery assessment can be raised at a later date to prevent the loss of tax.

The use of a discovery assessment is restricted where a self-assessment has already been made:

- Unless the loss of tax is due to fraud or negligence, a discovery assessment cannot be raised where full disclosure was made in the return, even if this is found to be incorrect.
- HMRC will only accept that full disclosure has been made if any contentious items have been clearly brought to their attention – perhaps in a covering letter or in the 'white space' on the tax return.
- Information lying in the attached accounts will not constitute full disclosure if its significance is not emphasised.

- Only a taxpayer who makes full disclosure in the self-assessment tax return therefore has absolute finality 12 months after the date the return is filed.

The time limit for issuing a discovery assessment is:

- four years from the end of the tax year (2009/10 by 5 April 2014)
- increased to six years if there is a careless error (2009/10 by 5 April 2016), or
- 20 years if there is a deliberate error or failure to notify a chargeability to tax (2009/10 by 5 April 2030).

A discovery assessment may be appealed against.

Information and inspection powers

- HMRC have unified powers to undertake compliance checks with one set of powers to inspect business records, assets and premises.
- The new regime covers income tax, capital gains tax, corporation tax, VAT and PAYE.
- HMRC will also have a single approach across all taxes to asking taxpayers for supplementary information, based on formal information notices with a right of appeal. They can also request information from third parties provided either the taxpayer or the new First tier Tax Tribunal agrees (see section 6).

Penalties

In addition to interest on the late payment of tax, HMRC can impose penalties.

Standard penalty

HMRC is standardising penalties across taxes and for different offences. For 2010 exams, the standard penalty applies to two areas:

- inaccuracies in returns – all taxes
- failure to notify liability to tax – income tax, CGT, corporation tax, VAT and PAYE/NIC.

The penalty is calculated as a percentage of 'potential lost revenue' which is generally the tax unpaid as a result of the error or failure to notify.

Taxpayer behaviour	Maximum penalty (% of revenue lost)
Genuine mistake	No Penalty
Failture to take reasonable care	30%
Serious or deliberate understatement	70%
Serious or deliberate understatement with concealment	100%

Penalties can be reduced where the taxpayer makes full disclosure and cooperates with HMRC to establish the amount of tax unpaid.

Offence	Penalty
Failure to notify chargeability to tax within 6 months of the end of the tax year	Standard penalty Based on a % of tax unpaid on 31 January following the end of the tax year
Late submission of income tax return	
– within 6 months of due date – between 6-12 months of filing date	£100 fixed penalty Further £100 fixed penalty These penalties cannot exceed the amount of tax due per the return
– delay > 12 months	Additional penalty of up to 100% of the tax due per the return
– upon direction by the tribunal	Additional £60 per day from : date of direction to: date return submitted
Failing to notify HMRC of an under assessment to tax	Standard penalty Based on a % of the amount of under assessed tax
Deliberately supplying false information to, or deliberately withholding information from, a person with the intention of making that person's document inaccurate	Standard penalty Based on a % of tax unpaid as a result of the error

Submission of an incorrect tax return or accounts leading to: – an understatement of tax liability – a false or inflated statement of a loss – a false or inflated claim for repayment of tax (see Note below)	Standard penalty Based on a % of tax unpaid as a result of the error
Fraud or negligence on claiming reduced payments on account	£ POAs actually paid X Less POAs if claims not made (X) — X —
Failure to keep and retain required records	Up to £3,000 per year of assessment

Note: HMRC may consider charging a penalty where tax has been under-assessed because of a person's failure to send a return, or where a person has discovered an inaccuracy in a document but has not taken reasonable steps to tell HMRC.

6 Appeals

Introduction

A taxpayer can appeal against a decision made by HMRC, but they must do so within 30 days of the disputed decision.

Most appeals are then settled amicably by discussion between the taxpayer and HMRC.

However, if the taxpayer is not satisfied with the outcome of the discussions, they can proceed in one of two ways:

- Request that their case is reviewed by another HMRC officer, or
- Have their case referred to an independent Tax Tribunal.

If the taxpayer opts to have their case reviewed but disagrees with the outcome, they can still send their appeal to the Tax Tribunal.

The taxpayer must also apply to postpone all or part of the tax charged. Otherwise they will have to pay the disputed amount.

Tax tribunals

The Tax Tribunal is an independent body administered by the Tribunals Service of the Ministry of Justice. Cases are heard by independently appointed tax judges and/or panel members. Each panel is appointed according to the needs of the case.

There are two tiers (layers) of Tax Tribunal system:

- First-tier Tribunal, and
- Upper Tribunal.

The First-tier Tribunal will be the first instance tribunal for most issues. They deal with:

- *Default paper cases:* simple appeals (e.g. against a fixed penalty) – will usually be disposed of without a hearing provided both sides agree.
- *Basic cases:* straightforward appeals involving a minimal exchange of paperwork in advance of a short hearing.
- *Standard cases:* appeals involving more detailed consideration of issues and a more formal hearing.
- *Complex cases:* some complex appeals may be heard by the First Tier however they will usually be heard by the Upper Tribunal.

The Upper Tribunal will mainly, but not exclusively, review and decide appeals from the First–tier Tribunal on a point of law.

In addition, they will also deal with:

- Complex cases requiring detailed specialist knowledge and a formal hearing – cases involving long and complicated issues, points of principle and large financial amounts which do not go through the First-tier Tribunal stage.
- Judicial review work delegated from the High Court and Court of Session.
- The enforcement of decisions, directions and orders made by Tribunals.

Hearings are held in public and decisions are published.

A decision of the Upper Tribunal may be appealed to the Court of Appeal. However, the grounds of appeal must always relate to a point of law.

The overriding objective of the tribunal rules is to allow cases to be dealt with fairly and justly. The tribunal system aims to avoid delays and unnecessary expense.

Costs of appeal

Each party (i.e. the taxpayer and HMRC) will normally pay their own costs.

However the Tribunal can award costs in two main situations:

- against a party who has acted unreasonably in bringing or conducting the case, and
- in complex cases (unless the taxpayer has requested that the proceedings be excluded from potential liability for costs or expenses).

Note that the costs of appeal incurred by the taxpayer are not allowable expenses for tax purposes.

7 The PAYE system

Introduction

Pay as you earn (PAYE) is the system used for collecting income tax and national insurance at source from the earnings paid to employees:

- All payments of earnings assessable as employment income are subject to deduction of tax under the PAYE system.
- In many cases, the PAYE system removes the need to file a formal self-assessment tax return since the correct amount of tax will have been deducted from earnings.
- All employers making payments of earnings are required to deduct the appropriate amount of tax from each payment (or repay over-deductions) by reference to PAYE tax tables.
- The aim of the tax tables is for the tax deducted from payments to date to correspond with the correct proportion to date of the total tax liability (after allowances and reliefs) of the employee for the year.

Coding notice

To enable the employer to match the tax collected with the particular tax affairs of the individual taxpayer, HMRC issues a tax coding.

The system enables different amounts of tax to be collected from different taxpayers according to their personal circumstances.

Coding notice

- From the information supplied in his or her tax return, each employee is sent a coding notice that sets out the total reliefs and allowances available to him for the year.
- The last digit is removed to arrive at the code number shown. Thus, allowances of £6,475 become 647.
- The employer is also notified of the code number.
- Using this code number and a set of tax tables, the employer can calculate the correct amount of tax each week or month.
- Most code numbers issued to the employer carry a suffix of which the most usual is L. The letter L denotes that just the ordinary personal allowance of £6,475 has been given.
- These letters are added in order to simplify the revision of codes, e.g. when the personal allowance is increased from one tax year to the next, all code numbers with the suffix L can easily be increased by the employer, so that PAYE can continue to operate effectively.
- Some code numbers carry a K prefix. This indicates that the deductions, such as benefits, to be made from allowances actually exceed the allowances. The code number is effectively 'negative'.
- Where an employee has not been allocated a code number (perhaps because the individual was previously self-employed), the employer must deduct tax under PAYE in accordance with an emergency code that reflects only the personal allowance (i.e. Code 647L). This code is applied until the correct code number is supplied by HMRC.

Tax code calculation

Allowances	£	**Deductions**	£
Personal allowance	X	Benefits	X
Allowable expenses	X	Adjustment for underpaid tax (must be less that £2,000)	X
Adjustment for overpaid tax	X	Other income	X
	—		—
Total allowances	X	Total deductions	X
	—		—

The tax code is:

(Total allowances less total deductions) × 1/10

The answer is then rounded down to the nearest whole number.

Calculation of deductions

PAYE is calculated on a tax deductions working sheet (P11), using tax tables provided by HMRC.

The tax tables are as follows.

Pay adjustment tables:	Based on an employee's tax code, this set of tables shows the cumulative amount of tax-free pay to which an employee is entitled for each week or month of the year.
Taxable pay tables:	Deducting tax-free pay from pay gives a figure for taxable pay. The taxable pay tables can then be used to calculate the amount of income tax due.

The tax is calculated for any given pay week or month on a cumulative basis (i.e. the tax for, say month five, is the difference between the cumulative total tax due at the end of month five compared with the cumulative total due at the end of month four).

Payments to HMRC

Employers are generally required to make monthly payments of income tax and NIC to HMRC as follows:

- The income tax and NIC that the employer deducts during each tax month is due for payment to HMRC not later than 14 days after the month ends.
- The tax month runs from sixth to fifth of each month.
- Therefore the payment due date is the 19th of each month.
- Employers whose average monthly payments of PAYE and NICs are less than £1,500 in total are allowed to make quarterly, rather than monthly, payments. Payments are due by the 19th of the month following the quarters ending 5 July, 5 October, 5 January and 5 April.
- Employers with 250 or more employees must make their monthly PAYE payments electronically on the 22nd of each month.

8 Key PAYE forms

Introduction

To standardise the correspondence with HMRC, specific forms are issued for use in certain circumstances. This ensures all appropriate information is gathered and simplifies the process.

They key forms that you are required to know are:

Form	Purpose of use	Timing
P45	When employee leaves	Ongoing with staffing changes
P46	When new employee joins without P45	Ongoing with new starters
P35	Year end summary	Annually following end of tax year
P14 – P60	Year end summary	Annually following end of tax year

Procedures on leaving or joining

Procedure to be adopted when an employee leaves

When an employee leaves an employment the PAYE system is interrupted. Forms P45 must be completed for each employee in order that either:

- a new employer can carry on making PAYE deductions using the appropriate code and cumulative totals from the last employment
- the employee can claim a tax repayment.

Procedure to be adopted when an employee joins

The operation of the PAYE system depends upon having a tax code for each employee. The form P45 details his or her tax code, pay to date and tax to date and will allow the new employer to operate PAYE for the employee's pay.

Where form P45 cannot be produced the employee has to complete form P46 to identify the individual's circumstances so that the appropriate amount of tax can be deducted.

Employers with 50 or more employees must file P45s and P46s online.

End-of-year procedure

The P35 and P14 returns will need to be completed at the end of each tax year.

Employers with 50 or more employees must file their end of year returns online.

P35 employer's annual statement, declaration and certificate

This has to be submitted by 19 May, and performs the role of:

- an overall summary of tax and NIC deducted by the employer for the year
- a questionnaire to ensure compliance with PAYE arrangements
- a declaration and certificate to be signed by the employer confirming that all year-end returns have been completed.

P14 – P60 certificate of pay and tax deducted

Not later than 19 May the employer must send the first two copies of the form (P14) to HMRC, showing for each employee:

- Employee's National Insurance number
- Employer's name and address
- Personal details
- Total earnings for the year
- Final PAYE code
- Total income tax deducted for the year
- Total NIC for the year.

The third part of the form (P60) is given to the employee by 31 May in order to complete the employment pages of his self-assessment return.

9 Chapter summary

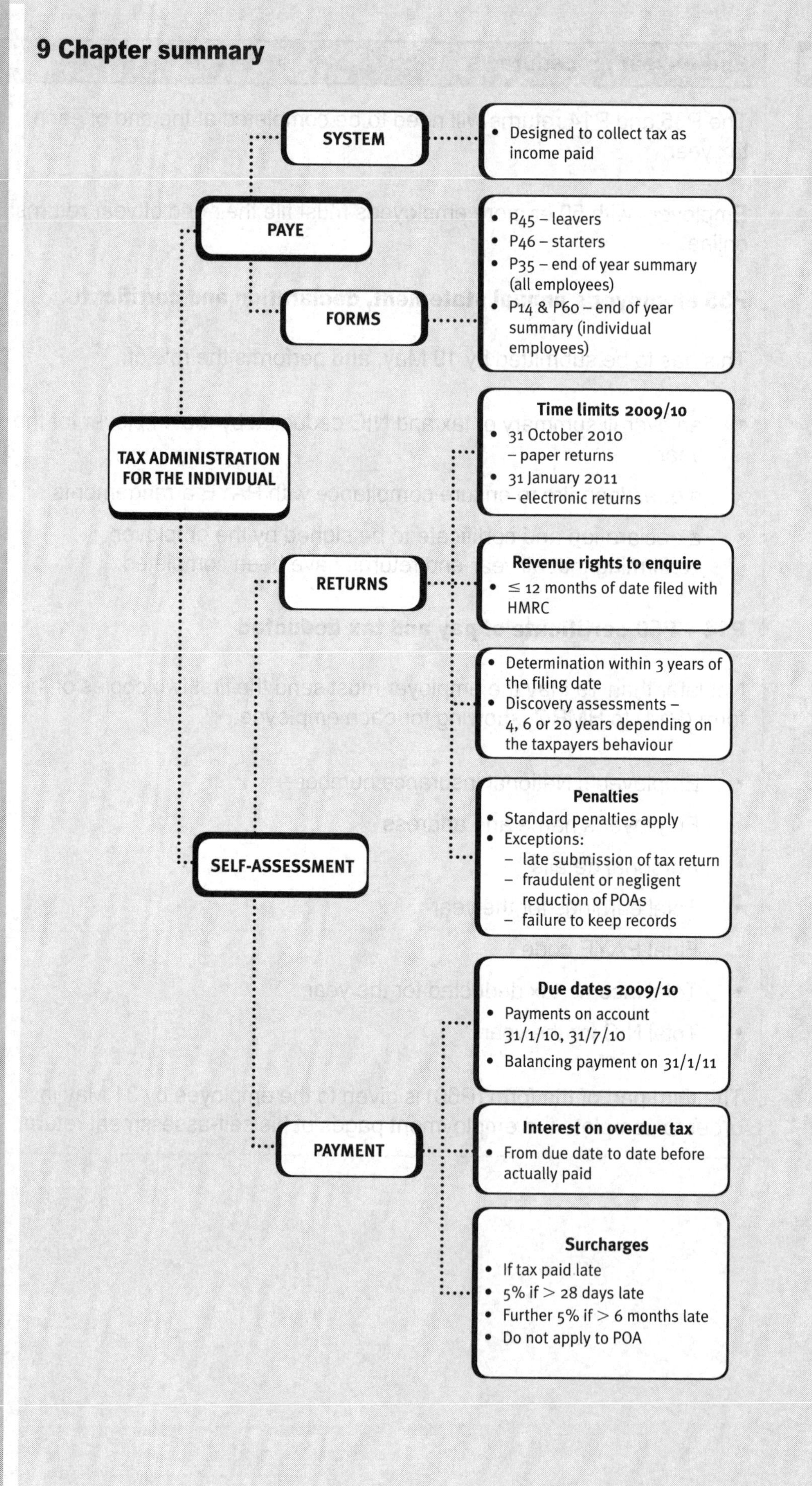

TAX ADMINISTRATION FOR THE INDIVIDUAL
PAYE
SYSTEM
• Designed to collect tax as income paid
FORMS
• P45 – leavers
• P46 – starters
• P35 – end of year summary (all employees)
• P14 & P60 – end of year summary (individual employees)
SELF-ASSESSMENT
RETURNS
Time limits 2009/10
• 31 October 2010 – paper returns
• 31 January 2011 – electronic returns
Revenue rights to enquire
• ≤ 12 months of date filed with HMRC
• Determination within 3 years of the filing date
• Discovery assessments – 4, 6 or 20 years depending on the taxpayers behaviour
Penalties
• Standard penalties apply
• Exceptions:
– late submission of tax return
– fraudulent or negligent reduction of POAs
– failure to keep records
PAYMENT
Due dates 2009/10
• Payments on account 31/1/10, 31/7/10
• Balancing payment on 31/1/11
Interest on overdue tax
• From due date to date before actually paid
Surcharges
• If tax paid late
• 5% if > 28 days late
• Further 5% if > 6 months late
• Do not apply to POA

Test your understanding answers

Test your understanding 1

Ahmed

The relevant amount is £8,000 (£7,300 + £700).

As this is > £1,000 and > 20% of the total tax liability (20% × (£9,400 + £700) = £2,020)), POAs are required.

POAs will be due for 2009/10 as follows:

31 January 2010 (£7,300 + £700 = £8,000 × 1/2)	£4,000
31 July 2010	£4,000

Note: No POAs of capital gains tax are ever required and it is ignored in the calculations.

Test your understanding 2

Peter

	£
Total tax liability	13,700
Less: POAs	(8,000)
Balancing payment due 31 January 2011	5,700

The balancing payment comprises:

	£
Income tax and National Insurance (£8,300 + £800 – £8,000)	1,100
CGT	4,600
Balancing payment	5,700

The first POA for 2010/11 will be 50% of the relevant amount using the 2009/10 position.

	£
2009/10 IT liability (after deducting PAYE)	8,300
Class 4 NIC	800
Relevant amount	9,100

The first POA is (£9,100 × 1/2) = £4,550

Summary:

	£
Balancing payment 2009/10	5,700
First POA 2010/11	4,550
Total payable on 31 January 2011	10,250

Test your understanding 3

Rodney

Periods on which interest is charged:

On first POA	31 January 2010 – 27 February 2010	28 days
On second POA	31 July 2010 – 30 August 2010	31 days
On final payment	31 January 2011 – 30 March 2011	59 days

Interest payable:

On first POA	(£2,100 × 2.5% × 28/365) = £4.03
On second POA	(£2,100 × 2.5% × 31/365) = £4.46
On final payment	(£1,000 × 2.5% × 59/365) = £4.04

Test your understanding 4

Rowena

The relevant date for balancing payments is 31 January 2011.

No POAs are ever required for CGT.

The amounts due were therefore as follows:

31 January 2011	Income tax	£2,000
	Capital gains tax	£3,000

Interest will run as follows:

Income tax	£2,000 from 31 January 2011 to 28 February 2011, i.e. 1/12 × 2.5% × £2,000 = £4.17
CGT	£3,000 from 31 January 2011 to 31 March 2011, i.e. 2/12 × 2.5% × £3,000 = £12.50

In addition a surcharge is due on the CGT and income tax (as they are more than 28 days late) of 5% of £5,000 = £250.

Total payable (£4.17 + £12.50 + £250) = £266.67.

The surcharge may be reduced if HMRC accept there was a reasonable excuse for late payment.

chapter

14

Computation of gains and tax payable

Chapter learning objectives

Upon completion of this chapter you will be able to:

- identify the persons and the transactions that are liable to UK tax on capital gains
- define 'residence' and 'ordinary residence' for an individual and state its relevance for capital gains tax
- identify which assets are exempt
- understand how to calculate the gain on the disposal of an asset
- calculate the chargeable gain on the disposal of an asset for an individual
- demonstrate how capital losses can be relieved against gains for an individual
- calculate the net chargeable gains on assets after losses
- compute the amount of capital gains tax payable.

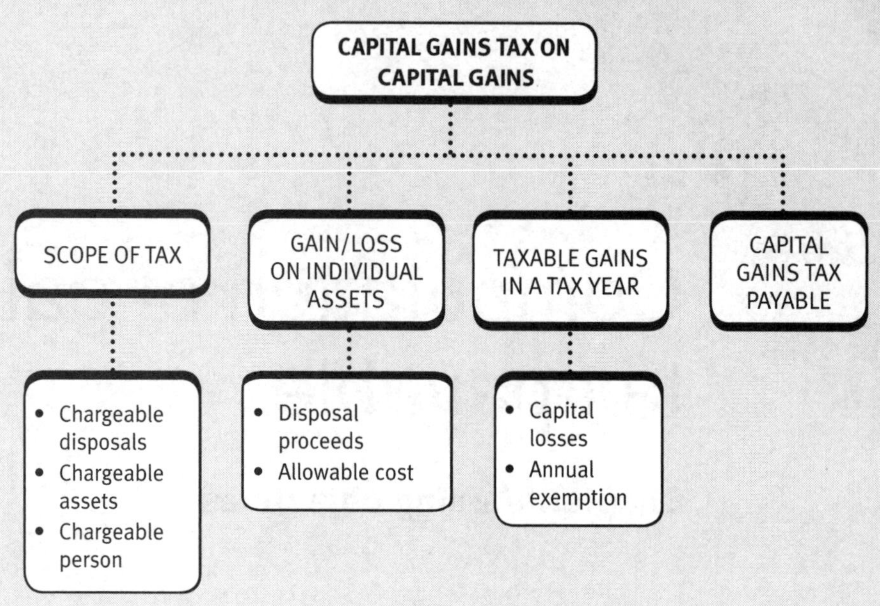

1 Introduction

This and the following three chapters deal with the way in which **individuals** are subject to tax on their capital gains.

The taxation of capital gains is an important topic as it will be the focus of question three, for **20 marks**, in the examination. Questions one and two may also contain an element of capital gains.

2 Scope of capital gains tax

Capital gains tax (CGT) is charged on gains arising on **chargeable disposals** of **chargeable assets** by **chargeable persons**.

Chargeable persons

Chargeable persons include individuals and companies.

In these CGT chapters we are only concerned with disposals by individuals.

- Only individuals who are either:
  - UK resident or
  - UK ordinarily resident

  in the tax year in which the disposal takes place are subject to capital gains tax on their gains.

- Chargeable individuals are subject to CGT on all disposals of assets, regardless of where in the world the assets are situated.
- An individual who is neither UK resident nor UK ordinarily resident does not pay UK CGT on any assets, not even those situated in the UK.

Definition of residence and ordinary residence

The definition of residence and ordinary residence for CGT is the same as for income tax purposes (see chapter 2).

Broadly, an individual will be a UK resident in a tax year if he is physically present in the UK for a period of six months or more.

An individual's ordinary residence is the place where the individual normally resides as opposed to his place of occasional residence.

Chargeable disposal	Exempt disposal
The following are treated as chargeable disposals: (i) sale or gift of the whole or part of an asset (ii) exchange of an asset (iii) loss or total destruction of an asset (iv) receipts of a capital sum derived from an asset, for example: • compensation received for damage to an asset • receipts for the surrender of rights to an asset.	Exempt disposals include: (i) disposals as a result of the death of an individual (ii) gifts to charities.

Chargeable assets	Exempt assets
All forms of capital assets, wherever situated, are chargeable assets. Common examples include: • Freehold land and buildings • Goodwill • Some types of leases • Unquoted shares • Quoted shares • Certain types of chattels - chapter 15 Note: Chattels are tangible moveable assets e.g. furniture, plant and machinery	Exempt assets include: • Motor vehicles (including vintage cars) • Main residence • Cash • Certain types of chattels - chapter 15 • Investments held within an ISA • Qualifying corporate bonds (QCBs) • Gilt-edged securities • National Savings Certificates • Foreign currency for private use • Debtors • Trading stock • Prizes and betting winnings.

Note that exempt assets are outside the scope of CGT. Consequently:

- gains are not taxable
- losses are not allowable.

Test your understanding 1

Which of the following disposals may give rise to a capital gain?

- **Sale of shares in an unquoted trading company.**
- **Gift of antique painting.**
- **Sale of 13% Treasury stock 2012.**
- **Exchange, with a friend, of a house for an apartment.**
- **Sale of a motor car to brother at less than market value.**
- **Gift of a London flat by an individual who is neither resident nor ordinarily resident in the UK.**

3 Calculation of capital gain/loss on individual disposals

An individual is subject to CGT on the total taxable gains arising on the disposal of all assets in a tax year.

The following steps should be carried out to compute the chargeable gains tax payable by an individual for a tax year:

Step 1 Calculate the chargeable gains/allowable loss arising on the disposal of each chargeable asset separately

Step 2 Calculate the net chargeable gains arising in the tax year = (chargeable gains less allowable losses)

Step 3 Deduct capital losses brought forward

Step 4 Deduct the annual exemption = taxable gains

Step 5 Calculate the CGT payable at a flat rate of 18%.

Pro forma – individual

The following basic CGT pro forma should be used to complete Step 1.

For each disposal by an individual calculate the chargeable gain/allowable loss as follows:

	£	£
Disposal proceeds		X
Less: Allowable selling costs		(X)
Net disposal proceeds		X
Less: Allowable expenditure		
Cost of acquisition	X	
Incidental costs of acquisition	X	
Additional (capital) enhancement expenditure	X	
		(X)
Chargeable gain/(allowable loss)		X/(X)

Net disposal proceeds

The disposal proceeds used in the computation is normally the sale proceeds received.

However, market value may be used in certain circumstances instead of the actual consideration.

- Market value is substituted for actual proceeds either because:
  - the deal was not made at arm's length (e.g. a gift)
  - the law assumes that it was not made at arm's length (e.g. transfers between connected parties).
- An individual is connected with family members, business partners and any company that he controls. For this purpose family members are:
  - ancestors, lineal descendants and their spouses/civil partners
  - brothers, sisters and their spouses/civil partners
  - his or her spouse/civil partner
  - the relatives (as above) of his or her spouse/civil partner.

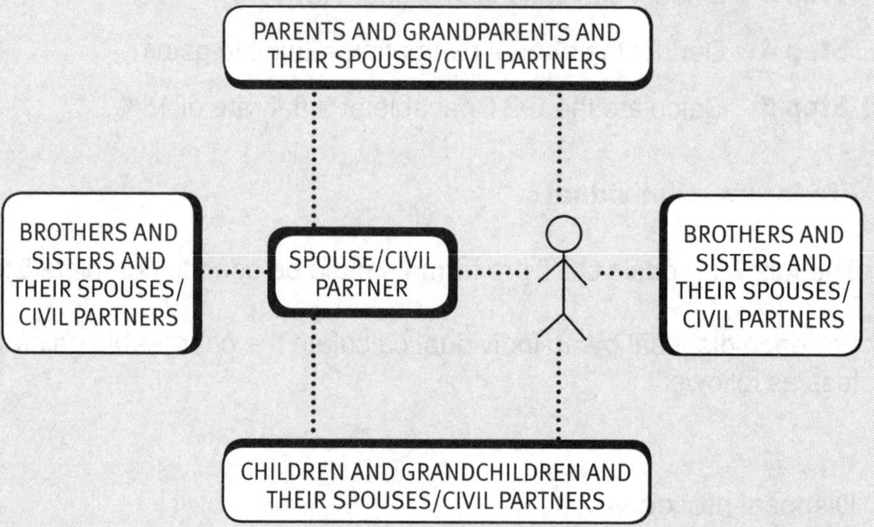

- Incidental costs arising on disposal are deducted from the gross proceeds, e.g. auctioneer's fees, estate agent fees.

Allowable expenditure

The types of expenditure that rank as allowable deductions are:

- cost of acquisition (e.g. purchase cost)
- expenditure on enhancing the value of the asset (improvement expenditure)
- expenditure incurred to establish, preserve or defend the taxpayer's title to the asset
- incidental costs arising on the acquisition of the asset.

Where an individual acquires an asset where the previous owner was required to use the asset's market value in calculating their own gain (e.g. gift of an asset) then that same market value is used by the current owner as their cost of acquisition.

Where an individual inherits an asset on death, the cost of acquisition when they later dispose of the asset is the asset's market value at the date of the death (i.e. probate value).

Example 1 - Calculation of net chargeable gains

On 1 May 2009 Sergei sold an antique vase for £12,000 and a painting for £20,000. He incurred auctioneer's fees of 1% of the proceeds. He acquired both assets on 1 July 1991 for £13,000 and £5,000, respectively.

Calculate the net chargeable gain arising in 2009/10.

Answer to example 1

	Vase	Painting
	£	£
Sale proceeds	12,000	20,000
Less: Allowable selling costs (1% auctioneer's fees)	(120)	(200)
Net sale proceeds	11,880	19,800
Less: Allowable expenditure		
Cost of acquisition	(13,000)	(5,000)
Chargeable gain/(allowable loss)	(1,120)	14,800
Net chargeable gain (£14,800 – £1,120)	13,680	

Test your understanding 2

On 1 May 2009, Margaret sold a holiday villa to her sister for £25,000. Its market value at that date was £100,000. Margaret had acquired the villa on 1 June 1997 for £20,000 and had paid legal fees on acquisition of £500. On 1 May 2002, she had added a conservatory at a cost of £10,000.

Calculate the chargeable gain arising on the sale of the villa.

Test your understanding 3

Amanda sold a holiday cottage for £75,000 on 13 August 2009. It cost £53,500 in May 1999 and was extended in September 2003 at a cost of £16,000. The estate agent and solicitor fees for the purchase totalled £2,300 and for the sale totalled £5,400.

She also sold her grandmother's engagement ring for £12,000. She had inherited the ring on the death of her grandmother in August 2005 when the ring was valued at £9,000.

Calculate the net chargeable gain arising in 2009/10.

4 Calculation of CGT payable

An individual is subject to capital gains tax on the total taxable gains arising on the disposal of all assets in a tax year.

The following proforma covers Steps 3 to 5 in the procedure to calculate the CGT payable by an individual.

Proforma capital gains tax payable computation – 2009/10

	£
Net chargeable gains for the tax year	X
Less: Capital losses brought forward (see later)	(X)
	X
Less: Annual exemption (2009/10)	(10,100)
Taxable gains	X
CGT payable (18% x taxable gains)	X

Annual exemption

Every individual is entitled to an annual exemption for each tax year.

- For 2009/10 the annual exemption is £10,100.
- If an individual's taxable gains for the tax year are:
  - ≤ £10,100; they are not chargeable to tax
  - > £10,100; they are chargeable to tax on the excess
- If the annual exemption is not utilised in any particular tax year, then it is wasted. It cannot be carried forwards or backwards against capital gains of another tax year.

For the purpose of the examination, **taxable gain** means the **chargeable gains after deducting capital losses and the annual exemption**.

Capital losses

Current year capital losses

Capital losses arising on assets in the current tax year are set off:

- against chargeable gains arising in the same tax year
- to the maximum possible extent (i.e. they cannot be restricted to avoid wasting all or part of the annual exemption).

Any unrelieved/unused capital losses are carried forward to offset against net chargeable gains in future years.

Brought forward capital losses

The maximum amount of brought forward losses that can be set off against gains in any tax year is restricted to the amount required to reduce the total net chargeable gains in the tax year to the level of the annual exemption.

Example 2 - Calculation of taxable gains in the tax year

Tom and Jerry made capital gains and allowable losses for the years 2008/09 and 2009/10 as set out below.

	Tom	Jerry
2008/09	£	£
Chargeable gains	12,000	4,000
Allowable losses	8,000	7,000
2009/10		
Chargeable gains	13,000	11,300
Allowable losses	2,000	1,000

Calculate the taxable gains for Tom and Jerry for both 2008/09 and 2009/10 and the amount of any losses carried forward.

Tom – 2008/09	£
Chargeable gains	12,000
Less: Allowable losses – current year	(8,000)
Net chargeable gains	4,000

Net chargeable gains are covered by the annual exemption. There are no losses to carry forward to 2009/10.

Tom – 2009/10	£
Chargeable gains	13,000
Less: Allowable losses – current year	(2,000)
Net chargeable gains	11,000
Less: Annual exemption	(10,100)
Taxable gains	900

Tom is taxed on gains of £900 in 2009/10.

Jerry – 2008/09	£
Chargeable gains	4,000
Less: Allowable losses – current year	(4,000)
Net chargeable gains	Nil

Jerry is unable to use his 2008/09 annual exemption since his gains are all covered by current year losses. He has losses of £3,000 (£7,000 – £4,000) to carry forward to 2009/10.

Jerry – 2009/10	£
Chargeable gains	11,300
Less: Allowable losses – current year	(1,000)
Net chargeable gains in the tax year	10,300
Less: Losses brought forward (2008/09)	(200)
	10,100
Less: Annual exemption	(10,100)
Taxable gains	Nil

Jerry used £200 of his losses brought forward, to reduce his chargeable gains to the level of the annual exemption. He still has losses of £2,800 (£3,000 – £200) to carry forward to 2010/11.

Test your understanding 4

Fred and Barney made chargeable gains and allowable losses for the years 2008/09 and 2009/10 as set out below.

	Fred	Barney
2008/09	£	£
Chargeable gains	15,000	5,000
Allowable losses	10,000	9,000
2009/10		
Chargeable gains	21,400	13,300
Allowable losses	11,000	2,500

Calculate the taxable gains for Fred and Barney for both 2008/09 and 2009/10 and the amount of any losses carried forward at the end of 2009/10.

5 Payment of CGT

CGT is due as follows:

- On 31 January following the tax year (i.e. for 2009/10 payment must be made by 31 January 2011).
- No payments on account are ever made.

Test your understanding 5

Jade sold an investment property on 1 May 2009 for £650,000. She had acquired the building for £80,000 in June 1995 and had extended it at a cost of £30,000 in June 1997.

Jade also disposed of a painting on 1 June 2009 for £20,000, incurring auctioneer's fees of 1%. She had acquired the painting for £35,000 in April 1997.

Jade had capital losses brought forward of £16,000.

Calculate Jade's capital gains tax payable for 2009/10 and state the due date for payment.

6 Chapter summary

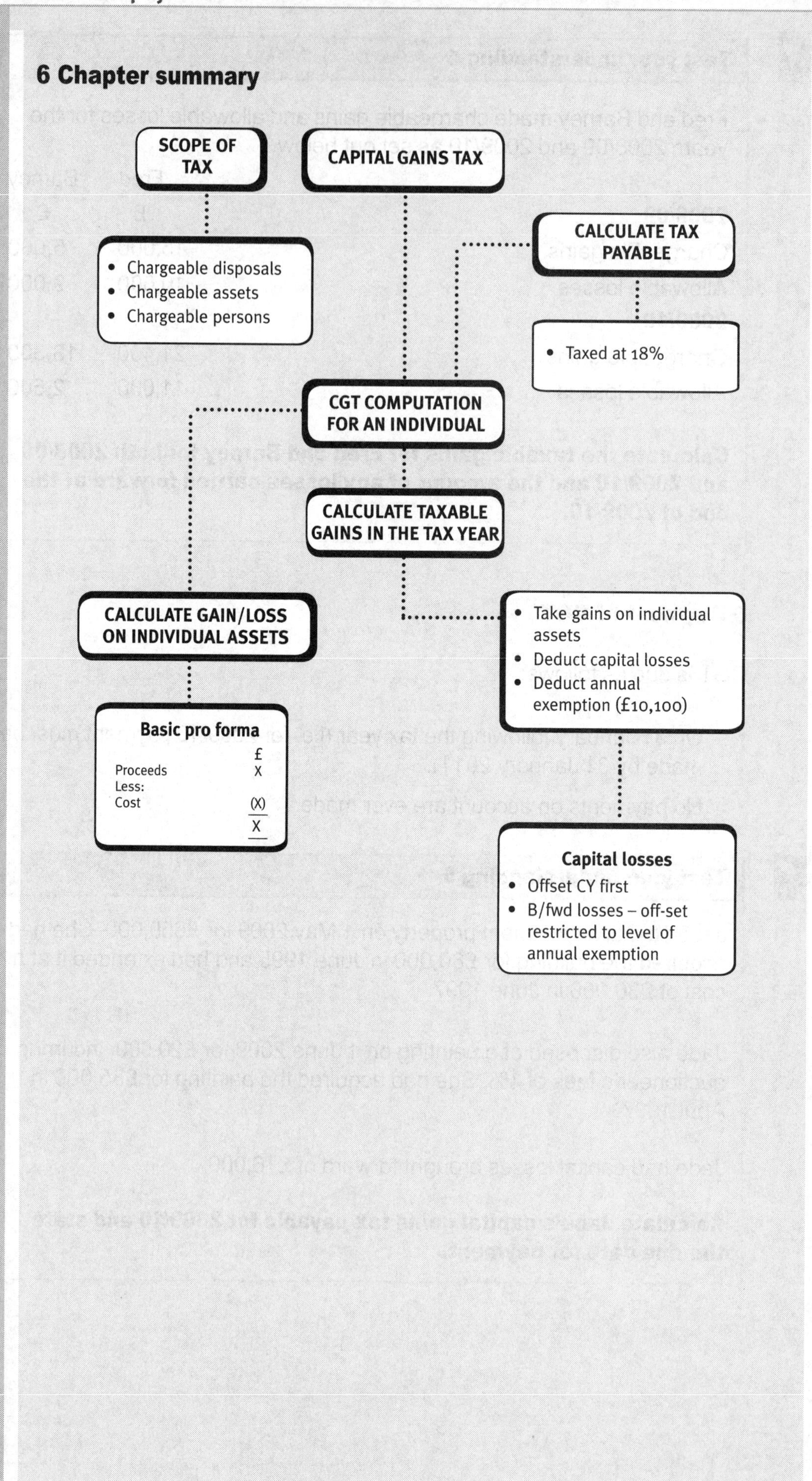

Test your understanding answers

Test your understanding 1

Not chargeable	Chargeable disposals
Sale of 13% Treasury stock 2012 (gilt-edged security – exempt asset)	Sale of shares in an unquoted trading company
Sale of a motor car to brother at less than market value (motor vehicle – exempt asset)	Gift of antique painting
Gift of a London flat by an individual who is neither resident nor ordinarily resident in the UK (not a chargeable individual)	Exchange, with a friend, of a house for an apartment

Test your understanding 2

Margaret

	£	£
Market value (Note 1)		100,000
Less: Allowable expenditure		
Cost of acquisition	20,000	
Incidental costs of acquisition – legal fees	500	
Enhancement expenditure (Note 2)	10,000	
		(30,500)
Chargeable gain in 2009/10		69,500

Notes

(1) Market value is substituted for actual proceeds as the sale was to a connected person (Margaret's sister) and is therefore deemed to not be an 'arm's length transaction'.

(2) The conservatory is allowable expenditure as it enhanced the value of the villa.

Test your understanding 3

Amanda

2009/10	Cottage £	Ring £
Sale proceeds	75,000	12,000
Less: Allowable selling costs	(5,400)	(Nil)
Net sale proceeds	69,600	12,000
Less: Allowable expenditure		
Cost of acquisition	(53,500)	
Incidental costs of acquisition	(2,300)	
Extension	(16,000)	
Probate value		(9,000)
Chargeable gain/(allowable loss)	(2,200)	3,000
Net chargeable gain (£3,000 – £2,200)	800	

Test your understanding 4

Fred

2008/09	£
Chargeable gains	15,000
Less: Allowable losses – current year	(10,000)
Net chargeable gains	5,000

Net chargeable gains are covered by the annual exemption. There are no losses to carry forward to 2009/10.

2009/10

	£
Chargeable gains	21,400
Less: Allowable losses – current year	(11,000)
Net chargeable gains	10,400
Less: Annual exemption	(10,100)
Taxable gains	300

Fred is taxed on gains of £300 in 2009/10.

Barney

2008/09

	£
Chargeable gains	5,000
Less: Allowable losses – current year	(5,000)
Net chargeable gains	Nil

Barney is unable to use his 2008/09 annual exemption since his gains are all covered by current year losses. He has losses of £4,000 (£9,000 – £5,000) to carry forward to 2009/10.

2009/10

	£
Chargeable gains	13,300
Less: Allowable losses – current year	(2,500)
Net chargeable gains for year	10,800
Less: Losses brought forward (2008/09)	(700)
	10,100
Less: Annual exemption	(10,100)
Taxable gains	Nil

Barney used £700 of his losses brought forward, to reduce his chargeable gains to the level of the annual exemption. He still has losses of £3,300 (£4,000 – £700) to carry forward to 2010/11.

Test your understanding 5

Jade

Capital gains tax computation – 2009/10

	£	£
Investment property		
Sale proceeds	650,000	
Less: Allowable expenditure		
Cost of acquisition	(80,000)	
Enhancement expenditure	(30,000)	
Chargeable gain		540,000
Painting		
Sale proceeds	20,000	
Less: Allowable selling costs	(200)	
Net sale proceeds	19,800	
Less: Allowable expenditure		
Cost of acquisition	(35,000)	
Allowable loss		(15,200)
Net chargeable gains arising in the tax year		524,800
Less: Capital losses brought forward		(16,000)
Net chargeable gains		508,800
Less: Annual exemption		(10,100)
Taxable gains		498,700
Capital gains tax payable (£498,700 x 18%)		89,766
Due date of payment		31 January 2011

chapter

15

Computation of gains: Special rules

Chapter learning objectives

Upon completion of this chapter you will be able to:

- show the tax treatment of a capital asset when the transfer is between spouses or registered civil partners
- calculate the chargeable gain when there is a part disposal of an asset
- define a wasting and non-wasting chattel
- identify when chattels and wasting assets are exempt
- compute the chargeable gain/allowable loss when a chattel is disposed of
- calculate the chargeable gain/allowable loss when a chargeable wasting asset is disposed of
- explain why the disposal of plant and machinery does not create a capital loss
- identify the tax treatment where an asset is lost/destroyed
- identify the tax treatment where an asset is damaged.

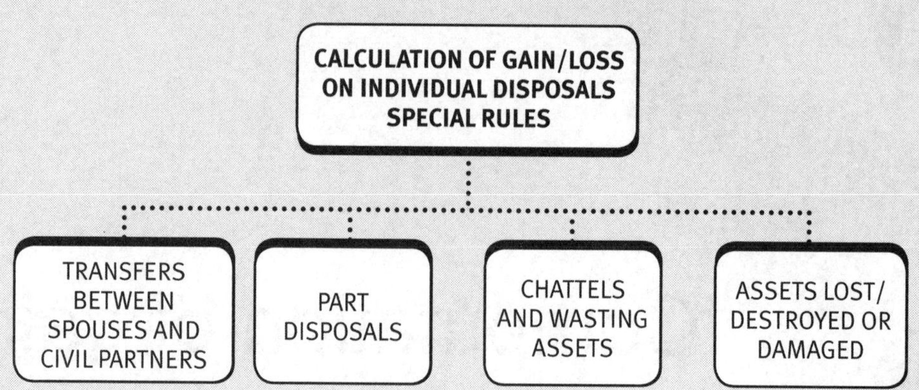

1 Introduction

The basic pro forma for calculating gains on the disposals of assets is adapted by special rules in the following circumstances:

- transfers between spouses and civil partners
- part disposals
- chattels and wasting assets
- assets lost or destroyed
- damaged assets.

2 Transfers between spouses and civil partners

Where an asset is transferred between spouses or civil partners:

- no gain or loss arises on the transfer
- any actual proceeds are ignored
- the transferor is deemed to dispose of the asset at its acquisition cost
- the deemed proceeds of the transferor are treated as the deemed acquisition cost of the transferee (i.e. the recipient spouse acquires the assets at its original acquisition cost).

However note that these rules only apply whilst the spouses/civil partners are living together (i.e. not separated).

Example 1 - Transfers between spouses and civil partners

David purchased some jewellery in August 1995 for £50,000. In June 2009 he gave it to his wife Victoria when it was worth £200,000.

Calculate the deemed sale proceeds of David's disposal and state Victoria's deemed acquisition cost.

Answer to example 1

David is deemed to have transferred the asset at its acquisition cost so that no gain or loss arises on the transfer.

The deemed proceeds are therefore £50,000 and Victoria's deemed acquisition cost is the same as David's deemed proceeds (i.e. £50,000).

Subsequent disposal by transferee

On a subsequent disposal of the transferred asset by the transferee, the deemed acquisition cost (often referred to as the base cost of the asset) is the original acquisition cost by the first spouse (i.e.deemed proceeds on the nil gain, nil loss transfer).

Example 2 - Subsequent disposal

Jack acquired a holiday cottage for £29,175 on 1 September 1987 and transferred it to his wife, Jill, on 31 August 2008. Jill sold the cottage to a third party on 31 January 2010 for £42,000.

Compute the chargeable gain on Jill's disposal in January 2010.

Answer to example 2

	£
Sale proceeds	42,000
Less: Deemed acquisition cost (Base cost)	(29,175)
Chargeable gain	12,825

Test your understanding 1

John acquired a warehouse for £100,000 on 1 September 1994. On 1 May 2008 he gave the warehouse to his wife, Tania, when it was worth £300,000. Tania sold the warehouse for £350,000 on 1 July 2009.

Tania had no other capital disposals in 2009/10, but has capital losses brought forward of £11,300.

Calculate Tania's capital gains tax payable in 2009/10.

Planning opportunities

Married couples and civil partners can transfer assets between them at no tax cost (i.e. the assets are transferred at no gain/no loss). This provides opportunities to minimise their total capital gains tax liability.

They can transfer assets between them to maximise the use of:

- each individual's annual exemption
- capital losses.

Example 3 - Planning opportunities

Adam, who is married to Kerry, made three chargeable disposals in the tax year 2009/10, as follows:

Asset 1	Chargeable gain	£10,000
Asset 2	Chargeable gain	£20,000
Asset 3	Chargeable gain	£14,800

(a) **Calculate Adam's CGT payable for 2009/10.**

(b) **Advise how savings could have been made by the couple, and calculate the revised CGT payable by the couple assuming they had taken your advice.**

Answer to example 3

(a) **Adam's CGT payable – 2009/10**

	£
Asset 1	10,000
Asset 2	20,000
Asset 3	14,800
Total chargeable gains	44,800
Less: Annual exemption	(10,100)
Taxable gain	34,700
CGT payable (£34,700 × 18%)	6,246

(b) **Advice**

As a married couple, Kerry and Adam can transfer assets between themselves at nil gain/nil loss (i.e. at no tax cost).

Accordingly, they should consider transferring assets between themselves to ensure that they both use their annual exemptions.

If Adam had transferred Asset 3 to Kerry, then the gain on the asset would be reduced by her annual exemption of £10,100, leaving only £4,700 chargeable to CGT.

Adam's revised CGT payable for the year is as follows:

	£
Asset 1	10,000
Asset 2	20,000
	30,000
Less: Annual exemption	(10,100)
Taxable gain	19,900
CGT payable (£19,900 × 18%)	3,582

Kerry's CGT payable would be:

	£
Asset 3	14,800
Less: Annual exemption	(10,100)
Taxable gain	4,700
CGT payable (£4,700 x 18%)	846
Total CGT payable (£3,582 + £846)	4,428
Tax saving (£6,246 – £4,428)	1,818

Alternative calculation:

Use of Kerry's annual exemption (£10,100 x 18%)	1,818

3 Part disposals

When there is a part disposal of an asset, we need to identify how much of the original cost of the asset relates to the part of the asset disposed of.

- The allowable expenditure of the part of the asset disposed of is calculated using the following formula:

  Cost x A / (A + B)

  Where:
  A = Value of the part disposed of
  B = Market value of the remainder at the time of the part disposal.

- The allowable expenditure, calculated using the formula, is then used in the basic capital gains tax computation as normal.

Example 4 - Part disposal

Yayha acquired 20 acres of land in March 1988 for £6,000. On 1 June 2009, he disposed of 8 acres for £8,000. The value of the remaining 12 acres at this date was £15,000.

On 1 September 2009, Yayha sold the reminder of the land for £18,000.

Calculate the chargeable gains arising on the disposals of land in 2009/10.

Answer to example 4

1 June 2009 disposal

	£
Sale proceeds	8,000
Less: Deemed cost of part disposed of	
£6,000 × £8,000/(£8,000 + £15,000)	(2,087)
Chargeable gain	5,913

Note that the number of acres is irrelevant in calculating the cost of the land disposed of.

Always use the (A/A + B) formula, which uses the **value** of the asset disposed of and retained.

1 September 2009 disposal

	£
Sale proceeds	18,000
Less: Deemed cost of the remainder (£6,000 – £2,087 (above))	(3,913)
Chargeable gain	14,087

Test your understanding 2

Jacob bought 10 acres of land for £8,000 in August 1992. He sold 3 acres of the land for £20,000 in January 2010. At that time the remaining land was worth £60,000.

In March 2010 Jacob sold the remaining acres for £75,000.

Calculate the capital gains tax payable for 2009/10 and state the due date of payment.

Test your understanding 3

Gemma bought an investment property in May 2000 for £50,000. On 1 July 2006 she disposed of part of the land attached to the property for £40,000. The value of the property and the remaining land at this date was £100,000.

On 1 August 2009 Gemma sold the property and remaining land for £200,000.

Calculate the capital gains tax payable for 2009/10.

4 Chattels and wasting assets

It is important to be able to identify a chattel and a wasting asset as there are special rules for calculating the gain or loss arising on them.

Chattels

Chattels are defined as tangible moveable property (e.g. a picture or table).

Note that the asset must be:

- moveable – therefore a building is not a chattel
- tangible – therefore shares are not chattels.

Wasting assets

A wasting asset is an asset with a predictable life not exceeding 50 years.

Chattels may be wasting or non-wasting as follows.

	Wasting chattels	**Non-wasting chattels**
Expected life	Not exceeding 50 years	More than 50 years
Examples	Greyhound Boat Plant and machinery Racehorse	Antiques Jewellery Paintings

Plant and machinery is deemed to have a useful life of less than 50 years and is therefore **always** a wasting chattel (but see below).

Chattels – exempt disposals

Certain disposals of chattels are exempt from capital gains tax as follows.

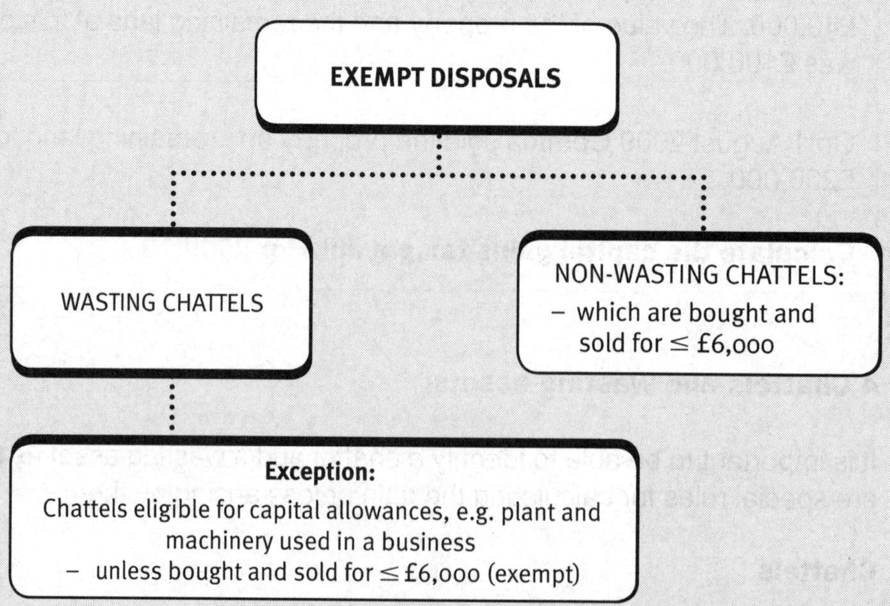

Example 5 - Chattels

Mr Windsor has made the following disposals in 2009/10.

(1) A painting was sold in July 2009 for £5,600. He originally bought it in February 1990 for £3,500.

(2) A piece of land, which he bought in April 2005 for £2,000 (an investment property), was sold in September 2009 for £5,000.

(3) He sold a vintage car for £25,000 in June 2009 that had originally cost him £5,500 in June 1999.

(4) He bought a moveable crane for £20,000 in August 1992, which he used in his haulage business. He sold the crane for £10,000 in January 2010.

(5) An antique vase was sold in August 2009 for £10,000. It originally cost £8,000 in April 2000.

(6) In May 2009 he sold his half share in a racehorse for £5,000, which he had acquired in June 2001 for £4,000.

For each of the above transactions, state whether they are chattels (wasting or non-wasting) and whether they will be subject to capital gains tax.

Answer to example 5

(1) The painting is a non-wasting chattel which was bought and sold for less than £6,000. This is therefore an exempt disposal.

(2) Land is not moveable property and is therefore not a chattel. The disposal is therefore chargeable to capital gains tax.

(3) Cars are always exempt assets for capital gains tax purposes.

(4) The crane is a wasting chattel which is eligible for capital allowances as it is used in a business. The disposal is therefore **not** an exempt disposal.

(5) The antique vase is a non-wasting chattel. As it was bought and sold for more than £6,000 it is chargeable to capital gains tax.

(6) A racehorse is a wasting chattel and is therefore exempt from capital gains tax.

Test your understanding 4

Which of the following disposals are exempt from, and which are chargeable to, capital gains tax?

(1) Gift of a necklace which was bought for £4,000. Its market value at the date of the gift was £7,000.

(2) Sale of shares in a quoted trading company for £2,000 which were bought for £1,000.

(3) Sale of a motor car, for £5,000, which was used for business purposes. It was acquired for £6,000.

(4) Sale of a boat for £20,000, which was acquired for £15,000.

(5) Sale of a painting for £5,000, which was acquired for £1,000.

(6) Sale of a greyhound for £10,000, which was acquired for £5,000

Non-wasting chattels

When a non-wasting chattel is disposed of the following rules apply:

(1) asset bought **and** sold for £6,000 or less = exempt

(2) asset bought and sold for more than £6,000 = the chargeable gain is computed in the normal way

(3) asset either bought or sold for £6,000 or less = then special rules apply:

- **Sold at a gain**

  Calculate the chargeable gain as normal but the gain cannot exceed a maximum of:

  5/3 × (gross disposal consideration – £6,000)

- **Sold at a loss**

  Sale proceeds are deemed to be £6,000.

The above rules are referred to as **the £6,000 rule**.

	Cost	
	£6,000 or less	**More than 6,000**
Sale proceeds: **£6,000 or less**	Exempt	Allowable loss but proceeds are deemed = £6,000
More than £6,000	Taxed on lower of: • Normal calculation. • 5/3 × (gross proceeds – £6,000)	• Normal CGT computation

Example 6 - Non-wasting chattel

Andrew sold a picture on 1 February 2010 for £6,600. He had acquired it on 1 March 2004 for £3,200.

Calculate the chargeable gain arising on the disposal.

Answer to example 6

As the picture is a non-wasting chattel, that was sold for more than £6,000, the disposal is not an exempt disposal.

	£
Sale proceeds	6,600
Less: Cost	(3,200)
Chargeable gain	3,400

Gain cannot exceed: 5/3 × (£6,600 – £6,000) = £1,000

Example 7 - Non-wasting chattel

Brian bought an antique table for £6,500 in September 2001 and sold it for £5,600 in December 2009. He incurred £250 to advertise it for sale.

Calculate the allowable loss arising, if any.

Answer to example 7

This is a disposal of a non-wasting chattel that cost more than £6,000 but which was sold for less than £6,000. The disposal is not an exempt disposal but the allowable loss is restricted as follows:

	£
Deemed sale proceeds	6,000
Less: Expenses of sale	(250)
Cost	(6,500)
Allowable loss	(750)

Test your understanding 5

Marjory bought two antique tables in March 1985 each for £1,000. She sold them both in June 2009 for £6,400 and £13,600 respectively.

Calculate the chargeable gains arising on the disposal of the two antique tables.

Test your understanding 6

Brian bought a picture in April 1983 for £10,000 plus purchase costs of £500. The market for the artist's work slumped and Brian sold the picture on 10 April 2009 for £500, less disposal costs of £50.

Calculate the allowable loss on disposal of the picture.

Test your understanding 7

During January 2010, Sally sold four paintings, which she had acquired in May 1999. Details were as follows.

Painting	Cost	Proceeds
	£	£
1	2,000	7,000
2	8,000	4,500
3	3,000	5,500
4	7,000	9,500

Calculate Sally's net chargeable gains for 2009/10.

Chattels – summary

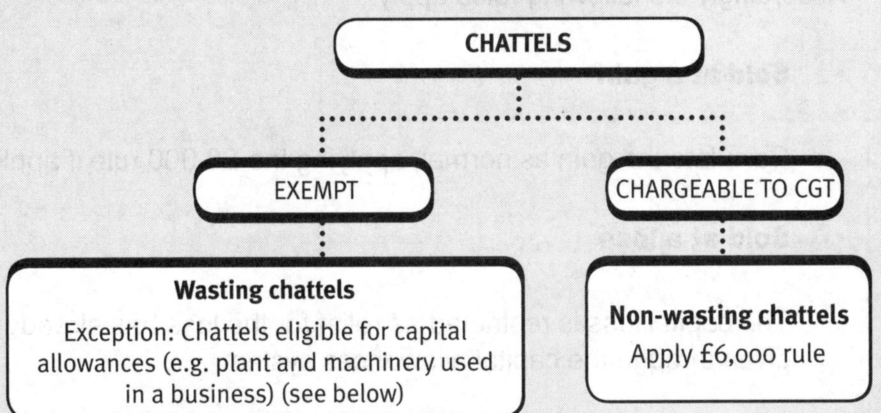

Wasting assets

Wasting assets (i.e. predictable life of less than 50 years) can be split into the following categories:

- Chattels not eligible for capital allowances = exempt from CGT.
- Chattels eligible for capital allowances.
- Other wasting assets.

Chattels eligible for capital allowances

For example, plant and machinery that has been used for the purposes of a trade.

Where capital allowances have been claimed on an asset we must take into account the tax relief for the actual cost of the asset, given through the capital allowances system, as follows:

- Where a trader acquires a machine for £10,000 and sells it for £7,000 he will receive capital allowances (net of any balancing adjustments) of £3,000. The net allowances match the actual £3,000 cash loss that he has realised.
- Where a trader acquires a machine for £10,000 and sells it for £14,000, proceeds of £10,000 will be used in calculating the net capital allowances (proceeds in the capital allowance computation are restricted to lower of sales proceeds and original cost). In this case, as the trader has made a gain the capital allowances given will be £nil (net of any balancing adjustments) and the gain will be subject to capital gains tax.

Accordingly the following rules apply:

- **Sold at a gain**

  Calculate the gain as normal, applying the £6,000 rule if applicable.

- **Sold at a loss**

  The capital loss is restricted as relief for the loss has already been given through the capital allowances system.

  In the capital loss computation, the net capital allowances given (i.e. net of balancing charges on disposal) are deducted from the asset's allowable expenditure.

Plant and machinery sold at a loss, which is eligible for capital allowances, results in a no gain/no loss situation for capital gains tax purposes.

Example 8 - Plant and machinery - Sarah

Sarah bought a machine for use in her trade for £35,000 in May 2006. In October 2009 she decided to replace it and sold the old machine for £40,000.

Calculate the chargeable gain arising on the disposal in October 2009.

Answer to example 8

The asset was sold at a gain. The capital gain is therefore calculated as normal.

	£
Sale proceeds	40,000
Less: Cost	(35,000)
Chargeable gain	5,000

Example 9 - Plant and machinery - Fred

Fred bought a machine for use in his trade for £35,000 in April 2002. In October 2009 he decided to replace it and sold the old machine for £26,500.

Calculate the chargeable gain or allowable loss arising.

Answer to example 9

Fred has sold the machine for a real loss of £8,500 (£35,000 – £26,500). He is compensated for this loss through the capital allowances system (i.e. he receives net capital allowances of £8,500 during his period of ownership of the machine).

The allowable capital loss computation is therefore adjusted to reflect the relief for the loss already given through the capital allowances system as follows:

	£	£
Sale proceeds		26,500
Less: Cost	35,000	
Less: Net capital allowances	(8,500)	
		(26,500)
Allowable loss		Nil

Other wasting assets

This category covers wasting assets that are not chattels (e.g. copyright). The allowable expenditure on these assets is deemed to waste away over the life of the asset.

Consequently, when a disposal is made:

- the allowable expenditure is restricted to take account of the asset's natural fall in value
- the asset's fall in value is deemed to occur on a straight line basis over its predictable useful life

- the allowable cost is calculated as:

$$C - \left[\frac{P}{L} \times C\right]$$

Where
P = the disposer's period of ownership
L = the asset's predictable life
C = the cost of the asset

Example 10 – Other wasting assets - Ian

On 1 February 2000 Ian bought a wasting asset at a cost of £24,000. It had an estimated useful life of 30 years. He sold the asset for £38,000 on 1 February 2010.

Calculate the chargeable gain or allowable loss arising.

Answer to example 10

	£
Sale proceeds	38,000
Less: Allowable element of acquisition cost (W)	(16,000)
Chargeable gain	22,000

Working: Allowable element of acquisition cost

	£
Cost	24,000
Less: Wasting asset depreciation (10/30 × £24,000)	(8,000)
	16,000

Example 11 – Other wasting assets - Jan

On 1 March 2005 Jan bought a wasting asset at a cost of £19,000. It had an estimated useful life of 40 years. She sold the asset for £30,000 on 1 March 2010.

Calculate the chargeable gain or allowable loss arising.

Answer to example 11

	£	£
Sale proceeds		30,000
Less: Purchase cost	19,000	
Less: Wasting asset depreciation (5/40 × £19,000)	(2,375)	
Allowable element of acquisition cost		(16,625)
Chargeable gain		13,375

Wasting assets – summary

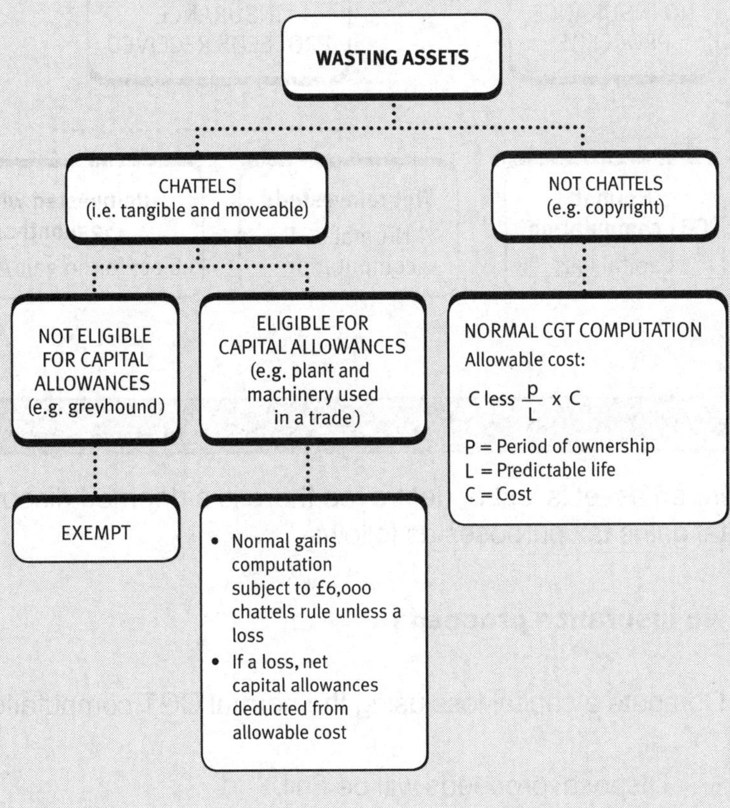

5 Assets lost or destroyed or damaged

Introduction

In most circumstances a capital transaction has two parties, a buyer and a seller.

However, when an asset is damaged, destroyed or lost and the asset's owner receives compensation (either from the perpetrator or an insurance company) the position is different. The owner has received a capital sum without disposing of the asset and the payer has received nothing in return. Consequently, a special set of rules is required.

The rules vary according to whether:

- the asset has been completely lost/destroyed or merely damaged
- the owner has replaced or restored the asset.

Asset lost or destroyed

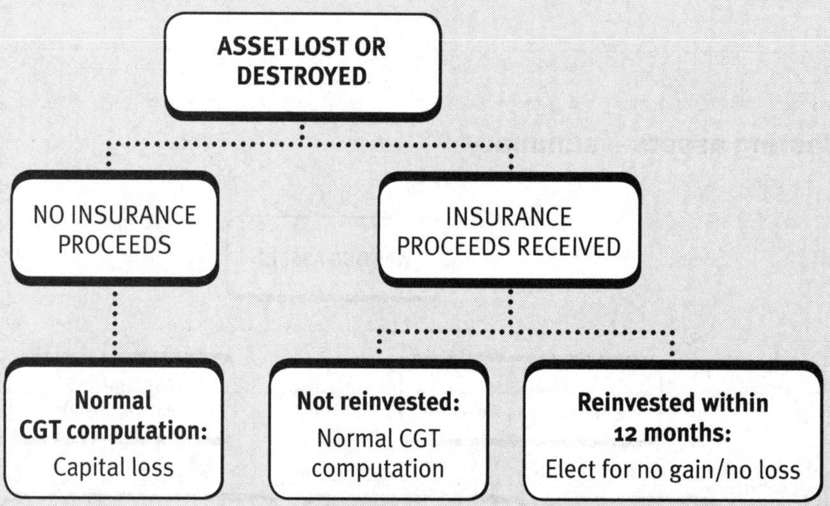

Assets lost or destroyed

Where an asset is lost or destroyed there is a deemed disposal for capital gains tax purposes as follows:

(a) **No insurance proceeds**

Compute a capital loss using the normal CGT computation:

- Disposal proceeds will be £nil.
- Deduction of the allowable expenditure will create a loss.

(b) **Insurance proceeds received – no replacement of asset**

Where an asset is lost or destroyed and insurance proceeds are not used to replace the asset, a chargeable gain/loss is computed using the normal capital gains tax computation proforma.

(c) **Insurance proceeds received – asset replaced**

Where an asset is lost or destroyed and the insurance proceeds are used to buy a replacement asset within 12 months the following rules apply:

- The taxpayer can claim that the destruction/loss of the asset is treated as a no gain/no loss disposal (as for husband and wife transfers).
- If the insurance proceeds are greater than the deemed disposal proceeds under the no gain/no loss computation, the excess is deducted from the replacement asset's allowable cost.

The date of disposal is the date that the insurance proceeds are received, not when the destruction or loss of the asset occurred.

Example 12 – Assets lost or destroyed – Nadir

Nadir purchased a business asset for £15,000 on 1 April 1990, which was destroyed by fire on 31 July 2009. The asset was not insured.

Calculate the allowable loss arising from the destruction of the asset.

Answer to example 12

	£
Proceeds	Nil
Less: Cost	(15,000)
Allowable loss	(15,000)

Example 13 – Assets lost or destroyed – Padma

Padma purchased an antique table for £35,000 on 1 May 1992, which was destroyed by fire on 30 June 2009. She received insurance proceeds of £50,000 on 1 September 2009. She did not replace the table.

Calculate the chargeable gain arising from the destruction of the antique table.

Answer to example 13

	£
Insurance proceeds	50,000
Less: Cost	(35,000)
Chargeable gain	15,000

Example 14 – Assets lost or destroyed – Silvio

Silvio purchased a painting for £57,000 on 1 June 1993, which was destroyed in a fire on 31 May 2009. He received insurance proceeds of £50,000 on 1 September 2009. He did not replace the painting.

Calculate the chargeable gain or allowable loss arising from the destruction of the painting.

Answer to example 14

	£
Insurance proceeds	50,000
Less: Cost	(57,000)
Allowable loss	(7,000)

Example 15 – Assets lost or destroyed – Bill

Bill purchased an asset for £25,000 on 1 October 1990, which was destroyed by fire on 30 September 2009. He received compensation of £35,000 from his insurance company on 1 January 2010. He purchased a replacement asset for £40,000 on 1 February 2010.

Assuming that Bill claims the loss by fire to be a no gain/no loss disposal, calculate the allowable expenditure (base cost) of the replacement asset.

Answer to example 15

	£	£
Cost of replacement asset		40,000
Less: Compensation	35,000	
Less: Deemed disposal proceeds of old asset (W)	(25,000)	
		(10,000)
Replacement asset base cost		30,000

Working – deemed disposal proceeds

Since the disposal of the old asset is assumed to be on a no gain/no loss basis. The disposal proceeds are the allowable cost of the asset.

	£
Allowable cost = Deemed disposal proceeds	25,000

Example 16 – Assets lost or destroyed – Belinda

Belinda purchased an antique necklace for £21,140 on 1 October 1996, which she lost on 30 June 2008. She received compensation of £45,000 from her insurance company on 1 October 2008 and purchased a replacement necklace for £50,000 on 1 November 2008.

She sold the replacement necklace for £65,000 on 1 March 2010.

Assuming that Belinda claims the loss of the necklace to be a no gain/no loss disposal, calculate the chargeable gain arising on the sale of the replacement necklace on 1 March 2010.

Answer to example 16

	£
Insurance proceeds	65,000
Less: Cost (W)	(26,140)
Chargeable gain	38,860

Working – Replacement asset base cost

	£	£
Cost of replacement necklace		50,000
Less: Insurance proceeds	45,000	
Less: Deemed disposal proceeds of lost necklace = Base cost	(21,140)	
		(23,860)
Replacement asset base cost		26,140

Asset damaged

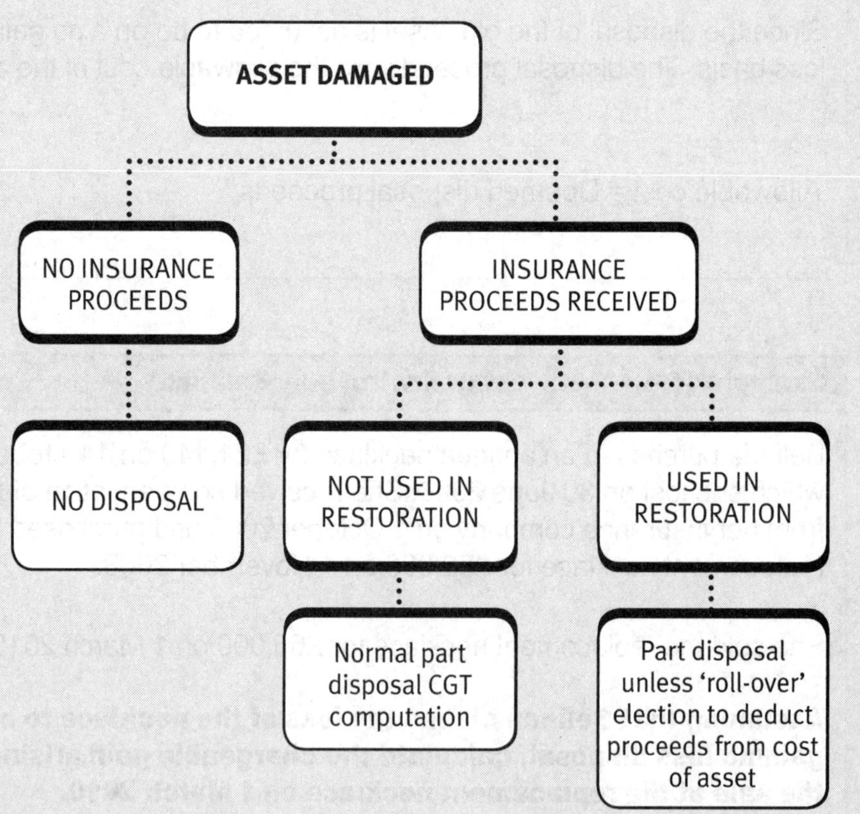

Asset damaged

Where an asset is damaged there are no implications for capital gains tax purposes unless compensation (e.g. insurance proceeds, is received).

Where an asset is damaged and compensation is received there is a part disposal for capital gains tax purposes.

The allowable cost is calculated using the normal part disposal formula:

Cost × A / A + B

Where

A = Compensation received
B = Market value of the remainder at the time of the part disposal.

The computation is varied depending on how the insurance proceeds are applied.

(a) **Proceeds not used in restoration work**

Normal part disposal capital gains computation is used. The value of the part retained is the value of the asset in its damaged condition.

(b) **Proceeds fully used in restoration work**

Where all of the insurance proceeds are used in restoring the asset the taxpayer may claim to deduct the proceeds from the cost of the asset rather than be treated as having made a part disposal of the asset. This is a form of 'roll-over relief' (see Chapter 17).

Example 17 – Asset damaged – Sasha

Sasha purchased a painting on 1 April 2000 for £10,000. The painting was damaged on 1 May 2009 when it was worth £50,000. After the damage the painting was worth £25,000. On 1 July 2009 insurance proceeds of £30,000 were received, which were not used to restore the painting.

Calculate the chargeable gain arising in respect of the painting.

Answer to example 17

	£
Insurance proceeds	30,000
Less: Deemed cost £10,000 × £30,000/(£30,000 + £25,000)	(5,455)
Chargeable gain	24,545

Example 18 – Asset damaged – Amy

Amy purchased a painting on 1 April 2000 for £10,000. The painting was damaged on 1 May 2009 when it was worth £50,000. After the damage the painting was worth £40,000. On 1 July 2009 insurance proceeds of £8,000 were received. All of the proceeds were used to restore the painting.

Assuming Amy elects for the insurance proceeds to be rolled over against the cost of the painting, calculate the revised base cost for CGT purposes of the painting after it has been restored.

Answer to example 18

There is no part disposal and the revised base cost of the painting is:

	£
Original cost	10,000
Insurance proceeds	(8,000)
Revised base cost	2,000

Example 19 – Asset damaged – Sari

Sari purchased an investment property on 1 May 2002 for £200,000. In June 2009 it was damaged by fire. On 1 August 2009 insurance proceeds of £100,000 were received which were used to restore the property. After the restoration the property was worth £500,000.

Assuming Sari elects for the insurance proceeds to be rolled over against the cost of the property calculate the revised base cost for CGT purposes of the property after it has been restored.

Answer to example 19

As the proceeds are fully used in restoration and the 'roll over' election is made, there is no part disposal and the revised base cost is:

	£
Original cost	200,000
Insurance proceeds	(100,000)
Revised base cost	100,000

6 Chapter summary

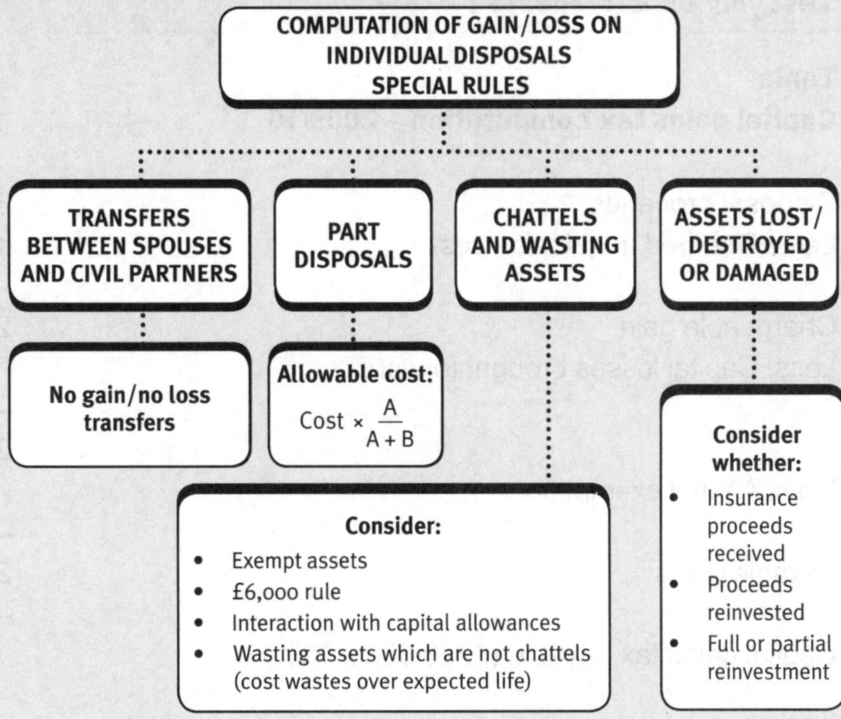
COMPUTATION OF GAIN/LOSS ON INDIVIDUAL DISPOSALS SPECIAL RULES
TRANSFERS BETWEEN SPOUSES AND CIVIL PARTNERS
PART DISPOSALS
CHATTELS AND WASTING ASSETS
ASSETS LOST/ DESTROYED OR DAMAGED
No gain/no loss transfers
Allowable cost:
Cost × A / A + B
Consider:
• Exempt assets
• £6,000 rule
• Interaction with capital allowances
• Wasting assets which are not chattels (cost wastes over expected life)
Consider whether:
• Insurance proceeds received
• Proceeds reinvested
• Full or partial reinvestment

Test your understanding answers

Test your understanding 1

Tania
Capital gains tax computation – 2009/10

	£
Disposal proceeds	350,000
Less: Deemed acquisition cost	(100,000)
Chargeable gain	250,000
Less: Capital losses brought forward	(11,300)
	238,700
Less: Annual exemption	(10,100)
Taxable gains	228,600
Capital gains tax payable (£228,600 x 18%)	41,148

Test your understanding 2

Jacob		
Disposal in January 2010	£	£
Sale proceeds	20,000	
Less: Deemed cost of part disposed of		
£8,000 × £20,000/(£20,000 + £60,000)	(2,000)	
		18,000
Disposal in March 2010		
Sales proceeds	75,000	
Less: Deemed cost of remainder (£8,000 – £2,000)	(6,000)	
		69,000
Total chargeable gains		87,000
Less: Annual exemption		(10,100)
Taxable gains		76,900
Capital gains tax (£76,900 × 18%)		13,842
Due date		31.1.2011

Test your understanding 3

Gemma

	£
Sale proceeds	200,000
Less: Deemed cost of remainder (£50,000 – £14,286) (W)	(35,714)
Chargeable gain	164,286
Less: Annual exemption	(10,100)
Taxable gain	154,186
Capital gains tax (£154,186 × 18%)	27,753

Working – Allowable expenditure

The allowable expenditure in relation to the part disposal of the land on 1 July 2006 was:

£50,000 × £40,000/(£40,000 + £100,000) = £14,286

Test your understanding 4

Exempt disposals	Chargeable disposals
(3) Motor car – exempt asset	(1) Necklace (deemed proceeds £7,000). Non-wasting chattel not sold and bought for ≤ £6,000
(4) Boat – wasting chattel	(2) Shares – not chattels (not tangible property)
(5) Painting – non wasting chattel bought and sold for ≤ £6,000	
(6) Greyhound – wasting chattel	

Test your understanding 5

Marjory

	Table A	Table B
	£	£
Sale proceeds	6,400	13,600
Less: Cost	(1,000)	(1,000)
Chargeable gains	5,400	12,600
Gains cannot exceed:		
5/3 × (sale proceeds – £6,000)	667	12,667
Decision = take the lower gain	667	12,600

Test your understanding 6

Brian

	£
Deemed sale proceeds	6,000
Less: Selling costs	(50)
Net sale proceeds	5,950
Less: Cost (including acquisition expenses)	(10,500)
Allowable loss	(4,550)

Note: It is the **gross** sale proceeds **before** deducting selling costs that are deemed to be £6,000. The £500 actual sale proceeds received are ignored.

Test your understanding 7

Sally

Net chargeable gains – 2009/10

Painting	1	2	4
	£	£	£
Sale proceeds	7,000		9,500
Deemed proceeds		6,000	
Less: Cost	(2,000)	(8,000)	(7,000)
Chargeable gain/(allowable loss)	5,000	(2,000)	2,500
Gain cannot exceed 5/3 × (£7,000 – £6,000)	1,667		

Net chargeable gains (£1,667 – £2,000 + £2,500) = £2,167

Note: Painting 3 is exempt as the cost and proceeds are both less than £6,000.

chapter

16

CGT: Shares and securities for individuals

Chapter learning objectives

Upon completion of this chapter you will be able to:

- identify the exemption for government securities and qualifying corporate bonds
- calculate the value of quoted shares where they are disposed of by way of a gift
- understand why identification rules are required when acquiring and disposing of shares
- apply the correct matching rules on a disposal of shares by an individual
- explain the pooling principle
- calculate a gain on the disposal of shares by an individual
- identify the treatment of a bonus issue
- identify the treatment of a rights issue
- explain the tax treatment on a takeover or reorganisation of a shareholding in exchange for other shares
- explain the treatment on a takeover where there is cash and shares consideration
- calculate the chargeable gain on the cash element on a takeover.

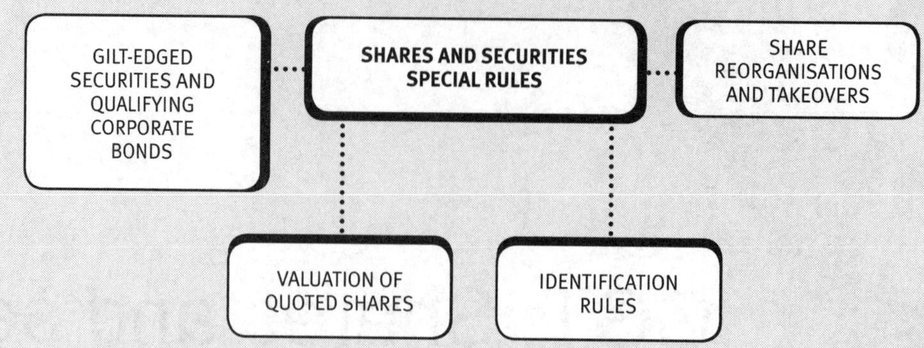

1 Introduction

The basic chargeable gain computation is used as normal on a disposal of shares or securities. However, because shares are indistinguishable from each other there are special rules to identify the allowable cost.

This chapter covers the rules as they apply to disposals by an individual.

2 Government securities and qualifying corporate bonds

All shares and securities disposed of by an individual are subject to capital gains tax except for the following, which are exempt:

- listed government securities (gilt-edged securities or gilts)
- qualifying corporate bonds (e.g. debentures and company loan notes)
- shares held in an Individual Savings Account (ISA).

Definition of a qualifying corporate bond

A qualifying corporate bond (QCB) is one that:

(a) represents a normal commercial loan;

(b) is expressed in sterling and has no provision for either conversion into, or redemption in, any other currency; and

(c) was issued after 13 March 1984 or was acquired by the disposer after that date (whenever it was issued).

Test your understanding 1

Which of the following shares and securities are exempt assets for CGT purposes when disposed of by an individual?

(1) £1 ordinary shares in the unquoted property development company, Sealand Ltd.

(2) 10½% Exchequer Stock 2016.

(3) 10% preference shares in the quoted trading company, Ace plc.

(4) 6% loan stock issued by Amble plc in 2007.

A (3) and (4) only

B (2) and (4) only

C (1) and (2) only

D (2), (3) and (4) only.

3 Valuation of quoted shares

On a sale of shares between unconnected parties, the actual proceeds are used in the capital gains computation.

However, it is necessary to identify the market value of quoted shares when shares are either:

- gifted
- transferred to a connected party.

Their market value is taken from prices quoted in the Stock Exchange Daily Official List and is:

the **lower** of:

- the value using the '¼ up method'
  i.e. lower quoted price + ¼ (higher price – lower price)
- the average of the highest and lowest recorded bargains.

Example 1 - Valuation of quoted shares

Shares in XYZ plc are quoted in the Stock Exchange Daily Official List at 230p to 270p. On the same day the highest and lowest recorded bargains were 224p and 276p.

If a disposal of XYZ plc shares were made on that day to a connected party, what would their value be for CGT purposes?

Answer to example 1

The value of XYZ plc shares is 240p, being the lower of:

(a) ¼ up rule:	
Lower price	230p
Add: (270p – 230p) × ¼	10p
	240p
(b) Average of lowest and highest recorded bargains	
(224p + 276p) × ½	250p

Test your understanding 2

Shares in Sawyer plc are quoted in the Stock Exchange Daily Official List at 460p to 540p.

On the same day the highest and lowest recorded bargains were 552p, 500p and 448p.

If a gift of Sawyer plc shares were made on that day, what would their value be for CGT purposes?

4 Identification rules

It is necessary to have identification (or matching) rules to determine which shares have been disposed of as:

- Shares and securities that are bought in a particular company of the same class are not distinguishable from one another.
- Each time shares are bought in any quoted company the price paid may be different.

- They enable you to decide which shares have been sold and to work out the allowable cost to use in the capital gains computation.

Identification rules for disposals by individuals

When shares are disposed of they are matched against shares acquired of the same class in the following order:

- Same day as the date of disposal.
- Within **following** 30 days.
- The share pool (shares acquired before the date of disposal are pooled together).

Shares acquired within the following 30 days

It may appear strange that a disposal is matched with acquisitions following the date of sale. The reason for this is that it prevents a practice known as 'bed and breakfasting'.

Typically, shares would have been sold at the close of business one day and then bought back at the opening of business the next day. A gain or loss would have been established without making a genuine disposal of the shares. It might have been useful for an individual to establish a capital loss, e.g. in the same tax year that he or she has chargeable gains, or a capital gain to use his or her annual exemption, if it had not been used already.

The 30-day matching rule makes the practice of bed and breakfasting much more difficult, since the subsequent acquisition cannot take place within 30 days.

Example 2 - Identification rules

Frederic had the following transactions in the shares of DEF plc, a quoted company.

			£
1 June 1986	Bought	4,000 shares for	8,000
30 July 1995	Bought	1,800 shares for	9,750
30 April 1999	Bought	500 shares for	4,000
20 May 2000	Bought	1,000 shares for	8,500
15 March 2010	Sold	3,500 shares for	36,000
28 March 2010	Bought	800 shares for	6,400

Identify with which acquisitions the shares sold on 15 March 2010 will be matched.

Answer to example 2

		Number of shares
Shares sold		3,500
1. Shares acquired on same day		(Nil)
2. Shares acquired in following 30 days		
28 March 2010		(800)
		2,700
3. Share pool		
(Shares pre 15 March 2010))		
1 June 1986	4,000	
30 July 1995	1,800	
30 April 1999	500	
20 May 2000	1,000	
	7,300	
The disposal from the share pool is therefore 2,700 out of 7,300 shares		(2,700)
		Nil

The share pool

The share pool is sometimes referred to as the 's104 pool' or the 'FA 1985 pool'.

For an individual, the share pool contains shares in the same company, of the same class purchased before the date of disposal.

- The share pool simply keeps a record of the number of shares acquired and sold and the cost of those shares.
- When shares are disposed of out of the share pool, the appropriate proportion of the cost which relates to the shares disposed of is calculated. The shares are disposed of at their average cost.

  Thus if there are 6,000 shares in the pool with a cost of £8,000 and 2,000 shares are disposed of:

  – the cost of the shares removed is £2,667 ((2,000/6,000) × £8,000).

5 Calculating the gain/loss on the disposal of shares

Once the identification rules have been used to identify which shares have been disposed of, the cost of those shares is used in the normal chargeable gains computation.

Example 3 - Calculating the gain/loss on the disposal of shares

Frances sold 11,000 ordinary shares in Hastings Co plc, a quoted company, on 18 December 2009 for £50,000. She had bought ordinary shares in the company on the following dates.

	Number of shares	Cost
		£
6 April 1998	8,000	7,450
12 December 1999	4,000	5,500
10 January 2010	2,000	6,000

Calculate the chargeable gain arising on the disposal of shares on 18 December 2009.

Assume that Hastings Co plc is not Frances' personal trading company.

Answer to example 3

Capital gains computation – 2009/10

Stage 1 Use the identification rules to identify the shares disposed of.

		Number
Shares sold		11,000
1	Shares acquired on same day	(Nil)
2	Shares acquired in following 30 days	
	10 January 2010	(2,000)
		9,000
3	Share pool (9,000 out of 12,000 shares)	(9,000)
		Nil

Stage 2 **Calculate the chargeable gain arising on each of the individual parcels of shares disposed of.**

(a) Shares acquired on 10 January 2010

	£
Sale proceeds (2,000/11,000 × £50,000)	9,091
Less: Acquisition cost	(6,000)
Chargeable gain	3,091

(b) Shares in the share pool

	£
Sale proceeds (9,000/11,000 × £50,000)	40,409
Less: Acquisition cost (W)	(9,712)
Chargeable gain	31,197
Total chargeable gains	34,288

Working: share pool

	Number	Cost £
Acquisition – 6 April 1998	8,000	7,450
Acquisition – 12 December 1999	4,000	5,500
	12,000	12,950
Disposal – 18 December 2009 9,000/12,000 × £12,950 (Note)	(9,000)	(9,712)
Balance carried forward	3,000	3,238

Note: The 'average cost' method is used to calculate the cost removed from the share pool on the disposal.

If the individual disposes of shares in his personal trading company and is also an employee of that company, Entrepreneurs' relief is available. This relief is covered in detail in Chapter 17.

Test your understanding 3

Zoe purchased 2,000 shares in XYZ Ltd on 16 April 1985 for £10,000.

In addition she acquired 1,500 shares in the company on 30 April 2009 for £18,000, and 500 shares on 31 May 2009 for £7,000. On 10 February 2010, Zoe bought a further 200 shares in XYZ Ltd for £3,600.

Zoe sold 3,500 shares in XYZ Ltd on 31 January 2010 for £70,000.

Calculate Zoe's chargeable gain on the disposal of shares on 31 January 2010.

Assume that XYZ Ltd is not Zoe's personal trading company.

6 Bonus issues and rights issues

Bonus issues

A bonus issue is the distribution of free shares to shareholders based on their existing shareholding.

For capital gains tax purposes they are treated as follows:

- For the purposes of the share identification rules the bonus shares acquired will be included in the share pool.
- The bonus shares are not treated as a separate holding of shares.
- The number of shares are included in the pool, but at Nil cost.

Example 4 - Bonus issues

Blackburn had the following transactions in the shares of Gray Ltd:

January 2009	Purchased 3,500 shares for £7,350
May 2009	Purchased 500 shares for £1,750
June 2009	Bonus issue of one for five
September 2009	Sold 2,600 shares for £10,400

Calculate the chargeable gain arising on the disposal in September 2009.

Assume that Gray Ltd is not Blackburn's personal trading company.

Answer to example 4

	£
Sale proceeds	10,400
Less Cost (Working)	(4,929)
Chargeable gain	5,471

Working: Share pool

		Number	Cost £
Jan 2009	Purchase	3,500	7,350
May 2009	Purchase	500	1,750
		4,000	9,100
June 2009	Bonus issue (1:5)	800	Nil
		4,800	9,100
September 2009	Sale	(2,600)	(4,929)
Balance c/f		2,200	4,171

Test your understanding 4

Kieran had the following transactions in Black plc shares:

January 2005	Purchased 3,000 shares for £6,000
May 2009	Bonus issue of one for three
June 2009	Purchased 500 shares for £1,500
February 2010	Sold 3,000 shares for £12,000

Calculate the chargeable gain arising on the disposal in February 2010.

Assume that Black plc is not Kieran's personal trading company.

Rights issues

A rights issue is the offer of new shares to existing shareholders in proportion to their existing shareholding, usually at a price below the market price.

Rights issues are similar in concept to bonus issues, however because money is paid for the new shares there are additional factors to consider:

- As for bonus issues, for the purposes of the share identification rules the rights shares acquired will be included in the share pool.
- The rights shares are not treated as a separate holding of shares.
- The number of shares are included in the pool, and the cost, in the same way as a normal purchase.

Example 5 - Rights issue

Carmichael had the following transactions in Rudderham Ltd shares:

January 2008	Purchased 2,700 shares for £5,400
May 2009	Purchased 600 shares for £1,500
June 2009	Took up 1 for 3 rights issue at £2.30 per share
August 2009	Sold 4,000 shares for £14,000

Calculate the chargeable gain on the disposal in August 2009.

Assume that Rudderham Ltd is not Carmichael's personal trading company.

Answer to example 5

	£
Sale proceeds	14,000
Less Cost (Working)	(8,573)
Chargeable gain	5,427

Working: Share pool

		Number	Cost £
Jan 2008	Purchase	2,700	5,400
May 2009	Purchase	600	1,500
		3,300	6,900
June 2009	Rights issue (1:3) @ £2.50 per share	1,100	2,530
		4,400	9,430
August 2009	Sale	(4,000)	(8,573)
Balance c/f		400	857

Test your understanding 5

Victor had the following transactions in the ordinary shares of Victorious Vulcanising plc, a quoted company:

April 1999	Purchased 1,000 shares for £11,000
September 1999	Rights issue of 1 for 2 at £6 each
August 2009	Sold 1,200 shares for £46,000

Calculate Victor's chargeable gain for 2009/10.

Assume that Victorious Vulcanising plc is not Victor's personal trading company.

7 Reorganisations and takeovers

Reorganisations

A reorganisation involves the exchange of existing shares in a company for other shares of another class in the same company.

Takeovers

A takeover occurs when one company acquires the shares in another company either in exchange for shares in itself, cash or a mixture of both.

Consideration: shares for shares

Where the consideration for the reorganisation or takeover only involves the issue of shares in the acquiring company, the tax consequences are:

- **No capital gains tax** is charged at the time of the reorganisation/ takeover.
- The cost of the original shares becomes the cost of the new shares.
- Where the shareholder receives more than one type of share in exchange for the original shares, the cost of the original shares is allocated to the new shares by reference to the market values of the various new shares on the first day of dealing in them.

This treatment is **automatic**.

However, the shareholder can elect for the event to be treated as a disposal for CGT purposes.

If the election is made, Entrepreneurs' relief may be available against the gain. This relief is considered in detail in Chapter 17.

Example 6 - Reorganisations and takeovers

Major purchased 2,000 ordinary shares in Blue plc for £5,000 in June 2002. In July 2009, Blue plc underwent a reorganisation and Major received two 'A' ordinary shares in exchange for each of his ordinary shares.

In December 2009, Major sold all his holding of 'A' ordinary shares for £8,000.

Calculate the chargeable gain or allowable loss arising on the disposal in December 2009.

Assume that Blue plc is not Major's personal trading company.

Answer to example 6

	£
Sale proceeds	8,000
Less: Cost (Note)	(5,000)
Chargeable gain	3,000

Note: The cost of the original ordinary shares (£5,000) becomes the cost of the new 'A' ordinary shares.

Example 7 - Reorganisations and takeovers

In July 2009, Craig sold his entire holding of ordinary shares in Corus plc for £75,000. Craig had originally purchased 20,000 £1 ordinary shares in BNB plc at a cost of £20,000 in April 2001.

In July 2004, BNB plc was taken over by Corus plc. Craig received one ordinary 50p share and one 50p 6% preference share in Corus plc for each ordinary share he held in BNB plc.

Immediately after the takeover the values of these new shares were quoted as:

50p ordinary share	£1.80 each
50p preference shares	£0.80 each

Compute the chargeable gain arising on the disposal by Craig in July 2009.

Assume that Craig has never worked for Corus plc or BNB plc.

Answer to example 7

	£
Sale proceeds	75,000
Less: Allocated acquisition cost (W)	(13,846)
Chargeable gain	61,154

Working: Acquisition cost

Following the takeover in July 2004 of BNB plc by Corus plc, Craig now owns the following shares in Corus plc as per the terms of the takeover:

	Total M.V.	Original cost
	£	£
20,000 50p ordinary shares @ £1.80	36,000	13,846
20,000 50p preference shares @ £0.80	16,000	6,154
	52,000	20,000

Allocate the original cost incurred in April 2001 to the shares now owned in July 2004, using the normal average cost method.

£36,000/£52,000 × £20,000 = £13,846
£16,000/£52,000 × £20,000 = £6,154

Test your understanding 6

In June 2009, Marie purchased 2,000 ordinary shares in Black Ltd for £5,000. In July 2009 Black Ltd was taken over by Red plc, and Marie received 2 ordinary shares and 1 preference share in Red plc for each ordinary share in Black Ltd.

Immediately after the takeover the ordinary shares in Red plc were valued at £2 and the preference shares in Red plc were valued at £1.

In December 2009, Marie sold all her holding of ordinary shares in Red plc for £8,000.

Calculate the chargeable gain or allowable loss arising on the disposal in December 2009.

Assume that Marie has never worked for Red plc or Black Ltd.

Takeovers: consideration in cash and shares

If the consideration for the takeover includes a cash element:

- there is a part disposal of the original shares
- a gain arises on the cash element of the consideration on the date the cash is received.

Cash proceeds – part disposal computation

In these circumstances the part of the cost of the original holding apportioned to the cash is calculated as:

$$\frac{\text{Cash received}}{\text{Cash received + M.V. of new shares}} \times \text{Cost of original shares}$$

Example 8 - Reorganisations and takeovers

Patrick bought 10,000 shares in Target plc in May 2004 for £20,000. On 3 November 2009, the entire share capital of Target plc was acquired by Bidder plc. Target plc shareholders received 2 Bidder plc shares and £0.50 cash for each share held. Bidder plc shares were quoted at £1.25.

Calculate the chargeable gain as a result of the takeover in November 2009.

Assume that Patrick has not worked for Target plc or Bidder plc.

Answer to example 8

The total consideration provided by Bidder plc is:

	£
Shares (20,000 @1.25)	25,000
Cash (10,000 × £0.50)	5,000
	30,000

As Patrick has received part of the consideration in cash he has made a part disposal of the original shares.

	£
Disposal proceeds (cash)	5,000
Less: Original cost	
£5,000/£30,000 × £20,000	(3,333)
Chargeable gain	1,667

Patrick's allowable cost on the future disposal of his shares in Bidder plc will be £16,667 (£20,000 – £3,333).

Test your understanding 7

Paula bought 25,000 shares in Tiny plc in May 2005 for £20,000. On 3 October 2009 the entire share capital of Tiny plc was acquired by Big plc. Tiny plc shareholders received 2 Big plc shares and £1.20 cash for each share held. Big plc shares were quoted at £1.75.

Calculate the chargeable gain as a result of the takeover in October 2009 and state the allowable cost of Paula's shares in Big plc.

Assume that Paula has not worked for either Tiny plc or Big plc.

8 Chapter summary

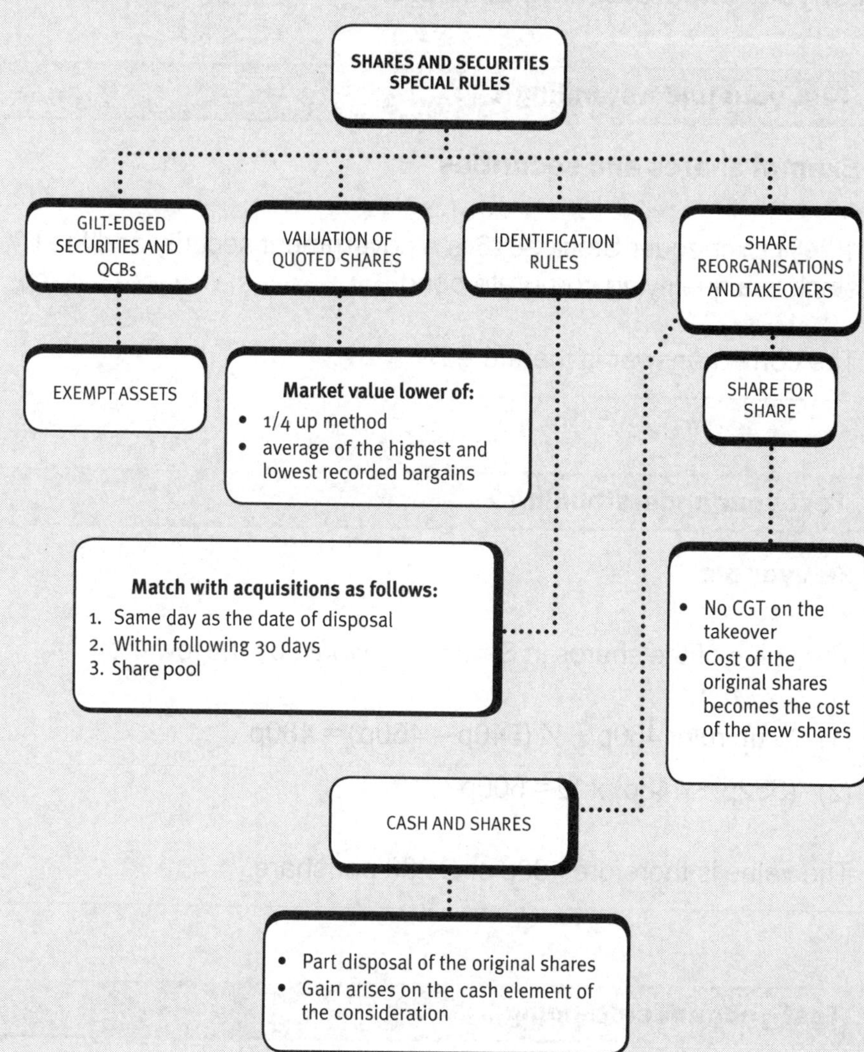
SHARES AND SECURITIES SPECIAL RULES
GILT-EDGED SECURITIES AND QCBs
VALUATION OF QUOTED SHARES
IDENTIFICATION RULES
SHARE REORGANISATIONS AND TAKEOVERS
EXEMPT ASSETS
Market value lower of:
• 1/4 up method
• average of the highest and lowest recorded bargains
SHARE FOR SHARE
Match with acquisitions as follows:
1. Same day as the date of disposal
2. Within following 30 days
3. Share pool
• No CGT on the takeover
• Cost of the original shares becomes the cost of the new shares
CASH AND SHARES
• Part disposal of the original shares
• Gain arises on the cash element of the consideration

Test your understanding answers

Test your understanding 1

Exempt shares and securities

10½% Exchequer Stock 2016 is a government security and the 6% loan stock is a qualifying corporate bond.

The correct answer is therefore B.

Test your understanding 2

Sawyer plc

The value of the shares in Sawyer plc would be the lower of:

(1) ¼ up rule: 460p + ¼ (540p – 460p) = 480p

(2) (552p + 448p) x ½ = 500p

The value is therefore 480p or £4.80 per share.

Test your understanding 3

Zoe

(a) Match with acquisitions within following 30 days (10 February 2010) (200 shares)

	£
Sale proceeds (£70,000 × 200/3,500)	4,000
Less: Purchase price	(3,600)
Chargeable gain	400

(b) Match with acquisitions in the share pool (balance of 3,300 shares)

	£
Sale proceeds (£70,000 × 3,300/3,500)	66,000
Less: Purchase price (W)	(28,875)
Chargeable gain	37,125
Total chargeable gains (£400 + £37,125)	37,525

Working – Share pool

	Number	Cost
Acquisitions		£
16/4/85	2,000	10,000
30/4/09	1,500	18,000
31/5/09	500	7,000
	4,000	35,000
Sale 31/1/10 (£35,000 x (3,300/4,000))	(3,300)	(28,875)
Balance carried forward	700	6,125

Test your understanding 4

Kieran

	£
Sale proceeds	12,000
Less Cost (Working)	(5,000)
Chargeable gain	7,000

Working: Share pool

		Number	Cost
			£
Jan 2005	Purchase	3,000	6,000
May 2009	Bonus issue (1:3)	1,000	Nil
June 2009	Purchase	500	1,500
		4,500	7,500
February 2010	Sale	(3,000)	(5,000)
Balance c/f		1,500	2,500

Test your understanding 5

Victor

	£
Sale proceeds	46,000
Less Cost (Working)	(11,200)
Chargeable gain	34,800

Working: Share pool

		Number	Cost
			£
April 1999	Purchase	1,000	11,000
September 1999	Rights issue (1:2) @ £6 per share	500	3,000
		1,500	14,000
August 2009	Sale	(1,200)	(11,200)
Balance c/f		300	2,800

Test your understanding 6

Marie

Capital gains computation – 2009/10

	£
Sale proceeds	8,000
Less: Cost (W)	(4,000)
Chargeable gain	4,000

Working – Cost of ordinary shares in Red Plc

Marie received:
4,000 ordinary shares, valued at (4,000 × £2) = £8,000
2,000 preference shares, valued at (2,000 × £1) = £2,000

Cost attributable to the ordinary shares is thus:
£5,000 × £8,000/£10,000 = £4,000

Test your understanding 7

Paula

The total consideration provided by Big plc is:

	£
Shares (50,000 × 1.75)	87,500
Cash (25,000 × £1.20)	30,000
	117,500

Paula has made a part disposal on 3 October 2009 in relation to the cash consideration.

	£
Disposal proceeds (cash)	30,000
Less: Original cost (£20,000 × (£30,000/£117,500))	(5,106)
Chargeable gain	24,894

Paula's allowable cost on the future disposal of her shares in Big plc will be £14,894 (£20,000 – £5,106).

chapter

17

CGT: Reliefs for individuals

Chapter learning objectives

Upon completion of this chapter you will be able to:

- define 'principal private residence'
- calculate the relief on disposal of a principal private residence
- calculate the gain when a principal private residence has been used partly for business purposes
- identify when letting relief is available on a principal private residence and calculate the relief
- explain and apply Entrepreneurs' relief
- explain and apply roll-over relief as it applies to individuals
- explain and apply hold-over relief for the gift of business assets
- explain when incorporation relief is available upon the transfer of a business to a company
- apply incorporation relief.

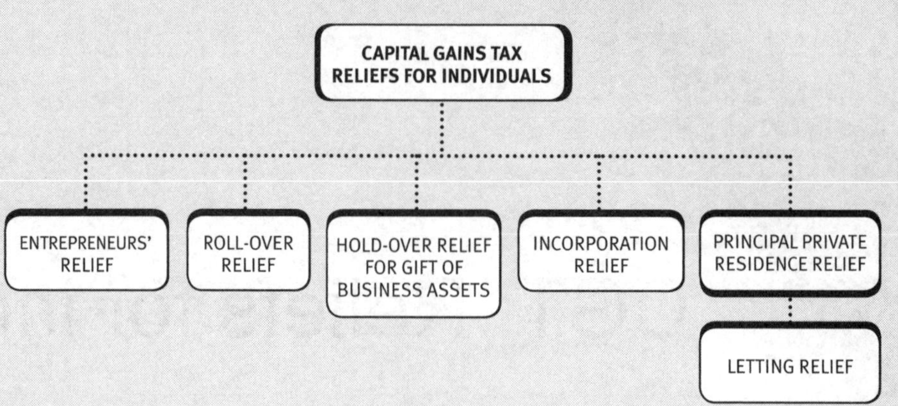

1 Introduction

In certain situations a gain on the disposal of an asset may be reduced or delayed by capital gains tax reliefs.

The reliefs are deducted from the gain **before** deducting capital losses.

The main reliefs available to individuals are as follows.

	Relief	**Available on:**
Non-business assets	Principal private residence relief	Individual's private residence
Business assets	Entrepreneurs' relief	Exemption on the disposal of certain business assets
	Roll-over relief	Reinvestment in new business assets
	Hold-over relief	Gift of business assets
	Incorporation relief	The incorporation of a business

2 Principal private residence relief

Principal private residence (PPR) relief applies when an individual disposes of:

- a dwelling house (including normally up to half an acre of adjoining land)
- which has at some time during his ownership been his only or main private residence.

The relief

The relief applies where the PPR has been occupied for either the whole or part of the period of ownership.

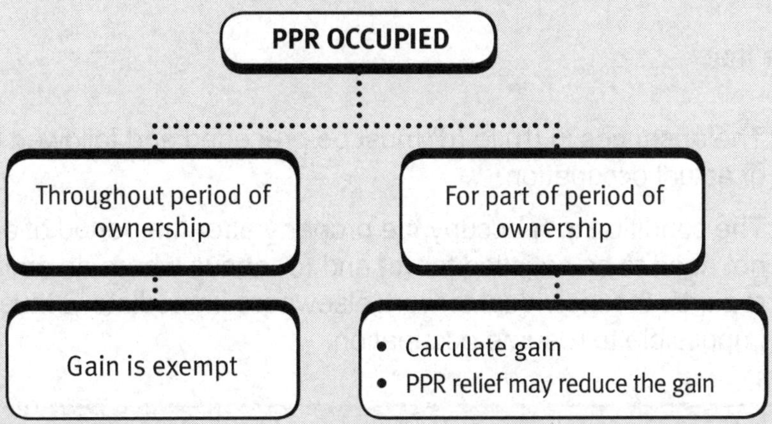

Calculating the relief

Where there has been a period of absence from the PPR the procedure is as follows.

- Calculate the gain on the disposal of the property
- Compute the total period of ownership.
- Calculate the periods of occupation (see below).
- Calculate the PPR relief as follows:

  Gain × (Periods of occupation/Total period of ownership)

- Deduct the PPR relief from the gain on the property.

Periods of occupation

The period of occupation includes periods of both:

- actual occupation
- deemed occupation.

Deemed occupation

Periods of deemed occupation are:

(a) the last 3 years of ownership

(b) up to 3 years of absence for any reason

(c) any period spent working abroad

(d) up to 4 years of absence while working in the UK.

Note that:

- The absences in (b) to (d) must be preceded and followed by a period of actual occupation.
- The condition to reoccupy the property after the period of absence does not need to be satisfied for (c) and (d) above where an employer requires the individual to work elsewhere immediately, thus making it impossible to resume occupation.

Further points

Ownership of more than one residence

Where an individual has more than one residence he is entitled to nominate which of them is to be treated as his principal residence for capital gains purposes by notifying HM Revenue and Customs in writing.

The election must be made within two years of acquiring an additional residence otherwise it is open to HMRC, as a question of fact, to decide which residence is the main residence.

Married couples/civil partners

Provided that they are not separated or divorced, a married couple (or civil partnership) is entitled to only one residence between them for the purposes of the principal private residence relief.

Example 1 - Principal private residence relief

On 1 May 1984 Mr Flint purchased a house in Southampton for £25,000, which he lived in until he moved to a rented flat on 1 July 1985.

He remained in the flat until 1 October 1987, when he accepted a year's secondment to his firm's New York office.

On coming back on 1 October 1988 he moved into a relative's house, where he stayed until he returned to his own home on 31 January 1989.

On 1 July 2001 he changed jobs and rented a flat near his new employer's offices in Newcastle. Here he remained until he sold his Southampton house on 1 February 2010 for £95,000.

Calculate the chargeable gain after reliefs, if any, arising on the disposal of the house on 1 February 2010.

Answer to example 1

	£
Sale proceeds	95,000
Less: Cost	(25,000)
	70,000
Less: Principal private residence (PPR) relief (W)	(54,209)
Chargeable gain after reliefs	15,791

Working – Chargeable and exempt periods of ownership

	Chargeable months	Exempt months
May 1984 – June 1985 (actual occupation)	–	14
July 1985 – September 1987 (absent – any reason)	–	27
October 1987 – September 1988 (absent – employed abroad)	–	12
October 1988 – January 1989 (absent – any reason)	–	4
Feb 1989 – June 2001 (actual occupation)	–	149
July 2001 – January 2007 (absent – see note)	67	–
February 2007 – January 2010 (final 36 months)	–	36
	67	242

Total period of ownership (67 + 242) = 309 months.

Exempt element of gain is £54,822 (242/309 × £70,000).

Notes

(1) After Mr Flint left his residence to work in Newcastle he never returned. Consequently the exemption for working away from home in the UK is not available as there is not actual occupation both before and after the period of absence.

(2) The remaining 5 months (3 years – 27 months – 4 months) for 'any reason' is also not available for exemption as Mr Flint never reoccupied the property after leaving for Newcastle.

(3) In contrast, the exemption for the final 36 months of ownership has no such restriction and is therefore still available.

Test your understanding 1

Arthur bought a house on 1 January 1990 and sold it on 30 September 2009 making a gain of £189,000.

He occupied the house as follows:

1 January 1990 – 31 December 1991	Lived in house
1 January 1992 – 30 June 1998	Employed overseas
1 July 1998 – 31 December 2002	Travels the world
1 January 2003 – 30 September 2009	Lived in house

Calculate the chargeable gain after reliefs, if any, arising on the disposal of the house on 30 September 2009.

Business use

Where a house, or part of it, is used wholly and exclusively for business purposes, this part loses its PPR relief and becomes taxable.

It should be noted that:

- The taxpayer cannot benefit from the rules of deemed occupation for any part of the property used for business purposes.
- However where part of the property was used for business purposes but was also at any time used as the taxpayer's main residence, the exemption for the last 36 months applies to the whole property.
- The 36 month exemption does not however apply to any part of the property used for business purposes **throughout** the period of ownership.

Example 2 - Principal private residence relief

On 30 June 2009 Alex sold his house for £125,000, resulting in a capital gain of £70,000. The house had been purchased on 1 July 1996, and one of the five rooms has always been used for business purposes.

Calculate the chargeable gain after reliefs arising on the disposal of the house.

Answer to example 2

Alex owned the house for 156 months and used 1/5th of the house (one of the five rooms) for business purposes. The 36 month exemption does not apply to the part of the property used for business purposes as it has never been used at any time for private purposes.

The chargeable gain is therefore: (£70,000 × 1/5) = £14,000

Alternative approach:

	£
Chargeable gain before reliefs	70,000
Less: PPR relief (£70,000 x 4/5)	(56,000)
Chargeable gain after reliefs	14,000

Test your understanding 2

On 30 April 2009 Todd sold his house for £150,000, resulting in a chargeable gain before reliefs of £60,000. The house had been purchased on 1 May 2001, and one of the seven rooms had always been used for business purposes.

Calculate the chargeable gain after reliefs arising on the disposal of the house.

Letting relief

Letting relief is available where an individual's PPR is let out for residential use.

It applies when:

- the owner is absent from the property and lets the house out, or
- the owner lets part of the property whilst still occupying the remainder.

It does not apply to let property which is not the owner's PPR (e.g. buy-to-let properties).

Letting relief is the lowest of:

- £40,000
- the amount of the gain exempted by the normal PPR rules
- the part of the gain (still in charge) attributable to the letting period.

Example 3 - Letting relief

Mr Hill bought a house in Luton on 1 April 1985. He occupied the house as follows:

1 April 1985 – 31 March 1986	Lived in as PPR.
1 April 1986 – 30 September 2000	Travelled the world Let the house from 1 April 1990 to 31 January 1999.
1 October 2000 – 1 May 2009	Lived in as PPR.

He sold the house on 1 May 2009 giving a chargeable gain of £209,730.

Calculate the chargeable gain after reliefs arising on the sale of the house.

Answer to example 3

	£
Chargeable gain before reliefs	209,730
Less: PPR relief (W1)	(109,582)
	100,148
Less: Letting relief (W2)	(40,000)
Chargeable gain after reliefs	60,148

Workings

(1) **PPR relief**

Total period of ownership/occupation:

1 April 1985 – 1 May 2009 = 24 years 1 month (289 months)

	Total	Exempt	Chargeable
1.4.85 – 31.03.06	12		
Actual occupation		12	
1.4.86 – 30.09.00	174		
3 years – any reason		36	
Rest of period – chargeable			138
1.10.00 – 1.5.09	103		
Last 3 years		36	
Rest of period – actual occupation		67	
Number of months	289	151	138

PPR relief = (£209,730 × 151/289) = £109,582

(2) **Letting relief**

The house was let from 1.4.90 to 31.1.99 and therefore, letting relief is available for this period of 106 months.

Letting relief = lowest of:

1 Maximum £40,000	
2 PPR = £109,582	
3 Gain on letting (£209,730 × 106/289) = £76,925	£40,000

Test your understanding 3

On 30 September 2009, Jane Smith made a gift of a house to her grandson Norman. The house had been bought by Jane on 1 September 1999 for £45,000, and was extended at a cost of £10,600 during June 2000. A market value of £140,000 at 30 September 2009 had been agreed by HM Revenue and Customs.

Jane occupied the house as her main residence until 30 September 2002 when she went to live with her sister. The house was rented out from 1 October 2003 to the date of the deemed sale.

Calculate the chargeable gain after reliefs arising on the gift.

Summary

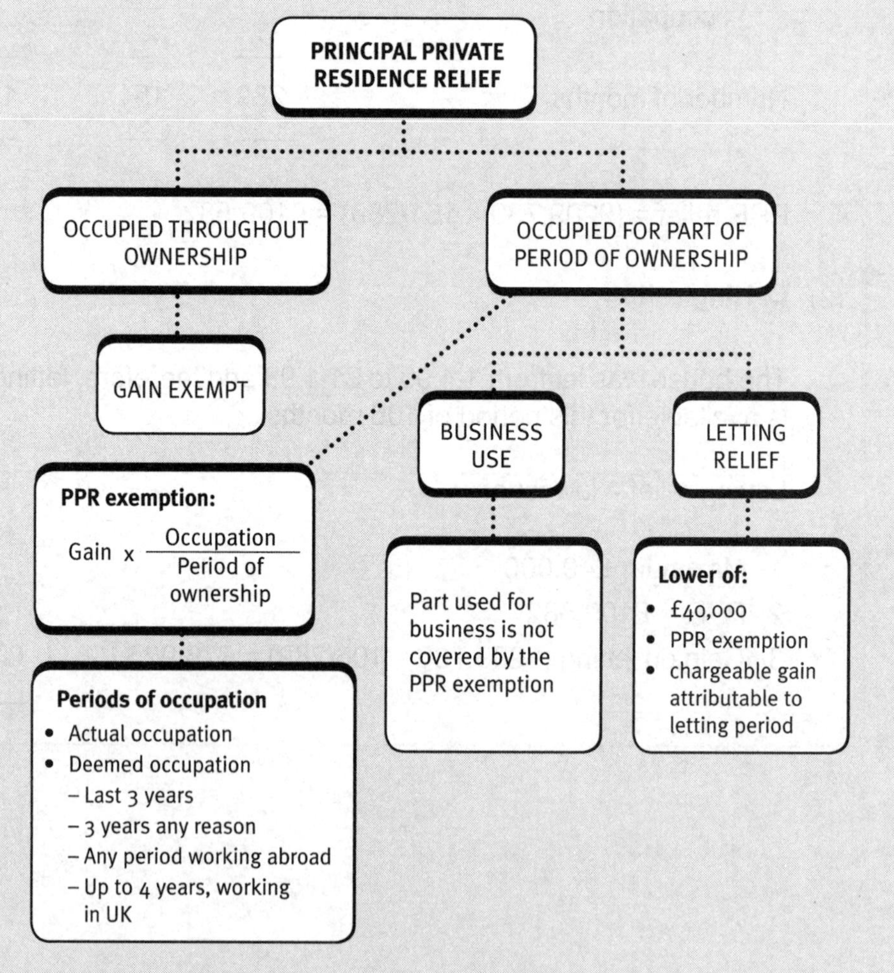

3 Entrepreneurs' relief

Entrepreneurs' relief reduces the capital gains tax payable on certain qualifying business disposals.

The relief operates as follows:

- The first £1 million of gains on 'qualifying business disposals' will be reduced by 4/9ths.
- The remaining 5/9ths are taxed at 18%, resulting in an effective rate of 10% on the first £1 million of gains (18% x 5/9 = 10%).
- Any gains above the £1 million limit are taxed in full at the 18% rate.

The relief is given **before** the deduction of:

- allowable losses (other than any losses on assets that are part of the disposal of the business), and
- the annual exemption.

The relief must be claimed within 12 months of the 31 January following the end of the tax year in which the disposal is made.

For 2009/10 disposals, the relief must be claimed by 31 January 2012.

The £1 million limit is a lifetime limit which is diminished each time a claim for the relief is made.

Qualifying business disposals

The relief applies to the disposal of:

- the whole or part of a business carried on by the individual either alone or in partnership
- assets of the individual's or partnership's trading business that has **now ceased**
- shares **provided**:
  - the shares are in the individual's 'personal trading company', **and**
  - the individual is an employee of the company (part time or full time).

An individual's 'personal trading company' is one in which the individual:

- owns at least 5% of the ordinary shares
- which carry at least 5% of the voting rights.

Note that:

- the disposal of an individual business asset used for the purposes of a continuing trade does not qualify. There must be a disposal of the whole or part of the trading business. The sale of an asset in isolation will not qualify.
- "Part of a business" is likely to be interpreted as meaning a "substantial part" which is "capable of independent operation".
- Where the disposal is a disposal of assets (i.e. not shares), relief is not available on gains arising from the disposal of those assets held for investment purposes.

Qualifying ownership period

The asset(s) being disposed of must have been owned by the individual making the disposal in the 12 months prior to the disposal.

Where the disposal is an asset of the individual's or partnership's trading business that has now ceased the disposal must also take place within three years of the cessation of trade.

Example 4 - Entrepreneurs' relief

In 2009/10, Katie sold her trading business which she set up in 1990 and realised the following gains:

	£
Factory	275,000
Goodwill	330,000
Warehouse	(100,000)
Investment property	200,000

All of the assets have been owned for many years.

Katie also sold her shares in an unquoted trading company and realised a gain of £600,000. She owned 25% of the ordinary shares of the company which she purchased ten years ago. She has worked for the company on a part time basis for the last three years.

Katie has not made any other capital disposals in 2009/10.

Calculate Katie's capital gains tax payable for 2009/10.

Answer to example 4

			£	£
Sale of trading business				
Factory			275,000	
Goodwill			330,000	
Warehouse			(100,000)	
	£		505,000	
Less: Entrepreneurs' relief	505,000	× 4/9	(224,444)	
				280,556
Sale of trading company shares				
Gain on shares			600,000	
Less: Entrepreneurs' relief	495,000	× 4/9	(220,000)	
	1,000,000			380,000
				660,556
Sale of investment property				200,000
Net chargeable gains				860,556
Less: Annual exemption				(10,100)
Taxable gains				850,456
Capital gains tax payable (£850,456 × 18%)				153,082

Test your understanding 4

In 2009/10 Paul sold shares in Dual Ltd, an unquoted trading company, and realised a gain of £430,000. Paul has worked for Dual Ltd for many years and has owned 10% of the ordinary shares of the company for the last five years.

Paul set up a trading business in 2003 and in 2009/10 he sold a warehouse used in the business, realising a gain of £245,000.

In 2010/11 Paul sold the rest of the business and realised gains of:

Factory	£495,000
Goodwill	£130,000

All of the assets in the business have been owned for many years.

He also sold an antique grandfather clock and realised a gain of £5,325.

Calculate Paul's CGT payable for 2009/10 and 2010/11.

Assume that the annual exemption for 2009/10 continues in the future.

Interaction with other reliefs

Note that other specific capital gains tax reliefs (e.g. gift relief, roll-over relief and incorporation relief) are given before Entrepreneurs' relief.

However, the interaction of Entrepreneurs' relief with other reliefs will not be examined.

Where relevant, a question will state that a particular relief is not available.

Interaction with takeovers

With a share for share exchange, it is possible that:

- the old shares would qualify for Entrepreneurs' relief if it were treated as a disposal
- but the new company is not the shareholder's personal trading company and so the later disposal of its shares would not qualify for relief.

Note that in this case, the shareholder can elect for the share exchange event to be treated as a disposal for CGT purposes such that Entrepreneurs' relief may be available against the gain.

4 Replacement of business asset relief (Roll-over relief)

Roll-over relief allows the gain arising on the disposal of a qualifying business asset to be rolled over (i.e. deferred) when the sale proceeds are reinvested in a new qualifying business asset.

The relief is available to both individuals and companies.

The relief

The relief operates as follows:

- The gain arising on the disposal of the qualifying business asset is deducted from (rolled over against) the acquisition cost of the new asset.
- Provided the proceeds are fully reinvested, no tax is payable at the time of the disposal.
- Roll-over relief effectively increases the gain arising on the disposal of the replacement asset, as its base cost has been reduced by the amount of deferred gain.
- Gains may be 'rolled over' a number of times such that a tax liability will only arise when there is a disposal without replacement.
- The relief is not automatic, it must be claimed.
- An individual must claim the relief within 4 years from the end of the tax year in which the disposal is made.
- A disposal in 2009/10 would require a claim by 5 April 2014.

Example 5 - Roll-over relief

Smith purchased an asset qualifying for roll-over relief in January 1987 for £160,000. In May 2009, he sold the asset for £180,000 and spent £200,000 in August 2009 on a new qualifying asset.

Calculate the chargeable gain arising on the disposal of the asset assuming that roll-over relief is claimed.

Calculate the base cost of the new asset acquired.

Answer to example 5

Gain on disposal of asset	£
Sale proceeds	180,000
Less: Cost	(160,000)
	20,000
Less: Roll-over relief	(20,000)
Chargeable gain	Nil

Base cost of new asset	
Acquisition cost	200,000
Less: Gain rolled over on asset disposed of	(20,000)
Revised base cost	180,000

Conditions

Where a **qualifying business asset** is sold at a gain, the taxpayer may roll over the gain provided the proceeds are reinvested in a replacement qualifying business asset within the **qualifying time period**.

Qualifying business assets

The main categories of assets qualifying for roll-over relief on a disposal by an individual are:

- goodwill
- land and buildings
- fixed plant and machinery (i.e. not moveable).

Both the old and the replacement assets must be qualifying business assets and have been used in a trade.

Qualifying time period

The replacement assets must be acquired within a period beginning **one** year before and ending **three** years after the date of sale of the old asset.

Example 6 - Rollover relief

Jones purchased a warehouse in February 1999 for £170,000. In July 2009, he sold the warehouse for £300,000. He used the warehouse for the purposes of his trade throughout the period of ownership.

In December 2011 Jones bought a new warehouse for £360,000 for the purposes of his trade. He plans to sell the warehouse in January 2013 for £550,000.

Calculate the chargeable gains arising on the sale of the two warehouses.

Answer to example 6

First warehouse – July 2009

	£
Sale proceeds	300,000
Less: Cost	(170,000)
	130,000
Less: Roll-over relief (Note)	(130,000)
Chargeable gain	Nil

Note: The full gain of £130,000 can be rolled over (i.e. deferred) as:

- the asset disposed of is a qualifying business asset
- the replacement asset is a qualifying business asset
- the reinvestment has been made in December 2011 (i.e. within the qualifying period of July 2008 to July 2012)
- the amount reinvested exceeds the sale proceeds received (i.e. purchase price of new warehouse of £360,000 exceeds the sale proceeds of £300,000).

Second warehouse – January 2013

	£	£
Sale proceeds		550,000
Less: Base Cost		
Cost	360,000	
Less deferred gain	(130,000)	
		(230,000)
Chargeable gain		320,000

Note: Entrepreneurs' relief is not available as this is the disposal of an individual asset used for the purposes of a continuing trade. The trade itself is not being disposed of.

Test your understanding 5

Chris acquired a freehold building in April 1995. In May 1998 he sold the building for £100,000 and realised a gain of £56,360. In August 1999, another freehold building was bought for £140,000 and this was sold in November 2009 for £380,000.

All of the buildings were used for the purposes of a trade by Chris.

Calculate the chargeable gain arising on the disposal of the second building in 2009/10.

Partial reinvestment of proceeds

Full roll-over relief is only available when all of the proceeds from the sale of the old asset are reinvested.

Where there is partial reinvestment of the proceeds, part of the gain is chargeable at the time of the disposal.

The gain which is chargeable (cannot be rolled over) is the lower of:

- the amount of the proceeds not reinvested
- the full gain.

Test your understanding 6

Jarvis bought a factory in September 1987 and in December 2009, wishing to move to a more convenient location, he sold the factory for £750,000. The gain arising on the disposal of the factory was £115,000.

Jarvis moved into a rented factory until March 2010 when he purchased and moved into a new factory.

Calculate the amount of the gain which is chargeable, if any, on the sale of the original factory and calculate the base cost of the new factory assuming the new factory was purchased for (a) £700,000, or (b) £550,000?

Non-business use

Full roll-over relief is only available where the asset being replaced (the old asset) was used entirely for trade purposes throughout the trader's period of ownership.

Where this condition is not met, roll-over relief is still available but it is scaled down in proportion to the non-trade use.

Example 7 - Roll-over relief

Robert acquired a freehold building in April 1995 for £65,500. He only used 60% of the freehold building for the purposes of his trade. The building was sold in November 2009 for £162,000.

A replacement building was acquired in January 2009 for £180,000 and this was used 100% for trade purposes by Robert.

The replacement building was sold for £250,000 in May 2010.

Calculate the gain rolled over and the chargeable gains arising on the disposals in November 2009 and May 2010.

Answer to example 7

First building – November 2009

	£
Sale proceeds	162,000
Less: Cost	(65,500)
Chargeable gain before reliefs	96,500

Note: The asset disposed of is a qualifying business asset, but as only 60% of the building has been used for trade purposes, the gain eligible for roll-over relief must be restricted by 60%

	Business portion	Non-business portion
	£	£
Split of chargeable gain before reliefs	57,900	38,600
Less: Rollover relief (Note)	(57,900)	(N/A)
Chargeable gain – 2009/10	Nil	38,600

Note:
- the replacement asset is a qualifying business asset, used 100% for the purposes of the trade
- the reinvestment has been made in January 2009 (i.e. within the qualifying period of November 2008 to November 2012).

- the amount reinvested for the purposes of the trade exceeds the sale proceeds received relating to the trade use of the building (i.e. purchase price of new warehouse of £180,000 exceeds the portion of the sale proceeds on the first building relating to the trade of £97,200 (£162,000 x 60%)).
- therefore roll-over relief is available on all of the business portion of the gain.

Sale of replacement building – May 2010

	£	£
Sale proceeds		250,000
Less: Base Cost		
Cost	180,000	
Less deferred gain	(57,900)	
		(122,100)
Chargeable gain – 2010/11		127,900

Note: Entrepreneurs' relief is not available as this is the disposal of an individual asset used for the purposes of a continuing trade.

Test your understanding 7

Hadley purchased a factory in November 1988 and not needing all the space, he let out 15% of it.

In August 2009 he sold the factory for £560,000 and realised a capital gain of £45,000.

In October 2009 Hadley bought another factory which he used 100% for business purposes for £500,000 claiming roll-over relief.

(a) **Calculate the chargeable gain arising on the disposal in August 2009**

(b) **Calculate the base cost of the new factory.**

Depreciating assets

Roll-over relief is modified where the new asset is a depreciating asset:

- If the replacement asset acquired is a depreciating asset, the gain cannot be rolled over, instead it is deferred until the earliest of the following three events:
  - Disposal of replacement asset.

  - The depreciating asset ceases to be used for the purposes of the trade.
  - Ten years from the date of acquisition of the replacement asset.
- The deferred gain is not deducted from the cost of the new asset.
- The deferred gain is just 'frozen' and becomes chargeable on the earliest of the three events above.

A depreciating asset is a wasting asset (i.e. with a predictable life of 50 years or less), or an asset that will become a wasting asset within ten years, (e.g. fixed plant and machinery or leasehold property with ≤ 60 years remaining on the lease).

- If prior to the deferred gain crystallising, a non-depreciating asset is bought, then the original deferred gain can now be rolled over.

Example 8 - Depreciating assets

Cooper purchased a freehold factory in June 1985 for £250,000. In May 2009 he sold it for £420,000 and in June 2009 bought fixed plant and machinery for £450,000. In March 2011, Cooper sold the fixed plant and machinery for £475,000.

Calculate the chargeable gains arising in 2010/11 assuming Cooper claims to roll over the gains where possible.

Answer to example 8

Freehold factory – May 2009

	£
Sale proceeds	420,000
Less: Cost	(250,000)
	170,000
Less: Deferred gain (see Note)	(170,000)
Chargeable gain – 2009/10	Nil

Note:
- the asset disposed of is a qualifying business asset
- the replacement asset is a qualifying business asset, but is a depreciating asset (fixed plant and machinery)
- the reinvestment has been made in June 2009 (i.e. within the qualifying period of May 2008 to May 2012)

- the amount reinvested exceeds the sale proceeds received (i.e. purchase price of new plant and machinery of £450,000 exceeds the sale proceeds on the factory of £420,000)
- therefore all of the gain can be deferred, but the deferred gain is not deducted from the base cost of the plant and machinery
- the gain of £170,000 is frozen and becomes chargeable on the earliest of:
  - the sale of the fixed plant and machinery (March 2011)
  - the date the plant and machinery ceases to be used in the trade (presumably March 2011)
  - ten years from the acquisition of the plant and machinery (June 2019)

Sale of plant and machinery – March 2011

	£
Sale proceeds	475,000
Less: Cost	(450,000)
Capital gain on plant and machinery	25,000
Deferred gain becomes chargeable	170,000
Chargeable gains – 2010/11	195,000

Note: Entrepreneurs' relief is not available as this is the disposal of an individual asset used for the purposes of a continuing trade.

Test your understanding 8

Amir purchased a freehold factory in May 1985 and in May 1997 he sold it for £350,000 realising a capital gain of £150,000. In June 1999 Amir bought fixed plant and machinery for £400,000. In March 2011 Amir sold the fixed plant and machinery for £500,000.

Calculate the chargeable gains arising in respect of the sale of the freehold factory and the fixed plant and machinery, assuming Amir claims to roll over the gains where possible.

Clearly identify in which tax year the gains arise.

Summary

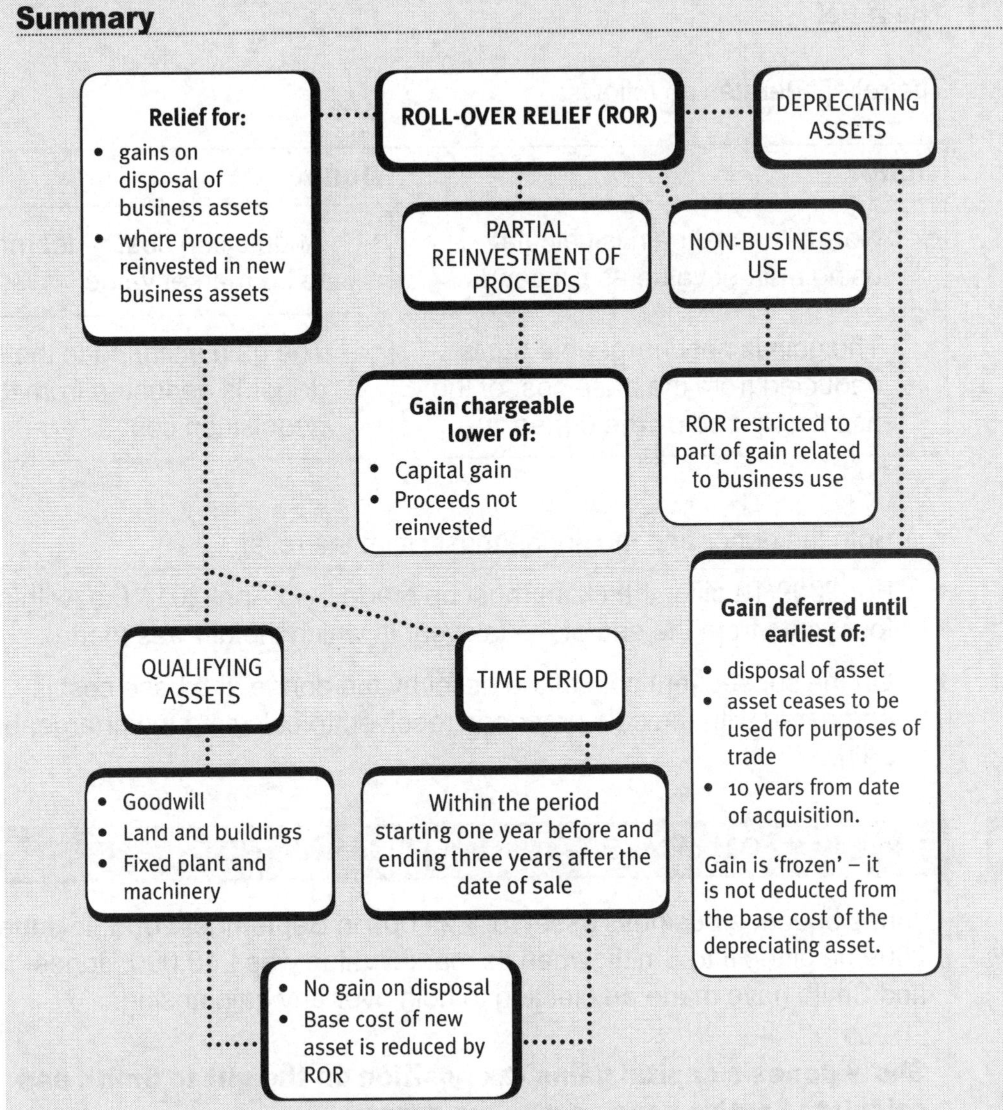

5 Gift of business assets – hold-over relief

The gift of an asset is a chargeable disposal which gives rise to a capital gains tax liability for the donor, however the donor has not received any funds with which to pay the tax.

Gift relief allows the gain arising on the gift of qualifying business assets to be held over (i.e. deferred) until the asset is eventually sold by the donee.

The relief however is only available for:

- qualifying business assets
- gifted by individuals.

The relief

The relief operates as follows:

Donor	Donee
• Normal capital gain is calculated using market value as proceeds	• Acquisition cost = deemed to be market value
• The gain is not chargeable but is deducted from the base cost of the asset acquired by the donee	• The gain accruing to the donor is deducted from the acquisition cost

- Both the donor and the donee must claim the relief.
- For 2009/10 gifts, the claim must be made by 5 April 2014 (i.e. within four years from the end of the tax year in which the gift was made).
- On the subsequent sale of the asset by the donee, the base cost is compared with the sale proceeds received to calculate the chargeable gain.

Example 9 - Gift of business assets – hold-over relief

Jones bought a business asset for £25,000 in September 2003. In June 2009 he gifted it to Smith, when its market value was £40,000. Jones and Smith have made an election to hold over any gain arising.

Show Jones's capital gains tax position on the gift to Smith and calculate Smith's base cost in the asset.

Answer to example 9

Gift to Smith – June 2009

	£
Market value of asset	40,000
Less: Cost	(25,000)
	15,000
Less: Hold-over relief for business assets	(15,000)
Chargeable gain	Nil

Smith's base cost

Smith has allowable expenditure to set against a future disposal, calculated as follows:

	£
Market value of asset acquired	40,000
Less: Held over gain	(15,000)
Base cost	25,000

Qualifying assets

The relief is only available where there is a gift of a qualifying asset.

The following are the main categories of qualifying asset.

- Assets used in the trade of:
  - the donor (i.e. where he is a sole trader)
  - the donor's personal company (this extends the relief to assets owned by the individual but used in the company by him directly for trading purposes).
- Unquoted shares and securities of any trading company.
- Quoted shares or securities of the individual donor's personal trading company.

A company qualifies as an individual's personal trading company if at least 5% of the voting rights are owned by the individual.

Note that, if applicable, gift relief is given **before** Entrepreneurs' relief. However, the interaction of Entrepreneurs' relief with other reliefs will not be examined.

Note, however, that

- the donor may **choose not to claim** gift relief in order to crystallise a gain and claim Entrepreneurs' relief instead if this is advantageous (i.e. if the donee will not qualify for the relief, for example if they would not satisfy the one-year ownership rule).
- the donee **may** be able to make his or her own claim to Entrepreneurs' relief on a subsequent disposal if the conditions are satisfied.

Sales at an undervalue

The relief applies not just to outright gifts but also to sales at an undervalue, where there is an element of gift.

For sales at an undervalue the relief is modified as follows:

- Any proceeds received which exceed the **original cost** of the asset gifted are chargeable to capital gains tax at the date of the gift.
- The gain held over is reduced by the amount chargeable.

Example 10 - Gift of business assets – hold-over relief

Ronald bought a business asset on 4 July 1998 for £20,000. He gave this asset to his son, Regan, on 1 September 2000 when the market value was £52,000. Ronald and Regan made a joint election to hold over any gain arising. Regan sold the asset on 18 December 2009 for £95,000.

(a) **Calculate the gain 'held over' and the chargeable gain arising on the eventual disposal by Regan in 2009/10.**

(b) **Calculate the gain eligible for gift relief and the base cost for Regan, assuming the same facts as above, but Regan pays his father on 1 September 2000:**

(i) **£28,000 or**

(ii) **£18,000.**

Answer to example 10

(a) **Ronald – Capital gains computation – 2000/01**

	£
Deemed disposal proceeds (MV at date of gift)	52,000
Less: Acquisition cost	(20,000)
Chargeable gain	32,000

As Ronald and Regan have made a joint election the gain of £32,000 can be 'held over' (i.e. deferred) from Ronald to Regan (under the gift relief for business assets provisions).

Therefore there would be no chargeable gain on Ronald in 2000/01.

Regan – Capital gains computation – 2009/10

	£	£
Sale proceeds		95,000
Less Base cost:		
MV at date of gift	52,000	
Less: Gain held over from Ronald	(32,000)	
		(20,000)
Chargeable gain		75,000

Note: Entrepreneurs' relief is not available as this is the gift of an individual asset, not the disposal of a whole or substantial part of a business.

(b) **Sale at undervaluation**

(i) **Ronald – Capital gains computation – 2000/01**

	£	£
Deemed disposal proceeds (MV at date of gift)		52,000
Less: Acquisition cost		(20,000)
Potential gain (as before)		32,000
Actual proceeds	28,000	
Less: Original cost	(20,000)	
Excess proceeds over cost chargeable now	8,000	
Less: Gain eligible to be held over		(24,000)
Chargeable gain – 2000/01		8,000

Regan – Base cost (for future disposal)

	£
Deemed acquisition cost (MV at date of gift)	52,000
Less: Gain held over from Ronald	(24,000)
Base cost	28,000

(ii) **Ronald – Capital gains computation – 2000/01**

	£
Deemed disposal proceeds (MV at date of gift)	52,000
Less: Acquisition cost	(20,000)
Potential gain (as before)	32,000
Actual proceeds of £18,000 are less than original cost of £20,000 therefore the entire gain is eligible for gift relief.	
Less: Gain eligible to be held over	(32,000)
Chargeable gain – 2000/01	Nil

Regan – Base cost (for future disposal)

	£
Deemed acquisition cost	52,000
Less: Gain held over from Ronald	(32,000)
Base cost	20,000

Test your understanding 9

Alice bought a business asset in May 2006 for £120,000. She gave this asset to her brother, Adam, on 1 June 2009 when the market value was £150,000. Alice and Adam made a joint election to hold over any gain arising. Adam sold the asset on 1 May 2010 for £180,000.

(a) **Calculate the gain 'held over' and the capital gain arising on the eventual disposal by Adam in 2010/11.**

(b) **Calculate the gain eligible for gift of business assets relief and the base cost of Adam if, instead of giving the asset to Adam, Alice had sold it to him for £130,000.**

Assets not used wholly for trade purposes

The relief is restricted where either:

- only part of an asset is used for trading purposes
- an asset is used for trading purposes for only part of the donor's period of ownership.

Assets apart from shares

Only the gain relating to the period that the asset was used in the trade or the part of the asset used for trading purposes is eligible for relief.

The restriction to the relief operates in the same way as roll-over relief where assets have not been wholly used in the trade.

Example 11 - Gift of business assets – hold-over relief

David acquired a freehold building in May 2005 for £160,000. He used 60% of the freehold building in his trade for business purposes. In June 2009 he gifted the building to his son, Ben, when its market value was £250,000. David and Ben signed an election to hold over the gain arising on the gift.

Calculate the gain held over and the chargeable gain arising on the gift of the building in June 2009.

Answer to example 11

David – Capital gains computation – 2009/10

	£
Market value at date of gift	250,000
Less: Acquisition cost	(160,000)
Potential gain	90,000
As only 60% of the building has been used for the purposes of a trade, the gain eligible to be held over must also be restricted by the same %.	
Less: Gain eligible to be held over (60% × £90,000)	(54,000)
Chargeable gain – 2009/10 (40% of £90,000)	36,000

Note: Entrepreneurs' relief is not available as this is the gift of an individual asset, not the disposal of a whole or substantial part of a business.

Shares

Where the assets being gifted are shares the gain eligible to be held over is restricted in the following situation:

- the shares are in the donor's personal company (at least 5% of the voting rights are owned by the donor) whether quoted or unquoted; and
- the company owns chargeable non-business assets.

In this situation the gain eligible for gift relief is:

$$\text{Total gain} \times \frac{\text{M.V. of chargeable business assets (CBA)}}{\text{M.V. of chargeable assets (CA)}}$$

Note that where the donor holds less than 5% of the voting rights:

- for unquoted shares - no restriction to the relief when shares are gifted
- for quoted shares - gift relief is not available at all.

Chargeable assets

A chargeable asset is one that, if sold, would give rise to a chargeable gain (or an allowable loss). Exempt assets such as motor cars are therefore excluded. Stocks, debtors, cash, etc. are also excluded as they are not capital assets and therefore not chargeable.

Chargeable business assets

These are defined as chargeable assets (as defined above) that are used for the purposes of a trade. Chargeable business assets therefore **exclude** shares, securities or other assets owned by the business but held for investment purposes.

Note that if the individual disposes of shares in a personal trading company:

- gift relief is available:
  - subject to the (CBA / CA) restriction above
  - regardless of whether or not the individual works for the company
- entrepreneurs' relief is also available provided:
  - the individual works for the company, and
  - it has been the individual's personal trading company
  - for the 12 months prior to the disposal.

Summary

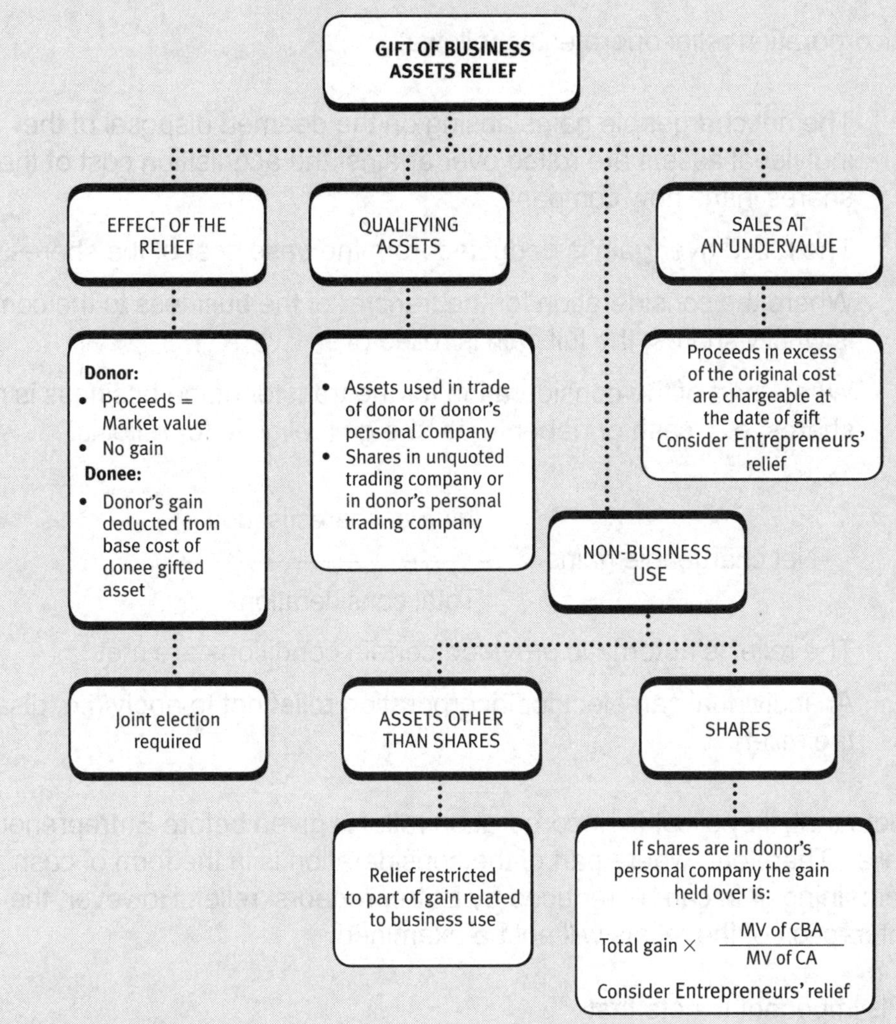

6 Incorporation relief

Where an individual transfers their business to a company, the individual assets of the business are deemed to have been disposed of at market value for capital gains tax purposes.

Incorporation relief is a form of roll-over relief to allow the gains arising on incorporation to be deferred until the shares in the newly formed company are disposed of.

The conditions

Incorporation relief is available where the following conditions apply:

- The unincorporated business is transferred as a going concern.
- All of the assets of the business (other than cash) are transferred.
- The consideration for the transfer of the business must be wholly or mainly shares in the company.

The relief

Incorporation relief operates as follows:

- The net chargeable gains arising on the deemed disposal of the individual assets are rolled over against the acquisition cost of the shares in the new company.
- The rolled over gain is deducted from the base cost of the shares.
- Where the consideration for the transfer of the business to the company is wholly shares, the full gain is rolled over.
- Where part of the consideration for the transfer of the business is not shares, e.g. cash or debentures, the gain eligible for relief is:

$$\text{Net chargeable gains} \times \frac{\text{Value of shares issued}}{\text{Total consideration}}$$

- The relief is automatic provided certain conditions are met.
- An individual can elect for incorporation relief not to apply (i.e. disapply the relief).

Note that, if applicable, incorporation relief is given before Entrepreneurs' relief. Therefore, where part of the consideration is in the form of cash, the remaining gain can be reduced by Entrepreneurs' relief. However, the interaction of the reliefs will not be examined.

It is important to note that :

- The subsequent disposal of the shares should normally qualify for Entrepreneurs' relief provided the conditions are satisfied.
- However, if this in unlikely, the individual may **disapply** incorporation relief in order to crystallise a gain and claim Entrepreneurs' relief instead if this is advantageous (i.e. if the individual plans to dispose of the shares within one year and fails the one-year ownership rule).

Example 13 - Incorporation relief

Sarah incorporated her sewing business on 1 June 2009. The assets transferred to the new company, Sarah Ltd, are set out below. In exchange for the transfer of the business she received 100,000 £1 ordinary shares.

Assets transferred	MV at 1.6.09	Original cost
	£	£
Freehold premises – acquired May 2000	150,000	70,000
Furniture and fittings	5,000	10,000
Plant and machinery	5,500	15,000
Stock	25,500	25,000
Goodwill	54,000	–
	240,000	120,000

All items of plant and machinery and furniture and fittings were bought and sold for less than £6,000.

Calculate the chargeable gains, if any, arising on the incorporation of Sarah's business and state Sarah's base cost in the shares in Sarah Ltd.

Answer to example 13

	£	£
Freehold premises		
MV on incorporation	150,000	
Less: Acquisition cost	(70,000)	
		80,000
Goodwill		
MV on incorporation	54,000	
Less: Acquisition cost	(Nil)	
		54,000
Total capital gains		134,000
Less Incorporation relief (Note)		(134,000)
Chargeable gain		Nil
Base cost of shares in Sarah Ltd		
Market value of shares		240,000
Less: Capital gains rolled over		(134,000)
Base cost		106,000

Note: As the consideration is wholly in shares the gains arising on incorporation can be rolled over in full.

Test your understanding 11

On 8 March 2010 Chandra incorporated a wholesale business that she had run as a sole trader since 1 May 2006. The market value of the business on 8 March 2010 was £250,000.

All of the business assets were transferred to a new limited company, with the consideration consisting of 200,000 £1 ordinary shares valued at £200,000 and £50,000 in cash.

The only chargeable asset of the business was goodwill and this was valued at £100,000 on 8 March 2010. The goodwill has a nil cost.

Calculate the chargeable gains arising from Chandra's disposals during 2009/10. Ignore Entrepreneurs' relief.

Example 14 - Incorporation relief

Sam started a retail business in 1985. On 1 May 2009 he transferred his business to a company, Sam Ltd. The assets transferred are set out below. In exchange he received 4,000 £1 ordinary shares, valued at £80,000 and £20,000 cash.

Assets transferred	M.V. at 1.5.09	Gain
	£	£
Freehold premises	35,000	25,000
Furniture and fittings	8,000	–
Plant and machinery	14,000	–
Stock	25,000	–
Goodwill	18,000	18,000
	100,000	43,000

On 1 February 2010 Sam sold his entire holding in Sam Ltd for £150,000.

Calculate Sam's chargeable gains for 2009/10 and consider any tax advice you may wish to give Sam.

Answer to example 14

Capital gain on transfer of business – May 2009

	£
Total gains	43,000
Less: Incorporation relief (£43,000 × £80,000/(£80,000 + £20,000)	(34,400)
Chargeable gain before Entrepreneurs' relief	8,600

Note: Entrepreneurs' relief is available on the remaining gain.

Disposal of shares – February 2010

	£	£
Sale proceeds		150,000
Less Base cost:		
Market value of shares	80,000	
Less: Rolled over gain	(34,400)	
		(45,600)
Chargeable gain (Note)		104,400

Note: Entrepreneurs' relief is not available on the disposal of the shares as Sam has owned them for less than 12 months.

Tax advice

In these circumstances it would be advantageous to disapply incorporation relief and claim Entrepreneurs' relief on the whole gain arising at the date of incorporation.

As a result the total chargeable gains in 2009/10 would be £93,889 (W) (£23,889 + £70,000).

Working

	£
Total gains on transfer of business	43,000
Less: Entrepreneurs' relief (£43,000 x 4/9)	(19,111)
Chargeable gain	23,889

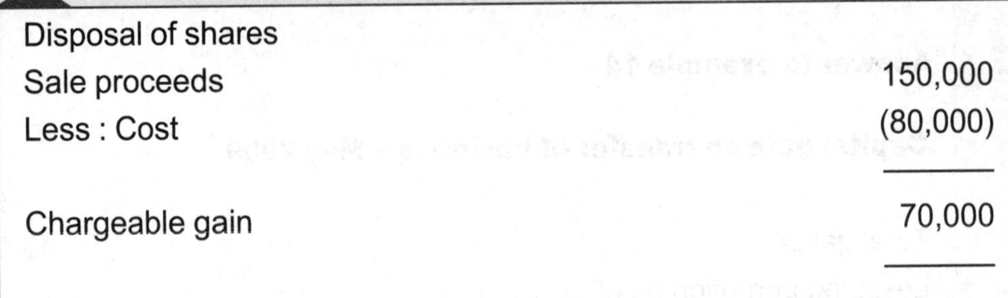

Disposal of shares	
Sale proceeds	150,000
Less : Cost	(80,000)
Chargeable gain	70,000

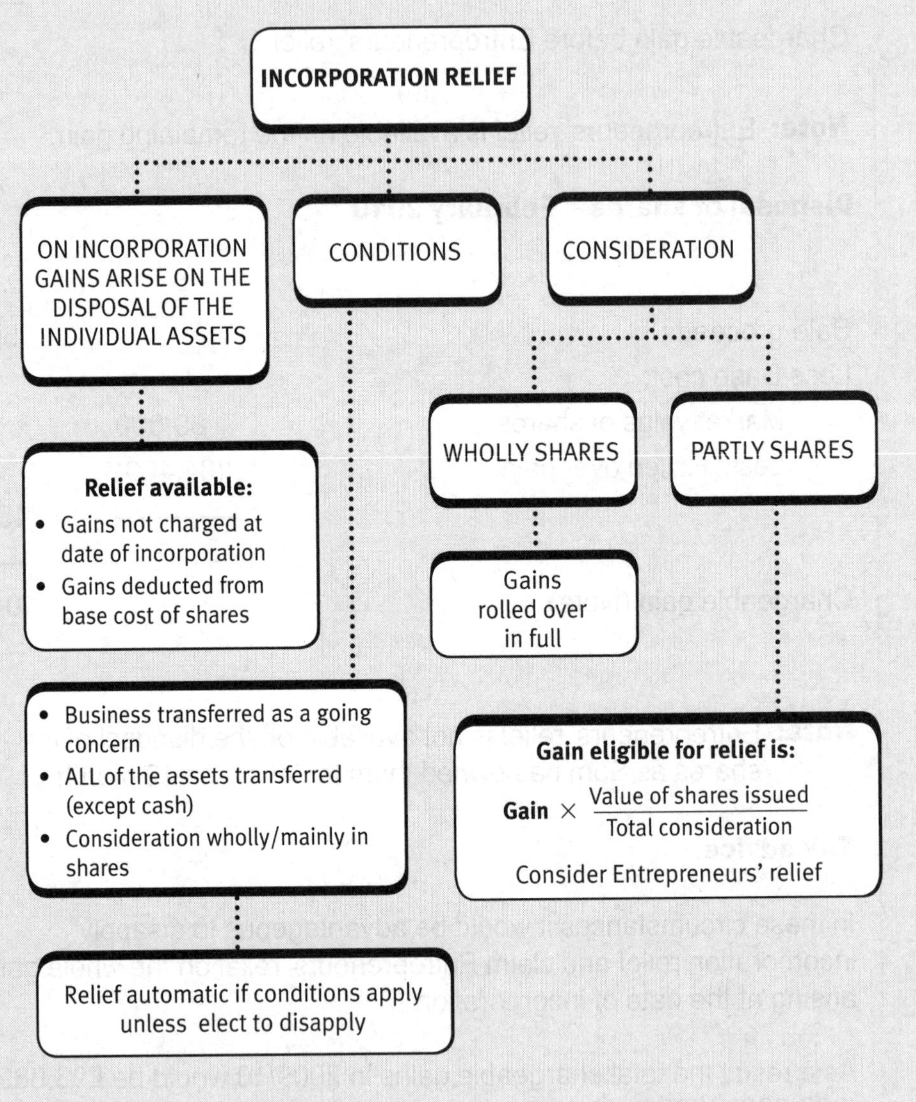

INCORPORATION RELIEF
ON INCORPORATION GAINS ARISE ON THE DISPOSAL OF THE INDIVIDUAL ASSETS
CONDITIONS
CONSIDERATION
Relief available:
• Gains not charged at date of incorporation
• Gains deducted from base cost of shares
WHOLLY SHARES
PARTLY SHARES
Gains rolled over in full
• Business transferred as a going concern
• ALL of the assets transferred (except cash)
• Consideration wholly/mainly in shares
Gain eligible for relief is:
Gain × Value of shares issued / Total consideration
Consider Entrepreneurs' relief
Relief automatic if conditions apply unless elect to disapply

7 Chapter summary

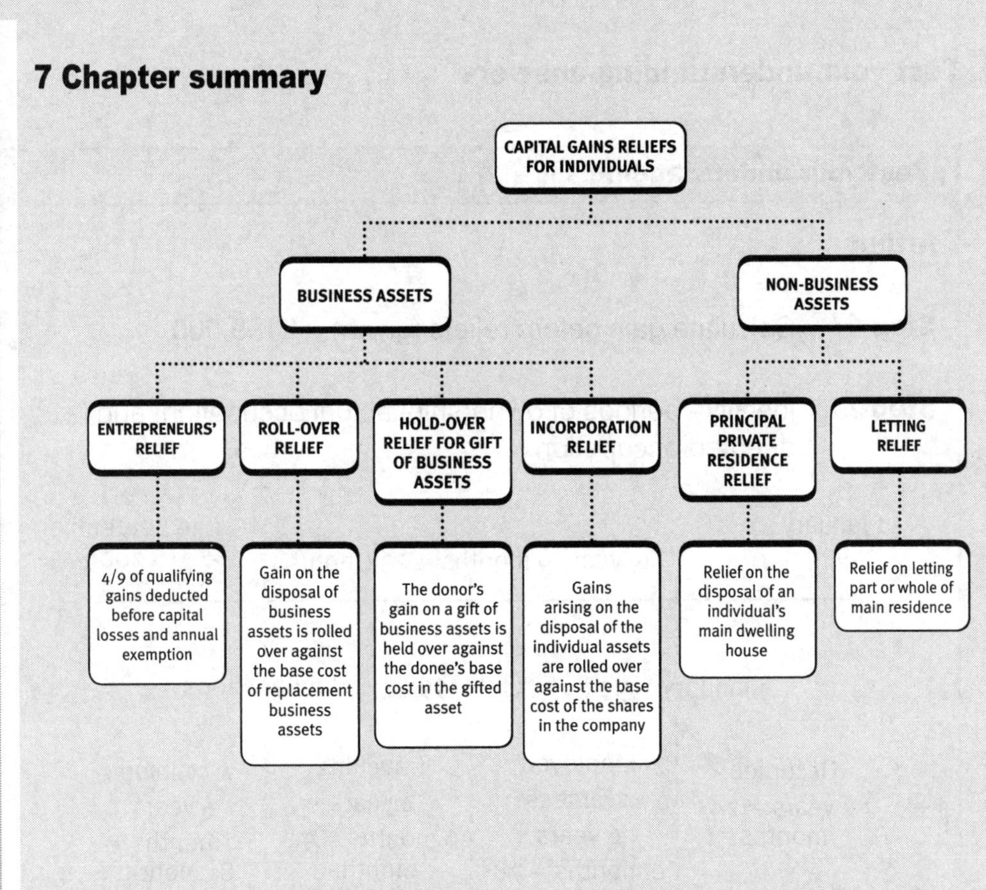

Test your understanding answers

Test your understanding 1

Arthur

Step 1 Calculate gain before reliefs (given) = £189,000

Step 2 Identify - periods of ownership, actual occupation, and deemed occupation.

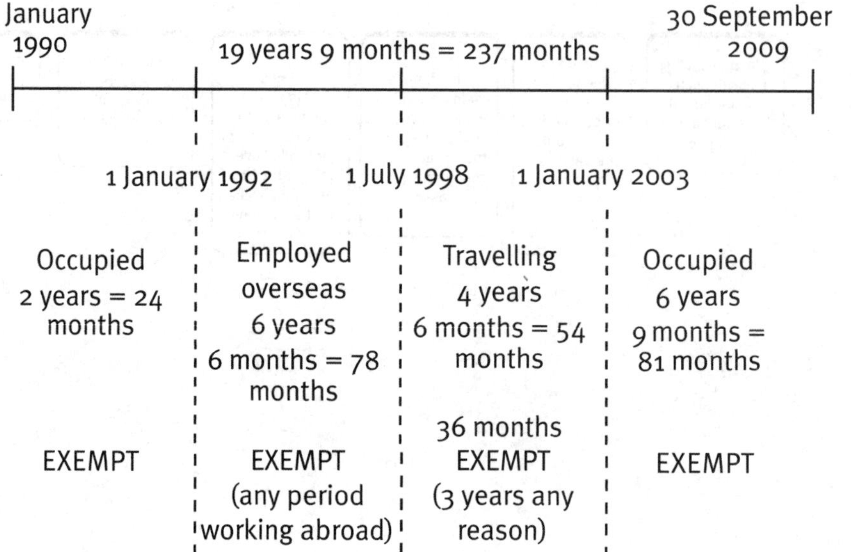

PPR exemption	Months	
Occupied	24	
Employed overseas	78	
Any reason	36	
Occupied	81	
PPR exemption	219	out of 237

The periods of occupation before and after deemed occupation do **not** need to be **immediately** before and after (for example the employment overseas ended on 30 June 1998 and is followed by actual occupation which did not start until 1 January 2003).

Step 3 Deduct PPR relief.

	£
Gain before reliefs	189,000
Less: PPR relief (219/237 × £189,000)	(174,646)
Chargeable gain after reliefs	14,354

Test your understanding 2

Todd

Todd owned the house for six years and used 1/7th of the house (one of the seven rooms) for business purposes.

The last 36 months exemption does not apply to the business element of the gain as this part of the house has never been used for private purposes.

The chargeable gain after reliefs = (£60,000 × 1/7) = £8,571.

Test your understanding 3

Jane Smith

	£
Market value	140,000
Less: Cost	(45,000)
Enhancement expenditure	(10,600)
Chargeable gain before reliefs	84,400
Less: PPR relief (£84,400 × 73/121) (W1)	(50,919)
	33,481
Less: Letting relief = lowest of:	
(a) Maximum = £40,000	
(b) PPR relief = £50,919	
(c) Letting gain = £84,400 × 36/121	(25,111)
Chargeable gain after reliefs	8,370

Working: PPR and letting relief

	Total	Exempt	Chargeable
1.9.99 –30.9.02	37		
Actual occupation		37	
1.10.02 – 30.9.03	12		
Empty – chargeable			12
1.10.03 – 30.9.09	72		
Last 3 years		36	
Rest of period – chargeable			36
Number of months	121	73	48

The property was let from 1.10.03 to 30.9.09; however the last 3 years are exempt under the PPR rules. Therefore letting relief is available for the remaining 36 months in that period.

Test your understanding 4

Paul

2009/10	£
Sale of trading company shares	
Gain on shares	430,000
Less: Entrepreneurs' relief (£430,000 × 4/9)	(191,111)
	238,889
Sale of warehouse (Note)	245,000
Chargeable gains	483,889
Less: Annual exemption	(10,100)
Taxable gains	473,789
Capital gains tax payable (£473,789 × 18%)	85,282

Note: The disposal of the warehouse in 2009/10 is the disposal of an individual business asset used for the purposes of a continuing trade. To qualify for Entrepreneurs' relief, there must be a disposal of the whole or part of the trading business. The sale of an asset in isolation will not qualify.

2010/11	£
Sale of trading business	
Factory	495,000
Goodwill	130,000
	625,000
Less: Entrepreneurs' relief - rest of the lifetime allowance (£1,000,000 – £430,000) = £570,000 × 4/9	(253,333)
	371,667
Sale of Grandfather clock	5,325
Chargeable gains	376,992
Less: Annual exemption	(10,100)
Taxable gains	366,892
Capital gains tax payable (£366,892 x 18%)	66,041

Test your understanding 5

Chris

Second building – November 2009	£	£
Sale proceeds		380,000
Less: Base cost		
Cost	140,000	
Less: deferred gain	(56,360)	
		(83,640)
Chargeable gain		296,360

Note: The full gain of £56,360 can be rolled over (i.e. deferred) as:

- the asset disposed of is a qualifying business asset
- the replacement asset is a qualifying business asset
- the reinvestment has been made in August 1999 (i.e. within the qualifying period of May 1997 to May 2001)
- the amount reinvested exceeds the sale proceeds received (i.e. purchase price of new warehouse of £360,000 exceeds the sale proceeds of £300,000).

Test your understanding 6

Jarvis

	(a)	(b)
New factory purchased for	£700,000	£550,000
	£	£
Chargeable gain now = Lower of:		
(i) Sale proceeds not reinvested		
(£750,000 – £700,000)	50,000	
(£750,000 – £550,000)		200,000
(ii) Gain on the disposal of original factory	115,000	115,000
Therefore, **chargeable in 2009/10** (Note)	**50,000**	**115,000**
Roll-over relief		
(£115,000 – £50,000)	65,000	
(£115,000 – £115,000)		Nil
Base cost of new replacement factory		
Cost	700,000	550,000
Less Roll-over relief	(65,000)	(Nil)
	635,000	550,000

Note: Entrepreneurs' relief is not available as this is the disposal of an individual asset used for the purposes of a continuing trade.

Test your understanding 7

Hadley

Disposal of factory – August 2009

The asset disposed of is a qualifying business asset, but as only 85% of the building has been used for trade purposes, the gain must be split and only 85% is eligible for roll-over relief.

	Business portion	Non-business portion
	£	£
Split of capital gain (85% : 15%)	38,250	6,750
Less: Rollover relief (Note)	(38,250)	(N/A)
Chargeable gain – 2009/10	Nil	6,750

Note:

- the replacement asset is a qualifying business asset, used 100% for the purposes of the trade
- the reinvestment has been made in October 2009 (i.e. within the qualifying period of August 2008 to August 2012)
- the amount reinvested for the purposes of the trade exceeds the sale proceeds received relating to the trade use of the building (i.e. purchase price of new warehouse of £500,000 exceeds the portion of the sale proceeds on the first building relating to the trade of £476,000 (£560,000 × 85%))
- therefore roll-over relief is available on all of the business portion of the gain.
- Entrepreneurs' relief is not available as this is the disposal of an individual asset used for the purposes of a continuing trade and the gain is arising on an investment asset.

Base cost of replacement factory – October 2009

	£
Cost	500,000
Less: Deferred gain	(38,250)
	461,750

Test your understanding 8

Amir

Freehold factory – May 1997

	£
Capital gain	150,000
Less: Deferred gain (see Note)	(150,000)
Chargeable gain – 1997/98	Nil

Note:

- the asset disposed of is a qualifying business asset
- the replacement asset is a qualifying business asset, but is a depreciating asset (fixed plant and machinery)
- the reinvestment has been made in June 1999 (i.e. within the qualifying period of May 1996 to May 2000)
- the amount reinvested exceeds the sale proceeds received (i.e. purchase price of new plant and machinery of £400,000 exceeds the sale proceeds on the factory of £350,000)
- therefore all of the gain can be deferred, but the deferred gain is not deducted from the base cost of the plant and machinery
- the gain of £150,000 is frozen and becomes chargeable on the earliest of:
  - the sale of the fixed plant and machinery (March 2011)
  - the date the plant and machinery ceases to be used in the trade (presumably March 2011)
  - ten years from the acquisition of the plant and machinery (June 2009)

Chargeable event – June 2009

	£
Deferred gain becomes chargeable – 2009/10	150,000

Sale of plant and machinery – March 2011

Sale proceeds	500,000
Less: Cost	(400,000)
Chargeable gain – 2010/11	100,000

Test your understanding 9

Alice

(a) **Alice – Capital gains computation – 2009/10**

	£
MV at date of gift	150,000
Less: Acquisition cost	(120,000)
Chargeable gain	30,000

As Alice and Adam made a joint election this gain of £30,000 can be 'held over' from Alice to Adam (under the 'gift relief' provisions).

Therefore there would be no chargeable gain on Alice in 2009/10.

Adam – Capital gains computation – 2010/11

	£	£
Sale proceeds		180,000
Less: Base cost		
MV at date of gift	150,000	
Less: Gain held over	(30,000)	
		(120,000)
Chargeable gain		60,000

Note: Entrepreneurs' relief is not available as this is the gift of an individual asset, not the disposal of a whole or substantial part of a business.

(b) **Alice – Capital gains computation – 2009/10**

	£	£
MV at date of gift		150,000
Less: Acquisition cost		(120,000)
Potential gain (as above)		30,000
Actual proceeds	130,000	
Less: Original cost	(120,000)	
Excess proceeds over cost	10,000	
Less: Gain eligible to be held over		(20,000)
Chargeable gain in 2009/10		10,000

Adam – Base cost (for future disposal)

	£
Deemed acquisition cost (MV at date of gift)	150,000
Less: Gain held over from Alice	(20,000)
Base cost	130,000

Test your understanding 10

Fred

Fred Ltd's chargeable business assets total £400,000 (premises), whilst the chargeable assets total £500,000 (premises and shares held as investments).

Therefore £336,000 (£420,000 × £400,000/£500,000) of the capital gain can be held over.

Fred's chargeable gain in 2009/10 is therefore £84,000 (£420,000 – £336,000).

Note: Entrepreneurs' relief is not available on the remaining gain as Fred did not work for the company in the 12 months before he disposed of the shares.

Test your understanding 11

Chandra

Capital gains computation – 2009/10

	£
Goodwill	
MV on incorporation	100,000
Less: Acquisition cost	(Nil)
	100,000
Less: Incorporation relief	
£100,000 × £200,000/£250,000 (Note 1)	(80,000)
Chargeable gain	20,000

Note: Entrepreneurs' relief would be available on the remaining gain, but the interaction of the other reliefs with Entrepreneurs' relief will not be examined.

chapter

18

Introduction to corporation tax

Chapter learning objectives

Upon completion of this chapter you will be able to:

- define the terms 'period of account', 'accounting period', and 'financial year'
- explain the rules for determining when an accounting period starts and ends
- identify the correct accounting period for corporation tax from information supplied
- define the rules of residence for a company and determine a company's residence using those rules
- identify the different taxable profits for a company and the basis of assessment
- explain the implications of receiving franked investment income
- compute the corporation tax liability for a single company.

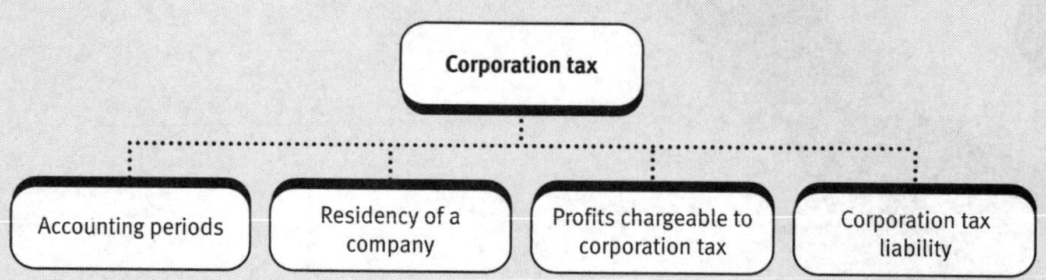

1 Introduction

UK resident companies are assessed to corporation tax on their worldwide income and chargeable gains arising in an accounting period.

This and the following five chapters deal with the way in which companies are assessed to corporation tax.

Corporation tax is an important topic as it will be the focus of question two in the examination, which will be either for either **25** or **30 marks**.

This first introductory chapter sets out the basis upon which companies are assessed to corporation tax and explains how a company's corporation tax liability is calculated.

2 Basis of assessment

- Corporation tax is assessed on a company's income and chargeable gains arising in an accounting period.
- The accounting period is not necessarily the same period as the company's set of accounts (period of account).

It is important when dealing with corporation tax to understand the terms 'period of account' and 'chargeable accounting period'.

Period of account

A period of account is any period for which a company prepares accounts. It is usually 12 months in length, but may be shorter or longer than this.

Chargeable accounting period

A chargeable accounting period (CAP) is the period for which a charge to corporation tax is made. It may never be longer than 12 months.

3 Chargeable accounting periods

When does CAP start?

A CAP period starts when:

- a company starts to trade (or receives income chargeable to corporation tax)
- the previous accounting period ends.

When does a CAP end?

The main situations where a CAP ends are:

- twelve months after the beginning of the accounting period
- the end of the company's period of account
- the date the company begins or ceases to trade.

Long periods of account

For corporation tax purposes, a CAP can never exceed 12 months.

Therefore, if a company prepares accounts for a period of more than 12 months, there must be two accounting periods for tax purposes.

The long period of account is divided into CAPs as follows:

- CAP for the first 12 months.
- a separate CAP for the balance.

A corporation tax computation is prepared for each CAP.

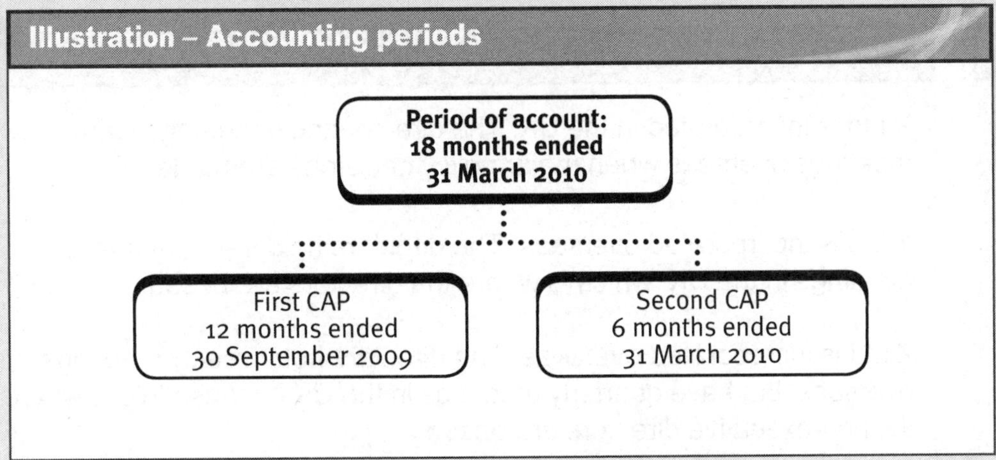

The method of allocating the accounting profits between the two CAPs is covered in chapter 19.

4 The tax residence of a company

Companies **resident** in the UK are chargeable to corporation tax on all profits and chargeable gains **wherever they arise** (i.e. on worldwide profits and gains).

It is therefore important to correctly determine where a company is resident.

Determining residence

A company is UK resident as follows:

- a company **incorporated** in the UK is resident in the UK for corporation tax purposes
- if a company is incorporated elsewhere, it is regarded as resident in the UK if it is **centrally managed and controlled** in the UK.

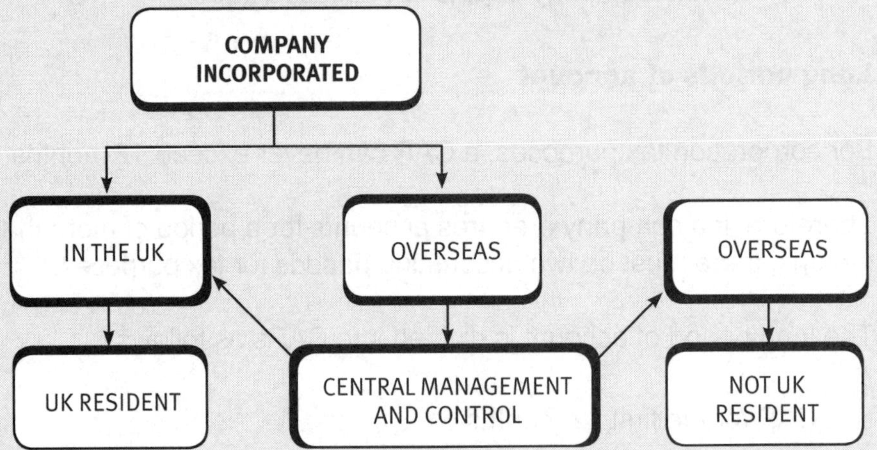

A company that is incorporated in the UK is resident in the UK regardless of where it is centrally managed and controlled.

Example 1 - The tax residence of a company

X Ltd is incorporated in the UK. The directors hold monthly board meetings overseas when major policy decisions are made.

Y Ltd is incorporated overseas. The directors hold frequent board meetings in the UK, which is where the directors are based.

Z Ltd is incorporated overseas. The directors hold weekly meetings overseas, but have quarterly meetings in the UK because this is where the non-executive directors are based.

State which of the above companies will be treated as resident in the UK.

Answer to example 1

- X Ltd is resident in the UK. If a company is incorporated in the UK it is irrelevant where meetings are held and decisions are made.
- Y Ltd would probably be treated as resident in the UK for corporation tax purposes. Although not incorporated in the UK, it would appear that the company is centrally managed and controlled from the UK.
- Z Ltd would probably not be treated as resident in the UK. The company is not incorporated in the UK, and it appears to be centrally managed and controlled from overseas.

Test your understanding 1

Matthew Ltd is a French company that holds all its board meetings in Germany. Its directors live in the UK most of the year.

Mark Ltd is an Italian company that holds its monthly board meetings in London. Other interim board meetings are held in Italy, where some of the directors are based. Most of the directors are based in the UK.

Luke Ltd is a UK company. Board meetings are held in France.

State which of the above companies will be treated as resident in the UK for corporation tax purposes.

5 Profits chargeable to corporation tax

Introduction

- A company's corporation tax liability for an accounting period is calculated by computing profits from all sources, and deducting Gift Aid payments.
- Included in the computation of profits are the world-wide income and chargeable gains of a company.
- The resultant figure is known as profits chargeable to corporation tax (or 'PCTCT' for short).

Layout of a corporation tax computation

Company name
Corporation tax computation for the year ended 31 March 2010

	£
Trading profit	X
Interest income	X
Property business profit	X
Chargeable gains	X
	—
Total profits	X
Less: Gift Aid	(X)
	—
Profits chargeable to corporation tax (PCTCT)	X
	—

Trading profit

Assesses all trading income net of trading expenditure. See Chapter 19 for detail.

Interest income

Assesses all interest receivable net of some interest payable. See Chapter 19 for detail.

Dividends

Dividends received from UK and overseas companies are exempt from corporation tax.

Although exempt from corporation tax, dividends received have an impact on the rate of corporation tax that is applicable (see section 6).

Property business profit

Assesses the profit (or loss) from letting furnished or unfurnished property and is calculated on the accruals basis. (See Chapter 19 for more detail.).

Chargeable gains/losses

- Corporation tax is also charged on any chargeable gains that a company makes during an accounting period.

It is essential to understand that companies pay **corporation tax** on their chargeable gains rather than capital gains tax.

- Chargeable gains for companies are covered in detail in Chapter 20.

Gift Aid

The tax treatment of Gift Aid payments made by a company is different from that applied to payments made by an individual.

- For companies, Gift Aid payments are simply deducted from total profits.
- See Chapter 19 for more detail of Gift Aid payments made by a company.

Example 2 - Profits chargeable to corporation tax

Westmorland Ltd has the following income and outgoings for the year ending 31 March 2010.

	£
Tax-adjusted trading profit	1,456,500
Property business profit	25,000
Interest receivable	10,000
Chargeable gains	35,000
Dividends from UK companies	14,400
Gift Aid donation	(10,000)

Compute the PCTCT for the year ending 31 March 2010.

Answer to example 2

	£
Tax-adjusted trading profits	1,456,500
Property business profit	25,000
Interest receivable	10,000
Chargeable gains	35,000
	1,526,500
Less: Gift Aid donation	(10,000)
PCTCT	1,516,500

Note: Dividends from UK companies are ignored when calculating PCTCT as they are exempt from corporation tax.

Test your understanding 2

Cumberland Ltd has the following income and outgoings for the year ended 31 March 2010.

	£
Tax-adjusted trading profit	81,500
Property business profit	1,300
Non-trading loan interest receivable	2,200
Chargeable gains	3,000
Dividends from overseas companies	3,500
Dividends from UK companies	900
Gift Aid donation	1,000

Compute the PCTCT for the y/e 31 March 2010.

6 The corporation tax liability

The company's corporation tax liability is calculated by applying the appropriate rate of corporation tax to the company's PCTCT.

Rate of corporation tax

The rate of corporation tax is determined by the:

(1) financial year, and

(2) 'profits' of the company.

Financial year

- The rate of corporation tax is fixed by reference to financial years.
- A financial year runs from 1 April to the following 31 March and is identified by the calendar year in which it begins.
- The year commencing 1 April 2009 is the financial year 2009 (FY 2009). Financial years should not be confused with the tax years for income tax, which run from 6 April to the following 5 April.
- The following rates apply to the 2009 financial year (FY 2009) (i.e. year ended 31 March 2010).

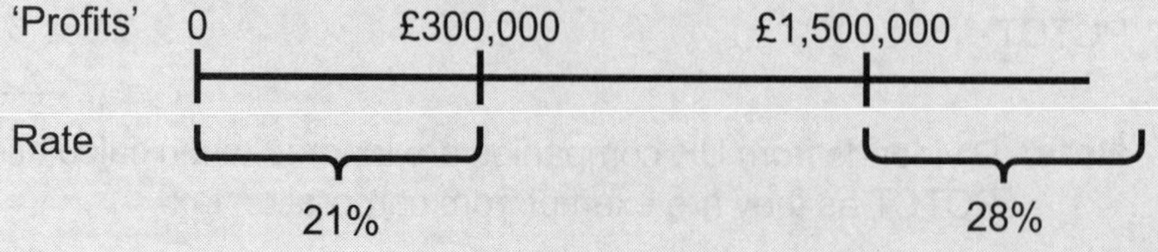

These rates and limits are provided in the Tax Rates and Allowances tables provided in the examination.

- If the 'profits' are below £300,000 (the 'lower limit') then the 'profits chargeable to corporation tax' are charged at the small company's rate of 21%.
- If the 'profits' exceed £1,500,000 (the 'upper limit') then the 'profits chargeable to corporation tax' are charged at the full rate of 28%.
- Where 'profits' are between £300,000 and £1,500,000 a special marginal relief applies.
- These limits for 'profits' are fixed for each financial year.

'Profits'

To determine the rate of corporation tax, a special definition of 'profits' applies as follows:

	£
PCTCT	X
Plus: Franked investment income (FII)	X
	—
'Profits'	X
	—

The 'profits' figure is compared to the 'profits limits' for the relevant financial year to determine the rate of corporation tax applicable. The appropriate rate of tax is then applied to the company's PCTCT.

Franked investment income

Although dividends received from UK and overseas companies are exempt from corporation tax, they can have an impact on the rate of corporation tax that is applicable.

- Dividends received plus the associated 10% tax credit are known as franked investment income (FII).
- To calculate FII, take dividends received and multiply by 100/90.
- FII is added to the PCTCT in order to arrive at the 'profit' figure.

- Although corporation tax is calculated on the PCTCT, it is the 'profit' figure that determines which **rate** of corporation tax is applicable.
- There is one type of dividend that is not included as FII:
  - a dividend received from a 51% group company (see Chapter 22).

Test your understanding 3

Zachary Ltd has profits chargeable to corporation tax of £148,000 in the year ended 31 March 2010, and dividends received from other UK companies of £4,500.

Calculate Zachary Ltd's corporation tax liability for the year ended 31 March 2010.

Test your understanding 4

Argo Ltd has profits chargeable to corporation tax of £1,450,000 in the year ended 31 March 2010, and UK dividends received of £72,000.

Calculate Argo Ltd's corporation tax liability for the year ended 31 March 2010.

Marginal relief

If 'profits' fall between the 'lower and upper limits' (i.e. between £300,000 and £1,500,000) then the company is 'marginal' and its PCTCT are charged as follows:

	£
PCTCT @ full rate (28%)	X
Less Marginal relief	
7/400 × (M – P) × I/P	(X)
Corporation tax liability	X

where:

M = Relevant 'profits' upper limit for the financial year
P = 'Profits'
I = PCTCT

Example 3 - The corporation tax liability

Small Ltd has the following PCTCT for the year ended 31 March 2010.

	£
Trading profit	260,000
Property business profit	40,000
	300,000
Less: Gift Aid paid	(10,000)
PCTCT	290,000

Calculate the company's corporation tax liability if:

(a) **no dividends are received.**

(b) **£9,000 of dividends are received.**

(c) **£45,000 of dividends are received.**

Answer to example 3

(a) No dividends received

PCTCT = 'Profits' (No FII)	£290,000

'Profits' are below the lower limit of £300,000 therefore:

Corporation tax liability = £290,000 × 21% = £60,900.

(b) Dividends received = £9,000

	£
PCTCT	290,000
Plus: FII (£9,000 × 100/90)	10,000
'Profits'	300,000

'Profits' are equal to the lower limit and therefore the small companies rate applies:

Corporation tax liability = £290,000 × 21% = £60,900, as before.

The 'profits' level has not altered the decision.

(c) Dividends received = £45,000

	£
PCTCT	290,000
Plus: FII (£45,000 × 100/90)	50,000
'Profits'	340,000

'Profits' are above £300,000 but below £1,500,000; therefore marginal relief applies:

	£
Corporation tax (£290,000 × 28%)	81,200
Less: Marginal relief	
7/400 × (£1,500,000 – £340,000) × £290,000/£340,000	(17,315)
Corporation tax liability	63,885

Test your understanding 5

Sycamore Ltd has the following results for the y/e 31 March 2010:

Tax-adjusted trading profit	£320,000
Chargeable gain	£10,000
Dividends received	£18,000

Calculate Sycamore Ltd's corporation tax liability for the year ended 31 March 2010.

Short accounting periods

- The upper and lower 'profits' limits of £1,500,000 and £300,000 apply for accounting periods of 12 months.
- If an accounting period is for less than 12 months, the limits must be reduced proportionately.

Example 4 - The corporation tax liability

Minnow Ltd has the following results for the three-month accounting period ended 31 March 2010:

	£
Tax-adjusted trading profit	250,000
Dividends from UK companies	18,000

Compute the company's corporation tax liability for the accounting period ended 31 March 2010.

Answer to example 4

Corportion tax computation – 3 m/e 31 March 2010

	£
PCTCT	250,000
Plus: FII (£18,000 × 100/90)	20,000
'Profits'	270,000
Corporation tax (£250,000 × 28%)	70,000
Less: Marginal relief	
7/400 × (£375,000 – £270,000) × £250,000/£270,000	(1,701)
Corporation tax liability	68,299

Note: As the accounting period is only three months long, the lower limit is reduced to £75,000 (£300,000 × 3/12) and the upper limit is reduced to £375,000 (£1,500,000 × 3/12).

As 'profits' fall between these reduced limits, marginal relief applies.

Note that the reduced upper limit of £375,000 is used in the marginal relief calculation.

Test your understanding 6

Petal Ltd has the following results for the 9 m/e 31 March 2010:

Tax-adjusted trading profit	£1,100,000
Chargeable gain	£60,000
Dividends from UK companies	£45,000

Calculate the company's corporation tax liability for the 9 m/e 31 March 2010.

Accounting periods straddling 31 March

Where a company's accounting period falls into two financial years then the corporation tax liability must be calculated for each financial year if either:

- the corporation tax rates, or
- the 'profits' limits have changed between the financial years.

The rates of corporation tax and the marginal relief fractions were different for the Financial years 2007 and 2008. Therefore a two-part computation is required for a CAP straddling 31 March 2008.

The corporation tax liability must be calculated for each financial year separately; applying the appropriate rates of tax to each.

However, there is no change in the rates or limits in financial year 2009, therefore only one computation is required for the whole CAP if it straddles 31 March 2009.

The following tables will be provided to you in the Tax Rates and Allowances section of the exam:

Financial year:	**2007**	**2008**	**2009**
Small companies rate	20%	21%	21%
Full rate	30%	28%	28%
Lower limit	£300,000	£300,000	£300,000
Upper limit	£1,500,000	£1,500,000	£1,500,000
Marginal relief fraction	1/40	7/400	7/400

Example 5 - Accounting periods straddling 31 March

Flute Ltd had profits chargeable to corporation tax of £400,000 and received dividends from UK companies of £45,000 in the year ended 30 September 2008.

(a) **Calculate Flute Ltd's corporation tax liability for the year ended 30 September 2008.**

(b) **Calculate the liability assuming exactly the same results but a year later (i.e. for the year ended 30 September 2009).**

Answer to example 5

(a) **Corporation tax computation – y/e 30 September 2008**

	£
PCTCT	400,000
Plus: FII (£45,000 × 100/90)	50,000
'Profits'	450,000

As 'profits' are between the small companies lower limit of £300,000 and the upper limit of £1,500,000 marginal relief applies.

The company's CAP straddles 31 March 2008. Six months (1.10.07 to 31.3.08) fall into FY 2007 and six months (1.4.08 to 30.9.08) fall into FY 2008.

The corporation tax liability is calculated for each FY as follows:

	£	£
FY2007		
(£400,000 x 30% x 6/12)	60,000	
Less: Marginal relief		
1/40 x (£1,500,000 – £450,000) x £400,000/£450,000 x 6/12	(11,667)	
		48,333
FY2008		
(£400,000 x 28% x 6/12)	56,000	
Less: Marginal relief		
7/400 x (£1,500,000 – £450,000) x £400,000/£450,000 x 6/12	(8,167)	
		47,833
Corporation tax liability		96,166

(b) **Corporation tax liability – year ended 30 September 2009**

The PCTCT and profits are identical, and marginal relief applies. However, as the CAP straddles 31 March 2009, one computation for the whole year can be performed as follows:

	£
(£400,000 × 28%)	112,000
Less: Marginal relief	
7/400 × (£1,500,000 – £450,000) × £400,000/£450,000	16,333
Corporation tax liability	95,667

Test your understanding 7

Oboe Ltd had profits chargeable to corporation tax of £100,000 and franked investment income of £20,000 for the year ended 31 December 2008.

(a) **Calculate Oboe Ltd's corporation tax liability for the year ended 31 December 2008.**

(b) **Calculate the liability assuming the year ended on 31 December 2009.**

Test your understanding 8

Bassoon Ltd had PCTCT of £850,000 and received dividends from UK companies of £16,200 in the year ended 30 June 2008.

(a) **Calculate Bassoon Ltd's corporation tax liability for the year ended 30 June 2008.**

(b) **Calculate the liability assuming the year ended on 30 June 2009.**

7 Chapter summary

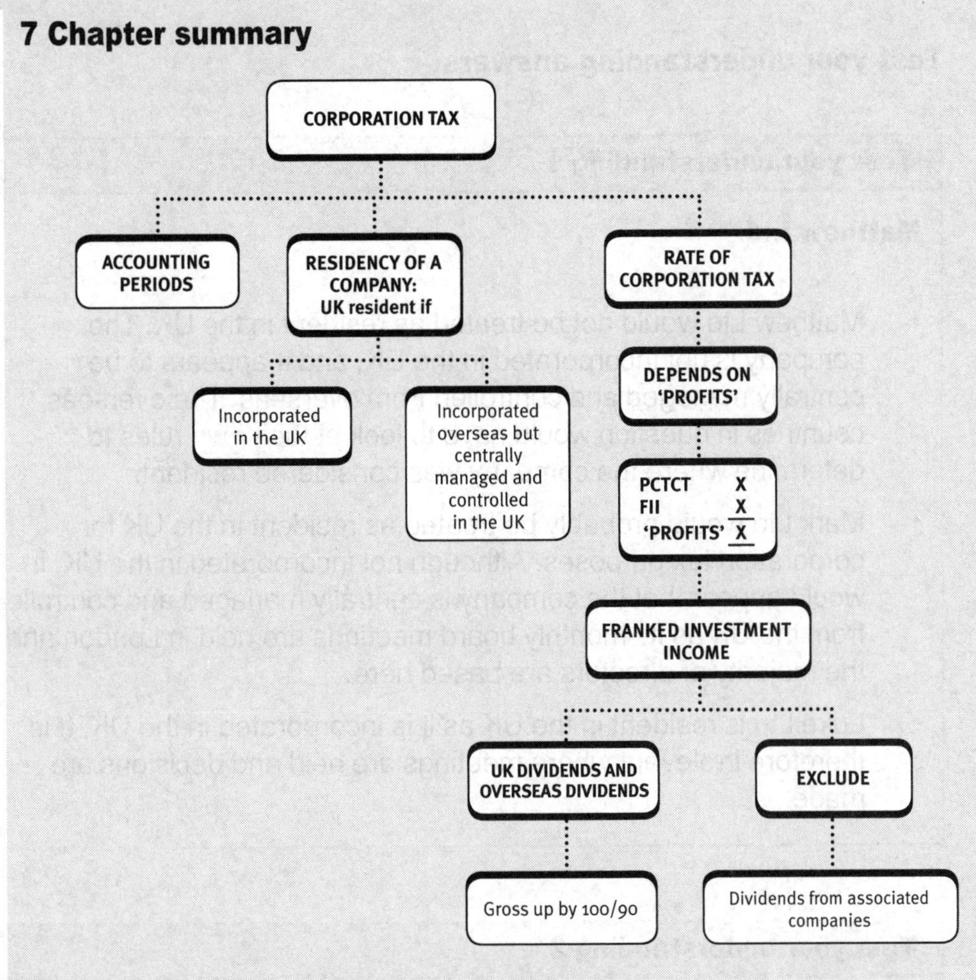

Test your understanding answers

Test your understanding 1

Matthew Ltd

- Matthew Ltd would not be treated as resident in the UK. The company is not incorporated in the UK, and it appears to be centrally managed and controlled from overseas. The overseas countries in question would have to look at their own rules to determine where the company was considered resident.
- Mark Ltd would probably be treated as resident in the UK for corporation tax purposes. Although not incorporated in the UK, it would appear that the company is centrally managed and controlled from the UK as its monthly board meetings are held in London and the majority of directors are based here.
- Luke Ltd is resident in the UK as it is incorporated in the UK. It is therefore irrelevant where meetings are held and decisions are made.

Test your understanding 2

Cumberland Ltd

	£
Tax-adjusted trading profits	81,500
Property business profit	1,300
Interest receivable	2,200
Chargeable gains	3,000
	88,000
Less: Gift Aid donation	(1,000)
Profits chargeable to corporation tax (PCTCT)	87,000

Note: Both UK and overseas dividends are exempt from UK corporation tax.

Test your understanding 3

Zachary Ltd

Step 1: Calculate 'profits':

	£
PCTCT	148,000
Plus: FII (£4,500 × 100/90)	5,000
'Profits'	153,000

Step 2: From 'profits' determine the rate of corporation tax:

As 'profits' are less than £300,000, then PCTCT is taxed at 21%.

Step 3: Apply rate to PCTCT:

Corporation tax liability (£148,000 × 21%) = £31,080.

Test your understanding 4

Argo Ltd

	£
PCTCT	1,450,000
Plus: FII (£72,000 × 100/90)	80,000
'Profits'	1,530,000

As 'profits' are more than £1,500,000, then PCTCT is taxed at 28%.

Corporation tax liability (£1,450,000 × 28%) = £406,000.

Note: The fact that PCTCT is below the limit of £1,500,000 is irrelevant. 'Profits' determine the tax rate.

Test your understanding 5

Sycamore Ltd

Corporation tax computation – y/e 31 March 2010

	£
Tax-adjusted trading profit	320,000
Chargeable gain	10,000
PCTCT	330,000
Plus: FII (£18,000 × 100/90)	20,000
'Profits'	350,000

The 'profits' are between £300,000 and £1,500,000 and therefore PCTCT is charged at the full rate with marginal relief.

	£
Corporation tax (£330,000 x 28%)	92,400
Less: Marginal relief	
7/400 × (£1,500,000 – £350,000) × £330,000/£350,000	(18,975)
Corporation tax liability	73,425

Test your understanding 6

Petal Ltd

Corporation tax computation – 9 m/e 31 March 2010

	£
Tax-adjusted trading profit	1,100,000
Chargeable gain	60,000
PCTCT	1,160,000
Plus: FII (£45,000 × 100/90)	50,000
'Profits'	1,210,000
Corporation tax liability (£1,160,000 at 28%)	324,800

Note: As the CAP is only nine months , the small company rate lower limit is reduced to £225,000 (£300,000 × 9/12) and the upper limit is reduced to £1,125,000 (£1,500,000 × 9/12). As 'profits' fall above the upper limit of £1,125,000 the tax rate is 28%.

Test your understanding 7

Oboe Ltd

(a) **Corporation tax computation – y/e 31 December 2008**

	£
PCTCT	100,000
Plus: FII	20,000
'Profits'	120,000

As 'profits' are below the lower limit of £300,000 the small companies rate applies.

The company's CAP straddles 31 March 2008. Three months (1 January 2008 to 31 March 2008) fall into FY 2007 and nine months (1 April 2008 to 31 December 2008) fall into FY 2008.

The CT liability is calculated for each FY as follows:

	£
FY 2007: (£100,000 × 3/12 × 20%)	5,000
FY 2008: (£100,000 × 9/12 × 21%)	15,750
Corporation tax liability	20,750

(b) **Corporation tax liability – y/e 31 December 2009**

As there is no change in rate, the liability can be calculated for the whole CAP as follows:

(£100,000 × 21%) £21,000

Test your understanding 8

Bassoon Ltd

(a) **Corporation tax computation – year ended 30 June 2008**

	£
PCTCT	850,000
Plus: FII (£16,200 × 100/90)	18,000
'Profits'	868,000

As 'profits' are between the small companies lower limit of £300,000 and the upper limit of £1,500,000 marginal relief applies.

The CAP straddles 31 March 2008. Nine months (1.7.07 to 31.3.08) fall into FY 2007 and 3 months (1.4.08 to 30.6.08) fall into FY 2008.

The CT liability is calculated for each FY as follows:

	£	£
FY2007		
(£850,000 x 30% x 9/12)	191,250	
Less: Marginal relief		
1/40 x (£1,500,000 – £868,000) x £850,000/£868,000 x 9/12	(11,604)	
		179,646
FY2008		
(£850,000 x 28% x 3/12)	59,500	
Less: Marginal relief		
7/400 x (£1,500,000 – £868,000) x £850,000/£868,000 x 3/12	(2,708)	
		56,792
Corporation tax liability		236,438

(b) **Corporation tax liability – year ended 30 June 2009:**
No change in rate, therefore CT liability is calculated for the whole CAP.

	£
(£850,000 × 28%)	238,000
Less: Marginal relief	
7/400 × (1,500,000 – £868,000) × £850,000/£868,000	(10,831)
Corporation tax liability	227,169

chapter

19

Profits chargeable to corporation tax

Chapter learning objectives

Upon completion of this chapter you will be able to:

- identify the different taxable profits for a company and the basis of assessment
- calculate the tax-adjusted trading profit or loss for a company
- explain how relief can be obtained for pre-trading expenditure
- compute capital allowances on plant and machinery and industrial buildings for companies
- compute property business profits
- distinguish between trading and non-trading loans and deposits
- identify the tax treatment of trade and non-trade interest and associated costs
- show the treatment of Gift Aid donations made by a company
- prepare a computation of profits chargeable to corporation tax for an accounting period
- calculate profits chargeable to corporation tax for a long period of account.

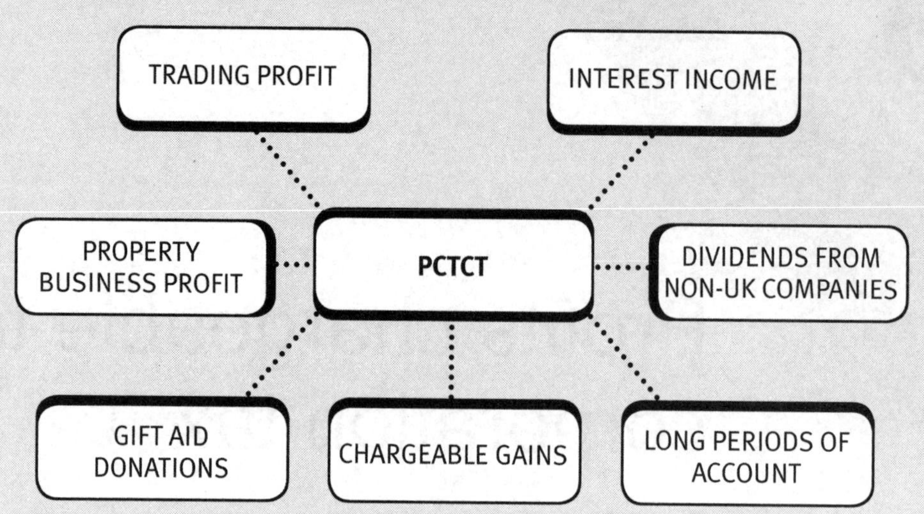

1 Profits chargeable to corporation tax

Companies pay corporation tax on their profits chargeable to corporation tax (PCTCT) for an accounting period.

As illustrated in Chapter 18, PCTCT is calculated as follows:

	£
Trading profit (section 2)	X
Interest income (section 3)	X
Property business profit (section 4)	X
Chargeable gains (Chapter 20)	X
Total profits	X
Less: Gift Aid (section 5)	(X)
Profits chargeable to corporation tax (PCTCT)	X

Chapter 18 briefly discussed the different elements which make up PCTCT and then showed how the corporation tax liability is calculated on PCTCT.

This and the following chapters show in detail how each item within PCTCT is calculated.

2 Trading profit

In Chapter 5 we studied how to adjust a sole trader's trading profit for tax purposes. The rules for companies are very similar.

For reference, a summary of the main adjustments is given below:

- Disallow expenditure which is not wholly and exclusively for the purposes of the trade.
- Disallow entertaining (except entertaining staff).
- Disallow expenditure on capital items.
- Adjust for leased high emission cars (CO_2 > 160 g/km)
- Adjust for gifts to customers.
- Disallow depreciation.
- Adjust for profits/losses on disposal of capital items.
- Add back Gift Aid donations.
- Adjust for non-trading income.

All the above rules apply for companies.

There are, however, a number of key differences which apply when computing the taxable trading profits for a company.

Differences relating to companies

The main differences are in relation to:

- private use adjustments
- interest payable/receivable
- dividends payable
- capital allowances.

Key differences

Private use adjustments – There are no private use restrictions for companies:

- Any private use of assets by a director or employee of the company is ignored in the capital allowances calculation. There is no restriction for private usage.
- Any private expenses of a director or employee of a company are fully allowable, when calculating the tax-adjusted trading profit.

The director or employee may however suffer income tax on the employment benefit received (Chapter 4).

Interest payable/receivable – Companies have special rules which cover interest payments and interest income. These are known as the loan relationship rules.

The detail of the rules is covered in section 3, however, when adjusting trading profits the following rules apply:

- Any interest payable relating to trading activities is allowable as a deduction against trading profits, therefore no adjustment is required.
- Any interest payable in relation to non-trading activities must be added back to trading profit.
- Any interest receivable must be deducted from trading profit.

Dividends payable – Dividends payable by a company are an appropriation of profit and are not allowable as a trading expense.

Example 1 - Trading profit

The accounts of Helen Ltd show the following for the year ended 31 December 2009

	£	£
Gross profit from trading		280,000
Interest receivable	6,320	
Rent income	2,850	
		9,170
		289,170
Less Expenses:		
Rent and rates	10,950	
Depreciation	6,730	
Interest payable (Note 1)	3,560	
Entertaining and gifts (Note 2)	7,420	
Delivery costs	2,890	
Motor expenses (Note 3)	5,480	
Miscellaneous (Note 4)	12,000	
		(49,030)
Profit before tax		240,140

Notes

(1) Interest payable was in respect of a loan to acquire the rental property (non-trading interest).

(2) Entertaining and gifts comprise:

	£
Gifts to customers (Christmas champagne: cost £25 per customer)	1,500
Staff Christmas party	3,430
Client Christmas party	2,490

(3) Motor expenses represent costs for the director's car. He uses the car 60% for private use.

(4) Miscellaneous includes a £3,500 gross charitable donation under the Gift Aid scheme.

Calculate the tax-adjusted trading profit before capital allowances for Helen Ltd, for the year ended 31 December 2009.

Answer to example 1

	£	£
Profit before tax		240,140
Add: Disallowable expenditure:		
Rent and rates	Nil	
Depreciation	6,730	
Non-trading interest payable	3,560	
Gifts to customers: Drink (Note 1)	1,500	
Client entertaining	2,490	
Delivery costs	Nil	
Motor expenses (Note 2)	Nil	
Gift Aid donation (Note 3)	3,500	
		17,780
		257,920
Less: Income not chargeable as trading income		
Non-trading interest receivable	6,320	
Property business income	2,850	
		(9,170)
Tax-adjusted trading profit		248,750

Notes

(1) Gifts to customers are disallowed unless they amount to £50 or less per customer during the year and display a conspicuous advert for the business. Gifts of food or drink or tobacco are disallowed irrespective of their cost.

(2) No adjustment is required for the private use motor expenses of the director. These are fully deductible when calculating company taxable trading profits. The director will be taxed on the benefit of private use as an employment benefit.

(3) As for a sole trader, Gift Aid is disallowable as trading expenditure but will be deductible when calculating PCTCT.

Tutorial note

The examiner will give credit for mentioning all items of expenditure and showing where there are no adjustments, as well as where an adjustment is required.

Test your understanding 1

You are presented with the accounts of Cornelius Ltd, for the year to 31 December 2009. Cornelius Ltd runs a small printing business and the managing director wishes to know the amount of the company's tax-adjusted trading profit for the year ended 31 December 2009.

Calculate Cornelius Ltd's tax-adjusted trading profit before capital allowances for the year ended 31 December 2009.

	£	£
Gross profit from trading		21,270
Interest receivable		4,350
Profit on sale of business premises (Note 1)		1,750
		27,370
Advertising	642	
Impaired debts (Note 2)	80	
Depreciation	2,381	
Light and heat	372	
Miscellaneous expenses (Note 3)	342	
Motor car expenses (Note 4)	555	
Rates	1,057	
Repairs and renewals (Note 5)	2,598	
Staff wages (Note 6)	12,124	
Telephone	351	
		(20,502)
Profit before tax		6,868

Notes

(1) The profit on the sale of premises relates to the sale of a small freehold industrial unit in which the company stored paper, before building the extension (see Note 5).

(2) The charge for impaired debts is made up as follows:

	£
Write-off of loan to customer	55
Write-off of trade debts	32
Increase in specific allowance for debtors	10
Recovery of trade debts previously written off	(17)
Charge to profit and loss account	80

(3) Miscellaneous expenses is made up as follows:

	£
Subscription to Printers' association	40
Contribution to national charity under Gift Aid	45
Gifts to customers:	
– Calendars costing £7.50 each and bearing the company's name	75
– Two food hampers bearing the company's name	95
Other allowable expenses	87
	342

(4) A director uses the motor car 75% for business purposes and 25% for private purposes.

(5) Repairs and renewals comprise the following expenditure:

	£
Redecorating administration offices	951
Building extension to enlarge paper store	1,647
	2,598

(6) Staff wages included an amount of £182 for a staff Christmas lunch.

Capital allowances

Chapters 6 and 7 covered the main principles of calculating capital allowances and industrial building allowances for sole traders.

The same rules apply for companies, but in addition, the following points should be noted when calculating capital allowances for companies:

Effective date for changes in FA 2009

The recent changes in rules in respect of capital allowances apply to companies in the same way as sole traders, however the effective date of implementation is 1 April 2009 (not 6 April 2009).

Therefore, expenditure incurred on:

- General pool plant and machinery items between 1 April 2009 to 31 March 2010, if not covered by the AIA, is eligible for the temporary FYA of 40%.
- Expenditure before 1 April 2009 and after 31 March 2010 is not eligible for the FYA but is eligible for WDA of 20%.
- Cars with effect from 1 April 2009 will be treated according to CO_2 emissions.
- Cars purchased before 1 April 2009 will continue to be dealt with under the old rules according to cost (i.e. expensive and inexpensive cars).

  The examiner has confirmed that there will not be any new purchases of these cars, although potentially there could be balances brought forward in relation to 'old' cars.

Short and long accounting periods

- Allowances are given for **accounting periods** by reference to acquisitions and disposals in that accounting period.
- If the accounting period is less than 12 months:
  - the annual investment allowance and the writing down allowance is proportionately reduced.
  - but first year allowances are always given in full. They are never reduced for a short accounting period.
- Where a company has a long period of account:
  - there will be two accounting periods
  - two capital allowances computations will be required; one for each of these accounting periods
  - the balance period will be a short accounting period.

Private use adjustments

- There are no private use adjustments where company assets are used by directors or employees, when calculating capital allowances for companies.

Example 2 - Trading profit

Bill Ltd prepares accounts to 30 April.

The company's tax written down values on 1 May 2009 were as follows:

General pool	£23,500
Expensive car	£16,600

The expensive car is used by the managing director for 25% of the time for private purposes.

In the two years ended 30 April 2011, the following transactions took place:

Year ended 30 April 2010

1 November 2009	Purchased plant costing £13,260.
10 November 2009	Sold two lorries (purchased for £8,450 each) for £2,500 each. Purchased two replacement lorries for £5,250 each.

Year ended 30 April 2011

1 November 2010	Purchased a motor car with CO_2 emissions of 149 g/km for £7,500.
1 December 2010	Sold the expensive car for £12,000.

Compute the capital allowances available to Bill Ltd for the years ended 30 April 2010 and 30 April 2011.

Answer to example 2

	£	General pool £	Expensive car £	Allowance £
Y/e 30 April 2010				
TWDV b/f (Note)		23,500	16,600	
Qualifying for AIA and FYA:				
Plant and machinery	13,260			
Lorries (£5,250 × 2)	10,500			
	23,760			
Less AIA	(23,760)			23,760
	Nil			
Disposal proceeds		(5,000)		
		18,500	16,600	
Less WDA (20%)		(3,700)		3,700
Less WDA (restricted)			(3,000)	3,000
Less FYA (40%)	(Nil)			
		Nil		
TWDV c/f		14,800	13,600	
Total allowances				30,460
y/e 30 April 2011				
No AIA or FYA: Cars		7,500		
Disposal proceeds			(12,000)	
		22,300	1,600	
Balancing allowance			(1,600)	1,600
Less: WDA (20%)		(4,460)		4,460
TWDV c/f		17,840		
Total allowances				6,060

Note: Private use of car by MD is not relevant for companies. Full capital allowances are available.

Test your understanding 2

Ellingham Ltd is a UK resident company that manufactures aeroplane components. The company has always prepared accounts to 31 March in each year and has now decided to change its accounts preparation date to 30 June, after having prepared accounts to 31 March 2009.

The results for the 15 m/e 30 June 2010, included the following.

On 1 April 2009, the TWDVs of plant and machinery were as follows:

	£
General pool	149,280
Short-life asset	13,440

The following assets were purchased during the 15 m/e 30 June 2010.

		£
1 April 2009	Heating system	12,800
5 June 2009	Equipment	100,800
22 September 2009	Motor car (CO_2 emissions 139 g/km)	11,760
18 November 2009	Fire alarm system	7,200
11 December 2009	Motor car (CO_2 emissions 104 g/km)	12,200
14 May 2010	Plant and machinery	50,000

Ellingham Ltd made the following sales:

15 January 2010	Lorry	(14,160)
12 March 2010	Short-life asset	(5,520)

The lorry sold on 15 January 2010 for £14,160 originally cost £21,600.

Compute the capital allowances for the 15 m/e 30 June 2010.

Pre-trading expenditure

The rules for pre-trading expenditure are the same for companies and sole traders (see Chapter 5) and are as follows:

- Any revenue expenditure incurred in the **seven years** before a company commences to trade is treated as an expense, on the day that the company starts trading.

- Any capital expenditure is treated as if bought on the first day, when the trade commences. Any capital allowances will be claimed in the first capital allowances computation.

3 Interest income – loan relationship rules

All interest paid or received by a company is dealt with under the loan relationship rules.

The rules apply to:

- Payments in connection with borrowing money, e.g. interest paid on overdrafts, bank loans, corporate debt (i.e. company debentures and loan stock) and other costs such as arrangement fees.
- Income received from the lending of money (i.e. interest income). This includes interest from deposits, loans, government stocks and corporate bonds.
- In order to apply the loan relationship rules correctly, all interest paid/received must first be distinguished as either 'trading' or 'non-trading'.

Trade v non-trade purposes

- Generally, all interest receivable by a company is non-trade interest, unless it is the company's trade to lend money (e.g. a bank).
- Examples would be:
  - interest receivable on investments such as gilts, debentures, loan stock and bonds.
- Examples of trading interest payable would be:
  - Interest on a loan taken out to purchase plant and machinery for the business.
  - Loan or overdraft to fund the daily operations (i.e. working capital).
  - Issue of debentures to fund trading operations.
- Examples of non-trading interest payable would be:
  - interest payable on a loan to purchase a commercially let property (where the rent would be taxable as property business income – section 4).
  - Interest payable on a loan to acquire the shares of another company.

Interest income

- All interest receivable by a company is normally assessable as non-trading interest income.
- Interest receivable should be deducted when calculating trading income and included in the corporation tax computation as interest income.
- Interest received and receivable is usually credited in the company accounts on an 'accruals' basis. As interest receivable is taxed on an accruals basis, the figure included in the accounts is the figure which is taxed as interest income.
- Interest income is received **gross** by companies. No grossing up calculations are therefore required in the corporation tax computation.

Interest paid

- Interest paid and payable on borrowings for a trading purpose is deductible as a trading expense.
- Interest payable on borrowings for a non-trading purpose is:
  - added back to trading profit
  - deducted from interest income.

Assessment in PCTCT

- All interest paid by a company is deductible on the accruals basis.
- As the company accounts are also prepared on the accruals basis, the figure included in the accounts is also the figure used for tax purposes.
- If only cash payments are provided, these would have to be adjusted for opening and closing accruals of interest payable/receivable.
- Where interest income exceeds interest payable
  - the net profit is assessed as interest income in PCTCT.
  - the situation where interest payable exceeds interest income is not examinable.

Example 3 - Interest income – loan relationship rules

Trinity Ltd, a clothing manufacturer, received bank interest of £2,800, on 14 December 2009 and paid debenture interest of £19,500, on 26 September 2009.

The debentures were issued in January 2009, to raise finance for the purchase of a new packing machine.

The company prepares accounts to 31 December each year. Accrued debenture interest payable at 31.12.09 was £9,000. There was no interest receivable at either 31.12.08 or 31.12.09.

Explain how the bank and debenture interest will be treated in the corporation tax computation for the year to 31 December 2009.

Answer to example 3

Bank interest receivable

The bank interest receivable in the period will be taxable as non-trading interest income. As there was no interest receivable at the beginning or end of the year, the taxable interest income will be the amount received of £2,800.

Debenture interest payable

The debenture interest paid relates to finance issued for the purposes of the trade (i.e. to purchase new machinery). It is therefore allowed as a trading expense. The interest will be recorded in the accounts on the accruals basis (i.e. interest payable of £28,500) (£19,500 paid + £9,000 accrued). No adjustment will therefore be required for tax purposes.

Note: The interest on the debentures is paid gross and the interest income is received gross.

Example 4 - Interest income – loan relationship rules

PQR Ltd prepares its accounts to 31 December.

The company issued £100,000 of 12% debentures on 1 May 2009. The proceeds of the issue were used to purchase a new factory.

Explain how the interest on the debentures is treated for tax purposes for the year ended 31 December 2009.

Answer to example 4

For the year ended 31 December 2009, PQR Ltd will be entitled to a deduction against trading profits of £8,000 (£100,000 at 12% × 8/12).

Provided this amount is included in the accounts, no adjustment will be necessary when calculating the tax-adjusted trading profit.

The amount of debenture interest actually paid is irrelevant as interest payable is deductible on the accruals basis.

Test your understanding 3

The net profit of Simon Ltd per the accounts for the year ended 31 December 2009, is £105,940, which includes:

	£
Depreciation	9,750
Debenture interest payable (on loan to purchase machinery)	12,760
Bank interest payable (on loan to purchase an investment property)	6,590
Bank interest receivable	15,860

Notes:

1 Bank interest receivable includes an accrual of £2,340 as at 31 December 2009 and £1,210, as at 31 December 2008. There were no accruals in respect of the debenture or bank interest payable at either the beginning or the end of the year.

2 The company's capital allowances for the year are £11,800.

Calculate Simon Ltd's PCTCT for the y/e 31 December 2009.

Summary – interest payable/receivable

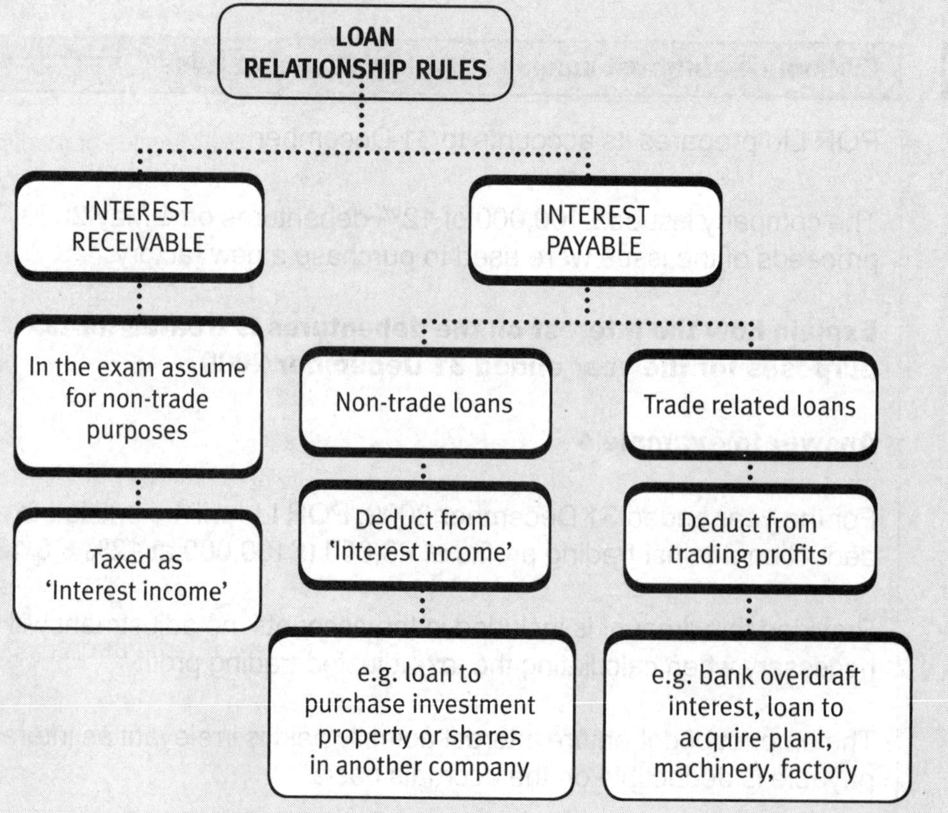

4 Property business profits

A trading company may hold property for investment purposes or have premises which are rented out, as they are surplus to the company's current trading requirements. The income from these properties is assessed as property business income.

Treatment for companies

The rules in connection with property business income for companies are basically the same as sole traders:

- Property business profits are taxed on the accruals basis.
- Allowable expenses are those associated with the normal running and upkeep of the property (generally revenue expenses, like property maintenance, repairs, insurance and irrecoverable debts).

There are, however, a few differences in the way that companies are assessed on their property business profits as follows:

- The company is assessed on the property business profit arising in the accounting period (not the tax year as for individuals).
- The treatment of interest payable.
- The treatment of capital losses.

Interest on loan to buy a property

- Interest payable on a loan to acquire or improve an investment property, is not allowed as a deduction from property business income. Instead, it is taxed under the 'Loan Relationship' rules and is therefore deducted from interest income (see section 3).

Property business losses

- Profits and losses on properties are 'pooled' together to obtain an overall 'property business profit or loss' for an accounting period.
- A property business loss is:
  - first set-off against total profits (before Gift Aid) of the same accounting period
  - then carried forward to be set against total profits (before Gift Aid) in the future.
  - is also available for 'group relief' (Chapter 22).

Lease premiums

Where a company receives a premium for the grant of a lease, an element of the premium is taxed as property business income in the same way as for sole traders (see Chapter 3).

Example 5 - Property business profits

Speed Ltd prepares accounts for the y/e 31 March 2010 and during the year received a premium of £12,000 on the grant of a seven-year lease.

The building was rented out from 1 September 2009, for an annual rent of £6,000. It lay empty until this date. Rent is received quarterly in advance.

Calculate the property business income for the y/e 31 March 2010.

Answer to example 5

	£
Premium £12,000 – (2% × (7 – 1) × £12,000)	10,560
Rent (£6,000 × 7/12)	3,500
Total property business profit	14,060

Test your understanding 4

Tasman Ltd is a UK resident company that manufactures components for washing machines. Tasman Ltd lets out two warehouses that are surplus to requirements.

The company's results regarding income from property for the year ended 31 March 2010, are as follows:

- The first warehouse was empty from 1 April to 31 August 2009, but was let from 1 September 2009. On that date the company received a premium of £47,000, for the grant of a seven-year lease, and the annual rent of £10,500, which is payable in advance.
- The second warehouse was let until 31 January 2010, at an annual rent of £11,200. On that date the tenant left owing three months' rent, which the company is not able to recover. The roof of the warehouse was repaired at a cost of £7,200, during March 2010.

Calculate the property business profit for the y/e 31 March 2010.

5 Gift Aid for companies

The tax treatment of Gift Aid payments is different for companies and individuals.

For **individuals**, Gift Aid payments are treated as follows:

- Gift Aid payments are paid net of basic rate tax.
- Tax relief is given by extending the basic rate band by the gross amount of the Gift Aid paid in the tax year.

For **companies**, Gift Aid payments are treated as follows:

- Gift Aid payments by companies are made gross.
- The amount **paid** in the accounting period is deducted from total profits in calculating a company's profits chargeable to corporation tax.
- If the amount of Gift Aid paid exceeds the total profits of the company, no relief for the excess is given.

6 Comprehensive examples

Test your understanding 5

Geronimo Ltd is a UK resident company that manufactures motorcycles. The company's summarised profit and loss account for the year ended 31 May 2010 is as follows:

	£	£
Gross profit		921,540
Operating expenses		
Impaired debts (Note 1)	22,360	
Depreciation	83,320	
Gifts and donations (Note 2)	2,850	
Professional fees (Note 3)	14,900	
Patent royalties (Note 4)	7,200	
Repairs and renewals (Note 5)	42,310	
Other expenses (all allowable)	136,520	
		(309,460)
		612,080
Other operating income (Note 6)		24,700
Operating profit		636,780
Income from investments		
Bank interest (Note 7)	2,800	
Loan interest (Note 8)	22,000	
Dividends (Note 9)	36,000	
		60,800
		697,580
Interest payable (Note 10)		(45,000)
Profit before taxation		652,580

Notes:

(1) Impaired debts

	£
Trade debts written off	19,890
Loan to customer written off	600
Increase in allowance for trade debtors	1,870
	22,360

(2) Gifts and donations

	£
Donation to national charity (made under the Gift Aid scheme)	1,800
Donation to national charity (not made under the Gift Aid scheme)	100
Donation to local charity (Geronimo Ltd received free advertising in the charity's magazine)	50
Gifts to customers (food hampers costing £30 each)	900
	2,850

(3) Professional fees

	£
Accountancy and audit fee	4,100
Legal fees re – the renewal of a 20-year property lease	2,400
Legal fees in connection with the issue of a debenture loan (see Note 10)	8,400
	14,900

(4) Patent royalties

The patent royalties were trade related. The figure for patent royalties payable is calculated as follows:

	£
Accrued at 1 June 2009	Nil
Paid 31 July 2009	3,500
Paid 31 January 2010	2,300
Accrued at 31 May 2010	1,400
	7,200

(5) Repairs and renewals

The figure of £42,310 for repairs includes £6,200 for replacing part of a wall that was knocked down by a lorry, and £12,200 for initial repairs to an office building that was acquired during the year ended 31 May 2010.

The office building was not usable until the repairs were carried out, and this fact was represented by a reduced purchase price.

(6) Other operating income

Other operating income consists of patent royalties derived from patents which the company registered in 2001 to protect a manufacturing technique it has developed.

Royalties of £8,900 and £15,800 were received on 30 November 2009 and 31 May 2010 respectively. The amounts received are the amounts accrued in the six months to that date.

(7) Bank interest received

The bank interest was received on 31 May 2010. The bank deposits are held for non-trading purposes.

(8) Loan interest received

The figure for loan interest received is calculated as follows:

	£
Accrued at 1 June 2009	(5,500)
Received 30 June 2009	11,000
Received 31 December 2009	11,000
Accrued at 31 May 2010	5,500
	22,000

The above figures are all gross. The loan was made for non-trading purposes.

(9) Dividends received

The dividends were received from other UK companies. The figure of £36,000 is the actual amount received.

(10) Interest payable

Geronimo Ltd raised a debenture loan on 1 July 2009. The loan was used for trading purposes. Interest of £30,000 was paid on 31 December 2009, and £15,000 was accrued at 31 May 2010.

(11) Plant and machinery

On 1 June 2009 the tax written down value of the general pool of plant and machinery was £66,000. There were no purchases or sales of plant and machinery during the year ended 31 May 2010.

(12) Other information

Geronimo Ltd has no associated companies.

(a) **Calculate Geronimo Ltd's tax-adjusted trading profit for the year ended 31 May 2010.**

(b) **Calculate the corporation tax payable by Geronimo Ltd for the year ended 31 May 2010.**

Assume that the FY 2009 tax rates continue in the future.

7 Long periods of account

Where a company has a period of account of more than 12 months, it must be split into two accounting periods as follows:

- First 12 months.
- Remainder of the period of account.

There are rules to determine how to allocate taxable income between these two accounting periods.

Allocation of taxable income

Income	Method of allocation
Trading profits before capital allowances	Adjust profit for period of account for tax purposes and then apportion on a time basis.
Capital allowances	Separate calculation for each accounting period. AIA and WDAs will be restricted if accounting period is less than 12 months.
Property income/Interest income/Other income	Calculate accrued amount for each CAP separately. If the information to apply the strict accruals basis is not available, then time apportion.
Chargeable gains	Taxed within the accounting period in which disposal takes place.
Gift Aid	Deducted from profits of the accounting period in which donations are paid.
Franked investment income	Allocate to the accounting period in which it is received.

Having allocated profits and Gift Aid to the two separate CAPs:

- two separate corporation tax computations are prepared
- with two separate pay dates.

Example 6 - Long periods of account

Oak Ltd prepared accounts for the 15 months period to 30 June 2010, with the following results:

	£
Trading profit (adjusted for tax purposes, before capital allowances)	383,880
Bank interest (received 31 December 2009)	22,000
Property business profit	10,000
Chargeable gain (asset disposed of 1 June 2010)	16,000
Gift Aid payment (1 February 2010)	24,000

Bank interest (income) accrued was as follows:

At 1 April 2009	5,200
At 1 April 2010	4,100
At 30 June 2010	9,780

The company bought plant costing £120,000, for use in its trade on 31 August 2009. The TWDV on the general pool on 1 April 2009 is £17,000.

Calculate Oak Ltd's PCTCT for the 15 m/e to 30 June 2010.

Answer to example 6

Oak Ltd – Profits chargeable to corporation tax

	y/e 31 March 2010	3 m/e to 30 June 2010
	£	£
Trading profit (12:3)	307,104	76,776
Less: Capital allowances (W)	(81,400)	(2,780)
Trading income	225,704	73,996
Interest income		
(£22,000 – £5,200 + £4,100)	20,900	
(£9,780 – £4,100)		5,680
Property income (12:3)	8,000	2,000
Chargeable gain	Nil	16,000
	254,604	97,676
Less: Gift Aid payment	(24,000)	
PCTCT	230,604	97,676

Working: Capital allowances computation

		General pool	Total allowances
	£	£	£
y/e 31 March 2010			
TWDV b/f		17,000	
Plant and machinery	120,000		
Less AIA (max)	(50,000)		50,000
	70,000		
Less WDA (20%)		(3,400)	3,400
Less FYA 40%	(28,000)		28,000
		42,000	
TWDV c/f		55,600	
Total allowances			81,400
3 m/e ended 30 June 2010			
Less WDA (20% x 3/12)		(2,780)	2,780
TWDV c/f		52,820	
Total allowances			2,780

Test your understanding 6

Ash Ltd prepared accounts for the 17 month period to 30 September 2010, with results as follows:

	£
Trading profit (adjusted for tax purposes but before capital allowances)	485,390
Bank interest (received 31 December 2009)	11,540
Property business profit	25,500
Chargeable gain (asset disposed of 1 March 2010)	12,995
Gift Aid payment (1 February 2010)	16,500

Bank interest (income) accrued was as follows:

At 1 May 2009	7,400
At 1 May 2010	5,600
At 30 September 2010	10,540

The company bought plant costing £90,000, for use in its trade on 1 January 2010. The tax written down value on the general pool on 1 May 2009 is £45,000.

Calculate Ash Ltd's PCTCT for the 17 month period.

8 Chapter summary

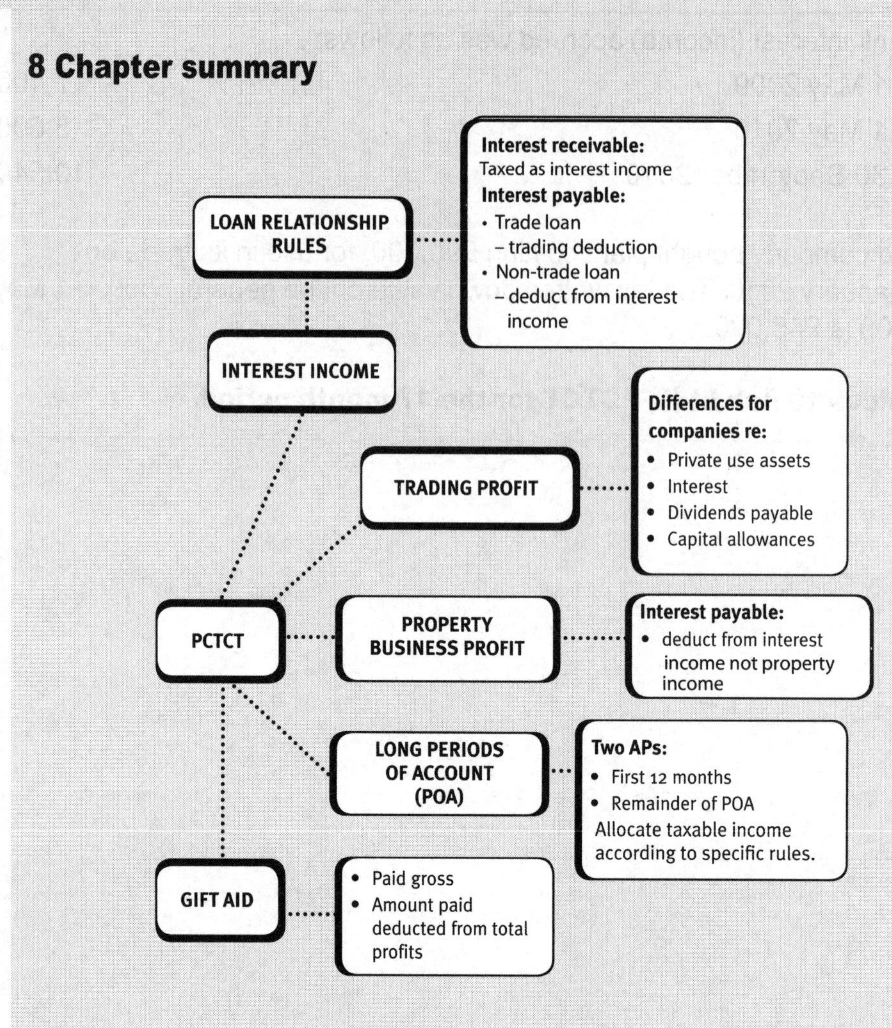
LOAN RELATIONSHIP RULES
Interest receivable:
Taxed as interest income
Interest payable:
• Trade loan
– trading deduction
• Non-trade loan
– deduct from interest income
INTEREST INCOME
TRADING PROFIT
Differences for companies re:
• Private use assets
• Interest
• Dividends payable
• Capital allowances
PCTCT
PROPERTY BUSINESS PROFIT
Interest payable:
• deduct from interest income not property income
LONG PERIODS OF ACCOUNT (POA)
Two APs:
• First 12 months
• Remainder of POA
Allocate taxable income according to specific rules.
GIFT AID
• Paid gross
• Amount paid deducted from total profits

Test your understanding answers

Test your understanding 1

Cornelius Ltd

Tax-adjusted trading profit for the year ended 31 December 2009

	£	£
Profit before tax		6,868
Add: Disallowable expenditure		
Advertising	Nil	
Depreciation	2,381	
Impaired debts (Note 1)	55	
Light and heat	Nil	
Gift Aid (Note 2)	45	
Gifts to customers (food hampers) (Note 3)	95	
Motor car expenses (Note 4)	Nil	
Rates	Nil	
Repairs (capital)	1,647	
Staff wages (Note 5)	Nil	
Telephone	Nil	
		4,223
		11,091
Less: Income not chargeable as trading income		
Interest receivable		(4,350)
Profit on sale of premises		(1,750)
Tax-adjusted trading profit		4,991

Notes

(1) The write-off of a non-trade debt (e.g. loan to a customer) is not an allowable trading deduction.

(2) Gift Aid is disallowable as trading expenditure but will be deductible when calculating PCTCT.

(3) Gifts to customers are disallowed, unless they amount to £50 or less per customer during the year and display a conspicuous advert for the business. Gifts of food or drink or tobacco are disallowed irrespective of their cost.

(4) Motor car expenses are all allowable for the company, although the director will be taxed as an employee on the private use of the car.

(5) The expenditure on the Christmas lunch is an allowable deduction for the employer.

Tutorial note

The examiner will give credit for mentioning all items of expenditure and showing where there are no adjustments, as well as where an adjustment is required.

Test your understanding 2

Ellingham Ltd

The 15 month period must be broken down into two chargeable accounting periods:

(1) FIrst 12 months: 12 m/e 31 March 2010

(2) Balance period: 3 m/e 30 June 2010

Capital allowances computation

		General pool	Short life asset	Special rate pool	Allowances
	£	£	£	£	£
Year ended 31 March 2010					
TWDV b/f		149,280	13,440		
Additions:					
Not qualifying for AIA or FYA:					
Cars		11,760			
Qualifying for AIA not FYA:					
Heating system	12,800				
Less AIA	(12,800)				12,800
	———			Nil	
Qualifying for AIA and FYA:					
Equipment	100,800				
Fire alarm system	7,200				
	———				
	108,000				
Less AIA (Note)	(37,200)				37,200
	———				
	70,800				
Disposal proceeds		(14,160)	(5,520)		
		———	———	—	
		146,880	7,920	Nil	
Balancing allowance			(7,920)		7,920
			———		
WDA (20%)		(29,376)			29,376
WDA (10%):				(Nil)	
FYA (40%)	(28,320)				28,320
	———	42,480			
Low emission car	12,200				
Less FYA (100%)	(12,200)				12,200
	———	Nil			
		———		—	
TWDV c/f		159,984		Nil	
		———		—	———
Total allowances					127,816
					———

Note: The AIA is allocated to the additions in the 'special rate pool' (WDA 10%) in priority to the addition in the general pool (WDA 20%).

	£	General pool £	Allowances £
TWDV b/f		159,984	
3 m/e 30 June 2010			
Additions:			
Qualifying for AIA but not FYA:			
Plant	50,000		
Less AIA (max x 3/12)	(12,500)		12,500
		37,500	
		197,484	
WDA (20% x 3/12)		(9,874)	9,874
TWDV c/f		187,610	
Total allowances			22,374

Note: Additions of plant and machinery on/after 1 April 2010 are not eligible for temporary FYA.

Test your understanding 3

Simon Ltd

	£	£
Profit per accounts		105,940
Add: Non-trading interest payable	6,590	
Depreciation	9,750	
		16,340
Less: Non-trading interest receivable		(15,860)
Capital allowances		(11,800)
Tax-adjusted trading profit		94,620
Interest income:		
Non-trading interest receivable	15,860	
Non-trading interest payable	(6,590)	
		9,270
PCTCT		103,890

Test your understanding 4

Tasman Ltd

Property business profit – Year to 31 March 2010

	£	£
Rent receivable		
(7/12 × £10,500)		6,125
(10/12 × £11,200)		9,333
Premium	47,000	
Less: 2% × (7 – 1) × £47,000	(5,640)	
		41,360
		56,818
Less: Allowable expenses		
Irrecoverable debt (3/12 × £11,200)		(2,800)
Roof repairs		(7,200)
Profit		46,818

Note: There is no need to calculate individual profits or losses for each property. Profit and losses are pooled to obtain an overall property business profit.

Test your understanding 5

Geronimo Ltd

(a) **Tax-adjusted trading profit – y/e 31 May 2010**

	£
Operating profit	636,780
Trade debts written off	Nil
Increase in allowance for trade debtors	Nil
Loan to customer	600
Depreciation	83,320
Gift Aid donation	1,800
Donation to national charity	100
Donation to local charity	Nil
Gifts to customers	900
Professional fees	Nil
Patent royalties	Nil
Repacing part of a wall	Nil
Initial repairs to office building	12,200
	735,700
Interest payable	(45,000)
Capital allowances (£66,000 @ 20%)	(13,200)
Tax-adjusted trading profit	677,500

Tutorial note

The alternative approach of commencing with the profit before taxation figure of £652,580 is acceptable, and would be awarded equivalent marks.

Notes:

(1) The loan to a customer is for non-trade purposes (money lending is not the company's trade). The write off of the loan is therefore not an allowable deduction in calculating taxable trading profits. The write off is allowable against interest income under the loan relationship rules.

(2) The Gift Aid donation is deducted in the corporation tax computation from total profits and is therefore added back in calculating trading profits.

(3) Costs of renewing a short lease (< 50 years) are allowable.

(4) The legal fees in connection with the issue of the debenture are incurred in respect of a trading loan relationship and are therefore deductible as a trading expense.

(5) The patent royalties paid are for trading purposes and are allowed as an expense on an accruals basis so no adjustment is required.

(6) The replacement of the wall is allowable since the whole structure is not being replaced. The repairs to the office building are not allowable, being capital in nature, as the building was not in a usable state when purchased and this was reflected in the purchase price.

(7) The patent royalties received are included in the trading profit (on an accruals basis) as they clearly relate to the company's trading activities – no adjustment is therefore needed.

(8) Interest on the debenture loan used for trading purposes is deductible in calculating the taxable trading profit on an accruals basis.

(b) **Geronimo Ltd**

Corporation tax computation – y/e 31 May 2010

		£	£
Trading profit			677,500
Interest income	– Bank interest	2,800	
	– Loan interest	22,000	
	– Customer loan written off	(600)	
			24,200
Total profits			701,700
Less: Gift Aid donation			(1,800)
PCTCT			699,900
Plus FII (£36,000 × 100/90)			40,000
Profits			739,900
Corporation tax (£699,900 @ 28%)			195,972
Less Marginal relief			
7/400 × (£1,500,000 – £739,900) × £699,900/£739,900			(12,583)
Corporation tax payable			183,389

Note: The year end straddles 31 March 2010. However it is assumed that there is no change in rates of tax therefore a separate calculation for each financial year is not required.

Test your understanding 6

Ash Ltd

Profits chargeable to corporation tax

	Year ended 30.4.10	5 months to 30.9.10
	£	£
Trading profit (12:5)	342,628	142,762
Less: Capital allowances (W)	(75,000)	(5,000)
	———	———
Trading income	267,628	137,762
Interest income		
(£11,540 – £7,400 + £5,600)	9,740	
(£10,540 – £5,600)		4,940
Property income (12:5)	18,000	7,500
Chargeable gain	12,995	Nil
	———	———
	308,363	150,202
Less: Gift Aid payment	(16,500)	Nil
	———	———
PCTCT	291,863	150,202
	———	———

Working: Capital allowances computation

		General pool	Allowances
	£	£	£
Year ended 30 April 2010			
TWDV b/f		45,000	
Additions:			
Qualifying for AIA and FYA:			
Plant and machinery	90,000		
Less AIA (max)	(50,000)		50,000
	40,000		
WDA (20%)		(9,000)	9,000
FYA (40%)	(16,000)		16,000
		24,000	
TWDV (c/f)		60,000	
Total allowances			75,000
3 m/e ended 30 September 2010			
WDA (20% x 5/12)		(5,000)	5,000
TWDV c/f		55,000	
Total allowances			5,000

chapter

20

Chargeable gains for companies

Chapter learning objectives

Upon completion of this chapter you will be able to:

- understand how to calculate the gain on the disposal of an asset by a company
- recognise when indexation is available for a company and calculate the indexation allowance
- calculate the indexed gain on the disposal of an asset for a company
- demonstrate how capital losses can be relieved against gains
- apply the correct matching rules for a company disposal of shares and securities
- calculate the gain on the disposal of shares by a company
- identify the treatment of a bonus issue
- identify the treatment of a rights issue
- explain the tax treatment on a takeover or reorganisation of a shareholding in exchange for other shares
- explain the treatment on a takeover where there is cash and shares consideration
- calculate the chargeable gain on the cash element
- explain and apply roll-over relief as it applies to companies.

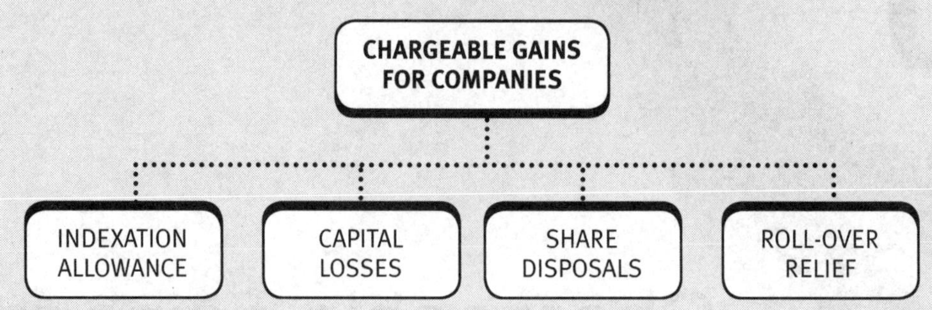

1 Introduction

The main principles of calculating chargeable gains for individuals were set out in Chapters 14 – 17. Some of the content is applicable to companies, but there are some notable differences in the calculation of chargeable gains for companies.

Chargeable gains for a company

- Any chargeable gains that a company makes during an **accounting period** are included in the PCTCT computation.

- It is important to note that companies pay **corporation tax** on their chargeable gains and not capital gains tax.

Calculation of chargeable gains for a company

The following steps should be carried out to compute the chargeable gains to be included in a company's PCTCT computation:

(1) Calculate the chargeable gains/allowable loss arising on the disposal of each chargeable asset separately

(2) Calculate the total net chargeable gains arising in the accounting period = (chargeable gains less allowable losses)

(3) Deduct capital losses brought forward = total net chargeable gains

(4) Include in PCTCT computation.

Note that there is no annual exemption available to companies, the total net chargeable gains is simply included in the company's PCTCT computation.

Proforma – companies

The following basic proforma should be used for the disposal of all assets by a company:

	£
Disposal proceeds	X
Less: Incidental disposal costs	(X)
Net proceeds	X
Less: Allowable expenditure (as for individuals)	(X)
Unindexed gain	X
Less: Indexation allowance (section 2)	(X)
Chargeable gain/(allowable loss)	X

Note that:

- The calculation of capital gains is the same as for individuals except that companies are entitled to an indexation allowance (see section 2).
- There are a few other key differences when dealing with the disposal of assets by companies. These include
  - the treatment of capital losses (section 3)
  - the treatment of shares and securities (section 4), and
  - the availability of reliefs (section 7).
- There is no annual exemption available to companies, the net chargeable gains are included in the PCTCT computation.

2 Indexation allowance

The indexation allowance (IA) gives a company some allowance for the effects of inflation in calculating a gain.

The aim is to ensure that the capital gains subject to tax represent the true increase in capital value in real terms.

The rules for the IA are as follows:

- the IA is based on the cost of the asset and the movement in the retail price index
- it is available:
  - **from** the month of purchase
  - **to** the month of disposal

- the IA is calculated separately for each item of expenditure (e.g. calculate a different IA for the original acquisition cost and any enhancement expenditure because they have different purchase dates).
- the IA cannot create or increase a capital loss.

Calculation of the indexation allowance

The IA is calculated as follows:

IA = (indexation factor x allowable cost)

The indexation factor is calculated as follows:

$$\frac{\text{RPI in month of disposal} - \text{RPI in month of expenditure}}{\text{RPI in month of expenditure}}$$

Note that the indexation factor must be rounded to three decimal places.

Example 1 - Indexation allowance

Kane Ltd sold a chargeable asset in June 2009, which it had bought in February 1987.

The RPI for February 1987 is 100.4 and for June 2009 it is 211.9.

Calculate the indexation factor to be used.

Answer to example 1

Indexation factor is:
(211.9 – 100.4)/100.4 = 1.111 (rounded to three decimal places).

Example 2 - Indexation allowance

Pye Ltd bought a factory for £250,000, on 1 April 1983. On 15 July 1986, the company spent £70,000 on an extension to the factory. The factory was sold on 30 September 2009, for £800,000.

Assume the relevant RPIs are as follows:

April 1983	84.28
July 1986	97.52
September 2009	212.5

Calculate Pye Ltd's chargeable gain.

Answer to example 2

	£
Sale proceeds	800,000
Less: Cost	(250,000)
Enhancement expenditure	(70,000)
Unindexed gain	480,000
Less: Indexation allowance (W)	
Cost (£250,000 × 1.521)	(380,250)
Enhancement expenditure (£70,000 × 1.179)	(82,530)
Chargeable gain	17,220

Working: Indexation factors

The indexation factor from April 1983 to September 2009 is:
(212.5 – 84.28)/84.28 = 1.521 (rounded to three decimal places)

The indexation factor from July 1986 to September 2009 is:
(212.5 – 97.52)/97.52 = 1.179 (rounded to three decimal places)

Test your understanding 1

Hobbit Ltd bought a factory for £175,000 on 1 June 1984. On 15 September 1990, the company spent £62,000 on an extension to the factory. The factory was sold on 31 August 2009, for £650,000.

Assume the relevant RPIs are as follows:

June 1984	89.20
September 1990	129.3
August 2009	212.3

Calculate Hobbit Ltd's chargeable gain.

- If there is a fall in the RPI between the month of purchase and the month of disposal, the indexation allowance in relation to that expenditure is £Nil.

3 Capital losses

Calculation of a capital loss

- A capital loss arises if the proceeds received for an asset, are lower than the allowable expenditure.
- Remember that indexation cannot create or increase a capital loss.

Test your understanding 2

JNN Ltd is considering selling a field at auction in July 2009. It acquired the field in August 1984, for £10,000 and the sale proceeds are likely to be one of three figures:

(a) £25,000

(b) £12,000

(c) £8,000

Calculate the chargeable gain or loss under each of these alternatives.

Assume the indexation factor from August 1984 to July 2009 is 1.358.

Utilisation of a capital loss

- Where allowable losses arise, they are set off against chargeable gains arising in the same accounting period.
- Any loss remaining, is carried forward against **chargeable gains** of future accounting periods, as soon as they arise.
- Capital losses can not be set-off against any other income of a company.

Example 3 - Capital losses

Jump Ltd prepares its accounts to 31 March.

For the year ended 31 March 2010, the company has a tax-adjusted trading profit of £65,000, and a chargeable gain of £3,600.

As at 1 April 2009, Jump Ltd had unused capital losses brought forward of £6,000.

Calculate Jump Ltd's corporation tax liability for the year ended 31 March 2010.

Answer to example 3

	£
Trading profit	65,000
Net chargeable gain (W)	Nil
PCTCT	65,000
Corporation tax (21% × £65,000)	13,650

Working: Net chargeable gain

	£
Chargeable gain	3,600
Less: Capital loss b/f	(6,000)
Capital loss c/f	(2,400)

Net chargeable gain in the accounting period is therefore £Nil.

Note: Capital losses can not be set against the trading income of the company in the year.

Test your understanding 3

High Ltd prepares its accounts to 31 December.

For the year ended 31 December 2009, the company has a tax-adjusted trading profit of £200,000, and a chargeable gain of £17,000.

As at 1 January 2009, High Ltd had unused capital losses brought forward of £23,000.

Calculate High Ltd's corporation tax liability for the year ended 31 December 2009.

4 Shares and securities

The issues regarding the disposal of shares by a company are similar to those set out in chapter 16 for disposals by individuals.

Remember that:

- Shares and securities present a particular problem for capital gains computations, because any two shares in a company (of a particular class) are indistinguishable.
- Matching rules are therefore needed, to solve the problem of being unable to identify acquisitions with disposals. They apply, when there has been more than one purchase of shares or securities, of the same class in the same company.

Matching rules

The matching rules for shares disposed of by companies, are different from those for an individual.

For a company, disposals are matched against acquisitions in the following order:

- Shares acquired on the same day (as the sale).
- Shares acquired during the nine days before the sale.
- Shares in the share pool (also know as the s104 pool or the 1985 pool).

Example 4 - Disposal of shares and securities

Minnie Ltd sold 3,000 shares in Mickey plc for £15,000, on 15 February 2010. The shares in Mickey plc were purchased as follows:

Date	Number	Cost
		£
1 July 1989	1,000	2,000
1 September 2000	1,000	2,500
8 February 2010	500	1,200
15 February 2010	1,500	6,000

Explain which shares Minnie Ltd sold.

Answer to example 4

Using the matching rules, the 3,000 shares sold are as follows:

		Number
(1) Same day purchases: 15 February 2010		1,500
(2) Previous 9 days purchases: 8 February 2010		500
		2,000
(3) Share pool:		
All other shares were purchased more than 9 days ago, therefore they must be in the share pool.		
1 July 1989	1,000	
1 September 2000	1,000	
Total number of shares in pool	2,000	
Disposal from the pool	(1,000)	
Left in share pool	1,000	
Shares disposed of		3,000

Calculation of gains on same day and previous 9 day purchases

There is no indexation available on either of these calculations, even if the dates of acquisition and disposal straddle a month. Hence, the gain is calculated as:

	£
Sale proceeds	X
Less: Allowable cost	(X)
Chargeable gain	X

Example 5 - Disposal of shares and securities

From the above example (Minnie Ltd), calculate the gains on the shares purchased:

(1) **on the same day**

(2) **in the previous 9 days.**

Answer to example 5

Calculate sale proceeds per share:

3,000 shares are sold for £15,000, therefore 1 share is sold for £5.00 (£15,000/3,000).

Gain on same day purchases (1,500 shares):

	£
Sale proceeds (£5 × 1,500)	7,500
Less: Allowable cost	(6,000)
Chargeable gain	1,500

Gain on previous 9 days, purchases (500 shares):

	£
Sale proceeds (£5 × 500)	2,500
Less: Allowable cost	(1,200)
Chargeable gain	1,300

The share pool for companies is different to the share pool for individuals as follows:

- it contains shares in the same company, of the same class, purchased **up to 9 days before** the date of disposal.
- The pool keeps a record of the:
  - number of shares acquired and sold
  - cost of the shares, and
  - indexed cost of the shares (i.e. cost plus indexation allowance)

- Each purchase and sale is recorded in the pool, but the indexed cost must be updated **before** recording the "operative event"
- When calculating the IA in the share pool, the indexation factor is **not** rounded to three decimal places.

  Note that this is the only situation where a non-rounded factor is used.

- When shares are disposed of out of the share pool, the appropriate proportion of the cost and indexed cost which relates to the shares disposed of is calculated on an average cost basis (as for individuals).

Pro forma for a company's share pool

The following pro forma, should be used to ensure that additions to and disposals from the share pool, are correctly dealt with.

	Number	Cost		Indexed cost
		£		£
Purchase	X	X	——→	X
IA to next operative event				X
Purchase	X	X	——→	X
	X	X		X
IA to next operative event				X
	X	X		X
Disposal	(X)	(X)		(X)
		W1		W2
Pool carried forward	X	X		X

Note:

(W1) Calculates the average pool cost of shares disposed of
(W2) Calculates the average indexed cost of shares disposed of

Workings 1 and 2 then feed into a normal gain computation, as follows:

	£
Sale proceeds	X
Less: Cost (W1)	(X)
Unindexed gain	X
Less: Indexation allowance (W2 – W1)	(X)
Chargeable gain	X

Example 6 - Disposal of shares and securities

Continuing the example of Minnie Ltd (above), calculate the gain on the disposal from the share pool.

Assume the RPIs are as follows:

July 1989	115.5
September 2000	171.7
February 2010	213.5

Answer to example 6

	£
Sale proceeds (£5 × 1,000)	5,000
Less: Allowable cost (W)	(2,250)
	2,750
Less: Indexation allowance (£3,403 – £2,250) (W)	(1,153)
Chargeable gain	1,597

Working: Share pool	Number	Cost	Indexed cost
		£	£
July 1989 purchase	1,000	2,000	2,000
IA to next operative event: (July 1989 to September 2000) (171.7 – 115.5)/115.5 × £2,000			973
September 2000 purchase	1,000	2,500	2,500
	2,000	4,500	5,473
IA to next operative event (September 2000 to February 2010) (213.5 – 171.7)/171.7 × £5,473			1,332
	2,000	4,500	6,805
February 2010 sale (1,000 out of 2,000)	(1,000)	(2,250)	(3,403)
Pool carried forward	1,000	2,250	3,402

Note: Half of the shares sold, therefore take out half of the cost and indexed cost.

Test your understanding 4

Braganza Ltd sold 10,000 ordinary shares in the FRP Co plc, a quoted company, on 20 December 2009, for £70,000.

Braganza Ltd always prepares its financial statements to 31 December each year.

The company had bought the ordinary shares on the following dates:

	Number of shares	Cost	Indexed cost
		£	£
1 April 1998 – Balance b/fwd	8,000	17,450	25,250
22 December 2000	4,000	7,500	

Calculate the chargeable gain arising on the disposal of the shares.

Assume retail price indices are:

April 1998	162.6
December 2000	172.2
December 2009	213.1

5 Bonus and rights issues

The key points to remember are as follows:

- A bonus issue is the distribution of free shares to shareholders, based on existing shareholdings.
- A rights issue involves shareholders paying for new shares, usually at a rate below market price and in proportion to their existing shareholdings.
- In both cases, therefore, the shareholder is making a new acquisition of shares.
- However, for matching purposes, such acquisitions arise out of the original holdings. They are not treated as a separate holding of shares.
- Bonus and rights issues therefore, attach to the original shareholdings, for the purposes of the identification rules.

Bonus issues

- As a bonus issue is free shares (i.e. no cost is involved), there is no indexation to be calculated.
- A bonus issue is not an operative event in the share pool.
- Simply, add the bonus issue shares to the share pool. When the next operative event occurs (e.g. next sale or purchase), index from the operative event before the date of the bonus issue.

Rights issue

- A rights issue is simply a purchase of shares (usually at a price below the market rate).
- Hence, it should be treated as an operative event, in the same way as a purchase in the share pool:
  - Index up to the date of the rights issue; then
  - Add in the number of shares and their cost.

Example 7 - Bonus issue

Alma Ltd acquired shares in S plc, a quoted company, as follows:

2,000 shares acquired in June 1987, for £11,500.

In October 1988, there was a 1 for 2 bonus issue.

Set up the share pool and deal with the events up to and including the bonus issue.

Answer to example 7

Share pool	Number	Cost	Indexed cost
		£	£
Purchase (June 1987)	2,000	11,500	11,500
Bonus issue (October 1988)			
(1 for 2) 1/2 × £2,000	1,000	Nil	Nil
	3,000	11,500	11,500

Note: DO NOT index up to the date of the bonus issue as no cost is involved. The next time there is an operative event, IA will be calculated from June 1987 (the last operative event).

Test your understanding 5

Michael Ltd sold 2,000 ordinary shares out of a holding of 5,000 shares in Ryan Ltd, on 30 September 2009, for £15,400.

Michael Ltd prepares accounts every year to 31 March. The holding of shares in Ryan Ltd had been built up as follows:

Date acquired	Number of shares	Cost £
May 1995	4,000	7,000
March 1996 – Bonus issue 1 for 4	1,000	Nil

Compute the chargeable gain arising on the sale of shares, in the year to 31 March 2010.

Assume the retail price indices are:

May 1995	149.6
March 1996	151.5
September 2009	212.5

Example 8 - Rights issue

Amber Ltd sold 2,600 shares in Pearl Ltd in December 2009 for £30,000.

Amber Ltd originally acquired 3,000 shares in Pearl Ltd in June 1987 for £11,500. In December 1994 Amber Ltd took up its entitlement to a 1 for 4 rights issue at £3 per share.

Calculate the chargeable gain arising on disposal of the shares, in December 2009.

Assume the following RPIs apply:

June 1987	101.9
December 1994	146.0
December 2009	213.1

Answer to example 8

	£
Sale proceeds	30,000
Less: Cost (W)	(9,533)
Unindexed gain	20,467
Less: Indexation (£18,952 – £9,533) (W)	(9,419)
Chargeable gain	11,048

Working: share pool	Number	Cost	Indexed cost
		£	£
Purchase – June 1987	3,000	11,500	11,500
IA to December 1994 (146.0 – 101.9)/101.9 × £11,500			4,977
	3,000	11,500	16,477
Rights issue (1 for 4) at £3 – December 1997	750	2,250	2,250
	3,750	13,750	18,727
IA to December 2009 (213.1 – 146.0)/146.0 × £18,727			8,607
	3,750	13,750	27,334
Disposal – December 2008 (2,600/3,750) × £13,750/£27,334	(2,600)	(9,533)	(18,952)
Balance to c/f	1,150	4,217	8,382

Note: The indexed cost is updated prior to the rights issue, because there is a purchase which involves additional cost (i.e. it is an operative event).

Following the disposal, there are 1,150 shares in the pool, with a cost of £4,217 and an indexed cost of £8,382.

This will be used as the starting point, when dealing with the next operative event.

6 Takeovers/reorganisations

Consideration: shares for shares

Where the consideration for the reorganisation or takeover, only involves the issue of shares in the acquiring company, the tax consequences are:

- No chargeable gain arises at the time of the reorganisation or takeover.
- The cost of the original shares becomes the cost of the new shares.
- Where the shareholder receives more than one type of share, in exchange for the original shares, the cost of the original shares is allocated to the new shares, by reference to the market values of the various new shares, on the first day of dealing in them.

Mixed consideration

When both cash and shares are received on a takeover:

- There is a part disposal of the original shares. A chargeable gain arises on the cash element of the consideration.

Example 9 - Takeovers/reorganisations

In June 1997, Major Ltd purchased 2,000 ordinary shares in Blue plc, for £5,000.

In July 2009, Blue plc was taken over by Red plc, and Major Ltd received 2 ordinary shares and 1 preference share in Red plc, for each ordinary share in Blue plc.

Immediately after the takeover, the ordinary shares in Red plc, were quoted at £2 and the preference shares in Red plc, were quoted at £1.

In December 2009, Major Ltd sold all of its holding of ordinary shares in Red plc, for £8,000. The indexation factor from June 1997 to December 2009, should be taken as 0.353.

Calculate the chargeable gain arising on the disposal in December 2009.

Answer to example 9

	£
Sale proceeds	8,000
Less: Cost (W)	(4,000)
Unindexed gain	4,000
Less: Indexation allowance (£4,000 × 0.353)	(1,412)
Chargeable gain	2,588

Working: Cost of ordinary shares in Red plc

Major Ltd received:

	£
4,000 ordinary shares, valued at £2	8,000
2,000 preference shares, valued at £1	2,000
	10,000

The cost attributable to the ordinary shares is therefore:
£5,000 × (8,000/10,000) = £4,000

Test your understanding 6

In July 2009, Concert Ltd sold its entire holding of ordinary shares in Corus plc, for £75,000. Concert Ltd had originally purchased 20,000 £1 ordinary shares in BNB plc, at a cost of £20,000, in April 1992.

In July 1998, BNB plc was taken over by Corus plc. Concert Ltd received one ordinary 50p share and one 50p 6% preference share in Corus plc, for each ordinary share it held in BNB plc.

Immediately after the takeover, the values of these new shares were:

50p ordinary share	£1.80 each
50p preference shares	£0.80 each

Compute the chargeable gain arising on the disposal by Concert Ltd, who has always prepared financial statements to 31 December each year.

The relevant indexation factor to be used is 0.528.

7 Reliefs available to companies

The **only** capital gains relief available to companies is Roll-over relief. The other reliefs covered in Chapter 17 are not applicable to companies.

Roll-over relief for companies

The detail of roll-over relief is covered in Chapter 17. There are generally no differences in the application of roll-over relief for companies. The rules are summarised in expandable text.

Summary of roll-over relief

- Roll-over relief exists to allow companies to replace assets used in their trade, without incurring a corporation tax liability on the related chargeable gains.
- The gain arising on the disposal of the business asset, is deducted from (rolled over against), the acquisition cost of the new asset.
- Provided the proceeds are fully reinvested, no tax is payable at the time of the disposal.
- The most common assets which qualify for roll-over relief in an exam are:
  - Land and buildings that are both occupied and used for trading purposes.
  - Fixed plant and machinery (in this context 'fixed' means immovable).
- The acquisition of the replacement asset, must occur during a period that begins **one year before** the sale of the old asset and ends **three years after** the sale.
- Where disposal proceeds of the old asset are not fully reinvested, the surplus retained, reduces the amount of chargeable gain that can be rolled over.
- When an asset has not been used entirely for business purposes throughout the company's period of ownership, the roll-over relief is scaled down in proportion to the non-business use.
- If reinvestment is in a depreciating asset, the capital gain is deferred until the earliest of:
  - disposal of the depreciating asset
  - depreciating asset ceases to be used for trading purposes
  - 10 years since the asset was acquired.

- Any asset with a predictable life of not more than 60 years, is a depreciating asset.
- If a new non-depreciating asset is acquired before the deferred gain becomes chargeable, roll-over relief can be reinstated.

The key differences in the rules for companes are as follows:

- **goodwill is not a qualifying asset** for companies
- the gain deferred is the 'indexed gain' (i.e. the gain **after** IA).

Test your understanding 7

Medway Ltd has been offered £160,000 for a freehold factory that it owns, and is considering disposing of the factory in January 2010.

The company acquired the factory on 15 March 1984, for £120,000 (this figure is already indexed to January 2010). The factory has always been used by Medway Ltd for business purposes.

Explain the capital gains implications of each of the following alternative courses of action that Medway Ltd is considering taking:

(a) **Acquiring a larger freehold factory in April 2010, for £170,000.**

(b) **Acquiring a smaller freehold factory in April 2010, for £155,000 and using the remainder of the proceeds as working capital.**

(c) **Using the proceeds to pay a premium of £180,000 in April 2010, for a 40-year lease of a new factory (it is possible that a freehold warehouse will be bought in the next two or three years for an estimated cost of £200,000).**

8 Chapter summary

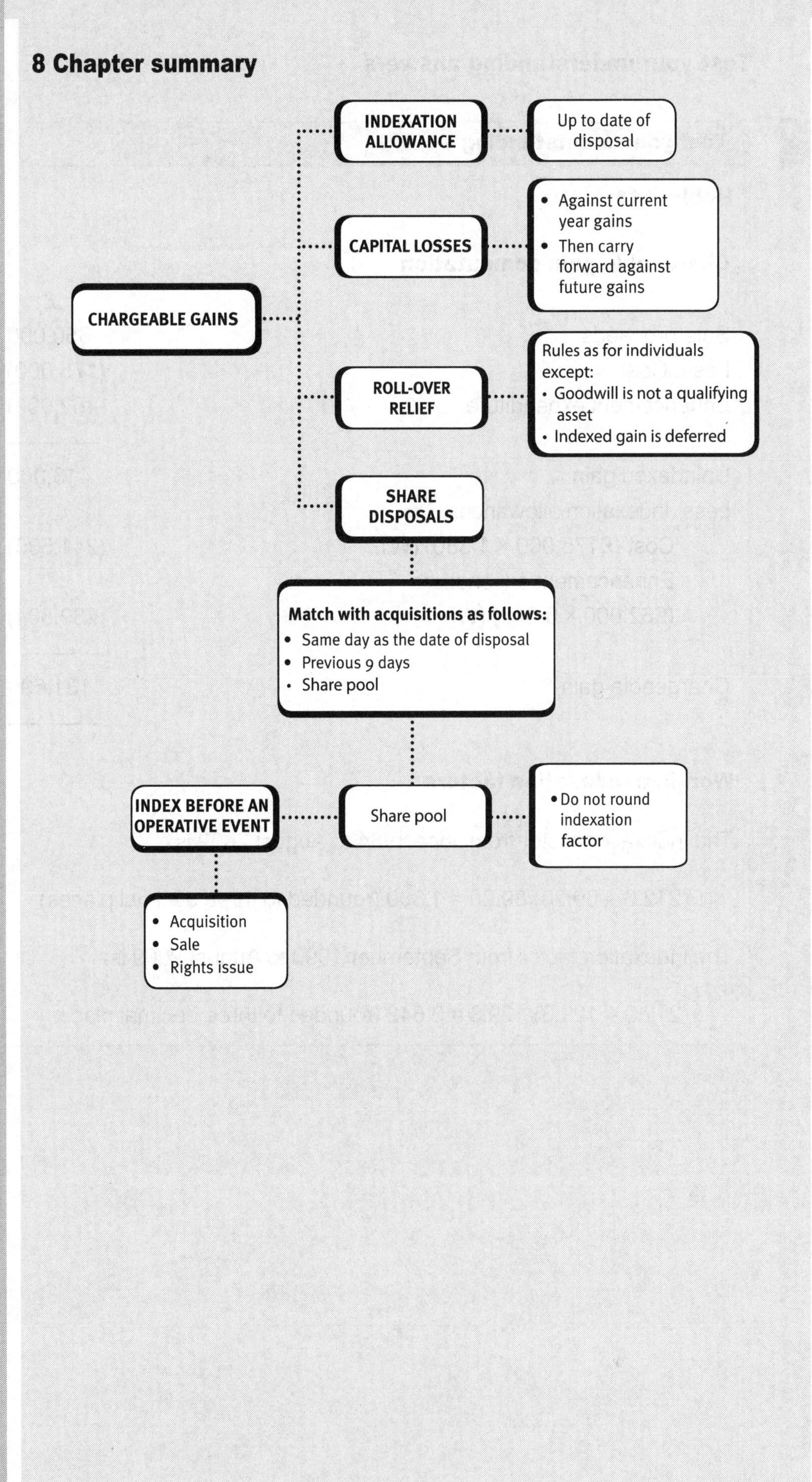

Test your understanding answers

Test your understanding 1

Hobbit Ltd

Chargeable gain computation

	£
Sale proceeds	650,000
Less: Cost	(175,000)
Enhancement expenditure	(62,000)
Unindexed gain	413,000
Less: Indexation allowance:	
Cost (£175,000 × 1.380) (W)	(241,500)
Enhancement expenditure (£62,000 × 0.642) (W)	(39,804)
Chargeable gain	131,696

Working: indexation factors

The indexation factor from June 1984 to August 2009 is:

(212.3 – 89.20)/89.20 = 1.380 (rounded to three decimal places)

The indexation factor from September 1990 to August 2009 is:

(212.3 – 129.3)/129.3 = 0.642 (rounded to three decimal places)

Test your understanding 2

JNN Ltd

	(a)	(b)	(c)
	£	£	£
Sale proceeds	25,000	12,000	8,000
Less: Cost	(10,000)	(10,000)	(10,000)
Unindexed gain/(loss)	15,000	2,000	(2,000)
Less: Indexation allowance			
£10,000 x 1.358	(13,580)		
Restricted (see note)		(2,000)	Nil
Chargeable gain/(allowable loss)	1,420	Nil	(2,000)

Note: Part (b): IA is restricted as indexation cannot create a loss.
Part (c): no IA as indexation cannot increase a loss.

Test your understanding 3

High Ltd

Corporation tax liability – year ended 31 December 2009

	£
Trading profit	200,000
Net chargeable gain	Nil
PCTCT	200,000
Corporation tax liability (£200,000 × 21%)	42,000

Working: Net chargeable gain

	£
Chargeable gain	17,000
Less: Capital loss b/f	(23,000)
Capital loss c/f	(6,000)

Therefore the net chargeable gain is Nil.

Test your understanding 4

Braganza Ltd
Chargeable gain computation – year to 31 December 2009

	£
Sale proceeds	70,000
Less: Acquisition cost (W)	(20,792)
Unindexed gain	49,208
Less: Indexation allowance (£35,312 – £20,792) (W)	(14,520)
Chargeable gain	34,688

Working: share pool	Number	Cost	Indexed cost
		£	£
Balance at 1.4.98	8,000	17,450	25,250
IA to December 2000			
(172.2 – 162.6)/162.6 × £25,250			1,491
December 2000 acquisition	4,000	7,500	7,500
	12,000	24,950	34,241
IA to December 2009			
(213.1 – 172.2)/172.2 × £34,241			8,133
	12,000	24,950	42,374
Disposal – December 2009	(10,000)	(20,792)	(35,312)
Balance c/f	2,000	4,158	7,062

Proportion of cost and indexed cost relating to the disposal:

Cost: (10,000/12,000) × £24,950 = £20,792
Indexed cost: (10,000/12,000) × £42,374 = £35,312

Test your understanding 5

Michael Ltd

Chargeable gain computation – year to 31 March 2010

	£
Sale proceeds	15,400
Less: Acquisition cost (W)	(2,800)
Unindexed gain	12,600
Less: Indexation allowance (£3,977 – £2,800) (W)	(1,177)
Chargeable gain	11,423

Working: share pool	Number	Cost	Indexed cost
		£	£
May 1995	4,000	7,000	7,000
March 1996 – bonus issue	1,000	Nil	Nil
	5,000	7,000	7,000
Index to September 2009 from May 1995 (212.5 – 149.6)/149.6 × £7,000			2,943
	5,000	7,000	9,943
Disposal (Note)	(2,000)	(2,800)	(3,977)
Balance c/f	3,000	4,200	5,966

Note: The proportion of cost and indexed cost relating to the disposal is calculated as: (2,000/5,000) × £7,000 and £9,943 respectively.

Test your understanding 6

Concert Ltd

Chargeable gain computation – year to 31 December 2009

	£
Sales proceeds	75,000
Less: Deemed acquisition cost (W)	(13,846)
Unindexed gain	61,154
Less: Indexation allowance (£13,846 × 0.528)	(7,311)
Chargeable gain	53,843

Working: Deemed acquisition cost

Following the takeover in July 1998 of BNB plc by Corus plc, Concert Ltd now owns shares in Corus plc as per the terms of the takeover.

	Total M.V.	Original cost
	£	£
20,000 50p ordinary shares @ £1.80	36,000	13,846
20,000 50p preference shares @ £0.80	16,000	6,154
	52,000	20,000

Allocation of original cost incurred in April 1992, to the shares now owned in July 1998, using the average cost method.

To ordinary shares: (£36,000/£52,000) × £20,000 = £13,846

To preference shares (£16,000/£52,000) × £20,000 = £6,154

Test your understanding 7

Medway Ltd

The chargeable gain on the disposal of the freehold factory is £40,000 (£160,000 – £120,000).

(a) **Larger freehold factory**

The gain will be rolled over against the base cost of the new factory as all the proceeds are reinvested:

	£
Cost of factory	170,000
Gain rolled over	(40,000)
Base cost of new factory	130,000

(b) **Smaller freehold factory**

As only part of the proceeds are reinvested, the capital gain element that cannot be rolled over will be £5,000 (£160,000 – £155,000).

This will be immediately chargeable to corporation tax. The balance of the gain will be rolled over as above.

	£
Cost of factory	155,000
Gain rolled over (£40,000 – £5,000)	(35,000)
Base cost of new factory	120,000

(c) **Lease**

All of the proceeds are being used to acquire a depreciating asset (one with an expected life of less than 60 years). The capital gain is therefore not rolled over, but is instead 'frozen'.

It will become chargeable to corporation tax on the earlier of:

– the date that the lease is sold

– the date the lease ceases to be used in the trade

– the expiry of ten years from April 2010.

Therefore, the base cost of the lease remains at £180,000.

If, before the 'frozen' gain becomes chargeable, a non-depreciating asset is acquired, the gain can be rolled over in the usual way.

In this question, if the freehold warehouse is acquired in the next 2 – 3 years, all the proceeds will be reinvested and so the roll-over claim would switch to the freehold warehouse cost of £200,000.

chapter

21

Losses for companies

Chapter learning objectives

Upon completion of this chapter you will be able to:

- determine a trading loss and explain the various ways of giving relief in a single company
- demonstrate the application of the trading loss reliefs in a corporation tax computation
- show how a trading loss is relieved on cessation of a trade
- identify the factors that influence the choice of a loss relief claim
- explain how relief for a property business loss is given
- demonstrate how capital losses can be relieved against gains.

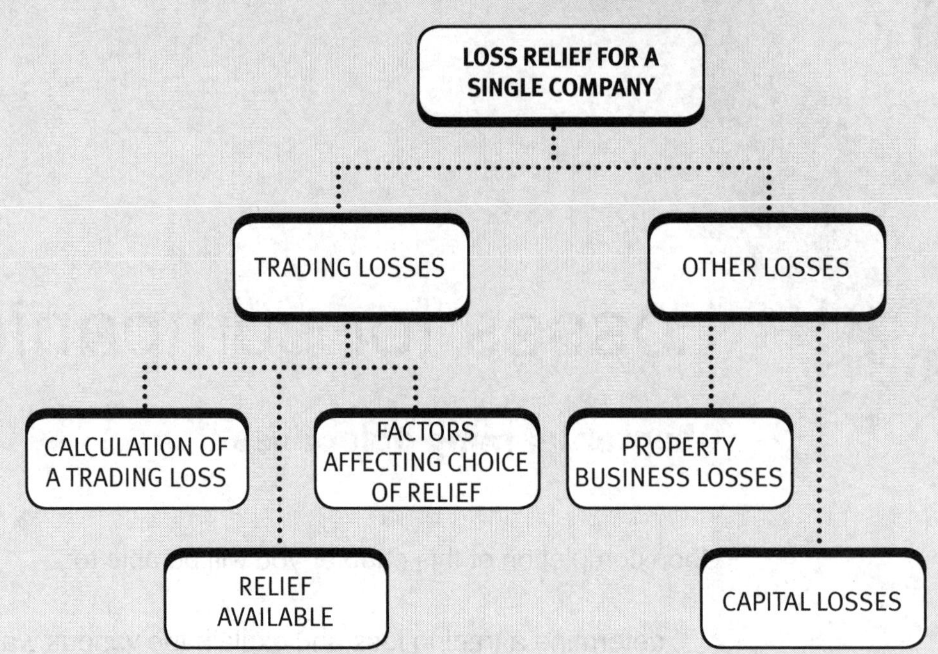

1 Introduction

This chapter covers the rules for loss reliefs available to a single company.

The following losses are dealt with:

- Trading losses (section 2).
- Property business losses (section 5).
- Capital losses (section 6).

2 Trading losses

Calculation of a trading loss

- Trading losses are computed in the same way as tax-adjusted trading profits:

	£
Tax-adjusted net profit/(loss)	X/(X)
Less: Plant and machinery capital allowances	(X)
Less: Industrial buildings allowances	(X)
Adjusted trading loss	(X)

- If a company has made an adjusted trading loss, £Nil is entered in the company's PCTCT computation for trading income for that period.

Example 1 - Trading losses

Carlos Ltd had the following results for its year ended 31 March 2010:

	£	£
Gross profit		30,000
Less: Expenditure		
Depreciation	5,000	
Allowable costs	12,000	
		(17,000)
Net profit per accounts		13,000

The capital allowances for the year amount to £21,000.

(a) **Calculate the tax-adjusted trading loss for the y/e 31 March 2010.**

(b) **Calculate the tax-adjusted trading loss for the y/e 31 March 2010 assuming the facts are the same except that the company made a net loss per the accounts of £10,000.**

Answer to example 1

(a) **Tax-adjusted trading loss – y/e 31 March 2010**

	£
Net profit per accounts	13,000
Add: Depreciation	5,000
	18,000
Less: Capital allowances	(21,000)
Tax-adjusted trading loss	(3,000)
Trading income included in PCTCT	Nil

(b) **Tax-adjusted trading loss**

	£
Net loss per accounts	(10,000)
Add: Depreciation	5,000
	(5,000)
Less: Capital allowances	(21,000)
Tax-adjusted trading loss	(26,000)
Trading income included in PCTCT	£Nil.

Relief for trading losses

There are four ways in which a company can offset trading losses:

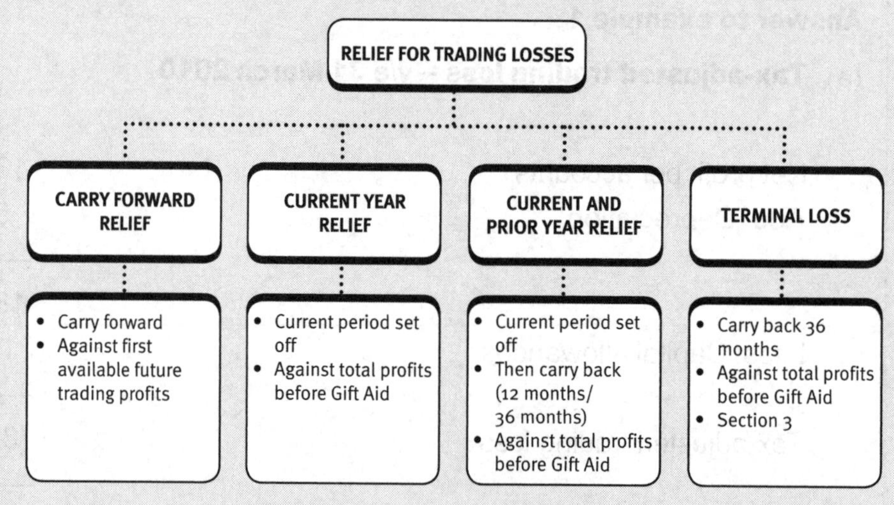
RELIEF FOR TRADING LOSSES
CARRY FORWARD RELIEF
CURRENT YEAR RELIEF
CURRENT AND PRIOR YEAR RELIEF
TERMINAL LOSS
• Carry forward
• Against first available future trading profits
• Current period set off
• Against total profits before Gift Aid
• Current period set off
• Then carry back (12 months/ 36 months)
• Against total profits before Gift Aid
• Carry back 36 months
• Against total profits before Gift Aid
• Section 3

Carry forward loss relief

The key features of this relief are:

- The loss is carried forward for offset in future accounting periods.
- The loss is set against the **first available** tax-adjusted profits from the **same trade**.
- The relief is automatic (i.e. no claim is required).
- The loss can be carried forward indefinitely.
- There is no need to make a current year or a prior year claim first.

Carry forward loss relief

- The loss can be carried forward indefinitely, but it must be set-off against the **first available** trading profits from the **same trade**.
- Therefore if the company changes their trading activity, any remaining losses are forfeited.
- Losses can be carried forward:
  - After a current year claim only.
  - After a current year and prior year claim.
  - If no claims are made.
- A claim to establish the amount of the loss available to carry forward should be made within four years of the end of the loss-making accounting period.
- The carry forward relief applies automatically against future trading profits as soon as they arise. They cannot be relieved against any other profits.

Example 2 - Trading losses

Poppy Ltd has a current year tax adjusted trading loss of £25,000, for the year ended 31 March 2010.

The company's projected trading profits are as follows:

	£
Year ended 31 March 2011	14,000
Year ended 31 March 2012	6,500
Year ended 31 March 2013	15,600

Poppy Ltd also receives property business income of £5,000 each year.

Calculate Poppy Ltd's PCTCT for the four years ended 31 March 2013 assuming that the loss for the year ended 31 March 2010, is carried forward.

Answer to example 2

Year ended 31 March	2010	2011	2012	2013
	£	£	£	£
Trading income	Nil	14,000	6,500	15,600
Less Loss relief b/f	–	(14,000)	(6,500)	(4,500)
	Nil	Nil	Nil	11,100
Property income	5,000	5,000	5,000	5,000
PCTCT	5,000	5,000	5,000	16,100

Working - loss memorandum

Loss - y/e 31.3.2010	25,000
Used in - y/e 31.3.2011	(14,000)
y/e 31.3.2012	(6,500)
y/e 31.3.2013	(4,500)
Carry forward to y/e 31.3.2014	Nil

Current year relief

If a current year loss relief claim is made, trading losses are set off against:

- total profits before deduction of Gift Aid
- of the same accounting period.

A current year claim must be made:

- for the whole loss; a partial claim is not allowed
- within two years of the end of the loss-making accounting period.

Example 3 - Trading losses

Sage Ltd had the following results for the y/e 31 March 2010.

	£
Tax-adjusted trading loss	(40,000)
Property business income	10,000
Chargeable gain	50,000
Gift Aid payment	10,000

(a) **Show how the trading loss could be relieved with a current period claim.**

(b) **Show how your answer would be different if the tax-adjusted trading loss was £60,000.**

Answer to example 3

(a) **PCTCT computation for the y/e 31 March 2010**

	£
Trading income	Nil
Property income	10,000
Chargeable gain	50,000
Total profits	60,000
Less Loss relief – current year	(40,000)
	20,000
Less: Gift Aid	(10,000)
PCTCT	10,000

Loss memorandum

Year ended 31 March 2010	40,000
Less Used in current period	(40,000)
	Nil

(b) **PCTCT computation for the y/e 31 March 2010**

	£
Total profits (as before)	60,000
Less Loss relief – current year	(60,000)
PCTCT	Nil
Gift Aid wasted (see Note)	(10,000)

Note: Gift Aid

As the loss is set off before the deduction of Gift Aid, the Gift Aid payments have become excess (i.e. not used), as there are insufficient profits. It is an important principle that, where there is an available loss, no restriction in set off is permitted.

This means that it would **not** have been possible here, to restrict the loss relief to (£50,000), so as to then relieve the Gift Aid payments of (£10,000), and find an alternative use for the remaining (£10,000) loss.

Excess Gift Aid donations cannot be carried forward or back and are therefore wasted.

Carry back relief

Any trading loss remaining after a current year claim can be carried back.

Under carry back loss relief, trading losses are set off against:

- total profits (before deduction of Gift Aid)
- of the previous 12 months
- on a LIFO (last in first out) basis.

A carryback claim can only be made, if a claim for current year loss relief has been made first.

The carry back claim:

- is optional
- must be made within two years of the end of the loss-making accounting period.

Extended loss relief

- A trading loss can normally be carried back and set against profits of the preceding 12 months.
- However, for loss making accounting periods ending between 24 November 2008 and 23 November 2010 this relief is extended to 36 months.
- The extended relief is restricted to a **maximum of £50,000**.
- The £50,000 limit is apportioned if a loss making period is shorter than 12 months. For example, for a 6-month loss making period the extended relief would be restricted to a maximum of £25,000 (6/12 x £50,000).
- The £50,000 restriction only applies to losses carried back past the normal 12 month carry back period.

Trading losses – pro-forma computation

When dealing with losses it is necessary to have a neat and logical layout for computations.

Pro forma: Corporation tax losses

(Loss arises in 2009)	2006	2007	2008	2009	2010
	£	£	£	£	£
Trading profit	X	X	X	Nil	X
Less Loss relief b/f					(X)
					X
Other income	X	X	X	X	X
Chargeable gains	X	X	X	X	X
Total profits	X	X	X	X	X
Less Loss relief					
– Current year				(X)	
– 12 month carry back			(X)		
– Extended carry back (Max £50,000)	(X)	(X)			
	X	Nil	Nil	Nil	X
Less Gift Aid	(X)	Wasted	Wasted	Wasted	(X)
PCTCT	X	Nil	Nil	Nil	X

Note: The carry back claims are on a LIFO basis (i.e. 12 m/e 31 December 2008, then 2007, then 2006).

Example 4 - Trading losses

Marjoram Ltd has the following results for the three accounting periods to 31 March 2010.

Year ended 31 March:	2008	2009	2010
	£	£	£
Trading profits/(loss)	111,000	99,000	(195,000)
Building society interest	500	500	500
Chargeable gains	–	–	4,000
Gift Aid payment	250	250	250

Calculate the PCTCT for all periods affected, assuming that loss relief is taken as soon as possible.

Answer to example 4

Marjoram Ltd – Corporation tax computations

Year ended 31 March:	2008	2009	2010
	£	£	£
Trading income	111,000	99,000	Nil
Interest income	500	500	500
Chargeable gain	–	–	4,000
Total profits	111,500	99,500	4,500
Less Loss relief (W)			
– Current year			(4,500)
– 12 month carry back		(99,500)	
– Extended carry back	(50,000)		
	61,500	Nil	Nil
Less: Gift Aid payment	(250)	Wasted	Wasted
PCTCT	61,250	Nil	Nil

Working – loss memorandum

	£
Loss for the year ended 31 March 2010	195,000
Less Used in current year – y/e 31.3.10	(4,500)
Less Used in 12 month carry back – y/e 31.3.09	(99,500)
Less Used in extended carry back relief – y/e 31.3.08	(50,000)
Loss carried forward	41,000

Note: The carry back for 12 months is not restricted in amount. However, the maximum carry back in the extended period is £50,000.

The Gift Aid payments in the years ended 31 March 2009 and 2010 are wasted.

Test your understanding 1

Alfred Ball Ltd has the following results:

Year ended 31 December:	2006	2007	2008	2009
	£	£	£	£
Adjusted trading profit/(loss)	48,000	32,000	119,000	(187,000)
Bank interest received	4,000	3,000	2,000	1,000
Chargeable gains	4,000	4,000	4,000	4,000
Gift Aid paid	10,000	10,000	10,000	–

Calculate the PCTCT, for all of the accounting periods shown above, clearly indicating how you would deal with the trading loss, to obtain relief as soon as possible.

Loss-making period of less than 12 months

The length of the loss-making period is usually not important:

- Full relief is given against the current period total profits.
- The remaining loss can be carried back in full in the normal way.

However, remember that the £50,000 maximum limit for the extended relief must be apportioned according to the length of the loss-making accounting period.

Test your understanding 2

Mint Ltd has the following results:

	y/e 31.3.08	y/e 31.3.09	9 m/e 31.12.09	y/e 31.12.10
	£	£	£	£
Adjusted trading profit/(loss)	60,000	15,000	(137,500)	40,000
Interest income	5,000	5,000	10,000	10,000
Chargeable gain	–	–	40,000	–

Calculate the PCTCT, for all of the accounting periods shown above, clearly indicating how you would deal with the trading loss, to obtain relief as soon as possible.

Short accounting periods prior to year of loss

If any of the accounting periods falling in the carry back period is less than 12 months:

- The profits of the accounting period that falls partly into the carry back period must be time apportioned.
- The loss can only be offset against those profits which fall within the carry back period.
- Remember, the loss is offset on a LIFO basis (i.e. against the later accounting period first).

Example 5 - Trading losses

Starbuck plc's recent results are as follows:

	y/e 31.12.05	y/e 31.12.06	5 m/e 31.5.07	y/e 31.5.08	y/e 31.5.09
	£	£	£	£	£
Trading profit/(loss)	40,000	24,000	10,000	16,000	(100,000)
Interest income	4,000	3,500	2,000	4,700	6,000

Calculate the PCTCT for all periods assuming the trading loss is relieved as early as possible.

Answer to example 5

	y/e 31.12.05	y/e 31.12.06	5 m/e 31.5.07	y/e 31.5.08	y/e 31.5.09
	£	£	£	£	£
Trading profit/(loss)	40,000	24,000	10,000	16,000	Nil
Interest income	4,000	3,500	2,000	4,700	6,000
Total profits	44,000	27,500	12,000	20,700	6,000
Less Loss relief					
– Current year					(6,000)
– 12 month carry back				(20,700)	
– Extended carry back	(10,500)	(27,500)	(12,000)		
PCTCT	33,500	Nil	Nil	Nil	Nil

Loss Memorandum

	£
Trading loss y/e 31.5.09	100,000
Less Used in current year claim – y/e 31.5.09	(6,000)
	94,000
Less Used in 12 month carry back – y/e 31.5.08	(20,700)
	73,300
Less Used in extended carry back (LIFO)	
– 5 months to 31.5.07	(12,000)
– y/e 31.12.06	(27,500)
– y/e 31.12.05	
Lower of:	
(i) Total profits × 7/12	
= (7/12 × £44,000) = £25,667	
(ii) Remaining maximum loss	
= (£50,000 – £12,000 – £27,500) = £10,500	(10,500)
Loss remaining to carry forward	23,300

Test your understanding 3

Catalyst Ltd has the following results:

	y/e 30.4.06	y/e 30.4.07	p/e 31.12.07	y/e 31.12.08	y/e 31.12.09
	£	£	£	£	£
Trading profit/(loss) before capital allowances	30,930	25,000	23,000	16,500	(75,000)
Capital allowances	5,430	5,000	5,400	4,050	6,550
Interest income	1,500	1,600	1,200	1,300	1,400
Chargeable gain/(loss)	Nil	Nil	(6,000)	Nil	15,000
Gift Aid donations	4,000	8,000	Nil	3,000	3,000

Calculate the PCTCT for all periods assuming the trading loss is relieved as early as possible. Show the amount of unrelieved losses at 31 December 2009.

3 Terminal loss relief

When a company incurs a trading loss during the **final 12 months of trading**, then it is possible to make a carry back claim.

The terminal loss can be carried back and set against **total profits** of the **three years** preceding the loss-making period on a **LIFO basis**.

The relief operates in the same way as the extended carry back relief, but there is no maximum limit.

Test your understanding 4

Brown Ltd has been trading for many years. The company prepared its annual accounts to 31 March, each year, but changed its accounting date to 31 December in 2009. The company ceased trading on 31 December 2010.

Period ended:	31.3.07	31.3.08	31.3.09	31.12.09	31.12.10
	£	£	£	£	£
Trading profit	450,000	87,000	240,000	45,000	Nil
Bank interest	9,000	3,000	6,000	1,500	1,500
Chargeable gain	7,500	–	–	–	–
Gift Aid donation	30,000	30,000	30,000	30,000	30,000

In the year ended 31 December 2010, Brown Ltd made a tax-adjusted trading loss of £525,000.

Calculate Brown Ltd's PCTCT, for all of the above accounting periods, assuming terminal loss relief is claimed for the trading loss for the accounting period ended 31 December 2010.

4 Choice of loss relief

Factors that influence choice of loss relief

Where there is a choice of loss reliefs available, the following factors will influence the loss relief chosen:

- Tax saving
- Cash flow
- Wastage of relief for Gift Aid payments.

In examination questions, it is usually the option that gives the most beneficial tax saving that is recommended.

Tax saving

The company will want to save (or obtain a refund at) the highest possible rate of tax.

- The effective rate of tax for profits in the margin is used to work out the tax saving.
- The effective rate of tax in the margin describes the rate of tax saved for each £1 of loss utilised.

The preferred order to claim relief to achieve the highest tax saving is against profits subject to tax at the:

(1) full rate, but obtaining marginal relief.

Losses being set against profits in the marginal band have an effective rate of tax relief for FY2008 and FY2009 of 29.75% (FY2007 32.5%).

(2) full rate.

Losses being set against profits taxed at the full rate have an effective rate of tax relief for FY2008 and FY2009 of 28% (FY2007 30%).

(3) small companies rate.

Losses being set against profits taxed at the small companies rate have an effective rate of tax relief for FY2008 and FY 2009 of 21% (FY2007 20%).

Note: The effective rates of tax in the margin (or marginal rate) are not provided in the exam. You need to learn the marginal rates for FY2008 and FY2009.

Marginal rate of tax

The example below demonstrates how a company in the 'marginal' band between the small company rate and the large company rate, pays tax of 29.75% in FY2009 on each extra £1 it earns above the lower limit.

Example 6 - Marginal rate of tax

A Ltd has PCTCT of £300,000, for the year ended 31 March 2010. B Ltd has PCTCT of £310,000, for the year ended 31 March 2010. Neither company received any dividends in the year.

Calculate the corporation tax liability payable by each company and the marginal rate of tax on the additional profits of £10,000 earned by B Ltd.

Answer to example 6

Year ended 31 March 2010	**A Ltd**	**B Ltd**
	£	£
PCTCT = Profits	300,000	310,000
Corporation tax:		
£300,000 @ 21%	63,000	
£310,000 @ 28%		86,800
Less: Marginal relief		
7/400 × (£1,500,000 – £310,000)		(20,825)
		65,975

Additional tax paid by B Ltd (£65,975 – £63,000) = £2,975

Additional PCTCT earned by B Ltd = £10,000

Effective extra rate of tax on extra profits over £300,000 (the small company lower limit):

£2,975/£10,000 × 100 = **29.75%**

Choice of loss relief

Cash flow

A company's cash flow position may affect its choice of loss relief.

A company may be prepared to accept loss relief at a lower marginal rate, if it results in an earlier receipt of cash.

Note that when a loss is carried back, it will probably result in a repayment of corporation tax, whereas carrying losses forward will only result in a reduction of a future tax liability.

Loss of relief for Gift Aid donations

Unrelieved Gift Aid donations cannot be carried forward and relieved against future trading profits. Therefore, certain claims for loss relief may lead to relief for Gift Aid being lost.

Approach to questions

Loss questions will often give you PCTCT information for a company for a number of years. This may initially appear daunting.

However, the following step by step approach will provide you with a logical way to attempt the question and ensure that you offset the losses correctly.

Step 1: Write out the skeleton PCTCT proforma remembering to leave space for loss relief claims, lay out the years side by side.

Step 2: Fill in the pro forma with the PCTCT information provided, ignoring loss relief. In the year of the loss, the trading income is £Nil.

Step 3: Keep a separate working for the 'trading loss'. Update the workings as the loss is relieved.

Step 4: Consider the loss relief options available.

- Where there is more than one loss to offset:
  - Deal with the earliest loss first.
  - Losses brought forward are offset in priority to current year and carry back claims.
- If a question states 'relief is to be obtained as early as possible', the order of set-off is:
  - Current year claim followed by a carry back claim to the previous 12 months (or 36 months).
  - Carry forward any remaining loss and offset against future trading profits.
- If a question asks you to identify the option that will save the most tax, consider in turn the three options:
  - Carry forward only.
  - Current year claim and then carry forward any excess.
  - Current year claim, followed by a carry back claim and then carry forward any excess.
- Identify the amount of tax saving and loss of relief for Gift Aid under each option and conclude as to which option saves the most tax.

Step 5: Work out the revised PCTCT after any carry back of the trading loss.

Example 7 - Choice of loss relief

Loser Ltd prepared its accounts to 31 March 2008 but has since changed to a 30 September accounting date and prepared a set of accounts to 30 September 2008.

The company forecasts a substantial tax-adjusted trading loss for the current year to 30 September 2009. A small trading profit is forecast for the following year to 30 September 2010, with steadily increasing profits thereafter.

Loser Ltd's tax-adjusted trading profits for recent years have been :

	£
Year ended 31 March 2008	550,000
Period ended 30 September 2008	70,000

Advise Loser Ltd as to which loss relief claims would save the most tax.

Answer to example 7

Loser Ltd has the following options regarding the trading loss arising in the year to 30 September 2009:

(1) **Carry the loss forward to off-set against the first available future trading profits.**

As the trading profits in the year to 30 September 2010, are expected to be small, relief for the loss is likely to be at 21% (assuming the small companies rate is unchanged in the future).

(2) **Current year off-set against the total profits of the year ended 30 September 2009 and balance carried forward.**

Assuming that the non-trading income of the company in the current year is small, relief for the loss will be small companies rate of 21%.

(3) **Current year off-set followed by a carryback claim**

The carry back will be initially to the period ended 30 September 2008 and then the year ended 31 March 2008.

Relief in the current year and the period ended 30 September 2008, will be at the small companies rate of 21%.

The significant level of profits in the year ended 31 March 2008, will mean that relief for the loss in this year will be at the marginal rate of 32.5%.

Conclusion

Option 3 will therefore save the most tax.

Summary of trading loss reliefs

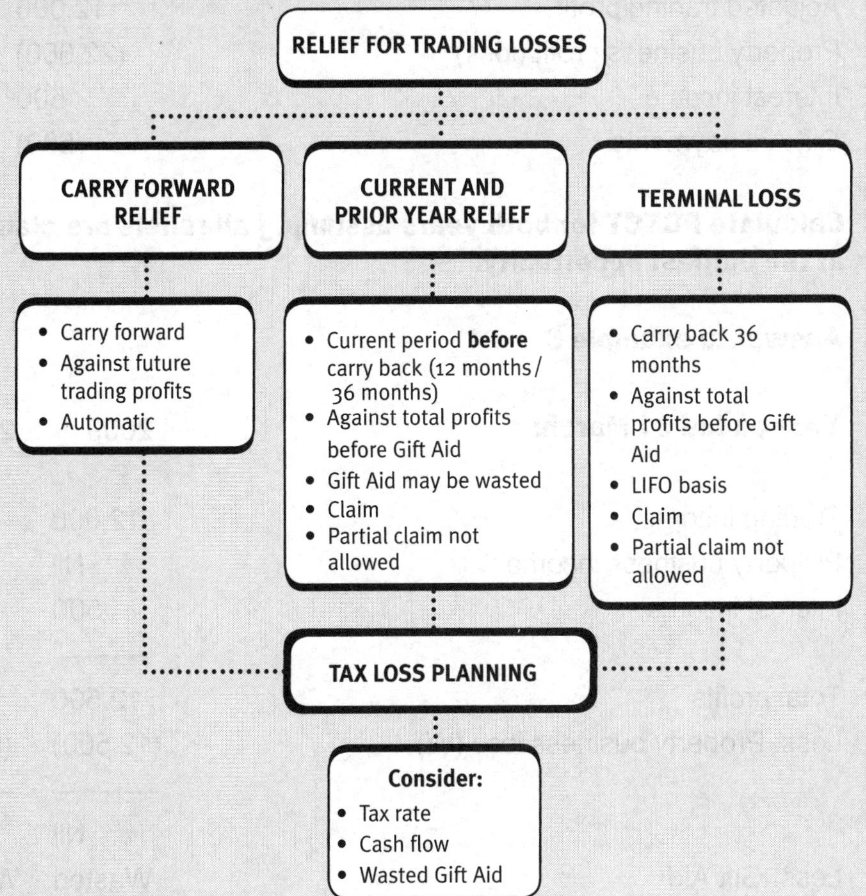
RELIEF FOR TRADING LOSSES
CARRY FORWARD RELIEF
CURRENT AND PRIOR YEAR RELIEF
TERMINAL LOSS
• Carry forward
• Against future trading profits
• Automatic
• Current period before carry back (12 months / 36 months)
• Against total profits before Gift Aid
• Gift Aid may be wasted
• Claim
• Partial claim not allowed
• Carry back 36 months
• Against total profits before Gift Aid
• LIFO basis
• Claim
• Partial claim not allowed
TAX LOSS PLANNING
Consider:
• Tax rate
• Cash flow
• Wasted Gift Aid

5 Property business losses

Property business losses are:

- off-set against **total profits (before Gift Aid)** for the current period.
- Any excess is carried forward and off-set against the **first available** future **total profits** of the company.

Note that:

- Relief is automatic – no claim is required.
- There is no carry back facility for property business losses.
- Partial loss claims are not allowed.
- If applicable, property business losses are set off before trading losses.

Example 8 - Property business losses

Reas Ltd has the following results:

Year ended 31 March:	2009	2010
	£	£
Adjusted trading profit	12,000	7,000
Property business profit/(loss)	(22,600)	800
Interest income	500	1,400
Gift Aid payments	(500)	(500)

Calculate PCTCT for both years assuming all reliefs are claimed at the earliest opportunity.

Answer to example 8

Year ended 31 March:	2009	2010
	£	£
Trading income	12,000	7,000
Property business income	Nil	800
Interest income	500	1,400
Total profits	12,500	9,200
Less: Property business loss (W)	(12,500)	(9,200)
	Nil	Nil
Less: Gift Aid	Wasted	Wasted
PCTCT	Nil	Nil

Working: Property business loss

	£
Loss in y/e 31 March 2009	22,600
Used in current period – y/e 31 March 2009	(12,500)
	10,100
Used in carry forward – y/e 31 March 2010	(9,200)
Unrelieved loss carried forward	900

Test your understanding 5

Comfy Ltd has the following results:

Year ended 31 December:	2007	2008	2009
	£	£	£
Adjusted trading profit/(loss)	12,450	(14,500)	4,000
Property business profit/(loss)	2,000	1,800	(500)
Interest income	1,000	600	1,000
Gift Aid payments	(400)	(400)	(400)

Calculate PCTCT for all three years assuming all reliefs are claimed at the earliest opportunity.

6 Capital losses

A capital loss incurred in an accounting period is:

- relieved against any chargeable gains arising in the same accounting period.
- Any excess losses are then carried forward for relief against gains arising in future accounting periods.

Note that:

- Relief is automatic – no claim is required.

- A capital loss may never be carried back and relieved against chargeable gains for earlier periods.
- Capital losses can only be set against gains, they may not be set against the company's income.
- Partial claims are not allowed.

Example 9 - Capital losses

Rose Ltd has the following results:

Year ended 31 March:	2009	2010
	£	£
Trading profit/(loss)	(20,000)	18,000
Interest income	6,000	9,000
Capital loss	(2,000)	
Chargeable gains		7,000

Calculate the PCTCT for the two accounting periods assuming that the trading loss is carried forward. Show any unrelieved losses carried forward at 1 April 2010.

Answer to example 9

Trading losses carried forward are relieved against the first available trading profits.

Capital losses can only be set against current or future chargeable gains.

Rose Ltd – PCTCT computations

Year ended 31 March	2009	2010
	£	£
Trading income	Nil	18,000
Less: Loss relief b/f	–	(18,000)
	Nil	Nil
Interest income	6,000	9,000
Chargeable gains (£7,000 – £2,000)	Nil	5,000
PCTCT	6,000	14,000
Trading loss carried forward at 31 March 2010 (£20,000 – £18,000)		2,000

Test your understanding 6

Coriander Ltd started to trade on 1 January 2007 and has the following results:

Year ended:	Trading profit/ (loss)	Interest Income	Gift Aid paid	Capital gains or (losses)
	£	£	£	£
31.12.07	37,450	1,300	3,000	(6,000)
31.12.08	(81,550)	1,400	3,000	
31.12.09	20,000	1,600	3,000	13,000

Calculate PCTCT for all relevant periods assuming loss relief is given as early as possible.

7 Comprehensive example

Test your understanding 7

Eagle Ltd is a UK resident company that manufactures components. The company's results for the y/e 31 March 2010 are:

	£
Trading loss (as adjusted for taxation but before taking account of capital allowances) (Note 1)	(225,484)
Income from property (Note 4)	56,950
Profit on disposal of shares (Note 5)	56,900
Donation to charity (Note 6)	(3,000)

Notes

(1) **Trading loss**

The trading loss includes £20,000 in respect of patent royalties which are paid for a trading purpose as follows:

	£
Payments made	20,600
Accrued at 31 March 2010	1,600
	22,200
Accrued at 1 April 2009	(2,200)
	20,000

(2) **Industrial building**

Eagle Ltd had a new factory constructed at a cost of £350,000 that was brought into use on 1 July 2008. The cost breakdown is :

	£
Land	87,500
Site preparation	12,000
Architect's fees	5,000
Canteen for employees	32,000
General offices	72,500
Factory	141,000
	350,000

(3) **Plant and machinery**

On 1 April 2009 the tax written down values of plant and machinery were as follows:

	£
General pool	64,700
Expensive motor car	14,700

The expensive motor car was sold on 15 February 2010 for £12,400. The following assets were purchased during the year ended 31 March 2010:

		£
20 October 2009	Lorry	32,400
15 December 2009	Equipment	25,640
18 March 2010	Motor car (CO_2 emissions 136 g/km)	11,300

(4) **Income from property**

Eagle Ltd lets out two warehouses that are surplus to requirements.

The first warehouse was empty from 1 April to 30 June 2009, but was let from 1 July 2009. On that date the company received a premium of £50,000 for the grant of an eight-year lease, and the annual rent of £12,600 which is payable in advance.

The second warehouse was let until 31 December 2009 at an annual rent of £8,400. On that date the tenant left owing three months rent which the company is not able to recover. The roof was repaired at a cost of £6,700 during February 2010.

(5) **Profit on disposal of shares**

The profit on disposal of shares relates to a 1% shareholding in a UK company that was sold on 22 December 2009 for £257,250.

The shareholding was purchased on 5 June 1997 for £112,800. Assume that the indexation allowance from June 1997 to December 2009 it is £39,818.

(6) **Donation to charity**

The donation to charity was made under the Gift Aid scheme.

(7) **Other information**

Eagle Ltd has no associated companies. Its results for the six-month period ended 31 March 2008 and for the year ended 31 March 2009 were as follows:

	p/e 31 March 2008	y/e 31 March 2009
	£	£
Trading profit	137,900	52,000
Property business profit/(loss)	(4,600)	18,700
Chargeable gain/(allowable loss)	(8,900)	18,200
Donation to charity (gross)	(2,300)	(2,600)

(a) **Calculate Eagle Ltd's tax-adjusted trading loss for the year ended 31 March 2010.**

You should assume that the company claims the maximum available capital allowances.

(b) **Assuming that Eagle Ltd claims relief for its trading loss as early as possible, calculate the company's PCTCT for the three accounting periods ended 31 March 2010.**

Your answer should show the amount of unrelieved trading losses as at 31 March 2010.

(c) **Describe the alternative ways in which Eagle Ltd could have relieved the trading loss for the year ended 31 March 2010.**

8 Chapter summary

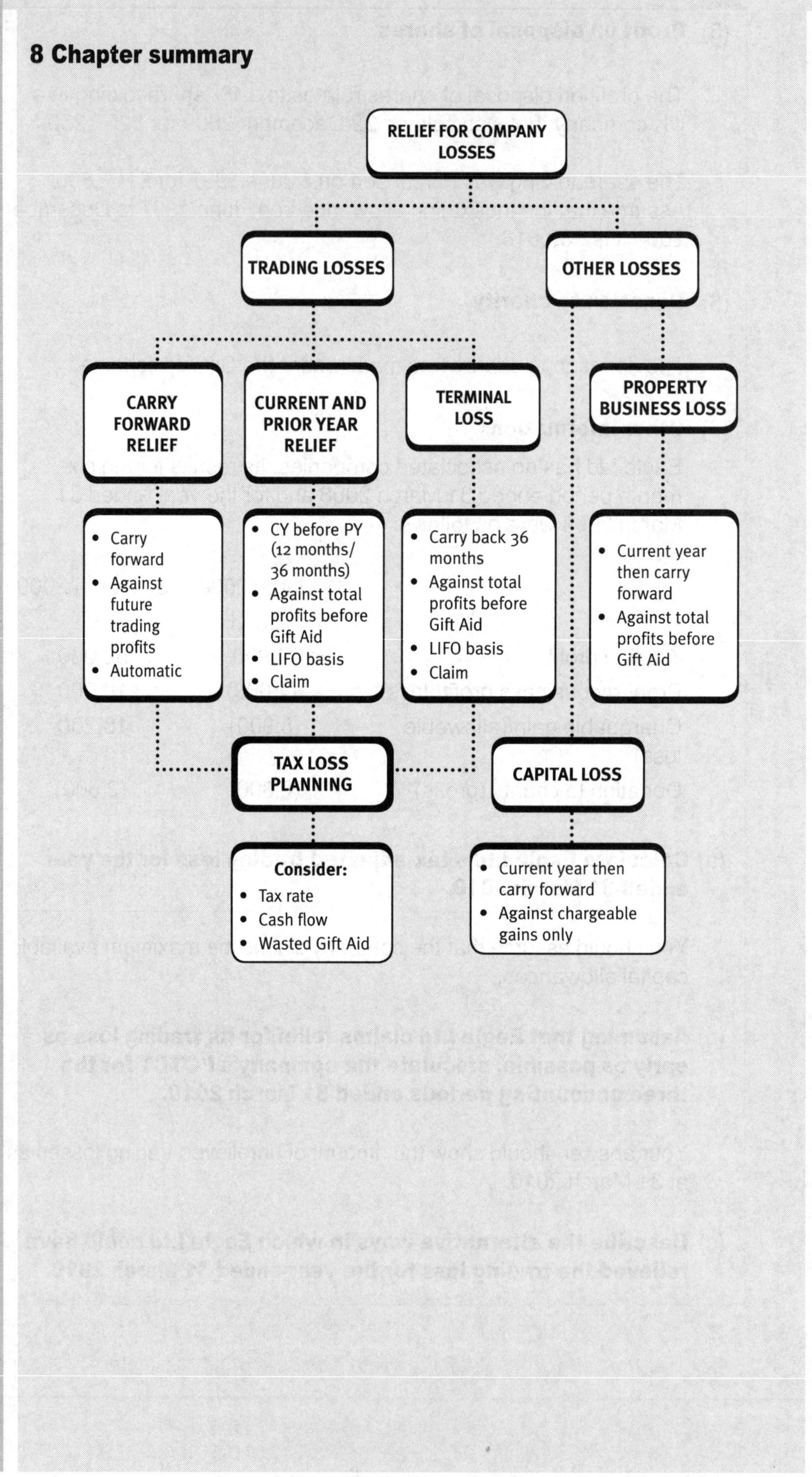
RELIEF FOR COMPANY LOSSES
TRADING LOSSES
OTHER LOSSES
CARRY FORWARD RELIEF
CURRENT AND PRIOR YEAR RELIEF
TERMINAL LOSS
PROPERTY BUSINESS LOSS
• Carry forward
• Against future trading profits
• Automatic
• CY before PY (12 months/ 36 months)
• Against total profits before Gift Aid
• LIFO basis
• Claim
• Carry back 36 months
• Against total profits before Gift Aid
• LIFO basis
• Claim
• Current year then carry forward
• Against total profits before Gift Aid
TAX LOSS PLANNING
CAPITAL LOSS
Consider:
• Tax rate
• Cash flow
• Wasted Gift Aid
• Current year then carry forward
• Against chargeable gains only

Test your understanding answers

Test your understanding 1

Alfred Ball Ltd

Year ended 31 December	2006	2007	2008	2009
	£	£	£	£
Trading income	48,000	32,000	119,000	Nil
Interest income	4,000	3,000	2,000	1,000
Chargeable gains	4,000	4,000	4,000	4,000
Total profits	56,000	39,000	125,000	5,000
Less Loss relief				
– Current year				(5,000)
– 12 month carry back			(125,000)	
– Exteded carry back	(11,000)	(39,000)		
	45,000	Nil	Nil	Nil
Less Gift Aid (Note)	(10,000)	Wasted	Wasted	–
PCTCT	35,000	Nil	Nil	Nil

Loss memorandum

	£
Year ended 31 December 2009	187,000
Used in current year – y/e 31.12.09	(5,000)
Used in 12 month carry back – y/e 31.12.08	(125,000)
Used in Extended carry back – y/e 31.12.07	(39,000)
– y/e 31.12.06	(11,000)
Loss carried forward	7,000

Notes

(1) The Gift Aid of £10,000 paid in the years ended 31 December 2007 and 2008 are wasted. Note that the amount of the loss off-set cannot be restricted to leave sufficient profits to be covered by the Gift Aid.

(2) The current period and 12 month carry back is unrestricted in amount. However, the maximum carry back in the extended period is £50,000.

(3) The unrelieved loss of £7,000 as at 31 December 2009 is automatically carried forward for off-set against the first available future trading profits of the same trade.

Test your understanding 2

Mint Ltd

	y/e 31.3.08	y/e 31.3.09	p/e 31.12.09	y/e 31.12.10
	£	£	£	£
Trading income	60,000	15,000	Nil	40,000
Less Loss relief b/f	–	–	–	(30,000)
	60,000	15,000	Nil	10,000
Interest income	5,000	5,000	10,000	10,000
Chargeable gain	–	–	40,000	–
Total profits	65,000	20,000	50,000	20,000
Less Loss relief				
– Current period			(50,000)	
– 12 month carry back		(20,000)		
– Extended carry back	(37,500)			
PCTCT	27,500	Nil	Nil	20,000

Loss memorandum

	£
9 months to 31 December 2009	137,500
Used in current period – 9 m/e 31.12.09	(50,000)
Used in 12 month carry back – y/e 31.3.09	(20,000)
Used in Extended carry back – y/e 31.3.08 (Note)	(37,500)
Carried forward	30,000
Used in y/e 31.3.10	(30,000)
	Nil

Note: Normally the length of the loss-making period is not important.

The current period and 12 month carry back is unrestricted in amount. However, the extended carry back is restricted to £50,000 for a 12 month loss making period.

Therefore, the maximum offset in the extended period is £37,500 (£50,000 × 9/12).

Test your understanding 3

Catalyst Ltd

	y/e 30.4.06	y/e 30.4.07	p/e 31.12.07	y/e 31.12.08	y/e 31.12.09
	£	£	£	£	£
Trading income	30,930	25,000	23,000	16,500	Nil
Capital allowances	(5,430)	(5,000)	(5,400)	(4,050)	Nil
Trading profit	25,500	20,000	17,600	12,450	Nil
Interest income	1,500	1,600	1,200	1,300	1,400
Chargeable gain	Nil	Nil	Nil	Nil	9,000
Total profits	27,000	21,600	18,800	13,750	10,400
Less Loss relief					
– Current year					(10,400)
– 12 month carry back				(13,750)	
– Extended carry back	(9,000)	(21,600)	(18,800)		
	18,000	Nil	Nil	Nil	Nil
Less Gift Aid	(4,000)	Wasted	–	Wasted	Wasted
PCTCT	14,000	Nil	Nil	Nil	Nil

Workings

(W1) Chargeable gain/capital loss

	£
CAP to 31.12.07 (Loss)	(6,000)
CAP to 31.12.09 Gain	15,000
Net gain – CAP to 31.12.09	9,000

Note that the capital losses can only be off-set against future chargeable gains (see section 6)

(W2) Tax-adjusted trading loss available and its utilisation

	£
Trading loss y/e 31.12.09	75,000
Capital allowances	6,550
Tax adjusted trading loss available	81,550
Used in current year claim – y/e 31.12.09	(10,400)
	71,150
Used in 12 month carry back – y/e 31.12.08	(13,750)
	57,400
Used in extended carry back (LIFO)	
– 8 months to 31.12.07	(18,800)
– y/e 30.4.07	(21,600)
– y/e 30.4.06	
Lower of:	
(i) Total profits × 4/12	
= (4/12 × £27,000) = £9,000	(9,000)
(ii) Remaining maximum loss	
= (£50,000 – £18,800– £21,600) = £9,600	
Loss remaining to carry forward	8,000

Test your understanding 4

Brown Ltd

	Y/e 31.3.07	Y/e 31.3.08	Y/e 31.3.09	P/e 31.12.09	Y/e 31.12.10
	£	£	£	£	£
Trading income	450,000	87,000	240,000	45,000	Nil
Interest income	9,000	3,000	6,000	1,500	1,500
Chargeable gain	7,500	–	–	–	–
Total profits	466,500	90,000	246,000	46,500	1,500
Less Loss relief					
– Current year					(1,500)
– Terminal loss	(116,625)	(90,000)	(246,000)	(46,500)	
	349,875	Nil	Nil	Nil	Nil
Less Gift Aid	(30,000)	Wasted	Wasted	Wasted	Wasted
PCTCT	319,875	Nil	Nil	Nil	Nil

Loss memorandum

	£
Tax-adjusted trading loss of final 12 months of trading	525,000
Used in current year – y/e 31.12.10	(1,500)
	523,500
Used in Terminal loss carry back (LIFO):	
9 months to 31.12.09	(46,500)
12 months to 31.3.09	(246,000)
12 months to 31.3.08	(90,000)
3 months of y/e 31.3.07 (3/12 × £466,500)	(116,625)
Balance of loss = lost	24,375

Note: With terminal loss claims there is no maximum £50,000 offset in the carry back period.

Test your understanding 5

Comfy Ltd

Year ended 31 December:	2007	2008	2009
	£	£	£
Trading income	12,450	Nil	4,000
Less Loss relief b/f	–	–	Nil
	12,450	Nil	4,000
Property income	2,000	1,800	–
Interest income	1,000	600	1,000
Total profits	15,450	2,400	5,000
Property business loss (W2)			(500)
Less Loss relief			
– Current year (W1)		(2,400)	
– 12 month carry back	(12,100)		
	3,350	Nil	4,500
Less: Gift Aid	(400)	Wasted	(400)
PCTCT	2,950	Nil	4,100

Workings

(W1) Trading loss

	£
Trading loss – y/e 31.12.08	14,500
Used in current year – y/e 31.12.08	(2,400)
Used in 12 month carry back – 31.12.07	(12,100)
Carry forward at 31 December 2008	Nil

(W2) Property business loss

	£
Loss in y/e 31 December 2009	500
Used in current year – y/e 31 December 2009	(500)
Carry forward at 31 December 2009	Nil

Test your understanding 6

Coriander Ltd

Year ended 31 December:	2007	2008	2009
	£	£	£
Trading income	37,450	Nil	20,000
Less: Loss relief b/f	–	–	(20,000)
	37,450	Nil	Nil
Interest income	1,300	1,400	1,600
Chargeable gains			
(£13,000 – £6,000 b/f)	Nil	Nil	7,000
Total profits	38,750	1,400	8,600
Less Loss relief			
– Current year		(1,400)	
– 12 month carry back	(38,750)		
	Nil	Nil	8,600
Gift Aid	Wasted	Wasted	(3,000)
PCTCT	Nil	Nil	5,600
Gift Aid = unrelieved	3,000	3,000	

Loss memorandum

	£
y/e 31 December 2008 – Loss	81,550
Used in current period	(1,400)
Used in 12 month carry back – y/e 31 December 2007	(38,750)
Loss relief to carry forward	41,400
Used in y/e 31 December 2009	(20,000)
Carry forward at 31 December 2009	21,400

Note: There is no extended relief as the company only commenced to trade on 1 January 2007.

Test your understanding 7

Eagle Ltd

(a) **Tax-adjusted trading loss for the year ended 31 March 2010**

	£
Trading loss before capital allowances	(225,484)
Capital allowances	
– IBA (W1)	(3,800)
– P & M (W2)	(70,716)
Trading loss	(300,000)

Note: The patent royalties are an allowable deduction against trading profits on an accruals basis, as they are paid for trade purposes. No adjustment is required to the trading loss figure as the amount has already been reflected in the trading loss given in the question.

Workings

(W1) Industrial buildings allowance

	£
Site preparation	12,000
Architect's fees	5,000
Canteen	32,000
Factory	141,000
Eligible expenditure	190,000
Industrial buildings allowance at (2%)	3,800

Notes:

(1) The cost of the land does not qualify

(2) The general offices do not qualify as they cost more than 25% of the total qualifying cost (£350,000 – £87,500 = £262,500 × 25% = £85,625

In practice some of the other costs may be treated as relating to the general offices and would therefore not qualify. This approach would be awarded equivalent marks.

(W2) Plant and machinery capital allowances computation

	£	General pool £	Expensive car £	Total CAs £
TWDV b/f		64,700	14,700	
Additions:				
No AIA or FYA:				
Car		11,300		
With AIA and FYA:				
Lorry	32,400			
Equipment	25,640			
	58,040			
Less AIA (Maximum)	(50,000)			50,000
	8,040			
Disposal			(12,400)	
		76,000	2,300	
Balancing allowance			(2,300)	2,300
Less WDA (20%)		(15,200)		15,200
Less FYA (40%)	(3,216)			3,216
		4,824		
TWDV c/f		65,624		
Total allowances				70,716

(b) **Corporation tax computations**

Period ended 31 March:	2008	2009	2010
	£	£	£
Trading income	137,900	52,000	Nil
Property income (W1)	–	18,700	49,950
Chargeable gains (W2)	–	9,300	104,632
Total profits	137,900	80,000	154,582
Less Property loss (W2)	(4,600)	–	–
	133,300	80,000	154,582
Less Loss relief			
– Current year (W4)			(154,582)
– 12 month carry back		(80,000)	
– Extended carry back	(50,000)		
	83,300	Nil	Nil
Less Gift Aid (Note)	(2,300)	Wasted	Wasted
PCTCT	81,000	Nil	Nil

Notes:

(1) A property business loss is set off automatically against total profits of the same period and takes priority over relief for trading losses.

(2) The current period and 12 month carry back is unrestricted in amount. However, the extended carry back is restricted to a maximum of £50,000.

Workings:

(W1) The property business profit for the year ended 31 March 2010 is calculated as follows:

	£
Premium received	50,000
Less: £50,000 × 2% × (8 – 1)	(7,000)
	43,000
Rent receivable	
– Warehouse 1 (£12,600 × 9/12)	9,450
– Warehouse 2 (£8,400 × 9/12)	6,300
– Irrecoverable debt (£8,400 × 3/12)	(2,100)
	56,650
Repairs to roof	(6,700)
Property income	49,950

(W2) **Property loss**

The property business loss in the six months to 31 March 2008 is set off against total income of that period in priority to utilising the trading loss.

(W3) **Chargeable gains**

The capital loss of the six months to 31 March 2008 is carried forward and set against the chargeable gain in the following period.

Chargeable gain in y/e 31 March 2009 = (£18,200 – £8,900) = £9,300

The chargeable gain in y/e 31 March 2010 is calculated as follows:

	£
Sale proceeds	257,250
Less: Cost	(112,800)
Unindexed gain	144,450
Less: Indexation allowance	(39,818)
Chargeable gain	104,632

(W4) **Loss relief**

	£
Loss in y/e 31.3.10	300,000
Used in current year	(154,582)
Used in 12 month carry back – y/e 31.3.09	(80,000)
Used in extended carry back – 6 m/e 31.3.08 (Maximum)	(50,000)
Loss available to carry forward	5,418

Note: The Gift Aid paid in the years ended 31 March 2009 and 2010 are unrelieved.

(c) **Alternative ways to relieve loss**

The claim against total profits need not be made. The total loss can be carried forward against future trading profits of the same trade.

The claim against total profits could be restricted to just a current year claim in the year ended 31 March 2010 and no carry back. The balance of the loss can be carried forward.

chapter

22

Groups of companies

Chapter learning objectives

Upon completion of this chapter you will be able to:

- define an associated company
- identify associated companies from information provided
- determine the effect of associated companies for corporation tax
- define a 75% group for group loss relief
- identify the members of a 75% group relief group from information provided
- explain and apply the rules for allowing surrender of losses between 75% group relief companies
- identify the key factors in using group losses to minimise corporation tax liabilities for the group
- define a 75% group for capital gains purposes
- identify a capital gains group from information provided
- explain and apply the reliefs available on capital transactions in a 75% capital gains group to minimise corporation tax liabilities.

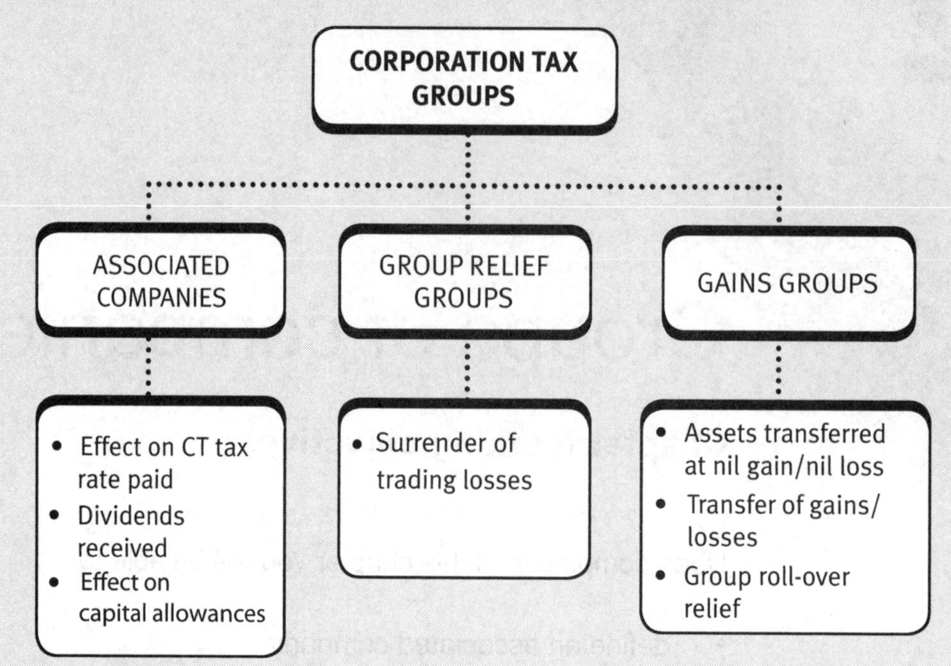

1 Introduction

This chapter deals with the tax position of groups of companies (i.e. where a company owns shares in another company).

For corporation tax purposes, each company within the group is treated as a separate entity and is required to submit its own tax return, based on its individual results.

Being a member of a group however, has other corporation tax implications and these vary, depending on the actual relationship of the group members.

This chapter sets out the corporation tax implications of:

- associated companies
- groups for group relief purposes
- capital gains groups.

2 Associated companies

Definition

For corporation tax purposes, two companies are 'associated' with each other if either:

- one of the companies is under the 'control' of the other; or
- they are both under the 'control' of the same person or persons (which can be a company, an individual or a partnership).

'Control' broadly means ownership of more than 50% of the company's issued ordinary share capital.

Control

For tax purposes 'control' means:

- ownership of over 50% of issued share capital, or
- holding over 50% of the voting rights, or
- entitlement to over 50% of the company's income, if all the income were to be distributed, or
- entitlement to over 50% of the company's assets, if the company were to wind up.

Points to note:

- Companies that are associated for only part of an accounting period are deemed to be associated for the whole of the accounting period.
- Both UK resident and overseas resident companies are included.
- Dormant companies are excluded.

Example 1 - Associated companies

A Ltd is the holding company for a group of four companies. The relationships between the companies in the group, are shown in the diagram below:

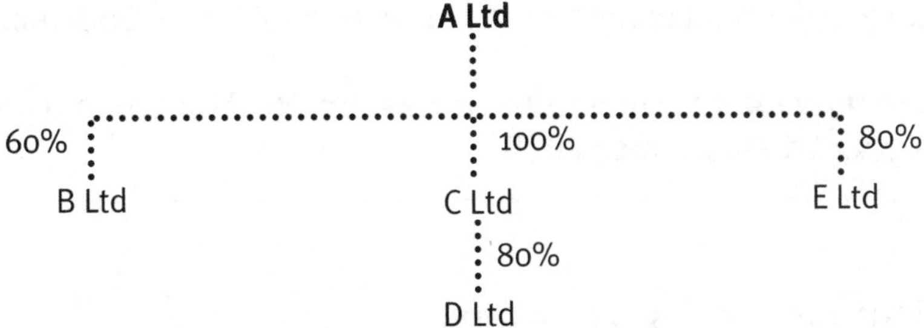

All of the companies are UK resident except for E Ltd, which is resident outside the UK and all its trading activities are conducted outside the UK. All of the companies have 31 December year ends.

B Ltd is a dormant company. D Ltd was bought by C Ltd on 1 July 2009.

State how many companies are associated for tax purposes in the year to 31 December 2009.

Answer to example 1

A Ltd is associated with:

- C Ltd (owns more than 50%).
- D Ltd (bought by C Ltd in the year, associated for the whole year).
- E Ltd (even though it is resident overseas).

A Ltd is not associated with B Ltd, as it is dormant.

Therefore, there are four associated companies in the year to 31 December 2009.

Test your understanding 1

W Ltd group has the following structure:

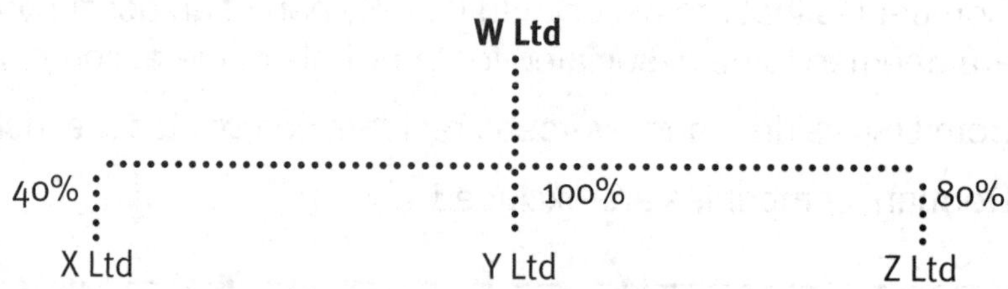

All of the companies are UK resident except for Y Ltd, which is resident outside the UK and all its trading activities are conducted outside the UK. All the companies have 31 December year ends.

Z Ltd is a dormant company. X Ltd was bought on 1 December 2009.

State how many companies are associated for tax purposes, in the year 31 December 2009.

Implications of being associated

The tax implications of being associated are:

- The upper and lower limits, used to determine the rate of corporation tax, are divided by the number of associated companies.
- Intra-group dividends (both UK and overseas) are not treated as franked investment income, for the purposes of calculating the company's 'profits'.

- Only one annual investment allowance (maximum £50,000 p.a.) is available for the group.

Tax rate

The identification of the number of associated companies, is the starting point for every 'group question', as this establishes:

- the applicable lower and upper limit for each company, and therefore
- the rate of corporation tax applicable to each company.

Example 2 - Associated companies

A Ltd, in Example 1, has tax-adjusted trading profits for the year ended 31 December 2009 of £750,000. A Ltd had no dividend income during the year.

Calculate the corporation tax payable by A Ltd, for the year ended 31 December 2009.

Answer to example 2

A Ltd controls more than 50% of C Ltd, D Ltd and E Ltd – therefore (including A Ltd), we have four associated companies under common control.

Therefore, the corporation tax rate limits are as follows:

Upper limit: £1,500,000/4 = £375,000.
Lower Limit: £300,000/4 = £75,000.

A Ltd's profits exceed the revised upper limit and therefore, it will pay corporation tax at the full rate.

A Ltd has a 31 December 2009 year end. As there is no change in rate of tax between FY 2008 and FY 2009, the corporation tax is calculated at 28% in one computation.

Corporation tax payable (£750,000 × 28%)	£210,000

Test your understanding 2

Cob Ltd prepares accounts for the year ended 31 January 2010. On 1 February 2009, the company acquired 60% of the shares of a company, that is resident overseas. On 1 May 2009, it acquired 75% of the shares of a company, that is resident in the UK.

Cob Ltd has profits chargeable to corporation tax of £140,000, for the year ended 31 January 2010, and also received franked investment income of £10,000, during the year.

Calculate Cob Ltd's corporation tax payable for the year ended 31 January 2010.

Dividends

- Dividends received by UK companies from other UK companies and overseas companies are not taxable.
- Normally they are grossed up by 100/90 and included as franked investment income (FII), when calculating the company's 'profits'. The company's 'profits' then determine the rate of corporation tax payable.
- Dividends received from associated companies however, do not form part of FII.

Example 3 - Associated companies

Holly Ltd is the parent company of two wholly owned subsidiaries, Berry Ltd and Sprig Ltd.

Holly Ltd had the following income for the y/e 31 December 2009:

	£
Trading profit	300,000
Interest income	50,000
Dividends received from Berry Ltd	60,000
Dividends received from Sprig Ltd	34,000
Dividends received from other UK companies	45,000

Calculate the corporation tax payable by Holly Ltd, for the year ended 31 December 2009.

Answer to example 3

Corporation tax computation – y/e 31 December 2009

	£
Trading income	300,000
Interest income	50,000
PCTCT	350,000
(£350,000 x 28%)	98,000
Less: Marginal relief	
7/400 x (£500,000 – £400,000) x £350,000/£400,000	(1,531)
Corporation tax payable	96,469

Note

- Only dividends received from non-associated companies, are included as FII.
- Dividends received from UK companies are not taxable.

Workings: Rate of tax

Holly Ltd has 2 associates and therefore, the limits for determining the corporation tax rate must be divided by 3, as follows:

Upper limit: £1,500,000/3 = £500,000
Lower limit: £300,000/3 = £100,000

	£
PCTCT	350,000
Plus FII (£45,000 × 100/90) (Note)	50,000
'Profits'	400,000

Therefore, Holly Ltd is a marginal relief company.

Note that the year ended 31 December 2009 falls into FY 2008 and into FY 2009, however there is no change in rate.

Therefore only one calculation for corporation tax payable is required.

Test your understanding 3

Bill Ltd is the parent company of one wholly owned subsidiary, Ben Ltd.

Bill Ltd had the following income for the year ended 31 August 2009:

	£
Trading profit	380,000
Interest income	25,000
Dividends from Ben Ltd	60,000
Dividends from other UK companies	76,500

Calculate the corporation tax payable by Bill Ltd, for the year ended 31 August 2009.

The annual investment allowance

For capital allowance purposes, only one AIA is available to a group of companies.

Note that:

- A 'group' for this purpose is where a parent company holds a simple majority shareholding (> 50%) in another company or companies at the end of the accounting period.
- Therefore if there are associated companies, the allocation of the AIA between the group members will need to be considered.

When allocating the AIA:

- the group members can allocate the maximum £50,000 AIA in any way across the group
- the AIA does not have to be divided equally between them
- all of the allowance can be given to one company, or any amount can be given to any number of companies within the group.

3 Group relief group

Group loss relief is available to members of a 75% group relief group.

Losses of one member of the group can be surrendered to other group companies, which may then relieve the losses against their own PCTCT.

Definition of a 75% group relief group

- Two companies are members of a 75% group relief group where:
  - one company is the 75% subsidiary of the other, or
  - both companies are 75% subsidiaries of a third company.
- One company is a 75% subsidiary of another if:
  - at least 75% of its ordinary share capital is owned directly or indirectly by the other company, and
  - it has the right to 75% or more of distributable profits, and
  - it has the right to 75% or more of net assets on a winding up.
- For sub-subsidiaries to be in a group, the holding company must have an effective interest in the sub-subsidiary of at least 75%.
- Groups can be created through companies resident anywhere in the world.
- For the purposes of the examination the companies claiming/ surrendering group relief must, however, be resident in the UK.

Example 4 - 75% group relief group

The following information relates to the Holding Ltd group:

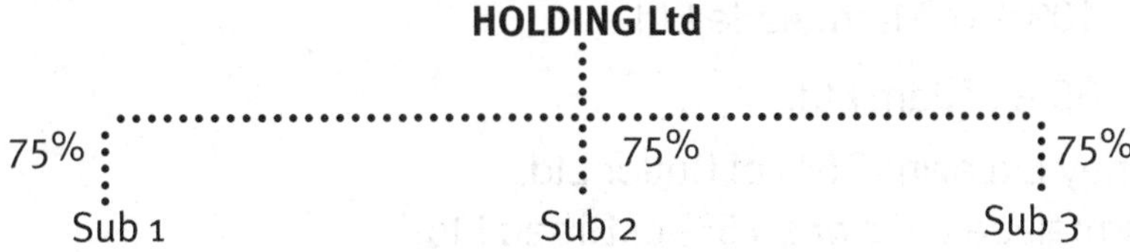

State which companies form a group for group relief purposes.

Answer to example 4

Holding Ltd has a 75% direct holding in Sub 1, Sub 2 and Sub 3 and therefore, all four companies are part of a 75% group for group relief purposes.

Example 5 - 75% group relief group

Beef Ltd owns 75% of Lamb Ltd. Lamb Ltd owns 75% of Bacon Ltd.

State which companies form a group for group relief purposes.

Answer to example 5

Beef Ltd and all its direct and indirect 75% holdings:

- Lamb Ltd (directly owns 75%)

Bacon Ltd does not belong to the same group relief group as Beef Ltd, as Beef Ltd only indirectly owns (75% × 75%) = 56.25%.

As Lamb Ltd directly owns 75% of Bacon Ltd, they will form a separate group relief group.

Therefore, there will be two group relief groups:

- Beef Ltd and Lamb Ltd.
- Lamb Ltd and Bacon Ltd.

Test your understanding 4

Toast Ltd owns:

- 75% of Honey Ltd.
- 100% of Marmalade Ltd.
- 65% of Jam Ltd.

Honey Ltd owns 75% of Butter Ltd.
Marmalade Ltd owns 75% of Bread Ltd.

State which companies form a group for group relief purposes.

Implications of being in a group relief group

Where a group of companies form a group relief group, losses of one group company may be surrendered to other companies in the group. The recipient company can then relieve the losses against its own PCTCT.

A loss may be surrendered by any member company to any other member of the same group, provided they are UK resident.

Example 6 - 75% group relief group

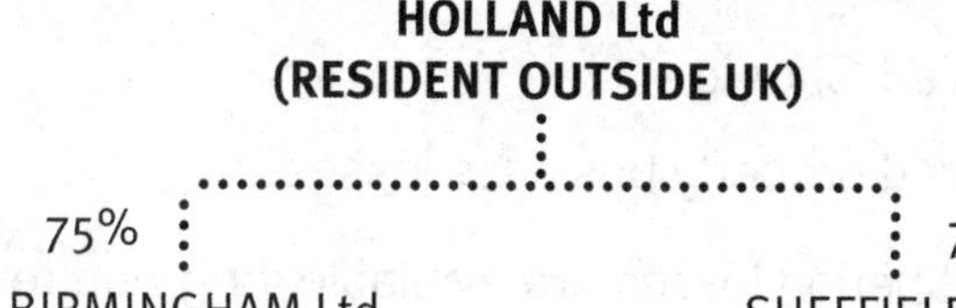

Birmingham Ltd and Sheffield Ltd are both UK resident companies.

State which companies form a group for group relief purposes and between which companies losses can be transferred.

Birmingham Ltd and Sheffield Ltd are within a 75% group, as both companies are 75% subsidiaries of Holland Ltd. Remember, that non-UK resident companies can be used to establish a group relief group.

Birmingham Ltd and Sheffield Ltd can therefore transfer losses between each other, (i.e. Birmingham Ltd to Sheffield Ltd or vice versa).

Losses cannot be transferred to or from Holland Ltd, as the company is resident outside of the UK.

Test your understanding 5

GROUP 1	GROUP 2
HOLDING Ltd	HOLDING Ltd
90%	80%
Sub 1 Ltd	Sub 1 Ltd
90%	80%
Sub 2 Ltd	Sub 2 Ltd

From the above structures, identify which companies form a group for group relief purposes and between which companies losses can be transferred.

Mechanics of group relief

- Companies which form part of the same group relief group can transfer losses between each other.
- The surrendering company is the company that surrenders its loss.
- The claimant company is the company to which the loss is surrendered.

- The losses which may be surrendered are:
  - trading losses
  - unrelieved Gift Aid
  - unrelieved property business losses.
- Only current period losses are available for group relief.
- Capital losses cannot be surrendered to group companies under these rules. See section 4 for the transfer of capital losses.

The surrendering company

- The surrendering company may surrender any amount of its current period losses.
- There is no requirement for the surrendering company to relieve the loss against its own profits first.

The claimant company

- Offsets the loss against PCTCT of its corresponding accounting period.
- The surrendering company may surrender any amount of its eligible loss. However, the maximum loss which can be claimed by the claimant company, is the company's profits (after Gift Aid), assuming that current year losses and losses brought forward of the claimant company, are offset first.
- The maximum loss which can be claimed is:

	£
Total profits	X
Less: Gift Aid	(X)
PCTCT	X
Less: Current year losses	(X)
Less: Brought forward losses	(X)
Maximum loss relief	X

Test your understanding 6

Red Ltd has trading losses for the year to 31 December 2009, of £65,000. It has brought forward trading losses of £12,000.

Red Ltd owns 85% of Pink Ltd.

Pink Ltd has tax-adjusted trading profits of £85,000, for the year to 31 December 2009. It has brought forward trading losses of £35,000 and brought forward capital losses of £5,000.

Show the maximum amount of group relief available in the year to 31 December 2009 and state the amount of any unrelieved losses.

Corresponding accounting periods

Losses surrendered by group relief, must be set against the claimant company's profits of a 'corresponding' accounting period as follows:

- A corresponding accounting period is any accounting period falling wholly or partly within the surrendering company's accounting period.
- Where the companies do not have coterminous (same) year ends, the available profits and losses must be time apportioned, to find the relevant amounts falling within the corresponding accounting period.
- In this situation, the maximum 'loss' that can be surrendered = lower of:

	£
(a) 'loss' in the surrendering (loss making) company for the corresponding accounting period, and	X
(b) 'PCTCT' in the claimant company for the corresponding accounting period	X

Example 7 - 75% group relief group

Sugar Ltd incurs a trading loss of £27,000, in its nine months accounting period to 31 March 2010.

The total 'profits' of Cup Ltd are £24,000 and £38,000 for the 12 months accounting periods to 30 September 2009 and 2010 respectively.

State the maximum amount of group relief which Cup Ltd can claim from Sugar Ltd, for the two accounting periods to 30 September 2010.

Answer to example 7

As the companies have non-coterminous year ends, firstly identify the corresponding accounting periods:

- 9 m/e 31.3.10 and y/e 30.9.09:

  The corresponding accounting period is 1 July 2009 to 30 September 2009 (i.e. three months).

- 9 m/e 31.3.10 and y/e 30.9.10:

  The corresponding accounting period is 1 October 2009 to 31 March 2010 (i.e. six months).

Cup Ltd can therefore claim the following group relief:

CAP to 30.9.09

			£
Sugar Ltd	can surrender	3/9 × £27,000 loss	9,000
Cup Ltd	can claim	3/12 × £24,000	6,000

Therefore maximum loss claim is £6,000

CAP to 30.9.10

Sugar Ltd	can surrender	6/9 × £27,000 loss	18,000
Cup Ltd	can claim	6/12 × £38,000	19,000

Therefore maximum loss claim is £18,000.

Test your understanding 7

White Ltd and Black Ltd are in a group relief group and had the following recent results:

	£
White Ltd – trading loss for the year to 30 June 2010	(24,000)
Black Ltd – taxable profits:	
For the year ended 30 September 2009	36,000
For the year ended 30 September 2010	20,000

Explain the amount of group relief Black Ltd can claim from White Ltd, for the two accounting periods ended September 2010.

Tax loss planning

The following points should be considered, when deciding how to offset a trading loss which arises within a 75% group relief group company:

- Whether the loss should be surrendered.
- Order of surrender.

Choosing whether to surrender

A group member suffering a loss, has the choice to make a claim against its own profits, or to surrender the loss to another group member.

Consideration should be given to:

- the rate of tax saved
- the cash flow position (a claim to carryback the loss under s393A ICTA 1988, could lead to a repayment of tax).

Order of surrender

Losses should be surrendered in the following order, in order to save the maximum amount of tax:

(1) To companies that are subject to a marginal tax rate of 29.75% in FY 2009 and 2008 (see Chapter 21), to bring their profits down to the 'small company rate limit'

(2) To companies that are subject to the full tax rate of 28% in FY 2009 and FY 2008, to bring their profits down to the small company rate limit.

(3) To companies that are subject to tax at the small companies rate of 21% in FY 2009 and FY 2008.

Remember, that the upper and lower limits that determine the rate of tax, will be adjusted for the number of associated companies.

Example 8 - 75% group relief group

A Ltd has four wholly owned subsidaries, B Ltd, C Ltd, D Ltd and E Ltd. The group companies had the following results for the year ended 31 March 2010.

		£
A Ltd	Loss	(100,000)
B Ltd	Profit	20,000
C Ltd	Profit	83,000
D Ltd	Profit	96,000
E Ltd	Profit	375,000

None of the companies received any dividends in the year.

Calculate the corporation tax payable by each of the companies:

(a) **if no election for group relief is made**

(b) **if an election for group relief is made, on the assumption that the loss is allocated in such a manner as to save the maximum amount of tax.**

Answer to example 8

(a) **If no group relief**

Calculate the upper and lower limits and calculate the tax payable by each company, assuming no election for group relief is made.

Upper limit £1,500,000/5 = £300,000
Lower limit £300,000/5 = £60,000

	A Ltd	B Ltd	C Ltd	D Ltd	E Ltd
	£	£	£	£	£
PCTCT	Nil	20,000	83,000	96,000	375,000
Corporation tax					
at 21%		4,200			
at 28%			23,240	26,880	105,000
Less: Marginal relief					
7/400 × (£300,000 – £83,000)			(3,798)		
7/400 × (£300,000 – £96,000)				(3,570)	
Corporation tax liability	Nil	4,200	19,442	23,310	105,000

(b) **With group relief**

In order to save the maximum amount of tax, the loss of A Ltd, should be allocated as follows:

- First to companies paying tax at the marginal rate of 29.75%, so as to bring their profits down to the lower limit, (i.e. to those companies with profits in the marginal rate relief band).
- Then surrender to companies paying tax at 28%.
- Any remaining loss should be surrendered to companies paying tax at the small companies rate of 21%.
- Remember the upper and lower limit have been revised for the number of associated companies.

  Accordingly, the loss is first surrendered to C Ltd and D Ltd to bring their profits down to £60,000 (revised lower limit), the balance of the loss is surrendered to E Ltd.

	A Ltd	B Ltd	C Ltd	D Ltd	E Ltd
	£	£	£	£	£
PCTCT	Nil	20,000	83,000	96,000	375,000
Less: Group relief			(23,000)	(36,000)	(41,000)
PCTCT after group relief	Nil	20,000	60,000	60,000	334,000
Corporation tax					
@21%	Nil	4,200	12,600	12,600	
@28%					93,520

Test your understanding 8

A Ltd is the holding company for a group of four companies. The relationships between the companies in the group, are shown in the diagram below:

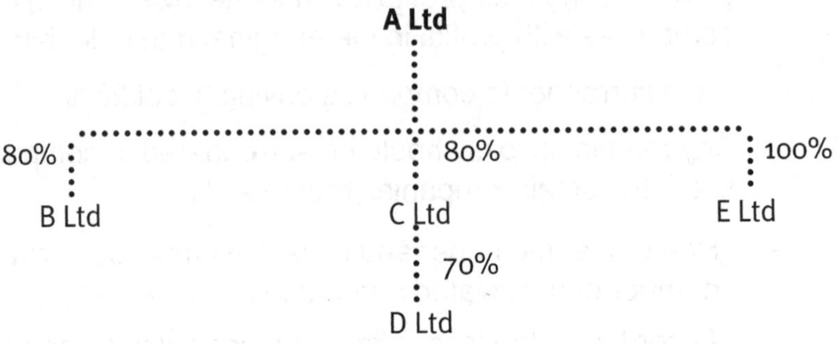

All of the companies are UK resident except for E Ltd, which is resident overseas and all its trading activities are conducted outside the UK.

All of the companies have an accounting year ended 31 March 2010 and their income/(losses) for this year, were as follows:

	Tax adjusted trading profit/(loss)	Bank interest (non-trade)
	£	£
A Ltd	100,000	–
B Ltd	110,000	15,000
C Ltd	(110,000)	12,000
D Ltd	(25,000)	–
E Ltd	15,000	–

On the assumption that the most efficient use is made by the group of any trading losses, compute the corporation tax payable by each UK resident company.

4 75% capital gains group

Special capital gains advantages are available to members of a capital gains group. They enable:

- assets to be transferred tax efficiently around the group
- the efficient use of capital losses within the group
- the advantages of roll-over relief to be maximised.

Definition of a 75% capital gains group

- A capital gains group comprises of the parent company and its 75% (direct or indirect) subsidiaries and also, the 75% subsidiaries of the first subsidiaries and so on.
- The parent company must have an effective interest of over 50%, in ALL companies.
- A company which is a 75% subsidiary, cannot itself be a 'parent company' and form a separate gains group.
- While applying the 75% test, the shares held by overseas companies can be taken into account. Non-UK resident companies, however, cannot take advantage of the special reliefs due to UK resident members.
- The 75% requirement only applies to the ordinary share capital.

It is important to note that the definition of a gains group, is different from that for a group relief group. It is essential to learn the different definitions.

Test your understanding 9

The A Ltd group consists of the following companies:

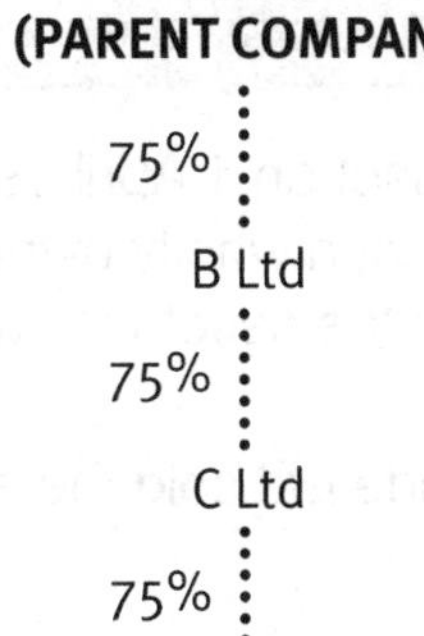

(a) **State which companies form a capital gains group.**

(b) **State which companies form a group relief group,**

Implications of being in a 75% capital gains group

The reliefs that are available to members of a 75% capital gains group, are as follows:

(1) Assets are transferred at nil gain/nil loss.

(2) Capital gains and losses can be transferred around the group.

(3) Roll-over relief is available on a group basis.

Transfer of assets within a group

- Assets transferred within a gains group, are automatically transferred at neither a gain nor a loss (i.e. without a chargeable gain or allowable loss arising).
- The transfer takes place at a price that does not give rise to a gain or a loss to the transferor company (i.e. at original cost plus indexation allowance to the date of the transfer).
- The transferor's deemed proceeds figure, is also the deemed cost of the acquiring company.
- No claim is made – the treatment is automatic and mandatory.
- When the acquiring company sells the asset outside of the gains group, a chargeable gain/loss arises on the disposal in the normal way.

Example 9 - Inter group transfer then sale outside group

Green Ltd acquired an asset on 1 April 1983, for £100,000. The asset was transferred to Jade Ltd, a wholly owned subsidiary, on 1 October 1993, for £120,000, when the asset was worth £180,000.

On 1 December 2009, Jade Ltd sold the asset outside of the group for £350,000.

Calculate the chargeable gain, if any, arising on the transfer of the asset in October 1993 and the sale of the asset in December 2009.

Assume the RPIs as follows:

April 1983	84.28
October 1993	141.8
December 2009	213.1

Answer to example 9

Transfer of asset – October 1993

The transfer from Green Ltd to Jade Ltd, takes place at such a price that gives Green Ltd, no gain and no loss as follows:

	£
Cost	100,000
Plus: Indexation allowance: April 1983 to October 1993:	
(141.8 – 84.28)/84.28 = 0.682 × £100,000	68,200
Deemed proceeds	168,200

Sale of asset – December 2009

When Jade Ltd sells the asset outside the group, its cost is deemed to be £168,200:

	£
Sale proceeds	350,000
Less: Deemed cost	(168,200)
Unindexed gain	181,800
Less: Indexation Allowance (Oct 1993 to Dec 2009):	
(213.1 – 141.8)/141.8 = 0.503 × £168,200	(84,605)
Chargeable gain	97,195

The gain is chargeable on Jade Ltd; the company selling the asset.

Example 10 – Inter group transfer and sale outside group

Orange Ltd acquired an asset on 1 June 1985, for £80,000. The asset was transferred to Amber Ltd, a wholly owned subsidiary, on 1 September 1991, for £115,000, when the asset was worth £160,000.

On 21 November 2009, Amber Ltd sold the asset outside the group for £385,000.

Calculate the chargeable gain, if any, arising in September 1991 and November 2009.

Assume the following RPIs:

June 1985	95.41
September 1991	134.6
November 2009	212.9

Answer to example 10

Transfer of asset – September 1991

The transfer from Orange Ltd to Amber Ltd, takes place at such a price as gives Orange Ltd no gain and no loss as follows:

	£
Cost	80,000
Indexation allowance: June 1985 to September 1991:	
(134.6 – 95.41)/95.41 = 0.411 x £80,000	32,880
Deemed proceeds	112,880

Sale of asset – November 2009

When Amber Ltd sells the asset outside the group, its cost is deemed to be £112,880:

	£
Sale proceeds	385,000
Less: Deemed cost	(112,880)
Unindexed gain	272,120
Less: IA (Sept 1991 to Nov 2009)	
(212.9 – 134.6)/134.6 = 0.582 x £112,880	(65,696)
Chargeable gain	206,424

Transfer of capital gains and losses

As shown above, assets can be transferred around a capital gains group with no tax cost (i.e. assets are transferred at nil gain/nil loss).

A company will transfer an asset if the other group company wants to use it in its business.

However, pre 1 April 2009, a group could 'use' the 'nil gain/nil loss' rule and transfer assets around the group, so that a capital gain/loss on the disposal of an asset outside of the group, was realised in another company.

This 'notional transfer' was useful for the following reasons:

- Transferring an asset before it was sold outside of the group at a gain, to a company with capital losses, enabled the capital losses to be utilised.
- Assets which were about to be sold outside of the group at a gain, could be transferred to the group member paying the lowest rate of tax on the gain.

Election to transfer capital gains and losses

With effect from 1 April 2009 however, members of capital gains groups can make a joint election to transfer capital gains or losses to any other company in the group.

As a result, a group can:

- plan to maximise the use of its capital losses as early as possible, and
- ensure gains crystallise in the company paying the lowest rate of tax,
- wlthout having to make an actual transfer of an asset.

The joint election:

- is available provided both companies are members of the gains group at the time the gain or loss arose
- must be made within 2 years of the end of the accounting period, in which the asset is disposed of outside of the group
- must specify which company in the group is to be treated for tax purposes, as having disposed of the asset.

Note, however, that only current year capital losses can be transferred, not brought forward losses.

Benefits of the joint transfer election

- As no actual transfer of assets is taking place within the gains group, there will be savings in legal and administrative costs.
- The two-year time limit for making the election, means that tax planning can be undertaken retrospectively.
- An election can apply to a specified portion of a disposal (i.e. effectively, only part of a gain or loss needs to be transferred). This gives increased flexibility with tax planning.

Example 11 - 75% capital gains group

Red Ltd has brought forward capital losses of £60,000.

Its 100% subsidiary Blue Ltd, disposed of an asset on 15 June 2009, that resulted in a chargeable gain of £55,000.

Both companies prepare accounts to 31 March.

Explain how Red Ltd and Blue Ltd can make an election to minimise the tax payable for the year ended 31 March 2010.

Answer to example 11

The two companies can make a Joint election to transfer Blue Ltd's gain to Red Ltd.

The election must be made by 31 March 2012 (i.e. two years after the year ended 31 March 2010). There is no need for the asset to actually be transferred from Blue Ltd to Red Ltd.

Red Ltd can then set-off its capital losses brought forward against the chargeable gain arising on the disposal outside of the group.

Note that capital losses brought forward can not be transferred around the group.

Test your understanding 10

In the accounting period to 31 March 2010, Alpha Ltd disposed of a chargeable asset which will result in a chargeable gain of £90,000.

Alpha Ltd also has a 80% subsidiary, Beta Ltd.

In the accounting period to 31 March 2010, Beta Ltd disposed of a chargeable asset, which resulted in a capital loss of £65,000.

Alpha Ltd and Beta Ltd are both UK resident companies.

Show how the tax liabilities of the Alpha Ltd group may be minimised.

Group roll-over relief

Roll-over relief was covered in detail in Chapters 17 and 20.

- Companies within a 75% gains group, are treated as if they form a single trade, for the purposes of roll-over relief.
- Roll-over relief can therefore be claimed, where one company within a gains group, disposes of an eligible asset and makes a gain and another company within the same gains group, acquires a replacement eligible asset.

Example 12 - 75% capital gains group

Cheese Ltd sold a factory for £600,000, in the year ended 31 December 2009. The original cost of the factory was £200,000 and indexation to the date of sale was £65,000.

Cheese owns 75% of Ham Ltd.

Ham Ltd bought a warehouse costing £750,000, in the year ended 31 December 2010.

(a) **Calculate the chargeable gain arising on the sale of the factory assuming all available reliefs are taken.**

(b) **Calculate the base cost of the warehouse.**

Answer to example 12

Gain on sale of factory for Cheese Ltd

	£
Proceeds	600,000
Less: Cost	(200,000)
Unindexed gain	400,000
Less: Indexation allowance	(65,000)
Indexed gain	335,000
Less: Roll-over relief	(335,000)
Chargeable gain	Nil

Note: Full roll-over relief is available, as all proceeds were reinvested by a member of the gains group, within the required time limit.

Base cost of the warehouse for Ham Ltd

	£
Original cost	750,000
Less: Roll-over relief	(335,000)
Base cost	415,000

5 Chapter summary

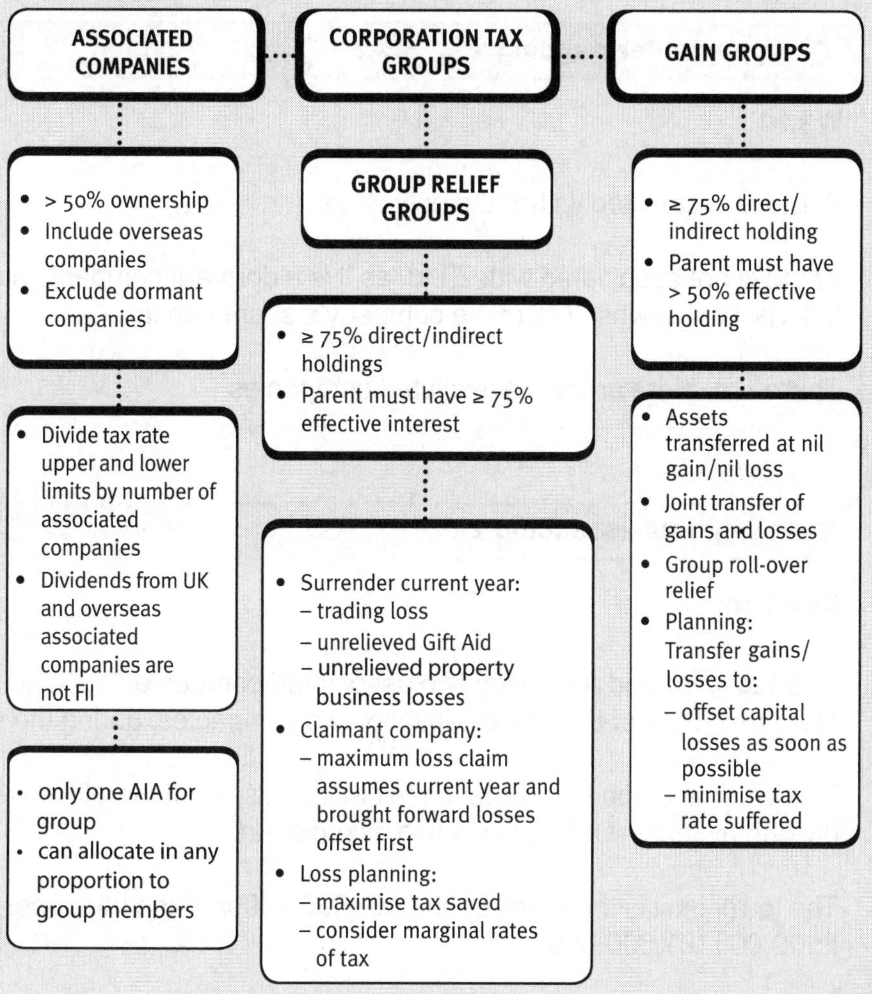

ASSOCIATED COMPANIES

- > 50% ownership
- Include overseas companies
- Exclude dormant companies

- Divide tax rate upper and lower limits by number of associated companies
- Dividends from UK and overseas associated companies are not FII

- only one AIA for group
- can allocate in any proportion to group members

CORPORATION TAX GROUPS

GROUP RELIEF GROUPS

- ≥ 75% direct/indirect holdings
- Parent must have ≥ 75% effective interest

- Surrender current year:
  - trading loss
  - unrelieved Gift Aid
  - unrelieved property business losses
- Claimant company:
  - maximum loss claim assumes current year and brought forward losses offset first
- Loss planning:
  - maximise tax saved
  - consider marginal rates of tax

GAIN GROUPS

- ≥ 75% direct/indirect holding
- Parent must have > 50% effective holding

- Assets transferred at nil gain/nil loss
- Joint transfer of gains and losses
- Group roll-over relief
- Planning: Transfer gains/losses to:
  - offset capital losses as soon as possible
  - minimise tax rate suffered

Test your understanding answers

Test your understanding 1

W Ltd

W Ltd is associated with Y Ltd only.

W Ltd is not associated with Z Ltd, as it is a dormant company, nor X Ltd, as it only owns 40% of the company's share capital.

Therefore, there are two associated companies.

Test your understanding 2

Cob Ltd

Cob Ltd is treated as having two associated companies, as it acquired more than 50% of the share capital of two companies, during the year.

The lower and upper corporation tax rate limits, must therefore, be divided by three (Cob Ltd plus two associates).

The lower limit is therefore £100,000 (£300,000/3) and the upper limit is £500,000 (£1,500,000/3).

Cob Ltd – year ended 31 January 2010	£
PCTCT	140,000
Plus FII	10,000
Profits	150,000

The profits of £150,000 lie between £100,000 and £500,000, so marginal relief applies.

As there is no change in rate of tax between FY 2008 and FY 2009, the corporation tax payable can be calculated in one computation.

	£
Corporation tax (£140,000 × 28%)	39,200
Less: Marginal relief	
7/400 × (£500,000 – £150,000) × £140,000/£150,000	(5,717)
Corporation tax payable	33,483

Note: The revised upper limit is used in the marginal relief calculation.

Test your understanding 3

Bill Ltd

Corporation tax computation – y/e 31 August 2009

	£
Trading income	380,000
Interest income	25,000
PCTCT	405,000
Corporation tax (£405,000 x 28%)	113,400
Less: Marginal relief	
7/400 x (£750,000 – £490,000) x £405,000/£490,000	(3,761)
Corporation tax liability	109,639

Working: Rate of tax

Bill Ltd has one associated company and therefore the limits for determining the corporation tax rate, must be divided by 2:

Upper limit: £1,500,000/2 = £750,000
Lower limit: £300,000/2 = £150,000

	£
PCTCT	405,000
Plus FII (£76,500 × 100/90)	85,000
'Profits'	490,000

Therefore, Bill Ltd is a marginal relief company.

Note that the year ended 31 August 2009 straddles 31 March 2009, however there is no change in rate of tax. Therefore only one calculation of corporation tax payable required.

Test your understanding 4

Toast Ltd

Toast Ltd and all its direct 75% holdings:

- Honey Ltd.
- Marmalade Ltd.

Toast Ltd only own 65% of Jam Ltd, therefore, it does not form part of the group.

Also include any 75% indirect holdings of Toast Ltd:

- Bread Ltd
  (Toast Ltd indirectly holds (100% × 75%) = 75% of Bread Ltd).

Note: Butter Ltd is not included, as Toast Ltd only indirectly holds (75% × 75% = 56.25%)

Honey Ltd owns 75% of Butter Ltd, so they will form a second group relief group.

Therefore, there are two groups:

- Toast Ltd, Honey Ltd, Marmalade Ltd and Bread Ltd.
- Honey Ltd and Butter Ltd.

Test your understanding 5

Group 1	**Group 2**
Holding Ltd (H), Sub 1 (S1) and Sub 2 (S2) are within a 75 % group.	Holding Ltd (H) and Sub 1 are within a 75% group; Sub 1 and Sub 2 are within another 75% group.
The direct shareholding links between the group are all 75% and over.	Holding Ltd and Sub 2 are **not** within a 75% group **because** H's effective holding in Sub 2, is only 64% (80% × 80%).
In addition, Holding Ltd has an indirect shareholding in Sub 2 Ltd, of over 75% (90% × 90% = 81%).	
Losses can be transferred from:	**Losses can be transferred between:**
H to S1 and S2	H to S1 or S1 to H,
S2 to S1 and H	S1 to S2 or S2 to S1
S1 to H and S2.	**but** not from H to S2 **or** S2 to H.

Test your understanding 6

Red Ltd

	£
Profits	85,000
Less: b/f trading losses	(35,000)
Maximum claim by Pink Ltd	50,000

Maximum group relief, the lower of:

• Loss of Red Ltd	£65,000
• Maximum claim by Pink Ltd	£50,000

Therefore, Red Ltd can group relieve £50,000 of its current year trading losses, to Pink Ltd.

Unrelieved losses

Red Ltd:

Assuming maximum group relief is claimed:

Red Ltd will have £15,000 of current year trading losses unrelieved. A current year or prior year claim, can be made to relieve these losses against total profits.

Alternatively, they will be carried forward against the first available future trading profits.

Red Ltd's brought forward trading losses of £12,000, will continue to be carried forward and set against the first available trading profits.

Pink Ltd:

Pink Ltd's brought forward trading losses of £35,000, will be utilised in the year to 31 December 2009.

The company's capital losses b/f, will be carried forward and used against the first chargeable gains of the company.

Test your understanding 7

White Ltd and Black Ltd

Firstly, identify the corresponding accounting:

- Y/e 30.9.09 and y/e 30.6.10:

  The corresponding accounting period is 1 July 2009 to 30 September 2009, (i.e. three months).

- Y/e 30.9.10 and y/e 30.6.10

  The corresponding accounting period is 1 October 2009 to 30 June 2010, (i.e. nine months).

Black Ltd can therefore claim the following group relief:

y/e 30 September 2009

			£
Black Ltd	can claim	(£36,000 × 3/12)	9,000
White Ltd	can surrender	(£24,000 × 3/12)	(6,000)

Black Ltd can claim group relief of £6,000 against its profits, for the year ended 30 September 2009.

y/e 30 September 2010

			£
Black Ltd	can claim	(£20,000 × 9/12)	15,000
White Ltd	can surrender	(£24,000 × 9/12)	(18,000)

Black Ltd can claim group relief of £15,000, against its profits for the year ended 30 September 2010.

Test your understanding 8

A Ltd

Associated companies

A Ltd controls more than 50% of B Ltd, C Ltd, D Ltd as well as E Ltd – therefore (including A Ltd), there are five associated companies in the A Ltd group.

Group relief group

A Ltd, B Ltd and C Ltd form a group of companies for group relief purposes.

D Ltd is not a group member, as it is not a 75% subsidiary.

E Ltd is non-UK resident and therefore, cannot participate in a group relief claim.

Note: Non-UK resident companies are treated as associated companies.

Corporation tax computations – y/e 31 March 2010

	A Ltd	B Ltd	C Ltd	D Ltd
	£	£	£	£
Trading income	100,000	110,000	Nil	Nil
Interest income	Nil	15,000	12,000	
Total profits	100,000	125,000	12,000	
CY claim – s393A (W2)			(5,000)	
Group relief (W2)	(40,000)	(65,000)		
PCTCT	60,000	60,000	7,000	Nil
CT @ 21%	12,600	12,600	1,470	Nil

Note: The trading loss of D Ltd (£25,000), can only be carried forward in D Ltd for set-off against its first available future trading profits as it is not a member of the group relief group.

Workings

(W1) Associated companies

There are five associated companies; therefore, the upper and lower limits applicable to each company are:

£1,500,000/5 = £300,000 and £300,000/5 = £60,000

The following would not be not required in the examination but is provided for you to understand the implications of the relevant limits applicable to each company.

When 'profits' are:	**PCTCT charged**
≤ £60,000	Small company's rate (21%)
> £60,000 and ≤ £300,000	Full rate and MR (29.75%)
> £300,000	Full rate (28%)

The loss of C Ltd, is utilised most efficiently by surrendering sufficient of the loss to A Ltd and B Ltd to reduce their profits to the lower limit of £60,000.

Relief for the loss will be at 29.75%. Any remaining loss can be relieved against C Ltd's other profits, where relief is obtained at 21%.

Note: Further loss relief to A Ltd or B Ltd would also save tax at 21%.

(W2) Utilisation of loss

Trading loss available in C Ltd and its efficient utilisation:

	£
Available loss in C Ltd	110,000
Utilisation: to A Ltd (Note)	(40,000)
to B Ltd (Note)	(65,000)
	5,000
in C Ltd	(5,000)
	Nil

Note: Loss given to bring the profits down to £60,000.

You could have started with B Ltd and then A Ltd, but in total you want to surrender £105,000 of the loss, from C Ltd to A Ltd and B Ltd.

The following would not be required in the examination but is provided to aid your understanding

If C Ltd had used its own loss and not transferred any loss under group relief to A Ltd and B Ltd, then it would not have any PCTCT and the loss available to carry forward would have been £98,000 (£110,000 – £12,000).

	A Ltd	B Ltd	C Ltd	D Ltd
	£	£	£	£
Trading income	100,000	110,000	Nil	Nil
Interest income	Nil	15,000	12,000	
Total profits	100,000	125,000	12,000	
Less: s393A – CY claim			(12,000)	
PCTCT = Profits	100,000	125,000	Nil	Nil

	A Ltd	B Ltd	C Ltd	D Ltd
	£	£	£	£
Corporation tax				
£100,000/£125,000 @ 28%	28,000	35,000		
Less: MR				
7/400 × (£300,000 – £100,000)	(3,500)			
7/400 × (£300,000 – £125,000)		(3,063)		
Corporation tax payable	24,500	31,937	Nil	Nil

From the 'group' viewpoint, the total corporation tax (CT) payable, **without** making any claim for group loss relief, is **£56,437** (£24,500 + £31,937).

In our answer with group relief, the total CT payable was **£26,670** (£12,600 + £12,600 + £1,470).

We have allocated group relief as follows:

To A Ltd: £40,000 (to bring the PCTCT down to £60,000)

	£
CT of A Ltd (without group relief)	24,500
CT of A Ltd (with group relief)	(12,600)
Difference	11,900

This means that we have relieved the loss of £40,000 at an effective rate of 29.75%. ((£11,900/£40,000) x 100)

To B Ltd: £65,000 (to bring the PCTCT down to £60,000)

	£
CT of B Ltd (without group relief)	31,937
CT of B Ltd (with group relief)	(12,600)
Difference	19,337

This means that we have relieved the loss of £65,000 at an effective rate of 29.75% ((£19,337/£65,000) x 100).

Test your understanding 9

A Ltd group

Gains group

- A Ltd, B Ltd and C Ltd are in a gains group, as there is 75% ownership at each level and A Ltd (the parent) owns more than 50% (75% × 75% = 56.25%) in C Ltd.
- A Ltd does not own more than 50% of D Ltd (75% × 75% × 75% = 42.19%) and therefore D Ltd does not form part of the gains group.
- C Ltd and D Ltd, cannot form a separate gains group, as C Ltd is part of the A Ltd gains group and cannot therefore, be itself a 'parent' company and form a separate gains group.

Group relief group

- A Ltd and B Ltd form a group relief group.
- B Ltd and C Ltd form a group relief group.
- C Ltd and D Ltd form a group relief group.

Remember, that for a group relief group the parent company (A Ltd), must have an effective interest in all companies of at least 75%.

Test your understanding 10

Alpha Ltd

As the two companies satisfy the criteria of a gains group, they can make a joint election to either:

- transfer Alpha Ltd's capital loss of £65,000 to Beta Ltd, or
- transfer Beta Ltd's capital gain of £90,000 to Alpha Ltd.

In both instances, the capital loss will be set-off against the chargeable gain, resulting in a net chargeable gain of £25,000, chargeable to corporation tax. It is therefore possible, to have the gain of £25,000, taxed in the company that is subject to the lower rate of corporation tax.

The time limit for making the election is 31 March 2012 (i.e. within two years from 31 March 2010).

chapter

23

Overseas issues for companies

Chapter learning objectives

Upon completion of this chapter you will be able to:

- explain the basis for charging overseas profits to UK corporation tax
- determine the amount of overseas chargeable profits
- explain the treatment of overseas dividends
- explain how relief is given for overseas tax suffered
- calculate double tax relief when withholding tax is suffered
- explain the purpose of the transfer pricing rules as they apply to transactions between a UK and overseas company.

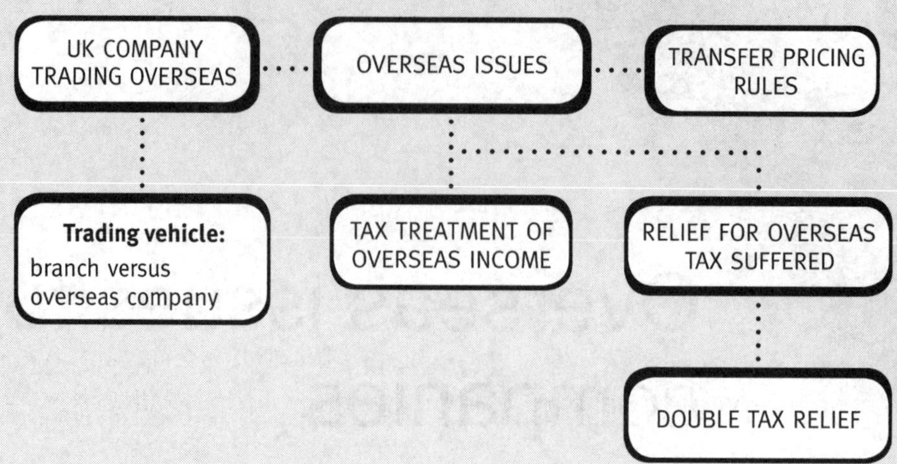

1 Overseas operations

Companies **resident** in the UK are chargeable to corporation tax on all profits and chargeable gains wherever they arise (i.e. worldwide profits including gains).

Definition – residency

The residency rules were covered in detail in Chapter 18. In summary, a company is resident in the UK if:

- it is incorporated in the UK, or
- it is 'centrally managed and controlled in the UK'.

A company which is incorporated in the UK or an overseas company which is centrally managed and controlled in the UK, will therefore be chargeable to UK corporation tax on their worldwide profits.

Overseas operations of a UK company

A UK resident company considering whether or not to set up an operation overseas must consider whether to operate through an overseas resident company or a branch. Each set up has different tax implications.

Overseas branch of a UK resident company

An overseas branch of a UK company is effectively an extension of the UK trade.

Accordingly, the tax implications of operating through an overseas branch, are as follows:

- 100% of the branch profits will be assessed to UK corporation tax. Whether profits are remitted to the UK or not is irrelevant.

- The branch profits will normally be taxed as UK trading profits.
- UK capital allowances are available on the branch's assets.
- Branch trading losses are eligible for UK loss relief, including group relief.
- UK trading losses can be offset against overseas branch profits.

Overseas resident company

To operate through an overseas resident company, the UK company must set up a separate legal entity abroad; separate from the UK company.

Accordingly, the tax implications of operating through an overseas resident company, are as follows:

- Dividends paid to the UK parent company are exempt from UK corporation tax.
- If the overseas company is controlled (> 50% ownership) by the UK company:
  - it will be classed as an associated company, for the purposes of determining the rate of UK corporation tax payable by the UK company.
  - dividend received is group income and therefore not included as FII.
- If the overseas company is not controlled by the UK company (≤ 50% ownership), cash dividends received are treated in the same way as UK dividends (i.e. grossed up at 100/90 and treated as franked investment income (FII)).

Note that the following benefits are not available:

- No UK capital allowances on the overseas company's assets.
- No relief in the UK for losses incurred by the overseas company.

Overseas chargeable profits

- Profits from an overseas branch are normally taxed as UK trading profits.
- Dividends received from an overseas company, are exempt.
- Overseas rental income is assessed as property income and overseas interest as interest income.

Example 1 - Overseas operations

Probe plc, a UK resident company, has a tax-adjusted trading profit of £1,400,000, for the year ended 31 March 2010.

The company has a 5% shareholding in Deep Inc, an overseas resident company. During the year ended 31 March 2010, Deep Inc paid a total dividend of £360,000. This is after the deduction of overseas tax at the rate of 3%.

Calculate the 'profits' used to determine the rate of corporation tax in Probe plc for the year ended 31 March 2010.

Answer to example 1

'Profits' computation – year ended 31 March 2010

	£
Trading profit = PCTCT	1,400,000
Plus: Franked investment income	
Dividend from overseas (£360,000 × 5% × 100/90)	20,000
'Profits' to determine rate of tax	1,420,000

Note: Overseas dividends are not grossed up for any overseas tax suffered. The dividend received is grossed up by 100/90.

Test your understanding 1

Happy Ltd, a UK resident company, has tax-adjusted trading profits of £1,650,000, for the year ended 31 December 2009.

The company has an 8% shareholding in Jolly Inc, an overseas resident company. During the year Jolly Ltd paid a dividend to Happy Ltd of £31,500 (after the deduction of 22% overseas tax).

Calculate the 'profits' used to determine the rate of tax of Happy Ltd, for the year ended 31 December 2009.

2 Double tax relief (DTR)

- Overseas dividend income is exempt from UK corporation tax.
- However, overseas branch profits, rental income and interest are chargeable and may be subject to both overseas tax and UK corporation tax.
- Relief for this double taxation is given by means of a 'tax credit' to the UK resident company.

Relief for overseas tax suffered

Relief for overseas tax suffered is given as follows:

- The overseas income is included gross of overseas tax in the PCTCT computation.
- Double tax relief (DTR) is given for the overseas tax suffered by way of credit against the corporation tax liability.
- The amount of DTR is limited to the lower of:
  - the amount of overseas tax on the overseas income
  - the UK corporation tax payable on that overseas income.

Operation of DTR

DTR must be calculated on a 'source by source' basis, not a global basis. Therefore, each source of overseas income and its related overseas and UK tax liability, must be dealt with separately (i.e. if a company has overseas branch profits and overseas rental income, separate DTR calculations are needed).

Approach a question with different sources of overseas income as follows:

- Include overseas income inclusive of overseas taxes as part of PCTCT. Use a columnar layout to recognise each different overseas source of income.
- The overseas income is included as PCTCT and therefore, taxed at the appropriate UK rate.
- Deduct from the UK corporation tax liability, the lower of:
  - attributable UK corporation tax on overseas profits; and
  - overseas tax suffered.

Example 2 - Double tax relief

A Ltd, a UK resident company, has taxable trading profits of £500,000, during the year ended 31 March 2010. Due to the number of associates in the A Ltd group, the company pays tax at the rate of 28%.

The company also had the following overseas income during the year:

- a dividend of £10,000 (gross) from ABC Inc. This has been taxed overseas at the rate of 20%. A Ltd has a 60% interest in ABC Inc.
- overseas branch profits of £10,000 (gross). These profits have been taxed overseas at the rate of 66%.
- overseas rental income of £7,000 (gross). This income was taxed at 25%.

Calculate A Ltd's UK corporation tax liability, after double tax relief for the year ended 31 March 2010.

Answer to example 2

	Total	UK income	Branch profits	Rental income
	£	£	£	£
PCTCT	517,000	500,000	10,000	7,000
UK CT at 28% (Note)	144,760	140,000	2,800	1,960
Less: DTR – lower of				
(i) Branch profit:				
UK CT: £2,800 (above)	(2,800)		(2,800)	
Overseas tax				
(66% × £10,000)				
= £6,600				
(ii) Rental income				
UK CT: £1,960 (above)				
Overseas tax:				
(25% × £7,000) = £1,750	(1,750)			(1,750)
UK CT liability	140,210	140,000	Nil	210

Note: The overseas dividends are exempt from UK corporation tax. As A Ltd owns a controlling interest in AB Inc, the dividends are group income and not treated as FII.

Gift Aid

When calculating PCTCT for a company with overseas income, Gift Aid may be allocated in the most beneficial manner, (i.e. first against UK profits and then against overseas income).

If we do not do this, then we are reducing the foreign income and as a result, reducing the UK tax due on foreign income and as a direct consequence reducing the DTR available.

Overseas tax suffered

Overseas tax suffered on overseas income is called withholding tax (WHT).

WHT is any direct tax imposed at source by the overseas country.

Note that:

- WHT can apply to any overseas income (e.g. branch profits, interest, rent).
- DTR for WHT is always available.

Example 3 - Double tax relief

Maxwell Ltd, a UK resident trading company, owns an overseas branch in Malawi. It received rental income from renting a property in Spain and owns 8% of the share capital of Zulu Inc.

Maxwell Ltd also has a controlling interest in two other UK resident companies.

The following information relates to Maxwell Ltd's y/e 31 March 2010:

	£
Tax adjusted trading profits	500,000
Overseas Income:	
Branch profits – after deduction of withholding tax of 30%	35,000
Rental income – after deduction of withholding tax of 5%	38,000
Dividend from Zulu Inc – after deduction of withholding tax of 20%	18,000
Gift Aid donation	10,000

Calculate the UK corporation tax payable for the above period by Maxwell Ltd, showing clearly your treatment of double taxation.

Answer to example 3

Corporation tax computation – year ended 31 March 2010

	Total	UK income	Branch profits	Rental income
	£	£	£	£
Trading income	500,000	500,000		
Overseas income (W1)	90,000		50,000	40,000
Total profits	590,000	500,000	50,000	40,000
Less: Gift Aid	(10,000)	(10,000)		
PCTCT	580,000	490,000	50,000	40,000
Corporation tax				
(£580,000 @ 28%) (W2)	162,400	137,200	14,000	11,200
Less: DTR (W3)	(16,000)		(14,000)	(2,000)
CT payable	146,400	137,200	Nil	9,200

Note: Overseas dividends from Zulu Inc are exempt from UK corporation tax but treated as FII.

Workings

(W1) Grossing up the overseas income

	Branch profits	Rental income
	£	£
Income required	35,000	38,000
Add: WHT (30/70)/(5/95)	15,000	2,000
	50,000	40,000

(W2) **Associated companies**

There are 3 companies under common control, as Maxwell Ltd has a controlling interest in 2 other UK resident companies (Zulu Inc is not an 'associated' company as Maxwell Ltd only has an 8% interest).

Limits for determining the tax rate:
£1,500,000/3 = £500,000
£300,000/3 = £100,000

	£
PCTCT	580,000
Plus FII (£18,000 × 100/90)	20,000
Profits	600,000

Therefore with profits of £600,000, the full rate of 28% applies.

(W3) DTR relief

	Branch profits	Rental income
Lower of:	£	£
(i) UK CT liability on overseas profits	14,000	11,200
(ii) Overseas taxes suffered	15,000	2,000

The following calculations would not be required in the exam – they are provided to aid your understanding.

If Gift Aid is not deducted from UK income first, then:

	Total	UK income	Branch profits	Rental income
	£	£	£	£
Trading income	500,000	500,000		
Overseas income	90,000		50,000	40,000
Total profits	590,000	500,000	50,000	40,000
Less: Gift Aid	(10,000)		(10,000)	
PCTCT	580,000	500,000	40,000	40,000
Corporation tax @ 28%	162,400	140,000	11,200	11,200
Less: DTR (Note 1)	(13,200)		(11,200)	(2,000)
CT payable	149,200	140,000	Nil	9,200

Notes

(1) The DTR has been reduced by £2,800 due to the amount of UK tax due on the income.

(2) The CT payable has now become £149,200, (i.e. more than the original answer) because having allocated the Gift Aid against overseas income, we have restricted the DTR.

Therefore:

- Gift Aid should be allocated against UK income first then against overseas income, with the lower effective rate of overseas tax.
- This should, therefore, give the maximum amount of DTR for overseas income, with the higher effective rate of overseas tax.

Test your understanding 2

London Ltd, a UK resident trading company, owns two overseas branches, one in Paris and one in Rome. It also owns 4% of the share capital of Berlin Gmbh, an overseas company. London Ltd also has a controlling interest in three other UK resident companies.

The following information relates to London's Ltd's year ended 31 March 2010:

	£
Tax-adjusted trading profits	400,000
Overseas income:	
Paris branch profits	54,000
– after deduction of withholding tax of 40%	
Rome branch profits	39,100
– after deduction of withholding tax of 15%	
Dividend from Berlin Gmbh	
– After deduction of withholding tax of 27%	2,700
Gift Aid donation	20,000

Compute the UK corporation tax payable for the above period by London Ltd, showing clearly your treatment of double taxation.

Summary

- Overseas income is included gross of overseas tax in the corporation tax computation.
- The amount of DTR is limited to the lower of:
  - the amount of overseas tax on the overseas income
  - the UK corporation tax payable on that overseas income.
- DTR is calculated on a 'source by source' basis.
- Relief for withholding tax is always available.

3 Transfer pricing

If a UK resident company has a 'controlling' interest in an overseas resident subsidiary, then it might try to sell goods to the subsidiary at an undervalue or buy goods from it at an overvalue in order to manipulate where the profits should arise.

The aim of these arrangements would be to move the profits to a country with a lower corporation tax rate than the UK.

Transfer pricing – rules

- The transfer pricing rules prevent UK companies from charging artificial prices for goods and services in order to gain a tax advantage.
- The basic rule for transfer pricing is that transactions between group members should be charged on an arms-length basis.
- An 'arms-length' price is what it could have been sold for to an independent third party dealing on commercial terms, e.g. market prices.
- For example, where sales are made to an overseas resident 'group' company at an undervalue, then its true market price should be substituted for the transfer price.
- Under self-assessment rules, if transactions are not made on an arms-length basis, an adjustment to substitute arms-length prices should be made by the UK resident company in its corporation tax return.
- There are detailed rules for establishing which companies are within the scope of the transfer pricing rules, but the basic test is one of control.
- Advance pricing arrangements are available to enable a company to agree in advance with HMRC, that its 'transfer pricing policy' is acceptable.
- The transfer pricing rules can also apply between two UK resident companies. However, the examiner has stated that any question on transfer pricing will involve an overseas company.

Example 4 - Transfer pricing

Focus plc, a UK resident company, is to export cameras that it manufactures, to its 100% overseas subsidiary, at a discount of 30% to their normal trade selling price.

The company wishes to maximise the subsidiary's profits, as these are only subject to corporation tax overseas at the rate of 15%.

Discuss the tax implications of the above arrangement.

Answer to example 4

- The invoicing of cameras by Focus plc at a discount of 30% to the normal trade selling price, will have the effect of reducing its taxable trading profits, and hence UK corporation tax.
- The sales are at an under-valuation to an overseas company which it controls. Therefore a market price must be substituted for the transfer price when calculating Focus plc's profits chargeable to UK corporation tax.
- The market price will be an 'arm's length' one that would be charged if the parties to the transaction were independent of each other.
- Under self-assessment, transfer pricing adjustments are not made by HMRC, but should be made by the company concerned, in this case, Focus plc.

4 Chapter summary

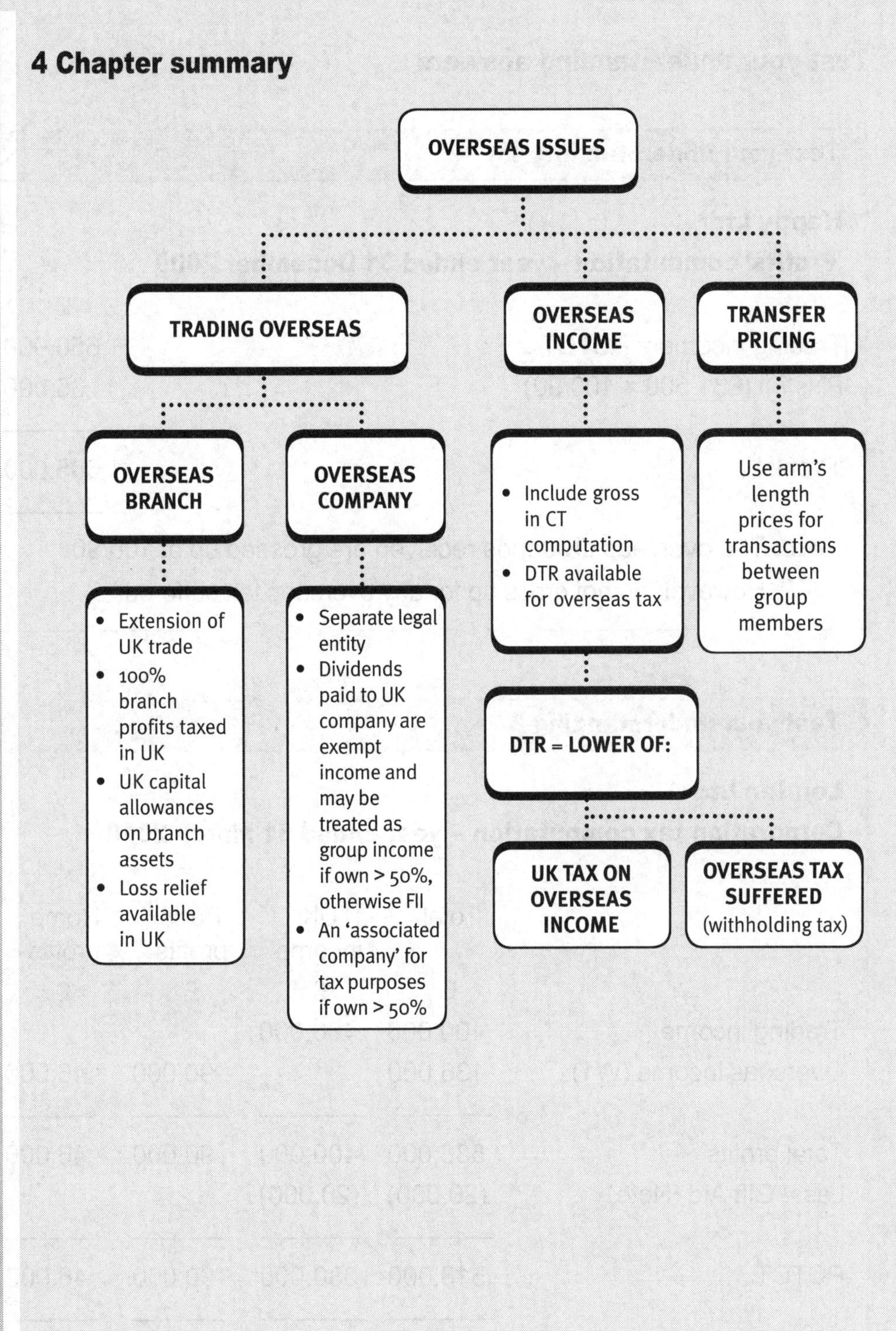

Test your understanding answers

Test your understanding 1

Happy Ltd

'Profits' computation – year ended 31 December 2009

	£
Trading income = PCTCT	1,650,000
Plus FII (£31,500 × 100/90)	35,000
'Profits'	1,685,000

Note: The overseas dividends received are grossed up at 100/90. However, do not gross up for any overseas tax suffered.

Test your understanding 2

London Ltd

Corporation tax computation – year ended 31 March 2010

	Total	UK income	Paris profits	Rome profits
	£	£	£	£
Trading income	400,000	400,000		
Overseas income (W1)	136,000		90,000	46,000
Total profits	536,000	400,000	90,000	46,000
Less: Gift Aid (Note)	(20,000)	(20,000)		
PCTCT	516,000	380,000	90,000	46,000
Corporation tax				
£516,000 @ 28% (W2)	144,480	106,400	25,200	12,880
Less: DTR (W3)	(32,100)		(25,200)	(6,900)
CT payable	112,380	106,400	Nil	5,980

Note: The Gift Aid is offset firstly against UK income in order to maximise the DTR available.

Workings

(W1) Grossing up the overseas income

Branch profits	Paris	Rome
	£	£
Income received	54,000	39,100
Add: WHT (40/60)/(15/85)	36,000	6,900
	90,000	46,000

(W2) Associated companies

There are three companies under common control, as London Ltd has a controlling interest in three other UK resident companies (Berlin Gmbh is not an 'associated' companies).

Therefore, the applicable limits for determining the tax rate for each company are:

£1,500,000/4 = £375,000
£300,000/4 = £75,000

	£
PCTCT	516,000
Plus FII (£27,000 × 100/90)	30,000
Profits	546,000

Therefore, with PCTCT of £546,000, the full rate applies.

(W3) DTR relief

	Paris	Rome
	£	£
UK CT on overseas profits	25,200	12,880
Overseas taxes suffered	36,000	6,900

chapter

24

Tax administration for a company

Chapter learning objectives

Upon completion of this chapter you will be able to:

- explain and apply the features of the self-assessment system as it applies to companies
- state the time limits for filing a tax return
- list the information and records that the company needs to retain for tax purposes together with the retention period.
- state when corporation tax is due for companies which are not large
- state the time limits for key claims
- define a large company and explain how they are required to pay corporation tax on a quarterly basis
- calculate interest on overdue tax
- state the penalties for late submission of tax returns/notification of liability
- state the penalties that can be charged on a late payment of tax
- explain the circumstances in which HM Revenue and Customs can enquire into a tax return

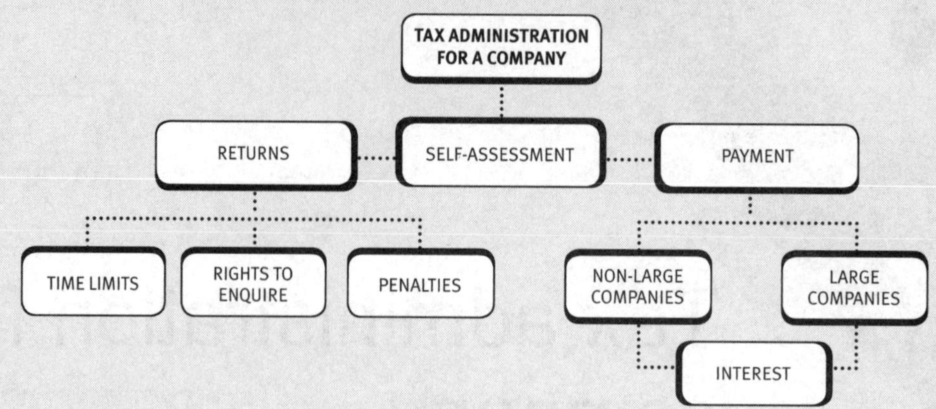

1 The self-assessment system for companies

Introduction

As with individuals, self-assessment exists for corporate taxpayers. Responsibility rests with the company to:

- calculate their own corporation tax liability for each accounting period
- submit a self-assessment corporation tax return **within 12 months** after the end of the accounting period
- pay any corporation tax due **within nine months** after the end of the accounting period.

Given the timing of the due date for payment of tax, in practice, many companies will aim to complete the self-assessment tax return prior to the nine-month deadline for paying the corporation tax.

The following session considers all aspects concerning the self-assessment system for companies and the related procedures.

The self-assessment tax return

The self-assessment tax return must be submitted either:

- **within 12 months** after the end of the accounting period; or
- **three months** after the issue of the return (if this is later than the normal submission date).

The return should contain all information required to calculate the company's profits chargeable to corporation tax.

A company has to submit a copy of its financial accounts together with the self-assessment tax return.

The return must include a self-assessment of the amount of corporation tax payable for that accounting period.

Mrs Steel – Capital gains tax computation – 2009/10

Icon	£	£
Deemed sale proceeds	6,000	
Cost	(6,300)	
Allowable loss		(300)
Plot of land		
Sale proceeds (3 acres)	15,000	
Less: Cost (3 acres)		
£4,500 × £15,000/(£15,000 + £25,000)	(1,688)	
Chargeable gain		13,312
Jade		
Sale proceeds	11,000	
Less: Cost	(6,500)	
Chargeable gain		4,500
Land		
Disposal proceeds	12,000	
Less: Deemed acquisition cost	(2,000)	
Chargeable gain		10,000
Net chargeable gains		27,512
Less: Annual exemption		(10,100)
Taxable gain		17,412
Capital gains tax (£17,412 x 18%)		3,134

Jasper

Answer 1 – Chapter 16

Jasper – Total chargeable gains – 2009/10

	£	£
Shares in Carrot plc		
Net sale proceeds	8,580	
Less: Cost (W1)	(3,928)	
		4,652
Takeover		
Cash received (W2)	4,800	
Less: Cost (W2)	(1,030)	
		3,770
Shares in Grasp plc		
Sale proceeds	3,600	
Less: Cost (W2) £9,008 x 400/12,000	300	
		3,300
Total chargeable gains		11,722

Workings

(W1) Carrot plc

		Number	Cost £
July 2005	Purchase	1,750	2,625
May 2006	Purchase	200	640
		1,950	3,265
June 2007	Rights issue (1:10) @ £3.40	195	663
		2,145	3,928
November 2009	Sale	(2,145)	(3,928)

(W2) Grasp plc

Apportionment of cost of Cawte plc securities to new securities and cash acquired at date of takeover.

	Purchase consideration	Cost allocation
	£	£
For 12,000 Cawte plc ord shares:		
12,000 Grasp £1 ord shares at 350p	42,000	9,008
24,000 Grasp 10% pref shares at 110p	26,400	5,662
Cash (12,000 × 40p)	4,800	1,030
	73,200	15,700

Jack Chan

Answer 1 – Chapter 17

CGT computation – 2009/10

	£	£
Goodwill		
Market value (Note 1)	60,000	
Less: Cost	(Nil)	
	60,000	
Less: Gift relief (£60,000 – £50,000) (Note 2)	(10,000)	
		50,000
Freehold office building		
Market value	130,000	
Less: Cost	(110,000)	
	20,000	
Less: Gift relief (Note 3)	(20,000)	
		Nil
		50,000
Less: Entrepreneurs' relief (£50,000 x 4/9)		(22,222)
		27,778
Freehold warehouse (Note 4)		
Market value	140,000	
Less: Cost	(95,000)	
		45,000
Motor cars (Note 5)		Nil
Net chargeable gains for the tax year		72,778
Less: Capital loss brought forward		(6,400)
		66,378
Less: Annual exemption		(10,100)
Taxable gains		56,278

	£
Capital gains tax (£56,278 x 18%)	10,130
Due date for CGT liability	31 January 2011

Notes:

(1) Jack and Jill are connected persons, and therefore the market values of the assets sold are used.

(2) The consideration paid for the goodwill exceeds the original cost by £50,000 (£50,000 – Nil). This amount is immediately chargeable to CGT.

(3) The consideration paid for the office building does not exceed the original cost, so full gift relief is available. Holdover relief is not restricted.

(4) The warehouse does not qualify for gift relief.

(5) Motor cars are exempt from CGT.

Sophie

Answer 2 – Chapter 17

(a) **Sophie – Capital gains computation – 2009/10**

	£	£	£
Freehold premises			
Market value	200,000		
Less: Acquisition cost	(80,000)		
		120,000	
Goodwill			
Market value	50,000		
Less: Acquisition cost	(Nil)		
		50,000	
		170,000	
Less: Entrepreneurs' relief		(75,556)	
Chargeable gain on incorporation			94,444
Sale of house			
Sale proceeds		450,000	
Less: Acquisition cost		(120,000)	
		330,000	
Less: PPR exemption (£330,000 x (96/120)) (W1)		(264,000)	
Chargeable gain			66,000
Total chargeable gains			160,444
Less: Annual exemption			(10,100)
Taxable gains			150,344
Capital gains tax (£150,344 x 18%)			27,062

Workings

(W1) PPR relief

	Total	Exempt	Chargeable
1.6.99 – 31.12.01	31		
Actual occupation		31	
1.1.02 – 31.5.03	17		
Part of 3 years for any reason		17	
1.6.03 – 31.5.04	12		
Actual occupation		12	
1.6.04 – 31.5.09	60		
Last 3 years		36	
Rest of period – chargeable			24
	—	—	—
Number of months	120	96	24
	—	—	—

Notes:

(1) The period spent living with her mother is deemed occupation, being part of the three years absence for any reason, as Sophie lived in the property both before and after the period of absence.

(2) The last three years of ownership represents a deemed period of occupation, even if the owner has elected for another property to be treated as his PPR in the same period.

(3) The remaining 24 month period of absence does not qualify as deemed occupation as the property was not reoccupied after the period of absence.

(b) **Incorporation relief**

Incorporation relief is available where the following conditions apply:

- The unincorporated business is transferred as a going concern.
- All of the assets of the business (other than cash) are transferred.
- The consideration for the transfer of the business must be wholly or mainly shares in the company.

(c) **Effect of incorporation relief**

Incorporation relief operates such that the gains arising on the deemed disposal of the individual assets are rolled over against the acquisition cost of the shares in the new company.

However where part of the consideration for the transfer of the business is not shares (e.g. cash), the gain eligible for relief is:

$$\text{Net chargeable gains x} \quad \frac{\text{Value of shares issued}}{\text{Total consideration}}$$

Therefore if Sophie had taken advantage of incorporation relief part of the gain would have been rolled over against the base cost of the shares in Sophie Ltd and would not have been chargeable in 2009/10.

The chargeable gains on incorporation would be:

	£
Total capital gains on incorporation	170,000
Less: Incorporation relief	
£170,000 x (£200,000/£322,000)	(105,590)
Chargeable gain after incorporation relief	64,410
Less: Entrepreneurs' relief (£64,410 x 4/9)	(28,627)
Chargeable gain on incorporation	35,783

Therefore if she had taken advantage of incorporation relief, Sophie's capital gains tax liability for 2009/10 would have been reduced by £10,559 ((£94,444 – £35,783) x 18%).

Earth Ltd

Answer 1 – Chapter 20

(1) **Venus plc – sale of 25,000 shares**

	£
Sale proceeds	115,000
Less: Cost (W)	(17,000)
Unindexed gain	98,000
Less: Indexation (£37,007 – £17,000) (W)	(20,007)
Chargeable gain	77,993

Share pool	Number	Cost	Indexed cost
		£	£
Purchase – June 1986	40,000	34,000	34,000
Bonus issue – October 2002 (£40,000 × ¼)	10,000	Nil	Nil
	50,000	34,000	34,000
Indexation to November 2009 £34,000 × (212.9 – 97.8)/97.8			40,014
	50,000	34,000	74,014
Disposal – November 2009 Cost/Indexed cost× (25,000/50,000)	(25,000)	(17,000)	(37,007)
Balance c/f	25,000	17,000	37,007

(2) **Saturn plc**

	£
Sale proceeds	52,500
Less: Cost (W)	(80,000)
Allowable capital loss	(27,500)

Share pool	Number	Cost	Indexed cost
	£	£	£
3 January 2010	30,000	97,500	115,950
Rights issue (1 : 2) @ £1.50	15,000	22,500	22,500
	45,000	120,000	138,450
Disposal – 22 January 2010	(30,000)	(80,000)	(92,300)
Balance c/f	15,000	40,000	46,150

Note: Indexation cannot be used to increase a capital loss.

(3) **Jupiter plc**

	£
Sale proceeds	55,000
Less: Cost	(11,200)
Unindexed gain	43,800
Less: Indexation allowance (£13,760 – £11,200)	(2,560)
Chargeable gain	41,240

Share pool	Number	Cost	Indexed cost
	£	£	£
7 March 2009	10,000	14,000	17,200

Takeover consideration	Value
	£
20,000 Ordinary shares @ £2.50	50,000
10,000 Preference shares @ £1.25	12,500
	62,500

Allocation of cost and Indexed cost

	Cost	Indexed Cost
	£	£
Ordinary shares		
(50,000/62,500) × £14,000/£17,200	11,200	13,760
Preference shares		
(12,500/62,500) × £14,000/£17,200	2,800	3,440
	14,000	17,200

Gold Ltd

Answer 1 – Chapter 22

(a) **Gold Ltd – Corporation tax liabilities**

Year ended	31.12.08	31.12.09
	£	£
Trading income	177,000	90,000
Property income	5,000	–
Chargeable gain	–	12,000
Total profits	182,000	102,000
Less: Gift Aid donation	(2,000)	(2,000)
	180,000	100,000
Less: Group relief	(70,000)	(50,000)
PCTCT	110,000	50,000
Corporation tax liability		
FY2007 (£110,000 x 20% x 3/12)	5,500	
FY2008 (£110,000 x 21% x 9/12)	17,325	
FY2008/FY2009 (£50,000 x 21%)		10,500
	22,825	10,500

Notes:

(1) The CAPs are not coterminous, so both Gold Ltd's PCTCT and Silver Ltd's trading loss must be time apportioned.

(2) For the y/e 31 December 2008 group relief is the lower of Gold Ltd's available profits of £90,000 (£180,000 × 6/12) and Silver Ltd's available loss of £70,000 (£140,000 × 6/12).

(3) For the y/e 31 December 2009 group relief is the lower of Gold Ltd's available profits of £50,000 (£100,000 × 6/12) and Silver Ltd's available loss of £70,000 (£140,000 × 6/12).

(4) Gold Ltd has one associated company so the small companies rate lower limit is £150,000 (£300,000/2).

(5) The y/e 31 December 2008 straddles 31 March 2008. As the small companies rate changed on 31 March 2008 the corporation tax liability must be calculated for each financial year seperately. However, there is no change in rate in the y/e 31 December 2009.

(b) **Maximising benefit of group relief**

(1) Relief should initially be claimed against profits subject to corporation tax at the marginal rate of 29.75% (FY2008 and FY2009) or 32.5% (FY2007) and then profits subject to the full rate of 28% or 30%.

(2) Where group relief is concerned, the amount surrendered should be sufficient to bring the claimant company's profits down to the small companies rate lower limit.

(3) Any remaining loss should be claimed against profits subject to corporation tax at the small companies rate of 21% (FY2008 and FY2009) or 20% (FY2007).

(4) Consideration should also be given to the timing of the relief obtained (an earlier loss relief claim is generally preferable), and the extent to which relief for Gift Aid donations will be lost if loss relief is carried back.

(c) **Most beneficial way to relieve Silver Ltd's trading loss**

(1) The group relief claim for the y/e 31 December 2008 should be restricted to £30,000 so that Gold Ltd's profits are reduced to exactly £150,000 (£180,000 – £30,000) and relief is obtained for the loss at the small companies marginal relief rate.

(2) No group relief claim should be made for the y/e 31 December 2009 since Gold Ltd's profits are already below the small companies rate lower limit and the losses are therefore only being relieved at 21%.

(3) The remaining £110,000 (£140,000 – £30,000) of the loss should be carried back to the y/e 30 June 2008 in order to reduce Silver Ltd's profits to £150,000 (£260,000 – £110,000), hence obtaining relief at the marginal rate.

Apple Group

Answer 2 – Chapter 22

(a) **Group relationship – Group relief** – One company must be a 75% subsidiary of the other, or both companies must be 75% subsidiaries of the holding company.

The holding company must have an effective interest of at least 75% of the subsidiary's ordinary share capital.

The holding company must have the right to receive at least 75% of the subsidiary's distributable profits and net assets (were it to be wound up).

(b) **Allocation of group relief** – Surrender should be made initially to companies subject to corporation tax at the small companies marginal rate of 29.75%.

Surrender should then be to those companies subject to the full rate of corporation tax of 28%.

The amount surrendered should be sufficient to bring the claimant company's PCTCT down to the small company rate limit.

(c) **Corporation tax liabilities – year ended 31 March 2010**

	Apple Ltd	Banana Ltd	Cherry Ltd
	£	£	£
Trading income	–	650,000	130,000
Chargeable gain	120,000	–	–
Total profits	120,000	650,000	130,000
Less: Current year loss relief	(20,000)		
Less: Group relief		(75,000)	(30,000)
PCTCT	100,000	575,000	100,000
CT @ 21%/28%/21%	21,000	161,000	21,000

Apple Ltd has two associated companies, so the relevant lower and upper limits for corporation tax purposes are £100,000 (£300,000/3) and £500,000 (£1,500,000/3) respectively.

Apple Ltd's chargeable gain can be rolled over against the reinvestment by Cherry Ltd. The proceeds not reinvested of £128,000 (£418,000 – £290,000) remain chargeable in the year ended 31 March 2010.

Banana Ltd and Apple Ltd should make a joint election to transfer the capital loss realised by Banana Ltd to Apple Ltd to be set against Apple Ltd's gain.

Net chargeable gain = (£128,000 – £8,000) = £120,000.

Apple Ltd's trading loss is relieved so as to reduce both its own and Cherry Ltd's profits down to the small company rate limit.

The order of the claims to use the losses would be as follows:

(1) Group relief to Cherry Ltd of £30,000.

(2) Group relief to Banana Ltd of £75,000.

(3) Current year relief against total profits of Apple Ltd of £20,000.

Ramble Ltd

Answer 1 – Chapter 24

(a) Self-assessment tax return

Ramble Ltd's self assessment corporation tax return for the year ended 31 March 2009 was due by 31 March 2010.

As the company did not submit the return until 15 October 2010 there will be a late filing penalty of £200 as the return was submitted more than three months late.

As a payment of tax was also made on 15 October 2010 there will also be a tax-geared penalty of 10% of the tax unpaid more than six months after the filing date.

(b) **Corporation tax payments**

Ramble Ltd's profits chargeable to corporation tax for the year ended 31 March 2010 exceed £1,500,000. It will therefore pay corporation tax at the full rate and be classed as a large company for the purposes of paying its corporation tax liability.

The company is therefore required to pay its corporation tax liability by quarterly instalments as follows:

– 14 October 2009 (month 7) (£2,456,000 × 28% × 1/4)	£171,920
– 14 January 2010	£171,920
– 14 April 2010	£171,920
– 14 July 2010	£171,920

Interest will be due on the late payment of corporation tax as follows:

– £171,920	– from 14 October 2009 to 30 April 2010
– £171,920	– from 14 January 2010 to 30 April 2010
– £127,060	– from 14 April 2010 to 30 April 2010
– £44,860 (W)	– from 14 April 2010 to 31 December 2010
– £171,920	– from 14 July 2010 to 31 December 2010

Working: underpayment	£
Outstanding payments (3 × £171,920)	515,760
Less: Payment on 1 May 2010	(470,900)
Underpayment	44,860

Mary

Answer 1 – Chapter 26

VAT return for the quarter ended 31 March 2010

	£
Output tax	
Standard-rated supplies (£230,000 x 97½%) = £224,250	
(17½ % × £224,250) (net of discount sales)	39,244
Zero-rated sales (0% × £50,000)	Nil
Car fuel charge (2/3 × £414 × 17.5/117.5)	41
	39,285
Input tax	
Standard-rated purchases (£102,440 @ 17.5%)	(17,927)
Standard-rated expenses (£18,000 - £5,000) @ 17.5%	(2,275)
Bad debt relief (£1,000 + £1,000) @ 17.5%	(350)
VAT payable	18,733

Due and payable date is 30 April 2010

Notes:

The car was bought on 1 February 2010 – therefore, in this quarter there are only two months of private use.

Relief for bad debts was available for the sales invoice issued on 1 May 2009 and 1 August 2009 as the payment for these invoices was due on 1 June 2009 and 1 September 2009 – debt written off and more than six months overdue. Relief is given on the discounted amounts.

Relief for invoice issued on 1 November 2009, the payment for which was due on 1 December 2009 is not possible as the debt is not over six months old.

Index

Index

Index

Index

Index

Index

Index